Elections in Times of a Pandemic – Dilemmas and Challenges

International Comparative Social Studies

VOLUME 59

The titles published in this series are listed at *brill.com/icss*

Elections in Times of a Pandemic – Dilemmas and Challenges

Experiences of the European Countries

Edited by

Magdalena Musiał-Karg
Izabela Kapsa

BRILL

LEIDEN | BOSTON

Originally published in hardback in 2024.

Cover illustration: Copyright 2023, Magdalena Musiał-Karg and Izabela Kapsa.

The Library of Congress has cataloged the hardcover edition as follows:

Names: Musiał-Karg, Magdalena, editor. | Kapsa, Izabela, editor.
Title: Elections in times of a pandemic - dilemmas and challenges :
    experiences of the European countries / edited by Magdalena Musiał-Karg,
    Izabela Kapsa.
Description: Leiden ; Boston : Brill, [2024] | Series: International
    comparative social studies, 1568-4474 ; volume 59 | Includes
    bibliographical references and index.
Identifiers: LCCN 2023052950 (print) | LCCN 2023052951 (ebook) | ISBN
    9789004690561 (hardback) | ISBN 9789004690622 (ebook)
Subjects: LCSH: Elections–Europe–History. | COVID-19 Pandemic,
    2020–Political aspects–Europe. | Europe–Politics and
    government–21st century.
Classification: LCC JN45 .E626 2024 (print) | LCC JN45 (ebook) | DDC
    324.94/0562–dc23/eng/20240116
LC record available at https://lccn.loc.gov/2023052950
LC ebook record available at https://lccn.loc.gov/2023052951

Typeface for the Latin, Greek, and Cyrillic scripts: "Brill". See and download: brill.com/brill-typeface.

ISSN 1568-4474
ISBN 978-90-04-73839-3 (paperback, 2025)
ISBN 978-90-04-69056-1 (hardback)
ISBN 978-90-04-69062-2 (e-book)
DOI 10.1163/9789004690622

Contents

Figures and Tables

Figures

Tables

Abbreviations

ACEEEO	Association of European Election Officials
ACHR	Inter-American Convention on Human Rights
ACHPR	African Charter of Human and Peoples' Rights
AfD	Alternative für Deutschland
ANO	Action of Dissatisfied Citizens
ArCHR	Arab Charter of Human Rights
ASL	Azienda Sanitaria Locale – Local Health Unit
BMPO	*Bulgarian* National Movement
BSP	*Bulgarian* Communist Party
C!	Cambiamo!
CBOS	Public Opinion Research Center in Poland
CD	Democratic Centre
CDU	*Christian Democratic Union* of *Germany*
CEC	Central Election Commission
CEE	Central and Eastern Europe
CFR	Charter of Fundamental Rights of the European Union
CNEL	National Council of Economics and Labour
CSCE	Commission on Security and Cooperation in Europe
CT	Constitutional Tribunal
ČSSD	Czech Social Democratic Party
DB	Democratic Bulgaria
DC	Christian Democracy
DemTech	Democracy & Technology
DPL	Die Demokraten pro *Liechtenstein*
DPS	the Movement for Rights and Freedoms
EC	Electoral Code
ECHR	European Convention on Human Rights
EOPM	Election Observation Mission
EP	European Parliament
EpI	Energies for Italy
EU	European Union
FBK	Foundation for Fighting Corruption
FBP	Progressive Citizens' Party, Fortschrittliche Bürgerpartei
FdI	Brothers of Italy
FDP	The Free Democratic Party
FdV	Federation of the Greens
FFP	Filtering Face Piece
FI	Forza Italia

FL	Die Freie Liste
ICCPR	International Covenant on Civil and Political Rights
GERB	Citizens for European Development of Bulgaria
IiC	Italia in Comune
International IDEA	International Institute for Democracy and Electoral Assistance
IP	Polish Initiative
IV	Italia Viva
KSČM	the Communist Party of Bohemia and Moravia
LACA	the 2000 Law on the Anti-Corruption Agency (
Lega	League
LEOM	Limited Election Observation Mission
LFPA	the 2011 Law on the Financing of Political Activities
LGBT	Lesbian, Gay, Bisexual, Transgender
LUVR	Law on the Unified Voter Register
M5S	Five Star Movement
MAIE	Associative Movement Italians Abroad
NAM	ODIHR Needs Assessment Mission
NATO	North Atlantic Treaty Organization
NEC	National Electoral Commission
ODIHR	The OSCE *Office for Democratic Institutions and Human Rights*
ODIHR SEAM	the ODIHR Special Election Assessment Mission
ODS	Civic Democratic Party
OSCE	Organization for Security and Co-operation in Europe
PaP	Power of the People
PATT	Trentino Tyrolean Autonomist Party
PB	Polling Board
PCI	Italian Communist Party
PD	Democratic Party
PeC	Fatherland and Constitution
PESEL	Universal Electronic System for Registration of the Population
PiS	Law and Justice
PMLI	Italian Marxist-Leninist Party
PORP	Civic Platform of the Republic of Poland
PP	We Continue the Change (political party)
PpA	Pact for Autonomy
PRC	Communist Refoundation Party
PSG	*Pokret slobodnih građana*
PSI	Italian Socialist Party
PSL	Polish People's Party
PsV	Party of Venetians

REC	Republican Electoral Commission RTRS Republika Srpska Television
SAC	Supreme Administrative Court
SDP	*Social Democratic Party* of *Germany*
SI	Italian Left
SLD	Self-Left Aliance
SNS	Srpska Napredna Stranka, Serbian Progressive Party
SPAS	Serbian Patriotic Union
SPOLU	the Czech alliance of ODS, KDU-ČSL and TOP-09 (
SP	Solidary Poland
SPS	Socialist Party of Serbia
SRNA	Republika Srpska News Agency
STAN	the Mayors and Independents
SVP	South Tyrolean People's Party
SVP-PATT, UV	the Brothers of Italy and the For the Autonomies
SzS	*Savez za Srbiju*
UDHR	Universal Declaration of Human Rights
UN	United Nations
UpT	Union for Trentino
USEI	South American Union Italian Emigrants
UV	Valdostan Union
US	United States
USA	United States of America
USSR	Union of Soviet Socialist Republics
VC	Venice Commission
VDD	Latvian State Security Service
VU	The Patriotic Union, Vaterländische Union
WHO	World Health Organization

Notes on Editors and Contributors

Ryszard Balicki
associate professor at the University of Wrocław, Faculty of Law, Administration and Economics. Author of many scientific publications on the issues
of freedom and human rights, the executive power of modern states, constitutional aspects of European integration, and the author of opinions prepared, inter alia, on behalf of the Sejm of the Republic of Poland, the Senate
of the Republic of Poland, the Chancellery of the President of the Republic
of Poland, the Ministry of Foreign Affairs and the European Parliament.
ORCID ID: 0000-0002-9192-908X e-mail: ryszard.balicki@uwr.edu.pl

Roman Bäcker
Professor of Political Sciences at Nicolaus Copernicus University, Toruń,
Poland, and the Head of the Department of the Theory of Politics. He was
the president of the Polish Political Science Association in 2010–2016. He has
published widely on Polish and Russian political thought, democratization,
totalitarianism, the theory of politics, and the methodology of political sciences. He is a co-investigator in the research project "Contentious Politics and
Neo-Militant Democracy" financed by the National Science Centre, Poland.
ORCID ID: 0000-0002-3796-3711 e-mail: backer@umk.pl

Piotr Chrobak
associate professor at the University of Szczecin, Institute of Political and
Security Sciences. Author of over 100 scientific publications published in
Poland and abroad, including 4 monographs and a dozen or so collective
works, which have been published by him or co-edited. He specializes in the
analysis of campaigns and electoral preferences in Poland, with particular emphasis on Western Pomerania. His research also concerns the political system
of Poland and Romania as well as the private sector in Poland in the first years
after World War II. ORCID ID: 0000-0002-6408-9396 e-mail: piotr.chrobak@
usz.edu.pl

Rafał Dudała
associate professor and lecturer at the Institute of International Relations and
Public Policy, Jan Kochanowski University of Kielce; head of the Department
of Political Science. He specializes in theory of politics, political system of Italy, democracy in crisis, the phenomenon of populism, relations between religion and politics. He published, among others, 'System polityczny współczesnych Włoch. Dynamika zmian' (The political system of contemporary Italy.

Dynamics of changes), Kielce 2019; 'The development of technopopulism in a globalized world', in *The Future of Political Leadership in the Digital Age. Neo-leadership, Image, and Influence*, Routledge 2021. ORCID ID: 0000-0002-9942-3470 email: rafal.dudala@ujk.edu.pl

Kamil Glinka
PhD, political scientist, assistant professor at the Institute of Political Science, University of Wrocław. He is investigator in various research projects financed by National Science Centre of the Republic of Poland, Ministry of Science and Higher Education of the Republic of Poland and International Visegrad Fund; METERX Bernd Steinacher Fellow 2022–2023. His research area includes: public governance, urban and regional policy, public communication, place branding and political marketing. ORCID ID: 0000-0002-4983-9697 e-mail: kamil.glinka2@uwr.edu.pl

Maciej Górny
political scientist, lawyer, currently a PhD student at the Department of Social and Economic Policy at the Faculty of Political Science and Journalism at the Adam Mickiewicz University, Poznań. His esearch interests focus on subjective well-being, the economy of happiness, positive psychology, social policy, digital state. ORCID ID: 0000-0003-1476-1049 e-mail: maciej.gorny@amu.edu.pl

Maciej Hartliński
an associate professor at the Institute of Political Science, University of Warmia and Mazury in Olsztyn. He conducts research on political leaders and political parties. He is particularly interested in intra-party democracy and the mechanisms regulating the functioning of political parties. He is the author of several books, chapters and articles in peer-reviewed journals on party politics, political leaders and party leadership in post-communist countries.ORCID ID: 0000-0003-3099-5806 maciej.hartlinski@uwm.edu.pl

Marcin Jastrzębski
PhD., assistant professor at the Department of Political and Administrative Systems at the Faculty of Political Sciences and Administration of the Kazimierz Wielki University in Bydgoszcz. His research interests focus on public international law, international and Polish systems protection of human rights, political rights and freedoms, including right to free elections, cyberspace, crisis of democracy, contemporary parties and party and political systems, with particular emphasis on electoral systems and their impact on the shaping of party systems and the position of political parties in individual countries. ORCID ID: 0000-0003-3403-261X e-mail: mjastrzebski@ukw.edu.pl

Izabela Kapsa

associate professor at the Faculty of Political Science and Administration, Kazimierz Wielki University in Bydgoszcz and Faculty Coordinator for International Cooperation. She has been involved as a team member in the research project on e-voting, financed by National Science Centre (Poland). She researches political and electoral systems, civic participation, public opinion, and voting behavior. She is an author of many publications on those topics, chiefly articles in Polish and international journals and chapters of monographs dedicated to e-voting and democracy. ORCID ID: 0000-0003-2342-3682 e-mail: izabela.kapsa@ukw.edu.pl

Agnieszka Kasińska-Metryka

professor of social sciences. A researcher specializing in political leadership, women's participation in politics, marketing and social communication. Author of numerous books on political problems in contemporary Spain. A member of IPSA (she was a member of the Executive Committee) and CEPSA. ORCID ID: 0000-0002-9172-4228 email: agnieszkakm@wp.pl

Joanna Kielin-Maziarz

an Associate Professor at the Department of Constitutional Law, Collegium of Law, Akademia Leona Koźmińskiego. Since 2009, she has been a member of the Polish Society of Constitutional Law and The International Association of Constitutional Law. She is the author of dozens of scientific publications, in Polish, English and French, including monographs, scientific articles, chapters in monographs, reviews, and co-editor of monographs. ORCID ID: 0000-0003-1728-3361 e-mail: jkielin@kozminski.edu.pl

Jakub Klepański

PhD student at the Institute of Political Science, University of Warmia and Mazury in Olsztyn. His research interests focus mainly on political leadership and parliamentary discourse. He also conducts research on the parliamentary activity of party leaders. ORCID ID: 0000-0002-3470-7288 jakub.klepanski@gmail.com

Oliwia Kowalik

political scientist, currently a PhD student at the Department of Social and Economic Policy at the Faculty of Political Science and Journalism at the Adam Mickiewicz University, Poznań. Her dissertation will address issues related to the development of electronic democracy in Estonia. Research interests: new technologies in democratic systems with particular emphasis on electoral processes (e-voting) and political participation. ORCID ID: 0000-0001-5753-2022 e-mail: oliwia.kuban@amu.edu.pl

Krzysztof Koźbiał

associated Professor, Director of the Institute of European Studies at the Jagiellonian University in Kraków. Research interests in political systems of European states, European micro-states (domestic and foreign policies) and the process of European integration. ORCID ID: 0000-0001-6124-5341 e-mail: krzysztof.kozbial@uj.edu.pl

Aleksandra Kuczyńska-Zonik

PhD, a research assistant at the John Paul II Catholic University of Lublin, Poland; Head of the Department of the Baltics at the Institute of Central Europe. She holds She is a Political Scientist and Archaeologist. She is a laureate of the "Mobility Plus" Program, over the period 2016–2017 she conducted research at Vilnius University, Lithuania, regarding Russian minorities in the Baltic States. Her recent research focuses on politics and security in East-Central Europe and the post-Soviet space, the Baltic states, Russian diaspora, and Soviet heritage. ORCID ID: 0000-0002-5672-9613 e-mail: kuczynska.a@gmail.com

Natalia Kusa

PhD at the Faculty of Political Sciences and Journalism at the University of Adam Mickiewicz University in Poznań. Her research interests focus on the political system of the Russian Federation, opposition activity in Russia, political activity of the society, non-standard forms of protest. ORCID ID: 0000-0001-8036-5322 e-mail: natalia.kusa@amu.edu.pl

Elżbieta Lesiewicz

associate professor of Adam Mickiewicz University in Poznań, historian of modern history and political scientist. Head of the Department of Recent Political History at the Faculty of Political Science, Adam Mickiewicz University (AMU). She specializes in research on European integration and equality policy. Her research interests also focus on women participation in public space, analysis of inter-generational dialogue, Polish-Czech relations, and history of the Wielkopolska Region. Coordinator of the Research Group on Diversity, Equality and (Re)Integration at the Faculty of Political Science and Journalism, AMU. ORCID ID: 0000-0002-6209-3455 email: elzbieta.lesiewicz@amu.edu.pl

Natasza Lubik-Reczek

PhD, assistant professor at the Department of Political Systems, Faculty of Political Science and Journalism, Adam Mickiewicz University in Poznań. In her research she focuses on innovative methods of citizen attitude formation. Her research interests also focus on the role of women in public space, political systems (with special focus on post-Yugoslav countries), and direct democracy. Member of the Polish Political Science Association, Polish Association for

European Studies and the Centre for European Research and Education.
ORCID ID: 0000-0003-4294-5064 e-mail: natasza.lubik@amu.edu.pl

Agnieszka Łukasik-Turecka
associate professor, political scientist and media expert, director of the Institute of Political Sciences and Public Administration of the John Paul II
Catholic University of Lublin. The area of her scientific and research interests
covers the broadly understood sphere of political communication. Author,
coauthor, and editor of 10 monographs and about 50 articles. Member of the
Polish Society of Social Communication and the Polish Society of Political
Sciences. Vice-chair of the Council of the Interdisciplinary Research Center of
the University of Warsaw "Identity-Dialog-Security." Editor-in-chief of the journal *Studies and Analyses of Political Science*. ORCID ID: 0000-0003-3657-9862
e-mail: agnieszka.lukasik-turecka@kul.pl

Martinas Malużinas
PhD, political scientist, assistant professor. His main research areas focus on
the evolution of political systems (especially Lithuanian political system), elections, alternative voting methods (e-voting) and contemporary political history. Author of many articles and chapters on Baltic states, quality of democracy.
ORCID ID: 0000-0002-2772-9534 e-mail: martiasmaluzinas@gmail.com

Paweł Malendowicz
Professor at the Kazimierz Wielki University (Bydgoszcz, Poland). Head of
the Department of Political Thought and Social Movements at the Faculty
of Political Science and Administration. Head of the Department of Political
Thought and Social Movements at the Faculty of Political Science and Administration. The main areas of his research interests: anarchism in Europe,
the hard left and the far right in Poland and in the world, the concepts of
the vision of future in the policy of political groups, Polish Americans in the
United States. ORCID ID: 0000-0003-2325-9966 e-mail: p.malendowicz@
ukw.edu.pl

Radosław Marzęcki
political scientist and sociologist; associate professor at the Pedagogical University of Kraków. From 2017 to 2020, he was leading a project funded by the
Polish National Science Centre: „First Free Generations: The Country, Patriotism, Democracy in the Context of the Social Awareness of Youth (Universi-
ty-Level Students) in Poland and Ukraine – Comparative Analysis". He is the
author of many publications (monographs and scientific articles) devoted
to youth citizenship and political culture. ORCID ID: 0000-0002-2915-8878
e-mail: radoslaw.marzecki@up.krakow.pl

Magdalena Musiał-Karg

Professor of Political Sciences, works at the Department of Political Systems, Faculty of Political Science and Journalism, Adam Mickiewicz University in Poznań, Poland. Her main research interests focus on direct democracy and the impact of modern technologies (ICT) on democratic systems, mainly on the electoral process (e-voting). She is the author of numerous publications devoted to electronic participation, alternative voting methods, and direct democracy. She is the Vice-Dean for Research and Scientific Cooperation at the Faculty of Political Science and Journalism, Adam Mickiewicz University in Poznań, and a former Vice-Dean for Research and Development (2016–2020). She is also the Vice-President of the Polish Political Science Association, member of the Political Sciences Committee of the Polish Academy of Sciences (2020–2023), and the President of the Center for European Research and Education. ORCID ID: 0000-0002-6089-1389 e-mail: magdalena.musial-karg@amu.edu.pl

Adam Pluszczyk

an assistant professor at the University of Silesia in Katowice. His research interests focus on sociolinguistics and pragmatics: linguistic variation, regional and social dialects, prestigious and stigmatized dialects and varieties (standard and non-standard varieties of English), speech styles, registers, genres, hedging devices / tropes, taboo language, gender differences, interruption, overlapping speech, communication and small talk; humour, theories of humour, verbal humour / linguistic humour studies, politeness theories. ORCID ID: 0000-0002-2940-9657 email: adam.pluszczyk@us.edu.pl

Agata Pyrzyńska

PhD., assistant professor at the Faculty of Law and Administration of the University of Szczecin. Her main research areas focus on electoral law, constitutional law, protection of human rights, administrative law. A special attention she pays to to the problems of Polish electoral law, including the functioning of the election administration, the legal foundations of the organization of the electoral process and the problems of making electoral laws. ORCID ID: 0000-0002-4573-4310 e-mail: agata.pyrzynska@usz.edu.pl

Marcin Rachwał

an associate professor at Adam Mickiewicz University Poznań, the Faculty of Political Science and Journalism. His research interests focus on such issues as democracy, political elites, election law, and civic society. His interests also involve around political transformation in Poland and Central and Eastern Europe. Editor for collective publications, author of dozens of academic articles, and two monographs. ORCID ID: 0000-0003-2949-1328 e-mail: marcin.rachwal@amu.edu.pl

Joanna Rak
an associate professor at the Faculty of Political Science and Journalism
of Adam Mickiewicz University, Poznań, Poland. In 2016–2020, she was a
visiting researcher at CEU San Pablo University in Madrid and Charles III
University of Madrid. She is the principal investigator of the research projects
"The Culture of Political Violence Dynamics of Anti-austerity Movements in
Europe" and "Contentious Politics and Neo-Militant Democracy" financed
by the National Science Centre, Poland. The laureate of the Barbara Skarga
Scholarship and START Scholarship by the Foundation for Polish Science.
ORCID ID: 0000-0002-0505-3684 e-mail: joanna.rak@amu.edu.pl

Kamila Sierzputowska
Phd., assistant professor at the Department of Security Policy, Faculty of Political Sciences and Administration Kazimierz Wielki University, Bydgoszcz. Her
main research interests focus on n: international relations. Research interests:
international relations, the Republic of Estonia, transatlantic security, NATO,
soft power. ORCID ID: 0000-0002-3974-8118 e-mail: kamila.sierzputowska@
ukw.edu.pl

Krzysztof Skotnicki
Professor, Head of the Department of Constitutional Law, Faculty of Law
and Administration, University of Lodz. Department of Constitutional and
Comparative Law, Faculty of Law and Economics, Jan Dlugosz University in
Czestochowa. ORCID ID: 0000-0002-9428-2103 e-mail: k.skotnicki@ujd.edu.pl

Jacek Wojnicki
Professor at the Faculty of Political Science and International Studies of the
University of Warsaw. His research interests focus on the political systems of
Central European and Balkan countries. ORICD ID: 0000-0002-4289-989X
e-mail: jacekwojnicki@uw.edu.pl

Piotr Walewicz
PhD, an assistant professor in the Department of International Relations
at the Faculty of Political Science and Administration at Kazimierz Wielki
University in Bydgoszcz. His research interests revolve around political theory,
including theory of International Relations, as well as the interrelations between the global ecological crisis, global political economy and political and
scientific discourses. ORCID ID: 0000-0001-6878-4380 e-mail: piotr.walewicz@
ukw.edu.pl

Waldemar Wojtasik
Professor at the University of Silesia in Katowice. His research focuses on elections, political parties, and party systems. His work has appeared in the *Journal for the Study of Religions and Ideologies,* the *Journal of Comparative Politics* and *East European Politics and Society: and Culture* ORCID ID: 0000-0001-9111-1723 email: waldemar.wojtasik@us.edu.pl

Elections in Times of a Pandemic: An Introduction

Magdalena Musiał-Karg and Izabela Kapsa

The COVID-19 pandemic has unprecedentedly impacted human lives, societies and states. It has also demonstrated that unexpected and unpredictable situations can hamper the organisation of general elections. In 2020 and 2021, most countries faced the challenge of organising local or national elections. Some were well prepared, and some were looking for accurate solutions. Most countries and territories have decided to hold national or subnational elections despite concerns related to COVID-19. However, some have decided to postpone elections and referendums. Furthermore, many have held initially postponed elections due to the pandemic. Analysing the election landscape across the world, the editors of this book are convinced that the pandemic has provided a pretext and, at the same time, an extremely effective stimulus for research on the functioning of states and state institutions during emergencies. It stimulated much broader and more detailed analyses of different aspects of the subject. Aiming to provide the reader with a publication in which he will find a comprehensive analysis of the issue, they invited to publish many authors who looked at the elections during the pandemic from different perspectives.

This book broadly analyses elections from theoretical and empirical perspectives. Next to the theoretical background, which refers to researching elections and using different theoretical perspectives to analyse them, it also presents an empirical analysis. The authors of the particular chapters have made case studies of the elections conducted in the European countries during the COVID-19 pandemic. Due to the limitations of the monograph, the analysis includes selected European countries where the solutions adopted were diverse and allowed for an overview of electoral solutions that could be used during the pandemic. Among them we have analysed established and young democracies, authoritarian countries as well as Western, Eastern and Southeast European countries. All of the analysed cases held elections in the first stages of the pandemic, but with the use of different solutions and different voting methods. As the pandemic progressed, the measures were relaxed and the organization of the elections could proceed without interruption. Italy, Lithuania and Serbia held elections in 2020; Liechtenstein, Latvia and the Czech Republic – electoral process ongoing in 2020 and 2021; and Germany, Bulgaria, Russia and Estonia – in 2021. The editors decided to pay special attention to the Polish example. In Poland, one of the countries where, despite the pandemic and the peak in cases, the electoral process initially planned for the end of April, the presidential elections scheduled for 10 May 2020 were not postponed. Moreover, it was decided to hold elections despite the lack of alternative election procedures. New solutions were introduced using special legal acts after announcing a new election date, which significantly impacted their course and evaluation.

The authors of the individual chapters adopted various research methods used in social sciences. In the theoretical part, a literature review was carried our as well as definition and conceptualization of state of emergency, elections in extraordinary situations and the concept of resilience of electoral systems were introduced. In this part the authors also used institutional and legal analysis to study alternative voting procedures and reports of OSCE missions monitoring elections in EU states in 2020–2021; comparative analysis (for neo- and quasi-militant democracy examples as well as populism patterns); media (also electronic, social media) and content analysis in the context of disinformation, populism and anarchism (here also content of treaties, program documents, propaganda); participant observation of the anarchist movement and case studies in the context of neo- and quasi-militant democracy. In this part the technique of reflexive thematic analysis served also to explore and interpret patterned meaning across the electoral laws and their drafts issued in the period from the introduction of lockdowns in the EU member states in March 2020 to the end of 2021. It is worth to add that the time frame applied for the first part of the book corresponds with the examples analyzed in the next part.

In the empirical part of the book, the main research method is a case study supported by wide range of other methods: an institutional-legal analysis of the election law and other specific legislation; a system analysis and decision-making method to illustrate the decision-making process related to elections; media content analysis with respect to campaigns, elections and implemented electoral solutions; comparative analysis of similarities and differences of political parties and their candidates in elections; and qualitative analysis of statistical data with respect to the number of COVID-19 cases, electoral participation and public opinion (secondary data or own research for the case of Poland).

The book is divided into three parts. In the first one, the authors present theoretical background for researching elections in extraordinary situations, introduce the concept of resilience into the study of electoral systems within political science and analyse the elections in the crisis as a political tool and their influence on the sovereignty of the political nations. They also make a theoretical analysis dedicated to radical criticism of the democratic state and general elections in anarchist political thought and populist governance, as

well as taking up the topic of disinformation and its role in the electoral process. Finally, the topic of alternative voting procedures and the right to free and
universal elections is also taken up here.

The elections were one of the crucial topics of post-2020 research. Their
organisation and feasibility in a situation where in-person voting was hampered due to social contact restrictions indicate different research perspectives. However, they also show the most frequently raised issues and scientific
considerations. That is why the authors provide an overview of issues related
to the state of research on elections during emergencies in the first chapter. An
overview of the main terms (states/emergency situations, elections/referenda
and alternative voting methods introduced to enhance the implementation of
universal suffrage), various perspectives, and challenges for holding elections
during emergencies show that there are many unknown factors about extraordinary situations and government response to them. Based on this review,
the next chapter calls for integrating resilience research into political studies,
including the study of electoral systems. The author introduces the concept of
resilience, gives some theoretical and historical background and shows why
and how it is helpful in electoral studies. He provides an intellectual inspiration for looking at electoral systems from a different perspective than the traditional one – now expanding the research on environmental challenges and
crises.

The further chapter, as a continuation of the analysis of elections in crisis,
presents the use of electoral laws in four central-east European countries as
a political tool and its influence on the sovereignty of the political nations.
Embedding in the theory of neo- and quasi-militant democracy, the authors,
explain to what extent the electoral laws adopted or proposed for adoption
during the COVID-19 pandemic reduced the scope of the sovereignty of the
political nations. In this part, there are also theoretical analyses dedicated to
radical criticism of the democratic state and general elections in anarchist
political thought, as well as the analysis of the mechanisms of populist governance and the cause-and-effect relationships between the pandemic and
populism in the context of elections. The authors also take up the topic of disinformation, considering it as one of several factors in the instrumentalisation
of the electoral process. Finally, at the end of this part of the book, there are
two chapters devoted the electoral law. The first one examines the nature and
significance of alternative voting procedures while trying to satisfy the electoral principle of universality during a pandemic. The second is an analysis of
the procedure and practice of holding elections in the exceptional situation
of the COVID-19 pandemic in a number of European countries in the context of
international standards of the right to participate in free elections (basing on

the reports of OSCE missions monitoring elections in European Union states
in 2020–2021) which is at the same time an introduction to the next part of the
monograph.

The second part of the book presents the empirical analysis of the elections
conducted during a pandemic in a few European countries. It opens with the
chapter that refers to the first infected country in Europe, presenting the electoral situation in Italy in the context of the constitutional referendum. The
author proves that the introduction of increased security measures impacted
the preparation of the elections, the campaign, the voting process itself, turnout and the final result. A fascinating case is the Lithuanian parliamentary
election of 2020, where electoral regulations adopted during the pandemic,
including the introduction of additional forms of voting, the specific nature
of the election campaign during the crisis, and the election process itself set
this country as a model in the ODIHR report that formulated many recommendations concerning various stages of the electoral cycle so as to enhance the
conduct of elections in Lithuania further and to support efforts to bring them
fully in line with OSCE commitments and other international obligations and
standards for democratic elections. On the other hand, a different solution was
chosen in Serbia, where the election process was suspended, and the elections
were postponed to later months in 2020.

Few European countries were to organise elections in 2020 and 2021, facing a completely different pandemic stage, including vaccination availability.
An example is Liechtenstein, where the election date was postponed during
the referendum vote in 2020. During the referendum and the parliamentary
elections in February 2021, an alternative voting technique was applied in the
form of postal voting, causing that the solutions adopted were both valuable
and effective, especially with regard to extreme situations such as the pandemic. Also, Latvian and Estonian local as well as German state elections that
were not organised in a state of emergency were affected by the pandemic and
took place under several restrictions. The pandemic had an essential impact
on elections held in the Czech Republic in 2020 and 2021, resulting in the
adoption of legal regulations defining new methods, precautions and voting
techniques under the sanitary regime, as well as issues raised by the political parties during the election campaign, and election results. As a result, the
Czech government decided to hold elections during the pandemic and introduced stricter hygiene measures and alternative voting methods for citizens in
quarantine.

Regarding elections held in 2021, in this book, the authors analyse four
countries: Germany, Bulgaria, Russia and Estonia. The state and federal elections held in Germany in 2021 met the highest democratic standards, proving

that it is possible even in such a difficult situation as the COVID-19 pandemic. Additionally, thanks to the popularity of postal voting and the success of the social campaign that explained the advantages of choosing this form of voting, there was an increase in voter turnout in elections to Landtag of Mecklenburg-Vorpommern as well as Bundestag. A completely different situation occurred in Bulgaria, where only the third parliamentary election held within eight months led to the formation of a stable government coalition. However, the pandemic significantly impeded the conduct of the parliamentary elections. Also, the parliamentary elections in Russia were exceptional. Not least because of the pandemic that affected the procedures and way of holding elections. The uniqueness of this election was also due to, inter alia, the lack of participation of the opposition, the difficult economic situation in Russia, problems in international politics, and low public support for the rulers. The last analysed in this part case concerns the potential impact of an emergency/pandemic situation on the elections that took place in October 2021 in Estonia. Although internet voting was used during the local elections held in autumn, it can undoubtedly be considered a set of solutions minimising the risks. Given that now, Estonian citizens have access to the widest range of alternative voting methods, the 2021 local elections can be described as among the safest in the world.

The authors' special attention is dedicated to the Polish case where despite the pandemic conditions, the government was determined to organise the elections, which encountered some legal, organisational and political difficulties and reactions of the international organisations. The 2020 presidential elections in Poland were to be held during the so-called peak of the first wave of the COVID-19 pandemic. Despite the coincidence of both dates, it was finally decided to hold presidential elections on 10 May 2020, based on specific legal provisions - in the form of all-postal voting. As it soon turned out, both Poland's minimal experience in using this alternative voting method and the legal and time constraints meant that the actions taken by the ruling body were ineffective, and it was impossible to hold elections within this timeframe in a pandemic. As a result, adopting a special law proved to be the case, which laid down specific rules for holding these elections at a new date. According to them, Poles in the country voted in person at polling stations under a sanitary regime (except for high-incidence constituencies), and voters voting outside the country - voted by post.

This part of the book starts with the procedural and legal review of the electoral law measures prescribed for the event of extraordinary situations, as well as the analysis of available voting methods in Poland. It seems crucial to understand the difficulties in organising the electoral process in Poland during the COVID-19 pandemic. As the most important limitation was the lack (a small

number) of alternative voting methods, the deep analysis of the electoral law
and its amendments during the pandemic is conducted in the next few chapters. It is concentrated on a few aspects. The first one concerns the guarantees
of the principle of universal voting and how these guarantees were affected
by the COVID-19 pandemic. The authors indicated which of the experiences
regarding solutions in the case of voting guarantees in the era of a pandemic
should be maintained and which should be intensified works, particularly on
electronic voting. The second evaluates which legislative solutions caused difficulties in the pandemic-related circumstances. It also determines whether
the experience from electoral practice stands a chance to translate into specific actions of the Polish legislator to ensure fair and democratic elections
should similar circumstances occur in the future. The last perspective consid-
ers the possibility of holding elections, and it indicates that the responsibility
of public authorities is a necessity to ensure realistic (but also safe) conditions
for making decisions by the sovereign.

Expanding the analysis of the 2020 presidential elections in Poland to
include political context, five further chapters refer to postal voting abroad,
participation of young voters in the elections, political communication during
the campaign and the position of the political parties and political leaders
on these particular elections. The first chapter contains an analysis of postal
voting in the presidential elections in Poland in 2020 from the perspective of
voters voting from abroad and the experience of postal voting in the country
so far. The next chapter discusses the political attitudes of young Poles who,
for almost three decades after 1989, were described as apathetic, alienated or
passive. And that must be revised, as the COVID-19 pandemic influenced the
politicisation of the young generation, changing their adaptation strategy and
attitude towards political elites: from conformism or withdrawal to rebellion
or innovation. In further analysis, the author presents one of the most characteristic features of the 2020 presidential election campaign in the Republic of
Poland – the emergence of a new type of political communication actor, i.e.,
medical experts. This chapter contains an analysis of the results of research,
the purpose of which was to show whether, and if so, how, the medical experts
present in the media in connection with the COVID-19 pandemic influenced
the content of the political messages of the main candidates for the presidency
of the Republic of Poland during the 2020 elections. At the end of this part, two
chapters are dedicated to the position of the political parties and political leaders in the 2020 presidential elections. One analyses the positions and actions
taken by the Law and Justice (PiS), the largest and most important party in
the ruling coalition, and the Civic Platform of the Republic of Poland (PO RP),
which is the largest and most important opposition group in Poland, in view

of holding elections for the office of the President of the Republic of Poland during the COVID-19 pandemic in 2020. Another one analyses Polish political leaders' views on holding the 2020 presidential election during the pandemic and the restrictions related to it.

The editors of this book believe that such a broad research perspective provides the readers with multifaceted knowledge about the elections during a pandemic. Furthermore, the research brings us closer to the specific solutions adopted in individual countries, allowing for conclusions to be drawn as to how to organise and not to organise elections in an extraordinary time.

PART 1

Elections in Extraordinary Situations

Dilemmas and Challenges

∵

CHAPTER 1

Research into Elections in Extraordinary Situations

Magdalena Musiał-Karg and Izabela Kapsa

1.1   Introduction

The COVID-19 pandemic has provided a pretext and, at the same time, an extremely effective stimulus for research on the functioning of states and state institutions during emergencies. Until 2020, a number of valuable publications had been produced on the subject of running elections under different emergencies, but the territorial scope and duration of the SARS-CoV-2 pandemic stimulated much broader and more detailed analyses of different aspects of the subject. One of the important topics of post-2020 research was elections, their organisation, and their feasibility in a situation where voting in-person was hampered due to social contact restrictions. Indeed, in many countries, due to the spread of the virus and the consequent threat to the life and health of citizens, social distancing and restrictions on access to public places have been introduced. Due to the importance of the subject, it seems extremely useful to outline the current state of research in the area. It does not only allow to indicate different research perspectives, but also indicate the most frequently issues raised and scientific considerations.

This chapter provides an overview of issues related to the state of research on elections during emergencies. An overview of the main terms, various perspectives, and challenges for holding elections during emergencies shows that there are many unknown factors pertaining to extraordinary situations and government response to them. There are clearly no single or simple solutions to guarantee credibility, integrity, and safety of elections, so the analysis of research contexts provides an excellent toolkit for further exploration of the topic.

1.2   Theoretical Background

As the main research problem discussed in the chapter focuses on answering the question of how to run elections under extraordinary circumstances, there is a need to define the most important terms used. It seems that the following themes are most frequently addressed in research on elections under extraordinary circumstances: states/emergency situations, elections/referenda (ensuring democratic standards and proper organisation), and alternative voting methods introduced to enhance the implementation of universal suffrage.

1.3   State of Emergency/Extraordinary Situations

The starting point for the analysis is the *state of emergency*. The most universal explanation of the term is that the state of emergency occurs in a situation of exceptional hazard to a state, resolution of which requires measures that are not permitted in regular circumstances, to ensure safety and protect citizens. In order to remove existing threats, the state has to use measures that normally would not be acceptable in a democratic society, or sometimes even contradict the basic principles of democracy itself (Prokop, 2005, p. 9). The state of emergency is imposed by a government decision in response to an emergency situation that poses a fundamental threat to the country and its citizens. Governmental decisions "may suspend certain normal functions of the government, request citizens to alter their normal behaviour, or authorise government agencies to implement crisis management plans, as well as to limit or suspend civil liberties and human rights" (DCAF, 2005). When imposing the state of emergency, state governments may also resort to such measures as the concentration of power in the executive branch, change of the structure and operation principles of state bodies, as well as change of the law-making system. The state of emergency translates into an internal order of the state in which part of binding constitutional regulations are suspended and replaced (for specified period) by extraordinary regulations. The government can announce the introduction of the state during a natural disaster, armed conflict, civil unrest, or health risk, such as pandemic/epidemic or other threat to biosecurity.

   According to the basic laws in most democratic countries, the state of emergency may be declared as a consequence of events defined as disastrous, i.e. sudden and unexpected events with negative impact, including material losses and severe injuries or multiple deaths. Disasters are divided into anthropogenic (of human origin) and non-anthropogenic (caused by natural forces, including natural disasters, calamities, and natural catastrophes). Anthropogenic catastrophes are primarily transport-related events (railways, roads, air and water transport). They also include industrial accidents, chemical disasters, fires, and building disasters. The literature refers to *technological accidents*, which are defined as sudden events with tragic consequences in which people suffer, die or which cause large material and ecological losses. Other extraordinary events, such as acts of terror, acts of war, or humanitarian disasters, should also be included here.

Then, non-anthropogenic catastrophes include *natural disasters* which occur as a result of natural forces and are the manifestation of natural processes in the atmosphere or inside the Earth. The following events should be mentioned: floods, droughts, extensive fires, earthquakes, volcanic eruptions, tsunamis, hurricanes, tornadoes, heavy snowfalls and snow avalanches, extreme heat or frost, especially in the long term, landslides and space disasters, e.g. meteorite fall, meteor explosion, and explosion of a close supernova. A natural disaster may lead to a calamity (Rokitowska, 2018, pp. 361–365).

The basic laws in many states provide for emergency situations in which routine governance is no longer possible. Thus, governments have the possibility to introduce the state of emergency. Regulations pertaining to the state of emergency vary as they ramp up restrictions and determine ways in which these and the state of emergency can be lifted. Since the state of emergency may restrict rights of individuals (restrictions are introduced temporarily), rules are defined in constitutions to prevent any abuse of power by the government devoid of social control (Grzybowska-Walecka & Wojtas-Jarentowska, 2020, p. 2). An interesting comparison related to emergency powers found in constitutions of European states has been offered by Anna Khakee. The author has placed constitutions of 28 states on a three-level scale: little, medium, and extensive. Details are presented in Table 1.1.

Constitutions of many Western European countries do not explicitly provide for any state of emergency at all, but rather contain references - often only *en passant* - to 'extraordinary circumstances', 'international crisis', 'particularly urgent situations' or 'times of war' (Khakee, 2009, p. 11). It is noteworthy that

TABLE 1.1   Codification of emergencies in European constitutions

Little or minimal degree	Austria, Belgium, Cyprus, Czech Republic, Denmark, Finland, Luxembourg, Norway, Switzerland
Medium degree	Bulgaria, Estonia, France, Ireland, Italy, Latvia, Lithuania, Malta, the Netherlands, Romania, Slovakia, Slovenia, Sweden
Extensive degree	Germany, Greece, Hungary, Poland, Portugal, Spain

SOURCE: KHAKEE, A. (2009). *SECURING DEMOCRACY? A COMPARATIVE ANALYSIS OF EMERGENCY POWERS IN EUROPE*, GENEVA CENTER FOR DEMOCRATIC CONTROL OF ARMED FORCES (DCAF), POLICY PAPER, NO. 30; P. 11. HTTPS://WWW.FILES.ETHZ.CH /ISN/99550/PP30_ANNA_KHAKEE_EMERGENCY_POWERS.PDF

more than half of the 28 countries analysed by Khakee regulate at least two forms of states of exceptions, usually making a distinction between situations of war (codified by martial law or 'state of war') on the one hand, and other types of emergencies on the other hand (Khakee, 2009, p. 11). In addition, it should be noted that former states under the influence of the USSR and those that have experienced authoritarian rule contain more detailed regulations in their constitutions[1].

In conclusion, we should refer to the opinions of Katarzyna Walecka and Kinga Wojtas who point out that some countries (e.g. Switzerland, Norway) have largely adopted the concept of extraordinary powers that are not regulated by constitutions, while other countries (e.g. Germany and Spain) precisely regulate and limit extraordinary powers (Grzybowska-Walecka & Wojtas-Jarentowska, 2020, p. 3).

Regulations on states of emergencyincluded in constitutions, as well as those included in special laws, are designed to safeguard democratic system and society against uncontrolled actions of a suddenly empowered executive branch (Grzybowska-Walecka & Wojtas-Jarentowska, 2020, pp. 7–8; Khakee, 2009, pp. 11–14).

1.4   Elections in Emergency Situations

General elections are undoubtedly the most important procedure in modern democracies, as the possibility to vote in an election is one of the fundamental citizen rights (Cześnik, 2003, pp. 43–44). Moreover, various issues related to the election procedure are frequently discussed in research into emergency situations or states.

Since the planning of elections usually requires extensive person-to-person contact and multidimensional preparations, organising popular votes during a crisis or an extraordinary situation has become a challenge. In many countries worldwide, various unexpected, extraordinary circumstances exposed the limits of legal and institutional solutions in the case of elections held in extraordinary situations when public health is at stake.

The debate about elections in extraordinary conditions that require special measures, the following terms are most often used: "election in a state of emergencies", "election in emergencies", "election under extraordinary state",

---

1 The Czech Republic and Estonia have not included provisions on states of emergency in their constitutions. In the Czech Republic, the legal order was supplemented by a constitutional law in 1997, and in Estonia by a law on emergency in 2017.

"election in extraordinary situations", or "emergency election". They are used to name elections (popular votes) that are held under extraordinary or exceptional conditions which are usually least expected by the government. In constitutions (and other legislation), these situations are most often referred to as a 'state of emergency'.

The introduction of the state of emergency undoubtedly affects the organisation of elections. One of the key features of democracy and the implementation of the popular sovereignty is the fact that people in power are chosen through periodic elections. This rule is not only a standard of intra-state arrangements, but it is also derived from international law, e.g. the Universal Declaration of Human Rights (UDHR). The latter reads: "The will of the people shall be the basis of the authority of government; this will shall be expressed in periodic and genuine elections which shall be by universal and equal suffrage and shall be held by secret vote or by equivalent free voting procedures" (Article 21 (3)).

Constitutions of many countries regulate the period during which national elections may be held following the end of a state of emergency. For example, in Poland and Lithuania, this period is 3 months, in Slovenia and Germany, 6 months (9 months for presidential elections), while in Greece, Hungary and Romania elections can be held immediately after the end of a state of emergency. Sweden has an interesting solution, namely if the parliament decides by a simple majority, elections may be held during the state of emergency. Elections there may be postponed for a maximum period of one year if such a decision is supported by ¾ majority in the parliament (Grzybowska-Walecka & Wojtas-Jarentowska, 2020, p. 12).

It should be stressed that the above-mentioned regulations aim to ensure the integrity of the electoral process and the possibility for those eligible to have a free, secret, equal, and universal vote. Countries where elections are held during states of emergency may need to determine when to hold the vote, what measures have to be put in place to guarantee freedom and fairness of the electoral processes, and how to mitigate the potential impact of election-related tensions that may be exacerbated by circumstances of the extraordinary situations and restrictions associated with them.

It is worth emphasising that when analysing states of emergency and elections or referenda, the introduction of alternative voting methods seems to be very relevant. The sovereignty of the nation is realised through various forms of collective decision-making while using representative democracy and direct democracy tools, such as elections and referenda. It should be noted that it has been considered to introduce various alternative ways of participation in elections and referendums during unforeseen crises and difficulties in conducting elections through traditional voting at polling stations. Such measures are designed to fulfil the principle of sovereignty of the nation and guarantee universal suffrage (Kapsa & Musiał-Karg, 2020, pp. 55–56).

It should be noted that the terms "alternative voting procedures" or "alternative voting methods" are understood as additional techniques of voting (in their physical sense) in elections and referenda. These additional techniques are treated as completely separate (and complementary) to the basic and traditional voting procedure, i.e. paper ballot at the polling station (Czaplicki, 2007, pp. 30–31).

The mechanisms that guarantee more complete fulfilment of the universal suffrage (i.e. people who, for various reasons, could not vote at a polling station enjoy possibility to participate in elections) (Korycki, 2017, p. 88) include, for example, voting by proxy, mobile ballot box, postal voting, and electronic voting (Kapsa & Musiał-Karg, 2020, pp. 55–80). It should be noted that the debate on the implementation of additional voting techniques in elections and referenda is dominated by views that justify the introduction of postal voting as a safe method. Recently, experience of some countries, mainly Estonia, also encourage other countries to consider the implementation of Internet voting as a convenient and safe election procedure. It should be noted that in some emergency situations the use of alternative voting techniques may be sufficient to hold democratic elections that are safe for voters and election committees.

1.5   Research on Elections in Emergency Situations

When analysing states of emergency, one of major issues to be solved is general election. It applies to parliamentary, presidential and local elections, as well as national and local referenda. These issues are discussed not only in terms of maintaining the continuity of power, but also in the context of respecting democratic principles, organisation of voting under emergency conditions, and guaranty of security and safety of voters and other people involved in the conduct of general elections. The wide range of topics raised by researchers allows us to state that research into elections held in emergency states or situations is interdisciplinary as it combines themes typical not only of various disciplines but also fields of science. Legal studies discuss legitimacy of the introduction of the state of emergency (Grogan, 2020; Clement, Alen, 1992), legal regulations on the organisation of elections in the state of emergency (Morley, 2018), and respect for electoral rules (Roy). Representatives of political science and administration analyse elections, among others, in terms of the political impact of calamities and natural disasters on the electoral behaviour during emergency elections (Campante, Depetris-Chauvin & Durante, 2020;

Vázquez-Carrero, Vázquez-Carrero, García, Jiménez, 2020). It is impossible to list all research contexts that deal with states of emergency, democracy, and elections. However, research in these areas has been carried out by historians, sociologists, psychologists, representatives of medicine and biology, as well as economists and specialists in management science, security, and social communication and media.

Considering analyses focusing on elections in emergency situations, it should be noted that we can divide them according to several criteria, which are briefly described in Table 1.2.

Elections in emergency situations can be considered while taking into account several criteria that allow to distinguish directions and perspectives of research in this area. Reasons to introduce the state of emergency divide underlying events into unexpected and unpredictable (e.g. armed conflicts, wars, natural disasters, catastrophes, technological disasters, epidemics, etc.). The criterion of a place distinguishes continents, countries, regions, territories where the event occurred and elections were held (or planned to be held). Moreover, some researchers focus their considerations on the election date, while others on alternative voting methods used in emergency elections. The analysis of literature on elections held during emergencies also reveals other perspectives adopted by researchers. They analyse the issue while taking into account electoral law reform, the context of electoral integrity or particular stages of the electoral cycle, as well as case studies and many more. Such a wide range of research perspectives allows us to conclude that the issue of elections held in emergency situations is an extremely important, frequently discussed, and multidimensional in terms of its scientific exploration.

1.6   Research on Elections during COVID-19

Governments around the world strive to ensure integrity, credibility, and security of elections held in crisis situations. Compared to other emergencies, the COVID-19 pandemic is a much larger phenomenon and a historic health crisis, both in terms of its territorial and temporal extent. For example, the extent of Ebola epidemics, earthquakes, hurricanes, and floods has covered smaller territories and affected a limited number of countries (or regions), and their duration was much shorter.

The search for an answer to the question about the role of elections is an important part of research into democracy in contemporary states. It is related to a common belief that holding regular elections is an essential part of democratic practices (R.A. Dahl, 1971; A. Przeworski, 1999). During the COVID-19

TABLE 1.2   Contexts for elections in the state of emergency according to different criteria

Criterion	Context for considering elections in a state of emergency
Reason for the state of emergency	1. Wars, armed conflicts 2. Extraordinary events (e.g. terrorist attack) 3. Natural catastrophes (e.g. tsunami, flood, tornado, earthquake) 4. Technological disasters 5. Epidemics/pandemics (Ebola, COVID-19, bird flu, etc.)
Location	1. Continents – Africa (Ebola, civil war) – Asia (tsunamis, earthquakes) – North America (hurricanes) – South America (floods) – Europe (floods, pandemic) – Australia (fires) 2. Regions – (Europe, Caribbean, „famine virus" in African countries 3. States (Indonesia, Haiti, Guinea, Sierra Leone, Rwanda, Liberia, DRC, USA, Cuba, Poland, Lithuania, France, Sweden, Germany, etc.) 4. Federal states, state regions, municipalities (Geneva, Bavaria, etc.)
Date of elections	1. Elections held as scheduled 2. Elections postponed
Voting procedure	1. Existing „standard" solutions 2. New, additional solutions introduced due to the emergency situation (special voting places, e.g. Lithuania, postal voting for specific groups of voters) 3. Completely new solutions (all-postal voting; e-voting, etc.)
Other approaches	1. Justification to postpone 2. Electoral reforms 3. Introduction of AVM 4. Election campaign 5. Electoral integrity 6. Stages of the electoral cycle 7. Role of state institutions and Election Administration Bodies (EAB) 8. Case studies

SOURCE: OWN STUDIES

pandemic, this has become even more evident, and the need to ensure election integrity, credibility, and safety during emergencies (extraordinary situations) is one of key tasks vested in authorities worldwide. Many researchers from different disciplines have been dealing with a range of issues related to the organisation and management of elections, electoral standards, and electoral law, especially in emergency situations. These topics have been addressed by T.S. James (2021), T. Landmann & L. Di Gennaro Splendore (2020), L.M. Eriksson (2016), A. Spinelli (2020), D. Duenas-Cid, R. Krimmer, J. Krivonosova (2020, 2021), L.A. Abad, N. Maurer (2020), A.F. Johnson, W. Pollock, B. Rauhaus (2020), D. Bol, M. Giani, A. Blais, P.J. Loewen (2021) and others. Some of the researchers analysed the impact of natural disasters on the electoral process and decline in voter turnout, others dealt with risks pertaining to election management, and democratic procedures in crisis situations. Although they highlight the need to prepare the electoral process for crisis situations, their conclusions and recommendations are rarely implemented (due to relatively infrequent nature of emergencies). Recently, research by the International IDEA focused on elections during COVID-19. Their studies show that since the global spread of COVID-19 has had a profound impact on public life and health of citizens around the world (International IDEA), decisions regarding elections during the pandemic will have a significant effect on the quality of democracy in the future. Undoubtedly, in recent months, we have observed a growing interest in the field.

The functioning of democracy and managing of extraordinary circumstances are more frequently the leading subjects of scholarly inquiries. The reason for this is not only the increase in natural disasters (epidemics, cyclones, wildfires, droughts, floods, hurricanes, tornadoes, etc.), but also the fact that they affect contemporary states and the election process. The COVID-19 pandemic has shown that holding elections in extraordinary circumstances is a major challenge for authorities (James, 2021, 2020; Aviña & Sevi, 2021; Repucci & Slipowitz, 2020, 2021; Krimmer, Duenas-Cid & Krivonosowa, 2021; Musiał-Karg & Kapsa 2021). Not only do democratic rules need to be guaranteed, but also the safety of voters (Quarcoo 2020; Amat, Arenas, Falcó-Gimeno & Muñoz 2020; Malużinas, 2021; Bol, Giani, Blais & Loewen 2021).

While natural disasters and other emergency situations pose similar challenges to democracy, they typically have a more local impact on elections, e.g. the global spread of COVID-19. Certainly, while there is abundance of publications on holding elections during natural disasters (Ebola, Swine Flu, hurricanes) (Debbage, Gonsalves, Shepherd & Knox, 2014) or in the face of terrorist attacks (Morley, 2018). Many of them are case studies of short-term disasters, which lack any detailed analysis of the experience in certain countries and tools implemented over such a long-lasting global epidemic (all disasters discussed in the majority of publications are much shorter and of limited territorial impact). Furthermore, new articles/chapters/reports were published in 2020 and 2021 (James, 2021); James and Alihodzic, 2020); Krimmer, Duenas-Cid & Krivonosova, 2021), but many of them may serve as starting points for further and much deeper analysis, since few of them provide detailed and multidimensional analysis of specific cases.

1.7   Contexts of Research on Elections During a Pandemic

Based on the above, we believe that the COVID-19 pandemic, due to its unprecedented territorial and temporal scope, has affected electoral processes around the world and disrupted and hindered them in many countries in Europe and beyond (James & Alihodzic, 2020; IFES, 2020; Landman & Di Gennero Splendore, 2020; Engler, Brunner, Loviat, Abou-Chadi, Leemann, Glaser & Kübler, 2021).

The COVID-19 pandemic has neither been the first nor the last global health issue. But without any doubt, it has disrupted practically every area of social life. Self-isolation and social distancing have also become a challenge for contemporary democracies and electoral procedures. The pandemic has shown that the implementation of democratic and safe elections can be demanding, sometimes even impossible.

The COVID-19 pandemic has placed elections in many countries between a rock and a hard place. Due to the very rapid spread of coronavirus, most national governments decided to introduce lockdowns and postpone their parliamentary, presidential, or local elections and referendums scheduled for 2020 (at least 79 countries and territories did so from 21st Feb. 2020 until 21st Nov. 2021, as reported by International IDEA 2021). States where elections were due to take place during the pandemic had to make important choices as to when to hold the poll, what measures should be put in place to reduce the risk of infection, and how to mitigate the potential impact of election-related tensions that may be exacerbated by the pandemic and restrictions associated with it. However, some countries decided to embark on a more dangerous path and hold elections as scheduled. They implemented special measures to guarantee a safe voting process - both for voters and the entire election administration involved.

The pandemic has caused unprecedented disruption to elections worldwide. In 2020 and 2021, COVID-19 changed everything – from how elections were designed and campaigns conducted to how people voted. COVID-19 cancelled hustings and party conferences, moved campaigning into the digital realm, and forced many authorities make rapid changes to how voters obtain and submit their ballots. Therefore, it required electoral authorities not only to prepare and implement additional participation methods, but also to take special security measures at polling stations. Over the past two years, the acute worldwide health crisis has moved such issues as public health, democratic principles, credibility of elections, as well as electoral procedure safety to the top of the agenda. Undoubtedly, the spread of the virus and various government responses have had a significant impact on the election process. The difficulties and challenges related to the outbreak of the pandemic can be seen practically on every stage of the process: (1) pre-electoral period (training, information, and voter registration), (2) electoral period (nominations, campaigns, voting, and results), and (3) post-electoral period (review, reform, and strategies) (Landman & Gennaro Splendore, 2020, p. 1062).

Consequently, research on elections during the COVID-19 pandemic focuses on a variety of strands, and research perspectives present a wide range of relevant issues.

The wide range of issues and perspectives in the research on elections during COVID-19 pandemic outlined in the graph represents the most frequently raised topics by representatives of social sciences, mainly political, legal, and media and social communications sciences. It should be remembered, however, that the vast majority of works on the 2020–2022 elections also touch upon other scientific disciplines – outside the social sciences, which undoubtedly makes the analyses in this area interdisciplinary and research multidimensional.

1.8   Conclusions

Every state, regardless of its political system, is exposed to various dangers and crises. A legal instrument for combating the most serious threats to the security of the state and its citizens are states of emergency, which are regulated in different ways in national constitutions. The COVID-19 pandemic has demonstrated that emergencies that are unexpected and unpredictable in their scope can translate into many difficulties in organising general elections, which in turn can bring many threats to democracy.

The COVID-19 has affected the organisation of elections around the world, both in mature and young democracies. The pandemic may put into question what constitutes the essence of democratic states, namely the popular vote. In the face of the historical health crisis, governments realised that when they

TABLE 1.3   Contexts of research on elections during the COVID-19 pandemic

Contexts of research on elections during the COVID-19 pandemic

	legal framework / electoral reform	safety measures during voting	organisation and management of elections	electoral campaigning and media	political parties' attitudes and political preferences	introduction of alternative voting methods	electoral turnout and results of the elections
democratic standards	stages of the electoral cycle	the role of national institutions and electoral management bodies	justifying and effects of postponing the elections	the role of experts in shaping public opinion	case studies	comparisons of the case studies	
electoral integrity							

SOURCE: OWN STUDY

are to decide whether to hold elections or not, they need to consider a variety of legal, technical, and health issues and implications. Moreover, they need to make constitutional arrangements to ensure that democratic institutions can continue their operation as normal and people's fundamental rights and freedoms are upheld.

The challenges related to the organization of safe and democratic elections in emergency situations show that there are many threats and unknown factors, and no simple solutions are available at hand. A review of research into elections in crisis situations proves that the pandemic has encouraged deeper and multidimensional analysis of the problem. The most important conclusion from the study is that in the face of the COVID-19 pandemic, effective solutions should be found and implemented to protect democratic principles and accountability of the electoral process. Moreover, electoral authorities should focus to develop such solutions and implement an election management plan in case crisis similar to the COVID-19 pandemic occurs in the future (Landman & Gennero Splendore, 2020, p. 1065).

References

Abad, L.A. & Maurer, N. (2020), "Do pandemics shape elections? Retrospective voting in the 1918 Spanish Flu pandemic in the United States", *SSRN*, http://dx.doi.org/10.2139/ssrn.3680286.

Agamben, G. (2005), *A Brief History of the State of Exception*, https://press.uchicago.edu/Misc/Chicago/009254.html.

Amat, F., Arenas, A., Falcó-Gimeno, A. & Muñoz, J. (2020), *Pandemics meet democracy. Experimental evidence from the COVID-19 crisis in Spain*, SocArXiv https://osf.io/preprints/socarxiv/dkusw/.

Aviña, M. M. & Sevi, S. (2021), "Did exposure to COVID-19 affect vote choice in the 2020 presidential election?", *Research and Politics*, vol. 8 no 1, https://doi.org/10.1177/20531680211041505.

Bol, D., Giani, M., Blais, A. & Loewen, P.J. (2021), "The effect of COVID-19 lockdowns on political support: Some good news for democracy?", *European Journal of Political Research*, vo. 60 no. 2, pp. 497–505.

Campante, F.R., Depetris-Chauvin, E. & Durante, R. (2020). The virus of fear: the political impact of Ebola in the U.S., National Bureau of Economic Research, Working Paper 26897, http://www.nber.org/papers/w26897.

Debbage, N., Gonsalves N., Shepherd J.M. & Knox J.A. (2014), "Superstorm Sandy and voter vulnerability in the 2012 US Presidential Election: a case study of New Jersey and Connecticut", *Environmental Hazards*, vol. 13, no 3.

Engler, S., Brunner, P., Loviat, R., Abou-Chadi, T., Leemann, L., Glaser, A. & Kübler, D. (2021), "Democracy in times of the pandemic: explaining the variation of COVID-19 policies across European democracies", *West European Politics*, vol. 44, no 5–6, pp. 1077–1102, DOI: 10.1080/01402382.2021.1900669.

Clement, J., Alen, A. (1992). "Emergency Laws". In A. Alen (Ed.), *Treatise on Belgian Constitutional Law*. Deventer-Boston.

Czaplicki, K.W. (2007). "Alternatywne sposoby głosowania (Zarys problemów)". In S. Grabowska, R. Grabowski (Eds.), *Alternatywne sposoby głosowania a aktywizacja elektoratu. Międzynarodowa Konferencja Naukowa. Rzeszów 26–27 marca 2007 r.*, Rzeszów: Poligrafia Wyższego Seminarium Duchownego.

Cześnik, M. (2003). Uczestnictwo wyborcze: teoretyczne przesłanki, modele wyjaśniania, analizy empiryczne. *Studia Socjologiczne*, no 2(169), pp. 43–78.

Dahl, R. (1971), *Polyarchy: Participation and Opposition*, NewHaven, CT: Yale University Press.

DCAF (2005), *State of emergency*, DCAF - Geneva Centre for Security Sector Governance. Retrieved from: https://www.files.ethz.ch/isn/14131/backgrounder_02_states_emergency.pdf.

Eriksson, L. M. (2016), "Winds of Change. Voter Blame and Storm Gudrun in the 2006 Swedish Parliamentary Election", *Electoral Studies*, no. 41, pp. 129–142.

Grogan, J. (2020), Analysing Global Use of Emergency Powers in Response to COVID-19, *European Journal of Law Reform* (22) 4, pp. 338–354; doi: 10.5553/EJLR/138723702021022004002.

Grzybowska-Walecka, K. & Wojtas-Jarentowska, K. (2020). *Lockdown w demokracjach w czasach pandemii COVID-19*, Raport, Konrad Adenaer Stiftung, https://www.kas.de/documents/279510/8099243/Raport+Lockdown.pdf/8eb86ae7-2a6c-7e06-6506-0b76386b2494?version=1.0&t=1610026523952.

IFES (2020). *Elections Held and Mitigating Measures Taken During COVID-19*, https://www.ifes.org/sites/default/files/elections_held_and_mitigating_measures_taken_during_COVID-19.pdf.

James, T.S (2021). *Comparative Electoral Management Performance, Networks and Instruments*, Routledge.

James, T. S. (2021), "New development: Running elections during a pandemic", *Public Money & Management*, vol. 41 no 1, pp. 65–68, https://doi.org/10.1080/09540962.2020.1783084.

James, T.S., Alihodzic S. (2020). "When Is It Democratic to Postpone an Election? Elections During Natural Disasters, COVID-19, and Emergency Situations", *Election Law Journal*, vol. 19, no 3;

Johnson, A.F., Pollock, W. & Rauhaus, B. (2020). "Mass casualty event scenarios and political shifts: 2020 election outcomes and the U.S. COVID-19 pandemic", *Administrative Theory & Praxis*, vol 42, no 2, pp. 249–264.

Khakee A. (2009). *Securing Democracy? A Comparative Analysis of Emergency Powers in Europe*, Geneva Center for Democratic Control of Armed Forces (DCAF), Policy Paper, No 30; https://www.files.ethz.ch/isn/99550/PP30_Anna_Khakee_Emergency _Powers.pdf.

Krimmer, R., Duenas-Cid, D., & Krivonosova, I. (2020). "Debate: Safeguarding democracy during pandemics. Social distancing, postal, or internet voting—the good, the bad or the ugly?", *Public Money & Management*, no 1.

Krimmer, R., Duenas-Cid, D. and Krivonosova, J. (2021), "New methodology for calculating costefficiency of different ways of voting: is internet voting cheaper?', *Public Money and Management*, vol. 41, no 1, pp. 17–26;

Landman, T., Di Gennero Splendore L. (2020). "Pandemic democracy: elections and COVID-19", *Journal of Risk Research*, vol. 23 no 7–8 (COVID-19 Special Issue), pp. 1060–1066.

Malużinas, M. (2021). "Parliamentary elections during the COVID-19 pandemic: The example of the Lithuanian elections in 2020", *Athenaeum. Polish Political Studies*, vol. 69, no. 1, pp. 216–233; https://doi.org/10.15804/athena.2021.69.13.

Morley, M. T. (2018). "Election Emergencies: Voting in the Wake of Natural Disasters and Terrorist Attacks", *67 Emory Law Journal*, vol. 67, no. 3, pp. 545–617; https://scholarlycommons.law.emory.edu/elj/vol67/iss3/6

Musiał-Karg, M. & Kapsa, I. (2021). "Debate: Voting challenges in a pandemic— Poland", *Public Money & Management*, vol. 41, no 1, pp. 6–8.

Prokop, K. (2005). *Stany nadzwyczajne w Konstytucji Rzeczypospolitej Polskiej z dnia 2 kwietnia 1997 r.*, Białystok: Temida 2.

Przeworski, A. (2019). *Crises of Democracy*, Cambridge: Cambridge University Press;

Quarcoo, A. (2020). *Can Elections Be Credible During a Pandemic?* Carnegie Endowment for International Peace.

Repucci S. & Slipowitz, A. (2020). *Democracy under Lockdown. The Impact of COVID-19 on the Global Struggle for Freedom*, Freedom House.

Repucci S., Slipowitz, A. (2021), "The Freedom House Survey for 2020: Democracy in a Year of Crisis", Journal of Democracy, vol. 32 no 2, pp. 45–60;

Rokitowska, J. (2018). *Katastrofy naturalne*, in: *Vademecum Bezpieczeństwa*, eds. O. Wasiuta, R. Klepka, R. Kopeć, Wydawnictwo LIBRON – Filip Lohne, Kraków. https://depot.ceon.pl/bitstream/handle/123456789/16615/Justyna_Rokitowska_Katastrofy _Naturalne_Vademecum_Bezpieczenstwa.pdf?sequence=1&isAllowed=y.

Roy, M. (2007). "The State of Democracy after Disaster: How to maintain the right to vote for Displaced Citizens", *Southern California Interdisciplinary Law Journal*, Vol. 17, pp. 203–230, https://gould.usc.edu/why/students/orgs/ilj/assets/docs/17-1%20Roy .pdf.

Spinelli, A. (2020). *Managing Elections under the COVID-19 Pandemic: The Republic of Korea's Crucial Test*, International IDEA, Technical Paper no 2.

Universal Declaration of Human Rights, United Nations, 1948.

Vázquez-Carrero, M., Artés, J., García C. & Jiménez, J. L. (2020), "Empirical evidence of the effects of COVID-19 on voter turnout", *COVID Economics*, CEPR PRESS, issue 50, 25 September, pp. 181–208). https://accedacris.ulpgc.es/bitstream/10553/106031/2 /empirical_evidence_effects.pdf.

CHAPTER 2

Towards Resilient Electoral Systems

Piotr Walewicz

2.1 Introduction

The importance of elections – a core element of almost every political system in modern states – is indisputable and explained thoroughly by numerous scholars (i.e., Przeworski, 2019) and authors of every chapter of this book. The other obvious fact is that modernity and globalization present us with more and more systemic risks (Goldin & Mariathasan, 2014), including more pandemics and global environmental threats (Price-Smith, 2009). Within this context the COVID-19 pandemic has shown us the vulnerability and fragility of electoral systems all over the world, including many developed democracies. The state often seemed to be unprepared, slow to mobilize and unable to deliver in many areas. It was not resilient enough. This can and should be treated as a prelude to what can come next when taking into account the continuous degradation of ecosystems and the still unsolved climate crisis. These will bring only more extraordinary situations and challenge the electoral systems of states and their capability to conduct fair and safe elections. This is because not only a pandemic can create circumstances when it is unsafe for certain citizens to leave their homes and take part in political activity. One can simply picture the record-breaking heat waves which occurred in many Western European countries in 2019 and took the lives of possibly more than one thousand people. If their origin is indeed anthropogenic and resulting form climate change (Vautard *et al.*, 2020) we should then be ready for more of such heat waves, each worse than the former. We should imagine a situation such as the one mentioned – but multiplied by a factor of ten – when the heat outside is so great and long-lasting that most if not all senior citizens (or citizens with cardiovascular or metabolic contraindications) cannot leave their homes for a whole summer. What then if there were general elections scheduled for this timeframe? Should they be conducted or are states going to once again scramble for intermediate and hasty solutions like they did in 2020 and 2021? And heat waves are only one of the many possible scenarios that will become more common and more severe in the next few decades. Some states will face unprecedented floods or hurricanes whereas others will need to deal with unforeseen migration waves.

© PIOTR WALEWICZ, 2024 | DOI:10.1163/9789004690622_004

Political systems – including their electoral subsystems – will need to be prepared for the unprecedented and unforeseen. We no longer live in a world of certainty where the state has the capability to deal with any crisis. We live in a world of the unknown, unstable, uncertain. Researchers are just now starting to ask questions about the viability, fairness and safety of voting during emergency situations (James & Alihodzic, 2020), but this area of study is still not explored fully. There is very little research on the adaptation of electoral systems for climate change. There is some scholarly interest in the relation between sustainable development and elections (Musiał-Karg & Kapsa, 2019), although the concept of sustainable development is something different than persevering and overcoming unforeseen crises. The COVID-19 pandemic was a catalyst for researchers and hundreds of publications are in print, but intellectual inspirations are still needed for the proper development of the field of studying and modeling better electoral systems against unforeseen crises. We need new concepts to not only analyze state behavior in such circumstances but also evaluate it critically and provide advice. Resilience can be one such concept – it is already gaining traction in social sciences. It is very visible in policy making at the international level, including the European Union (Council of the European Union, 2013) or the United Nations (UNFCCC, 2021). It is very capacious and able to incorporate many aspects and dimensions of socio-ecological life. It is a concept of achieving security through embracing change and seeking the sources of security within the state by focusing attention inward and through self-organizing adaptation to external shocks (Dalby, 2020). Obviously, it is difficult to imagine a secure and resilient state without the ability to conduct safe and fair elections under any difficult circumstances. However, elections and electoral systems themselves are rarely discussed within the resilience discourse and probably not given enough priority. Even a sample search through scientific databases returns little to no publications with both 'resilience' and 'elections' among their keywords. The most prevalent topics for social sciences are climate, urbanization, technology, inequality, violence, migration, food, health, education and culture. Thus, both scholars of electoral systems as well as those interested in resilience could gain from looking towards each other's fields of study.

This chapter builds on the call for integrating resilience research into political studies that had already been made (Brassett *et al.*, 2013). It can serve as an intellectual inspiration for incorporating the concept of resilience into electoral research in both political science and security studies centered on elections. It may provide some arguments against the perceived impotence of many methodologies and models when faced with unprecedented and global challenges that disturb many layers of social life at the same time. If anything, the scale, consequences and duration of the current pandemic did come as a surprise not only for political decision-makers but for social scientists as well. The uncertainty and instability ensuing from the epidemiological necessitates embracing new concepts and models that will not only let us analyze what went wrong, but also provide clear prescriptions for not only re-stabilizing electoral systems but improving and preparing them for the next unforeseen crisis.

2.2 Resilience and Its Relevance to Political Studies

Resilience as a practical concept seems quite intuitive and most of us have some idea about its possible meaning. Many of these ideas will in fact fit into the frame of meaning of resilience even its analytical dimension. What is problematic is that there are multiple usable definitions and a lack of clarity (Wakefield, Grove & Chandler, 2020). Nevertheless, the concept – as used by scholars and practitioners – needs specifying. History matters here, because the intellectual roots of resilience come from natural sciences while its path brought it into policymaking on a global level.

A detailed history of resilience in all sciences is neither necessary nor possible within the limited scope of this chapter and may be found elsewhere (i.e. Chandler & Coaffee, 2017). Sufficient to say, many different disciplines or areas of study have adapted it or came up with their own versions of it. Those belong to a whole spectrum from natural to social sciences and include environmental science, geography, medicine, psychology, pedagogy, sociology, security studies, economics and many more (Gruszczak, 2016). The most important aspect of the concept's history are its roots in systems ecology and the study of ecosystem balance and stability. It was first used and propagated by C. S. Holling (1973), who observed that an ecosystem can still maintain its basic features and functions even when under constant or incidental perturbations of outside origin that throw it out of balance. Resilience is the feature that makes this possible and it is measured by the durability of relations within the ecosystem and their ability to absorb the unexpected shifts in its functioning. It opposes the traditional ecosystem stability paradigm in that it sees the ecosystem not through the lens of a constant return to homeostasis but through the lens of constant development. The absorption of perturbations and shifts of outside origin gives the ecosystem the ability to survive in the dynamic and uncertain environment (Stępka, 2021).

Recollecting the divergent development of the concept in different disciplines in unnecessary here. The more interesting part of its history – at least for political scientists – is its emergence in policymaking circles at the turn of the century. Wakefield, Grove and Chandler (2020) see the turning point at the numerous social, geopolitical, technical, economic and ecological processes and events that challenged and undermined the modernist mode of controlling reality. Among those were the end of the Cold War, a new wave of terrorism, the Asian financial crisis, as well as the United Nations Framework Convention on Climate Change's alerts about the severity and danger of climate change coupled with the rising number of grand natural disasters around the world. It was also when Crutzen and Stoermer (2000) introduced the concept of Anthropocene, while others declared that we had been living in the time of a Great Acceleration for the last five decades (Steffen *et al.*, 2004). It was in these circumstances that scholars and policymakers alike noticed the limits of modernity and the inadequacy of the idea of security as a homeostasis that the system can always bounce back to. Resilience – seen until then as a property of an (eco)system to absorb and embrace change – was found to be an attractive alternative to the traditional ideas of security in a world that is no longer predictable.

In resilience thinking it is accepted that change has already happened and will be happening (although its pace still depends on our actions). It is thus pointless to reject it as well as reject the ever-increasing interconnectivity within the world and try to repeatedly return to a point of stability that is no longer attainable – reality is constantly shifting away from it. The more prudent solution seems to be to affirm this kind of reality, reflect on it, learn and adapt. On the political level it means a reconfiguration of socio-ecological relations, integrating adaptive management and welcoming institutional change. This is one possible explanation of resilience that is usable in political science. A more coherent definition might be possible although it is not necessary (Wakefield, Grove & Chandler, 2020).

Of course, resilience is not without its critics. It is said to have become so universalized that it is often the first, but not always the best answer to many contemporary problems (Nadasdy, 2007). Some also claim its natural propensity towards sustaining neoliberalism, because both have a lot in common, including their liberal genealogy and underlying logic of security (O'Malley, 2010; Walker & Cooper, 2011). Many of these critiques however are losing ground or substance against a new generation of resilience scholars who uncover more questions to be explored or have begun interrogating resilience not only within its traditional paradigm of liberalism (Schmidt, 2017). Whether or not the critiques are valid – which depends on certain philosophical and social-theoretical assumptions – the prevalence of resilience thinking in contemporary global governance is an undeniable fact. Thus relating it to electoral research in the context of crises and the challenges they create seems only logical. One does not need to agree with resilience as a governance principle, but knowing it might provide valuable analytical insight.

Even though resilience is said to be difficult to grasp for social scientists compared to natural scientists, scholars of political systems will probably be in a better position than many other political scientists. This is because their common use of systems analysis prepares them well for understanding that system ontology is essential in resilience thinking (Olsson *et al.*, 2017). This kind of system ontology might be controversial in today's social sciences, very much departed from their naturalistic roots, because it presupposes that "ecological and social domains of social-ecological systems can be addressed in a common conceptual, theoretical, and modeling framework" (Walker *et al.*, 2006). Moreover the kind of system analysis required is more like that of Talcott Parsons' rather than Niklas Luhmann's or Immanuel Wallerstein's (Olsson *et al.*, 2017). A social entity such as an institution, city or state will be analyzed similarly to a forest or a coral reef – like an ecosystem rather than an isolated autopoietic system with no links to its environment. Social ontology will not be distinct from the ecological one. This is not to mean that concepts from natural sciences should be inappropriately extended onto society in all its complexity – which is a trend already halted in most of social science some decades ago. It simply means that the relations within society and relations within ecology overlap and isolating them is an ontological as well as an analytical problem, especially when it comes to relations between environmental crises and society. This kind of integrated social-ecological thinking and analysis is somewhat similar to popular eco-philosophies like 'deep ecology' (Naess, 1973) or 'social ecology' (Bookchin, 1982). From a political-scientific perspective it should be assumed that "all socio-political projects are ecological projects and vice versa" (Harvey, 1996, p. 174). To talk about a resilient state we must then acknowledge it as a state-in-ecology as well as an ecology-within-a-state, but not necessarily analyze it through a naturalistic lens.

Of course in the sphere of policy-making the specifics of the term or its intellectual background and philosophical affinity are rarely mentioned. Most of the time resilience is talked about as something obvious, not requiring any detailed explanation. One very current example is the *Race to Resilience* – a campaign led by the United Nations Framework Convention on Climate Change since 2021. The campaign's call-to-action is about a "resilient world where we don't just survive climate shocks and stresses, but thrive in spite of them" (UNFCCC, 2021). Resilience, as understood by the UN, is the ability to survive and develop in spite of the unavoidable consequences of climate change, as well as actively trying to reduce emissions so that those consequences do not get worse (Climate Champions, 2022). For the conditions of public discourse, this simple yet vivid definition that touches on the main points of resilience without delving into details is both adequate and common.

2.3   A Resilient State

There is a noticeable amount of literature on resilient governance (Erickson, 2015), resilient local governments (Shaw & Theobald, 2011) or resilient cities (Jabareen, 2013), because they correlate best to the most common understandings of socio-ecological resilience with its bottom-up focus and locality. It is however difficult to point at a specific body of scientific literature that uses 'resilient state' as an analytical category, although there are studies that try to describe it based on its usage in political discourse and practice. One such study is by Pospisil and Kühn (2016) who analyzed what kind of model of resilient state stems from contemporary state-building policy papers. The authors emphasized that they were not trying to form a new definition of a 'resilient state' but rather study how resilience was now aimed at all levels of social life: social orders, state-society relations as well as state institutions. They concluded that in the sphere of state-building resilience is understood and supported as the vision opposite to fragility. What is important is that the discourse they had analyzed was focused on failed and fragile states or states on the brink of becoming fragile – ones that required state-building interventions. Thus, it is not exactly the domain of the kind of resilience thinking described earlier in the chapter, with its ecological roots and socio-ecological focus. Other than the one mentioned, there are not many accessible scientific publications that try to describe a 'resilient state' or a 'resilient political system' as climate-change-durable or pandemic-durable entities.

An interesting, readily available and quite comprehensive model of such a resilient state as a model to aspire to – one that can withstand shocks like the pandemic – can be generalized from a collection of essays by thinkers from the British think tank Reform (Cadman *et al.*, 2020). Drawing inspiration from their government's flawed response to the COVID-19 pandemic, the authors not only point out the mistakes and shortcomings but also give specific guidelines for turning their state into a fully resilient one. All of those always relate to the basic understandings of resilience in science mentioned earlier in the chapter. Firstly, the authors underline the aspect of having the ability to learn and implement the newly gained knowledge without delay. Secondly, they claim that a resilient state is able to emerge from a crisis stronger than before, which distinguishes it from a merely competent state – which recovers to its previous level – and a fragile state that breaks down under external pressure. This ability to not only *bounce back* but *bounce forward* (see Siambabala *et al.*, 2011) is achieved through a certain set of practices: learning from one's own and others' mistakes, having a trained and trusted staff, preparing well during times of stability, properly distributing power and managing resources as well as building international coalitions of mutual support. What is important is that these practices must be in force over long periods of time since one-off interventions do not induce lasting changes. Another emphasized aspect of building a resilient state is ensuring public compliance with emergency directives – or any directives that must be followed to maintain resilience even outside of crises. This goes hand in hand with citizens' faith in the competence of their government and its capability to induce change for the better. All in all, the model of a resilient state assumes a strong and well-prepared state on every level (Cadman *et al.*, 2020). As an aside one should notice that none of the authors of these essays included electoral systems or any voting practices in their analysis – the emphasis was on the functioning of the current government rather than ensuring that the next one can be elected fairly and safely. This is a recurrent issue in most of practical and scientific resilience literature in which pandemic-resilient or climate-resilient electoral systems are rarely emphasized as an important part of a resilient state.

2.4   A Resilient Electoral System

One can easily see how all of these practices of a resilient state could actually be practices of a well-functioning democratic electoral system as well. It would be a system ready to withstand and *bounce forward* after any crisis it encounters from pandemics to heat waves. After all, there were already numerous postponed or cancelled elections all over the world, caused by natural or other disasters, the so-called 'non-elections' (James & Alihodzic, 2020). Out of all possible reasons for postponing or cancelling elections, humanitarian postponement or technical delays fit best into the domain of a resilient electoral system. Technical delays stem from an inadequate level of institutional and technological preparedness, when the technical systems fail to deal with an unforeseen shift in circumstances. Other reasons – power-grabs, constitutional crises, or violence – could also be taken into account as possibilities, even if a really resilient state should never have to deal with those in the first place. Including those would shift the understanding of resilience more towards the resilient-fragile axis of state-building discourse and farther from the climate-resilience and pandemic-resilience discourse of the UN.

The reasons for non-elections that this chapter focuses on are emergency situations that call for humanitarian interventions and legislative changes, when citizens would have to risk their lives or health in order to vote. The catalogue of natural disasters that could affect an electoral cycle is vast, ranging from geophysical (earthquakes, volcanic activity), through meteorological (extreme temperature, storm), hydrological (flood, wave action), climatological (drought, wildfire), biological (epidemic, insect infestation) to extraterrestrial (asteroid impact). Unfortunately, many of those will most probably be getting more common, longer or more severe because of the ongoing climate change (Van Aalst, 2006; Banholzer *et al.*, 2014). This has been confirmed by every report from the Intergovernmental Panel on Climate Change (IPCC, 2021) and should definitely find its way into political science and the study of electoral systems. Moreover, public health experts have also been warning about the increasing possibility of pandemics in the globalized world (Bjørkdahl & Carlsen, 2019), and political scientists know well how the current one disturbed numerous electoral systems around the world.

If we know what can come – keeping in mind that there may be threats that we have not even imagined yet – can we provide a model for a resilient electoral system or assess the degree of resilience of existing ones? The most obvious way to do it is to use the same set of guidelines, indicators and measures that we would use for assessing the resilience of societies and states as a whole. These could be loosely categorized as: learning, building capabilities, adapting and trust. Because numerous states have already faced the challenge of organizing elections during the COVID-19 pandemic, there is much to learn from other's successes and failures. The book that this chapter belongs to gives all the examples one needs, including analyses of Poland, United Kingdom, Estonia, Russian Federation, Italy, Lithuania, North Macedonia, Latvia, Czech Republic and Serbia. Going into detail on each of those cases is thus not deemed necessary, although some thought must be given to those here as well. Learning from the readily available and well-studied experience of different countries already forms a quite coherent image of what a resilient electoral system could look like and what flaws it should definitely not have.

None of the states that faced the need to organize elections during the pandemic obviously had any past experiences to learn from, because the scale of the current challenge is unlike anything they might have known. Each state came up with solutions that it deemed best for its circumstances and those choices already reflect how different the capabilities of those states were. For some (i.e. Poland) switching into special voting arrangements came up short because the capabilities of the system were not in place – they required building up when it was already too late (Musiał-Karg & Kapsa, 2020). On the other hand others (i.e. Estonia or the German federal state of Bavaria) have shown that it had indeed been possible to build those capabilities during stable times (Krimmer *et al.*, 2020; Wagner, 2020), which allowed or will allow them to conduct elections in a safe way and with high voter turnout. Without delving into detail, the more alternatives to traditional practices a state had the easier it was to conduct elections or referendums during the pandemic with the least controversies and doubts from health experts.

Possibly the best matrix of risk mitigation practices that include special voting arrangements during times of crisis is given by Landman and Di Gennaro Splendore (2020), who propose a set extraordinary measures that could be implemented on each and every step of the electoral cycle. Amongst their suggestions for the pre-electoral and post-electoral period are limiting physical meetings (planning, training, review) in favor of on-line meetings or switching from physical candidate registration to on-line and postal registration. For the electoral period they propose that both primaries and elections be held through postal, on-line or hybrid voting, while the campaigns could also be run mostly via the Internet (Landman & Di Gennaro Splendore, 2020). Importantly, these special arrangements are applicable not only during a pandemic, but should become staples of an electoral system that also wants to be resilient during climate-related natural disasters or any other difficult external conditions. Improving the electoral system's resilience should definitely take into account the fact that elections are not simply voting day. They include infrastructure preparations, candidate appointment, campaigns etc. – each of those elements can be affected by a crisis. Thus a resilient electoral system should be able to provide efficient and safe alternatives to all elements and on every step of the electoral cycle. For example simply providing citizens with i-voting options will not be sufficient if candidates are not provided with equal and fair campaign opportunities via the Internet.

It probably does not come as a surprise that the capabilities required for achieving resilience of an electoral system mostly include limiting physical contact and the use of methods that work at a distance, be it via post or the Internet. This is because having those available assures that another key element of resilience – adaptability – can be achieved. It should not be expected of every state to conduct each elections with special voting arrangements, although expecting having viable alternatives for times of crisis does not seem exorbitant. The example of Bavaria which was able to quickly adapt to the crisis using the already built-in capabilities and organizing the first full postal vote during the COVID-19 pandemic is very instructive (Wagner, 2020). However, adaptability will not only need to rely on using special voting arrangements or alternative means of communications between institutions, but also on elastic legislation. In 2020 and 2021 states had to improvise and they came up with different legal solutions and amendments to electoral laws (Wass *et al.*, 2021). What is important is that since resilience is not a one-size-fits-all solution, there also should not be a universal electoral law that will be able to withstand any crisis anywhere. We need not a model of electoral law but a model of transformation of said law that will make the system more resilient, but always geared towards state-specific conditions. The counter-example of Poland and its failure to legislate meaningful changes might serve as a good lesson (Musiał-Karg & Kapsa, 2020).

The last key element of a resilient electoral system will be trust. It should be mutual trust between the state and its citizens. Without it, even if provided with procedural solutions and physical conditions that allow safe voting, citizens may opt not to take advantage of those if they mistrust their government and fear some form of power abuse. Inversely the government may not introduce alternative – and always costly – solutions if it fears that the citizens will be uninterested in voting anyway. Like James and Alihodzic (2020) conclude, states where trust is embedded into political institutions are better able to weather any storm. However, building citizens' trust toward new alternative voting arrangements might still be difficult even in such states, because it depends on trust towards many different institutions and ways of communication, i.e. the postal service (Wass *et al.*, 2021). What this means for most states is that creating a resilient electoral system will likely not take months but years of building that mutual trust. Any single situation when that trust is betrayed or power is abused in any way will push those efforts back several years. A resilient electoral system will thus be built not only on institutional and technological solutions but on values as well. One can go further and say that this axiological basis is the most fundamental component of electoral resilience, while any other is secondary to it. This is because the kind of proposed solution (i.e. i-voting, longer voting periods etc.) becomes unimportant as long as the values underlying the system make all of them unattractive or trustworthy for citizens and governments alike. Moreover, trust in alternative measures could be lower than expected even because of failure to inform citizens and communicate with them during the crisis. What this means is that resilience of an electoral system will never be limited to material and institutional levels, but will need to transcend and also result from an adequate political culture.

2.5   Conclusion

We will most probably be facing more, not less, difficult and unprecedented crises that disturb electoral cycles, and thus we should be analytically prepared for assessing the effectiveness of electoral systems as well as giving expert guidelines for improving them. Because the concept of resilience is here to stay – especially in global policy and development circles – it might as well become one of the concepts we use as political scientists to assess reality and give meaningful advice. This is important for democracy itself, because having ways of conducting elections during crises might be better for its health than postponing them – especially during prolonged crises such as the COVID-19 pandemic. The latter carries more risk of seeking partisan advantage, pushing for further dates when poll ratings are low or even seeking to permanently cancel elections. Opportunities for gaining partisan advantage might also present themselves during non-traditional elections in extraordinary circumstances – for example manipulating campaign opportunities for candidates that are not backed by the government (James & Alihodzic, 2020) – but a resilient electoral system will also have foreseen those and removed or minimalized that possibility.

To conclude, for political scientists resilience can be used as a filter through which one can observe a political system. It is not a whole new feature, but allows one to see the interconnectedness of multiple existing features of a system. It makes it easier to pinpoint the weakest link in an electoral system – whether it is the lack of technological alternatives, lack of political will or lack of trust – and is fully compatible with any sustainable model of development of political systems. Analytically it is something more than just a new set of indicators and practically it is more than just crisis management.

It must be repeated, that there will never be a single model of a climate-resilient and pandemic-resilient electoral system given as a set of institutions and procedures. It will only be a model of transformation, which should be carried out by each state mostly independently, using its already built capabilities, its strengths, traditions and social capital. If anything the elements of resilience should become staples in all future electoral reforms as the advantages are numerous and disadvantages are difficult to pinpoint. Any electoral system will benefit from learning from its own and others' experience, expanding its institutional and technological capabilities, being able to adapt to changing circumstances and maximizing mutual trust between voters and the system. All of these are necessary to transform into a resilient electoral system, but each of them is going to be beneficial even by itself. Mere thinking about what might happen and trying to prepare for it both analytically and practically will be a decent first step towards resilient electoral systems. Moreover, the science and expert knowledge is already here – this book adds to it substantially – and only needs to be analyzed synthetically and holistically in order to be able to point at obvious flaws of existing electoral systems and provide guidelines on how to make them more resilient against future challenges.

References

Banholzer, S., Kossin, J., & Donner, S. (2014). The Impact of Climate Change on Natural Disasters. In Zommers, Z., & Singh, A. (eds.), *Reducing Disaster: Early Warning Systems For Climate Change* (21–49). Dordrecht: Springer. DOI: https://doi.org/10.1007/978-94-017-8598-3.

Bjørkdahl, K., & Carlsen, B. (eds.). (2019). *Pandemics, Publics, and Politics: Staging Responses to Public Health Crises.* Basingstoke: Palgrave Macmillan.

Bookchin, M. (1982). *The Ecology of Freedom: The Emergence and Dissolution of Hierarchy.* Palo Alto.

Brasset, J., Croft, S., & Vaughan-Williams, N. (2013). Introduction: An Agenda for Resilience Research in Politics and International Relations. *Politics,* 33(4), 221–228. DOI: https://doi.org/10.1111/1467-9256.12032.

Cadman, D., Crewe, I., Goldin, I., Haldane, A., Hall, S., Kruger, D., Morgan, N., Pearce, N., Pickles, Ch., Thornton, R., Miron, M., & Wallace, W. (2020). *Building a resilient state: a collection of essays.* Reform.

Chandler, D., & Coaffee, J. (eds). (2017). *The Routledge Handbook of International Resilience.* London – New York: Routledge.

Climate Champions (2021, February 28). IPCC: We must build resilience to the impacts we cannot prevent. *Climate Champions.* Retrieved from: https://climatechampions.unfccc.int/ipcc-we-must-build-resilience-to-the-impacts-we-cannot-prevent/.

Council of the European Union (2013). *Council Conclusions on an EU Approach to Resilience.* 3241st External Relations Council meeting. Brussels: European Union.

Crutzen, P. J., & Stoermer, E. F. (2020). The 'Anthropocene'. *IGBP Global Change Newsletter,* 41, 17–18.

Dalby, S. (2020). Resilient Earth: Gaia, geopolitics and the Anthropocene. In Chandler, D., Grove, K., & Wakefield, S. (eds.), *Resilience in the Anthropocene: Governance and Politics at the End of the World* (22–36). London – New York: Routledge.

Erickson, A. (2015). Efficient and resilient governance of social–ecological systems. *Ambio,* 44(5), 343–352. DOI: https://dx.doi.org/10.1007%2Fs13280-014-0607-7.

Goldin, I., & Mariathasan, M. (2014). *The butterfly defect: how globalization creates systemic risks, and what to do about it.* Princeton – Oxford: Princeton University Press.

Gruszczak, A. (2016). Resilience and mitigation in security management: concepts and concerns. *Forum Scientiae Oeconomia,* 4(special issue no. 1), 7–23.

Harvey, D. (1996). *Justice, Nature and the Geography of Difference.* Cambridge – Oxford: Blackwell Publishers.

IPCC (2021). *Climate Change 2021: The Physical Science Basis. Contribution of Working Group I to the Sixth Assessment Report of the Intergovernmental Panel on Climate Change.* Cambridge University Press.

Jabareen, Y. (2013). Planning the resilient city: Concepts and strategies for coping with climate change and environmental risk. *Cities*, 31, 220–229. DOI: https://doi.org/10.1016/j.cities.2012.05.004.

James, T. S., & Alihodzic, S. (2020). When Is It Democratic to Postpone an Election? Elections During Natural Disasters, COVID-19, and Emergency Situations. *Election Law Journal*, 19(3), 344–362. DOI: https://doi.org/10.1089/elj.2020.0642

Krimmer, R., Duenas-Cid, D., & Krivonosova, I. (2020). Debate: safeguarding democracy during pandemics. Social distancing, postal, or internet voting—the good, the bad or the ugly?. *Public Money & Management*, 41(1), 8–10. DOI: https://doi.org/10.1080/09540962.2020.1766222.

Landman, T., & Di Gennaro Splendore, L. (2020). Pandemic democracy: elections and COVID-19. *Journal of Risk Research*, 23(7–8), 1060–1066.

Musiał-Karg, M., & Kapsa, I. (2019). Citizen e-Participation as an Important Factor for Sustainable Development. *European Journal of Sustainable Development*, 8(3), 210–220. DOI: https://doi.org/10.14207/ejsd.2019.v8n3p210.

Musiał-Karg, M., & Kapsa, I. (2020). Debate: Voting challenges in a pandemic – Poland. *Public Money & Management*, 41(1), 6–8. DOI: https://doi.org/10.1080/09540962.2020.1809791.

Nadasdy, P. (2007). Adaptive Co-management and the Gospel of Resilience. In Armitage, D. R. (ed.), *Adaptive Co-management: Collaboration, Learning, and Multi-level Governance* (208–227). Vancouver, BC: University of British Columbia Press.

Naess, A. (1973). The Shallow of the Deep, Long Range Ecology Movement. *Inquiry*, 16, 95–100.

Olsson, L., Jerneck, A., Thorén, H., Persson, J., & O'Byrne, D. (2017). A social science perspective on resilience. In Chandler, D., & Coaffee, J. (eds), *The Routledge Handbook of International Resilience* (49–62). London – New York: Routledge.

Pospisil, J., & Kühn, F. P. (2016). The resilient state: new regulatory modes in international approaches to state building?. *Third World Quarterly*, 37(1), 1–16.

Price-Smith, A. T. (2009). *Contagion and Chaos: Disease, Ecology, and National Security in the Era of Globalization*. Cambridge, MA: MIT Press.

Przeworski, A. (2019). *Crises of Democracy*. Cambridge: Cambridge University Press.

Schmidt, J. (2017). Resilience and the inversion of possibility and reality. In Chandler, D., & Coaffee, J. (eds), *The Routledge Handbook of International Resilience* (119–131). London – New York: Routledge.

Shaw, K., & Theobald, K. (2011). Resilient local government and climate change interventions in the UK. *The International Journal of Justice and Sustainability*, 16(1), 1–15. DOI: https://doi.org/10.1080/13549839.2010.544296.

Siambabala, B. M., O'Brien, G., O'Keefe, P., & Rose, J. (2011). Disaster resilience: a bounce back or bounce forward ability?. *Local Environment*, 16(5), 417–424.

Steffen, W. L., Eliott, S., & IGBP. (2004). Global change and the earth system: A planet under pressure: executive summary. Stockholm: IGBP Secretariat.

Stępka, M. (2021). Rezyliencja jako paradygmat bezpieczeństwa w czasach przewlekłych kryzysów. *Przegląd Politologiczny*, (2), 105–117. DOI: https://doi.org/10.14746/pp.2021.26.2.7

UNFCCC (2021). Join the Race. *Race to Resilience*. Retrieved from: https://racetozero.unfccc.int/join-the-race-to-resilience/.

Van Aalst, M. K. (2006). The impacts of climate change on the risk of natural disasters. *Disasters*, 30(1), 5–18.

Vautard, R., van Aalst, M., Boucher, O., Drouin, A., Haustein, K., Kreienkamp, F., van Oldenborgh, G. J., Otto, F., Ribes, A., Robin, Y., Schneider, M., Soubeyroux, J-M., Seneviratne, S., Vogel, M., & Wehner, M. (2020). Human contribution to the record-breaking June and July 2019 heatwaves in Western Europe. *Environmental Research Letters*, 15(9), 094077. DOI: https://doi.org/10.1088/1748-9326/aba3d4

Wagner, R. (2020). *Responding to COVID-19 with 100 percent Postal Voting: Local Elections in Bavaria, Germany*. Stockholm: International Institute for Democracy and Electoral Assistance.

Wakefield, S., Grove, K., & Chandler, D. (2020). Introduction: The power of life. In Chandler, D., Grove, K., & Wakefield, S. (eds.), *Resilience in the Anthropocene: Governance and Politics at the End of the World* (1–21). London – New York: Routledge.

Walker, J., & Cooper, M. (2011). Genealogies of resilience from systems ecology to the political economy of crisis adaptation. *Security Dialogue*, 42(2), 143–60.

Wass, H., Peltoniemi, J., Weide, M., & Nemčok, M. (2021, April 28). *How to run pandemic-sustainable elections: Lessons learned from postal voting* (preprint). DOI: https://doi.org/10.31235/osf.io/v2cq5.

CHAPTER 3

Electoral Laws during the COVID-19 Pandemic as a Tool of Quasi-Militant Democracies: Comparative Perspective

Roman Bäcker and Joanna Rak

3.1 Introduction

The outbreak of the COVID-19 pandemic in 2019 and the subsequent introduction of lockdowns in many states quickly resulted in the emergence of firm opinions about the impact of COVID-19-induced actions on the evolution of political regimes. Larry Diamond ventured one of the most emphatic opinions with the sentence, "The coronavirus is emboldening autocrats the world over" (Diamond, 2020). Is it invariably true? The following supposition seems much more accurate: the situation in each political system is so varied that it cannot be argued that one, even a powerful stimulus, can always act in the same way (cf. Guasti, 2020; Rak & Bäcker, 2022).

This chapter has far less ambition than to verify the two contradictory statements in their entirety. Instead, it seeks to test to what extent they account for the changes in the peculiar states whose mechanisms of system change are not fully explained. Those states are pretty far from the ideal types of autocratic and democratic regimes. Moreover, they are particularly susceptible to change; and how these systems respond to the use of various political tools remains a puzzle. This situation applies to four post-communist member states of the European Union (EU), i.e., Hungary, Poland, Bulgaria, and Romania. According to the EIU Democracy Index (2020), their political regimes are the most distant of all EU member states from the ideal type of democracy. Their positions, Poland – 50, Hungary – 56, Bulgaria – 52, and Romania – 62, are classified as flawed democracies (Democracy Index, 2020). In all these states, very strong authoritarian tendencies are visible in political and legal structures. Nonetheless, at the same time, a significant potential of the empowered political nations incessantly influences the course and efficiency of anti-democratic actors' political actions (cf. Kovács, 2021; Navrátil & Kluknavská, 2020).

Although the vast field of clashes between democratic and authoritarian forces, or more precisely between neo-militant democracy and quasi-militant democracy (Rak & Bäcker, 2022), involves the use of various political tools, this

© ROMAN BÄCKER AND JOANNA RAK, 2024 | DOI:10.1163/9789004690622_005 chapter focuses on the electoral laws that were carried out or planned to be implemented in these four countries. Consequently, the study addresses the following research question: to what extent did the electoral laws adopted or proposed for adoption during the COVID-19 pandemic reduce the scope of the sovereignty of the political nations? By doing so, it contributes empirically to studies on militant democracy. The contribution lies in recognising the role of the changes in the electoral laws in shaping the sovereignty of the political nations. It uncovers the results of clashes between democratic and anti-democratic actors in times of the pandemic-induced social, political, and economic crisis in the still insufficiently recognised in terms of systemic shifts region of the EU.

The remainder of the chapter consists of seven sections. The first one presents the literature review and locates the study against contemporary research on militant democracy. The second section establishes a research framework by delimitating a research field as well as discussing a method, technique, and tool used to tackle the research question. It also determines a corpus of sources. The following four sections deliver research results from the case studies of Poland, Hungary, Romania, and Bulgaria, respectively. They shed light on the peculiarities of the electoral laws and their drafts as the neo-militant democratic and quasi-militant democratic tools in the individual states. Adopting a comparative perspective, the final section concludes on the nature and consequences of attempts to influence the sovereignty of the political nations.

3.2   Literature Review

Karl Loewenstein formulated the category of militant democracy in the 1930s to stimulate the development of studies on democratic vulnerability to anti-democratic threats and the weak self-defence mechanisms of liberal democracies (Loewenstein, 1937). The researcher observed that the Weimar Republic proved susceptible to fascist danger due to its state structure's lack of militancy and democratic fundamentalism. Loewenstein argued that "general elections are manifestly a perfectly legitimate device of constitutional government" (1937, p. 418). Nevertheless, subversive actors exercise the democratic freedom to be elected, gain social support, and thus access and maintain power with legal means, through an electoral process, to establish their own political agenda (Cavanaugh & Hughes, 2016, p. 629). As a result, the power competencies of anti-democratic forces increase while the quality of democracy declines. To protect democracy from this threat, the Loewensteinian idea of militant democracy entails using anti-democratic legislative measures against subversive individual and collective subjects. As it assumes, democratic freedoms of speech, the press, assemblies, universal suffrage, organisation in associations and political parties can be limited to defend democracy from its enemies (Loewenstein, 1937, p. 431).

Electoral laws might become the militant democracy measure that efficiently protects democracy from those who try to undermine or overthrow it (cf. Müller, 2016). In addition, this measure may be designed and implemented, among others, to strengthen the position of ruling actors by increasing their power competencies, to prevent the replacement of the ruling elite, and to weaken democracy (Invernizzi Accetti & Zuckerman, 2017). However, as contemporary students of militant democracy argue, one cannot assume that the militant democracy means designed to defend democracy will be used following their original intended purpose (Malkopoulou, 2019, p. 1–2; Macklem, 2006, p. 490). Accordingly, militant democracy measures can be misused or abused for political purposes, especially in unstable democracies (Tyulkina, 2015, p. 7).

In its original wording, the theoretical category of militant democracy is analytically inefficient in distinguishing the indicated nuances (Balthasar, 2021; Elkins, 2022). However, to overcome this weakness, researchers differentiate between neo-militant democracy and quasi-militant democracy (Rak & Bäcker, 2022). A neo-militant democracy is a legal principle established in a democratic system by the government, the parliament, and the judiciary (cf. Beširević, 2021). It rests on restricting democratic freedoms to protect the democratic order against anti-democratic actors. The inherent part of the democratic order is the sovereignty of a political nation. Here, a political nation is defined as a group of equals who can uninterruptedly, freely, and independently participate in decision-making processes concerning the significant matters of the state. In turn, the very sovereignty is understood as a political nation's potential to make final political decisions. The potential is shaped by the other members of a political nation, including the ruling. As a result, the potential has no constant value but changes over time. A political nation is sovereign if its decisions are final and not based on coercion (Bäcker, 2020, p. 35–46.). Accordingly, what makes a neo-militant democracy unique is the imposition of Loewensteinian anti-democratic measures, i.e., the restrictions of political rights, to protect, preserve, or expand the sovereignty of a political nation.

A quasi-militant democracy is also a legal principle established in a democratic system by the government, the parliament, and the judiciary. Nevertheless, it differs from a neo-militant democracy in its influence on the democratic order. In contrast to a neo-militant democracy, a quasi-militant democracy does not seek to protect but impair or destroy the democratic order. A quasi-militant democracy emerges when democratic freedoms are limited to challenge, undermine, and eliminate the sovereignty of a political nation. Loe-wensteinian anti-democratic measures serve anti-democratic purposes since political actors extend their own political sovereignty at the expense of the sovereignty of a political nation as a whole.

The dyad of theoretical categories of neo-militant democracy and quasi-militant democracy constitutes an efficient theoretical framework for studying the consequences of implementing Loewenstein's tools of militant democracy. It allows researchers to differentiate between the detrimental and beneficial influence of legal means on the sovereignty of a political nation. Therefore, it provides the theoretical grounding for the study on the impact of electoral laws on the Polish, Hungarian, Romanian, and Bulgarian political nations.

3.3   Research Framework

To what extent did the electoral laws adopted or proposed for adoption during the COVID-19 pandemic reduce the scope of the sovereignty of the political nations in Poland, Hungary, Romania, and Bulgaria? In order to address this research question, the study draws upon the theoretical framework of neo- and quasi-militant democracy and the method of qualitative source analysis. The source selection is deliberate and theory-grounded. The essential sources for the research are documents published on the websites of the most import-ant public offices, mainly parliaments and constitutional courts, in the states under scrutiny. The corpus of sources includes the documents concerning changes to the electoral laws implemented into the legal order or remaining in the sphere of projects processed by state institutions. In the case of Poland, it is the act on special rules for holding presidential elections in 2020, which was brought as a parliamentary bill to the Sejm on 6 April 2020. An important doc-ument for the Hungarian case is a draft amendment to the electoral law to par-liament on 10 November 2020 created by the government led by Victor Orbán. In Romania, the Election Law, Political Finance Law, and the Law on Postal Voting were simultaneously significantly changed in September 2020, just before the parliamentary elections scheduled for 6 December 2020. Finally, in Bulgaria, the Constitutional Court ruled on 4 May 2021 that the amendments to the electoral law introduced in 2020 are unconstitutional.

The complementary sources are reports and expert analyses from European Network of National Human Rights Institutions, European Platform for Demo-cratic Elections, Heinrich-Böll-Stiftung, Office for Democratic Institutions and

Human Rights, The Economist Intelligence Unit, Verfassungsblog – On Matters Constitutional, and journalistic texts concerning the bills and the results of the implementation of the electoral laws in the individual states.

The technique of reflexive thematic analysis serves us to explore and interpret patterned meaning across the electoral laws and their drafts issued in the period from the introduction of lockdowns in the EU member states in March 2020 to the end of 2021. The analysis starts with marking data that deals with the research question, i.e., identifying the changes or attempted changes in the electoral laws. The following step involves labelling the pieces of data with a label indicating whether a change is aimed at the sovereignty of a political nation or not. Then, the evaluators focus on those data extracts that contain such attempts. Each attempt undergoes further assessment in terms of the nature and consequences of the change it entails. More precisely, by drawing on the corpus of sources, the evaluators decide whether the theme of neo-militant democracy or quasi-militant democracy prevails in each attempt. The electoral law is a tool of a neo-militant democracy when a change seeks to defend, preserve, or expand the sovereignty of a political nation. In turn, when a change leads up to challenge, undermine, and eliminate the sovereignty of a political nation, the electoral law is a tool of a quasi-militant democracy.

At the next stage of the analysis, the study uses an original theoretical tool in the form of a set of detailed questions to identify and understand the extent of the influence of neo-militant and quasi-militant democratic tools on sovereignty of the political nations. The questions are asked to the electoral laws or their bills. They concern three issues. The first one relates to a procedure for introducing changes to the electoral law, i.e., whether they are made with procedures and bodies that are legal or not provided for in the fundamental laws. The second question addresses the scope of inclusion or exclusion of citizens who have electoral rights, due to facilitation or difficulties, especially in the case of socially excluded people or people staying outside the country. The third question deals with the institutions conducting the elections and approving their results. Accordingly, it asks whether those institutions ensure the impartial organisation of elections and fair accounting of the results, and then the independent and fair settlement of any doubts related to their conduct.

The analysis of Poland, Hungary, Romania, and Bulgaria will allow us to examine the extent to which COVID-19 was the determining incentive for presenting and pushing through the solutions that limited or abolished the sovereignty of the political nations. Although conclusions will concern only these four countries, they can inspire further research into the democratisation or autocratisation of political regimes during the COVID-19 pandemic.

3.4   Poland: Between the Struggle for Democracy and the Failure of the
        Rule of Law

The presidential elections in Poland, following the election calendar, were
scheduled for 10 May 2020. However, after setting this date, the Council of Ministers imposed a lockdown on 23 March 2020 by the regulation. This freezing
of direct social contacts, combined with the restriction of the right to associate and organise public gatherings, should have been introduced through
the procedure for states of emergency. However, if the state of emergency had
been imposed, the presidential election date would have been postponed by
three months after the end of this state. In such a case, an incumbent president
descending from the governing Law and Justice party (Prawo i Sprawiedliwość,
PiS) would have been at risk of losing these elections (Schultheis, 2020).

On 6 April 2020, a group of deputies from the ruling party submitted a draft
amendment to the electoral law (Ustawa z dnia 6 kwietnia 2020). It provided
for the organisation of elections only by correspondence. Adding oneself to
the list of voters could take place no later than on the date of entry into force
of this act (Article 4). It meant the actual exclusion from the list of voters of all
those who recently changed their place of residence, and especially all those
who were abroad for work purposes. As a result, a significant part of young and
educated voters, who usually had not voted for PiS (Turska-Kawa, 2016), was
excluded from the political nation.

Responsibilities related to the organisation of elections were transferred
from the National Electoral Commission (Państwowa Komisja Wyborcza) to
the minister's competence, not even the minister of administration, but dealing with state assets. Such competencies are not typical of a minister managing
state-owned companies. Thus, this decision resulted from the trust of the PiS
decision-making elite in the loyalty of Marek Suski, the minister of state assets.
An election commissioner, i.e., an official appointed at the request of the minister of internal affairs, was the only body mentioned in this act that determined the composition of municipal electoral commissions. The latter's task
was to count the votes thrown into mailboxes located in a given municipality.

The Act of 6 April 2020 (Ustawa z dnia 6 kwietnia 2020) handed over the
elections' entire organisation to the ruling party's politicians, allowing for any
manipulation of election results. It excluded a significant part of voters from
the Polish political nation.

Before the parliament passed the law, the Polish postal service Poczta Polska
demanded the lists of voters from mayors of local governments on 23 April
2020. A significant part of them refused to provide these data due to the lack of
legal grounds. On 5 May 2020, the Senate passed a resolution to reject this bill;

on 7 May 2020, the Sejm rejected the Senate's veto; and the next day, the president signed the bill. The act's entry into force on the new electoral law two days before the date of the elections meant that there was no longer any possibility to organise them (Kustra-Rogatka, 2020). The National Electoral Commission announced that the presidential election would not be held on the scheduled date due to the inability to organise them, which was tantamount (sic!) to the lack of candidates. Thus, it was necessary to schedule new elections. Meanwhile, the Marshal of the Sejm should have decided that it was impossible to hold elections and simultaneously set a new date for them (Ustawa z dnia 6 kwietnia 2020, Article 20, Paragraph 2).

Moreover, the National Electoral Commission established the legal regulations regarding presidential elections scheduled for a new date, in the 1st round, on 28 June 2020. It was the case, for example, with the decision that there was no need to register candidates if they were registered in the elections scheduled at the first date. In addition, the presidential election, whose first round was held on 28 June 2020, was conducted under the ordinance in force before the adoption of the Act of 6 April 2020. The latter, however, has so far been treated as a binding legal act appearing in the Journal of Laws (Dziennik Ustaw). This dual legal order is possible in a situation of legal anarchy, or it is peculiar to a prerogative state, antinomic to the rule of law.

In sum, the Act of 6 April 2020 sought to deprive the Polish political nation of sovereignty. However, the attempt failed due to the use by the opposition-controlled Senate of the maximum time limit for processing bills. The second reason was the resistance of local self-governments. An equally important reason was the internal tensions in the ruling coalition and the opposition of Jarosław Gowin, the chairman of the marginal party, Agreement (Porozumienie), who has thus far accepted all PiS's actions undermining democracy. The course of events related to the presidential elections with a turnout of 0% on 10 May 2020, called "ghost election" (Schultheis, 2020), proves the intention to take away the political nation's sovereignty, and thus to destroy democracy. It also uncovers the failure of the ruling politicians to observe the elementary principles of the rule of law.

3.5 Hungary: Softly and Efficiently

In 2020–2021, no parliamentary elections were held in Hungary. However, the ruling party was preparing for the parliamentary elections scheduled for spring 2022. In the fall of 2020, an amendment to the electoral regulations was proposed. Deputy Prime Minister Dr Zsolt Semjén submitted the draft amendment to the parliament on 10 November 2020 at 11:59 pm. On the same day, late in the evening, a general ban on assembly was ordered from the following day, and a ban on moving from 8:00 pm to 5:00 am in the entire territory of Hungary. The draft was not consulted with opposition parties, election experts, and non-governmental organisations (Elemzésünk, 2020).

The critical issues in the draft amendment concerned the parliamentary elections. Paragraph 3 proposed the following amendment: "(1) A party list may be drawn up by a party which has nominated independent candidates in at least fifty individual constituencies in at least nine counties and in the capital" ((1) Pártlistát az a párt állíthat, amely – legalább kilenc megyében és a fővárosban – legalább ötven egyéni választókerületben önállóan jelöltet állított") (Törvény, 2020). This provision meant that the list of parties participating in the elections was entered only by those that had registered at least fifty candidates in single-member constituencies located in at least ten regions, including the capital city. So far, there was a threshold of twenty-seven candidates. It should also be added that Hungary has a mixed electoral system with single- and multi-seat constituencies. Thus, voters have two votes, i.e., one for majority elections the other for proportional elections.

Such a proposal to increase the requirements for parties turned out to be relatively neutral for the election results, mainly due to the emergence of a broad coalition of six opposition parties, regardless of their position on the ideological and political scene. The increase in the electoral threshold for a coalition to 15% in the case of proportional elections also proved insignificant (Végh, 2020). The coalition of opposition parties receives roughly half of the votes in all polls.

Since the above-mentioned legislative changes failed to lead to the results desired for the ruling party, in mid-November 2021, the Hungarian parliament adopted another amendment to the electoral law. The change involved resigning from criminal liability towards people abroad and having a fictitious residential address in Hungary just to be able to vote. Until then, Hungarian citizens living abroad (e.g., in Slovakia or Ukraine) were deprived of the right to vote in single-member constituencies because they did not live in them, and if they wanted to vote nevertheless by registering themselves, they committed a crime against the elections. The depenalisation of this phenomenon, which has already occurred in the 2018 elections, enables legal electoral tourism to appear. Thus, in single-member constituencies, where the advantage of the united opposition will be minimal, and therefore a majority of several hundred votes is enough to win, the ruling party may move its voters from abroad or from other constituencies, and thus artificially secure a victory for itself. At the same time, it is not necessary to organise particular actions. Approximately

90% of voters who voted by e-mail because of being abroad supported the ruling party (Döbrentey, 2021).

In order to increase the governing party's electoral chances, the level of polarisation in Hungarian society was intensified by holding a referendum on the prohibition of LGBTQI promotion and gender reassignment in schools on the day of the parliamentary elections (Siad & Kottasová, 2022). Scheduling a referendum on which the majority of Hungarians supported the government's position aimed to significantly increase the ruling party's chances of gaining a majority in parliament.

To sum up, the party led by Orbán uses amendments that are of a technical nature to change the electoral law. Therefore, it is difficult to treat those changes as obviously depriving the Hungarian political nation of its sovereignty. However, the knowledge of the context, everyday practice and, above all, the recognition of the entirety of influences on more or less objectified social masses, and thereby democratic order, allow for the formulation of different conclusions.

3.6   Romania: Weakly and Largely Inefficiently

The electoral law is regulated in Romania by the Constitution and other laws, including the acts of two-chamber parliamentary elections, political parties, Law on Financial Activity of Political Parties and Electoral Campaigns (Political Finance Law), Law on Postal Voting, and Law on Radio and Television Broadcasting. Notably, the electoral laws in Romania were changed in 2018, 2019, and 2020. However, the most significant changes concerned the Election Law, Political Finance Law, and the Law on Postal Voting and were adopted in 2020. The 2019 and 2020 changes were introduced rapidly and without prior social consultation (Selejan-Gutan, 2021). They mainly resulted from the epidemiological situation. Such changes include, for example, extending the voting time in voting districts abroad to two days in order to avoid queues since about 3.5 million citizens reside permanently outside Romania. In addition, the number of signatures required to register a candidate was halved and made it possible to submit them electronically. The number of representatives of political parties in sub-electoral administration bodies was increased. The competencies of the president of the Permanent Electoral Authority in resolving the organisational matters of this institution were extended (Office for Democratic Institutions and Human Rights, 2020, p. 5). The changes can be treated as technical, improving, and, at the same time, increasing the participation of competitive political entities in the organisation of elections.

Some of these changes were introduced by the government in February 2020, when the epidemic broke out, by being included in the government emergency ordinance. The Constitutional Tribunal found this method of changing the electoral law unconstitutional with the judgment of 12 March 2020, and thus this legal act ceased to apply (Decizia, 2020; European Network of National Human Rights Institutions, 2021, p. 6).

As a result, the changes to the electoral laws in Romania did not reduce the sovereignty of the political nation. Some of them, e.g., postponing local elections, followed the logic of ensuring that the political nation could decide after the state of emergency. Nevertheless, the manner of introducing changes, their speed, and the lack of social consultations reduced the level of deliberativeness in making decisions by the political nation. Such a manner of proceeding by the government came, as it was argued, from the sense of lack of time when an extreme and unrecognised threat emerged. However, the political position of the minority government in parliament was fragile, and in addition, the Constitutional Tribunal was entirely independent of the government (cf. Selejan-Gutan, 2020). Consequently, despite the state of emergency, the sovereignty of the Romanian political nation did not decrease in this respect.

3.7   Bulgaria: Corruption and Fight?

Bulgaria is the most corrupt state in the EU. It is primarily due to the substantial remnants of a traditional patriarchal society with strong family ties and social relationships peculiar to communal groups. Therefore, Bulgarians treat changes in the law, including the electoral law, as an attempt to change the procedures for the functioning of social life and, to some extent, having a façade character. In each case, however, their adoption results from the clashes of many different interests.

Since the changes to the electoral law introduced in 2019 turned out to be insufficient, further amendments were proposed in the following year. The most significant change was the introduction of voting machines to polling stations in which more than 300 voters were registered. The second change involved simplifying the election protocols by removing the column for the number of unused and invalid ballots (Office for Democratic Institutions and Human Rights, 2021). Nonetheless, the president vetoed these amendments due to the excessive complexity of the election process and the lack of explicit provisions regarding the preparation of voting protocols. In turn, the parliament rejected the president's veto (The Sofia Globe, 2020). However, on 4 May 2021, the Constitutional Tribunal found the changes to the electoral law unconstitutional (Constitutional Court of the Republic of Bulgaria, 2021, p. 120–137). Introducing these changes was characterised by a rapid process of adoption and a lack of social consultations (Vassileva, 2021).

In sum, the changes to the Bulgarian electoral law were not substantial. Their introduction might have altered the speed of service to voters during the voting activity and thus reduced queues to the polling station. However, at the same time, it would mean a significant increase in the cost of handling elections and the emergence of public procurement for a company offering voting machines for polling stations. The course of the legislative process also reveals significant political divisions between the government and the president. The proposed changes to the electoral law did not change the sovereignty of the Bulgarian political nation.

3.8   Conclusions

Despite being located close to each other on the line between the ideal types of neo-militant democracy and quasi-militant democracy, on the latter's side, the analysis of themes across the attempts to shape the sovereignty of the political nations uncovered no significant similarities between Poland, Hungary, Romania, and Bulgaria. Additionally, each of these political systems is different from all others.

If the presidential elections in Poland had been held under the so-called envelope act of 6 April 2020, the Polish political nation would have lost its sovereignty. It would be up to the ruling party's officials to organise these elections and determine their results. To a large extent (this assumption applies mainly to Poles staying abroad), the political nation could not participate in the decision-making process. Furthermore, paradoxically, holding elections according to the law that was no longer in force at the moment meant that Poland became a prerogative state to an even greater extent than before.

The Hungarian ruling party took advantage of more subtle methods to increase its electoral chances. It does not mean, however, that it was a fair game. Prime Minister Orbán's party aimed to achieve a parliamentary majority by appropriate changes to the electoral law and holding a referendum, i.e., a classic tool for gaining support by autocratic leaders.

The Romanian minority government could not amend the electoral law under the procedures in force in the rule of law. Nonetheless, it is not equivalent to ineffective action. At the same time, changes to the electoral law did not limit the sovereignty of the Romanian political nation. Without more detailed analyses, it is impossible to decide whether it was the result of the weakness of the ruling political camp or the ruling elites' interiorised consciousness of the rule of law.

The Bulgarian parliament introduced, in any case, inefficiently, insignificant changes to the electoral law. Those changes neither increased nor decreased the scope of the Bulgarian political nation's decision-making freedom. At the same time, the nature of these changes raised the cost of holding the elections.

In all these four cases, changes to the electoral laws were introduced in a hurry, in the privacy of ministerial offices, and without social consultation. Such a way of proceeding with changes in the law did not result either from the epidemiological threat or the work overload of the most influential politicians. It stemmed from the need to change the law as soon as possible and thus avoid or reduce the resistance from the political opposition, other centres of public authority, and non-governmental organisations.

Acknowledgements

This chapter is a result of the research project *Civil Disorder in Pandemic-ridden European Union*. It was financially supported by the National Science Centre, Poland [grant number 2021/43/B/HS5/00290].

References

Balthasar, A. (2021). "The Austrian Path to the Constitution Of 1 May 1934 – An Applica-
    tion of the Paradigm of 'Militant Democracy' Just Avant La Lettre!?". *Hungarian Jour-
    nal of Legal Studies*, 61(2), 159–209. DOI: https://doi.org/10.1556/2052.2021.00268.
Bäcker, R. (2020). "Kategoria narodu politycznego". In J. Wojnicki, J. Miecznikowska, &
    Ł. Zamęcki (Eds.), *Polska i Europa w perspektywie politologicznej*, 35–46. Warszawa:
    Oficyna Wydawnicza ASPRA-JR.
Beširević, V. (2021). "Thinking Outside the Politics Box: Framing a Judicial Role in
    Shaping Militant Democracy in the European Union". In M. Belov (Ed.), *Courts and
    Judicial Activism under Crisis Conditions: Policy Making in a Time of Illiberalism and
    Emergency Constitutionalism*, 74–98. London and New York: Routledge.
Cavanaugh, K., & Hughes, E. (2016). "Rethinking What is Necessary in a Democratic
    Society: Militant Democracy and the Turkish State". *Human Rights Quarterly*, 38(3),
    623–654. DOI: https://doi.org/10.1353/hrq.2016.0045.
Constitutional Court of the Republic of Bulgaria (2021). "Конституционен Съд На
    Република България Годишник 2021". Retrieved from: https://constcourt.bg/en
    /YearBook.

Decizia nr.150 din 12 martie 2020 referitoare la excepţia de neconstituţionalitate a dispoziţiilor Ordonanţei de urgenţă a Guvernului nr.26/2020 privind modificarea şi completarea unor acte normative în materia alegerilor pentru Senat şi Camera Deputaţilor, precum şi unele măsuri pentru buna organizare şi desfăşurare a alegerilor parlamentare anticipate. Publicată în Monitorul Oficial nr.215 din 17.03.2020 (2020). Retrieved from: http://www.ccr.ro/wp-content/uploads/2020/05/Decizie_150_2020-1.pdf.

Democracy Index (2020). "In Sickness and in Health?". *The Economist Intelligence Unit.* Retrieved from: https://www.eiu.com/n/campaigns/democracy-index-2020/.

Diamond, L. (2020). "Democracy Versus the Pandemic: The Coronavirus Is Emboldening Autocrats the World Over". *Foreign Affairs.* Retrieved from: https://www.foreignaffairs .com/articles/world/2020-06-13/democracy-versus-pandemic.

Döbrentey, D. (2021). "Legalised Voting Tourism and Other Rules Threatening the Chances of Transparent Elections". *Heinrich-Böll-Stiftung.* Retrieved from: https:// cz.boell.org/en/2021/12/13/legalized-voting-tourism-and-other-rules-threatening -chances-transparent-elections.

Elemzésünk az egyes választási tárgyú törvények módosításáról szóló T/13679. számú törvényjavaslatról (2020). Retrieved from: https://tasz.hu/elemzesunk -az-egyes-valasztasi-targyu-torvenyek-modositasarol-szolo-t-13679-szamu -torvenyjavaslatrol.

Elkins, Z. (2022). "Militant Democracy and the Pre-emptive Constitution: From Party Bans to Hardened Term Limits". *Democratisation*, 29(1), 174–198. DOI: https://doi.org /10.1080/13510347.2021.1988929.

European Network of National Human Rights Institutions (2021). "Romania. Romanian Institute for Human Rights". *ENNHRI.* Retrieved from: https://ennhri.org /wp-content/uploads/2021/07/Romania.pdf.

Guasti, P. (2020). "The Impact of the COVID-19 Pandemic in Central and Eastern Europe: The Rise of Autocracy and Democratic Resilience". *Democratic Theory*, 7(2), 47–60. DOI: https://doi.org/10.3167/dt.2020.070207.

Invernizzi Accetti, C., & Zuckerman, I. (2017). "What's Wrong with Militant Democracy?". *Political Studies*, 65(1), 182–199. DOI: https://doi.org/10.1177/0032321715 614849.

Kovács, K. (2021). "Hungary and the Pandemic: A Pretext for Expanding Power". *VerfBlog.* Retrieved from: https://verfassungsblog.de/hungary-and-the-pandemic-a-pretext -for-expanding-power/.

Kustra-Rogatka, A. (2020). "Between Constitutional Tragedy and Political Farce: On the Postponement of the Presidential Elections in Poland". *VerfBlog.* Retrieved from: https://verfassungsblog.de/between-constitutional-tragedy-and-political-farce/.

Loewenstein, K. (1937). "Militant Democracy and Fundamental Rights, I". *The American Political Science Review*, 31(4), 417–432.

Macklem, P. (2006). "Militant Democracy, Legal Pluralism, and the Paradox of Self-Determination". *International Journal of Constitutional Law*, 4(3), 488–516. DOI: https://doi.org/10.1093/icon/mol017.

Malkopoulou, A. (2019). "Introduction: Militant Democracy and Its Critics". In A. Malkopoulou & A. Kirshner (Eds.), *Militant Democracy and Its Critics: Populism, Parties, Extremism*, 1–12. Edinburgh: Edinburgh University Press.

Müller, J. W. (2016). "Protecting Popular Self-Government from the People? New Normative Perspectives on Militant Democracy". *Annual Review of Political Science*, 19, 249–265. DOI: https://doi.org/10.1146/annurev-polisci-043014-124054.

Navrátil, J., & Kluknavská, A. (2020). "Civil Society Trajectories in CEE: Post-Communist 'Weakness' or Differences in Difficult Times?". *Politologicky Casopis*, 27(2), 101–118. DOI: https://doi.org/10.5817/PC2020-2-101.

Office for Democratic Institutions and Human Rights (2020). "Romania Parliamentary Elections. 6 December 2020. ODIHR Needs Assessment Mission Report, 14–18 September 2020". *OSCE*. Retrieved from: https://www.osce.org/files/f/documents/f/c/466779_0.pdf.

Office for Democratic Institutions and Human Rights (2021). "Republic Of Bulgaria. Parliamentary Elections. 4 April 2021. ODIHR Needs Assessment Mission Report, 14–18 December 2020". *OSCE*. Retrieved from: https://www.osce.org/files/f/documents/6/o/476866_0.pdf.

Rak, J., & Bäcker, R. (Eds.) (2022). *Neo-militant Democracies in Post-communist Member States of the European Union*. London and New York: Routledge.

Schultheis, E. (2020). "What Poland's 'Ghost Election' Can Teach Us About Pandemic-Era Democracy". *CNN*. Retrieved from: https://edition.cnn.com/2020/05/29/opinions/what-polands-ghost-election-can-teach-us-about-pandemic-era-democracy/index.html.

Selejan-Gutan, B. (2020). "Romania in the COVID Era: Between Corona Crisis and Constitutional Crisis". *VerfBlog*. Retrieved from: https://verfassungsblog.de/romania-in-the-COVID-era-between-corona-crisis-and-constitutional-crisis/.

Selejan-Gutan, B. (2021). "Romania: COVID-19 Response in an Electoral Year". *VerfBlog*. Retrieved from: https://verfassungsblog.de/romania-COVID-19-response-in-an-electoral-year/.

Siad, A., & Kottasová, I. (2022). "Hungary Sets a Date for Referendum on Controversial LGBTQ Law". *CNN*. Retrieved from: https://edition.cnn.com/2022/01/11/europe/hungary-lgbtq-law-referendum-intl/index.html.

The Sofia Globe (2020). "Bulgarian MPs Overturn President's Veto on Electoral Code Amendments". *The Sofia Globe*. Retrieved from: https://sofiaglobe.com/2020/10/08/bulgarian-mps-overturn-presidents-veto-on-electoral-code-amendments/.

Törvény egyes választási tárgyú törvények módosításáról (2020). Retrieved from: https://www.parlament.hu/irom41/13679/13679.pdf.

Turska-Kawa, A. (2016). "Preferowane wartości podstawowe a zachowania wyborcze w elekcji parlamentarnej 2015 roku". *Political Preferences*, 12, 105–119. DOI: https://doi.org/10.6084/m9.figshare.4128963.

Tyulkina, S. (2015). *Militant Democracy: Undemocratic Political Parties and Beyond.* London and New York: Routledge.

Ustawa z dnia 6 kwietnia 2020 r. o szczególnych zasadach przeprowadzania wyborów powszechnych na Prezydenta Rzeczypospolitej Polskiej zarządzonych w 2020 r., Dziennik Ustaw, 2020, poz. 827. Retrieved from: https://isap.sejm.gov.pl/isap.nsf/download.xsp/WDU20200000827/T/D20200827L.pdf.

Vassileva, R. (2021). "COVID-19 in Autocratic Bulgaria: How the Anti-Corruption Protests Temporarily Limited the Abuse of Questionable Legislation". *VerfBlog.* https://verfassungsblog.de/COVID-19-in-autocratic-bulgaria/.

Végh, Z. (2020). "Concerns over Hungary's Pending Electoral Code Amendment". *European Platform for Democratic Elections.* Retrieved from: https://www.epde.org/en/news/details/concerns-over-hungarys-pending-electoral-code-amendment.html.

CHAPTER 4

Elections in Times of a Pandemic – the Context of Political Disinformation

Waldemar Wojtasik and Adam Pluszczyk

4.1   Introduction

After President Donald Trump was sworn in, White House spokesperson Sean Spicer repeated several times during his first press conference that the attendance at the inauguration was the highest in U.S. history. Such a claim was not supported by the numbers, which indicated that there were one-third more attendees at Barack Obama's inauguration in 2009. A day later, Kellyanne Conway, an advisor to the president, defending Spicer during a television program, claimed that he provided "alternative facts" (Wight, 2018, pp. 17–19). The described event can be considered a symbolic moment in which the phenomenon of post-truth was constituted as a tool of political competition. The phenomenon itself is not new in the communication space, but the form of this kind of description of reality has changed, brought by the development of new media in the last few years. Indeed, the changes associated with mass communication favor the intensification of the occurrence of the phenomenon itself, but also tend to foster the systematic use of post-truth by politicians with the intention of achieving specific, particular goals (Pawełczyk & Jakubowski, 2017, pp. 198–199). Spicer's example reveals another mechanism relevant to political communication. In the Internet age, governments have finally lost their dominant position in creating, controlling, and accessing information and, most significantly, in fact interpretation. How a single piece of information delivered over the Internet will be decoded by an individual recipient is no longer determined primarily by the sender, who has influence over the shape of the message, but by someone able to impose their own interpretation. Therefore, a growing problem in contemporary political communication is also the phenomenon of systemic disinformation, which involves the dissemination of false or unverified information (Jerit & Zhao, 2020, pp. 77–94) that can be used to achieve political goals.

The growing role of disinformation in politics is caused by new opportunities for its dissemination, which is linked to the emergence of several previously absent phenomena. The first is the rapid acceleration of the use of the Internet and new types of media (especially social media) as tools of social communication, favoring the demassification of political communication. With them, it is possible to develop the technique of algorithmic targeting of the audience of campaign messages, allowing the autonomization of networked political communication from the previous mainstream election campaigns (Pomerantsev, 2019). Instead of one large election campaign, millions of microcampaigns are run in an integrated fashion, managed in large part by artificial intelligence (O'Neil, 2016). The web also allows for the creation of unconventional forms of political participation, triggering a far deeper type of engagement than just the often ritualistic participation in voting (Lilleker & Koc-Michalska, 2017). The increasingly rapid shift to the network of the most effective forms of electoral communication is due not only to the increasing prevalence of Internet use, but in particular to the ability to aggregate large data sets for campaign purposes (Issenberg, 2012). Another aspect favoring the development of electoral disinformation is related to the processes of personalization of politics. Focusing on the personal aspect of electoral campaigns allows the competing parties not only to nuance their messages in terms of individual social expectations, but also to reach (usually through the Internet) a single voter.

Finally, not without significance is the rapid development of big data aggregation-based electoral marketing techniques, which are increasingly effective not only in diagnosing voters' needs, but also, through the use of artificial intelligence, in generating the impressions expected by them and, with the help of network tools, reaching their awareness. The purpose of the study is to demonstrate the occurrence of disinformation in the elections in Europe during COVID-19 between 2020 and 2021. In other words, we argue that the COVID-19 pandemic offers an opportunity to instrumentalize elections. More specifically, it can be argued that the pandemic crisis constitutes a tool which can be utilized by politicians with a view to conducting disinformation, including electoral campaigns via the Internet and social media. In this chapter it will be shown that through the application of various disinformation strategies by the politicians who allegedly combat the negative consequences of the pandemic, the pandemic crisis can constitute a tool to apply particular disinformation activities. The research methods will be based on identifying selected examples of disinformation which occurred in the elections in Europe. The specific examples which will be analyzed and discussed will be taken from the websites.

4.2 Electoral Disinformation

The use of post-truth and alternative facts in contemporary electoral discourse shows the core of the difference between traditional and networked electoral disinformation. The essence of the latter is the combination of possibilities offered by online communication with the knowledge of neurobiology, especially the ability to consciously stimulate voters with stimuli that evoke expected emotional reactions, influencing the consolidation or change of presented opinions. The Internet communication revolution, therefore, must have brought about rapid changes in relations between politicians and voters, based on the increased possibility of instrumental influence on the latter, also through the possibility of using disinformation. This regularity follows from two observations about political behavior. First, political orientation is usually consistent and dependent on the professed value system in the form of a set of ideological abstracts used to give interpretations. Second, political orientation is generally not directly related to specific political issues (Sapolsky, 2021). These assumptions allow us to see that a voter's change in attitude toward specific political issues results from the evolution of his or her value system, as he or she replaces some abstracts with others. An effective mechanism for this substitution is the stimulation of the voter's consciousness (in some cases also subconsciousness) by Internet communication (Bruter & Harrison, 2017), based on using intentional disinformation.

The prevalence of disinformation tools is confirmed by regular research carried out by a team from Oxford University, which in the framework of a research project entitled Democracy & Technology (DemTech) produces an annual report on the manipulation of public opinion in social media, treating this phenomenon as a critical threat to democracy. The system of global organization of social media manipulation is monitored based on a specially designed methodological framework. The 2020 study of the prevalence of election disinformation and manipulation in 81 countries found that social media platforms and instant messaging play a key role in creating and sharing news, in campaigns and elections, and in political communication for nearly two billion voters worldwide. While network technologies have created many new opportunities for political involvement, they have also ushered in new challenges, as disinformation and state-sponsored trolling undermine human rights, degrade the quality of political news in circulation and undermine the legitimacy of democratically elected governments. Manipulation of public opinion is carried out by four main types of actors: government agencies, political parties, private companies and online communities and political influencers (DemTech, 2021).

In general, four types of manipulative strategies involving disinformation and deliberate misleading of the voter can be distinguished. The first is pro-government or pro-party communication, which involves using Internet propaganda to artificially amplify messages supporting the state or a political party. The second type of strategy concerns the creation and publication of messages aimed at attacking the opposition or supporting a smear and slander campaign against political opponents. The third type of communication strategy is aimed at suppressing participation in political debate through discouragement, trolling or harassment. Using negatively charged and exclusionary vocabulary, manipulators engage in subtle harassment of opposition-minded individuals in order to silence voices of political dissent and influence free speech. Finally, the fourth disinformation strategy, utilizing intentional hyperbolization of the arguments used, involves the use of narratives that fuel divisions and increase political polarization. Implemented externally (e.g. by foreign states), it is supposed to facilitate creating socio-political conflicts that are difficult to resolve, while the internal motivation for its use may be the electoral mobilization or demobilization of selected segments of society (Bradshaw et al., 2021).

4.3 Electoral Disinformation in the Era of COVID-19

One of the political consequences of the COVID-19 pandemic is the activation of attitudes and movements based on conspiracy theories. Belief in conspiracy theories is fostered by a societal crisis of trust in science, which fuels movements based on disinformation (Blokker & Anselmi, 2019). Research on the causes and consequences of belief in conspiracy theories points to their role in undermining trust in authorities and political institutions (Wahl et al., 2010, p. 386). In light of their findings and due to the unprecedented scope of conspiracy theories on COVID-19, there are reasons to presume their significant impact on social activism (Eberl et al., 2020). In general, conspiracy beliefs can have the effect of undermining general support for the government (Prooijen & Douglas, 2018, pp. 898–899) and reducing respect for existing laws (Imhoff & Bruder, 2014, p. 29), which can provide fertile ground for the conduct of disinformation. Additionally, belief in conspiracy theories may be associated with important life decisions e.g. questioning the legitimacy of vaccinations is associated with reduced propensity to vaccinate a child (Jolley & Douglas, 2014) and questioning the safety of technology is associated with a general reluctance to use modern technology (Bodner et al., 2020).

In an era of demassified communication, misinformation is pervasive and is further exacerbated in times of crises and emerging uncertainty about the future. The COVID-19 outbreak has created a favorable environment for disinformation activities that are organized and can be observed particularly online, as the Internet provides individuals and groups with autonomy beyond the control of regulatory bodies and governments. In addition, one of the effects of the pandemic has been shifting much of people's activity to the web, where they seek information about what was previously unknown and unpredictable (e.g. the SARS-CoV-2 virus), which, in turn, increases the likelihood of encountering disinformation. Social networks support the process of integration of spatially dispersed supporters of specific theories or social movements. They are a platform for information exchange, mutual support. It should be noted that also modern technologies facilitate the formulation of claims and demands based on false premises (Cömert, 2019, p. 14). At the same time, the literature emphasizes that the dynamic development of the Internet creates new forms of group membership. These groups are able to self-organize using information networks, omitting or minimizing the role of formal organizational leaders (Anduiza et al., 2014, p. 756). Virtual space (e.g. in the form of websites, or closed groups on social media) is a platform not only for the transmission of information between supporters of such initiatives, but also a place to raise material funds for activities or receive legal assistance (Wojtasik et al., 2021).

However, the effectiveness of manipulation in this respect may be increased considerably, only if one has influence over the media content formulated for the public (not only over disinformation activities). The asymmetry we are discussing may also be noted on this level. It is those in power (in the vast majority of cases) who will be able to exert greater influence on the media and the messages they formulate. Sometimes this is done with the use of budgetary means, as in the case of the intentional creation of content on the activities of the Polish Ministry of Justice, where under the guise of an information campaign on the changes introduced in the judicial system, this institution provided funds to the wp.pl news portal to promote the ministry's activities, thus influencing the shape of the content presented (Bradshaw et al., 2021). In the case of opposition parties, a circumstance that facilitates the formulation of socially attractive media messages is an event (e.g. an economic crisis, a natural disaster, a terrorist attack), which forces those in power to take unpopular actions. The COVID-19 pandemic crisis along with its social consequences was certainly such an occasion. In political and electoral terms, it was most often used by extreme and populist parties that questioned the goals and methods of combating the virus, as exemplified by the German *Alternative für Deutschland* (AfD). It was the only German parliamentary party to instrumentally politicize the pandemic in a systemic way. This provided an opportunity not only to criticize the government and blame it for the negative socio-economic situation, but also to actively support often illegal and violent social protests (Wondreys & Mudde, 2020, pp. 9–12)we expect the responses to reflect the main ideology and the internal heterogeneity of the contemporary far right as well as to show the increasing mainstreaming of its positions. We analyze four different, but related, aspects: (1. Another disinformation incident involving the AfD came to light in 2019, when the party's official account was caught in what is sometimes called the "fake account fail". It consists of failing to switch between accounts when having a discussion with oneself. The party's AfD profile praised its own post, although the content showed that someone else was commenting. Internet users noticed this error and the comment was quickly deleted, confirming that it is likely that the site administrator forgot to log in to another profile when commenting on the post (Bradshaw et al., 2021).

To put it briefly, the spread of disinformation in Germany was also commonplace. As a result, according to "COVID-related measures spawned protests and inspired online groups. Some of the discussions leading to these protests were laced with disinformation and contributed to an ill-informed radicalization. This bled over into campaign-related disinformation, when candidates were attacked for doing too much or too little regarding the pandemic, for instance" (Jarusch, 2021). In Spain, various social media, such as Facebook and Twitter contributed to the promotion of various conspiracy theories associated with COVID and furthermore protests. The spread of fake news also contributed to the reluctance of taking a vaccine by Spaniards. On other words, as a result, there were a number of people who did not want to get vaccinated (CERTH, 2021).

Similarly, in France, for instance, as soon as the application of vaccinations started, a number of instances of disinformation appeared. More specifically, there were even some politicians and political candidates, but also a number of organizations, companies who came up with and spread misinformation about the justified use and thus the right decision of taking a vaccine. As a result, "Since Macron's July 12, 2021 announcement of vaccine health passes, various far-right French media organizations, political candidates, and inauthentic accounts have amplified anti-vaccination and anti-health-pass messages [...]. In particular, Les Patriotes, an offshoot of Marine Le Pen's Rassemblement National (formerly Front National) used the opportunity to push untested COVID-19 cures and announce its leader Florian Philippot's candidacy for the French presidency" (Hanley, 2021). This was based on spreading the news about the allegedly unjustified use of vaccines and, in the course of time, contributed to anti-vaccine protests and at the same time discouraging citizens from getting vaccinated (Hanley, 2021). There are also cases of disinformation with reference to COVID-19 in Greece. More specifically, these were some TV and radio stations which contributed to the promotion of the alleged inaccuracy of the information about COVID-19. There were even some webpages which provided disinformation and fake news concerning various aspects connected with COVID-19. Moreover, the problem of immigration was used with a view to stressing and emphasizing the assumption that that these are the immigrants who contributed to the unnecessary spread of the virus (CERTH, 2021, pp. 69–70).

Italy is a country where the spread of disinformation about COVID-19 is also very visible. As a result, "This large amount of disinformation shared in Italian media has led the Italian government to create a page that showcases the most popular false information spread on the web" (CERTH, 2021, p. 75). In the case of Italy, there are also foreigners who contributed to the formation of disinformation, such as Russia and China which accused the European Europe of poor commitment and giving insufficient assistance to Italy. More specifically, Russia and China took advantage of the relatively low support that the European Union has given to Italy while they were in a vulnerable position in the beginning of the pandemic.

In Poland, disinformation was also used by the government to achieve electoral goals. The message can also be analyzed in the context of what Prime Minister M. Morawiecki had said before: "I'm glad we are not afraid of the virus and the epidemic as much as we used to. It's a good approach, because the virus is in retreat now. We don't need to fear it any more. We have to go to the polling stations on 12 July. Seniors, I appeal to you, don't be afraid, let's all go cast our votes!" In the context of Prime Minister Morawiecki's utterance, it is worth noting that a few weeks after the 2nd round of the election, a new wave of the epidemic occurred in Poland, with record daily numbers of new COVID-19 infections (Tatarczyk & Wojtasik, 2022).

Sometimes, as in the case of Bosnia and Herzegovina, when the authorities of this ethnically divided country, under the guise of fighting disinformation about the COVID-19 pandemic, have introduced manipulative varied restrictions on the free expression of political views in the media sphere. On the other hand, however, the nature of the influence of the traditional media makes it necessary for the authorities of this post-Yugoslav republic to defend themselves against the disinformation policy applied by Republika Srpska Television (RTRS), Republika Srpska News Agency (SRNA) or Sputnik Srbija Agency, whose disinformation activity increases especially in the pre-election period (Jusić et al., 2021) converting mouthpieces of the regime into public

forums in which various interests and standpoints could be shared and deliberated. There is general agreement that this endeavor has not been a success.
Formally, the countries adopted the legal and institutional requirements of
public service media according to European standards. The ruling political
elites, however, retained their control over the public media by various means.
Can this trend be reversed? Instead of being marginalized or totally manipu-
lated, can public service media become vehicles of genuine democratization?
A comparison of public media services in seven countries (Albania, Bosnia &
Herzegovina, Croatia, Kosovo, Montenegro, North Macedonia, and Serbia).

4.4   Conclusions

The spread of online communication has given politicians the opportunity to
create a new type of disinformation strategies. Unlike their conventional form,
which relies on generalized communication through traditional media, online
disinformation enables effective association of voters with effectively influencing content. Three factors underlie this effectiveness. The first is the Internet
ubiquity; in developed democracies, over 90% of households (and often close
to 100%) have access to broadband Internet (Correa et al., 2020). The second
factor is the ability to collect (primarily through the web) such information
about users that enables effective psychographic profiling. The third reason
for the effectiveness of online disinformation is the possibility of reaching an
individual user with an electoral message addressed to him or her. If we add to
this the use of artificial intelligence as a tool for optimizing the effectiveness
of such manipulations, some researchers are beginning to postulate the need
for new regulation of this field. As Max Tegmark (Tegmark, 2019, p. 177) notes,
legislation needs to be rapidly updated to keep up with the development of
artificial intelligence, and this raises difficult legal questions about privacy, liability and regulation. Shoshana Zuboff points out the same problem. All the
traces that people leave online generate behavioral data about them. These
can be used to improve the quality of the services offered, but they can also be
traded or exchanged, also for manipulation. This latter possibility is referred
to as behavioral surplus, which, together with data analysis and engineering
(data science), increasing computing power, algorithmic systems and automated network communication platforms, have become the basis of a system
called surveillance capitalism, in which "Google will no longer dig into behavioral data solely to improve the quality of its service to users, but rather to read
their minds in order to tailor advertising to their interests, as these interests
can be deduced from the by-products – the traces of their online activities. [...]

it will now be possible to find out what a particular person, at a particular time and place, is thinking, feeling and doing" (Zuboff, 2020, p. 114).

Social media's attempts to self-regulate against misinformation and online communication manipulation have, so far, proved unsuccessful. Statements made by the majority shareholder of Facebook, Mark Zuckerberg, in the Cambridge Analytica case before the joint committees of the US Senate or the hearing of Alexander Nix before a committee of the British House of Commons showed that online media are not able to effectively oppose such manipulations and that it simply is not profitable for them to do so, because they earn money on traffic generated online and paid advertisements related to it. Instead, they have brought to light the actual power of social media, as Donald Trump found out when Twitter and Facebook blocked his official profiles after people questioning the legitimacy of Joe Biden's election stormed the Capitol. That event demonstrated yet another threat to the electoral communication process - the possibility of politicians being censored not only by the state, but also by solely private entities.

With free media, fair elections and an open internet, liberal democracies are more vulnerable than autocracies to external interference, especially from other states wishing to pursue their international goals (Bartlett, 2019, p. 94). Today's highly ineffective and illusory control over the distribution of online content will be further weakened when Elon Musk's Starlink and other global networks of communication satellites become widespread (although, on the other hand, this will severely limit the prospects for systemic Internet censorship currently being implemented in their territories by states such as China, Iran and Russia) (Vatandoost & Salehi, 2021, pp. 55–57). The process of undermining democratic principles can be intentionally reinforced from the outside, for example through online interference by hostile states in order to create disinformation, chaos and polarization of attitudes in society. An audit by the US administration forced Facebook to reveal that in this case alone, 470 pages and profiles were redirected to the disinformation-mongering Internet Research Agency, which is linked to the Russian secret service. Paid advertisements (often paid for in Russian rubles) reached over 126 million Americans, urging them to participate in actions supporting Donald Trump or protests against the establishment of mosques (Vaidhyanathan, 2018, pp. 281–282) many pointed to the liberating potential of platforms like Facebook andTwitter. Yet five years later, as many Americans reeled in shock from the election of an authoritarian bullshit artist (using philosopher Harry Frank's technical definition of the term. The DemTech report identifies dozens of other interferences in the electoral process (including in Australia, the Netherlands, Germany, Nigeria, Venezuela and Italy) that were carried out by Russian state services in countries deemed vital to the country's vital interests (Bradshaw et al., 2021). Other states that are suspected of global manipulation and disinformation include Iran, China, North Korea and Israel (Tenove, 2020, p. 521), that is primarily those states that are either non-democratic or in conflict with other countries.

References

Anduiza, E., Cristancho, C., & Sabucedo, J. M. (2014). Mobilization through online social networks: The political protest of the indignados in Spain. *Information, Communication & Society*, 17(6), 750–764. https://doi.org/10.1080/1369118X.2013.808360

Bartlett, J. (2019). *Ludzie przeciw technologii: Jak internet zabija demokrację (i jak ją możemy ocalić)*. Katowice: Sonia Draga

Blokker, P., & Anselmi, M. (2019). *Multiple Populisms: Italy as Democracy's Mirror*. New York: Routledge.

Bodner, J., Welch, W., & Brodie, I. (2020). *COVID-19 Conspiracy Theories: QAnon, 5G, the New World Order and Other Viral Ideas*. Jefferson: McFarland.

Bradshaw, S., Campbell-Smith, U., Henle, A., Perini, A., Shalev, S., Bailey, H., & Howard, P. N. (2021). *Country Case Studies Industrialized Disinformation: 2020 Global Inventory of Organized Social Media Manipulation*. https://demtech.oii.ox.ac.uk/wp-content/uploads/sites/127/2021/01/CyberTroop-Report-2020-v.2.pdf

Bruter, M., & Harrison, S. (2017). Understanding the emotional act of voting. *Nature Human Behaviour*, 1(1), 1–3. https://doi.org/10.1038/s41562-016-0024

CERTH. (2021). *Online Disinformation in Europe*. https://left.eu/content/uploads/2022/01/disinformation-study-24112021_compressed.pdf

Cömert, N. Ç. (2019). Postmodern Status of New Social Movements: A Research on Yellow Vests. *Connectist: Istanbul University Journal of Communication Sciences, 56*, 1–29.

Correa, T., Pavez, I., & Contreras, J. (2020). Digital inclusion through mobile phones?: A comparison between mobile-only and computer users in internet access, skills and use. *Information, Communication & Society*, 23(7), 1074–1091. https://doi.org/10.1080/1369118X.2018.1555270

DemTech. (2021). *DemTech | Industrialized Disinformation: 2020 Global Inventory of Organized Social Media Manipulation*. https://demtech.oii.ox.ac.uk/research/posts/industrialized-disinformation/

Eberl, J.-M., Huber, R. A., & Greussing, E. (2020). *From Populism to the 'Plandemic': Why populists believe in COVID-19 conspiracies*. SocArXiv. https://doi.org/10.31235/osf.io/ejpw7

Hanley, H. (2021). *Misinformation regarding France's COVID-19 "health passes" spread on Twitter*. https://medium.com/dfrlab/misinformation-regarding-frances-COVID-19-health-passes-spread-on-twitter-ba344920bc16

Imhoff, R., & Bruder, M. (2014). Speaking (Un-)Truth to Power: Conspiracy Mentality as a Generalised Political Attitude. *European Journal of Personality*, 28(1), 25–43. https://doi.org/10.1002/per.1930

Issenberg, S. (2012). *How Obama's Team Used Big Data to Rally Voters*. MIT Technology Review. https://www.technologyreview.com/2012/12/19/114510/how-obamas-team -used-big-data-to-rally-voters/

Jarusch, J. (2021). *Disinformation in the 2021 German Federal Elections: What Did and Did Not Occur*. https://www.institutmontaigne.org/en/blog/disinformation-2021 -german-federal-elections-what-did-and-did-not-occur

Jerit, J., & Zhao, Y. (2020). Political Misinformation. *Annual Review of Political Science*, 23, 77–94.

Jolley, D., & Douglas, K. M. (2014). The Effects of Anti-Vaccine Conspiracy Theories on Vaccination Intentions. *PLOS ONE*, 9(2), e89177. https://doi.org/10.1371/journal .pone.0089177

Jusić, T., Puppis, M., Herrero, L. C., & Marko, D. (2021). *Up in the Air?: The Future of Public Service Media in the Western Balkans*. Wien: Central European University Press.

Lilleker, D. G., & Koc-Michalska, K. (2017). What Drives Political Participation? Motivations and Mobilization in a Digital Age. *Political Communication*, 34(1), 21–43. https://doi.org/10.1080/10584609.2016.1225235

O'Neil, C. (2016). *Weapons of Math Destruction: How Big Data Increases Inequality and Threatens Democracy*. New York: Crown.

Pawełczyk, P., & Jakubowski, J. (2017). Postprawda i nowe media. Czy potrzebujemy postprawdy? *Środkowoeuropejskie Studia Polityczne*, 1, 197–212.

Pomerantsev, P. (2019). *This Is Not Propaganda: Adventures in the War Against Reality*. New York: Faber & Faber.

Prooijen, J.-W. van, & Douglas, K. M. (2018). Belief in conspiracy theories: Basic principles of an emerging research domain. *European Journal of Social Psychology*, 48(7), 897–908. https://doi.org/10.1002/ejsp.2530

Sapolsky, R. M. (2021). *Zachowuj się: Jak biologia wydobywa z nas to, co najgorsze, i to, co najlepsze*. Poznań: Media Rodzina.

Tatarczyk, D., & Wojtasik, W. (2022). The Incumbency Advantage during the COVID-19 Pandemic: Examining the 2020 Polish Presidential Election. *East European Politics and Societies*. https://doi.org/10.1177/08883254221085307

Tegmark, M. (2019). *Życie 3.0. Człowiek w erze sztucznej inteligencji*. Warszawa: Prószyński i S-ka.

Tenove, C. (2020). Protecting Democracy from Disinformation: Normative Threats and Policy Responses. *The International Journal of Press/Politics*, 25(3), 517–537. https:// doi.org/10.1177/1940161220918740

Vaidhyanathan, S. (2018). *Antisocial Media: How Facebook Disconnects Us and Undermines Democracy*. Oxford: Oxford University Press.

Vatandoost, O., & Salehi, E. (2021). *The Role of Star Link Mission on Degrading Authoritarian Governments' Power Across the Middle East* (SSRN Scholarly Paper ID 3815549). Social Science Research Network. https://papers.ssrn.com/abstract=3815549

Wahl, I., Kastlunger, B., & Kirchler, E. (2010). Trust in Authorities and Power to Enforce Tax Compliance: An Empirical Analysis of the "Slippery Slope Framework". *Law & Policy, 32*(4), 383–406. https://doi.org/10.1111/j.1467-9930.2010.00327.x

Wight, C. (2018). Post-Truth, Postmodernism and Alternative Facts. *New Perspectives, 26*(3), 17–29. https://doi.org/10.1177/2336825X1802600302

Wojtasik, W., Muster, R., & Buszman, K. (2021). Religiosity and New Populism. *European Journal of Science and Theology, 17*(5), 79–94.

Wondreys, J., & Mudde, C. (2020). Victims of the Pandemic? European Far-Right Parties and COVID-19. *Nationalities Papers*, 1–18. https://doi.org/10.1017/nps.2020.93

Zuboff, S. (2020). *Wiek Kapitalizmu Inwigilacji: Walka O Przyszłość Ludzkości Na Nowej Granicy Władzy*. Poznań: Zysk i S-ka.

CHAPTER 5

Populism in Times of Pandemic – When Difficult Questions Find Simple Answers. An Analysis of the Phenomenon Taking into Account Selected Choices

Agnieszka Kasińska-Metryka

5.1   Introduction

The crisis of liberal democracy is a widely discussed problem, which has attracted the attention of researchers from many fields and disciplines for over a decade. The erosion of political systems that have for years been considered models of democracy raises questions about its future. Forecasting the transformations of democracy has been extremely difficult since 2020 by the emergence of a factor that can be considered the so-called game changer, i.e. a pandemic caused by the COVID-19 virus. Apart from the threats to the life and health of citizens, there were unforeseen circumstances for verifying the effectiveness of the functioning of states. One of the threats to global security, which until now had functioned in the collective imagination as an abstract scenario, has become a reality.

Under these extraordinary conditions, some phenomena present in democracies, including new populisms, have been strengthened. Numerous studies in the form of indexes of populism prove that - by increasing the number of voters, the number of populist parties that govern alone or in coalitions in many countries, is increasing.

There are many definitions of populism in the literature, which essentially reduce it to the dimension of ideology (e,g, Mudde), "unique set of ideas" (Hawkins, Kaltwasser 2019) or action. Nowadays populisms should be considered both conceptually and as specific activities. Considering the changes within populisms and, above all, their entry into the mainstream, the concept of Takis Pappas was chosen for the purpose of this analysis. *Populism is an omnipresent, multifaceted, and ideologically boundless phenomenon. What, then, distinguishes its various manifestations in Europe, Latin America, the United States, and elsewhere across time (old vs new populisms), region (western vs eastern; but also Nordic, Alpine, Baltic, and Southern European), regime type in which they develop (democracy vs non-democracy), and ideological hue (right vs left populisms)* (Pappas 2015).

The purpose of this theoretical analysis is to confirm or deny the existence of a cause-and-effect correlation between the pandemic and populist sentiment and actions. There are the emotions of voters, which populists also managed during the pandemic time, that translated into concrete electoral results. Many political analysts expected that the pandemic elections would mark the end of the march to power for the populist parties, but this did not happen. It is therefore worth analyzing these correlations.

The field of reflection is both the forms of political activity of entities that are political actors (individual and / or collective) and the society subjected to populist influences. The hypothesis put forward in the text boils down to the statement that under the threat of a pandemic, populist parties initially lost support in order to finally regain their influence on the political reality, and even strengthen their position. The examples cited in the analysis concern elections during the pandemic, as their results verify the research hypothesis.

In an emergency, the narrative based on reference to science was not dominant, and the number of people doubting the existence of a pandemic increased proportionally to its duration. Populists formulated simple 'recipes and recommendations' that were often in response to rising or falling support in the polls. The same politicians refused to wear face masks or encouraged them, demanded the introduction of restrictions and then were their opponents. Thus, the pandemic revealed the cynical and opportunistic dimension of the actions of many populist actors, especially in those countries where elections took place.

The basic method used in this chapter is the comparative method, which is supplemented by the content analysis referring to the quoted fragments of statements of selected political actors as exemplification. A critical review of the existing sources allowed to conclude that while populism and its successive versions are often undertaken in scientific works, there has not been too many analysis of these phenomena against the background of a pandemic, especially in the theoretical dimension. The most comprehensive in this regard is the collective study entitled *Populism and the Politicization of the COVID-19 Crisis in Europe*, edited by Giuliano Bobb and Nicolas Hubé (Bobb & Hubé, 2021). This work relates primarily to the assessment of the support or loss of social support of populist parties in selected European countries during a pandemic and the strategy of political influence on the new *demos*. Equally interesting, although focused on the role of the media in the processes of populist influence, is the study entitled *Populism, the Pandemic and the Media. Journalism in the age of COVID, Trump, Brexit and Johnson*, edited by John Mir, Tor Clark, Neil Fowler, Raymond Snoddy and Richard Tait (Mir et al., 2022), The third book worth mentioning is Michael Burleigh's monograph *Populism Before and After the Pandemic* (Burleigh, 2021). The author makes a macroanalysis of the 'age of anger', referring to global examples. Interesting books, however more relate to the phenomenon of populism than to populism in times of pandemic, are also: Benjamin Moffitt *The Global Rise of Populism: Performance, Political Style, and Representation* (Moffitt, 2017), Alberto Martinelli, *Beyond Trump: Populism on the Rise* (Martinelli, 2017), Roger Kimball *Vox Populi: The Perils and Promises of Populism* (Kimball, 2017).

5.2   Populist Leaders and Their Influence on Elections

Understanding the phenomenon of populism is not possible without considering the question of leadership and changes within it. Analyzing elections during the pandemic, the question of what role populist party leaders played emerges as a key question. Whether in Central and Eastern Europe, Western Europe or the US, it was the leaders who played the most important role in mobilizing the electorate. Donald Trump in the US, Matteo Salvini in Italy, Santiago Abascal in Spain, Jaroslaw Kaczynski in Poland, Victor Orban in Hungary are just the most spectacular examples supporting the thesis that a strong leader is necessary for populists to win elections. Personalized leadership can be understood after Jean Blondel, who defines leadership in this way: It is the power of a person or several persons enabling a group to be persuaded to adopt a particular line of policy (Blondel, 1987:321).

To understand why populist leadership was effective during the pandemic, one must look at the two concepts of "change" (within leadership models) and "anger" (as "fuel" for populists).

Changes within liberal democracies take place at all levels of their functioning. The axiological, institutional and functional dimensions are changing. Much of the changes are dictated by the anger felt by the ruled. Anger towards reality and the elite who are responsible for the loss of public trust.

The category of anger is one of the most important for understanding contemporary changes and means experienced dissatisfaction, emotional turmoil and sometimes even a starting point for aggressive behavior. In literature, apolitical anger, politically destructive anger and politically constructive anger are most often indicated. In the case of the last two types, one can speak of the reverse and the obverse of the same coin. The destruction of the old order is usually associated with an attempt to build a new one. It is these circumstances that are also conducive to the 'exchange of leaders' and the emergence of such leaders who would not have had a chance to take power in the period leading up to the changes. The definition of this new type of leadership is the so-called 'neoleaders' characterized by abandoning traditional marketing tools in favor of direct communication using social media (Kasińska & Gajewski, 2021). Communication, which grew out of the subsoil of new populism, uses a simplified message distributed directly by leaders, freed from the principles of political correctness, changes both the existing democracies from the inside and directly affects the relations between the citizen and the state.

Although political rivalry is always based on making promises and trying to gain the greatest possible support among voters, populist leaders who have been brought to power by the greatest wave of the democratic crisis, represent a specific type of leadership and environmental impact. Unlike the leaders who represented the so-called classical, that is, having a left-wing populism, contemporary populists combine various axiological systems in their activities. The new populisms have got primarily right-wing roots, and as examples are right-wing populist parties, which at the end of 2018 had the support of over 50% in as many as three European countries, based on the results of recent elections, i.e. in Hungary (Fidesz), Greece (Syriza) and Italy (Five Star Movement). The term 'national populisms' is used more and more, and demagogic presidents such as Donald Trump (USA), Jair Bolsonaro (Brazil), Rodrig Duerte (Philippines) confirm both the importance of simplified message in the campaign and the role of new media.

This does not mean, however, that in their message they do not use left-wing or center rhetoric, while avoiding clear ideological declarations. The strength of the message of populist leaders is not ideologically anchored content, but simple slogans organizing the image of an increasingly complex and dangerous world. As examples, Marine Le Pen's statements regarding international politics and Russia-Ukraine relations (several months before the outbreak of the war) can be cited: "I don't think Putin made such a mistake. But I also believe that the Union played the role of a firefighter-pyromaniac in this matter. You can say what you like, but Ukraine belongs to Russia's sphere of influence. By trying to violate this sphere of influence, tensions and fears are created, and they lead to the situation we are witnessing today. And we should all fight together against the real threat that looms over Europe: Islamism" (Bielecki, 2021). When asked about the possibility of Ukraine joining NATO, she said: "First, Turkey needs to be moved out of it" and: "I also do not think that in the present state of NATO, it could accept any new states" (Bielecki, 2021). A content analysis of statements of Polish politicians as well confirms these tendencies – nowadays populism is right-wing and populist slogans appeared during the pandemic time to increase the number of electorates. Polish president Andrzej Duda was at an advantage over other candidates in the presidential campaign. Although the candidates have officially suspended their campaigns, Duda has an opportunity to show himself to Poles as a president and "caring father of the nation". Secondly, he might gain from the demobilization of opposition voters, a large percentage of whom are residents of the largest cities, most exposed to the virus. Also, the leader of the ruling populist party Law and Justice, repeatedly stressed that holding elections is a priority. Jaroslaw Kaczynski has also told many times, that religious practices should be continued even during a pandemic time: *If it doesn't create danger, if all these rules are followed, then I think it's okay to go to church* (PAP, 2020).

For the purposes of the above considerations, the perspective of populism was adopted after Jan-Werner Müller, i.e. as an anti-establishment and anti-pluralist phenomenon in which the real will of the nation is replaced by the so-called true will, that is the will established in an authoritarian, non-liberative manner and beyond the formal, rational election procedure (Werner-Müller, 2022). The author also draws attention to the fact that populists are not actually interested in increasing participation but want to replace it with plebiscite acclamation.

It is the simple answer to difficult questions that generate the popularity of populist leaders and parties. The Authoritarian Populism Index noted in relation to 2019 that in 33 surveyed countries, the total support for populists was as high as 22%, and in 11 of them they ruled independently or co-governed (Timbro Authoritarian Populism Index, 2019). The same source indicates how the nature of populist groups has changed over the three decades, i.e. how the dominance of right-wing populist parties has evolved since the 1990s. Currently, left-wing populisms are marginal in Europe and these phenomena concern mainly southern countries. The consolidation of populist groups is already visible at the level of various groupings in the European Parliament. The common denominator of these entities is the creation of conflicts ('people' versus 'elites'), nationalism, striving to remove institutional restrictions on power, anti-capitalism and anchoring most of them in Catholicism ('rebuilding the bulwark of Christianity in Europe').[1]

---

1   On December 4, 2021, the leaders of several European right-wing parties that can be classified as populist met in Warsaw. The chairman of the National Front, Marine Le Pen, Hungarian Prime Minister Viktor Orban and the leader of the Spanish party Vox Santiago Abascal, met with the PiS president. Earlier, i.e. in July 2021, members of right-wing conservative groups whose representatives sit in the European Parliament had signed a joint ideological declaration. The declaration was signed, inter alia, by: PiS president Jarosław Kaczyński, the president of the Brothers of Italy Giorgia Meloni, the president of the Spanish Vox Santiago Abascal, the president of Fidesz Viktor Orban, the leader of the League, Matteo Salvini, and representatives of several other center-right parties. The aim of the cooperation was described as 'a profound reform of the EU'. (Białkowski & Małecki, 2021).

What paradigm of populist leadership can be constructed on the evoked characteristics? Referring to the theory of leadership, they should be defined as 'neoleaders' who use a populist narrative and are endowed with communication skills. In practice, this means leaders who do not have the classically understood competences to be a leader (qualifications, experience, background) but are characterized by an above-average ability to read social moods and adequately respond to them. Having abandoned political correctness, these leaders establish not only new rules of behavior on the ruler-ruled line, but also new rules of the political game. Understanding the real impact of populists on reality requires emphasizing that they are the initiators of the transformation of legal systems, in those countries where they govern independently or in a coalition. The initiated reforms (for example in Hungary or Poland) violate the existing legal order and introduce the elements into it that allow us to speak of 'authoritarian populism'. In this way, there is a legitimation of undemocratic elements (changes in the judiciary, media, education) within systems that preserve the façades of democracy. These actions mean a restriction of the political freedom of citizens, but - as is the paradox - they are distributed under the slogans of actions for the benefit of the people (*populus*).

5.3   Elections Overshadowed by the Pandemic – the Example of the USA and Other Countries

The aforementioned Pappas pointed out the differences in populism depending, among other things, on geographical location. When writing about populism in Central and Eastern Europe, it is worth having a point of reference in the form of the US political system. Elections during the pandemic time in the United States created a certain matrix for comparisons. Many authors point to Central and Eastern Europe as the "new mecca" of populism, but on the other hand, it is in the US, the cradle of democracy, that populism has the most voters. Therefore, it is worth comparing the different levels of elections in some countries, and make the largest of them, the US, the reference point.

After all, writing about elections in pandemic time, it is impossible to avoid the question - how is it possible that the consolidated US democracy has not escaped the influence of a populist leader? The election of the 46th president of the United States was marked by exceptional drama related to the way Donald Trump left his office. The course of the campaign and the 'twists and turns' that took place during the voting also make it unique, and the figure of the president-populist seeking re-election confirms the correctness of the thesis that the American elections of 2020 can be treated as a lens focusing the phenomena arising at the meeting point of politics and pandemic.

Before the outbreak of the pandemic, the political situation in the US had indicated a possible re-election of D. Trump. Although the society remained polarized (which was favored by the president's populist narrative), the economic indicators were optimistic. However, already in November 2020, the number of cases (about 8 million) and deaths (about 220,000) verified the social perception of priorities and, above all, sharpened the differences between the attitude of D. Trump and his greatest rival from the Democratic Party, Joe Biden (Econ, 2021). It can be said that regardless of extraordinary circumstances, Trump used a strategy that had repeatedly brought him success, i.e. minimizing the problem. Already at the first meeting with voters, the US president declared that it was time to return to normality and defrost the economy. At the same time, he contested the actions of other leaders (including Angela Merkel), accusing them, inter alia, of too many tests performed to find out one is sick. One of the most unfortunate statements was D. Trump's statement that "Tests are a double-edged sword – when we perform a lot of them, we find more cases" (Krzysztofek, 2020). Although the president's backstage tried to joke this statement, it can nevertheless be interpreted as an expression of true intentions. Both the president himself and his supporters appeared at the rallies without face masks, even when some people turned out to be infected.

Despite the increasing number of victims of the pandemic, Trump has consistently 'cursed reality' with repeated statements that 'the virus is in retreat' and even pointing to a time when the pandemic will end. It was one of the rhetorical measures typical of populists, reinforced by messages that the US government was doing a great job of containing the threat. "According to Gallup, Trump's approval rating fell from a 2020 high of 49% on March 22 to 38% on June 30.8 Polls showed nearly 60% of Americans disapproved of Trump's response to the pandemic, with very little variation in the 5 months leading up to the election" (Econ, 2021) .

Contrary to the president's assurances, citizens noticed the rapidly spreading threats and criticized the administration's actions in the fight against the pandemic. At the same time, drastic changes affected the economy - the costs of hospitalization and the limitations resulting from the *lock down* irreversibly changed the image of *prosperity.*

The course of the pandemic has weakened Trump's chances of re-election, and the economic effects that were most noticeable to citizens resulted in a decline in support for the president and a clear increase in support for Joe Biden (in June 2020 his lead in the poll increased to around 10%). In the following months, this situation began to change, i.e. Trump was making up for losses, but in the most critical period of the election, that is in October, there was another economic slump and a drop in the ratings of the incumbent head of state. In addition to Trump's populist narrative and his tactics of negating threats, the attitude towards far-right groups, i.e. the lack of a strong condemnation, was also not without significance. Summing up, it should be stated that the president's strategy was directed primarily to supporters, in which it was to consolidate support for the candidate. The polarization of the message, highlighting economic successes, and emphasizing the need to care primarily for the interests of the USA, could guarantee success, but in pre-pandemic conditions.

Faced with the threat of COVID-19, especially just before the autumn elections, voters turned to the classically democratic values represented by Joe Biden. The rule of law, minority rights, climate policy and, most of all, self-control in hazardous conditions translated into electoral success.

For comparison, it is worth referring to presidential elections in Poland, parliamentary elections in Lithuania and local elections in Bavaria.

In the case of the presidential elections in Poland, the issue of the should of the state of emergency and mail-in voting, which they wanted to introduce for every voter, was important. In April and May, there was a discussion in Poland on the legitimacy of correspondence voting and it was never resolved. President Andrzej Duda's victory over Rafał Trzaskowski was only a few percent (51.2%), but in reality, it was a choice between two visions of Poland. During the pandemic, Poles heard that as a country they had to help themselves. This was emphasized by the president, the prime minister, and the leader of PiS. *Duda fought a divisive campaign in which he promised to back "family values" at the expense of LGBT rights and frequently used homophobic rhetoric* (Walker 2020). In retrospect, it can be said that this decision was not sufficiently analyzed from either a legal or financial perspective. Most important was the need to organize elections and mobilize the electorate to participate. Such a strategy is characteristic of populists, as goals achieved here and now are more important than future scenarios. It can be concluded that such a message reached the electorate - despite the pandemonium, turnout was over 68 percent, almost as high as in the 1995 presidential election.

In Lithuania, low turnout proved to be a problem during the 2020 elections. Despite the appropriate adjustment of the law and the use of security measures during the elections, citizens participated in the elections in such small numbers for the first time in many years (Malużinas 2021). The geographic proximity of Poland and Lithuania does not mean similarities in the mentality of citizens. The level of political rationality, resistance to right-wing populism, different models of coexistence between secular and ecclesiastical authorities

(Mačiulis 2021) and different historical experiences (Lithuania as a former Soviet republic) contributed to the formation of different electoral attitudes during the threat of the COVID-19 pandemic.

The example of Bavaria is another confirmation of the differences between countries, including in the level of political culture and the ability to achieve consensus, beyond the influence of populists. Local elections were held in Bavaria in March 2020, i.e. during the COVID-19 pandemic: March 15 - the first round of elections (in traditional form and by mail), and March 29 - the second round (by mail only). It is worth noting that the change in the voting formula was accompanied by consensus of all factions in parliament. The second round was organized in districts where the vote in the first round was inconclusive. Researchers of these elections also highlight the differences, between elections in Poland and Bavaria: *the Bavarian consensus of all parliamentary factions is in stark contrast to the sharp political dispute in Poland. For this reason, the example of Bavaria was also interpreted differently by each side of the dispute, to support a narrative favorable to that side. The credibility of the referenced data was for particular groups of voters depended on who was citing the data. It shows the erosion of public debate, since the feuding parties were unable to agree with each other not only on values or interpretations, but also on facts* (Radwan, Horonziak, 2022: 122).

The described election in the US, as well as the cited examples of neighboring countries (Poland, Germany, Lithuania) and three different types of elections during the pandemonium, show the correlation between the populism of power and the conduct of elections. The correlation relates to the strength of the influence of right-wing populism on political systems before the pandemic, the degree of cooperation between the state and the Church, and the mentality of voters.

Poland and the U.S. are countries whose power during the period under analysis can be classified as populist, while Lithuania and Germany are countries less affected by populism (the populist party only came third in the 2020 elections). Thus, a correlation can be identified - the higher the level of populism, the greater the problems with the organization of elections (Poland) or recognition of their legitimacy (USA).

5.4   Pandemic and Populism

As it has already been mentioned, the activities of populists are conducive to times of destabilization, threats, and a deficit in trust towards those in power. The restrictions related to the pandemic, which were introduced in the spring of 2020 by the governments of individual countries, have shown how much interdependence connects the countries of the European Union and the importance of solidarity in times of threat to the health and life of citizens. Paradoxically, it could be assumed that joint actions of states to research a vaccine against COVID, mobilization of funds for counteracting a pandemic or medical aid between states would confirm how valuable the values on which democracy is based and weaken populists. In practice, there has been no retreat from populist parties as their leaders have adopted various strategies to use the pandemic to strengthen their position on the political scene. The aforementioned author, Brett Meyer, compiled a list of the activities of the most important European populist leaders during the pandemic, and based on this description, it can be concluded that two attitudes were dominant, i.e. neglecting the threat and an anti-liberal attitude. Disregard for the threat (although these attitudes evolved in different phases of the pandemic) was shown by the already described Donald Trump, and anti-liberal attitudes by Victor Orban or Mateusz Morawiecki. Since the effectiveness of fighting the pandemic was disappointing, and the imposed restrictions irritated some of the ruled, populists very easily used proven communication matrices, including division into us-them. In order to emphasize their belonging to the 'people', populist leaders occasionally broke anti -pandemic orders (for example by not wearing face masks in public places). In this way, they both distanced themselves from formal centers of power and from scientists. It was therefore a message addressed to the 'people', although - as the example of Matteo Salvini is well illustrated - it was dependent on the ratings of support. This Italian politician was in favor of a complete lockdown and the closure of borders in just two months, calling for the complete opening of the country a week later, and the following week for the closure of the Schengen area. In early April, however, he called for the opening of churches for Easter, which even the center-right opposed (Krzysztofek, 2021).

These declarations resulted from changes in the support polls. A similar volatility of attitudes was presented by Donald Trump, whose campaign took place during the pandemic. In one of his speeches, he declared that wearing face masks was not effective, and in the following month he stated that it was 'an expression of patriotism' (Kolecka, 2020).

The wave of the pandemic did not slow down - as expected by some researchers - populist moods, although it made the citizens aware that their health and life depended on the effective mechanisms of the functioning of the state. However, despite these particular conditions, the DNA of populism, which Roger Eatwell referred to as 4D, has not changed. The first factor is distrust - lack of trust. It grows out of the belief that the elite are in the distance from the people, and even despise them. In Poland, such attitudes of the rulers led to the defeat of the Platforma Obywatelska (The Civic Platform, PO RP) in 2015, and in the US presidential elections, Hillary Clinton was accused of being insensitive to the needs of ordinary people. Another 'D' is destruction. Liberal democracy, focused on the development needs of an individual, posed a threat to traditional values and a fixed way of life for a part of society. The migration crisis has shown the difficult to accept side of multiculturalism, for which homogeneous societies were not mentally prepared. Exclusive behaviors and attitudes emerged as a defensive strategy, especially regarding persons of a different race or religion. In these circumstances, the populist narrative put in order the overly complex world and restored the vision of the old order. In the axiological area - which should be emphasized - populist parties often have the support of religious institutions when disputes concern such rights as, for example, the right to abortion (Black Marches of Women in Poland) (Gessen, 2020).

The third factor is deprivation i.e. the belief of citizens that they are cut off from the financial resources that a small financial elite holds in its possession. Deprivation also applies to opportunities for promotion and professional development, which applies to both people already present on the labor market and young people who are said to be in the precariat. The Glast component of the 'populism drive' is dealignment or loss of identification. "Even in mature democracies, more and more people no longer feel strongly identified with the main parties and they leave off voting for them" (Eatwell, 2021). The pendulums of the elites, which for many years marked the direction of the drift of old democracies, ceased to be a reliable mechanism at a time when change was needed. Paradoxically, it was the populists who turned out to be the force which, under the banner of antisystemism, penetrated into political systems, allowing the ruled to see the possibility of a 'new' in politics. Countries that have resisted populism for years (Spain, Germany, Portugal) are no longer an exception. In Spain, the far-right VOX party came to the fore, the existence of which the Spaniards themselves did not know existed for years. In Portugal, Chega's party leader André Ventura won 12%. votes in the presidential elections, which can be treated as an excellent result. "In Brazil, where Bolsonaro initially gained the support of a rather middle and wealthy class, state support from the public during the coronavirus crisis increased his popularity in areas belonging to the former leftist party" (Eatwell, 2021).

The pandemic highlighted the role of governments and experts in fighting it, but it certainly did not eliminate populist power. A significant number of researchers agree with the thesis that the pandemic was the leading cause of Donald Trump's failure to run for re-election. It was she who thwarted the time of economic prosperity, which was to secure the president's re-election. Fighting the pandemic dominated the presidential campaign in 2000, and the opponent Joe Biden accused Trump of downplaying the threats, and thus contributing to the deaths of over 200,000 COVID-19 patients in the US. From the beginning of the pandemic, Trump tried to free the economy from constraints, and he often appeared at meetings without a mask. Only the president's infection during the campaign and his hospitalization changed the image of the politician who places freedom, especially economic freedom over the epidemic. Trump's extreme style of politics has proved attractive enough in times of economic growth, but the pandemic factor has exposed real social needs, including security that does not depend on race, religion or education.

5.5   Populism - a Victim of the Pandemic?

Expectations about the limitation of the role of populist parties due to the pandemic, and even beliefs about their possible disappearance, have been negatively confronted with reality and it can be argued that two years after the outbreak of COVID-19, populist entities are returning to the political game with the existing rights. While, at the start of the pandemic, much of the public hoped for a vaccine to be developed quickly, distrust of the very concept of vaccination began to grow over time. The development of anti-vaccination movements was evident in every country, and the attitude towards vaccination became another tectonic trench between social groups. This threat was noted, among others, by Chancellor Angela Merkel – "I can only guess how bitter for those who mourn a loved one who has been lost to COVID-19 or are still struggling strenuously with the effects of this viral disease, must be some incorrect statements that deny the existence of the coronavirus and spread lies about it. Conspiracy theories are not only untrue and dangerous, but also cynical towards these people" (*Noworoczne orędzie*, 2021).

Such circumstances constitute the natural environment for the activities of populists who, as has already been mentioned, primarily use a strategy of dividing citizens and blaming narrow groups (elites) for everything. In this narrative, only populists represent 'the real society'. In this way, mechanisms that destroy democracy are created, because, as Jan Werner Muller notes, "their claim to a national monopoly has two negative consequences for democracy. First, the populists argue that all other contenders for power are not in principle entitled to power. It's not about programme or even axiological differences – other politicians are just bad" (Werner-Müller, 2020).

The temporary limitation of the populists' activity (Matteo Salvini in Italy, the AfD party in Germany) does not mean, however, that they have lost the 'war for the souls of voters'. The ideas of representing the 'true nation' can be combined with both anti-vaccination and vaccination rhetoric, depending on the conditions of a particular political system. Its functioning is significantly influenced by the media, because in those countries where free media have been reduced (for example Hungary), the message regarding both the pandemic and the effectiveness of the rulers depends entirely on the latter. Prime minister Orban, even before the outbreak of the pandemic, had a qualified majority in parliament, he could introduce convenient legal and institutional changes, so pandemic restrictions only strengthened the undemocratic governance mechanisms.

Populism, therefore, did not become another victim of the pandemic, but rather a patient who had fallen ill, but recovered quickly. Fears of populism generate ideas to combat it, which, however, appears to be impossible, but also unfounded. Apart from the parties that can be described as representing 'populist authoritarianism', there are many groups with populist concepts embedded in their programs (social democratic, Christian Democrats or others). Therefore, it seems that strategic actions on the political scene should focus on strengthening the rule of law of EU countries, especially regarding the protection of the judiciary, protection of minorities against repressive actions and ensuring the possibility of the functioning of free media.

5.6   Conclusions

Populism and the pandemic are two phenomena which, coming from different sources but with similar severity, attacked the seemingly stable world of Western democracies. Populist parties gradually grew in power, gaining influence in other countries (France, Spain, the Netherlands, Switzerland, Germany, Poland, Hungary, etc.) and creating a strong force in the European Parliament. Thus, the impact of populists can be compared to a disease that slowly unfolds the weakened organism of democracy. A disease so difficult to overcome that the cure could only be even more populist actions on the part of the rulers. This rivalry, however, would be deadly to democracy. It is more effective, though time-consuming, to rebuild lost social trust and to repair those mechanisms that have turned out to be dysfunctional. However, this scenario was disrupted by the outbreak of the COVID-19 pandemic in spring 2020. It diverted the attention of public opinion from traditional political problems, focusing on priority issues, i.e. protection of life and health. Populists seemed to have nothing to offer in circumstances that required the mobilization of state resources and the support of the scientific world in developing and implementing a COVID-19 vaccine as soon as possible. However, it soon turned out that the lack of a sense of security among citizens was conducive to the spread of anti-vaccine theories around which the pan-European movement was built. Easy access to content that undermines the existence of the COVID-19 virus or questions the need for vaccination contributes to building a narrative based on rumors, myths, and prejudices. Therefore, they are rhetorical narratives also used by populists, whose aim is not to actually involve the 'people' in the mechanisms of co-government, but to create a common belief that only populist parties are unique, and their postulates are right.

Thus, the hypothesis of the lack of a lasting impact of populism on elections during the pandemic and the subsequent functioning of political systems is confirmed. While the first wave of the pandemic caused populists to „stop" and citizens to seek reassurance in the mechanisms and institutions of traditional democracy, this was a temporary state. Ongoing research indicating the development of populism shows that there has been a steady rise in right-wing populism since 2000.

The problem of democratic systems is responding to the threats posed by populism. Bidding for electoral promises can lead to an escalation of the phenomenon, so the antidote to the disease of populism remains public education, especially in the field of critical information management.

References

Białkowski, R. & Małecki, M. (2021, December 4). „Orban, Le Pen, Kaczyński. W Warszawie trwa spotkanie liderów europejskich partii prawicowych". *Forsal.pl*. Retrieved from: https://forsal.pl/gospodarka/polityka/artykuly/8306322,orban-le-pen-kaczynski -w-warszawie-trwa-spotkanie-liderow-europejskich-partii-prawicowych.html

Bielecki, J. (2021, December 6)." Le Pen: „Ukraina należy do sfery wpływów Rosji". *Rzeczpospolita*. Retrieved from: https://www.rp.pl/polityka/art19168311-le-pen-ukraina -nalezy-do-sfery-wplywow-rosji

Blondel, J. (1987) Leadership, [In:] The Blackwell Encyclopaedia of Political Institutions, ed. V. Bogdanor, Oxford.

Bobb, G., Hubé, N. (Eds.) (2021). *Populism and the Politicization of the COVID-19 Crisis in Europe*. Palgrave Macmillan.

Burleigh, M. (2021). *Populism Before and After the Pandemic*. Hurst Publisher.

DPA, DW/jak (2020, December 30). „Noworoczne orędzie Angeli Merkel: „Stanęliśmy przed wyzwaniem na miarę stulecia".Retrieved from: https://www.dw.com/pl

/noworoczne-or%C4%99dzie-angeli-merkel-stan%C4%99li%C5%9Bmy-przed
-wyzwaniem-na-miar%C4%99-stulecia/a-56100743

Eatwell, R. (2021). „Fala populizmu się nie skończyła, choć pandemia lekko ją wyhamowała". Retrieved from: https://wszystkoconajwazniejsze.pl/prof-roger -eatwell-fala-populizmu-sie-nie-skonczyla-choc-pandemia-lekko-ja-wyhamowala/

Econ, J. P. (2021). "The COVID-19 pandemic and the 2020 US presidential election". Retrieved from: https://www.ncbi.nlm.nih.gov/pmc/articles/PMC7809554/

Gessen, M. (2020). "The Abortion Protests in Poland Are Starting to Feel Like a Revolution". Retrieved from: https://www.newyorker.com/news/our-columnists /the-abortion-protests-in-poland-are-starting-to-feel-like-a-revolution

Hawkins KA, Kaltwasser CR (2019) Introduction: the ideational approach. In: Hawkins KA, et al. (eds) The Ideational Approach to Populism. London: Routledge

Kasińska-Metryka, A., Gajewski T. (Eds.) (2021). *The Future of Political Leadership in the Digital Age. Neo-Leadership, Image and Influence.* Routledge.

Kimball, R. (2017). *Vox Populi: The Perils and Promises of Populism*, Encounter Books.

Kolecka, E. (2020). „Donald Trump w maseczce hitem sieci. Teraz tłumaczy, dlaczego ją założy". Retrieved from: https://www.o2.pl/informacje/donald-trump-w-maseczce -hitem-sieci-teraz-tlumaczy-dlaczego-ja-zalozyl-6534426338347808a

Krzysztofek, A. (2020). „Wybory 2020 w USA: Trump wznawia kampanię. Koronawirusa nazywa … „kung-flu". 6 chorych wśród organizatorów". Retrieved from: https://www .euractiv.pl/section/polityka-zagraniczna-ue/news/usa-trump-tulsa-koronawirus -COVID19-wybory2020-wybory-prezydenckie-w-usa-kung-flu/

Krzysztofek, J. (2020). Retrieved from: https://www.euractiv.pl/section/bezpieczens two-i-obrona/news/salvini-wlochysarscov2-COVID19-pandemia/

Krzysztofek, J. (2021). „Salvini zmienia zdanie ws. epidemii i wzywa do noszenia maseczek. Przyczyną spadające notowania Ligi". Retrieved from: https://www.euractiv.pl /section/bezpieczenstwo-i-obrona/news/salvini-wlochysarscov2-COVID19 -pandemia/

Mačiulis, D. (2021) Wkład Kościoła Katolickiego w Republice Litewskiej (1918–1940) w narrację o tworzeniu nowoczesnej Litwy (In:) Archiwa Biblioteki i Muzea Kościelne (115).

Mair, J., Clark T.,Fowler N. , Snoddy R., Tait R. (Eds.) (2022). *Populism, the Pandemic and the Media. Journalism in the age of COVID, Trump, Brexit and Johnson.* Routledge.

Malużinas, M., *Parliamentary Elections During the COVID-19 Pandemic: An example of Lithuanian Elections in 2020*, Atheneum 69/2021.

Martinelli, A. (2017). *Beyond Trump: Populism on the Rise*. Edizioni Epoké.

Moffitt, B. (2017). *The Global Rise of Populism: Performance, Political Style, and Representation.* Stanford University Press.

Mudde, C., Kaltwasser C.R, *Populism. A very short introduction*, Oxford University Press, 2017.

PAP (2020), "Jarosław Kaczyński o chodzeniu do kościoła w czasie pandemii: Biskupi nie zakazali", Retrieved from: https://wydarzenia.interia.pl/raport-koronawirus-chiny /news-jaroslaw-kaczynski-o-chodzeniu-do-kosciola-w-czasie-pandemii,nId,4394761

Pappas, T (2015) Populism, Retrieved from: https://www.academia.edu/9048351 /Populism

Radwan A., Horonziak S., Wybory korespondencyjne w Bawarii 29 marca 2020 r. a COVID-19. Analiza empiryczna na tle debaty o zasadności organizacji wyborów w czasie pandemii (In:) Public Policy Studies vol. 9, No 1/2022.

Timbro Authoritarian Populism Index (2019). Retrieved from: https://populismindex .com/

Walker S. (2020) "Duda narrowly re-elected in Poland in boost for ruling national-ists". Retrieved from: https://www.theguardian.com/world/2020/jul/13/incumbent -andrzej-duda-wins-polish-presidential-election-commission.

Werner-Müller, J. (2016). "Co to jest populizm?". Retrieved from: https://www.research gate.net/publication/326040527_JanWerner_Muller_Co_to_jest_populizm

Werner-Müller, J. (2020). "Populiści w pandemii zyskują". Retrieved from: https://oko .press/jan-werner-muller-populisci-w-pandemii-zyskuja/

A Radical Criticism of the Democratic State: The Case of the Anarchist Movement in Pandemic Times

Paweł Malendowicz

6.1   Introduction

The subject of the study is anarchism as a current of radical political thought. The precursors of anarchism in the nineteenth century, modern leaders of the anarchist movement and its followers are opposed to all forms of power and domination. Opposition to authority and social hierarchy is a basic negative value in anarchism. It was founded on the positive value, which is the idea of freedom. In anarchism, freedom is a maximized or absolutized value. For anarchists, the institution that limits people's freedom is primarily the state, including the democratic state.

The scope of the research includes anarchism as a current of contemporary political thought that criticizes the democratic state. Jacek Bartyzel, a Polish scholar of political thought, used the division into two types of critiques to analyze the criticism of democracy: substantial and accidental. The study of anarchist criticism of the state includes the substantial criticism, i.e. concerning the essence of the criticism of the democratic state, as an institution in which the essential 'evil' lies and which cannot be repaired. From this comes the call for the abolition of the state. The research also includes an accidental criticism of the democratic state, i.e. an analysis of the arguments formulated against the democratic state, which are the 'errors' of democracy that can nevertheless be corrected (Bartyzel, 2009, p. 11). The anarchist criticism of the democratic state is a substantial criticism, although in their criticism of the state anarchists also make use of the arguments inherent in accidental criticism. Anarchism is a current of political thought that seeks to annihilate the state, including the democratic state, as an oppressive institution based on coercion, violence, hierarchy, and capitalist exploitation. Other ideologies, anarchists argue, including the three major political ideologies – Liberalism, Marxism and Fascism – share a common assumption of the necessity of the state, which makes them authoritarian in nature (*On New Evil*, 2001, p. 16). Moreover, anarchism is not populism, although both movements sometimes use similar arguments to criticize democracy and refer to the myth of good people and bad elites. But anarchists do not want power. They do not create political parties. They do not want to change the state, but to destroy it, even if it were a democratic state based on electoral democracy. This determined the choice of anarchism for the following analysis. The attitude of anarchism to the institution of the state distinguishes this current of political thought from other currents. Other currents of political thought usually contain postulates for the repair of the state or changes in its political system, but not for the liquidation of the state itself. The only exceptions are currents of political thought that are on the margins of politics, such as primitivism, tribalism or national anarchism. These currents were influenced in different ways by the very anarchism formed back in the 19th century.

Contemporary research on anarchism covers a range of topics (see e.g.: Marshall, 1992; Gordon, 2007; Skirda, 2002; Malendowicz, 2007, 2013; Manfredonia, 2001; McLaughlin, 2007; Purkis & Bowen, 2004; Franks & Wilson, 2010; Franks & Kinna, 2014; Shantz, 2002; Epstein, 2001; Williams, 2009a, 2009b, 2017; Williams & Lee, 2012), primarily the history and present day of anarchist thought and the anarchist movement in particular countries or continents, new trends and transformations in anarchist thought, the philosophy of anarchism, anarchism in theories of social movements, the formation of new currents of anarchism, the differences between currents of anarchism, the relationship between anarchism and the anti-globalization movement, shifts in emphasis in anarchist rhetoric, the subject of anarchist criticism, and visions of the future. However, research aimed at recalling and clarifying the position of anarchists towards the nation-state as traditionally understood and democracy, whose institutional feature is the parliamentary system and general elections, is increasingly rare. Such research, however, may serve to determine the constructive functions of radical criticism of democracy performed for the improvement of the quality of democracy. And it is anarchism, understood as a thought formed in the nineteenth century and unchanged today in terms of core values, despite changes in the rhetoric, using non-modern language, as a thought in opposition to social hierarchy and any authority, also in a democratic state, that can be used as a lens for analyzing contemporary societies (Williams, 2009, p. 189). The time of the COVID-19 pandemic did not cause grassroots social movements to fade away and end their struggle for a more just world (Pleyers, 2020). This time also updated the anti-state aspects of anarchist thought. This was manifested in the criticism of the democratic state, including parliamentarism and general elections.

The research was based on interpretative theory. In the author's opinion, it is impossible to know the world properly, including the principles, values and nature of a democratic state, without learning about its various interpretations. Western societies learn about the world through the dominant interpretive frameworks and thinking patterns formed in the process of upbringing, by the education system and mass media, and perpetuated in social relations. Their interpretative frameworks and thinking patterns have been based on material values, on which the value of freedom (according to the logic of the free market – freedom to acquire goods) has been based. In the process of interpreting the world, Western societies give the democratic state the meaning of an obvious necessity and indispensability. For them, a democratic state is a guarantee of freedom to satisfy their needs, mainly material ones, while the need for non-material freedoms is satisfied by, for example, universal suffrage of governing bodies or the possibility to practice various religions and function in different subcultural circles. Anarchists, on the other hand, interpret the world through a different hierarchy of values and assigning different meanings to its elements. In their political thought, the value of freedom is maximized and taken holistically. It is also a value interpreted radically, which excludes the possibility of compromise. It implies the necessity of abolishing the state rather than reforming it. This is a postulate consistent with the concept of substantial criticism of the democratic state in anarchist thought. This, in turn, means that the postulates and demands of the anarchist movement are in fact a manifestation of the struggle to give commonly used concepts, such as 'state' and 'democracy', different meanings. The time of the COVID-19 pandemic perpetuated the dominant meanings given to these terms in the dominant narrative, but it also became a pretext for undermining them and for strengthening the criticism of democracy. This in anarchism is interpreted as a fiction of the power of the people. This was demonstrated during the pandemic, in which the authority in the democratic state appeared to be even more alienated from the people, expanding its reach and employing undemocratic means of wielding power, including manipulation and violence. Elections legitimized it, but declining voter participation raised questions about the level of legitimacy of power. Low participation rates were seen by anarchists as a premise for the social negation of the democratic state.

With reference to the above assumptions, the author formulated the following research questions:

1.   How do anarchists interpret the term 'state' and what meaning do they give to it?
2.   What is democracy as a political system functioning within the state for anarchists?
3.   What arguments do anarchists use in opposing democracy and in the criticism of general elections?

4. Which of these arguments are substantial and which are accidental?
5. How did the pandemic affect anarchist criticism of the democratic state?
6. What did anarchists propose as an alternative to representative democracy?
7. What functions can anarchist criticism of democracy have in relation to democracy itself?

Answering the above questions, the author used qualitative research. He applied content analysis of treaties, program documents, propaganda and journalistic articles, the authors of which were anarchists. The analysis made it possible to identify the arguments of anarchists used against the democratic state. The author also used participant observation of the anarchist movement in his long-term research on the anarchist movement. It allowed to 'feel' anarchism in order to understand it. Understanding different ways of interpreting the world, including the anarchist interpretation of the democratic state, may serve democracy itself, improve its quality and overcome the crisis of democracy. The author is aware that the applied interpretative strategy may cause the danger of creating a new interpretation of the studied concepts. However, he is convinced that the analysis of various interpretations, true for their authors, brings the researcher closer to the knowledge of objective reality. Its essence is the multiplicity of interpretations of democracy, including the motives for making choices and participating in elections.

6.2   The Contemporary Anarchist Movement and Anarchist Thought

The sources of modern anarchism lie in the thought and activity of the precursors of anarchism from the 19th century and the beginning of the 20th century. Contemporary anarchists in their program documents, propaganda and journalistic texts most often refer to the thought created by Pierre-Joseph Proudhon (1809–1865), Mikhail Bakunin (1814–1876), Élisée Reclus (1830–1905), Peter Kropotkin (1842–1921), Errico Malatesta (1853–1932), Emma Goldman (1869–1940). These, however, are only selected names of those among the anarchists of the turn of the nineteenth and twentieth centuries, which most often appear in the contemporary journalism of the anarchist movement. The anarchist movement, which developed in the late nineteenth century, existed in an organized international form until World War I. In the interwar period, only the International Workers' Association, which was founded in 1922, functioned at the international level. After World War II, attempts were made to reactivate the international activity of the movement, but it was not until 1968 that the International of Anarchist Federations was established (Manfredonia,

2001). Today, the anarchist movement includes hundreds of small and often ephemeral groups, mainly in Europe and the Americas, but also in Australia, Asia and Africa. Anarchism in the organizational and communication dimension also includes hundreds of titles of the anarchist press, Internet portals and actions, protests and demonstrations organized in defense of individual and social freedoms. They are part of the anti-globalization protest. However, the radical demands of anarchists dissolve in the anti-globalization protest, and the multiplicity of unorganized groups perpetuates the marginalization of the movement. This is facilitated by the diversity of currents in anarchism, among which the dominant currents are: anarcho-communism, anarcho-syndicalism, ecological anarchism (green anarchism), insurrectional anarchism, and anarcho-feminism. Anarchism also influences other currents of political thought, such as transhuamanism and primitivism, creating anarchotranshumanism and anarchoprimitivism. Since in some currents of political thought, in which the word 'anarchism' appears in their names, the idea of positive freedom (freedom to) is not treated as primary, they cannot be counted as anarchist thought. This applies, for example, to national anarchism, which has fascist connotations (Sunshine, 2008).

6.3   An Anarchist Interpretation of the State

Regardless of the doctrinal differences of the currents of anarchism, the characteristic feature of its core is the idea of maximized freedom and opposition to all coercive and violent organizations. Despite the transformation of the functions and tasks of the state in the era of globalization, it still remains such an organization for anarchists.

Anarchists are opponents of states, regardless of their systemic forms. Polish anarchists claimed to believe that the concentration of power in a system of state communism must lead to a narrow power elite controlling the rest of society by means of administrative coercion. However, they also recognized that the concentration of capital in a capitalist system leads to an equally narrow elite controlling society by means of economic coercion. Since neither of these situations can be reconciled with the anarchists' idea of freedom, they advocated the abolition of all hierarchical social and economic structures. They also recognized that today's society is dominated by a narrow ruling class with administrative power or capital. They rule over the rest of society in their own interests. The ruling class, even if it exercises power by democratic appointment, the moment it gains it, is no longer interested in maintaining the democratic rules of the game. Such an organized society cannot exist without coercion and repression, because maintaining the privileges of a narrow elite is only possible through the existence of a police apparatus ready to defend the status quo (*Płaszczyzna ideowa* ...).

Anarchist critique of the state covers both democratic and undemocratic states. In both, elections are held that perform specific functions. In undemocratic countries, elections do not select the party that best represents the people's will. Instead, elections serve as internal propaganda and are used to shape the image of power outside the state. Undemocratic countries, apart from using force against society, organise elections also to verify the level of public support. The support obtained in the elections is used to create a narrative about the legitimacy of power. Besides, elections are a form of interaction between the authorities and society. Voters can submit complaints and wishes against the authorities, written on election cards, which allows for assessing social moods and accurate opinions about the authorities (Żyromski, 2016, p. 109–116). Elections in non-democratic countries create the impression of the legitimacy of power, not its actual legitimation.

In democratic countries, elections are one of the primary conditions for the legitimacy of power. However, these must be general, equal and secret elections (Żukowski, 1997, pp. 21–34). They must also be based on the pluralism of programs and the competitiveness of political parties, free access to information by voters, and the ability to control the conduct of elections by independent observers. Elections in democratic countries perform specific functions (Szymanek, 2021, p. 40–41). First of all, it is a creational function consisting in filling specific positions by selected candidates. The elections provide an opportunity to perform the articulatory function, which rests upon revealing candidates' views and expressing the needs and interests of social groups. The recruitment function, in turn, is the selection and recruitment of political elites. The mobilisation function manifests itself in mobilising the electorate's support for political ideas, values and programs. The educational function concerns increasing the knowledge and awareness of society about political activities and processes. Beyond them, elections perform functions that, for anarchists, confirm that it is right to challenge democracy. It is primarily a control function, manifested in the fact that the ruled can control the rulers and replace them by voting. According to anarchists, however, this exchange always takes place within the circle of the dominant political elite, which, accepting electoral democracy, agrees with the very principle of power that limits human freedom. This entails the function of "creating power". As a result of the elections, a ruling majority emerges. For anarchists, it is evidence of the creation of social divisions, the conflicting nature of the political system and the state ignoring the needs and interests of those who, as a mathematical minority, found themselves in the opposition. The elections also play a legitimisation role, which legitimises the future actions of the authorities. From the anarchists' point of view, these actions may not be compatible with the will of the losing minority, but even with the intention of the majority that voted for the winning political party. Finally, the elections have a channelising function. It relies on channelling (channelling emotions and ordering) tensions and social conflicts. According to anarchists, social conflicts and tensions are specific to a capitalist state in particular. Elections understood in this way in a democratic and capitalist state serve to direct the activity of voters towards the election process, which is to prevent them from taking action against the government. According to the anarchist concept, elections thus serve to keep the dominant classes in power through the exchange of elites within these classes.

Related to this was the anarchist criticism of capitalism, which as an economic system was part of the democratic state. According to anarchists, capitalism is based on economic coercion and social inequality, forcing the majority of society to renounce its own desires and give up the realization of its own needs for the sake of the interests of the holders of the means of production. Since the capitalist system is unable to satisfy the needs of the majority of society at a satisfactory level, it is necessary to have a repressive apparatus to safeguard the interests of the dominant classes (*Płaszczyzna ideowa* ...). According to the editors of an anarcho-syndicalist magazine *Direct Action:* "The state does not hinder the working of capitalism as the free market right would have it, nor does it restrict or limit it, as the left would have it: The state works only in the interest of capitalism" (*Globalisation* ..., p. 18–19). In the era of globalization, states have become the lackeys of big business, and governments are unable to pursue effective intervention policies in economic markets, deliver social welfare benefits, and defend workers' rights. Already in the early stages of capitalism, the new capitalist class took control of the state as an instrument of political power. This enabled it to maintain privileges. Since then, the state has always served capitalism (*Globalisation* ..., p. 18–19). States with a system of parliamentary democracy, on the other hand, protect the interests of capitalists in a way that is legitimized by general elections.

A feature of states is social inequality. This is especially true in democratic and capitalist states at the same time. Therefore, as a publicist of *Rojo y Negro* from Spain recognized, talking about democracy as a system that promotes freedom is not justified. Political freedom without economic equality is a lie and self-deception (Peiró, 2010, p. 7).

Securing the interests of the power and ruling classes in states also manifests itself in fencing off the multitudes of migrants who try to enter Europe and North America (*Fortress Freedom* ..., p. 4–5), as well as in the military policy of Western countries. Both the migration policy and military policy of modern states are the consequence of globalization processes. The object of criticism of anarchists in the field of military and imperialist policy was mainly the United States, which after the collapse of the Soviet Union pretended to be the only superpower in the world, which was also served by the ideology of the free market (*Apocalypse soon* ..., p. 31–33). Apart from the military policies of nation-states, their maintenance was also served by the dominant mass culture, religions, media and educational systems, which, according to anarchists, gave such terms as 'state' the meaning of necessity and indispensability.

6.4   Criticism of State Democracy

In 2001, an article was published in the British journal *Direct Action* which stated: "Democracy is necessary. It is the only way we can hope to eradicate oppression and inequality. But the term has been misused and abused to the point of losing any specific meaning" (*Democracy without parties* ..., p. 2).

Electoral democracy within the state has been criticized by anarchists as an essentially undemocratic system, in which general elections legitimize the government and its right to limit the freedom of the people. In their criticism of democracy, modern anarchists invoked the words of anarchist Emma Goldman: "If voting changed anything, they'd make it illegal" (Goldman, no date). This claim reflects the anarchists' attitude toward general elections and, more broadly, towards democracy. It also shows that, according to them, the achievement of anarchist goals cannot be accomplished through acts of voting.

Anarchists are against taking part in elections and usually advocate boycotting them. For them, parliamentary democracy is not democracy. They call themselves democrats, but in the sense of supporting a democracy in which every individual has the right to participate permanently and not once every few years. Gregor Kerr – publicist for *Red & Black Revolution: A magazine of libertarian communism* from Ireland wrote in 2001: "The main reason why anarchists are so opposed to parliamentary elections is because we are fervent believers in democracy – in real democracy. What passes for democracy in terms of how parliament operates is in fact the complete opposite. You only have to look at the recent USA Presidential election for proof of that – the person who got the most votes didn't win the election, tens of thousands of people intimidated out of voting because of the colour of their skin, ballot papers laid out so confusingly that some people didn't know who they were voting for – and of course the result being declared before all the votes are counted. Now this didn't take place in some backward 'banana republic' where they're only starting to get the hang of this democracy thing. This was in the supposed 'greatest democracy in the Western World'. Oh and of course almost half of the people didn't bother to vote at all" (Kerr, 2001, p. 11). This author also pointed out the dependence of candidates in democratic elections on the business community. He reasoned that if any of them wanted to pursue a program of radical change, before they could do so, the owners of business and capital would transfer their financial resources, leading to economic disaster and mass unemployment. While the capitalist state can take the form of a welfare state, it is only if the ruling class fears losing power (Kerr, 2001, p. 12).

Fidel Manrique, on the pages of *Andalucía Libertaria*, accused democracy of being corrupt. He considered that there are people who join political parties in order to improve their lives and there are political parties that are created only to benefit from public assets. In this context, he believed that democracy is a fiction, and voting legitimizes the power of an organized minority for its own benefit (Manrique, 2010, p. 23).

Whereas in Polish journalism, criticism of democratic elections was based on ten arguments, identical to anarchist criticism of parliamentary democracy:

- everyone has the right not to vote,
- the basis of democracy is direct participation in political decision-making, and representation should rather be the exception, participation in elections is therefore an acceptance of the increasing alienation of power,
- participation in elections is an endorsement of representative democracy, which has led to oligarchic rule in which opposition is a fiction and the political system is a cause of social apathy,
- whole spheres of social life have been excluded from democratic principles, e.g. workplaces, so it is necessary to recognize democratic principles in real spheres of life, and not in spheres that are abstract for the majority
- people do not take part in elections because nobody represents their interests,
- democracy as a game of interests and not as a procedure of common decision making is a reason for its rejection, but moreover the democratic system does not give a possibility of proper identification of interests, which is connected with the message of media and education,
- calling for a vote against anti-democratic groups gives the illusion that the deepening authoritarianism can be resisted through parliamentary elections and legal means, while only a slight correction can be hoped for,
- calling for a vote may result in the victory of groups connected with the business world,
- people naively believe that there are politicians and parties that are trustworthy, while trust in politicians can only come from social control of their actions and not from a belief in their personal qualities,

- increasing voter absenteeism is a refusal to legitimize the system (Urbański, 2007; Malendowicz, 2013, p. 327–328).

The author of a publication in *Red & Black Revolution* magazine, summarizing criticisms of the general election, wrote: "The very act of going into a polling booth and putting a number or an x on a piece of paper is in itself an act of disempowerment, it is an acceptance that someone else has the right to make decisions on our behalf. In every situation in which decisions have to be made, there are basically two options – either the decision is made by the people affected by it or it is made by someone else. Capitalist society being what it is, usually our decisions are made for us by someone else" (Kerr, 2001, p. 13). According to him, being an anarchist means rejecting the right of those in power to rule. He proposed that instead of electing representatives, one should use one's energy to attempt to build a new society in which one can make decisions oneself, rather than through representatives who are not bound by instructions to the voters anyway (Kerr, 2001, p. 13).

Less frequently, anarchist journalism referred to the real problems related to violating the rules and fairness of elections in democratic countries. Meanwhile, they may manipulate election procedures, e.g. the size and boundaries of electoral districts, which results in the deformation of the election results (Żukowski, 1997, p. 131–141). More often, however, anarchists highlighted the problems of disinformation and voter manipulation. It manifests itself in spreading fake news, false accusations, rumours and discrediting opponents in the election fight. In addition, anarchists assessed the election campaigns to preach mutual slander and marketing activities aimed at promoting a specific product - a candidate. However, advertising such a candidate is based not on promoting his competence to take the position for which he is to be elected but on superficial features, attracting voters. In the candidates' opinion, these voters are guided by their impressions and not by an in-depth reflection on the competencies of politicians. According to anarchists, however, the most important thing is that every person and every social group are capable of independently shaping their lives and organising themselves into communities. For this, power in the relationship of leadership and subordination is not needed, nor is there any election to emerge this power.

6.5   Impact of the COVID-19 Pandemic on the Anarchist Criticism of the Democratic State

Negative opinions of anarchists about the democratic state and parliamentary democracy were consolidated in the period of the COVID-19 pandemic.

In the journalism and documents of the anarchist movement, emphasizing the dichotomy between society (the governed) and power (the governing) became increasingly clear. The anarchists' assessment of the actions taken by the authorities in democratic states is reflected in the March 2020 report on the spread of the coronavirus and the role of states in its 'fight'. In it, the authors of the report stated: "From one side, our lives are threatened by a new virus; from the other side, our freedom is menaced by nationalists and authoritarians intent on using this opportunity to set new precedents for state intervention and control. If we accept this dichotomy – between life and freedom – we will continue paying the price long after this particular pandemic has passed" (*Against the Coronavirus ...*, 2020).

According to anarchists, the authorities in the state always act according to their own interests and the interests of big business. In their opinion, the strategy adopted by the authorities during the pandemic was not aimed at protecting people from the virus, and those in power did not intend to save the lives of all those affected, including the poor. It was therefore a mistake to blindly trust in the authorities that they were acting to save people. For if those in power spoke of health, it was in relation to the health of the economy, as exemplified by the subsidies from state budgets directed to financial entities such as banks (*Against the Coronavirus ...*, 2020).

According to participants in the anarchist movement, the time of the pandemic was to be used by the authorities to intensify their control over society. Such opinions of anarchists justified numerous restrictions, including restrictions on the movement of people and orders to 'lock' people in their homes. Anarchists in Poland even called for resistance to 'the state of emergency'. They argued that the introduction of emergency laws is often accompanied by abuses of power (*Ruch anarchistyczny ...*, p. 4). This gave rise to the threat of a 'democratic state' turning into a 'totalitarian state'. Jarosław Urbański warned on the website of the Polish Anarchist Federation that what seemed to be an inevitable affliction for two weeks or months of the epidemic, over two years could mean the establishment of a new totalitarian regime (Urbański, 2020a). That is why banners with slogans appeared on the streets of one Polish city: 'Power is a virus' and 'Restrictions are a symptom of prison' (Pasterczyk, 2020).

Anarchists analyzed that most of the society believes that one of the primary roles of the state is to help the weakest and those affected by some crisis. Meanwhile, in crisis situations, the state fails (Urbański, 2020b). The crisis caused by the pandemic has hit the excluded, the poor and the vulnerable most of all (*Ruch anarchistyczny ...*, p. 4). Therefore, argued one of the publicists of the anarchist press, society cannot count on the state, but must 'help itself'. Realistically, helping each other turns out to be much more valuable (also in financial terms) than what the government can give people (Urbański, 2020b). 'Mutual help' – a key slogan for anarchists, and also the title of a book by the precursor of anarchism Peter Kropotkin (1915), would therefore be an alternative to state action during a pandemic.

However, the democratic state granted itself a monopoly on managing the crisis of the pandemic. Elections held during the pandemic were seen by anarchists as legitimizing the state's restriction of freedoms and civil rights and confirming the alienation of power from society – the public's trust in power was seen by anarchists as a failure of their propaganda and the result of manipulation and state violence, but on the other hand, increasing voter absenteeism was seen as a belief in the lack of social acceptance of power.

One of the examples of the lack of trust of part of the society in the state was the scandal called 'envelope elections', which took place in Poland in 2020. The government in Poland then tried to organise the elections using ballot papers, which were to be sent by post. However, this procedure raised doubts as to the observance of the secrecy of voting. Moreover, it was not based on the provisions of the law in force at that time. All voters, e.g. those in quarantine, could not participate in the elections, violating the universal suffrage principle. The National Electoral Commission, an institution established to organise elections in Poland, was to be eliminated from the election procedure. During the pandemic, elections were to be organised not by an independent institution but by a minister representing the party in power. If this happened, it would be inconsistent with the elementary principles of democracy (Jędrzejczyk, 2021). Analysing the events in Poland in 2020 in the context of anarchist political thought, it can be concluded that, from the anarchist perspective, they would prove that the ruling elites exercise power for their own benefit and, above all, for the sake of maintaining power. Power elites are also able to sacrifice the principles of a democratic state for the sake of maintaining power.

6.6   Substantial and Accidental Criticisms of the Democratic State

Among the arguments used by anarchists in criticizing the democratic state were those that were substantial in nature and those that were accidental in nature.

'State', 'democracy', 'elections' in the state are concepts that have been given the meaning of necessary and indispensable by the authorities. For anarchists, their meaning is different and boils down to the fact that the democratic state restricts freedom. It must be stressed, however, that the different meaning given to these concepts by anarchists does not depend on their sociopolitical characteristics and their material situation. Anarchist groups are formed by people of different ages, although young people and the so-called young adults predominate in them, there are people with different levels of education and different material situations. What they have in common, however, is a high sensitivity to social problems and a rebellion, usually youthful, against coercion resulting from the maximization of the idea of freedom in their respective thought processes. Therefore, in their view, elections are always elections of some kind of power and the relinquishment of freedom for it. This is also why anarchists believe that only the abolition of the state can lead to the liberation of individuals and whole societies. This is a criticism of the state with a substantial character. According to it, on the example of analyses published by German anarcho-syndicalists, it can be concluded that the choice between the main liberal and social parties will not change anything because 'socially just' capitalism is much less likely than a classless society (Webin, 2005, p. 12–13). Also, voting for political parties that would like to radically change the political system in the state is a mistake, according to anarchists. This is why anarchists criticized parties of the left whose programs were concepts of replacing one form of capitalism with another, in this case a form of bureaucratic state control (*Fascism and democracy* ..., p. 8–9). They also criticized anti-globalization movement activists and politicians who called: "Vote me, so I can save our democracy from the big companies". For they claimed that: "anarchists know that the role of the State is to serve those companies: this is what the State does!" And they added: "This is where we part ways with those who think the state is an ally of labor and the poor in the fight against capitalist globalization" (Walt van der, 2001, p. 19).

The pandemic provided an opportunity for anarchists to repeat substance-based arguments against the democratic state. During it, however, anarchists more often used accidental arguments. The author of a publication on the website of the Polish Anarchist Federation wrote about the government's reactions to the pandemic, which were late, exaggerated, inadequate to the situation, and dictated by the ignorance of those in power: "The government does not want to admit that it responded to the virus too late, that two months were wasted (...) to prepare the health service and society for the epidemic. It could have produced (purchased) a sufficient number of masks, suits, respirators, tests, designated infectious disease hospitals, set up laboratories, prepared personnel and procedures. It could have protected the elderly, and all the preparatory steps could have been subjected to public consultation, and written into democratic rules" (Urbański, 2020a).

Anarchists informed the recipients of their publications about the mistakes of government in managing the pandemic crisis. This did not mean, however, that the election of a different political party by popular vote would eliminate those mistakes. Electing a different party would only mean electing a different power. And any power, in the anarchist view, is opposed to expanding the freedom of individuals and social groups. This shows the connection between the accidental criticism and the substantial criticism of the democratic state and justifies the creation of alternative to state democracy concepts of direct democracy.

6.7 Anarchist Alternative to Electoral Democracy in the State

Democracy as a system operating within the state was criticized by anarchists. Anarchists rejected the rule based on the principle of mathematical majority and in the system of parliamentary democracy negated the rule of representation, i.e. the rule of minorities legitimated by elections. Related to this is the alternative concept of direct and participatory democracy leading to anarchy (Lundström, 2018). It can also be interpreted as simply a method of democratic self-organization of society. This conception is based on the interpretative radicalism of the term 'democracy'. It means precisely directness, individual and collective activity and, importantly, an uncompromising nature. The latter refers to the negative interpretation of the idea of freedom in electoral democracy. For, according to the anarchist interpretation, one cannot relinquish some freedom in a system of state democracy without losing it completely.

This is the justification for the concept of direct democracy. Anarchist documents and journalism point out that direct democracy is based on delegation and not representation. The difference between delegation and representation is that delegates are only elected to make certain decisions. Delegates do not have the right to change a decision previously made by an assembly of the people. Delegates (as opposed to representatives) can be dismissed immediately if they fail to fulfill their tasks. Decisions are made on the principle of 'from the bottom up', a principle formulated in the 19th century by Mikhail Bakunin, one of the precursors of anarchism. Direct democracy is also based on the assumption that people know best what they want. That is why the initiative and ideas of individuals and social groups are so important. In representative democracy, voting is merely approving the ideas of those in power. Finally, direct democracy involves both workplaces and entire communities. State democracy does not include workplaces. In direct democracy, factories or offices should be managed with the participation of all workers. They would decide on working conditions or the choice of managers who organize and coordinate work (Doyle, no date; Kerr, 2001, p. 14).

Proving the validity of their ideas, anarchists gave historical examples of their implementation, for example in Spain or Russia (Anarchist Federation, 2010, p. 14–15). British anarchists, firm believers in the stated goals, claimed: "Anarchist communism is socialism without government, based on workers' control and direct democracy, arrived at by workers and oppressed acting for themselves, together, freely and as equals. Only anarchist communism is built around the self-activity and autonomy of actual living people rather than ideological stereotypes. Through self-directed revolution and the creation of organisations after the revolution based upon free association, federation and equality, a free and better world can be made" (*Capitalism vs. humanity* ..., p. 1).

One method of implementing revolutionary change and achieving the anarchist goal was to be the creation of communities of anarchists as examples to the rest of society. Another method was to be direct action, interpreted as a prelude to direct democracy. Direct action is for anarchists the only democratic method of struggle. Parliamentary democracy, on the other hand, has never brought radical change for workers and oppressed people, and has led their struggles down blind alleys (Doyle, no date).

6.8   Discussion with Anarchist Concepts

From the perspective of the narrative dominant in Western societies, anarchists' views of the state, electoral democracy, and direct democracy contain errors, gaps, and paradoxes. They also reveal numerous inconsistencies in their criticism of state democracy and their projects for the future.

Anarchists disagree about whether decisions in an anarchist society would be made by majority or unanimous vote. Making decisions by majority, even though it would be preceded by deep reflection and discussion, would result in the danger of the minority being dominated by the majority. And this is the same argument used by anarchists in their criticism of electoral and parliamentary democracy. In turn, unanimous decision-making would have the effect of making it difficult or even impossible for society to function smoothly.

The pandemic was not a time for anarchists to search for new solutions resulting from criticism of electoral democracy. It has not become a pretext, for example, to reflect on the possibility of using electronic voting in political practice. One of the reasons for this was that while the internet provided opportunities for people to participate in the decision-making process directly, electronic democracy also had disadvantages. These include, for example, the complexity of public affairs, which means that they should be entrusted to experts, deficits in society's knowledge of public affairs, and obtaining knowledge by voters from television and other commercial media. In addition, the reluctance of people to devote their time to public affairs and the alienation of voters staying alone in front of computer monitors limits the possibilities of discussion, reaching a compromise on disputed matters and creating a community (Marczewska-Rytko, 2001, p. 190–191).

With this comes the problem of widespread participation in decision-making processes. An anarchist society would have to consist of individuals who are willing to take the time to participate in the decision-making process. These individuals would have to give up entertainment and other pleasures in favor of solving difficult and time-consuming problems. Anarchists do not explain how a person living in an age of materialism and consumerism would be persuaded to make such a transition.

Anarchists also fail to take into account that many of the issues that require decision-making about social groups are so complex that they require expertise and expert knowledge. People making decisions would therefore either have to be experts in many fields or they would have to listen to experts and be guided by their opinions. The time of the pandemic proved that people do not always want to listen to experts, and prefer to be guided by theories and beliefs that explain complex problems in simple terms. In designing the future, however, anarchism does not take into account the antisocial, the lonely, the uninvolved, and the lazy. Perhaps such individuals would not exist in an anarchist society because, according to anarchist beliefs, all people would want to participate in decision-making processes of their own free will in their own interest. But if such antisocial individuals existed, then decisions would have to be made for them, on their behalf, and would have to be imposed on them. And this is already contrary to the basic principles of anarchism.

Parliamentary democracy is a system based on compromise between large groups of people with diverse needs and interests. This is the essence of politics in a democratic state. The reconciliation of sometimes contradictory interests of large social groups is ensured by democratic procedures and institutions. Anarchist thought, on the other hand, is dominated by the belief that natural human tendencies, based on the balance of egoism and altruism, will lead to a compromise between different individuals and social groups. This is to be facilitated by the abolition of private property, social classes, and institutions of power. Anarchism is characterized by a belief in the goodness of human individuals and that freedom maximized in a society without authority would unleash man's natural inclination to do good.

Therefore, anarchism ignores the problem of pathological individuals and groups. Anarchists even recognized that the proper functioning of a democratic community requires a high level of ethics and responsibility from its members (*Płaszczyzna ideowa* ...). Such a postulate places anarchism among the currents of utopian political thought. It is utopian to require from everyone the same high level of morality, responsibility, commitment, participation and having similar desires, feelings and emotions. After all, their differentiation would be a source of conflict, which an anarchist society does not assume. This exposes anarchism to the accusation of formulating concepts that uniformize society, not on a local or regional scale, but on a global one. The concept of building a society based on new moral standards requires its implementation on a global scale. After all, the 'new individuals' could not function alongside societies operating according to the old principles. This would risk their anni-hilation by states with imperialistic characteristics. Moreover, 'new individ-uals' could not tolerate injustice in neighboring societies. The 'new people' would therefore have to populate the entire globe. Besides, the very idea of the creation of a 'new people' is a concept that exposes anarchism to the accusa-tion of being totalitarian and undemocratic.

6.9   Conclusions: The Functions of Anarchist Criticism of the Democratic State

Although anarchism is not free of paradoxes, and anarchist thinking shows a predilection for utopianism, this does not mean that it is unnecessary for reflection on contemporary democracy.

Anarchism as a realized political thought would be destructive to demo-cratic states. It would also be destructive to society. This is demonstrated by the wave of anarchist terrorism at the turn of the 20th century (Tuchman, 2014). This, in turn, would set back democratization processes by increasing repres-sion of anarchist activists and supporters of anarchism.

However, anarchism as unrealized thought, as an element of social and political pluralism, remaining one of many political ideologies, can serve to improve the quality of democracy.

One of the functions performed for the societies of democratic countries may be to inform them about the problems of the modern world that are not attractive to the mainstream media, and therefore they do not devote space and time to them. An example can be the first symptoms of the migration crisis in Europe, which the anarchist press drew attention to long before the problem was addressed by the mainstream media. The same applies to other problems, including those that directly affect the functioning of the political systems of democratic states.

Therefore, another function of radical ideologies is to sensitize societies to the problems of the modern world and to warn of their consequences. If the authorities of European countries had reacted in time to the symptoms of the migration crisis, perhaps it would not have happened. Similar conclusions apply to democracy. Its problems are related to the disappearance of the middle class, which is the mainstay of democracy, growing social apathy and voter absenteeism, growing isolation of individuals and disappearance of community, disappearance of social activism and civil society, treating the intangible values of democracy as self-evident and given once and for all, domination of material values and consumerism, which are equated with freedom. These symptoms intensified during the pandemic period. However, if democratic states take timely action to resume and accelerate democratization processes, then they will solve the problems associated with growing popularity of movements representing radical ideologies. These movements exploit the paradoxes and rhetoric of democracy, and by using demagogy based on democratic values they actually pose a threat to democracy.

This instead requires another function, which is to reform democracy. Democracy is not static. It is a process that requires constant transformation. Failure to do so means democracy is going backwards. However, reforming involves the ruling elites taking seriously the arguments contained in radical currents of political thought that criticize democracy based on general elections, including those that may be utopian.

References

Against the Coronavirus and the Opportunism of the State. Anarchists in Italy Report on the Spread of the Virus and the Quarantine (2020). *CrimethInc.* Retrieved from: https://pl.crimethinc.com/2020/03/12/against-the-coronavirus-and-the-opportunism-of-the-state-anarchists-in-italy-report-on-the-spread-of-the-virus-and-the-quarantine.

Anarchist Federation (2010, March). "Introduction to Anarchist Communism". Pamphlet 21. London: Anarchist Communist Editions.

Apocalypse soon (2001, Winter). *Direct Action*, 21, 31–33.

Bartyzel, J. (2009). *Śmiertelny bóg Demos: Pięć wykładów o demokracji i jej krytykach.* Warszawa: Fijorr Publishing.

Capitalism vs.humanity (2004, May). *Resistance: Anarchist bulletin*, 61, 1.

Democracy without parties (2001, Spring). *Direct Action*, 18, 2.

Doyle, K. (no date). "Parliament or democracy?". *The Struggle Site.* Retrieved from: http://struggle.ws/once/pd_chap9.html.

Epstein, B. (2001, September). "Anarchism and the anti-globalization movement". *Monthly Review: An Independent Socialist Magazine*, 53(4). Retrieved from: https://monthlyreview.org/category/2001/volume-53-issue-04-september-2001/.

Fascism and democracy –Two cheeks of the same arse (2008, Summer). *Organise! ... for revolutionary anarchism*, 70, 8–9.

Fortress Freedom (2003, Spring). *Direct Action*, 26, 4–5.

Franks, B & Kinna, R. (2014). "Contemporary British Anarchism". *La Revue LISA / LISA e-journal*, 12(8). Retrieved from: https://journals.openedition.org/lisa/7128.

Franks, B. & Wilson, M. (Eds.) (2010). *Anarchism and Moral Philosophy*. Basingstoke: Palgrave Macmillan.

Globalisation: Neither Left nor Right (2004/2005, Winter). *Direct Action*, 33, 18–21.

Goldman, E. (no date). "If voting...". *BrainyQuote*. Retrieved from: https://www.brainyquote .com/quotes/emma_goldman_107325.

Gordon, U. (2007). *Anarchy Alive!: Anti-authoritarian Politics from Practice to Theory*. London; Ann Arbor, MI: Pluto Press.

Jędrzejczyk, A. (2021). "Jak Rzecznik Praw Obywatelskich wyjaśnił sprawę wyborów kopertowych w 2020 r. i co udało się mu ustalić?". *Biuletyn Informacji Publicznej Rzecznika Praw Obywatelskich*. Retrieved from: https://bip.brpo.gov.pl/pl/content /rzecznik-praw-obywatelskich-i-wybory-kopertowe.

Kerr, G. (2001, Summer). "Anarchism and Elections". *Red & Black Revolution: A magazine of libertarian communism*, 5, 11–15.

Kropotkin, P. (1915). *Mutual aid, a factor of evolution*. London: Heinemann.

Lundström, M. (2018). *Anarchist Critique of Radical Democracy: The impossible argument*. Cham: Palgrave Macmillan.

Malendowicz, P. (2007). *Polski ruch anarchistyczny wobec współczesnych wyzwań politycznych*. Piła: Państwowa Wyższa Szkoła Zawodowa.

Malendowicz, P. (2013). *Ruch anarchistyczny w Europie wobec przemian globalizacyjnych przełomu XX i XXI wieku*. Warszawa: Difin.

Manfredonia, G. (2001). *L'anarchisme en Europe*. Paris: Presses Universitaires de France.

Manrique, F. (2010, May-June). "De la corrupción política". *Andalucía Libertaria*, 4, 23.

Marczewska-Rytko, M. (2001). *Demokracja bezpośrednia w teorii i praktyce politycznej*. Lublin: Wydawnictwo Uniwersytetu Marii Curie-Skłodowskiej.

Marshall, P. (1992). *Demanding the Impossible: A History of Anarchism*. London: HarperCollins.

McLaughlin, P. (2007). *Anarchism and Authority: A Philosophical Introduction to Classical Anarchism*. Aldershot, Hants; Burlington, VT: Ashgate Publishing Limited.

On New Evil (2001, Winter). *Direct Action*, 21, 16.

Pasterczyk, J. (2020). "Władza to wirus. Obostrzenia to symptom więzienia. O co chodzi z transparentami w Rzeszowie?". *Wyborcza.pl Rzeszów*. Retrieved from: https:// rzeszow.wyborcza.pl/rzeszow/7,34962,25876970,wladza-to-wirus-obostrzenia -to-symptom-wiezienia-o-co.html.

Peiró, J. (2010, March). "Los partidos de izquierda y los anarquistas". *Rojo y Negro: Anarcosindicalismo en Acción*", 233, 7.

Pleyers, G. (2020). "The Pandemic is a battlefield. Social movements in the COVID-19 lockdown", *Journal of Civil Society*, 16(4), 295–312. DOI: https://doi.org/10.1080/1744 8689.2020.1794398

Płaszczyzna ideowa Federacji Anarchistycznej (no date). *Federacja Anarchistyczna*. Retrieved from: https://federacja-anarchistyczna.pl/plaszczyzna/.

Purkis, J. & Bowen, J. (Eds.). (2004). *Changing Anarchism: Anarchist Theory and Practice in a Global Age*. Manchester; New York, NY: Manchester University Press.

Ruch anarchistyczny w czasie pandemii (2020). *A-tak: Ogólnopolskie Pismo Anarchistyczne*, 13, 4.

Shantz, J. (2002). "Green syndicalism: An alternative red-green vision". *Environmental Politics*, 11(4), 21–41. DOI: https://doi.org/10.1080/714000644

Skirda, A. (2002). *Facing the Enemy: A History of Anarchist Organization from Proudhon to May 1968*. (P. Sharkey, Trans.). Edinburgh; Oakland, CA: AK Press in conjunction with Kate Sharpley Library.

Sunshine, S. (2008, Winter). "Rebranding fascism: National-anarchists". *Public Eye*, 23(4), 1, 12–19. Retrieved from: https://politicalresearch.org/sites/default/files/2018 -10/PE-Winter-2008.pdf.

Szymanek, J. (2021). *Wstęp do prawa wyborczego*. Lublin, Warszawa: Wydawnictwo Naukowe Episteme, Wydawnictwo Szkoły Wyższej Wymiaru Sprawiedliwości.

Tuchman, B. W. (2014). *The proud tower: A portrait of the world before the war, 1890–1914*. New York, NY: Random House Trade Paperback Edition.

Urbański, J. (2007). "10 argumentów na rzecz bojkotu wyborów". *Rozbrat*. Retrieved from: https://www.rozbrat.org/publicystyka/polityka/394-10-argumentow-na-rzecz -bojkotu-wyborow.

Urbański, J. (2020a). "Koronawirus i cybernetyczny łagier". *Federacja Anarchistyczna*. Retrieved from: https://federacja-anarchistyczna.pl/2020/04/19/koronawirus-i -cybernetyczny-lagier/.

Urbański, J. (2020b). "Epidemia koronawirusa – państwo zrzuca odpowiedzialność na społeczeństwo". *A-tak. Ogólnopolskie Pismo Anarchistyczne"*, 13, 3.

Walt van der, L. (2001, Summer). "Revolutionary Anarchism & the Anti-Globalization Movement", *Red & Black Revolution: A magazine of libertarian communism*, 5, 18–20.

Webin, T. (2005, September/Oktober). "Goldene Türme wachsen nicht endlos...". *Direkte Aktion: Anarchosyndikalische Zeitung"*, 171, 12–13.

Williams, D. M. & Lee, M. T. (2012). "Aiming to overthrow the state (without using the state): Political opportunities for anarchist movements". *Comparative Sociology*, 11(4), 558–593. DOI: https://doi.org/10.1163/15691330-12341236

Williams, D. M. (2009a). "Red vs. green: Regional variation of anarchist ideology in the United States". *Journal of Political Ideologies*, 14(2), 189–210. DOI: https://doi .org/10.1080/13569310902925816

Williams, D. M. (2009b). "Anarchists and labor unions: An analysis using new social movement theories". *Working USA: The Journal of Labor and Society*, 12(3), 337–354. DOI: https://doi.org/10.1111/j.1743-4580.2009.00242.x

Williams, D. M. (2017). *Black flags and social movements: A sociological analysis of movement anarchism*. Manchester: Manchester University Press.

Żukowski, A. (1997). *Systemy wyborcze: Wprowadzenie*. Olsztyn: Wyższa Szkoła Pedagogiczna.

Żyromski, M. (2016). "Rola i funkcje wyborów w systemach niedemokratycznych". *Przegląd Politologiczny*, 3, 109–116. DOI: 10.14746/pp.2016.21.3.7

CHAPTER 7

Alternative Voting Procedures and Universal Suffrage during a Pandemic

Marcin Rachwał

7.1   Introduction

In democratic states, the highest authority (the sovereign) is vested in citizens who decide about the direction of the state's policy and elect their representatives. Nowadays, the model of representative democracy prevails, with elections that result in the appointment of representatives of the sovereign. These representatives actually exercise power, while the role of citizens is to control political elites through elections (Rachwał, 2013, pp. 69–82). In other words, via elections the principle of sovereignty is implemented, and the most important political decisions are seen as those which - though in fact taken by representatives - derive from the citizens' will. Elections to be considered democratic need to be held according to certain standards. In this respect, the principles of electoral law and features of elections are particularly important. The principles of electoral law include: universality, equality, directness, secrecy of vote, and the manner in which mandates are distributed. "As a rule, the principles of electoral law are defined by the constitution, and this guarantees the basic democratic nature of the system used to appoint elected representatives. (...) Irrespective of the fact that principles of electoral law are formulated in the legal act of the highest order, the process of its expansion by means of ordinary legislation can also be observed" (*Polskie*, 2000, p. 214). Moreover, elections in democratic states are free,[1] periodical (representatives are chosen for a specific term of office), and competitive (voters can choose one of at least two independent electoral proposals).

---

1 "The principle of free elections is more political than legal in its nature. It is related to the principle of political pluralism which means the freedom to establish political parties and their competition expressed in the freedom to nominate candidates. On the other hand, the freedom of elections implies that the voter is free to participate in voting (there are countries where voting is civic duty) and to cast a ballot" (*Polskie*, 2015, p. 124).

As regards the methodology, the chapter highlights a key importance of universal suffrage, i.e. the principle defining "the group of citizens who fulfil conditions set out by the law and enjoy the right to elect and be elected (active and passive electoral right)" (*Polskie*, 2000, p. 215). There is no doubt that the COVID-19 pandemic caused a number of very serious predicaments of social, political and economic nature. "Around the world, COVID-19 has disrupted societies, economies and lives" (*Managing* ..., p. 4). It has also affected electoral processes in many countries by hampering elections due to restrictions on mobility. Of course, restrictions were imposed to prevent the spread of the pandemic. "The pandemic could be defined as an increase in the number of acute infectious diseases in the human population, which spreads over several countries or the whole world" (Michalski, 2009, p. 19).

The pandemic hampered the implementation of the constitutional principle of universal suffrage, which is extremely important to meet the standards of a democratic state. Consequently, various decisions were taken, e.g. elections were postponed, alternative voting procedures were used. The latter allowed the vote to be cast electronically, the voter did not have to go to a polling station. These are certainly procedures that may increase the universal nature of elections at any time, but in particular during a pandemic. To what extent have the alternative voting procedures affected the principle of universal suffrage during the pandemic? The attempt to address the research problem provided further motivation to proceed with the research, results of which are presented in this chapter. The following specific questions were identified regarding the research problem: 1) What is the essence of alternative voting procedures? 2) How can the principle of universal suffrage be ensured during a pandemic? And 3) What conditions need to be met so that changes to the electoral law during a pandemic may gain social acceptance (legitimacy)? Several research methods were applied to develop the chapter, among which the following methods were crucial: critical analysis of literature (sources), institutional and legal method, and the systemic review.

After initial assumptions regarding definitions and methodology have been formulated, the focus shifted to the synthesis of the nature and forms of alternative voting procedures. Then, the chapter discusses the principle of universal suffrage during a pandemic, which is followed by the analysis of the role of alternative voting procedures while implementing this principle. In this part, special attention is paid to conditions that should be met when establishing new or amending existing election rules. In its conclusion, the chapter addresses methodological assumptions set in the introduction.

7.2   Alternative Voting Procedures – Literature Review

The basic voting method involves direct participation of citizens who go to polling stations to cast votes. However, this is not always possible, for example voters may have mobility restrictions due to illness or voting may coincide with their working time. Therefore, it has been decided that it is justified "to allow voting without the need for the voter to be physically present in the polling station. The literature on the subject describes the following alternative techniques. The point of reference for the 'alternative' is the traditional, basic mode of voting at a polling station" (Zbieranek, 2013, p. 15). Thus, we can distinguish between the basic (traditional) mode of voting, i.e. at polling stations, and an alternative procedure. The latter category is not uniform and includes several ways of citizen participation in voting.

Four main alternative voting procedures can be distinguished in electoral legislation: proxy voting, postal voting, electronic voting, and by using a mobile ballot box. All these solutions enable the voter to cast his/her vote without going to the polling station. Two issues can be raised regarding the methods: namely types of alternative voting procedures and a factor that distinguishes (defines) the essence of alternative voting procedures. At this point it is worth noting that the essence of the voting procedures is the possibility to exercise the active voting right beyond a polling station.

Voting by proxy means that "a voter who, for various reasons, cannot go to a polling station, authorises another voter to cast a vote on his/her behalf according to instructions given. (...) The institution of proxy was established to facilitate voting for a narrow group of voters. Usually, such solutions apply to the elderly, the sick, the disabled, as well as the military or civil servants who at the time of the election are away at work in the country or abroad" (Kapsa, Musiał-Karg, 2020, p. 55).

It is worth noting that voting by proxy raises some doubts. Firstly, there is a concern that the proxy will not vote according to the will of the voter. Secondly, the solution raises a question whether it does not infringe two principles of electoral law, namely directness and equality (Venice Commission, 2002).

The principle of directness means that we have one-step elections. Voters vote directly for their MP candidates. (...) There is an opinion that direct elections also mean that citizens need to vote in person (*Prawo*, 2000, p. 159). If such an interpretation is adopted, the conclusion would be that proxy voting violates the principle of direct election. However, as noted later in the monograph quoted above, directness applies to "the expression of will only, and not the entire election process and the relationship between the principal and the mandatary" (*Prawo*, 2000, p. 159). According to the quoted interpretation, an opinion can be formulated that voting by proxy does not violate the principle of direct elections. An analogous conclusion follows from the ruling of the Constitutional Court, in which the Court emphasises that directness applies to elections and not the voting itself. "Therefore, the principle of the directness provides indications that need to be taken into account when the legislator develops the electoral system. The directness of elections determines their one-step character, i.e. that voters vote directly for their candidates (...) and not for the electors, who will then make the final choice. (...) Direct elections (...) are elections where a representative is chosen by voters and not by other bodies (intermediate levels in electoral process). From the point of view of the direct election, the way of casting votes (in person or by proxy) does not matter. (...) Voting by proxy does not infringe the principle of directness, as the latter does not imply voting in person" (*Wyrok*).

The principle of equality "is understood nowadays in two ways - formal and substantive. The principle of equality in the formal sense means that each voter has an equal number of votes (...). The principle of equality in the substantive sense has a different meaning. It means that the power of each vote is equal, and each vote has the same influence on the final outcome" (*Polskie*, 2000, p. 217). Thus, formal equality means that each voter has an equal number of votes (usually one), while substantive equality refers to the influence of each citizen's vote on the final outcome. In order to guarantee substantive equality, a uniform standard of representation is applied, so the division into constituencies and the determination of the number of seats to be allocated need to ensure that the number of voters per seat is the same or at least similar (in practice, perfect substantive equality is difficult to achieve).

In the case of voting by proxy, a doubt is raised as to whether this solution infringes formal equality, since the proxy has a larger number of votes (e.g. two, while the other voters have one). As emphasised in the Constitutional Tribunal's ruling quoted above, "in order to address this objection, it is first necessary to establish the nature of the vote that the proxy casts on behalf of his/her principal. In particular, it has to be decided whether voting by proxy means that actually the principal votes, or whether the right to which he/she was originally entitled is transferred to the proxy. In the latter case, the proxy would indeed have two votes, and this would lead to the conclusion that this method of voting violates the principle of equality in the formal sense" (*Wyrok*). The conclusion by the Constitutional Court states that voting by proxy does not violate the principle of formal equality. "The analysis of the provisions of the Electoral Code leads to the conclusion that the proxy casts the vote on behalf of the voter and not on his/her own behalf. The authorisation of the proxy to vote does not deprive the voter of his/her electoral rights (...), as the proxy does not vote on his/her own behalf, but on behalf of the voter who granted the authorisation (...). The allegation that the proxy has two votes as an elector is therefore unsubstantiated" (*Wyrok*).

Another alternative voting procedure is voting by post (Funk, 2006; Wagner, 2020; Musiał-Karg, 2021). The voter receives a voting package by mail, which includes, among other things, a ballot paper, a declaration on casting a vote in person and by secret ballot, and an envelope to send back the abovementioned documents. After filling in the ballot paper and the statement, the voter sends back the documents, or someone collects them from him/her and delivers them to the address of the relevant election committee.

Reservations have also been formulated with regard to postal voting. These include the following: voting outside the polling station violates the principle of secret ballot, it creates a possibility of irregularities during the transmission of ballots, and it violates the requirement to hold elections within one day (Cf. *Wyrok*). In this context, it should be noted that the Constitutional Court provided a broad argumentation indicating that the objections cited are unsubstantiated (*Wyrok*).

The development of the Information and Communications Technology (ICT) has enabled yet another alternative voting procedure, i.e. electronic voting. While proxy voting and postal voting are closely related to the very act of casting a vote (model of representative democracy), the development of ICT and electronic voting offer a completely different prospects for the development of democracy as a means of public decision-making. The essence of the most far-reaching predictions is the electronic democracy with a digital agora. While taking into account only the technological aspect, it is possible to fundamentally restructure democratic political systems including the reduction or elimination of the institution of representation in favour of direct rule by the sovereign in the strict sense of the word (digital direct democracy). However, such a revolutionary change would also require a number of other changes, including those in the area of citizens' participation in politics. However, the topic extends beyond the scope of this study (Rachwał, 2019, pp. 23–35).

Electronic voting itself (e-voting) can be defined as voting by electronic means (Krimmer, 2010; Musiał-Karg, 2020, pp. 30–37). The term encompasses the possibility to cast a vote over the Internet, as well as via other electronic means, such as telephones. The definition of e-voting is very broad and includes the use of digital technologies in election-related procedures, and these must include at least the act of casting a vote. Under this broad understanding, e-voting includes: 1) voting with a digital machine (...) at a polling station (or at polling point, e.g. polling kiosk), 2) voting with a personal computer connected to the Internet, 3) voting with a mobile phone (using text messaging), and 4) voting with interactive television. In this context, it should be emphasised that in essence alternative voting procedures should enable to exercise the active electoral right outside the polling station, so voting procedures analysed in this chapter should not include voting by means of a digital machine. The remaining forms of electronic voting meet the conditions, and thus they can be included in alternative voting procedures.

Voting with a mobile ballot box involves the delivery of "a ballot box to the voter's residence and casting a vote there. (...) The voter casts his/her vote on a traditional paper ballot after ticking the appropriate option. Then, he/she puts the ballot into the ballot box" (Kapsa, Musiał-Karg, 2020, pp. 61–62).

In summary, the essence of alternative voting procedures is the possibility of casting a vote outside the polling station. Thus, we distinguish between the traditional voting method (at polling station) and alternative procedures. The last category includes: voting by proxy, postal voting, electronic voting, and voting with a mobile ballot box.

7.3   The Principle of Universal Suffrage in the Context of the Pandemic

Voter absenteeism can be either culpable or compulsory. Culpable absenteeism occurs when citizens consciously renounce their right to participate. Thus, they do not participate in voting for various reasons, but the common denominator is that it is based on a voluntary decision. This may be because, for instance, they do not trust politicians, they believe that one vote means nothing, they do not believe to be able to change the functioning of the state through elections (Zbieranek, 2011, p. 94). The situation, however, is different when a citizen expresses the will to vote but he/she is unable to do so due to, for example, illness, mobility problems, or professional duties. Such a citizen wants to exercise his/her active right to vote but is prevented from doing so as they are required to go to a polling station. The indicated situation is called a compulsory absence. Both forms of absenteeism result in lower voter turnout, but to counteract them we need specific measures. The introduction of alternative voting procedures will not reduce the level of culpable absenteeism, but it can definitely reduce compulsory absenteeism.

The pandemic necessitated the introduction of a series of measures, the common denominator of which was a significant reduction in people's mobility and opportunities to meet each other, chiefly to counteract the spread of the virus. Until the development of preventive vaccination, it was one of the basic strategies for combating the pandemic. Even after vaccination began, it still played a very important role. The ban on public gatherings, restrictions on citizens' mobility and the risk of contamination at polling stations are just some of the reasons behind the postponement or cancellation of elections in many countries. Other strategies have also emerged, such as the introduction of alternative voting procedures that allow elections to be held while the possibility of contamination with the virus is reduced.

Restrictions on movement of people, quarantines, isolations, large numbers of sick people are the order of the day during a pandemic. The implementation of elections during such a period with the use of basic voting methods (possibly supplementing them with alternative voting procedures available to some narrow groups of voters) would deprive many citizens of the opportunity to exercise their active voting right. Thus, the principle of universal suffrage would be considerably limited, which could even question the legitimacy of the entire electoral procedure and undermine the legitimacy of elected representatives. To counteract this, a number of measures were taken, as indicated above, including the introduction of alternative voting procedures. In this context it should be noted that such measures (changes in the rules of conducting elections) must also be accepted by the citizens so that the election results are not questioned. This issue is further elaborated on in the next section of this chapter.

7.4   Discussion

The tenure of elected representative bodies is one of the main principles in democratic states. As mentioned above, elections in a democratic state are free, cyclical, and competitive, and must also be conducted according to the principles of electoral law. The cyclical nature of elections means that candidates are elected to a given representative body or to hold office for a strictly defined period, called the term of office (Rachwał, 2017, pp. 54–55). In this respect, no changes should be made, especially those that are unjustified. Of course, some special circumstances, such as the state of emergency justify changes in the duration of the term of office. However, the principle of holding election in cycles is a feature of a democratic state.

The pandemic made disrupted the cyclical nature of elections due to the abovementioned restrictions on mobility. For example, "between February 21 and August 18, 2020, elections in at least 70 countries and territories across the globe had postponed some elections" (James, Alihodzic, 2020, pp. 344–345). The cancellation or postponement of elections clearly compromised their cyclical nature. Some countries, however, decided to hold elections within the constitutional deadline, but changed the way citizens cast their votes from traditional to alternative solutions, or they extended already existing possibilities to use alternative voting procedures. The situation required, among other things, legislative changes and adjustment of technical conditions to hold elections. Nevertheless, it was also needed to legitimise the new electoral law.

Legitimisation of power is a process of "gaining the approval of the governed for the rules defining ways power is acquired and exercised, as well as for institutions and persons exercising it. Moreover, legitimised power is the one that is recognised and approved by the people, which means that it excludes coercion and fear as means to subordinate people" (*Leksykon*, p. 235). In the case of democratic states, elections play a key role in gaining approval for the power, although the process concerned is much broader. The power must not only be gained through elections that meet certain conditions mentioned above, but it also need to be "exercised in accordance with the constitution of the state, other universally binding legal acts and procedures" (*Leksykon*, p. 237).

Thus, in a democratic state, the legitimacy of power depends, inter alia, on its acquisition through universal suffrage. In the context of the methodological assumptions and changes in the principles of holding elections during the pandemic, it is worthwhile to discuss the multifaceted concept of legitimacy of power by D. Beetham. According to the concept, "ideally, legitimacy manifests itself simultaneously at three levels: rules, beliefs, and behaviours. Firstly, it is necessary to ascertain that the acquiring and exercising of power complies with formal and informal rules established in a given political system; if such conformity exists, then power is legitimate. Secondly, both the governing and the governed need to believe in the acceptance of the said rules underpinned by positive effects of political practice. (...) Thirdly, the governed must manifest their approval of power in their behaviour" (Sobkowiak, 1998, p. 157).

The introduction of alternative voting procedures needs to be accepted by citizens. Otherwise, the legitimacy of elections can be questioned. As the above concept shows, the legitimisation of power occurs simultaneously at three levels: rules, beliefs and behaviours. Elections must be conducted in accordance with established rules. Although the rules may change, citizens should share a belief that they are rational and legal. Only then the second level of legitimacy of power can be achieved, i.e. acceptance of the established rules. As a result, we move to the final level of the process when citizens express their approval of existing solutions through their behaviour (by taking part in elections).

New solutions and rules for the conduct of elections established during the pandemic should not be opposed by citizens, as this threatens the legitimisation of the electoral procedure. As an example we could mention the 2020 presidential election in Poland, which, according to the new legal regulations, was to be held using only one of the alternative voting procedures, i.e. postal voting. It is worth recalling that the election was scheduled for 10th May 2020 (*Postanowienie Marszałka Sejmu Rzeczypospolitej Polskiej z dnia 5 lutego 2020 r....*). As it turned out, after the election had been announced, the pandemic started in Poland followed by extensive restrictions to the mobility of people. Accordingly, the Act of 6 April 2020 on special rules to hold the general election for the President of the Republic of Poland ordered in 2020 was enacted. According to its Article 2, "the election of the President of the Republic of Poland ordered in 2020 shall be conducted exclusively by postal voting" (*Ustawa*). The enactment of the law and the vigorous attempts of the ruling party to hold elections were confronted with numerous objections and protests from various circles. Protests were expressed, among others, by scientists, politicians (even in the United Right there was no agreement on such election method), and citizens. Objections applied not only to the postal voting, which in its adopted form posed a risk of numerous irregularities, but also to the way the new law was drafted (Musiał-Karg & Kapsa, 2021). The bill was submitted to the Sejm on 6th April 2020. On the same day, it went through the entire legislative procedure in the lower chamber and the adopted act went to the Speaker of the Senate (*Druk*). This is certainly contradicted the proper legislative process, especially concerning such an important issue as electoral law.

Without recalling the entire public debate on the adoption of law, it is worth to highlight selected objections. Representatives of the science community pointed out that the conduct of elections under the new law would, among other things, contradict electoral principles. "Voting conducted under this law will not be secret. Each voter can be identified (...). These elections will not be universal, as many voters will not receive a ballot paper. (...) These elections will not be transparent as votes will not be counted in the PECs, which immediately after counting announce the outcome in the district, in which each candidate may have his/her steward. (...) This means that the election will be invalid. As a result, the mandate of the person elected can be effectively challenged" (*Wybory*). Essentially, similar objections were raised by former presidents of Poland and some prime ministers, who in the conclusion of their statements indicated that they would not participate in such an election. "The postal voting pushed through by the Law and Justice Party was adopted in violation of the Constitution and Sejm regulations. They will be neither universal nor equal. They do not guarantee that all voters receive ballot papers. They create the possibility to cast votes while substituting other people. They do not ensure the secrecy of ballot. (...) The procedure of postal voting in such a form and at such time as the ruling party proposes leads to a pseudo election.

We will not take part in them. We hope that candidates and voters who share our concern for the democratic future of Poland will do the same" (*Wszyscy ...*). Ultimately, the elections scheduled for 10th May 2020 did not take place (*Uchwała*). After the failure, the Speaker of the Sejm ordered new presidential elections (*Postanowienie Marszałka Sejmu Rzeczypospolitej Polskiej z dnia 3 czerwca 2020 r....*).

The presidential election in Poland based on legal grounds indicated above could be questioned regarding its legitimacy not only in terms of its procedure but also possible delegitimization at the level of the political system. The example provides the basis for a general conclusion. It should be borne in mind that the legitimacy of government depends not only on the election that follows established rules, but the rules themselves need to be legitimised.

7.5   Conclusions

Elections in a democratic state must follow certain standards, among which is universal suffrage as one of the electoral law principles. The pandemic and the need to significantly reduce social contact posed a major challenge to hold elections. It had to be determined how to conduct elections and maintain the sanitary regime and, at the same time, avoid the violation of the universal suffrage principle. The legislators paid special attention to alternative voting procedures, which in essence provide the possibility to cast votes without the need to go to a polling station. The introduction of alternative voting procedures creates an opportunity to hold elections during a pandemic while meeting the principle of universal suffrage, but we should remember that the situation in individual countries may differ. If a given electoral system already provided for broad use of, for example, postal or electronic voting, then such voting is natural for citizens and a possible extension of the group of eligible voters does not require action to legitimise the process. The situation, however, is different in countries where such solutions have not been used before or they have been actually criticized. Then, the legislators need to implement measures to ensure that new electoral rules are accepted and legitimised. Elections held with the use of solutions that are not accepted by a significant part of the society threatens not only to the legitimacy of the electoral procedure itself, but it also poses a risk of delegitimization of the political system.

Alternative voting procedures enable to hold elections during a pandemic in compliance with the principle of universal suffrage, which in essence provides the possibility to cast votes without the need to go to a polling station. Postal voting and electronic voting are of particular importance in this context, as they significantly reduce the risk of contamination with the virus. In the case of voting by proxy and a mobile ballot box, we cannot avoid direct contact between the proxy or the voter and members of the electoral committee. Therefore, the legislators should pay particular attention to the development of postal voting and electronic voting, so in the future electoral systems are prepared for various emergency situations that hamper or prevent the use of traditional voting methods.[2]

When establishing new solutions, we should remember that it is necessary to legitimise such solutions at the level of rules, beliefs, and behaviours. The mere establishment of rules (alternative voting procedures) is only the first step in the legitimisation process; the next step is social acceptance of rules, which manifests itself at the level of behaviour, i.e., participation of the sovereign in voting.

References

Asplund, E. (ed.), "Global overview of COVID-19: Impact on elections". International IDEA, 18 March 2020 (and updated). Retrieved from: https://www.idea.int /news-media/multimedia-reports/global-overview-COVID-19-impact-elections.

Birch, S. et al. (2020). "How to hold elections safely and democratically during the COVID-19 pandemic". The British Academy. Retrieved from: https://www.thebritishacademy .ac.uk/documents/2632/How-to-hold-elections-safely-democratically-Shape-the -Future.pdf.

Casas-Zamora, K., Cliffe, S., Noel, N. (2020). „COVID-19, Election Governance, and Preventing Electoral Violence". Center on International Cooperation. Retrieved from: https://cic.nyu.edu/sites/default/files/cic-idea_COVID-19_election_governance _and_preventing_electoral_violence.pdf.

"COVID-19 and democracy". International IDEA. Retrieved from: https://www.idea.int /our-work/what-we-do/COVID-19-and-democracy.

Druk nr 328, Sejm RP IX kadencji.

---

2   The results of the experiment carried out in the Czech Republic can be cited in the context raised. "We exploit a natural experiment from the Czech Republic, which biannually renews mandates in one-third of Senate constituencies that rotate according to the 1995 election law. We show that in the second and third weeks after the 2020 elections (held on October 9–10), new COVID-19 infections grew significantly faster in voting compared to non-voting constituencies. A temporarily related peak in hospital admissions and essentially no changes in test positivity rates suggest that the acceleration was not merely due to increased testing. (...) Our results have implications for postal voting reforms or postponing of large-scale, in-person (electoral) events during viral outbreaks" (Palguta, Levínský, Škoda, 2022, p. 197).

"Elections during pandemic COVID-19. What to do with the democratic process?". Retrieved from: https://www.minsait.com/ideasfordemocracy/en/elections-during -pandemic-COVID-19.

Funk, P. (2006). "Modern Voting Tools, Social Incentives and Voter Turnout: Theory and Evidence". *Working Paper.* Retrieved from: https://pdfs.semanticscholar.org/5e67 /62d1210aae-ab395814d414d23b2c0d4cfa22.pdf.

James, T. S., Alihodzic, S. (2020). "When Is It Democratic to Postpone an Election? Elections During Natural Disasters, COVID-19, and Emergency Situations". *Election Law Journal,* Volume 19, Number 3, pp. 344–362, DOI: 10.1089/elj.2020.0642.

Kapsa, I., Musiał-Karg, M. (2020). *Alternatywne metody głosowania w opiniach Polaków. Postawy i poglądy względem wybranych form partycypacji w wyborach.* Poznań: Wydawnictwo Naukowe Wydziału Nauk Politycznych i Dziennikarstwa UAM.

Krimmer, R. (2010). "*E-voting as a New Form of Voting*". In *A. Balci, C. Can Ac-tan, O. Dalbay* (Eds.), *Explorations in eGovernment & eGovernance. Volume2: Selected proceedings of the Second International Conference on eGover-nment and eGovernance.* Antalya: The International Satellite and CableOperator (TURKSAT) and Social Sciences Research Society (SoSReS).

Leksykon wiedzy politologicznej (2018). J. Marszałek-Kawa, D. Plecka (Eds.). Toruń: Wydawnictwo Adam Marszałek.

"Managing Elections in the Context of COVID-19: Perspectives from the Commonwealth" (2020). Retrieved from: https://production-new-commonwealth-files.s3.eu -west-2.amazonaws.com/migrated/inline/Elections%20and%20C19%20Perspectives %20from%20CW%20FN.pdf.

Michalski, Z. C. (2009), „Pandemia – zagrożenie o zasięgu światowym". *Wiedza Obronna,* No. 3, pp. 18–27.

Musiał-Karg, M. (2020). *Elektroniczne głosowanie w opiniach Polaków. Postawy i poglądy na temat e-voting.* Poznań: Wydawnictwo Naukowe Wydziału Nauk Politycznych i Dziennikarstwa UAM.

Musiał-Karg, M. (2021). „*Głosowanie korespondencyjne podczas pandemii COVID-19. Doświadczenia z polskich wyborów prezydenckich w 2020 r.*" Przegląd Prawa Konstytucyjnego, nr 2 (60), pp. 31–48. DOI 10.15804/ppk.2021.02.02;

Musiał-Karg M., Kapsa I. (2021). "Debate: Voting challenges in a pandemic—Poland". *Public Money & Management,* vol. 41 no 21/1, pp. 6–8.

Palguta, J., Levínský, R., Škoda, S. (2022). "Do elections accelerate the COVID-19 pandemic? Evidence from a natural experiment". *Journal of Population Economics,* Volume 35, Issue 1, pp. 197–240. DOI: https://doi.org/10.1007/s00148-021-00870-1.

Polskie prawo konstytucyjne (2000), W. Skrzydło (Eds.). Lublin: MORPOL.

Polskie prawo konstytucyjne (2015), D. Górecki (Eds.). Warszawa: Lex a Wolters Kluwer business.

Postanowienie Marszałka Sejmu Rzeczypospolitej Polskiej z dnia 5 lutego 2020 r. w sprawie zarządzenia wyborów Prezydenta Rzeczypospolitej Polskiej, Dz. U. 2020, poz. 184.

Postanowienie Marszałka Sejmu Rzeczypospolitej Polskiej z dnia 3 czerwca 2020 r. w sprawie zarządzenia wyborów Prezydenta Rzeczypospolitej Polskiej, Dz. U. 2020, poz. 988.

Prawo konstytucyjne (2000), Z. Witkowski (Eds.). Toruń: TNOiK.

Rachwał, M. (2013). „Władza ludu czy elit politycznych? Próba zdefiniowania współczesnej demokracji". *Przegląd Politologiczny*, No 1, pp. 69–82. DOI: https://doi.org /10.14746/pp.2013.18.1.5

Rachwał, M. (2017). „Wybory we współczesnym państwie demokratycznym". In M. Rachwał (Eds.), *Uwarunkowania i mechanizmy partycypacji politycznej* (pp. 51–86). Poznań: Wydawnictwo Naukowe Wydziału Nauk Politycznych i Dziennikarstwa UAM.

Rachwał, M. (2019). "Electronic political participation and the model of democracy". In M. Musiał-Karg (Eds.), *E-voting and e-participation. Experiences, challenges and prospects for the future* (pp. 23–35). Poznań: Wydawnictwo Naukowe Wydziału Nauk Politycznych i Dziennikarstwa UAM.

Sobkowiak, L. (1998). „Legitymizacja władzy". In A. W. Jabłoński , L. Sobkowiak (Eds.), *Studia z teorii polityki*, vol. II (pp. 149–162). Wrocław: Wydawnictwo Uniwersytetu Wrocławskiego.

Uchwała nr 129/2020 Państwowej Komisji Wyborczej z dnia 10 maja 2020 r. w sprawie stwierdzenia braku możliwości głosowania na kandydatów w wyborach Prezydenta Rzeczypospolitej Polskiej, Dz. U. 2020, poz. 967.

Ustawa z dnia 6 kwietnia 2020 r. o szczególnych zasadach przeprowadzania wyborów powszechnych na Prezydenta Rzeczypospolitej Polskiej zarządzonych w 2020 r., Dz. U. 2020, poz. 827.

Venice Commission (2002). "Code of Good Practice in Electoral Matters: Guidelines and Explanatory Report – Adopted by the Venice Commission at its 51st and 52nd sessions. Venice, 5–6 July and 18–19 October 2002". CDL-AD(2002)023rev2-cor. Retrieved from: https://www.venice.coe.int/webforms/docu-ments/?pdf=CDL-AD (2002)023rev2-cor-e.

Wagner, R. (2020). "Responding to COVID-19 with 100 per cent Postal Voting: Local Elections in Bavaria, Germany. Case study, September 2020". Stockholm: International Institute for Democracy and Electoral Assistance, Stockholm. Retrieved from: https://www.idea.int/sites/default/files/responding-to-COVID-19-with-postal -voting-local-elections-in-bavaria.pdf.

„Wszyscy byli prezydenci oraz byli premierzy: Nie weźmiemy udziału w pseudowyborach korespondencyjnych". Retrieved from: https://for.org.pl/pl/a/7722,wszyscy -byli-prezydenci-oraz-byli-premierzy-nie-wezmiemy-udzialu-w-pseudowyborach -korespondencyjnych (14.03.2022).

„Wybory będą nieważne. Ponad 400 wykładowców prawa podpisało się pod apelem do rządu". Retrieved from: https://wiadomosci.onet.pl/kraj/wybory-korespondencyjne -ponad-400-wykladowcow-prawa-podpisalo-sie-pod-apelem-do-rzadu/402j7eb (14.03.2022).

Wyrok Trybunału Konstytucyjnego z dnia 20 lipca 2011 r. sygn. akt K 9/11, Dz. U. 2011, Nr 149, poz. 889.

Zbieranek, J. (2011). „Alternatywne procedury głosowania w Polsce na tle państw Unii Europejskiej". *Studia Biura Analiz Sejmowych*, No 3 (27), pp. 93–120.

Zbieranek, J. (2013). *Alternatywne procedury głosowania w polskim prawie wyborczym – gwarancja zasady powszechności wyborów czy mechanizm zwiększania frekwencji wyborczej?* Warsaw: Difin.

CHAPTER 8

Pandemic Elections in European Union Countries in the Assessment of OSCE Observing Missions Reports

Marcin Jastrzębski

8.1   Introduction

11 March 2020 WHO Director-General's officially declared growing number of recognized cases of COVID-19 disease spreading around as pandemic. This pestilence influenced existing world in majority, if not in all, areas of human activity. This also applied to the sphere of broadly understood politics and legal regulations, especially in areas such as human rights or issues related to fair and free elections.

Before the pandemic, North America and Europe were rated as two of the most democratic areas in the world by the International Institute for Democracy and Electoral Assistance (IDEA) - respectively 100% and 93% of countries of both regions were classified as democracies (IDEA, 2019, p. 27). Unfortunately, the quality of democracies around the world, including North America and Europe, has been declining for the past few years, especially due to weaker checks on government and human rights guarantees, but also to such factors as limited civic space, and the rise of populist and extremist parties (Russack, 2021, p. 1).

Faced with a one of most serious threat, countries have adopted radical and previously unthinkable policies to counter the spread of the coronavirus pandemic. Exercising COVID-19 pandemic and her impact on political systems has shown that while in some states the human rights, democratic institutions and electoral processes have proved robust and flexible, but many of them not. Outstanding democratic issues across numerous states are: an overly powerful executive, limited checks on government, and the side-lining of parliaments, lack of trust in political elites and, consequently, also the increasing number of violations of the rights and freedoms of individuals.

The experiences with the COVID-19 pandemic so far led to pessimistic conclusions that it fosters the rise of authoritarianism around the world including several European states. It is an opportunity, particularly for populist leaders, to consolidate power and suppress civil society activity and human rights.

Actually, the COVID-19 era put pressure on many democratic tenets. Fundamental political and civil liberties – such as freedom of movement, freedom of enterprise, and freedom of assembly and also right to free and fair elections – have been severely restricted. Democratic life has also been curtailed, including through the postponement of elections and suspension of parliamentary work (Belin, Di Mayo, 2020, p. 1).

The COVID-19 pandemic represents a new and stress test for the already disrupted liberal-representative democracies also in the context of holding of free elections in accordance with the basic electoral principles (Guasti, 2020, p. 48).

In these circumstances, the actual possibility of exercising one of the fundamental political rights - the right to participate in free elections is of great importance. This right is regulated both by the norms of domestic law and by international public law (more precisely by international human rights law). The former characterize (or at least should) the discussed freedom in a detailed and exhaustive manner, the latter describe the basic principles of the right to free elections - establishing its minimum, impassable, democratic standard. It is particularly relevant because international human rights law particular individual rights, including the right to free elections, create minimum standards, specific *ultima ratio*, the violation of which indicates failure to comply with the basic electoral principles.

Of course, legal regulation is of practical importance when it is actually implemented. The basic method of checking whether the right to participate in fair and free elections is actually implemented in individual states is the procedure of monitoring these elections carried out by various international organizations. The most recognized of them, based on extensive criteria and supported by many years of experience, is the monitoring of elections in various countries carried out under the Organization for Security and Cooperation in Europe - OSCE (exactly the responsible entity for its implementation is Office for Democratic Institutions and Human Rights - ODIHR).

The chapter discusses the procedure and practice of holding elections in the exceptional situation of the COVID-19 pandemic in a number of European Union (EU) states in the context of international standards of the right to participate in free elections. The main goal is to answer the following research question: whether and to what extent these elections met the above-mentioned standards? The approach is institutional and is based on the analysis of documents and legal frames and their comparison with particular practices in the electoral process. The main used research methods are institutional-legal and analysis of the content of reports of OSCE missions monitoring elections in EU states in 2020–2021.

The main anticipated finding is reconstruction of international standards for holding free elections in extraordinary and exceptional circumstances of fighting with global pandemic.

8.2   The International Legal Basis for the Right to Free and Fair Elections

Along with the development of the scientific discipline known as international human rights law, the catalog of rights and freedoms guaranteed under various systems of their protection expanded, mainly due to international judicial and quasi-judicial bodies, and the level of precision and scope of interpretation of individual freedoms protected in in various international treaties regulating the rights of the individual. It was no different in the case of the right to participate in the government / to participate in elections (Jastrzębski, 2021, pp. 52–53)[1].

This right is protected to a different extent in Article 21 of the Universal Declaration of Human Rights (UDHR), Article 25 of the International Covenant on Civil and Political Rights (ICCPR), Article 3 of Protocol I to the European Convention on Human Rights (Protocol No. I of the ECHR), Article 39 and 40 of the Charter of Fundamental Rights of the European Union (CFR, Official Journal of the European Union 2012, C 326/391). The title right is established not only within the universal and European systems of protection human rights but also in other regional human rights systems, that fall outside the scope of this article: Article 23 of the Inter-American Convention on Human Rights (ACHR), Article 13 of the African Charter of Human and Peoples' Rights (ACHPR) and Article 24 of the Arab Charter of Human Rights (ArCHR, Rishmawi 2010, pp. 169–178)[2].

One of the basic principles of the electoral law that determines the democratic nature of elections is the principle of free and fair elections. It has been expressed in numerous acts of international law mentioned above. The significance of this principle for determining other basic electoral principles (such

---

1   One of the widest databases, probably practically complete, concerning the case law of international bodies concerning right to free and fair elections can be found on the website Election Observation and Democracy Support – EODS: https://www.eods.eu/elex-table.

2   One of the most extensive databases on the legal basis of the right to participate in free and fair elections in international law is available on the website EODS: https://www.eods.eu/election-standards/.

as universal and equal suffrage, direct elections, secret ballot and electoral formulas – both majority and proportional representation systems) is crucial. Although the principle of free and fair elections is not uniformly understood in the electoral law doctrine, its indisputable meaning can be reduced to a few basic elements:

1. freedom to nominate candidates,
2. freedom of conducting an election campaign,
3. freedom to express electoral preferences - free and pressure-free voting.
4. In addition, each election process should be conducted by an independent and politically neutral election administration, and - which is extremely important - subject to control mechanisms - preferably carried out by independent bodies, such as courts.

Thus, the principle of free elections enables both voters and candidates for elected office to participate freely in the election process, both actively and passively (rights to vote and to be elected), which is the essence of the right to free and fair elections both in international law and in the legal and political systems of modern democratic states (Tuccinardi, 2014, pp. 39–44; Goodwin-Gill, 2006, pp. 15–18 and 71–74; Binder, 2007, pp. 135–140).

The above-mentioned provisions, together with the jurisprudence of the relevant treaty bodies, which explain their content and scope, constitute legal obligations for subjects of international law – states and international organizations, being part of the so-called hard law. Unfortunately, from a formal point of view, they do not apply to OSCE participating countries. In practice, however, these solutions constitute one of the foundations of a broad, international standard of free and fair elections created within this organization.

In addition, the source of reconstruction of the international right to free and fair elections are documents that do not generate legal obligations – soft law – these are various resolutions, recommendations, opinions of bodies of various international organizations. Therefore, none of the signatories of this type of legislation has the power to impose sanctions for non-compliance with its provisions. The essential is here Council of Europe's European Commission for Democracy through Law, better known as the Venice Commission, and especially its Code of Good Practice in Electoral Matters and its others documents.[3]

---

3   See: https://www.venice.coe.int/WebForms/pages/?p=02_Opinions_and_studies

8.3   Framework of Basic Criteria for Recognizing Elections as Free and Fair in OSCE Observation Missions

The institution of international observation is one of the essential guarantees of the practical functioning of the right to free and fair elections. It consists of two main areas. First of all, this institution serves to guarantee appropriate regulations governing the rights of voters and subjects of election competition during the election process, in line with generally accepted international standards. On the other hand, the role of international observers is to verify compliance with these provisions in practice, and thus to create effective control mechanisms (Bader, 2012, pp. 21–24). As can be seen, the main part of the issues related to election observation under the OSCE, and thus most of the regulations, mainly concern organizational and technical issues related to the procedures and practical operation of various kinds of long and short-term monitoring missions.

The most commonly used legal act defining the essence and principles of election observation is the Declaration of Principles for International Election Observation with an appendix - Code of Conduct for International Election Observers. Both of these documents were adopted on October 27, 2005 in New York and belong to the group of soft law acts.

A number of organizations that have decided to adopt this act are guided by the assumptions of the Declaration in their observation missions, which have been developed by a body of particular importance for election observation - the OSCE Office for Democratic Institutions and Human Rights (ODIHR). It is this body that coordinates all the quite frequent monitoring missions that take place in cooperation with the OSCE. The Declaration of Principles for International Election Observation is, as mentioned, a key, albeit not the only, piece of legislation relating to international election observation. For example, the observations carried out under the OSCE must also comply with the rules set out in the Election Observation Handbook, which was one of the foundations for the creation of the above-mentioned Declaration.

However, the original legal basis establishing the possibility of election observation missions under the CSCE / OSCE (and also the first such missions in the international system) is adopted in 1990 Document of the Copenhagen Meeting of the Conference on the Human Dimension of the CSCE (The Copenhagen Document). It contains not only very general provisions concerning the organizational and technical conditions for establishing monitoring missions, but also the material criteria for assessing the observed election processes. The first of them considered that : "The participating States consider that the presence of observers, both foreign and domestic, can enhance the electoral process for States in which elections are taking place. They therefore invite observers from any other CSCE participating States and any appropriate private institutions and organizations who may wish to do so to observe the course of their national election proceedings, to the extent permitted by law. They will also endeavour to facilitate similar access for election proceedings held below the national level. Such observers will undertake not to interfere in the electoral proceedings" (para. 8).

The basic material criteria for recognizing the elections as free and fair to this day Copenhagen Document offers in paragraph fifth and seventh. The first of these lists the basic electoral principles and the obligation of OSCE participating states to act in accordance with the rule of law. Free elections should be held at "reasonable intervals by secret ballot or by equivalent free voting procedure, under conditions which ensure in practice the free expression of the opinion of the electors in the choice of their representatives". States are obliged to establish a representative form of government in which "the executive is accountable to the elected legislature or the electorate". The main duty of the government and public authorities, also and mainly in the context of democratic election, is to act in a manner consistent with law and comply with the constitution (paras 5.1–5.3).

The latter legal provision contains a comprehensive list of conditions for the conduct of free and fair democratic elections:

a.   Periodicity of elections held at "reasonable intervals", as established by law. MP's in at least one chamber of the national legislature have to be freely contested in a popular vote.

b.   Guarantee of universal and equal suffrage to adult citizens. All citizens reaching the age of majority must be able to exercise the right to vote without any discrimination whatsoever.

c.   Secrecy of ballots or by equivalent free voting procedure.

d.   Transparency of vote counting and final results. Votes must be counted honestly and the official results made public.

e.   Guarantee of the right to be elected. The right of citizens to seek political or public office, individually or as representatives of political parties, must be respected without any discrimination.

f.   Guarantee of political pluralism and free competition of political parties on a non-discriminatory basis. Individuals must be able to establish, in full freedom, political parties enjoying legal guarantees to enable them to compete with one another on a basis of equal treatment before the law.

g.   Freedom from violence or intimidation. Legislation must guarantee that political campaigning be conducted in an atmosphere in which neither administrative action, nor violence, nor intimidation bar the parties/candidates from freely presenting their views and, or prevent the voters from learning about and discussing them or from casting their votes free of fear of retribution.

h. Non-discriminatory access to the media. No legal or administrative obstacles should stand in the way of access to the media on a nondiscriminatory basis for all political groupings and individuals wishing to participate in the electoral process.

i. Effective implementation and respect of the result of the election. Candidates elected in conformity with electoral procedures must be duly installed in office and permitted to remain there until their term expires or is otherwise terminated in a manner that is regulated by law in conformity with democratic parliamentary and constitutional procedures (paras 7.1–7.9; Ghebali, 2006 pp. 216–217).

The "Copenhagen" criteria are also the basis for assessing the emergency measures established by OSCE countries for which there was a need to hold elections during the COVID-19 pandemic.

8.4 Assessment of Extraordinary Election Solutions Adopted during a Pandemic in the Reports of OSCE Observation Missions

The effects of the COVID-19 pandemic affected not only the legal basis, organization and practice of holding elections in individual states, but, as already mentioned above, affected all areas of human activity. This also applied to the election observation missions themselves, including such activities undertaken as part of the OSCE. It is true that the average annual number of OSCE ODIHR election observation missions decreased slightly compared to the period of 5 years before the plague – from 23 (2019–26, 2018–21, 2017–22, 2016–21, 2015–24; OSCE ODIHR Elections) to 21,5 (2020–21, 2021–22; OSCE ODIHR Elections). Admittedly, the annual average decreased slightly, but not so much that it could be explained by the fact that the global pandemic particularly intensified. However, it must be taken into account that in his press release on March 17, 2020 the representative ODIHR stated that election observation activities of the OSCE are being temporarily limited in some places, as countries around the OSCE region restrict cross-border travel in response to increased health risks and emphasized that the primary importance of the organization is always the safety of the office's staff.[4] Problems in organizing

---

4 ODIHR election observation activities temporarily limited as health risks increase. Retrieved from: https://www.osce.org/odihr/elections/448531

recommended measures or election observation missions due to the pandemic were later confirmed in practice. For example, monitoring the parliamentary elections in Bulgaria of April 2021, ODIHR Needs Assessment Mission (NAM) had recommended the deployment of an Election Observation Mission (EOM), with 14 long-term observers to follow the process countrywide, as well as 200 short-term observers (STOS) for the observation of election day procedures. However, the deployment of STOS was considered not feasible due to the extraordinary circumstances caused by the COVID-19 pandemic and subsequent travel restrictions across the OSCE region. Therefore, ODIHR changed the format of the observation activity from an EOM to a less numerous Limited EOM (LEOM) (OSCE ODIHR Report Bulgaria 04.2021, p. 5).

The analysis of the conclusions from the OSCE election observation reports on extraordinary electoral solutions related to the COVID-19 pandemic is limited in this chapter to European Union member states in the period from March 2020 to the end of 2021. During this time, ODIHR established various observation missions in eleven EU states (two times in Bulgaria), the activities of which resulted in the formulation of twelve various reports. They concerned in majority on parliamentary elections (ten) but also two elections of heads of state and without any local elections. In general, considerations related to the COVID-19 pandemic in the analyzed reports can be either on four subject areas. They are: amendments to the electoral law, alternative/extraordinary voting methods, the impact of the pandemic on the election campaign and the applied preventive measures against COVID-19.

The scope of changes to the electoral law related to the pandemic in the analyzed countries was varied. No significant amendments to the Lichtenstein electoral law have been registered. Although the vote in this country is compulsory by law, but traditionally, over 95% of the voters vote by post which is available from up to two weeks until two days before the election day and without any justification and this type of voting will help overcome challenges posed by the COVID-19 pandemic (OSCE ODIHR Report Lichtenstein, p. 2). In the context of the two parliamentary elections in Bulgaria and Cyprus in the run-up to the pandemic, no significant changes were noted, apart from the non-plague related optional voting by machines in polling stations of at least 300 voters or procedure of replacement of vacant parliamentary seats (OSCE ODIHR Report Bulgaria 04.2021, p. 6; OSCE Report ODIHR Bulgaria 06.2021, p. 6; OSCE ODIHR Report Cyprus, p. 4). A similar situation occurred in Croatia, which was criticized by ODIHR and recommended for local legislators to "review the electoral legal framework and sub-legal acts to assess to what extent they cover and allow adapting to extraordinary emergency situations, such as health pandemics, and to fill in the gaps in preparation for such situations in the future by developing and maintaining contingency plans" (OSCE ODIHR Report Croatia, p. 18). In several other countries, changes to the electoral law in response to the COVID-19 pandemic were minor. For example, in Germany, electoral law was amended to reduce the number of required signatures for the registration of party lists to one quarter of number required in the law (OSCE ODIHR Report Germany, p. 4). A similar regulation was introduced before the parliamentary elections in Romania on 6 December 2020, but in this country the scale of changes to the electoral law was much larger and also concerned, among others, alternative voting methods (OSCE ODIHR Report Romania, pp. 3, 9). Additionally, the described elections were held in a broad legal context – the state of emergency established in connection with the plague (OSCE ODIHR Report Romania, p. 14; similarly OSCE ODIHR Report Portugal, p. 1). Some doubts in this context of local entities and the observation mission were raised by temporary restrictions on freedom of information were introduced following a state of emergency decree (OSCE ODIHR Report Romania, p. 9)

In the 4 analyzed countries, the scale of legislative changes was much larger. In Czech Republic Election Law has been amended on several occasions, including in 2021 when parliament approved a government bill on special voting methods with regards to three alternative voting methods, the latter in response to the COVID-19 pandemic. Similarly, in Lithuania, multiple amendments were made to a number of election-related laws. Changes included the establishment wide range of different voting forms especially for voters abroad and in self-isolation due to COVID-19. Comprehensive amendments have also been made in the Netherlands by the Temporary COVID-19 Elections Act was enacted on 4 November 2020, to address measures for local elections. Subsequently, this Act was amended to introduce measures for parliamentary elections and introduce temporary deviations from the Elections Act. (OSCE ODIHR Report Czech Republic, p. 1, 5; OSCE ODIHR Report Lithuania, p. 1; OSCE ODIHR Report Netherlands, p. 4)

A separate matter, both among the states that have introduced a broad amendment to the electoral law, and among all analyzed countries, is the case of Polish presidential elections, which were finally held on 28 June and 12 July 2020. The presidential election was originally scheduled for May 10. Due to the outbreak of the COVID-19 pandemic, no elections were held on May 10. This was related to the pushing through their original deadline by the ruling coalition, which at the same time led to the adoption of a periodic, special electoral law introducing universal postal voting and depriving the NEC of oversight of the electoral process in favor of the government. A new election date was scheduled for 3 June following the adoption of a new temporary law on 2 June on "Special regulations for general elections of the President of the Republic of Poland ordered in 2020 with the possibility of postal voting" governing the presidential election (2 June Act). Ultimately, the election was called for 28 June with a second round on 12 July (Vashchanka, 2020 pp. 6–10).

In the opinion of the members of the OSCE observation mission, the ad hoc changes of legal basis of the process of electing the Polish president meant that "the legal uncertainty during the electoral process. The constitutionally mandated election coincided with the outbreak of the COVID-19 pandemic, and the decision to continue with the holding of the election necessitated legal and practical adjustments. The changes jeopardized the stability and clarity of the otherwise suitable election legislation and had practical implications for candidate registration, campaigning and campaign finance, voting methods, and resolution of election disputes". Above mentioned amendments were "adopted in an expedited manner without meaningful consultation, which is at odds with OSCE commitments". Even so, it was considered ultimately that the election was administered professionally and legal framework was generally suitable for the holding of democratic elections, despite of above mentioned problems (OSCE ODIHR Report Poland, p. 1–2).

The conclusions of the ODIHR monitoring reports on the changes to the election framework of legal basis during the pandemic period generally recognized their compliance with the standard of the right to free and fair elections. A great deal of flexibility was shown here, especially with regard to the often significant changes to the law just before the elections, which in most cases was justified by a pandemic. It should be remembered that the guidelines of the Venice Commission, often taken into account by OSCE, as well as by the Council of Europe and the EU institutions, recognize that essential electoral regulations cannot be changed in principle one year before the election date. Minor comments in this field were directed to the Romanian government, and much more serious to the Polish government.

The second aspect in which subject reports mention the COVID-19 pandemic is the issue of various alternative or / and extraordinary voting methods. They were introduced in various analyzed countries to a different extent. In Germany and Lichtenstein before the pandemic, postal voting had already been introduced and used on a large scale - so in these countries the amendments were only related to additional facilities enabling the use of this alternative method (OSCE ODIHR Report Germany, p. 7; OSCE ODIHR Report Lichtenstein, p. 2). In Poland, limited optional postal voting was introduced (OSCE ODIHR Report Poland, p. 6).

On the other hand, in several of the cases studied, individual countries introduced a wide range of alternative/extraordinary voting methods. Mobile voting lists/mobile ballot box were introduced in Bulgaria, Romania, Cyprus and Croatia (with problems here). (OSCE ODIHR Report Bulgaria 04.2021, p. 13; OSCE Report ODIHR Bulgaria 06.2021, p. 28; OSCE ODIHR Report Romania, p. 9; OSCE ODIHR Report Croatia, p. 18; OSCE ODIHR Report Cyprus p. 4). Portugal law amendments expanded the possibilities for early voting and allowed for voting in self-confinement. In the Czech Republic, it was possible vote from the vehicles in drive-through polling stations, mobile voting of eligible voters in the quarantine residence and mobile ballot box at home (OSCE ODIHR Report Portugal, p. 5–6). Dutch temporary act introduced expanded voting by proxy, introduced early voting and voting by post for elderly voters (OSCE ODIHR Report Netherlands, p. 4). In Lithuania, in addition to the previously mentioned postal voting, mobile ballot box and early voting, the remote electronic voting (REV) were created (OSCE ODIHR Report Lithuania, p. 3, 9–11).

It should be noted that none of the alternative / extraordinary voting methods mentioned above and used in different configurations have been challenged by monitoring missions and found to be inconsistent with international standards for holding free elections.

Two other issues mentioned in the context of a pandemic in the analyzed OSCE reports - the impact of the pandemic on the election campaign and the applied preventive measures against plague - are treated similarly in individual documents. The recurring impact of the pandemic on the election campaign limited scale and number of events (especially meetings with voters) observed in her time (OSCE ODIHR Report Czech Republic, p. 1; OSCE ODIHR Report Lichtenstein, p. 2) The campaigns were often low key, in part because of the COVID-19 pandemic and related restrictions on the assemblies (OSCE ODIHR Report Lithuania, p. 12). Often the public health limitations on freedom of movement combined with restrictive campaign rules had an effect to an anaemic campaign"(OSCE ODIHR Report Romania, p. 1). In Poland "the uncertain legal basis of not holding an election on 10 May meant that campaigning and campaign finance were in a legal limbo between 10 May and the passing of the 2 June Act. Campaigning after the passing of the 2 June Act was able to take place generally uncurtailed as restrictions of public gatherings were eased on 29 May allowing for up to 150 participants". Despite these restrictions, candidates toured around the country and hold a large number of direct meetings with more numerous groups of voters (OSCE ODIHR Report Poland, p. 12–13).

These reports state that the applied preventive measures against plague were widely used in all of the countries surveyed. They most often recognized that state services are well equipped with election materials and personal protective equipment against COVID-19. (OSCE ODIHR Report Netherlands, p. 13; OSCE ODIHR Report Lichtenstein, p. 6). It was also noted that in several countries, most notably in Central and Eastern Europe, social distancing measures against the COVID-19 pandemic were not fully respected by participants. (OSCE ODIHR Report Bulgaria 04.2021, p. 5; OSCE Report ODIHR Bulgaria 06.2021, p. 10; OSCE ODIHR Report Czech Republic, p. 1; OSCE ODIHR Report Poland, p. 12–13).

It should be noted that in the documents examined, none of them directly formulate any priority or other ones recommendations relating to practical or legal electoral solutions regarding the pandemic. This proves that these solutions are within the limits of international standards of free and fair elections. However, in two cases, among the analyzed countries, such a recommendation appears indirectly.

Apart from a small mention of the possibility of a significant restriction of the freedom of speech in Romania under the provisions of the state of emergency, the problem concerns Poland to a much greater extent. Although the OSCE observation mission ultimately found the Polish presidential elections were "administered professionally", it did not said that they were considered "elections fundamental freedoms were respected" and "the legal framework provides for an adequate conduct of democratic elections" (OSCE ODIHR Report Bulgaria 04.2021, p. 4; OSCE Report ODIHR Bulgaria 06.2021, p. 3; OSCE ODIHR Report Romania, p. 1). This does not mean, of course, that the Polish elections did not fully meet the OSCE standards, but the report on them emphasized that "setting a new election date outside the constitutionally defined timeframe is at odds with paragraph 5.3 of the 1990 OSCE Copenhagen Document" (OSCE ODIHR Report Poland, p. 5) – which highlights "the duty of the government and public authorities to comply with the constitution and to act in a manner consistent with law."

This situation resulted in the fact that the Polish state was the only one of the eleven analyzed EU countries to which ODIHR addressed a priority recommendation regarding COVID-19 related measures related to the presidential elections. Polish government should consider that "any changes to the electoral legislation, including under emergencies, should ensure, that they are formulated and adopted well in advance, as a result of an open process allowing sufficient time for a meaningful public debate and ensuring the principle of stability of law" (OSCE ODIHR Report Poland, p. 26).

8.5   Conclusions

The COVID-19 pandemic was a significant factor in the timing of all above-described elections. In the light of the conclusions expressed in the analyzed reports of observation missions, EU states which were forced to conduct the election process after the outbreak of the COVID-19 pandemic, they passed the exam and by introducing various extraordinary electoral solutions and protective measures, they did not violate the international election standards formulated by OSCE, Council of Europe and EU.

This is evidenced by the statements from some reports which mention that in the monitored countries *"elections fundamental freedoms were respected", "the elections were competitive and pluralistic"* (OSCE ODIHR Report Croatia, p. 1; OSCE ODIHR Report Romania, p. 1) and *"the legal framework generally provides for an adequate conduct of democratic elections"* (OSCE ODIHR Report Bulgaria 04.2021, p. 4; OSCE Report ODIHR Bulgaria 06.2021, p. 3; OSCE ODIHR Report Romania, p. 1). However, electoral observers also occasionally make general comments criticizing states for some aspects of elections conducted during a pandemic. They concern, among others "longstanding concerns pertaining to key aspects of the process still remain to be addressed". (OSCE ODIHR Report Bulgaria 04.2021, p. 4; OSCE Report ODIHR Bulgaria 06.2021, p. 3) or "numerous amendments affected by quality [of elections] and contributed to legal uncertainty" (OSCE ODIHR Report Romania, p. 1).

However, the most far-reaching criticism, described above, was addressed by the OSCE bodies monitoring the elections to the Polish government. The low quality of the election process of the President of the Republic of Poland against the background of the elections in ten other EU countries seems to at least partially confirm the theses of numerous scientists who recognize Poland as a backsliding democracy, aiming or already being a hybrid regime - consensual / electoral authoritarianism (Sadurski, 2018; Guasti, 2020, pp. 49, 53–54; Holesch, Kyriazi, pp. 7–15; IDEA 2019, p. 212). It is wonder what the observation of the elections of the second EU country showing similar trends to Poland will look like - Hungary, where the parliamentary elections will be held on 3 April 2022.

References

Bader, M. (2012). OSCE electoral assistance and the role of election commissions, *Security and Human Rights, 23*(1), p. 19–29. doi: https://doi.org/10.1163/1875023128000 79728

Belin C., Di Mayo G., (2020). *Democracy After Coronavirus: Five Challenges For The 2020s.* Retrieved from: https://www.brookings.edu/research/democracy-after-coronavirus -five-challenges-for-the-2020s/

Binder, Ch. (2007). "International Election Observation by the OSCE and the Human Right to Political Participation", *European Public Law, volume 13* (issue 1), pp. 133–158

Declaration of Principles for International Election Observation and Code of Conduct for International Election Observers. Retrieved from: http://www.ndi.org/files/1923 _declaration_102705_0.pdf

Document of the Copenhagen Meeting of the Conference on the Human Dimension of the CSCE (The Copenhagen Document). Retrieved from: https://www.osce.org/files/f /documents/9/c/14304.pdf

Election Observation Handbook OSCE. Retrieved from: https://www.osce.org/files/f /documents/5/e/68439.pdf

Ghebali V. Y., (2006). "Debating Election and Election Monitoring Standards at the OSCE: Between Technical Needs and Politicization". In IFSH (ed.), *OSCE Yearbook 2005* (pp. 215–229). Baden-Baden: Nomos Verlagsgesellschaft.

Goodwin-Gill, G. S. (2006). *Free and Fair Elections.* Geneva. Inter-Parliamentary Union.

Guasti P. (2020). "The Impact of the COVID-19 Pandemic in Central and Eastern Europe. The Rise of Autocracy and Democratic Resilience". *Democratic Theory* (Volume 7: Issue 2), pp. 47–60. DOI: https://doi.org/10.3167/dt.2020.070207

Holesch A., Kyriazi A. (2022). "Democratic backsliding in the European Union: the role of the Hungarian-Polish coalition". *East European Politics*, Vol. 38 Nb.1, pp. 1–20. https://doi.org/10.1080/21599165.2020.1865319

IDEA (2019). *The Global State of Democracy 2019. Addressing the Ills, Reviving the Promise.* Stockholm: International Institute for Democracy and Electoral Assistance. DOI: https://doi.org/10.31752/idea.2019.28

Jastrzębski, M. (2021). „Pomiędzy równością a „efektywnością". Zasada równości materialnej wyborów w systemie Europejskiej Konwencji Praw Człowieka [Between Equality and „Efficiency". The Principle of Material Equality of Elections in The System of The European Convention on Human Rights]". In M. Malaczyńska – Biały, *Bezpieczeństwo, prawa człowieka, stosunki międzynarodowe, tom IV*, Rzeszów: Wydawnictwo Uniwersytetu Rzeszowskiego.

OSCE ODIHR Final Report on Bulgaria early parliamentary elections 6 July 2021. Retrieved from: https://www.osce.org/odihr/elections/

OSCE ODIHR Final Report on Bulgaria parliamentary elections 4 April 2021. Retrieved from: https://www.osce.org/odihr/elections/

OSCE ODIHR Final Report on Croatia parliamentary elections 5 July 2020. Retrieved from: https://www.osce.org/odihr/elections/

OSCE ODIHR Final Report on Cyprus parliamentary elections 30 May 2021. Retrieved from: https://www.osce.org/odihr/elections/

OSCE ODIHR Final Report on Czech Republic parliamentary elections 8–9 October 2021. Retrieved from: https://www.osce.org/odihr/elections/

OSCE ODIHR Final Report on Germany parliamentary elections 26 September 2021. Retrieved from: https://www.osce.org/odihr/elections/

OSCE ODIHR Final Report on Lichtenstein parliamentary elections 7 February 2021. Retrieved from: https://www.osce.org/odihr/elections/

OSCE ODIHR Final Report on Lithuania parliamentary elections 11 October 2020. Retrieved from: https://www.osce.org/odihr/elections/

OSCE ODIHR Final Report on Netherlands parliamentary elections 17 March 2021. Retrieved from: https://www.osce.org/odihr/elections/

OSCE ODIHR Final Report on Poland presidential elections 28 June and 12 July 2020. Retrieved from: https://www.osce.org/odihr/elections/

OSCE ODIHR Final Report on Portugal presidential elections 24 January 2021. Retrieved from: https://www.osce.org/odihr/elections/

OSCE ODIHR Final Report on Romania parliamentary elections 6 December 2020. Retrieved from: https://www.osce.org/odihr/elections/

OSCE ODIHR Office for Democratic Institutions and Human Rights Elections. Retrieved from: https://www.osce.org/odihr/elections/. Retrieved from: https://www.osce .org/odihr/elections/

Rishmawi, M., (2010), "The Arab Charter on Human Rights and the League of Arab States: An Update", *Human Rights Law Review vol.10* (issue1). Retrieved from: http:// www.refworld.org/cgi-bin/texis/vtx/rwmain?docid=3ae6b38540.

Russack, S., (Ed.) (2021). *The effect of COVID on EU democracies.* Retrieved from: https:// epin.org/wp-content/uploads/2021/04/EPIN-REPORT_The-effect-of-COVID-on-EU -democracies-1.pdf

Sadurski, W. (2018). "How Democracy Dies (in Poland): A Case Study of Anti-Constitutional Populist Backsliding". *Rule of Law.* Retrieved from: https://ruleoflaw.pl/how -democracy-dies-in-poland-a-case-study-of-anti-constitutional-populist -backsliding/

Tuccinardi D. Ed. (2014). *International Obligations for Elections: Guidelines for Legal Frameworks.* Stockholm: IDEA.

Vashchanka, V. (2020). *Political manoeuvres and legal conundrums amid the COVID-19 pandemic: the 2020 presidential election in Poland. Case study.* Stockholm: International Institute for Democracy and Electoral Assistance.

Venice Commission (2003), Code of Good Practice in Electoral Matters, Opinion No 190/2002. Retrieved from: http://www.venice.coe.int/webforms/documents/CDL -AD(2002)023rev.aspx

PART 2

Elections during a Pandemic

European Experiences – Case Studies

∴

CHAPTER 9

Italy: First Infected Country in Europe and Constitutional Referendum

Rafał Dudała

9.1 Introduction

The first European country after China and Thailand to discover cases of acute infectious respiratory disease COVID-19 caused by the SARS-CoV-2 virus was France: on January 24, 2020, two people were found in the country. A few days later (January 31), two Chinese tourists staying in Rome showed positive results of the test: the 67-year-old and the 66-year-old flew to Milan from Wuhan on January 23, 2020. As a result, on February 1, the Council of Ministers headed by the Prime Minister Giuseppe Conte announced blocking air traffic with China and introducing a state of emergency in the country. On February 21, the first fatal case was confirmed: it was a 78-year-old man from the small town of Vo' Euganeo (Padua province). On the same day, the first significant increase in cases was recorded in Lombardy, where 16 cases were confirmed, a day later – another 60 cases and more fatalities. At the turn of February and March, Italy, according to data published by the WHO, became the most affected region in the world (WHO): on the night of March 7–8, 2020, the prime minister issued a decree under which restrictions were placed on the entirety of Lombardy and 14 provinces of the north-central part of the country (in total, 16.5 million people were quarantined) (World Health Organization, 2020).

This situation directly influenced the social life in the country, also influencing political and administrative decisions. One of the consequences of the epidemic of COVID-19 cases and the growing number of deaths were the changes introduced both in the election calendar and in the form of the elections scheduled for 2020. The introduction of increased security measures had an impact on the preparation of the elections, the campaign, as well as the voting process itself, turnout, and the result. Considering all the above variables, a special - in this respect - case, also in comparison with the elections in other European countries, is the constitutional referendum held in Italy during this period.

The aim of the chapter is to present the electoral situation in Italy, the first country in Europe to face the coronavirus pandemic. The research area is the

situation before the constitutional referendum and the process of adopting
the act to amend the constitution; then preparations for the consultation,
conduct (including discussion and polls) and referendum results. The legislation introduced at that time, adjusting legal, sanitary, and administrative
standards to the then pandemic threat, will also be analysed. The study will be
carried out based on the method of source analysis, considering the opinions
of experts on the proposed changes to the constitution, a comparison of the
number of parliamentarians with other European Union countries, analysis
of survey data, analysis of the positions of Italian parties and political groups.
Considering the simple form of a referendum, the research question is: Has the
pandemic affected the election process, turnout, and the result?

9.2   Constitutional Referendum Background

An important place among the political determinants, characteristic of the
Italian state, is the institution of a referendum (Fisichella, 2009). In states
that have adopted the model of representative democracy, where collective
supremacy is exercised by elected representatives, its «supplement» in direct
forms appears more and more often (Krasnowolski, 2016, p. 3; Antoszewski &
Herbut, 1997, p. 211). In the history of Italy, the institutions of direct democracy gained an important systemic position only under the constitution (1948),
constituting an element modifying the classical parliamentary-cabinet system and enriching the principles of representative government (Bokszczanin,
2003, p. 350). The Basic Law introduced three types of them: people's petition
(art. 50), people's legislative initiative (art. 71) and referendum (art. 75 repealing referendum; art. 132 referendum on regions; art. 138 constitutional referendum). The first two forms of direct democracy exercised at the national level
have not yet been confirmed in Italian political practice (Grabowska, 2005,
p. 19); while the basic and most frequent one is the referendum consisting of
in "voting opinions on the subjects being voted on and concerning the affairs
of the entire state or a specific part thereof. The essence of a referendum is
to give it a form of voting, which is based on the basic principles of electoral
law (universality, equality, directness, and secrecy) and the formulation of an
alternative («yes» or «no») or an option to which the voter gives preferences in
voting" (Garlicki, 2006, p. 179).

    As already mentioned, the Italian Basic Law provides for three types of refer-
enda: abrogative (annulment) convened for the purpose of the total or partial
repeal of a law or an act establishing a law; consultative on the amalgamation of

existing or the creation of new regions, or on the detachment from one region and attachment to another of the provinces or municipalities that request so; optional constitutional of a ratification nature and concerns the acts amending the constitution and other constitutional acts which did not obtain the approval of a majority of 2/3 of the members of each chamber. The laws are submitted to a referendum at the request of 1/5 of the members of one of the chambers or 500,000 voters or five regional councils. It is worth adding that the provisions in the above scope at the national level were only implemented after 22 years. The reason for this situation was the reluctance of the two largest political parties at the time - Christian Democrats and Communists - towards any control over the legislative process. It was also accompanied by the fear that any form of direct democracy or popular initiative might expose the lack of the necessary syntony with the electorate (Pasquino, 2002, p. 192; Feola, 2001).

The constitutional referendum scheduled for 2020 was the fourth such consultation in the history of the Italian Republic. It should be noted that in the case of a confirming constitutional referendum, unlike the repealing referendum, no valid quorum is expected: the result of the referendum is in each case valid regardless of the voter turnout. The first constitutional referendum was held in 2001 and concerned the change of Title V of Part II of the constitution («yes» won with a turnout of 34%). The second was held in 2006 and concerned the amendment of the second part of the constitution («no» won with a turnout of 52.5%). The third was carried out in 2016 and concerned the disposition to abolish equal bicameralism, reduce the number of parliamentarians, reduce the operating costs of public institutions, liquidate the National Council of Economics and Labour (CNEL) and revise paragraph 5 of Part II of the constitution (the so-called Renzi-Boschi reform, 2016) (the «no» won with a turnout of 65.47%). The constitutional referendum discussed here was the 23rd referendum held in Italy and the 73rd inquiry to voters (Dudała, 2019b, p. 115–123).

The purpose of the introduced changes was twofold: on the one hand, to improve the decision-making process of the chambers so that they could better respond to the needs of citizens; on the other hand, to reduce the cost of the policies pursued by the legislature (estimates envisaged savings of around EUR 500 million). Moreover, the reform was supposed to bring the standards closer to those of other European countries. Well, according to the current constitution, in Italy there are a total of 945 parliamentarians (630 deputies and 315 senators). This group consists of life senators at most 5 and life senators by operation of law, i.e., former presidents of the Republic.

The above figures, based on the records from before the last constitutional referendum, prove that in Italy there are 1.6 MPs per 100,000 inhabitans (Table 9.1), which gives the 23rd place among all 28 European Union Member States. On the other hand, the comparison in absolute values (Table 9.2) confirms the high second position (after Great Britain) with 951 deputies and senators. On the other hand, the title of the leader belonged to Italy as the country with the largest number of parliamentarians (945) elected directly by the nation (Table 9.3).

The issue of the referendum and its role in the Italian political system is widely discussed in the source literature as evidenced by Polish-language

TABLE 9.1   Number of parliamentarians per 100,000 inhabitants

1.	Malta	14,5
19.	Great Britain	2,2
23.	**Italy**	**1,6**
25.	France	1,4
28.	Germany	0,9

SOURCE: DIPARTIMENTO PER LE RIFORME ISTITUZIONALI (2020)

TABLE 9.2   Number of parliamentarians – Absolute data

1.	Great Britain	1430
2.	**Italy**	**951**
3.	France	925
4.	Germany	778
5.	Spain	616

SOURCE: DIPARTIMENTO PER LE RIFORME ISTITUZIONALI (2020)

TABLE 9.3   Number of directly elected parliamentarians

5.	**Italy**	**945**
6.	Germany	709
7.	Great Britain	650
8.	France	577
9.	Poland	560

SOURCE: DIPARTIMENTO PER LE RIFORME ISTITUZIONALI (2020)

studies: I. Bokszczanin, A. Krasnowolski, M. Lorencka. The legal norms in force in the Italian Republic regarding the referendum remain a separate and extremely important section: articles of the Italian Constitution, resolutions of the parliament, decrees of the President. Studies referring directly to the 2020 referendum on reducing the number of parliamentarians are a necessary complement. In addition to scientific studies (R. Feola, A. Mannino, S. Curreri), the preceding polls, the study of the reasons for the turnout and the description of the results should be mentioned, taking into account the preferences of party voters. The last section in the source literature covering the topics discussed in the chapter are legal norms in the field of electoral law and constitutional rights created during the coronavirus pandemic and in force in Italy. These include legal acts signed by the President of the Italian Republic, the President of the Council of Ministers, the Minister of Health and the Minister of the Interior.

9.3 Legal Changes Made in the Context of the Pandemic

Admittedly, the text of the constitutional act was published in October 2019, and was to be submitted to a general referendum, however, it encountered a few difficulties (A.V., 2019). On March 16, 2020, the Council of Ministers approved the Decreto#CuraItalia following the state of emergency Coronavirus-COVID-19. to art. 81 Six-month postponement of the announcement of the confirmatory referendum. It was considered justified to postpone the referendum deadline until autumn: in the face of a short postponement, the citizens' right to full information will be better guaranteed and the right of social and political groups to organize the election campaign more efficiently (President of the Republic, 2020d).

The Decree on the time limit for calling a confirmatory referendum specified two hundred and forty days from the adoption of the ordinance that allowed it, despite the sixty-day law in force so far. Therefore, the referendum had to be announced by September 19, 2020, and held on Sunday between the 50th and 70th day of its announcement, therefore no later than November 22, 2020.

The date of the referendum, previously scheduled for March 29, 2020 (President of the Republic, 2020a), was cancelled. Then, the Act of June 19, 2020 (President of the Republic, 2020e). ordered the application of the principle of concentration of election dates, i.e., election day. The elections were to be held on Sunday and Monday between September 15 and December 15, 2020. Finally, the Council of Ministers, at its meeting on July 14, 2020, at the request of Prime Minister Giuseppe Conte, set the date of September 20–21, 2020, for the convening of a general confirmation referendum in on the approval of the text of the Constitutional Act containing "Amendments to Articles 56, 57 and 59 of the Constitution concerning the reduction of the number of parliamentarians" (President of the Council of Ministers (2020c). July 18, 2020 a presidential decree calling for a general referendum was published (President of the Republic, 2020f).

During the elections held during the pandemic, the *Rosatellum* law was in force, which was passed by the parliament at the end of the 2013–2018 legislature, introducing a new system for both houses. It is a mixed electoral system: 61% of members of parliament are elected in the proportional system and in multi-member constituencies, and 37% in the majority system and in single-member constituencies; 2% are assigned to foreign constituencies where only the proportional system applies. Under this law, the territory of the country was divided into electoral districts: 20 for the Senate and 28 for the Chamber of Deputies.

For the functioning of the *Rosatellum* system, the difference in the normative scope is important due to two types of circuits. In single-mandate constituencies, parliamentarians are elected by the majority system in one round (first-past-the-post): the candidate who receives the largest number of valid votes in the constituency is directly elected. In the event of a tie between more candidates in a single-member constituency, an additional round is not organized, as is the case, for example, during mayoral elections in communes with less than 15,000 inhabitants. residents: the younger candidate is considered the winner. In the event of a vacancy in a single-member constituency, by-elections are held. In the case of distribution of seats in the proportional system, the only difference between the chambers of parliament concerns the provisions of Art. 57 of the Constitution – the Senate takes into account the results in individual regions, not at the national level. In multi-member proportional system precincts, the lists of candidates are short and blocked in numerical order (no preference), and the names of the candidates on each list are listed on the card. Except as provided by law for individual districts, at the local level, three to eight deputies are elected to the Chamber for each district, and to the Senate from two to eight senators for the district. In addition, the ordinance also provides for the possibility of creating coalitions that must be homogeneous throughout the country. Then, different parties present a common candidate for all related lists within a single-member district. However, despite the coalition established for the majority system, the parties compete on their own under the proportional system (Dudała, 2019a, p. 120–122).

Due to the pandemic situation in the country, the updated guidelines were also published by the Ministry of Health on measures to prevent the risk of

COVID-19 infection during the upcoming election and referendum consultations. The measures referred to in Circular No. 49/2020 of the Central Directorate of Electoral Services concern three issues. First, on the vote of patients in home or quarantine treatment and in fiduciary isolation, only a doctor appointed by the local health unit (ASL - Azienda Sanitaria Locale) could certify a relapse as a condition for voting at home, one of the conditions for an infection viral. The issued certificate had to be attached to the application, which the voter sent to the competent mayor together with the declaration of willingness to vote in his own apartment (Ministry of Health, 2020a).

Second, the staff that make up the special electoral commission and are responsible for picking up house votes must be properly secured and trained. Members must wear a disposable gown / shirt, gloves, visor with a surgical mask, or face protection to collect voter votes for home treatment or fiduciary isolation. Gloves and a surgical mask are enough to collect the votes of the quarantined voters. Similar attention should be paid to the training of the personnel forming the special electoral commission, especially non-medical personnel. The Ministry of Health ordered the territorially competent health protection authorities in the days immediately preceding the referendum (September 18–19) to properly train members (from outside the health service) of the hospital constituency and special premises, which enable collecting and counting voting votes cast during home treatment, during quarantine or in isolation. It is imperative that these personnel, in addition to having the appropriate personal protective equipment, receive training in their proper use (dressing, undressing, removal procedures, etc.) and the correct procedures to be followed throughout the home voting process (Ministry of Health, 2020b).

Thirdly, there are also detailed instructions on collecting votes in health and social care institutions, where it must be done as soon as possible and in dedicated rooms, large enough to keep a distance and equipped with air exchange devices (Ministry of Health, 2020c).

Stringent safety measures are envisaged, ranging from devices to be used, to self-certification of health status for staff at special polling stations, while respecting the general duty of hygiene and distance.

To prevent the risk of contracting COVID-19 and at the same time ensure the correct course of the election procedure, the Minister of the Interior and the Minister of Health signed a health and safety protocol to be used during referendum consultations and supplementary, provincial, and municipal elections on September 20–21, 2020. Document. established operational and preventive procedures for members of election commissions and voters, reconciling constitutionally guaranteed electoral rights and the right to health (Ministry of Health, 2020c).

The means of preparation for and access to polling stations are to include conditional access to buildings with separate access and exit routes, distance between electoral commission members and between them and voters, especially when they need to remove their mask for identification, numbering, and voting. the availability of voting booths, considering the space available and the need for movement. To get to the polling station, each person with this right must wear a mask. The protocol also includes guidelines for maintaining hygiene in these places and for counting votes (Ministry of the Interior and Ministry of Health, 2020).

9.4   Analysis of Preparations for the Referendum, Voting and Results

Seven months after the first coronavirus infection was discovered in Italy, a so-called election day (20–21 September 2020), in which several votes were accumulated. On these days, by-elections were held for the Senate of the Italian Republic in the single-member constituencies of the Region of Sardinia (Sassari District) and the Veneto Region (Villafranca di Verona District) (Ministry of the Interior. (2020). The authorities of seven out of twenty regions were also elected (Tuttitalia, 2020a). On January 26, 2020, regional elections were held in Calabria and Emilia-Romania; the next ones, between March and June, were to be held in Campania, Liguria, Marche, Puglia, Tuscany, Veneto, and on April 19 in the Aosta Valley. However, due to the COVID-19 pandemic, voting in these regions was postponed to September 2020. In other regions, administrative elections were held later in the same year: in Sicily – October 4–5 (2nd round – October 18–19), and Sardinia – October 25–26 (2nd round – November 8–9).

In addition, municipal elections were held in 18 provincial capitals (including three regional capitals): Agrigento, Andria, Aosta, Arezzo, Bolzano, Chieti, Crotone, Enna, Fermo, Lecco, Macerata, Mantua, Matera, Nuoro, Reggio Calabria, Trani, Trento and Venice. Then the elections covered 156 larger communes (over 15,000 inhabitants) and 1,028 smaller communes (less than 15,000 inhabitants, except for the autonomous province of Trento, where communes with more than 3,000 inhabitants are considered larger) (Tuttitalia, 2020b).

On the indicated days, a constitutional referendum was also held on the law on limiting the number of parliamentarians adopted by the parliament in 2019. The referendum was initially planned for March 29, 2020, but was postponed due to the pandemic, which then entered a critical phase.

On May 18, 2018, the Five Star Movement and the League signed the "Agreement for the government of change", establishing the first government of

Giuseppe Conte (ilPost, 2018). The agreement provided for a few institutional reforms, including a "drastic reduction" in the number of parliamentarians. The next Conte government, created in September 2019 based on a programmatic agreement between the Five Star Movement, the Democratic Party and Free and Equal, put forward a proposal to limit the number of parliamentarians while starting the road to increasing appropriate constitutional guarantees and democratic representation, ensuring political and territorial pluralism. Including by changing the electoral law in the event of a positive referendum result.

The draft constitutional act by reducing the number of MPs in the Parliament by 36.5% was finally approved by the Chamber of Deputies at its meeting on October 8, 2019 in its second resolution. 569 deputies were present in the hall: 567 «voted», 553 «for», 14 «against», 2 «abstaining». The proposed constitutional law envisaged a drastic reduction in the number of parliamentarians by modifying Art. 56 and 57 of the Constitutions from the present 630 deputies to 400 and from the present 315 to 200 senators.

The act on amending the constitution was adopted in double reading by both houses by an absolute majority of votes, pursuant to Art. 138 sec. 1 of the Constitution. In the second Senate resolution of July 11, 2019, the act was de facto adopted by an absolute majority of votes without obtaining a qualified majority of ⅔ (due to the opposition of the then opposition parties – the Democratic Party and Free and Equal and the absence of Senators Forza Italia during the vote). In turn, in the last reading in the Chamber of Deputies on October 8, 2019, after obtaining the consent of all majority and opposition parliamentary groups (except for some members of the Mixed Group), the text reached a qualified majority of ⅔ votes. However, this did not affect the process of adopting the bill: without obtaining similar support in the Senate, pursuant to paragraph 2 of Art. 138 of the Constitution, the provision was not explicitly promulgated, thus making it possible to apply for a confirmation referendum within the next three months. On January 10, 2020, 71 senators belonging to almost all parliamentary groups and parties (except for the Brothers of Italy and the For the Autonomies (SVP-PATT, UV) submitted a request to the Supreme Court of Cassation to hold a referendum on the text of the constitutional law approved by Parliament.

The question put in the referendum, in accordance with the Presidential Decree of 17 July 2020, was: "Do you approve the text of the Constitutional Law concerning« Amendments to articles 56, 57 and 59 of the Constitution concerning the reduction of the number of parliamentarians »Approved by Parliament and published in the Official Gazette no. 240 of 12 October 2019?" (President of the Republic, 2020f).

Following the announcement of the referendum, successive political parties and movements represented in the Italian and / or European Parliaments announced their position (Table 9.4).

During preparations for the election, several referendum committees were established, both supporters (Comitato per Sì al taglio dei Parlamentari) and opponents of limiting the number of parliamentarians (Comitato per il No del referendum sulla riduzione del numero dei Parlamentari, Comitato noiNO, NOstra – Comitato Giovanile per il No al Referendum Costituzionale, 3 Motivi per il No, Democratici per il NO).

Opponents of the proposed changes pointed to the disproportionate and unreasonable dimensions of the reduction in the number of parliamentarians, which was to determine a drastic reduction in the representativeness of the Houses, creating serious problems in their functioning. The significant risk of not the planned reduction of the party's role, but of strengthening ties between the parties and parliamentarians, was also emphasized. Finally, they pointed to the anti-parliamentary spirit which animated the proposed changes, leading to the depreciation of the role of the Parliament. Others, on the other hand, pointed to the apparent clarity of the referendum question, the inadequacy of the «promised» recruitment method (electoral right) to the reduced political representation and the «blind» rationalization of the form of government based on the premise that a smaller amount will facilitate negotiations and increase functionality (Onida et al., 2020).

Supporters, on the other hand, saw the reduction in the number of parliamentarians as an opportunity to raise the debate in the Houses and the implementation of a few improvements to their functionality. They rejected the allegation that «representativeness» was weakened by the argument that it is now linked not to a quantitative factor, but to the personal relationship between voters and their representatives and the effectiveness of the instruments used by political parties and large social organizations. Although it is true that with a smaller number of elected representatives, the likelihood of small political groups entering parliament decreases, de facto it is supposed to be an argument for limiting excessive political fragmentation of the Parliament. The argument concerning the lack of representation of certain territories, e.g., small regions, was also considered untrue. In fact, parliamentarians «represent the people» and not the territory from which they were elected. The more so as the proposed reform maintains the minimum number of senators for each region, regardless of the population. Moreover, it was pointed out that the failure of the Italian parliament also had an impact on the proper functioning of the community institutions, and its constitutional role was weakened not only by the poor quality of representation, but also by its exaggerated

TABLE 9.4   Positions held by political parties represented in the Italian and/or European Parliaments

Choice	Parties
Yes	Five Star Movement (M5S)
	League (Lega)
	Democratic Party (PD)
	Brothers of Italy (FdI)
	Article One (Art. 1)
	South Tyrolean People's Party (SVP)
	Alternativa Popolare
	Cambiamo! (C!)
	Die Freiheitlichen
	Fatherland and Constitution (PeC)
	Party of Venetians (PdV)
	Valdostan Union (UV)
Uncertain	Italia Viva (IV)
	Forza Italia (FI)
No	Action (Azione)
	Italian Left (SI)
	More Uurope (+Eu)
	Federation of the Greens (FdV)
	Italia in Comune (IiC)
	Power of the People (PaP)
	Italian Socialist Party (PSI)
	Energies for Italy (EpI)
	Volt Italia
	Associative Movement Italians Abroad (MAIE)
	South American Union Italian Emigrants (USEI)
	Communist Party (PC)
	Democratic Centre (CD)
	Communist Refoundation Party (PRC)
	Christian Democracy (DC)
	Italian Communist Party (PCI)
	Pact for Autonomy (PpA)
	Italian Marxist-Leninist Party (PMLI)
	Trentino Tyrolean Autonomist Party (PATT)
	Venetian Left (Sanca)
	Union for Trentino (UpT)

SOURCE: OWN STUDY

composition. Many parliamentarians exacerbate the tendency of the political class to share logics by presenting micro-amendments that precisely identify recipients in strictly defined interest groups. Moreover, the progress of multi-level governance requires that the Chambers also adjust in terms of numbers: the decrease in the number of parliamentarians should also be seen in the light of decentralization and the transfer of powers to other places of representation, such as the European Union or the Regions (Onida et al., 2020).

All the polls published at that time indicated that the supporters of change were winning. For example, in a survey conducted on January 13, 2020 by Demos for "La Repubblica": «yes» (86%), «no» (12%), «uncertain» (2%) (Turco, 2020); in a survey conducted on August 25, 2020 by Winpoli-CISE for "Il Sole 24 ORE": «yes» (66%), «no» (34%), «uncertain» (0%) (Cipolla, 2020); in the study conducted on August 31, 2020 by Eumetra MR for Gruppo Mediaset: «yes» (74%), «no» (10%), «uncertain» (16%) (Eumetra, 2020); in a survey conducted on September 4, 2020 by Ipsos for "Corriere della Sera": «yes» (71%), «no» (29%), «uncertain» (0%) (Pagnoncelli, 2020).

The voting in Italy took place on Sunday, September 20 from 7:00 am to 11:00 pm and on Monday, September 21 from 7:00 am to 3:00 pm. Italian citizens living abroad who chose to vote in their country of residence voted by correspondence in the weeks before the vote in Italy. The control of the postal ballots took place in the afternoon of September 21, along with the ballots in Italy, in specially prepared premises in the Fiera di Roma area. The result did not differ significantly from the polls preceding the referendum.

When analysing the results of the referendum by region, the "yes" voters constituted the majority in each of the regions and in each of the foreign

TABLE 9.5   Detailed voting results

Results	Preferences	Percentage of valid votes	Percentage of voters	Percentage of electors
Yes	17 913 089	69,96	68,77	35,16
No	7 692 007	30,04	29,53	15,11
Blank votes	218 093	–	0,84	0,42
Invalid votes	226 568	–	0,86	0,43
Total voters	26 050 226	–	–	51,12
Registered voters	50 955 985	–	–	100,00

SOURCE: HTTPS://ELEZIONI.INTERNO.GOV.IT/REFERENDUM

districts. The constitutional law received the lowest support in Friuli Venezia Giulia (59.57%), and the highest in Molise (79.89%). Admittedly, higher support was recorded in two foreign districts, but with a much lower turnout.

After the general approval of the changes, the President of the Italian Republic promulgated the Constitutional Act, which entered into force on

TABLE 9.6   Results by region

Region	Yes (%)	No (%)	Turnout (%)
Abruzzo	73,76	26,24	50,78
Aosta Valley	67,96	32,04	73,44
Apulia	75,22	24,78	61,91
Basilicata	75,84	24,16	49,83
Calabria	77,53	22,47	45,21
Campania	77,41	22,59	61,01
Emilia Romagna	69,54	30,46	55,37
Friuli Venezia Giulia	59,57	40,43	50,22
Lazio	65,86	34,14	45,68
Liguria	63,78	36,22	59,17
Lombardy	68,12	31,88	51,36
Marche	69,19	30,81	66,39
Molise	79,89	20,11	47,52
Piedmont	68,41	31,59	51,55
Sardinia	66,84	33,16	35,71
Sicily	75,88	24,12	35,39
Trentino-Alto Adige/Südtirol	70,89	29,11	70,96
Tuscany	65,96	30,04	65,89
Umbria	68,72	31,28	48,75
Veneto	62,44	37,56	67,55
Total Italy	**69,64**	**30,36**	**53,84**
Europe	80,07	19,93	23,39
South America	74,19	25,81	23,95
North and Central Americas	81,07	18,93	22,49
Africa, Asia, Oceania, Antarctica	79,46	20,54	19,75
Total Abroad	**78,24**	**21,76**	**23,30**
Total	**69,96**	**30,04**	**51,12**

SOURCE: HTTPS://ELEZIONI.INTERNO.GOV.IT/REFERENDUM

November 5, 2020 (President of the Republic, 2020g). The provision amending Art. 59 of the Constitution, which defines the limit of the coexistence of five life senators with life senators by operation of law, i.e. retired presidents of the Republic. However, according to Art. 4 reforms, provisions amending Art. 56 and 57 (regarding the number of parliamentarians) will apply from the next dissolution of parliament, but not earlier than January 4, 2021, i.e. on the sixtieth day after the entry into force of the act on amending the constitution.

9.5   Conclusions

The so-called the election day organized on September 20–21, 2020 included as many as four elections: supplementary elections to the Senate, regional elections, municipal elections and a constitutional referendum. It was also the first political test for the government during the pandemic, at a time when the day before the elections the highest daily number of deaths since the beginning of July 2020 (24) was recorded and more than 1,500 infections were detected daily.

An important place in the modern history of Italy was occupied by the constitutional referendum on the reduction of the number of parliamentarians, the effects of which will affect subsequent areas of the political system. In the light of the above, answering the research question posed in the introduction: "did the pandemic affect the election process, turnout and the final result?", One should answer positively regarding the election process in terms of determining the date and course of voting. It related to the introduced pandemic restrictions and the resulting difficulties in the implementation of the election law.

Regarding the turnout: comparing with the previous referenda on constitutional changes, we can talk about the maintenance of a certain level (2001 – 34%; 2006 – 52.5%; 2016 – 65.47%; 2020 – 53.84%). In the constitutional referendum on the reduction of the number of parliamentarians, the approval «yes» reached almost 70%, confirming previous polls. The turnout finally exceeded 53%, but on that occasion, it was necessary to distinguish between regions where also renewing mayor and council elections were held, and those where elections were scheduled at a different date. Well, in the former the turnout was 63.8%, in the latter – 48.2%. It is therefore justified to conclude that the turnout would probably not have reached 50% without aggregating these elections; and while this referendum did not require a confirmatory quorum, it would nevertheless be a «symbolic» rather than a decisive threshold. This can also be explained by the low popularity of the constitutional vote, in which the victory of the supporters of change seemed inevitable (Quorum/YouTrend, 2020).

Then, as for the result, it is not related to the pandemic situation at that time but should be related to another data. Well, many more voters in favour of reducing the number of parliamentarians found themselves in the south of the country, where in some provinces the support reached or even exceeded 80%, than in the centre or in the north. This is in line with the dynamics of support for the Five Star Movement, the main instigator of the reform submitted to the referendum, expressed when the 2018 elections. There is therefore a correlation between «yes» and voting for the M5S on the one hand, and «no» and voting for centre-left parties. The figures show that 92% of M5S voters voted «yes», as did 75–78% of centre-right voters, while most centre-left voters voted «no», ranging from 55% of PD voters to 77% of Italia Viva voters (Quorum/YouTrend, 2020).

Considering all the above remarks, it is necessary to emphasize the importance of the law, which received a lot of support from the Parliament (almost unanimous in the second vote in the Chamber of Deputies), being the result of a complex process, when the majority was formed under the two governments of Giuseppe Conte, and the disputes were reduced to minimum. In the process of adopting the law, the consent of virtually all political, ruling and opposition forces was revealed: a condition that should always be met in the case of a constitutional amendment was fulfilled to avoid the risk of «majoritarian» reforms.

As the crisis related to the coronavirus pandemic has proved, a functional and efficient parliament is needed. Thus, it is intended to perpetuate the conviction that fundamental decisions concerning social life will not be taken elsewhere, by means of executive measures removed from parliamentary control, but will remain anchored in guarantees provided for by law: from the verification of the head of state during promulgation to the control of the legitimacy of the Constitutional Tribunal. This functional credibility of the new, smaller parliament was tested by the next parliamentary elections in Italy, which took place on 25 September 2023.

References

A.V. (1970). *Norme sul referendum previsti dalla Costituzione e sulla iniziativa legislativa del popolo.* "Gazzetta Ufficiale della Repubblica Italiana", June 15, 1970, no 147.

A.V. (2019). *Testo di legge costituzionale approvato in seconda votazione a maggioranza assoluta, ma inferiore ai due terzi dei membri di ciascuna Camera, recante: «Modifiche agli articoli 56, 57 e 59 della Costituzione in materia di riduzione del numero dei par-lamentari».* "Gazzetta Ufficiale della Repubblica Italiana", October 12, 2019, no 240, 1–2.

Antoszewski, A., & Herbut, R. (1997). *Demokracje zachodnioeuropejskie. Analiza porównawcza,* Wrocław: Wydawnictwo Uniwersytetu Wrocławskiego.

Bokszczanin, I. (2003). „Referendum we Włoszech". In E. Zieliński & I. Bokszczanin & J. Zieliński (Eds.), *Referendum w państwach Europy* (347–388). Warszawa: Fundacja Europea.

Cipolla, A. (2020). "Sondaggi referendum taglio parlamentari: il Sì oltre il 70%". *Money.it.* Retrieved from: https://www.money.it/Sondaggi-referendum-2020-taglio -parlamentari-si-oltre-70.

Dipartimento per le Riforme Istituzionali. (2020). "Analisi comparata". *Dipartimento per le Riforme Istituzionali.* Retrieved from: https://www.riformeistituzionali.gov.it /media/1342/confrontointernazionale_27agosto2020.pdf.

Dudała, R. (2019a). Rosatellum – *włoski system wyborczy i jego wpływ na wynik wyborów parlamentarnych.* „Roczniki Nauk Społecznych", tom 11(47) – numer 1, 113–134.

Dudała, R. (2019b). *System polityczny współczesnych Włoch. Dynamika zmian* [The political system of contemporary Italy. Dynamics of changes]. Kielce: Wydawnic-two Uniwersytetu Jana Kochanowskiego.

Eumetra MR. (2020). "Referendum Costituzionale". *Sondaggipoliticoelettorali.it.* Retrieved from: http://www.sondaggipoliticoelettorali.it/GestioneSondaggio.aspx

Feola, R. (2001). *Il referendum nel sistema politico italiano.* Bracigliano: Jovene.

Fisichella, D. (2009) "Ordinamento elettorale". In N. Bobbio & N. Matteucci & G. Pas-quino (Eds.), *Il Dizionario di Politica* (124–127). Torino: UTET.

Garlicki, L. (2003). *Polskie prawo konstytucyjne. Zarys wykładu.* Warszawa: Wolters Klu-wer.

Grabowska S. (2005). *Instytucja ogólnokrajowej inicjatywy ludowej w wybranych państ-wach europejskich. Studium prawno-porównawcze.* Rzeszów: Wydawnictwo Uniwer-sytetu Rzeszowskiego.

ilPost. (2018). "La versione finale del «contratto» M5S-Lega". *ilPost.it.* Retrieved from: https://www.ilpost.it/2018/05/18/contratto-m5s-lega-versione-finale/

Krasnowolski, A. (2016). *Referendum jako instytucja demokracji bezpośredniej w państ-wach europejskich.* Wrocław: Kancelaria Senatu.

Mannino, A & Curreri, S. (2019). *Diritto parlamentare.* Milano: FrancoAngeli.

Ministry of Health. (2020a). *Indicazioni sulle misure di prevenzione dal rischio di infezi-one da SARS-CoV-2 per lo svolgimento delle elezioni referendarie, suppletive, regionali e comunali del 20–21 settembre 2020, con particolare riferimento al voto di pazienti in quar-antena e in isolamento domiciliare – Aggiornamento.* September 11, 2020. Retrieved from:https://www.trovanorme.salute.gov.it/norme/renderNormsanPdf?anno=2020 &codLeg=76163&parte=1%20&serie=null.

Ministry of Health. (2020b). *Indicazioni sulle misure di prevenzione dal rischio di infezione da SARS-CoV-2 per lo svolgimento delle elezioni referendarie, suppletive, regionali e comunali del 20–21 settembre 2020, con particolare riferimento alla formazione del personale dedicato alla raccolta del voto presso il domicilio di elettori sottoposti a trattamento domiciliare o in condizioni di quarantena o di isolamento fiduciario per COVID-19, nonché nelle strutture sanitarie con Reparti COVID19 con meno di 100 posti letto.* September 11, 2020. Retrieved from: https://www.trovanorme.salute.gov.it /norme/renderNormsanPdf?anno=2020&codLeg=76164&parte=1%20&serie=null.

Ministry of Health. (2020c). *Indicazioni sulle misure di prevenzione dal rischio di infezione da SARS-CoV-2 per lo svolgimento delle elezioni referendarie, suppletive, regionali e comunali del 20–21 settembre 2020, con particolare riferimento alla raccolta del voto presso le strutture residenziali sociosanitarie e socioassistenziali (RSA).* September 11, 2020. Retrieved from: https://www.trovanorme.salute.gov.it/norme/renderNormsan Pdf?anno=2020&codLeg=76165&parte=1%20&serie=null,

Ministry of the Interior and Ministry of Health. (2020). *Protocollo sanitario e di sicurezza per lo svolgimento delle consultazioni elettorali e referendarie dell'anno 2020.* August 7, 2020. Retrieved from: https://www.trovanorme.salute.gov.it/norme/render NormsanPdf?anno=2020&codLeg=75942&parte=1%20&serie=null.

Ministry of the Interior. (2020). "Oltre 46 milioni di elettori alle urne il 20 e 21 settembre". *Ministero dell'Interno.* Retrieved from: https://www.interno.gov.it/it/notizie /oltre-46-milioni-elettori-urne-20-e-21-settembre.

Onida, V. & Nicotra, I. & Morelli, A. & Trucco, L. (2020). *Giustizia Insieme.* "Il referendum sulla riduzione dei parlamentari: tre ragioni per il sì e tre per il NO. Forum dei costituzionalisti". Retrieved from: https://www.giustiziainsieme.it/it/news/92-main /la-nostra-costituzione/1292-il-referendum-sulla-riduzione-dei-parlamentari-tre -ragioni-per-il-si-e-tre-per-il-no-forum-dei-costituzionalisti-valerio-onida-ida -nicotra-alessandro-morelli-e-lara-trucco?hitcount=0.

Pagnoncelli, N. (2020). "Il sondaggio: taglio dei parlamentari, il 71% dice Sì al referendum. Tra gli elettori del Pd 1 su 3 è contrario". Retrieved from: https://www.corriere .it/elezioni/referendum-2020/notizie/referendum-taglio-parlamentari-sondaggio -si-no-7e158dc2-eeof-11ea-8e1d-a2467c523c28.shtml.

Pasquino, G. (2002). *Il sistema politico italiano.* Bologna: il Mulino.

President of the Council of Ministers. (2020a). *Disposizioni attuative del decreto-legge 23 febbraio 2020, n. 6. recante misure urgenti in materia di contenimento e gestione dell'emergenza epidemiologica da COVID-19.* "Gazzetta Ufficiale della Repubblica Italiana", February 23, 2020, no 45, 3–4.

President of the Council of Ministers. (2020b). *Ulteriori disposizioni attuative del decreto-legge 23 febbraio 2020, n. 6. recante misure urgenti in materia di contenimento e gestione dell'emergenza epidemiologica da COVID-19.* "Gazzetta Ufficiale della Repubblica Italiana", March 8, 2020, no 59, 1–6.

President of the Council of Ministers. (2020c). *Ulteriori disposizioni attuative del decreto-legge 25 marzo 2020, n. 19, recante misure urgenti per fronteggiare l'emergenza epidemiologica da COVID-19, e del decreto-legge 16 maggio 2020, n. 33, recante ulteriori misure urgenti per fronteggiare l'emergenza epidemiologica da COVID-19.* "Gazzetta Ufficiale della Repubblica Italiana", July 14, 2020, no 176, 1–70.

President of the Republic. (2020a). *Indizione del referendum popolare confermativo della legge costituzionale, recante: «Modifiche agli articoli 56, 57 e 59 della Costituzione in materia di riduzione del numero dei parlamentari», approvata dal Parlamento.* "Gazzetta Ufficiale della Repubblica Italiana", January 29, 2020, no 23, 32.

President of the Republic. (2020b). *Misure urgenti in materia di contenimento e gestione dell'emergenza epidemiologica da COVID-19.* "Gazzetta Ufficiale della Repubblica Italiana", February 23, 2020, no 45, 1–2.

President of the Republic. (2020c). *Conversione in legge, con modificazioni, del decreto-legge 23 febbraio 2020, n. 6, recante misure urgenti in materia di contenimento e gestione dell'emergenza epidemiologica da COVID-19.* "Gazzetta Ufficiale della Repubblica Italiana", March 9, 2020, no 61, 6–7.

President of the Republic. (2020d). *Misure di potenziamento del Servizio sanitario nazionale e di sostegno economico per famiglie, lavoratori e imprese connesse all'emergenza epidemiologica da COVID-19.* "Gazzetta Ufficiale della Repubblica Italiana", March 17, 2020, no 70, 1–67.

President of the Republic. (2020e). *Conversione in legge, con modificazioni, del decreto-legge 20 aprile 2020, n. 26, recante disposizioni urgenti in materia di consultazioni elettorali per l'anno 2020.* "Gazzetta Ufficiale della Repubblica Italiana", June 19, 2020, no 154, 1.

President of the Republic. (2020f). *Conversione in legge, con modificazioni, del decreto-legge 19 maggio 2020, n. 34, recante misure urgenti in materia di salute, sostegno al lavoro e all'economia, nonché di politiche sociali connesse all'emergenza epidemiologica da CO- VID-19.* "Gazzetta Ufficiale della Repubblica Italiana", July 18, 2020, no 180, 1–61.

President of the Republic. (2020g). *Modifiche agli articoli 56, 57 e 59 della Costituzione in materia di riduzione del numero dei parlamentari.* "Gazzetta Ufficiale della Repubblica Italiana", October 21, 2020, no 261, 1–2.

Quorum/YouTrend. (2020). "Referendum costituzionale. Il dossier di Quorum/You Trend". *Youtrend.it.* Retrieved from: https://www.youtrend.it/wp-content/uploads/2016/12/Dossier-Referendum-Costituzionale.pdf.

Rossi, E. (2020) *Meno parlamentari, più democrazia?.* Pisa: University Press.

Senato della Repubblica e Camera dei deputati. (2019). "Riduzione del numero di parlamentari: elementi per l'esame in Assemblea (A.C. 1585-B). Dossier". Retrieved from: http://documenti.camera.it/leg18/dossier/pdf/AC0167f.pdf.

Severgnini, C. (2020). Coronavirus, primi due casi in Italia «Sono due cinesi in vacanza a Roma». Sono arrivati a Milano il 23 gennaio. *Corriere della Sera*. Retrieved from: https://www.corriere.it/cronache/20_gennaio_30/coronavirus-italia-corona -9d6dc436-4343-11ea-bdc8-faf1f56f19b7.shtml.

Turco, A. (2020). "Sondaggi politici Demos: taglio parlamentari, 86% italiani favorevole". *Termometropolitico.it*. Retrieved from: https://www.termometropolitico .it/1487114_sondaggi-politici-demos-taglio-parlamentari-86-italiani-favorevole.html? cn-reloaded=1.

Tuttitalia. (2020a). "Elezioni Amministrative 2020". *Tuttitalia.it*. Retrieved from: https://www.tuttitalia.it/elezioni-italiane/elezioni-amministrative-2020/.

Tuttitalia. (2020b). "Elezioni regionali in Italia". *Tuttitalia.it*. Retrieved from: https:// www.tuttitalia.it/elezioni-italiane/elezioni-regionali/.

World Health Organization. (2020). "Italy". *who.int*. Retrieved from: https://www.who .int/countries/ita/.

CHAPTER 10

The 2020 Parliamentary Election in Lithuania. Between Participation and Quality of Democracy during Pandemic

Magdalena Musiał-Karg and Martinas Malužinas

10.1 Introduction

The first round of election to the Parliament of the Republic of Lithuania (Seimas) was held on 11th October 2020 and the second on 25th October 2020. Citizens of the Republic of Lithuania, living in Lithuania and abroad, had the opportunity to elect 141 Members of the Parliament. Despite the pandemic, the parliamentary election was held on the date announced by President Gitanas Nausėda in spring 2020 - still during the lockdown. However, while monitoring the pandemic, the government decided to extend the so-called early voting to four days. In the parliamentary election held 7 months after the outbreak of the pandemic, the voter turnout reached 47.6% (first round) and was slightly lower than during the election four years earlier.

The aim of this chapter is to analyse the impact of the COVID-19 pandemic on the Lithuanian parliamentary election in 2020. Based on the example of Lithuania's election held during the pandemic, the authors intend to answer questions regarding electoral regulations adopted during the pandemic, including the introduction of additional forms of voting (and their use), specific nature of the election campaign during the crisis, and the election process itself. The point of reference for the deliberations is the emergency in Europe and in the world in 2020, as countries were forced to either postpone or proceed (under sanitary regime) with planned elections, as it was decided in Lithuania. An important reference in relation to the research is the extent to which the pandemic may have affected the quality of Lithuanian democracy, with particular emphasis on electoral participation. For this purpose, the chapter uses indicators of the quality of democracy. In combination with the analysis of the election and its results, conclusions are drawn regarding the impact of the pandemic on election and democracy in Lithuania.

Elections in emergency situations have previously been analysed from a scientific point of view. Many researchers in the world considered the establishment of special legal regulations, organization, conduct, and outcome of elections held in the state of natural disasters, natural calamities, or armed conflicts (Abad, Maurer, 2020; Debbage, Gonsalves, Shepherd, Knox, 2014; Eriksson, 2016; Morley, 2018).

Research on elections in the Republic of Lithuania has been conducted by many researchers, both Lithuanian (Ramonaitė, 2006, 2021; Kluonis, 2009; Jurkynas, 2017; Ulinskaitė, 2020, 2021; Ulinskaitė & Pukelis 2021; Jurkynas 2021; Malužinas 2021a, 2021c, 2022), as well as those from other countries (Clark, 1995; Csergő, Regelmann, 2017; Zielinski, 2000; Jagusiak, 2013; Kuczyńska-Zonik, 2021; Preece, 2014). However, even though the election took place during the pandemic, the 2020 election has not been analysed from the political science perspective. It seems, therefore, that the topic discussed in this chapter deserves an in-depth scientific exploration, as it concerns elections held in special circumstances on the originally planned date (while many countries decided to postpone elections) but under a stricter sanitary regime (due to spread of SARS-CoV-2 virus). The election involved the use of additional forms of voting, and it was held at the time of a perceived increased risk to public health and, consequently, increased tensions in social and political spheres.

10.2   The Electoral System

The principles of the Lithuania's electoral law are determined by the Constitution. These are classical principles characteristic for democratic states. According to Article 55 of the Constitution, the Parliament of the Republic of Lithuania is elected every five years. It represents the will of the nation. Importantly, the regularity of elections is also considered to be a sovereign electoral principle. Although it is not the intention of this chapter to analyse generally recognised electoral rules, it is worth noting that the Lithuanian legislator emphasised that elections in Lithuania should fulfil democratic principles of equality, secrecy, universality, as well as they should be free and fair. In principle, Lithuanian elections guarantee that the electoral process is free and transparent.

According to the Electoral Law, the active right to vote is granted to all citizens of the Republic of Lithuania who are at least 18 years old. The passive suffrage, or the right to stand for election to the Parliament, is vested in all citizens who are over 25 years of age. Citizens who have been deprived of their right to vote by a court of law do not take part in elections. Every eligible citizen has one vote in single-member and multi-member constituencies. Lithuania has a mixed electoral system (Sześciło, p. 4). A characteristic feature of the model are two overlapping levels of constituencies. Furthermore, the distribution of seats at both levels takes place independently (Massicotte, 1999). At the first tier, 71 MPs are elected in 71 single-member constituencies created based on the number of voters. Elections are held according to a mixed electoral system. At the second tier, 70 MPs are elected in a single state-wide constituency, and elections are held according to the principle of proportional representation. Political parties which have received more than 5% of votes in the first round ('barrier clause') are admitted to the Seimas from party lists. Coalitions have to pass the threshold of seven percent of all votes cast. A different rule applies to single-member constituencies. If in the first round none of the candidates obtains more than 50% of votes with a 40% turnout, the two candidates who obtained the largest number of votes in the first round compete in the second round.

It should be noted that all eligible citizens can vote in one multi-member constituency which covers the whole territory of the Republic of Lithuania. This means that the Lithuanian electoral system is mixed, which is the youngest form of electoral systems in democratic theory and practice.

During elections to the Seimas, voters have the right to vote either in their district or in any electoral district of their constituency, if both units (district where the voter lives and district where the voter is present) are connected via the IT communications system of the Central Election Commission.

From the point of view of a voter, the voter receives two ballots. The first one - intended for a single-member constituency - includes an alphabetical list of candidates. The voter marks one name on the ballot. The ballot paper for a multi-member constituency contains the party list. The order of names is random and determined by each political party. The voter may choose five candidates from the list, indicating the order of preference (Zielinski, 2003, pp. 19–20).

10.3 Legal and Political Response to COVID-19 in the Context of Parliamentary Elections

Due to the spread of the COVID-19 pandemic, many countries decided to postpone their elections to a later date. They assumed that it would happen after the peak when the pandemic would be in retreat (International IDEA, 2022). In Lithuania, however, the decision was made to hold the election on the date scheduled.

While observing experience of many countries around the world, the pandemic revealed that organising general elections in emergency situations is a major challenge. Likewise, Lithuania realised that it might be difficult to guarantee voters health and lives due to the growing number of infections and deaths, especially that the biggest wave of the disease was expected in autumn and winter of 2020. Apart from the need to secure health, no less important was to respect the principles of democratic elections. This could be problematic in the case of infected voters (universal suffrage and possibility to exercise active electoral rights). The same applied to the possibility to ensure campaigning (candidates were not able to hold direct campaigns).

Acting under the existing emergency legislation, the Lithuanian government decided to respond to the crisis by imposing two nationwide quarantines without declaring a constitutional state of emergency. The aim of the quarantines was to limit the spread of contagion by introducing special conditions, restrictions, and procedures for work, life, leisure, movement of people, and economic and other activities (Lietuvos Respublikos žmonių užkrečiamųjų ligų profilaktikos ir kontrolės įstatymas, 1996 m. rugsėjo 25 d. Nr. I-1553). The first quarantine was introduced at the very beginning of the pandemic and lasted three months (16th March to 17th June 2020). The second quarantine was introduced on 4th November 2020 (Dėl karantino Lietuvos Respublikos teritorijoje paskelbimo, 2020 m. lapkričio 4 d. Nr. 1226) and continued until 1st July 2021.

While the initial restrictions were introduced under conditions of great uncertainty, mainly as a precautionary measure (Lithuania had only a few confirmed cases at the time), the second quarantine was a response to a rapidly deteriorating health situation. Interestingly, just weeks after the 2020 elections, the number of new COVID-19 cases increased to the point where Lithuania became the most affected country in the world.

The government responded to the pandemic by implementing measures based on the pre-existing emergency legal framework. However, the Parliament had to amend existing primary legislation to expand their executive powers.

Therefore, the Government took up the challenge to organise elections to the Seimas while mitigating the above-mentioned risks. First, they maintained special security rules and tried to secure possibly the highest turnout (fear of contagion should not translate into higher absenteeism than in previous elections). Moreover, the government decided to adopt new legal regulations.

While analysing legal regulations introduced in connection with the parliamentary election planned during the pandemic, it should be noted that after 2016 a special constituency was established for citizens permanently or temporarily residing abroad. Additionally, measures were introduced to enable voting for people with disabilities, as well as provisions on candidate registration, alternative voting methods, and voting abroad. This was intended to allow the

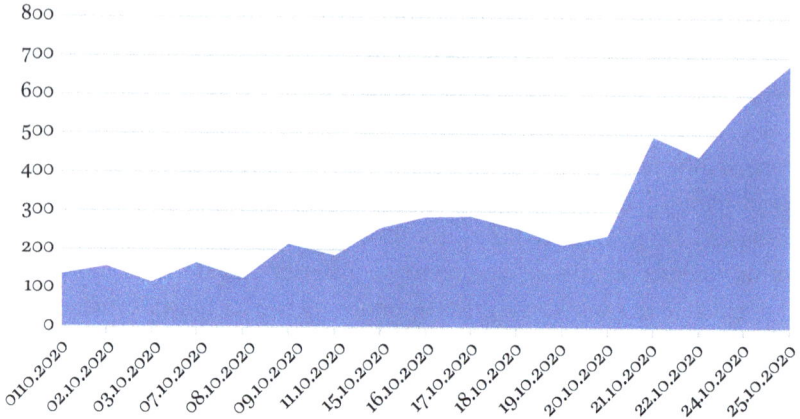

FIGURE 10.1   New Daily COVID-19 cases (1st October – 25th October 2020)
SOURCE: AUTHORS' STUDY BASED ON HTTPS://WWW.WORLDOMETERS
.INFO/CORONAVIRUS/COUNTRY/LITHUANIA/, ACCESSED: 10.02.2022

widest possible group of people to cast their votes in special circumstances of
the pandemic.

At the beginning of October 2020, with the rapid increase of COVID-19 cases
and the daily expansion of outbreaks, the second wave of coronavirus started
in Lithuania, spreading from regions to big cities. According to the Lithuanian
Department of Statistics, the number of new infections, deaths among hospi-
talised COVID-19 patients rapidly increased.

The first days of October 2020 saw the highest number of new COVID-19
infections since the beginning of the pandemic. With the increase in the number of infections, the country faced a shortage of hospital beds and the medical
staff. Moreover, from 21st October until 4th November, the government implemented colour-based zones in the country. The rise in new coronavirus cases
and related restrictions may have affected voter turnout. Growing unemployment and problems in the health care system led to nationwide dissatisfaction
with the coalition government (*Lithuania: Surging COVID-19...*).

10.4   Electoral Campaigning during a Pandemic

It is believed that one of key elements of the democratic process affected by
the pandemic was campaigning. Campaigns provide the opportunity for candidates and political parties to disseminate their views on the national policy
and convince the public that their approach is better than their political opponents. Campaigning enables citizens to have more informed assessment of

options when they go to the ballot box. It is widely believed that the pandemic (introduction of a state of emergency, lockdown, restrictions, sanitary regime, as well as public concerns about health, etc.) may have significantly affected the course of electoral campaigns (and election results). Not only were possibilities for electoral agitation and direct contact with voters limited, but also public access to information restricted due to the lack of direct contact with candidates and imbalance in the use of the media by politicians and opposition parties (campaigning moved to the Internet). However, there was also risk that campaigns could spread not only ideas but also the virus. There were loud and lengthy debates whether campaigning should be restricted to protect public health, especially during the first and second waves of the pandemic in 2020. It is therefore important to balance public health protection and democratic discussion and contestation.

While examining the experience with restrictions on traditional campaigning in different countries ahead of the 2020 elections, three groups can be distinguished: a) countries which restricted the number of public assembly participants, b) countries where political rallies and events were banned, and c) countries where no information about restrictions or bans on campaigning could be found (Asplund, 2021).

Officially, the campaigning period began with the announcement of elections by the President of the Republic of Lithuania in April 2020. Campaigning was not as intense as usual, partly because of the COVID-19 pandemic and related restrictions on assembly (restrictions began to be progressively lifted on 1st September, but alternative safety precautions were introduced for mass events, outdoor events included). Candidates were able to reach out to voters, and most of them advertised through traditional and online media, and to a lesser extent through posters, billboards, and banners. Some candidates decided to conduct door-to-door campaigning, while others refrained from direct contact with voters due to the COVID-19 pandemic. The public broadcaster organized candidate "debates," also available online, with an identical set of questions and the same time available for each candidate (ODIHR, 2021, p. 12). Since not every voter had access to the Internet, voters did not have full access to information about candidates, their political agendas, etc. At the same time, it should be noted that not all candidates had equal access to traditional media. As post-election reports indicate, candidates of ruling parties, who were promoted in the public media, were in the lead (Malużinas, 2021c, p. 224).

Therefore, it can be assumed that the election campaign conducted before the Lithuanian elections of 2020 could raise concerns related to, among other things, the principles of free and equal elections. This manifested itself in limitations for candidates to campaign, as well as unequal access to information about the candidates (e.g. no access to the Internet and the campaign content online, or unequal access candidates had to the public media).

Regarding the topics raised during the election campaign, it should be noted that the public debate was dominated by economic and social issues, energy and environmental problems, health issues, as well as issues related to crisis management during the COVID-19 pandemic (ODIHR, 2021, p. 12).

10.5   Specific Electoral Arrangements during a Pandemic

The Lithuanian parliamentary elections of 2022 were held between the first and the second lockdowns introduced by the state. After consulting the Ministry of Health, the Central Election Commission approved the extraordinary electoral procedure that set fundamental rules of conduct, which included the need to cover mouth and nose, keeping physical distance, frequently disinfect hands and surfaces touched in polling stations, control over the flow of voters to avoid crowding and guarantee safe voting (Kuczyńska-Zonik, 2020).Approximately 2.4 million citizens in more than 1,900 election districts enjoyed the active voting right. Due to the epidemiological situation, it was decided that correspondence voting was to be available for voters staying abroad with 51 polling stations established at Lithuanian embassies and consulates. For the first time ever, a single-member constituency of the Lithuanians of the World was established for Lithuanian citizens living outside the country. It was also decided that the group of voters eligible to vote at home would be extended. These extended group included those taking caring of the disabled at home and, in the first round, those in COVID-19 isolation (voting at home).

Regarding alternative voting methods, it should be noted that the Lithuanian law "provides for a wide range of alternative voting methods, including in any polling station within or outside the constituency of residence (absentee), early voting, homebound and institution-based" (ODIHR, 2021, p. 8). Due to the COVID-19 pandemic, Central Electoral Commission proposed an extension on early voting (four days instead two days). Voters could cast votes in any of the 73 early voting centres established in municipalities and other places from Monday to Thursday prior to each round. "A voter could vote multiple times during early voting and once more on the election day (ODIHR, 2021, 8).[1]

---

1   The electronic voter identification system allows for the printing of several ballot papers. In the first round, 33 voters cast ballots twice during early voting.

Interestingly, during the second round of the national election, Lithuania introduced COVID-19-friendly voting booths as citizens headed to the polls. In municipalities of Vilnius, Kaunas, and Šiauliai, and the Raseiniai District, early voting stations were opened specifically for voters in self-isolation from 19th to 22nd October. According to the Ministry of Health, self-isolated voters who returned from abroad or who had contact with persons affected by COVID-19 were allowed to leave their homes for up to 2 hours in order to be able to reach an early voting station (*Saviizoliacijoje esantiems ...*, 2020). Moreover, the Lithuania's Health Ministry allowed voters in self-isolation to vote in special drive-in polling sites set up in several municipalities from 19th–22nd October. Voters were instructed to come alone in their cars, put on facial masks, and cast their votes at four stations across the country. Only those in isolation and on the official list could vote this way until Thursday (22nd October) (*Lithuanians with coronavirus...*, 2020).

The concept of opening mobile polling stations was a kind of response to the great interest in early voting. The procedure required a citizen to stay in the car to keep the secrecy of voting. After establishing the identity of a voter, a member of election commission handed over ballots which, after being filled in, were put in an envelope, sealed, and returned (*Mobile ...*, 2020).

10.6   Results and Turnout in the 2020 Elections

In the first round on 11th October, about a half of seats in the 141-member parliament were filled under a proportional representation voting system, whereas the other half during the second round in single-member constituencies (based on the majority system).

Undoubtedly, the pandemic had an impact on the results of the autumn general elections, but the economic situation was also one of the factors influencing citizens' attitudes. Although the number of deaths caused by coronavirus in Lithuania was well below the EU average, and Lithuania's economy shrank by 4% year-on-year in the second quarter of 2020, many Lithuanians felt that the government focus on fighting the virus left thousands of patients without access to healthcare. Others said the government took insufficient action to help businesses during the first months of the pandemic, during which the unemployment rate rose from 9% to more than 14% in October. Poverty levels and income inequality in Lithuania were among the highest in the EU (*Lithuania: Surging COVID-19...*, 2020).

As for the results of the Seimas elections, it is worth noting that 17 parties and coalitions participated in the elections. Seventeen of them put forward their party lists in multi-member districts. Moreover, twenty-three independent candidates took part in the elections in single-member constituencies.

As in previous elections, no party or electoral coalition won the majority of seats, and a coalition had to be formed. On 15th October, four days after the first round, the leaders of the Homeland Union - Lithuanian Christian Democrats, the Liberal Movement, and the Freedom Party declared that all three parties nominate Ingrida Šimonytė as their joint candidate to be the Prime Minister of Lithuania. She was appointed Prime Minister on 24th November.

According to the Central Election Commission, the parliamentary seats were distributed among political parties as follows: Homeland Union - Lithuanian Christian Democrats - 50 seats, Lithuanian Farmers and Greens Union - 32 seats, Liberals Movement - 13 seats, Lithuanian Social Democratic Party - 13 seats, Freedom Party - 11 seats, Labour Party - 10 seats, Electoral Action of Poles in Lithuania - Christian Families Alliance - 3 seats, Lithuanian Social Democratic Labour Party - 3 seats, 'Freedom and Justice'- 1 seat, and Lithuanian Greens Party - 1 seat (*Seimas 2020–2024*). It is worth noting that right-wing parties won most seats in both the majority and proportional pools.

In the context of the COVID-19 pandemic, the 2020 Lithuanian parliamentary election had the second-lowest turnout in the first round since the Republic of Lithuania was restored in the early 1990s: 47.80% in the first round and 38.2% in the second round. While the turnout of the second round was comparable to the average turnout in the second round of the historic Seimas elections (37%), the participation of voters in the first round was much lower than the average of all previous elections (54.5%) (*Lietuvos Respublikos Seimo Rinkimai, 2020*).

When considering the reasons for the low voter turnout, attention should be drawn to the public fear of infection by the virus and the pandemic-related restrictions introduced during the election campaign. Although held on the scheduled date, the parliamentary election was held just before the peak of the second wave, and practically two weeks after the second round another the national lockdown was introduced. Additionally, there was negative public sentiment related to the worsening economic situation and rising unemployment rates. The turnout was probably also weakened by voters' negative attitude towards political parties which were unable to solve pandemic related problems effectively.

In the context of citizens' participation, results of alternative methods of voting were interesting. Postal voting was used in the first round by 826,758 people out of 2,411,617 eligible to vote (11.64%) and in the second round by 875,637 people out of 2,310,860 eligible to vote (11.29%).

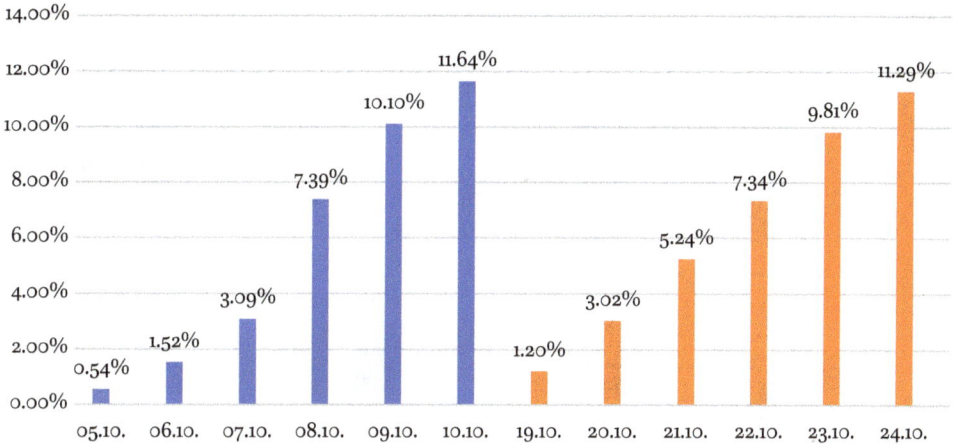

FIGURE 10.2 Postal voting before the first (5–10.10.2020) and second (19–24.10.2020) rounds of parliamentary elections
SOURCE: OWN COMPILATION BASED ON DATA FROM THE CENTRAL ELECTORAL COMMISSION OF THE REPUBLIC OF LITHUANIA

TABLE 10.1 Postal voting before the first (5–10.10.2020) and second (19–24.10.2020) rounds of parliamentary elections

05.10.	06.10.	07.10.	08.10.	09.10.	10.10.	19.10.	20.10.	21.10.	22.10.	23.10.	24.10.
0,54%	1,52%	3,09%	7,39%	10,10%	11,64%	1,20%	3,02%	5,24%	7,34%	9,81%	11,29%
12980	36759	74537	178145	243520	280817	27630	69752	121079	169616	226609	260951

SOURCE: OWN COMPILATION BASED ON DATA FROM THE CENTRAL ELECTORAL COMMISSION OF THE REPUBLIC OF LITHUANIA

While analysing the above data, it can be concluded that postal voting was a popular voting method among Lithuanian voters, and the pandemic further increased confidence in this voting method, as proved by the 2016 and 2020 election results.

As mentioned above, due to the COVID-19 pandemic, to avoid larger concentration of people, early voting was extended from the traditional two days to four. As for the other forms of voting allowed during the pandemic, the idea of opening a mobile polling station resulted from the high interest in early voting (early voting lasted from 5th to 8th October). Only during two days, almost 37 thousand (1.5%) of voters used the opportunity. There was also considerable interest in drive-in vote. In order to maintain the secrecy of voting, voters were required to be alone in the car. After establishing the driver's identity, a

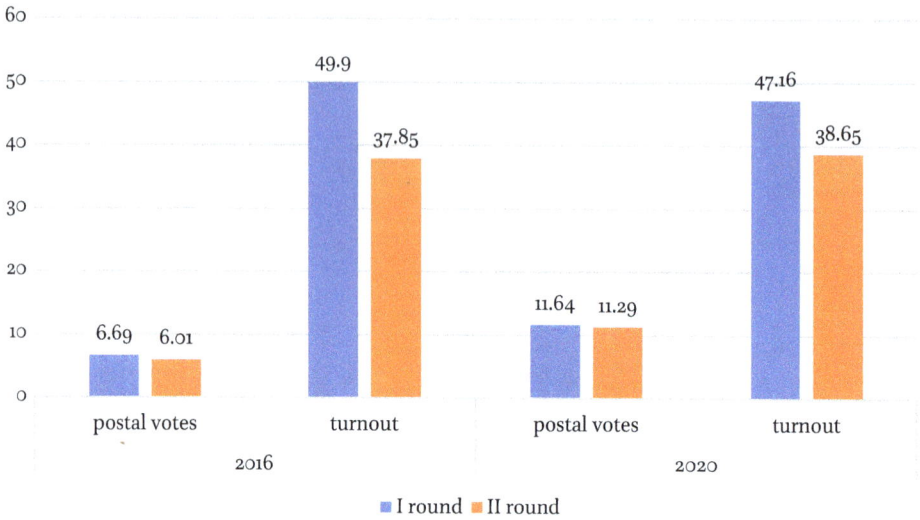

FIGURE 10.3   Postal voting in the first and second rounds of the 2016 and 2020 general
elections
SOURCE: OWN COMPILATION BASED ON DATA FROM THE CENTRAL
ELECTORAL COMMISSION OF THE REPUBLIC OF LITHUANIA

member of the electoral commission handed over ballots, which after filling in, the voter put into an envelope, sealed, and returned.

Two days before the actual election day (Friday and Saturday), voting was also possible from home. This time, the possibility to vote from home was available not only for people with disabilities or 70+, but also for those who went down with COVID-19 and had to stay in self-isolation (*W Wilnie działa....*, 2020).

In conclusion, mainly due to the pandemic (sanitary restrictions, increasing number of infections and thus health concern among voters), but also unfavourable public sentiment resulting from the weakening economic situation, the 2020 election failed to produce a high turnout. We need to admit that the COVID-19 pandemic had a significant impact on people's lifestyles, trust in institutions, voting intentions, and participation in elections (Picchio, Santolini, 2021, p. 3). People knew that going to the polls to exercise their right could indeed boost infections and the incidence of COVID-related mortality, especially among elderly people (Bertoli, Guichard, Marchetta, 2020; Santana, Rama, Casal Bértoa, 2020). The occurrence of a pandemic is one of these extraordinary circumstances in which citizens trust the national government to effective action to eradicate the pandemic and rapidly restore normal life (Picchio, Santolini, 2021, p. 3). If this does not happen and the government is ineffective, public attitudes deteriorate.

In addition, direct campaigning, i.e. attending assemblies and rallies, can make gatherings risky and spread viral infection among political candidates (Bach, Guillouzouic, Malgouyres, 2020) and voters. Thus, voters are making a choice between abstaining and fulfilling their civic duties and running the risk of contracting the infection. The decision depends on the voter's perception of infection risk. In areas where the risk seems to be higher and residents observe higher number of positive cases and deaths from COVID-19, there may be a sharp decline in voter turnout due to the fear of being infected at the polling station (Picchio, Santolini, 2021, p. 2).

10.7   Conclusion

The COVID-19 pandemic has complicated the electoral process around the world. The 2020 parliamentary elections in Lithuania have been affected by the COVID-19, which put the Lithuanian government to the test. Opinion polls have shown that the public seemed to be generally satisfied with Prime Minister Saulius Skvernelis' handling of the pandemic. However, some economic problems, unemployment, managing the crisis, and the fear of the pandemic helped the opposition to have better results in the elections.

The Lithuanian case converges with recent empirical evidence that the COVID-19 outbreak has mixed effects on trust in institutions. The pandemic has not only changed citizens' support for the government, but it also altered electoral participation. Many people could have been concerned about being infected in the polling station, which may have increased the number of abstentions. "Moreover, voting abstention may be higher in areas where the COVID-19 outbreak has had a more severe impact, because people perceive a greater risk to their health" (Santana, Rama, Casal Bértoa, 2020).

The Lithuania's case is consistent with opinions presented by Freedom House in its special report on *Democracy under Lockdown* stating that "since the coronavirus outbreak began, the condition of democracy and human rights has grown worse in 80 countries" (Repucci, Slipowitz, 2020). In support of this, we can refer to the *Democracy Index* by the Economist Intelligence Unit.

The 2016–2020 democracy indexes show that the Republic of Lithuania saw their index decreasing every year, and over the 5-year period the average value of the Democracy Index for Lithuania dropped by 0.34 points (Figure 10.4).

According to the data presented in the figure, Lithuania dropped from 36th to 42nd place in 2020 (down 0.37 points compared to 2019). It recorded the largest declines in categories of political culture (-0.62), political participation

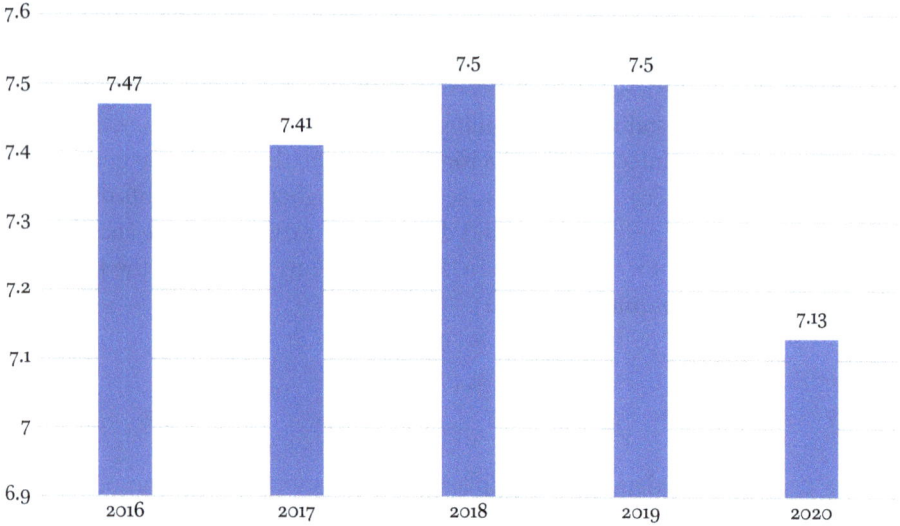

FIGURE 10.4   *Economist Intelligence Unit* democracy index for Lithuania (2016–2020)
Scale from 0 to 10, higher value of the indicator means better rating
SOURCE: OWN ELABORATION BASED ON: *ECONOMIST INTELLIGENCE
UNIT*, 2020

(-0.55), and government functioning (-0.36), with unchanged ratings for the electoral process and political pluralism (Maluzinas, 2021b, p. 74).

Political participation includes citizens' participation in elections, their interest in politics, and their ability to choose the political force that represents them.

Concluding, we need to admit that the coronavirus pandemic posed an unprecedented challenge for the Lithuanian society and the decision-makers. These considerations are subject to two conditions that must be kept in mind. First, the onset of the pandemic, the subsequent first lockdown, the October surge in infections, and the timing of the election did not allow for a widespread public information campaign about new alternative voting methods. Second, mail-in voting became more popular due to public health concerns, and both mobile and drive-thru polling stations proved to be effective as infected and isolated people could cast their ballots.

As the final remark, it is worth noting that the ODIHR in its report on the Lithuanian elections has formulated a number of recommendations concerning various stages of the electoral cycle so as to further enhance the conduct of elections in Lithuania and to support efforts to bring them fully in line with OSCE commitments and other international obligations and standards for

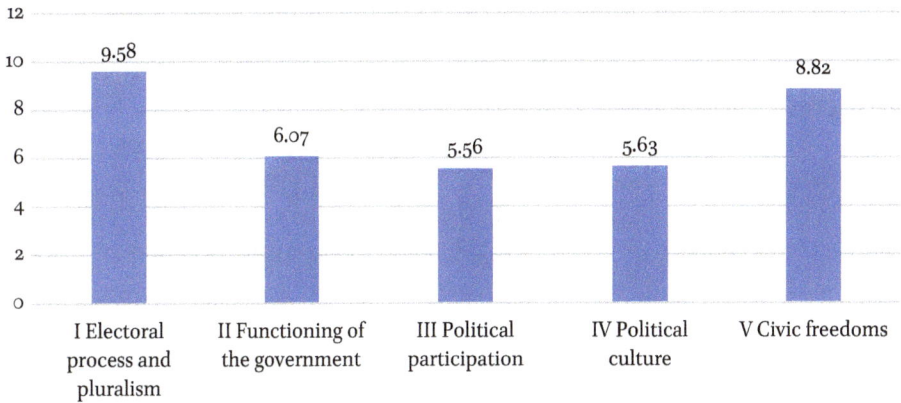

FIGURE 10.5   Categories included in the Democracy Index for Lithuania in 2020
SOURCE: OWN ELABORATION BASED ON: *ECONOMIST INTELLIGENCE UNIT*, 2020

democratic elections. Some of these recommendations concern the legislative process and the care taken to ensure democratic elections, as well as the conduct of the campaign, voting itself, and the counting of votes. These elements often raised concerns during pandemic elections, not only in Lithuania but also in other countries of the world (ODIHR, 2021, pp. 16–17).

References

Abad, L.A., Maurer, N. (2020). "Do pandemics shape elections? Retrospective voting in the 1918 Spanish Flu pandemic in the United State". *SSRN*. http://dx.doi.org/10.2139/ssrn.3680286.

Asplund, E. (2021). *Elections and COVID-19: How election campaigns took place in 2020*. International Institute for Democracy and Electoral Assistance (International IDEA). Retrieved from: https://docs.google.com/document/d/1LCtHGGJUOL8Uce6pXnm8NDoAfozDtj1I/edit#heading=h.jgi3jaw75r8.

Bach, L., A. Guillouzouic, Malgouyres, C. (2020). "Does holding elections during a COVID-19 pandemic put the lives of politicians at risk?". *Working Paper No. 2020–45*, Paris School of Economics.

Bertoli, S., Guichard, L., Marchetta, F. (2020). "Turnout in the municipal elections of March 2020 and excess mortality during the COVID-19 epidemic in France". *IZA Discussion Papers* No. 13335. Bonn: Institute of Labor Economics.

Clark, T.D. (2009). "The Lithuanian Political Party System. A Case Study of Democratic Consolidation". *East European Politics and Societies*, vol. 9, no 1, pp. 41–62.

Csergő, Z., Regelmann, A-Ch. (2017). "Europeanization and Collective Rationality in Minority Voting. Lessons from Central and Eastern Europe". *Problems of Post-Communism,* vol. 64, no. 5, pp. 291–310. https://doi.org/10.1080/10758216.2017.1330659.

Dagilytė, E., Padskočimaitė Q. (2021). *Lithuania's Two COVID-19 Quarantines: Challenges and Lessons for the Rule of Law and Human Rights. VerfBlog,* 2021/4/23. Retrieved from: https://verfassungsblog.de/lithuanias-two-COVID-19-quarantines/. DOI: 10.17176/20210423-101204-0.

Debbage, N., Gonsalves, N., Shepherd, J.M., Knox, J.A. (2014). "Superstorm Sandy and voter vulnerability in the 2012 US Presidential Election: a case study of New Jersey and Connecticut". *Environmental Hazards,* vol. 13, no. 3.

Dėl karantino Lietuvos Respublikos teritorijoje paskelbimo, 2020 m. lapkričio 4 d. Nr. 1226

Jagusiak, B. (2013). *Systemy polityczných krajów nadbałtyckic*h, Warszawa: Difin.

International IDEA (2022). *Global overview of COVID-19: Impact on elections.* Retrieved from: https://www.idea.int/news-media/multimedia-reports/global-overview-COVID-19-impact-elections.

Jurkynas, M. (2014). "The parliamentary election in Lithuania, October 2012". *Electoral Studies,* vol. 34, pp. 334–338. https://doi.org/10.1016/j.electstud.2013.08.019.

Jurkynas, M. (2021). "Change in a time of pandemic: the 2020 parliamentary elections in Lithuania", *Journal of Baltic Studies*, vol. 52, no. 2, pp. 269–278; https://doi.org/10.1080/01629778.2021.1901754.

Jurkynas, M. (2017). "The 2016 Parliamentary Elections in Lithuania", *Electoral Studies*, no. 47, pp. 46–50. DOI:10.1016/j.electstud.2017.04.001.

Duvold, K., and M. Jurkynas. (2013). "Lithuania". In S. Berglund, J. Ekman, K. Deegan-Krause, and T. Knutsen (Eds.), *The Handbook of Political Change in Eastern Europe*, 3rd ed. (pp. 125–166). Cheltenham: Elgar.

Eriksson, L. M. (2016). "Winds of Change. Voter Blame and Storm Gudrun in the 2006 Swedish Parliamentary Election". *Electoral Studies*, no. 41, pp. 129–142.

Kluonis. M., (2019). "2009 metų Europos Parlamento rinkimų Lietuvoje rezultatai: aplinkybės ir prognozę". *Parlamento Studijos,* no. 8. Retrieved from: http://www.parlamentostudijos.lt/Nr8/8_politika_1.htm.

Kuczyńska-Zonik, A. (2021). "The Influence of New Technologies on the Election Process in Lithuania". *Przegląd Prawa Konstytucyjnego,* no. 6(64), pp. 175–188, DOI: 10.15804/ppk. 2021.06.14.

Lietuvos Respublikos Seimo Rinkimai 2020. Retrieved from: https://rinkimai.maps.lt/rinkimai2020/aktyvumas/.

Lietuvos Respublikos žmonių užkrečiamųjų ligų profilaktikos ir kontrolės įstatymas, 1996 m. rugsėjo 25 d. Nr. I-1553 (Law on Prevention and Control of Infectious Diseases in Human Beings, 25 September 1996, No I-1553).

"Lithuania: Surging COVID-19 infections overshadow first round of parliamentary elections". DW.de. Retrieved from: https://www.dw.com/en/lithuania-surging -COVID-19-infections-overshadow-first-round-of-parliamentary-elections/a -55233998.

"Lithuanians with coronavirus vote at drive-in polling stations". Euronews.com. Retrieved from: https://www.euronews.com/2020/10/19/lithuanians-with-coronavirus -vote-at-drive-in-polling-stations.

Malużinas, M. (2021a). "Lithuanian Democracy under the State of Emergency: Will the COVID-19 Pandemic Affect the Assessment of the State of Democracy in the Country? - System Analysis". *Athenaeum. Polish Political Studies*, vol. 72, no 4, pp. 88–105. https://doi.org/10.15804/athena.2021.72.05.

Malużinas, M. (2021b). "Indicators of the quality of democracy in the regions of Europe 2016–2020. Towards the erosion of democracy in the countries of Central and Eastern Europe?". *Przegląd Politologiczny*, no. 2, pp. 71–87. DOI: 10.14746/pp.2021.26.2.5.

Malużinas, M. (2021c). "Parliamentary elections during the COVID-19 pandemic: The example of the Lithuanian elections in 2020". *Athenaeum. Polish Political Studies*, vol. 69, no. 1, pp. 216–233. https://doi.org/10.15804/athena.2021.69.13.

Massicotte, L., Blais, A. (1999). "Mixed electoral systems: a conceptual and empirical survey". *Electoral Studies*, no 3, pp. 341–366.

Musiał-Karg, M, Kapsa, I. (2020). „All-postal voting (universal correspondence voting) in the 2020 presidential election in Poland. On how not to proceed during a pandemic?" In K. Hajder, M. Musiał-Karg, M. Górny (Eds.), *Konsekwencje pandemii COVID-19. Państwo i społeczeństwo* (pp. 135–145). Poznań: Wydawnictwo Naukowe Wydziału Nauk Politycznych i Dziennikarstwa UAM.

Musiał-Karg, M., Kapsa, I. (2020). *Alternative voting methods in the opinions of Poles. Attitudes and views towards selected forms of participation in elections.* Poznań: Wydawnictwo Naukowe Wydziału Nauk Politycznych i Dziennikarstwa UAM.

Musiał-Karg, M., Kapsa, I. (2021). „Debate: Voting challenges in a pandemic – Poland". *Public Money & Management*, vol. 41(1), pp. 6–8. DOI:10.1080/09540962.2020.1809791.

Musiał-Karg, M. (2016). "Alternative Voting Methods Through the Example of Postal Voting and E-Voting in Switzerland". *Białystok Legal Studies*, vol. 20/A en, pp. 13–23. DOI: 10.15290/bsp. 2016.20A.en.01.

ODIHR (2021). "Republic of Lithuania, Parliamentary Elections, 11 and 25 October 2020". ODIHR Election Expert Team Report. Warsaw: Office for Democratic Institutions and Human Rights. Retrieved from: https://www.osce.org/files/f/documents /e/a/477730_0.pdf.

Picchio M., Santolini R., "The COVID-19 Pandemic's Effects on Voter Turnout", *Discussion Paper IZA DP*, No. 14241. IZA Institute of Labor Economics. Retrieved from: https://docs.iza.org/dp14241.pdf.

Prasidėjo išankstinis balsavimas Seimo rinkimuose. Balsuoti iš anksto bus galima net keturias dienas. 5.10.2020. Retrieved from: http://www.voruta.lt/prasidejo -isankstinis-balsavimas-seimo-rinkimuose-balsuoti-is-anksto-bus-galima-net -keturias-dienas/.

Ramonaitė, A. (2021). "The Phenomenon of the Freedom Party: the Effect of Newness or the Beginning of a New Value Cleavage?". *Politologija* 102:2, pp. 8–37.

Ramonaite, A. (2006), "The development of the Lithuanian party system: from stability to perturbation" In S. Jungerstam-Mulders (Ed.), *Post-Communist EU Member States: Parties and Party Systems* (pp. 69–88). Abingdon: Routledge.

Repucci, S., Slipowitz A, (2020). *Democracy under Lockdown. The Impact of COVID-19 on the Global Struggle for Freedom.* Freedom House.

Rinkimų dieną saviizoliacijoje būsiantys rinkėjai jau dabar raginami registruotis, 18.10.2020, Kurjeris.lt. Retrieved from: https://kurjeris.lt/aktualijos/rinkimu-diena -saviizoliacijoje-busiantys-rinkejai-jau-dabar-raginami-registruotis/.

Robinson Preece, J. (2014). "How the Party Can Win in Personal Vote Systems: the "Selectoral Connection" and Legislative Voting in Lithuania". *Legislative Studies Quarterly*, XXXIX, 2, pp. 147–167; DOI: 10.1111/lsq.12040.

Santana, A., J. Rama, and F. Casal Bértoa (2020). "The coronavirus pandemic and voter turnout: Addressing the impact of COVID-19 on electoral participation". *SocArXiv,* https://doi.org/10.31235/osf.io/3d4ny.

Saviizoliacijoje esantiems rinkėjams - specialios balsavimo vietos, 15.10.2020. Retrieved from: https://www.vrk.lt/naujienos/-/content/10180/2/saviizoliacijoje-esantiems -rinkejams-%E2%80%93-specialios-balsavimo-vietos.

Seimas 2020–2024. Retrieved from: https://www.lrs.lt/sip/portal.show?p_r=35354&p _k=2&p_kade_id=9.

Szczeszczło, D. (2016). "Mixed electoral system in Central and Eastern European countries". Retrieved from: https://www.batory.org.pl/upload/files/Programy%20o peracyjne/Masz%20Glos/Policy%20Paper%20Dawida%20Szescilo.pdf.

Ulinskaitė, J. (2021). "Lietuvos politinės partijos populizmo amžiuje: 2016 ir 2020 m. Seimo rinkimų programų turinio analizė". *Vilniaus universiteto leidykla & VU Tarptautinių santykių ir politikos mokslų institutas,* no. 1, pp. 52–77.

Ulinskaitė, J. (2020). "The Populist Discourse on Representation in Lithuania". *European Review* 28, no. 5 (2020 m. October), pp. 744–60. https://doi.org/10.1017 /S1062798720000216.

Ulinskaitė, J. & Pukelis, L. (2021). "Populizmo Lietuvos politinių partijų diskurse paieška". *Pranešimas nacionalinėje konferencijoje Lietuva po 2020 m. Seimo rinkimų,* 2021 m. kovo 26 d.

"W Wilnie działa mobilny punkt wyborczy ". Wilnoteka.lt, 7.10.2020. Retrived from: http://www.wilnoteka.lt/artykul/w-wilnie-dziala-mobilny-punkt-wyborczy?fbclid =IwAR2kdXMT213rfYWnoIiCQJ_4iWaoozoYsJFDUIzVCmRCb-MwGrr7jyHPVXQ.

CHAPTER 11

The First 'Pandemic' Election in Europe: Remarks Regarding the 2020 Election to the National Assembly of the Republic of Serbia

Natasza Lubik–Reczek

11.1 Introduction

The Republic of Serbia was established on 5th June 2006 as the successor to the state of Serbia and Montenegro, which broke up after Montenegro declared independence on 3rd June 2006. The Serbia and Montenegro union was proclaimed on 4th February 2003. It replaced the Federal Republic of Yugoslavia, created on 27th April 1992, which consisted of the Republic of Serbia and the Republic of Montenegro.

Since the break-up of the union, the Republic of Serbia, as an independent state, has continued to struggle with system changes. Undoubtedly, the most important of these are the rebirth of its own statehood, ongoing process of democratisation, and the transformation of the socialist to the free market economy. Thus, the above-mentioned issues have determined the specific nature of the transformation (Bujwid-Kurek, 2012, p. 59).

After Montenegro declared independence, the Serbs adopted the Basic Law on 8th November 2006. Therefore, the most important legal act regulating the political system of the Republic of Serbia is the Constitution of 30th September 2006 (Ustav Republike Srbije). Its introduction followed a referendum called for 28th and 29th October (Bujwid-Kurek, Mikucka-Wójtowicz, 2015, p. 240).

The key objective of the deliberations is to answer the question of what future awaits Serbia and whether the 2020 election to the National Assembly, organised during a pandemic, have changed the current politics and balance of power in the country? Moreover, the impact of the COVID-19 pandemic on the electoral process itself are also an important issue of the deliberations included in the chapter. To achieve the intended research objective, the systemic method, institutional and legal method, and the historical method are used to show the electoral system and the functioning of political and systemic institutions. The research also uses statistical data from the 2020 National Assembly election and the early election in 2022. The entire chapter is based on the case study of Serbian elections during the pandemic.

© NATASZA LUBIK–RECZEK, 2024 | DOI:10.1163/9789004690622_013

Serbia is a parliamentary republic with legislative power vested in a unicameral parliament - the National Assembly of the Republic of Serbia, consisting of 250 deputies elected by universal suffrage for a 4-year term of office (Constitution of the Republic of Serbia; Grabowska, Grabowski (Eds.), 2008). It is a public authority distinguished in terms of its organisation and competence, which has decision-making power over other legislative entities (Bujwid-Kurek, 2012, p. 70).

Executive power is vested in the government and the president. The former is headed by a prime minister appointed by the parliament, and the latter plays a key role in the system. Members of the government are appointed by the Parliament and candidatures are proposed by the Prime Minister. The government is responsible for the adoption and implementation of tasks related to current domestic and foreign policies. In addition, the government submits draft laws and other normative acts to the National Skupština and gives its opinion on reform proposals submitted by relevant entities. Currently, the position of Prime Minister is held by Ana Brnabić, known for her liberal views. It is worth noting that she is the first woman in the history of Serbia to be appointed to this office (Kokoszczyński, 2017). The President is the head of state, elected for a five-year term, with a limit of two terms.

The decision to call elections is taken by the President 90 days before the end of his term. The Serbian Constitution still refers to Kosovo as an integral part of Serbia. Since mid-1999 Kosovo has been an autonomous region of Serbia under the administration of the UN. Months of negotiations on the status of Kosovo had been futile. On 17th February 2008, the Kosovo Parliament adopted by acclamation a declaration of independence. One day later, on 18th February 2008, the Serbian Parliament rejected Kosovo's proclamation of independence. it has not recognised the proclamation to this day (Reynolds, 2008).

11.2   Literature Review

While developing the study, we have analysed monographs and other concise scientific works (including edited papers) on the formation of a democratic system in the Republic of Serbia after the declaration of independence by Montenegro. The chapter used the analyses by think tanks dealing with the evolution of the socio-political situation in the Republic of Serbia under the rule of the Serbian Progressive Party and Aleksandar Vučić (reports by Centre for Eastern Studies, Institute of Central Europe, Polish Institute for International Studies, and Institute of Eastern Studies). Other publications include communications from the Commission to the European Parliament and the

Council, OSCE/ODIHR reports, as well as press articles and reports that analyse the social and political situation in the country ("Rzeczpospolita", Reuters, BBC, N1 TV).

11.3   Legal and Organisational Changes during the Pandemic

Campaigning for the election to the National Assembly of the Republic of Serbia, regional (the Parliament of the Autonomous Province of Vojvodina), and local elections scheduled for 26th April 2020, was hampered by the COVID-19 pandemic. The elections were postponed to 21st June as the state declared the state of emergency. These were the first mid-epidemic elections in Europe. The outbreak of the pandemic coincided with the official start of the election campaign (4th March 2020). The Serbian authorities initially downplayed the danger. However, the situation changed on 6th March when the first case of coronavirus infection was confirmed. Under these circumstances, the election campaign could not continue and the election could not be held as scheduled. On 15th March 2020, President Vučić declared a state of emergency throughout the country. Consequently, the Republican Election Commission (Protest inspired Republičke izborne komisije, 2022) announced that all activities regarding the election campaign were suspended for the duration of the state of emergency. The SNS cancelled all election rallies, and so did the largest opposition parties (*Savez za Srbiju* (SzS) and *Pokret slobodnih građana* (PSG)). The Constitution of the Republic of Serbia regulates the state of emergency in minute detail. Article 200 of the Constitution states that when "the survival of the state or its citizens is threatened by public danger", the National Assembly may declare the state of emergency for a maximum period of 90 days, extendable for another 90 days by a majority vote of the total number of deputies. The National Assembly may also adopt measures that violate human and minority rights (Constitution of Republic of Serbia). A declaration of a state of emergency by the President must be confirmed by the National Assembly within 48 hours, or as soon as it is able to convene. Without such confirmation, it ceases to have effect at the end of the first session of the National Assembly held after the declaration of the state of emergency. If the National Assembly cannot convene, the state of emergency is declared by the President of the Republic, together with the Chair of the National Assembly, and the Prime Minister. Then, the Government may take "measures that violate human and minority rights" (Constitution...).

Representatives of the opposition accused the President of acting without the approval of the National Assembly, as well as of using the COVID-19 pandemic to build his own political capital for the election campaign. On 29th April, however, the National Assembly of Serbia confirmed the decision to impose the state of emergency, as well as all decrees with legal force adopted by the government during the state of emergency, jointly signed by the President of Serbia and the Prime Minister. Measures to prevent the spread of the COVID-19 pandemic introduced by government decrees affected the freedom of movement (Article 39 of the Constitution provides for the restriction of the right in order to "prevent the spread of infectious diseases or to defend the Republic of Serbia"), freedom of assembly (Article 54 of the Constitution, which allows to restrict the right "if it is necessary for the protection of public health") (Constitution…).

Amendments to the election law were adopted by Parliament shortly before the election (February 2020). They were not subject to public consultation, which is contrary to international standards and accepted practices. Besides, the changes came into effect immediately, rather than eight days after they were published in the Official Gazette. It was argued that the changes were introduced for particularly justified reasons. This practice violates the well-known democratic rule of not changing election laws in the election year, particularly not directly before an election.

Several important changes were introduced, including, among other things, changes to voter lists and election observers to counteract any abuse on the part of the state. The changes included a reduction in the electoral threshold from 5% to 3% (in both general and local elections) and were expected to contribute to better representation of national minority lists (Section XI, Participation of National Minorities, Constitution…). The lowering of the electoral threshold could have been seen as an opportunity for smaller and local political parties or citizen groups to have representatives in local parliaments. At the same time, it was intended to reduce the effect of the previously announced boycott of elections by the opposition (Nastić, 2020).

It was stressed that this measure was democratic in its nature and would contribute to the multiple party representation in the Assembly. Representatives of the opposition, however, argued that changing voting rules before the election was not in line with democratic standards. A similar decision was made by the Assembly of Vojvodina on 21st February 2020. The changes were accompanied by an awareness campaign led by the government.

Electoral rules at the local level are a continuation of the ones in parliamentary elections. Local elections can be seen as second-order national elections (Clark, Krebs, 2012). A proportional electoral system using party lists means that citizens only choose a political party whose central board gives the final word on the order of the lists. Thus, in local elections, citizens elect their representatives, who will be able to conduct local politics depending on central politics.

At the invitation of the REC, on 6th June the OSCE/ODIHR established a special group (SEAM ODIHR) to observe the parliamentary elections scheduled for 21st June 2020. It was headed by Urszula Gacek and consisted of eight experts from seven OSCE countries (ODIHR election reports on Serbia).

On 4th May 2020, at a meeting with representatives of all parties involved in the elections, the President of the Republic of Serbia announced that parliamentary, local government, and Assembly of Vojvodina elections postponed due to the pandemic would be held on 21st June 2020 (Elections in Serbia). The state of emergency was lifted by the National Assembly on 6th May 2020. Decisions were also taken to resume the election campaign on 11th May. However, the opposition demanded that the elections should be postponed for the safety of citizens. At this stage of the pandemic, vaccination against COVID – 19 was still not available.

11.4   Elections in the Shadow of the COVID-19 Pandemic

The elections took place with political groupings being highly polarised. The opposition had boycotted parliament meetings since 2019, claiming that no meaningful debate and oversight of the executive were in place. Opposition politicians and NGOs monitoring the government have repeatedly accused Vučić and his party of authoritarian inclinations, use of violence against political opponents, electoral fraud, corruption, nepotism, and links to organised crime, which was always vehemently denied by the government (Reuter). "The Serbian opposition was not present in the public media for eight years, and Vučić appeared there 292 times more often than all opposition leaders combined," said Dragan Djilas, leader of the Freedom and Justice Party (SSP), one of the groups comprising the Alliance for Serbia, the strongest coalition of opposition parties (Head of the European People's Party...). The European Commission's 2019 Progress Report on Serbia states that "there is an urgent need to create space for genuine cross-party debate and conditions for the opposition to participate meaningfully in the parliament. The role of independent bodies needs to be urgently guaranteed and supported" (Commission Progress Report on Serbia). An annual report published in April 2020 by the US NGO Freedom House listed Serbia among "hybrid regimes" with authoritarian power and which could no longer be considered democratic. Belgrade strongly rejected the report, claiming that it was based on inadequate research and criteria. Serbia also went from very strict restrictions due to the pandemic to lifting them almost completely in early June. According to the president's opponents, this was a deliberate move just so Vučić could hold elections, originally scheduled for April and postponed because of the pandemic. The president "introduced the strictest possible measures, including an 84-hour ban on leaving the place of residence (...) and then the measures were lifted as if nothing had happened, it's unbelievable," says Djilas (Head of the European People's Party...).

Parliamentary elections are regulated by the 2006 Constitution, the 2000 Law on the Election of Members of Parliament (election law, last amended in 2020), the 2009 Law on the Unified Voter Register (LUVR), the 2011 Law on the Financing of Political Activities (LFPA, last amended in 2019), and the 2000 Law on the Anti-Corruption Agency (LACA, last amended in 2020). The legal framework is supplemented by the REC Rules of Procedure, regulations, instructions, and decisions.

The elections were organised by a two-tier election administration consisting of the Republican Electoral Commission (REC) and 8433 Polling Boards (PBS). The REC also established 161 ad hoc Working Bodies (WBS) to ensure a smooth flow of information between the REC and PBS. In the opinion of observers, the State Election Commission acted in accordance with the law (ODIHR SEAM). Decisions were taken collegially during sessions that were open to observers and streamed online. However, there was a lack of substantive discussion and prior information about the agenda.

The Register of Voters was maintained by the Ministry of Public Administration and Local Self-Government. The Republican Electoral Commission announced that there were 6,584,376 voters listed. 21 candidate lists were registered, which had to be confirmed by at least 10,000 certified signatures. Each voter could support only one list. In order to facilitate the candidate registration procedure (following legislative changes introduced in May 2020), the power to certify signatures was vested in local authorities. Lists also had to meet a gender parity requirement of at least 40% in order to be registered. In addition to registering candidate lists, the REC also handled election complaints and announced election results.

The right to vote applies to all citizens who are at least 18 years of age on the polling day and have their permanent residence. Exceptions are those who have been deprived of their legal capacity by a court ruling. Every voter has the right to stand for election. Lists of candidates may be proposed by political parties, coalitions of parties, and groups of at least ten eligible voters.

The candidate registration period began on 4th March and ended on 5th June. It was interrupted by a state of emergency from 15th March to 11th May 2020. The election campaign proceeded without major disruptions. Due to the pandemic restrictions imposed by the Serbian authorities (state of emergency, restrictions on movement and assembly), the main source of political information was television (public channels - RTS, RTV; several private channels), and social media (Facebook, Twitter). Campaigning focused on the COVID-19 pandemic and containment of coronavirus, with the ruling parties claiming that they had managed to control the virus and the opposition accusing the government of using the crisis for electoral gains. Other topics included the status of Kosovo, foreign policy, corruption, and the economy.

The involvement of President A. Vučić, as the head of state and leader of the Serbian Progressive Party (SNS), showed his dominance on the Serbian political arena. Boundaries between the campaign of the Serbian Progressive Party and media coverage of the President and the Government on the threats of COVID-19 were blurred. This was not in line with point 5.4 of the 1990 Copenhagen Meeting Document - "a clear separation between the State and political parties; in particular, political parties shall not be equal to the State" (Dokument...). The electoral law sets out basic rules for media coverage, including the obligation on the media to provide equal information about all participants in the elections and the right of citizens to be informed about election programmes and candidates' activity (LEM).

On the election day, polling stations were equipped with masks and gloves to protect citizens from the spread of COVID-19. However, according to the ODIHR SEAM, some polling stations were too small and ran the risk of overcrowding. They were also inadequately adapted for people with disabilities.

For the fourth time in a row, the winning parties included the SNS (Srpska Napredna Stranka, Serbian Progressive Party), in power since 2012 (Lubik-Reczek, 2016) and led by President Aleksandar Vučić. According to the final election results, announced on 5th July, the electoral list headed by the SNS "Aleksandar Vučić - for our children" received 60.65% of votes compared to 48.3% in 2016 (Pawłowski, 2020). Thus, it held 188 seats in the 250-member unicameral National Assembly. The Serbian Progressive Party achieved the highest results in Serbia's history to date, winning a constitutional majority in the parliament (Ruling conservatives claim victory in Serbian parliamentary vote).

The co-ruling Socialist Party of Serbia (SPS), together with several smaller groupings led by Foreign Minister Ivica Dačić, won 10.4% of the vote and 32 seats (11% in the last election) (Zornaczuk, no. 46/2020). As a result of the reduction of the electoral threshold from 5% to 3%, the debutant Serbian Patriotic Union (SPAS) gained 11 seats in the parliament. As a result, an unusual situation took place in Serbia. The party in power (SNS) encouraged small political parties to participate in the elections in order to strengthen political pluralism. It can also be presumed that the Serbian authorities hoped to break up the unity of the opposition. The Assembly was to be completed by 19 MPs from four conservative regional minority parties: the Union of Hungarians from Vojvodina, Muamer Zukorlić's list, Sulejman Ugljanin's list, and a coalition of Albanian parties. Other parties did not reach the electoral threshold. The ultranationalist Serbian Radical Party (22 seats in the previous election) was outside the parliament. The State Election Commission of Serbia released information that the voter turnout was 50.32% (IEE Comments, 115/2020). It was low because most opposition parties considered that in the then situation there was no chance of holding democratic election and called to boycott it. "The turnout was definitely lower than in the 2008 elections," - stressed analyst Cvijetin Miliovojevic on N1 TV. In addition to the opposition boycott, the lack of independent media and corruption had an impact. The opposition accused the ruling party of seeking victory even at the cost of citizens' health and of not being able to conduct a fair campaign based on democratic principles. Criticism was also levelled at President Aleksandar Vučić, who was accused of having totalitarian tendencies. However, the boycott of the election did not change the situation, as was hoped by the part of the opposition that did not participate in the vote. As a result, the opposition disappeared from parliament, and President Aleksandar Vučić strengthened his position.

The election results mark the continuation of the SNS and SPS governments. The period since the last elections (2016) has emphatically showed the consolidation of the personal power of Aleksandar Vučić, who, despite becoming president in 2017, has not given up his position of a party leader. With his control over the party and the state, he is the most powerful politician in Serbia. The last election campaign (in which other SNS politicians were hardly visible) and the name of the electoral list can testify to this. He also owes his position to the appointment of people who are completely dependent on him to the most important positions in the state. An example was the appointment of Ana Brnabić as the prime minister in 2017. The system of power he built is based on the control of the media, media which belong to the state or oligarchs who favour the government. This effectively allows Vučić to build his personal popularity. The only television station critical of the government is available only on certain cable networks. The president has also perfectly subordinated resources of the state to the interests of the party. Getting a job in the public sector depends on supporting the ruling party. Another factor favouring power is the weakness of the conflicted opposition. In addition, the government tries to limit the activity of opposition parties. Supporting the opposition very often means losing one's job. The opposition is unable to agree on their political struggle. It has also failed to create a common strategy towards elections, wondering whether to participate in a process that does not meet democratic standards.

Both the European Commission and the OSCE have highlighted numerous irregularities concerning the parties' sources of funding, the use of state institutions by party structures, as well as the already mentioned media and their biased coverage of the elections. NGOs together with members of the European Parliament mediated between the government and the opposition. In this way, attempts were made to find democratic rules for the conduct of the elections. However, this failed to produce results. The opposition accused the government and the president of mere interest in the strengthening of their position on the international arena.

The National Assembly was established on 3rd August 2020. The inaugural session of the newly elected Parliament of Serbia was held one day before the constitutional deadline (Constitution of the Republic of Serbia, Article 101). However, the Speaker of the Assembly was not appointed during this session. The prolonged inaugural session of the National Assembly ended with the election of a new speaker on 22nd October 2020. The new speaker of the Assembly was the head of the SPS Ivica Dačić, who resigned from his position of the Minister of Foreign Affairs on the same day. As a result of the election boycott by the largest opposition parties, the Assembly lacks representatives of the real opposition. The only symbolic opposition consists of 6 members of the United Valley - Sandžak SDA parliamentary group who represent the Bosnian and Albanian minorities. The stall in the talks on the formation of the government coalition were also caused by President Vučić's involvement in international affairs. On 16th July, negotiations between Serbia and Kosovo resumed under the auspices of the EU. On 4th September 2020, an agreement was signed in Washington. These events led to the President entrusting Prime Minister Ana Brnabić with the mission to form a new government as late as on 5th October 2020. A government coalition was formed consisting of SNS, SPS, SPAS and several smaller parties. The official composition of the new government was announced on 26th October 2020. Two days later the Prime Minister delivered her exposé and received a vote of confidence. The second cabinet of Prime Minister Ana Brnabić consists of 23 ministers and, noteworthy, ten positions were taken up by women.

11.5   Serbia's EU Integration from the Perspective of Elections

The process of Serbia's integration with the European Union has been going on for quite some time (Republika Srbija u proces pridruživanja i pristupanja Evropskoj uniji). The Serbs wanted to complete their negotiations in 2019 in order to formally join the European Union in 2020. Although President Aleksandar Vučić promised to complete the negotiations precisely by 2020, no significant progress has been recorded in recent years. A serious obstacle on Serbia's path to the European Union is the Kosovo issue. The EU has repeatedly made it clear that it is not prepared to accept Serbia as a member unless it can sort out its relations with Kosovo.

Serbia began negotiations with the EU in 2014. EU reports highlighted problems that were also noticed during the National Assembly election. In their statements, the High Representative of the Union for Foreign Affairs and Security Policy Josep Borrell and the Commissioner for Neighbourhood and Enlargement Olivér Várhelyi expressed hope that the newly elected government would continue to introduce reforms necessary for Serbia's further integration with EU structures. Support for the Serbia's EU membership remains at around 50%. However, this is a very difficult issue, due to the integration process, which has already continued for quite a long time. Moreover, the Serbs also perceive the EU through the support for Aleksandar Vučić by at least some European capitals. This triggers a strong criticism in the liberal part of Serbia.

Formally, Serbia is still interested in the EU membership, although it has pursued a multi-vector policy. Cooperation with China, as well as Russia and Turkey, has deepened much in recent years. Particularly close relations are between Belgrade and Beijing. Diplomatic relations between the two countries have significantly intensified. PRC companies have acquired key Serbian companies in the heavy industry, including the Železara Smederevo steel mill (Hesteel) and the RTB Bor mining and metallurgical company (Zijin). An ongoing project is the construction of a high-speed railway linking Belgrade with Budapest. China is a new and important economic player in the region (Góralczyk). Within the framework of various forms of cooperation (China has offered countries of Central and Eastern Europe (CEE) regional cooperation in the "16+1" formula) or the concept of the Belt and Road Initiative and the construction of transport routes to Europe, China has chosen Serbia as its main partner. Belgrade was chosen as a site for one of the largest infrastructure investments, i.e. the new bridge over the Danube built thanks to preferential loans and low-cost labour from China. Relations with Russia have also been strengthened. The TurkStream gas pipeline is under construction in Serbia to transport Russian crude oil through Turkey to EU countries. The project has been implemented under non-transparent rules and in violation of EU Energy regulations.

11.6   Conclusions

Shortly after the election, Serbia has faced several challenges, such as the continued fight against the crisis caused by the coronavirus pandemic and the resolution of dispute with Kosovo. In the longer term, in the context of the international community's concerns expressed in the European Commission's report about the dominance of the sns on the Serbian political scene, Serbia is facing early elections. The decision was announced on 20th October by President Aleksandar Vučić. Consequently, early parliamentary elections, combined with presidential election, were to be held in Serbia by 3rd April 2022 at the latest. And this has actually happened. The decision was a consequence of the prolonged political crisis in the country, strengthened by the opposition's boycott of the elections. This meant that the second cabinet of Prime Minister A. Brnabić would rule for maximum several months. It could therefore be assumed that no decision would be made that could reduce the support for the current government. Serbia has been facing another election campaign that, as could be expected, raises many controversies on the opposition side. The opposition pointed to its marginalisation or even restriction in the media, as well as to the use of the state apparatus by the president and his ruling party as a tool to gain votes. On 3rd April 2022, the day of the election, representatives of the opposition pointed to the slow performance of election commissions in the largest cities. This resulted in many people queuing in front of polling stations. According to the opposition, this was supposed to discourage opposition supporters from voting. While announcing his and his party's victory without waiting for official results, Aleksandar Vučić assured that during his second presidential term he would continue his efforts to help Serbia join the European Union and maintain good relations with its neighbours (including, of course, Russia and China). On the one hand, Serbia is one of the most pro-Russian states in Europe, which support Russian military operation in Ukraine. On the other hand, President Vučić has repeatedly stressed his desire to join the EU.

References

Bujwid-Kurek. E. (2012). *Serbia w nowej przestrzeni ustrojowej: dzieje, ustrój, konstytucja.* Kraków: Księgarnia Akademicka.

Bujwid-Kurek, E., Mikucka-Wójtowicz D. (2015). *Transformacja ustroju politycznego wybranych państw Europy Środkowej i Południowo-Wschodniej. Podręcznik akademicki.* Kraków: Wydawnictwo Libron.

Clark A., Krebs T. B. (2012). *Elections and Policy Responsiveness.* In The Oxford Handbook of Urban Politics. Eds. Karen Mossberger, Susan E. Clarke, Peter John. Oxford: Oxford University Press.

Constitution of the Republic of Serbia. Retrieved from: http://www.srbija.gov.rs /cinjenice_o_srbiji/ustav.php?change_lang=en.

Dokument spotkania kopenhaskiego konferencji w sprawie ludzkiego wymiaru KBWE. Retrieved from: https://bisnetus.wordpress.com/2016/07/31/dokument-spotkania-kopenhaskiego-konferencji-w-sprawie-ludzkiego-wymiaru-kbwe/.

Draft Law on the unified register of Voters of Serbia. Retrieved from: https://www.legislationline.org/documents/id/15646.

Elections in Serbia. 2020 Parliamentary Elections. IFES. Retrieved from: https://www.ifes.org/sites/default/files/ifes_faqs_elections_in_serbia_2020_parliamentary_elections_june_2020.pdf

European Commission Progress Report on Serbia 2019. Retrieved from: https://ec.europa.eu/neighbourhood-enlargement/system/files/2019-05/20190529-serbia-report.pdf.

Grabowska, S., Grabowski, R. (Eds.) (2008). *Zasady zmian konstytucji w państwach europejskich*. Warszawa: Wolters. Kluwer.

Góralczyk, B. „Bałkany będą się radykalizować. Sytuacje mogą wykorzystać Chiny". Forsal.pl. retrieved from: http://forsal.pl/artykuly/942689,balkany-o-ktorych-nie-przypomni-sobie-europa-beda-sie-radykalizowac.html.

Kaczmarski, M. (2015). „Nowy Jedwabny Szlak: uniwersalne narzędzie chińskiej polityki". *Komentarze OSW*. Retrieved from: https://www.osw.waw.pl/pl/publikacje/komentarze-osw/2015-02-10/nowy-jedwabny-szlak-uniwersalne-narzedzie-chinskiej-polityki.

Kokoszczyński. K. (2017). „Serbia: nowa premier Ana Brnabić obejmuje wł*adzę*". Euractiv.pl. Retrieved from: https://www.euractiv.pl/section/polityka-zagraniczna/news/serbia-nowa-premier-ana-brnabic/.

Law on the Election of Members of the Parliament. Retrieved from: https://www.legislationline.org/download/id/4225/file/SER_law_Election%20_members_parliament_2000_am2011_en.pdf.

Law on Electronic Media (LEM). Retrieved from: https://wipolex.wipo.int/en/legislation/details/17054.

Law on Financing Political Activities. Retrieved from: https://www.venice.coe.int/webforms/documents/default.aspx?pdffile=CDL-REF(2014)035-e.

Law on Prevention of Corruption. Retrieved from: https://www.acas.rs/law-and-regulations/laws/law-acas/.

Lubik-Reczek, N. (2011). *Państwa postjugosłowiańskie wobec członkostwa w Unii Europejskiej i NATO (Analiza porównawcza)*, Toruń: Wydawnictwo Adam Marszałek.

Lubik–Reczek, N. (2016). „Serbian elections: The path towards Europe?" *Przegląd Politologiczny*, no 4.

MPALSG. Retrieved from: www.vladars.net/eng/vlada/ministries/MALS/Pages/default.aspx.

Musiał-Karg, M., (2008). *Referenda w państwach europejskich jako instytucja demokracji bezpośredniej*. Toruń: Wydawnictwo Adam Marszałek.

ODIHR election reports on Serbia. OSCE. Retrieved from: https://www.osce.org/files/f /documents/a/3/466026.pdf.

Pawłowski, K. (2020). „Wybory w Serbii: spodziewane zwycięstwo Serbskiej Partii Postępowej". *Komentarze IEŚ*, no 212 (115).

Protest ispred Republičke izborne komisije: Branićemo svaki glas. Retrieved from: https://www.glasamerike.net/a/srbija-izbori-izbori2022-protest-rik/6514722.html.

Reynolds, P. (2008). "Legal furore over Kosovo recognition". 16.02.2008. BBC, http:// news.bbc.co.uk/2/hi/europe/7244538.stm.

Centre for Research on Direct Democracy (c2d). Retrieved from: http://www.c2d .ch/detailed_display.php?lname=votes&table=votes&page=1&parent_id= &sublinkname=results&id=38916.

Republika Srbija u procesu pridruživanja i pristupanja Evropskoj uniji. Retrieved from: http://www.parlament.gov.rs/aktivnosti/evropske-integracije.4520.html.

Ruling conservatives claim victory in Serbian parliamentary vote. Euractive.com. Retrieved from: https://www.euractiv.com/section/enlargement/news/ruling -conservatives-claim-victory-in-serbian-parliamentary-vote/.

Stanisławski, W. (2008). „Serbia". In *Bałkany Zachodnie a integracja europejska. Perspektywy i implikacje.* Warszawa: UKIE.

„Szef Europejskiej Partii Ludowej wzbudził kontrowersje poparciem dla prezydenta i rządu Serbii". Kresy24.pl. Retrieved from: https://kresy24.pl/szef-europejskiej-partii -ludowej-wzbudzil-kontrowersje-poparciem-dla-prezydenta-i-rzadu-serbii/

Wojnicki, J. (2005). *System konstytucyjny Serbii i Czarnogóry.* Warszawa: Wydawnictwo Sejmowe.

Wojnicki, J. (2010). „Instytucja Rządu Republiki Serbii w systemie organów władzy". *Przegląd Prawa Konstytucyjnego*, no 2–3.

Żornaczuk, T. (2020). „Bezprecedensowe zwycięstwo partii rządzących w wyborach parlamentarnych w Serbii". PISM. Retrieved from: https://www.pism.pl/publikacje /Bezprecedensowe_zwyciestwo_partii_rzadzacych__w_wyborach_parlamentarnych _w_Serbii.

CHAPTER 12

Elections and Referenda in the Principality of Liechtenstein during the Coronavirus Pandemic

Krzysztof Koźbiał

12.1 Introduction and Background

The coronavirus pandemic has had numerous consequences in many spheres of human life and the limitation of human activity affected electoral processes on various levels. As a result, it was almost impossible to conduct the elections on the previously planned date and in the usual manner. Various solutions were considered to ensure that the electoral process would be as smooth and effective and possible.

As in other countries, the COVID-19 pandemic in the Principality of Liechtenstein in 2020 and in the first half of 2021 became the main problem, affecting societal, economic and political life.

The first information regarding the presence of the novel coronavirus in the Duchy appeared in February 2020. On February 11, a governmental crisis committee was established under the chairmanship of Mauro Pedrazzini, the member of the government who heads the Health Office.[1] The tasks of the staff included monitoring the pandemic situation as well as undertaking and coordinating actions aimed at combatting the coronavirus pandemic.

Medical testing on possible cases of COVID-19 was carried out in the only hospital in Liechtenstein - in the capital. The first positive case was diagnosed on March 3, 2020, in a person who came into contact with the virus outside the country. In its announcements, the government mainly emphasized the risk posed both by and to people returning from ski resorts. On March 17, two weeks after the first case was discovered, the number of cases reached 19, and at the end of March it was over 60. This was what could be called the first wave of the pandemic, and which lasted until the beginning of summer. In May, the number of cases reached 82, with cases diagnosed in all municipalities of this country.

---

1 The government of the Principality consists of 5 members, each of whom manages the work of 3 ministries.

In the analyzed period (i.e. from the beginning of the pandemic to the end of June 2021), the highest daily numbers of cases were recorded from mid-October 2020 to mid-January 2021 (a record-breaking 63 cases on December 24, 2020) and in the second half of April 2021 (www.worldometers...). The increase in the number of cases at the turn of autumn and winter 2020 was particularly noticeable. On October 15, there were a total of 183 cases, on November 1 already 551, on December 1 already 1,286 and on January 1, 2021. 3,039, 59 deaths were recorded. In June 2021, there were only isolated cases. Subsequent pandemic waves generally unfolded in a similar manner to other countries. It should be emphasized that during the course of the pandemic, the so-called excess death rate was noted in 2020, with 26% more people dying during the whole year when compared to the period of the last ten years (Übersterblichkeit).

The very dynamics of the pandemic and fluctuation in the number of patients reflected trends of a pan-European nature in general. The number of cases can be compared to other countries, taking into account the disease and death rates per 1 million inhabitants on average. In terms of the number of cases per 1 million inhabitants (data as of June 30, 2021), Liechtenstein was ranked 37th in the global scale, and 31st in terms of death rate. Taking into account the statistical data, the course of the epidemic did not differ from what was happening elsewhere in this part Europe. The total number of cases from the beginning of the pandemic is shown in Figure 12.1.

Liechtenstein can also be compared in terms of disease and death rate to other European micro-states (Table 12.1). Against this backdrop, the pandemic rates in this alpine country seem better than those of San Marino and Andorra, considering the number of cases as compared to Monaco (although the death rate in the latter case is lower than in Liechtenstein).

Since Liechtenstein is a country with close ties to Switzerland, the Helvetic epidemic legislation of September 28, 2012 also entered into force and thus in many ways the authorities in by decisions taken in Switzerland (Frommelt & Schiess Rütimann, 2021, pp. 4–5). In the event of a severe course of the disease, the inhabitants of the Duchy were dependent on Swiss hospitals (Frommelt & Schiess Rütimann, 2021, p. 5). On February 28, 2020, a state of emergency was declared, and the regulation related to combating COVID-19 entered into force (Verordnung vom 28. Februar 2020). It was forbidden to organize private or public events in the Duchy with participants exceeding 1,000 people. In the case of smaller gatherings of people, it had to be determined (in consultation with the Health Office) whether such an event was necessary.

The initial regulation was introduced for two weeks but over time this number was limited to 100 people, and later to only five. Any larger gatherings were banned. The original restrictions also did not differ from those applied in other

linear   logarithmic

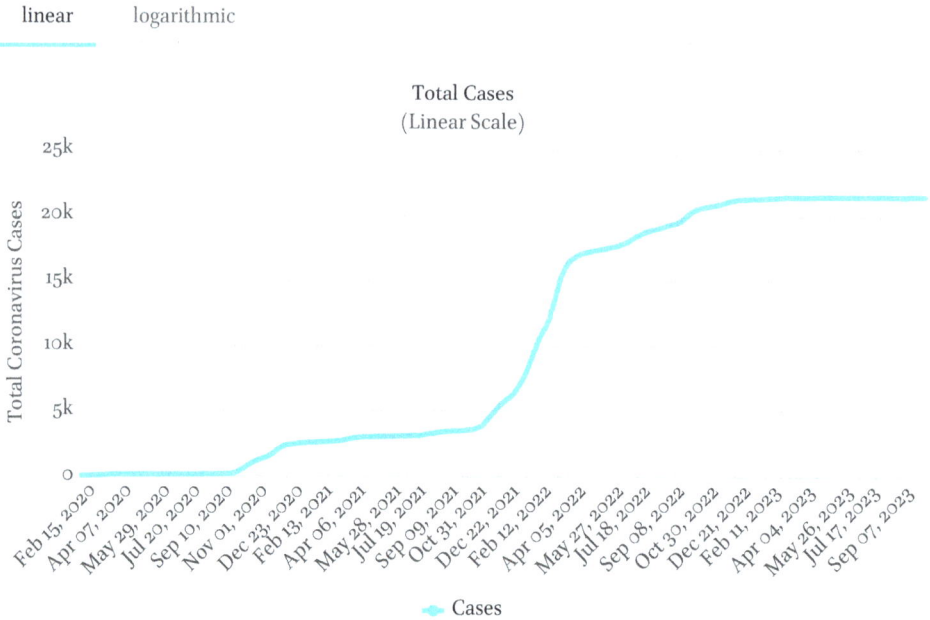

FIGURE 12.1   Total number of COVID-19 cases in Liechtenstein (February 2020–June 2021)
               SOURCE: HTTPS://WWW.WORLDOMETERS.INFO/CORONAVIRUS/COUNTRY/
               LIECHTENSTEIN/, 30.06.2021

TABLE 12.1   Number of coronavirus cases and deaths in European micro-states (average per
              1 million inhabitants)

Country	Terms of disease	Death rate
Andorra	181 860	1 641
Liechtenstein	79 912	1 543
Monaco	66 325	835
San Marino	149 743	2 647

SOURCE: HTTPS://WWW.WORLDOMETERS.INFO/CORONAVIRUS/#MAIN_TABLE, 01.07.2021

countries. These were the following: a ban on visiting elderly people and entering nursery care centers, a lockdown affecting swimming pools, museums,
casinos and amusement arcades, sport halls as well as the ski center in Malbun.
The number of guests in bars, restaurants and discos was initially limited to 50
but later on all these places were locked down. Schools and educational institutions were also closed and commercial activity was also limited, with the

exception of grocery stores, pharmacies and gas stations. Initially, the wearing of masks was recommended, but with time it became obligatory.

Restrictions on crossing the Liechtenstein border were also introduced. From March 13, the entry of people from the so-called high-risk countries (where the number of cases was high) was banned (Verordnung vom 13. März 2020). The regulation provided for many exceptions, including the right of residence in the Principality, a certificate of residence in Liechtenstein or Switzerland, the provision of goods transport services or unspecified „necessary situations". On March 17, the border between Liechtenstein and the Austrian federal state of Vorarlberg was essentially closed, although, it could be crossed by people working in the Duchy who commuted there daily (Grenzübergänge ...). The decisions concerning the Liechtenstein-Austrian border were of considerable importance for the Duchy since it is heavily dependent on employees who do not live permanently in Liechtenstein, but commute to work every day. Any complete closure of the border would in practice have meant a far-reaching regression in the economy of the micro-state.

Various social initiatives were discernible as they positively contributed to combatting the progress of the pandemic. These included, among others, a call for children to not visit their grandparents if unnecessary, and the police campaign "Stay home" (Zuhause bleiben!). Both were launched in March 2020 and other important actions were undertaken to help neighbors in need and people in quarantine. These actions were initiated by the private network Corona Hilfe Liechtenstein and approximately 500 volunteers took part in the campaign (https://www.corona-hilfe.li).

The government of the Duchy also took steps to mitigate the economic consequences of the pandemic. In mid-March, funds amounting to 50 million francs were allocated to payments for part-time workers. For the so-called small enterprises, the parliament accepted emergency, non-returnable aid in the amount of 4,000 Swiss francs. These were activities analogous to those undertaken in other European countries.

A gradual loosening of the restrictions from mid-May 2020 was made possible by falling infection rates. At that time, enterprises providing catering services were allowed to reopen, and events for 300 people were allowed to be organized.

A subsequent return to restrictions took place in the late autumn of 2020, when there was a drastic increase of infections. Between December 20, 2020 and January 10, 2021, the Liechtenstein government introduced a winter lockdown (*Winterruhe*), which meant the suspension of all activities in the public and private sphere. These restrictions were extended until mid-February (https://www.vaterland.li). Vaccinations against the virus began in January 2021 and by June 30, the number of those vaccinated with at least their first dose was almost 19,000, i.e. over 51% of the population of the micro-state (COVID-19-Impfungen ...).

At the end of June 2021, due to the declining number of infections, the Liechtenstein government decided to ease most of the restrictions. From July 5, the following actions, among others, were implemented: the obligation to wear anti-virus masks in public spaces was abolished (with the exception of public transport only); if the minimum distance of 1.5 m was kept, gatherings of up to 1,000 persons were permitted; the maximum number of people for private gatherings was lifted, and the number of guests for bars and restaurants lifted if the minimum distances were respected. The 12–15 age group was also allowed to be vaccinated.

12.2   Methodology and Results

To tackle the research problem investigated in this chapter, statistical data on the results of referendum votes and parliamentary elections were used since they are crucial for any assessment of the methods used during the election process. The data resulting from the public opinion polls conducted on the evaluation of the activities of the Duchy's government in the period of the COVID-19 pandemic were also significant.

The state-of-the art on the political system of Liechtenstein was also provided since system analysis is indispensable for the research conducted. I also consider personal experiences and observations as a result of numerous research stays in Liechtenstein to be of no less importance and thus the participatory observation method turned out to be particularly useful in this respect.

In the analyzed period of the pandemic, voting in Liechtenstein took place twice, namely: on August 30, 2020, during the referendum, the citizens of the Principality answered 3 questions, and on February 7, 2021 when the parliament was elected.

12.3   August 30, 2020 Referendum

In terms of the scale of the application of the instruments of direct democracy, Liechtenstein comes second in Europe, with Switzerland being the leader. The development of this form of decision-making in salient matters is, moreover, a derivative of political ties with its Western neighbor. This instrument, incorporated into the constitution adopted in 1921, has been put into practice from the very beginning. By the end of 2012, the number of referendum questions submitted to citizens was exactly 100 (Koźbiał, 2013, p. 82). Currently (as of

June 30, 2021) there have been 109. This is a characteristic feature of the country's political system. Voting on a given matter may be requested by citizens, the assemblies of individual communes, and the head of state (Article 66 of the Constitution) (Koźbiał & Stankowski, 2009, pp. 76–77. The range of topics deliberated in referenda in Lichtenstein to date has been very extensive. The referendum is believed to be an essential instrument for solving important problems, including local ones.

Taking into account the pandemic situation, in April 2020 the government of the Duchy postponed the date of the referendum (Verordnung vom 3. April 2020). Originally, the vote was supposed to take place on June 7. Due to the spread and progress of the pandemic, this turned out to be an unrealistic deadline that would increase the risk of the further acceleration of the pandemic. Therefore, the vote was postponed to 30 August and this decision should be seen as the right one in light of the situation. The new date was undeniably safer because by then there had been a profound reduction in the problems related to the pandemic. The turnout in the referendum was 83.5% (https://www.abstimmungen.li), a high figure, although it must be remembered that such voting is mandatory in the Duchy.

As much as 97% of the votes were cast by postal ballot, with polling stations only open on voting days between 10.30 am and noon (similar to the subsequent parliamentary elections). Traditional voting was made available to citizens who abided by the regulations in force at the time regarding the minimization of the risk of the transmission of the virus. At the time, in addition to general sanitary recommendations, wearing masks indoors was required. Taking into account the fact that the referendum took place at the time of the de facto summer termination of the virus activity, the vote was held without any hurdles.

In the above-mentioned referendum, voters - for the first time in history - answered three questions. The questions revealed the spectrum and salience of problems subject to this type of resolution. The first question was related to the amendment of the constitution - (*HalbeHalbe Initiative*) - specifically Art. 31 on the equality between women and men. The advocates of this amendment called for more balanced representation of both genders in political bodies (Informationen zu ..., pp. 2–3), assuming at the same time that this would essentially only be a first step towards the full equality participation (numerical) of women and men in the public sphere of the Principality and in its political institutions[2] (Koźbiał, 2010, pp. 55–76). The outcome of the vote saw 78.8% of those taking part rejecting this proposal. The second question was related

---

2 It was not until 1984 that women obtained the right to fully participate in parliamentary elections in Liechtenstein.

to the initiative on the possibility of having two nationalities upon acquiring citizenship of the Duchy (*Doppelte Staatsbürgerschaft*). To date, in the case of the acquisition of citizenship of the Duchy, proof of having resigned one's previous citizenship needed to be presented (Informationen zu ..., pp. 4–5). The outcome of this vote was 61.5% of voters rejecting the proposal. The third question, on the other hand, concerned infrastructure issues (S-Bahn) and was part of the complex of changes in this respect in the perspective of 2030. It concerned the reconstruction of a section of the railway line running through the northern part of the Duchy, connecting Austrian Vorarlberg with Switzerland (Feldkirch-Buchs connection) (Informationen zu ..., pp. 6–7). The idea was related to the fact that the roads in Liechtenstein are increasingly congested, which is also related to the fact that a significant number of people commute to work in Liechtenstein from neighbouring countries using their own car. Voters did not share these fears, however, and more than 62% of those participating in the referendum were against this initiative.

12.4   Parliamentary Elections of February 7, 2021

The *Landtag* or the parliament of the Principality of Liechtenstein, is composed of 25 deputies and is elected by universal, equal, secret and direct elections. The deputies represent the two historical regions that formed the Principality: Unterland and Oberland (they correspond to the former counties of Schellenberg and Vaduz) (Koźbiał, 2013, p. 106). Parliamentary elections are held every 4 years. The constitution stipulates that this should take place in February or March, except for earlier elections. The elections in 2021 were carried out on the original date, when the 4-year term of the Landtag was due to expire.

Details on the manner of conducting elections are laid down in the Act on the Exercise of Political Rights in Matters Concerning the State (VRG - Volksrechtegesetz) (Gesetz vom 17. Juli 1973). Article 3 of this law stipulates that voting is mandatory of the citizens of the Duchy. Since 2005, this obligation can be fulfilled by voting by post. In subsequent elections, this method of voting became increasingly popular, as shown in Table 12.2.

Postal voting is possible on an official ballot paper in a special voting envelope delivered in the so-called delivery envelope. It can be handed over to the commune office[3] in person or sent by post. The vote must reach the office by 5.00 p.m. on the Friday preceding the Sunday voting. All those eligible to vote

---

3   The principality is divided into 11 communes.

TABLE 12.2   Percentage of votes cast by post in the parliamentary elections in Liechtenstein since 2005 (percentage)

Election year	Percentage of votes cast by post
2005	49,0
2009	80,5
2013	95,6
2017	95,9
2021	97,3

SOURCE: OWN STUDY

receive ballot papers no later than 2 weeks before the election day (Koźbiał, 2013, p. 107). Formally, the government of the Duchy may allow electronic voting, but this solution has not been practiced to date, therefore it is difficult to talk about any experience in this area but should be considered a potential option in the future.

The postal voting option has been in use since 2005 and it undoubtedly proved to be extremely useful during the pandemic and the elections that were held in this period. It was a well-tested solution, very popular among voters and - most importantly - ensured safe voting.

The parliamentary elections in Liechtenstein were held on the originally planned date, i.e. February 7, 2021. The elections were won by VU (The Patriotic Union, Vaterländische Union) - 35.89% of votes. The FPB (Progressive Citizens' Party, Fortschrittliche Bürgerpartei) came second with - 35.87% of votes. Both political factions received fairly similar levels of support, with only 42 votes being the difference (sic!), an unprecedentedly small number. The remaining factions received accordingly: FL (Die Freie Liste) - 12.9% of the vote, DPL (Die Demokraten pro Liechtenstein)- 11.1% and an Independent - 4.2% of the vote (Ergebnisse ...). The latter did not join the newly elected parliament, as the electoral threshold is 8% of the vote (Koźbiał, 2013, p. 110).

The turnout in the elections was 78% despite the ongoing epidemic. Importantly, it did not differ from the number of voters in the previous elections (77.8% voted in 2017 and 79.8% in 2013). Postal voting was practiced by as many as 97.3% of voters, which meant another increase compared to 2017 (by 1.4 percentage points).

Since postal voting was adopted by the vast majority of voters, polling stations were only open on election Sunday between 10.30 am and 12.00 pm. The relatively short time was perfectly sufficient for those who chose to vote in the traditional way. However, due to the fact that polling stations were open for public access, pandemic restrictions were applied. As a result, a one-way system was organized so that the voters entering the polling station did not interact with those leaving, tables and cabins were regularly disinfected and rooms frequently ventilated. The polling station staff wore masks, mainly of the FFP-2 type. Undoubtedly, the fact that a referendum was held earlier on during the sanitary regime also contributed to the efficient conduct of the election.

In the advent of the vote, the number of infections was clearly lower than before, with it oscillating around 2–5 cases a day. This was another conducive factor in the course of the elections since in December and January - as already mentioned - the situation was much more serious.

Following the vote on February 7, a new government was formed, composed of the two leading political parties. It was headed by Daniel Risch, representing the VU and it was also the first national government where the majority were women (3 out of 5 members of the government are women).[4]

12.5   Conclusions

Despite the pandemic, both the referendum and the parliamentary elections in Liechtenstein proceeded in a relatively smooth manner. The vote on the three referendum questions took place at the end of summer 2020, when the number of cases was significantly reduced. In turn, the elections to the *Landtag* took place just after the biggest wave of cases and for this reason the election in February 2021 undoubtedly presented a greater challenge.

In both cases, however, the pandemic restrictions did not reduce popular interest in voting, with turnout similar to previous referenda and elections. Maintaining a high level of interest in voting in this country was possible thanks to the alternative voting techniques that have been in use since 2005 in the form of postal voting. This is certainly an experience that Liechtenstein can share with other countries. This voting instrument seems valuable and it can be used elsewhere, although one naturally has to take into account the small size of the Duchy, and thus the relatively small number of votes that are received by election commissions. In the case of countries with a larger number of voters, voting by post would require the development of the relevant technical and logistical infrastructure. A specific type of political culture and

---

4   It is worth adding that if the FBP had been victorious, a female candidate would have been the prime minister.

the high level of confidence in the election result obtained in this way is no less important.

It is worth paying attention to the fact that the Duchy's governmental pandemic crisis management was regarded favorably by its citizens. In a survey conducted at the beginning of September 2021, as many as 69% of respondents assessed the government's actions very well or rather good, while the opposite opinion was expressed by 27% of respondents (mainly unvaccinated people or those rejecting the severity of the pandemic). Additionally, 53% of respondents positively assessed the government's communication policy in this respect (Milic et al., 2021, pp. 24, 27). The high level of public trust in the government and a positive assessment of postal voting plays a very important role here. It is equally significant that we are dealing with a very small country, which means that the distance between the voter and politicians is relatively small. As a consequence, trust in political institutions decreased very little during the pandemic (Frommelt, 2020).

It is impressive that over 97% of those eligible to vote chose postal voting. This would not be possible without the previous 16 years of experience in this field and, in an extreme situation, this experience turned out to be very useful.

Considering the dynamics of both electoral processes, in particular the governmental elections, it should be noted that the pandemic undoubtedly influenced the course of the election campaign itself as it was utterly different from what had happened before. The campaign only took place in the media, through the printed press, radio and via the internet, with no bigger, face-to-face meetings held. Voters and candidates could not meet directly as the pandemic prevented this from happening. Taking this into account, however, it is difficult to avoid the conclusion that postal voting is seen as the norm – it is simply a kind of voting that the inhabitants of Liechtenstein are used to.

Liechtenstein will probably continue to use best practices, including voting postal voting. The next elections - at the level of 11 municipalities - will be held in 2023, with a referendum vote theoretically possible earlier. Also, postal voting has been allowed during local government elections since 2011 and it may very well be that postal voting will be a popular method in the upcoming elections.

References

COVID-19-Impfungen in Liechtenstein. *Liechtensteinische Landesverwaltung*. Retrieved from: https://www.llv.li/inhalt/118804/amtsstellen/sonderseite-COVID-19.

Ergebnisse Landtagswahlen 2021. Landtagswahlen. Retrieved from: https://www.landtagswahlen.li/resultat/12.

Frommelt C. (2020), *Die Politisierung der Coronakrise muss nicht mit Vertrauensverlust einhergehen*, „Liechtensteiner Vaterland" November 30.

Frommelt C., Schiess Rütimann P. M. (2021), *Die Rolle des Landtages in der Corona-pandemie. Kurzbericht*, Gamprin-Bendern.

Gesetz vom 17. Juli 1973 über die Ausübung der politischen Volksrechte in Landesangele-genheiten, „LLGB" 1973, no. 50, November 23, 1973.

Grenzübergänge in die Schweiz ab Dienstag dicht. Retrieved from: https://www.kleinezeitung.at/international/corona/5785371/Coronavirus_Grenzuebergaenge-in-die-Schweiz-ab-Dienstag-dicht.

Ergebnisse der Abstimmungen. Retrieved from: https://www.abstimmungen.li.

Liechtensteiner Vaterland. Retrieved from: https://www.vaterland.li/liechtenstein/politik/ein-jubilaeum-auf-das-alle-gerne-verzichtet-haetten;art169,443675.

Worldometers. Retrieved from: https://www.worldometers.info/coronavirus/country/liechtenstein/.

Informationen zu den Volksabstimmungen vom 30. August 2020, https://www.abstimmungen.li/files/attachments/22/GzD-Regierungskanzlei-Informationsbroschuere.pdf

Koźbiał K. (2010). *„Prawa wyborcze kobiet w Liechtensteinie".* In M. Musiał-Karg, B. Secler (Eds.) *Kobiety we współczesnym świecie*, pp. 55–76. Poznań: Wydawnictwo WNPiD UAM.

Koźbiał K. (2013). *System polityczny Księstwa Liechtensteinu.* Kraków: Wydawnictwo UJ.

Koźbiał K., Stankowski W. (2009). *Konstytucja Księstwa Liechtensteinu. Naród-państwo -polityka.* Kraków: Wydawnictwo UJ.

Milic T., Rochat P., Frommelt C. (2021). *Die COVID-19-Pandemie in Liechtenstein: ein Stim-mungsbild. Ergebnisse einer Umfrage.* Gamprin-Bendern: Liechtenstein-Institut.

Regierung lockert Corona-Massnahmen weiter. Retrieved from: https://www.presseportal.ch/de/pm/100000148/100873447.

Übersterblichkeit in Liechtenstein 2020. Retrieved from: https://www.llv.li/files/as/uebersterblichkeit-liechtenstein-2020.pdf

Verordnung vom 13. März 2020 über Massnahmen zur Bekämpfung des Coronavirus (COVID-19), „LLGB" 2020, no. 94, March 13, 2020.

Verordnung vom 28. Februar 2020 über Massnahmen zur Bekämpfung des Coronavirus (COVID-19), „LLGB" 2020, no. 72, Februar 28, 2020.

Verordnung vom 3. April 2020 über befristete Massnahmen im Bereich der Ausübung der politischen Volksrechte in Landesangelegenheiten in Zusammenhang mit dem Coronavirus (COVID-19), „LLGB" 2020, no. 124, April 3, 2020.

CHAPTER 13

Local Elections under Lockdown: The Case of Latvia

Aleksandra Kuczyńska-Zonik

13.1 Introduction

After regaining independence, the electoral system in Latvia, like several state institutions, underwent a number of changes. At that time, there was a transition from the electoral system used in the Soviet Socialist Republic of Latvia to the proportional electoral system that was used during the first Republic of Latvia in the 1920s and 1930s. Since 1991, the Supreme Council, and later the Saeima, tried to improve the electoral system that existed in pre-war Latvia without changing the constitutional norm. In 1993, after an almost 62-year hiatus, the first democratic parliamentary elections were held in Latvia (Osóbka, 2016). Later, the multi-party system was stabilized, and the mechanism of the electoral process was restored and improved. At that time, several significant changes regarding the issues of the election rights, the procedure for submitting and registering lists of candidates, the rights and restrictions of candidates, the conduct of elections, calculating results, creating electoral commissions, and the procedure for appeals against commission decisions were introduced.

Nowadays, Latvia is a democratic parliamentary republic. The Saeima is a unicameral, 100-member parliament, which is "directly democratically legitimised". This means that the Saeima, in accordance with the Constitution, may act in exercising the State's power in the name of the people of Latvia. Taking into account the proportion of the number of deputies and the size of its population, Latvia, similarly to other Baltic states, is characterized by the highest percentage in the Baltic Sea region - 5.2, while in Estonia the percentage is 7.6; in Lithuania - 5; and in Poland - 1.2 (*Jundzis,* 2012). The Latvian elections are based on *universal, equal, proportional,* and *direct* suffrage by *secret* ballot, with parliamentary elections held every four years on the first Saturday in October. Latvia has the lowest number of constituencies compared to other countries in the Baltic Sea region, which means a high proportionality of election results as a greater number of members from each multi-member constituency are included in parliament. The territory of Latvia is divided into five districts according to cultural and historical areas - Kurzeme (Courland),

Vidzeme (Livonia), Latgale (Latgale), Zemgale (Semigalia), and Riga. The number of deputies elected in each of the districts is determined by the Central Election Commission (CEC) according to the number of voters registered in each constituency.

Generally, the Latvian electoral system works correctly. Elections are held in a professional manner and the election administration enjoys great public trust. Since 2004, no large-scale protests have been observed over the organization of the Saeima elections. Participants are free to operate in a competitive and pluralistic environment where fundamental freedoms are usually respected. The legal framework is comprehensive and provides a sufficient basis for elections. The election administration works at all levels in a timely and professional manner. Various voting options, including early voting and special procedures for citizens living abroad, are available for voters (OSCE, 2019). Since 1991, Latvia has been represented in the Association of European Election Officials (ACEEEO), working to ensure the independence of elections, exchange information on elections and political processes between election officials, experts, and academics to support free, democratic, and fair elections in the member states. Despite some rules such as restrictions for candidates and parties in Latvia, which may not be compatible with the OSCE commitments and international standards for democratic elections, the Group of States against Corruption (GRECO, 2017) has pointed to Latvia's success in implementing the recommendations on counteracting electoral violations.

In order to identify and prevent possible efforts to unlawfully influence the course and results of the elections, several state institutions in Latvia have intensively monitored the information space, cooperated and exchanged information with other involved institutions, analysed the information obtained from various sources as well as carried out operational activities. They have been responsible for reacting toward foreign as well as internal risks threatening the safety of elections. Moreover, to secure free and democratic elections, the involvement of every person is important. So far, high civic activity has been observed as people provide information about the conformity of the course of elections with the regulations in certain polling stations. Particularly, in 2020–2021 the COVID-19 pandemic caused certain challenges to the course and security of elections as the institutions responsible for the course of these elections had to pay additional attention to the organization of work according to the epidemiological safety requirements as well as having to secure that voters also observe all safety measures. For example, the Latvian State Security Service (VDD) carried out inspections based on a few dozen reports received from residents, of which the majority were received during election days. Most of the reports related to possible breaches of election procedure and possible agitation breaches. There were only two reports on possible influencing of voters, being suspicions about so-called vote buying, however, the verification of this information did not confirm such activities. Also in connection with possible unlawful activities during the elections in 2020, four criminal proceedings were launched, however, in all cases the investigation established only negligence and unintentional mistakes by officials, and finally, due to a lack of real elements of a criminal offence, all criminal proceedings were terminated. In general, the 2020–2021 elections in Latvia were peaceful and no foreign influence was established. Society mostly showed a high level of responsibility and followed the epidemiological safety recommendations during the elections, with only a few exceptions.

At the same time, several debates were started about online public services involving the electoral system. They included the development of electronic procedures as part of the modernisation of public administration, aimed at reducing face-to-face contact between officials and citizens. As the pandemic highlighted a new issue in elections – physical safety – several states started to consider digital alternatives to protect the health of their citizens while governing in the face of the current and upcoming crises. As a result, the coronavirus pandemic has intensified disputes over electronic voting. For example, Lithuania has seen hot debate about online voting as the "digital alternative" to protect the health of the citizens and enable effective governance. The Central Election Commission, therefore, started considering measures for safe voting and finally, in June 2020, the Lithuanian government backed an amendment under consideration in parliament that would allow for the casting of ballots online in general elections. Because it was impossible to develop and apply such a system before the parliamentary election which took place in October 2020, the measure was not implemented for those elections. However, it could be used in municipal, presidential, EP elections, and referenda in the future. In contrast to Lithuania, there has been no serious debate over electronic voting in Latvia over the past few years, and residents should not expect to be able to emulate the country soon. In 2018, the issue was discussed by the Central Election Commission in Latvia when creating an electronic voter registry to make voting with an ID card easier, and the benefits and risks of online voting were discussed. However, opponents stressed the various risks of online voting due to security concerns based on the experience of other countries such as Switzerland or Australia.

The aim of this study is to investigate the effects of the COVID-19 outbreak on local elections in Latvia during 2020–2021. Specifically, the intention is to analyse the pre-election campaign, electoral procedures, acts of voting under the pandemic restrictions as well as the results of elections. When the extraordinary elections for Riga Council[1] were originally planned for April, following the state of emergency introduced on 13 March 2020, the date was changed several times until it was set to August 29. Moreover, ordinary local government elections were scheduled for 5 June 2021. Despite the fact that none of them was organized in a state of emergency in Latvia, they were both affected by the pandemic and took place under several restrictions.

The Author argues that the pandemic had a twofold impact on elections; firstly, a technical aspect that concerned epidemiological limitations during the pre-election period and at the polling stations. Restrictions were introduced on the basis of Cabinet Regulation, including location and layout of the polling stations, members of commissions and employees as well as a procedure of voting. Thus, several debates were started about online public services including the modernization of the electoral system aimed at reducing face-to-face contact between citizens such as e-voting as an effective tool used in the process of democratic development. However, more risks than benefits were underlined during the discussion. Secondly, a political aspect included the impact on participation in elections and the political preferences of voters. In fact, the voter turnout in the local elections in June 2021 was among the lowest since 1991. The study reveals, however, that while low voter turnout resulted from the fact that numerous citizens refused to vote due to safety reasons, it is also a consequence of factors that arose long before the pandemic outbreak such as distrust and discontent among various social groups against the political elite. Finally, the study uncovers how both the results of public discussion about new methods of voting and the results of the elections held in the pandemic in Latvia have deep socio-economic, political, cultural, and historic contexts. For the theoretical approach, the concept of "democratization of technology", which assumes the dissemination and use of new technologies by society in order to increase stability and security is discussed, according to which, new technologies are to meet specific social needs and serve the development of the idea of democracy. From a methodological point of view, this study is based on quantitative research on local elections in Latvia.

The Author mainly uses the method of critical analysis of media content and systemic analysis as well as the institutional-legal method to identify the documents of the state institutions regarding electoral procedures and mechanisms. They allow for a greater understanding of the process of an election

---

1   In early 2020, the Saeima decided to dismiss the Riga City Council because of its inability to make decisions, following three successive council meetings at which a quorum was not obtained.

conducted in the time of a pandemic. In a practical sense, this perspective provides a broader context for any election held at a time when residents are facing rapid challenges.

13.2 Research Framework

Latvia's highly distinctive proportional electoral system, based on the democracy of inter-war Latvia (Millard, 2011) has, since 1991, been a type of proportional representation party-list system with some distinctive features, particularly the arrangements for preference voting. Parties are usually centralized and leader-oriented, which to some extent resulted from the oligarchic nature of Latvian political parties and the trumping of ideology by personality politics (Pabriks, Purs, 2002). Overall, post-independence elections to Saeima were held in accordance with applicable legislation and international standards of free and fair elections, based on the opinions and reports of international organizations. The essence of the political system in Latvia is a deep ethnic division, which is manifested by the fact that the majority of political parties participating in the elections clearly emphasized their priorities with regard to national identity. Moreover, the emergence of new parties resulted from the dissatisfaction of the public with the ineffective government and a lack of implementation of election postulates by political parties (Ikstens, 2014). The relative instability is related to the socio-economic status of the voters, but also the electoral system operating in Latvia (Saarts, 2011). Nonetheless, the transfer of power usually took place peacefully, without causing any violent reactions either by the political actors or the voters, and also the country's pro-European political course.

The Latvian electoral system does have its weak points, as many young democracies do. Voters are rarely aware of the intricacies of electoral systems and their workings and many did not understand the basic elements of the system (Millard, 2011). Institutions provide incentives and disincentives; they shape developments but they rarely function as effective mechanisms and many irregularities have appeared. Also, corruption continues to make waves in Latvia's politics (Ikstens, 2020).

Political participation is crucial to democracy. But civic education appears to have been badly neglected in Latvia (Millard, 2011), thus, for several years political trust and self-assessed efficacy in Latvia have been much lower than in developed democracies. While at the beginning of the 90s, mass mobilization resulted from exhilaration after the collapse of the Soviet regime and restoring Latvia as an independent state, since the end of the decade, there has been increasing evidence of both political disenchantment, apathy, and alternative modes of political participation (Karklins, 2001).

Some claim that the best way to deal with low political participation is by "democratization of technology" (Piątek, 2018), which assumes the dissemination and use of ICT by society in order to increase stability and security. According to this concept, new technologies meet specific social needs and serve the development of democracy. This means that people have access to technology and this leads to more rapid developments and innovations within the democratic system. It has the power to change people's lives because it opens up new opportunities and possibilities and provides the innovative environment which enables citizens to participate meaningfully in its advancement. Appropriate legislation and testing, as well as increasing social competencies in the use of technology, can contribute to strengthening the mechanisms of protection against the negative effects of these tools. Thus, they can indirectly contribute to the growth of social trust in political systems. At the same time, some researchers (Karlovitz, 2020) point out that there are many risks and dangers. The democratization of technology is a formidable challenge to existing political systems that are trying to limit or hinder people's suddenly enormous freedom. Thus, information and communication technology raise a number of questions about security as well as human rights. They include concerns of interference in the electoral process, cyberattacks, or privacy and data protection. Moreover, it should be emphasized that digitalisation can create inequalities and exacerbate digital divides, particularly in education and labour markets. The need to apply new technologies as a remedy to boost productivity and sustain inclusive economic growth is significant for Latvia, where the development of ICT has not been a priority so far.

13.3   Results: Technical (r)evolution and Political Participation

Since the WHO announced a decision on the state of the COVID-19 pandemic (WHO, 2020), Latvia has held extraordinary elections for Riga Council (2020) and ordinary local elections (2021). The first of them was postponed several times due to the COVID-19 pandemic and took place only at the end of August 2020. The second was peculiar for several reasons; for the first time, local elections took place in 41 newly-formed constituencies: 35 districts and 6 state-level cities, with the new district within new borders after the administrative-territorial reform which officially came into force in July that year. There were also additional changes in the election process: no longer

could voters' associations participate in the elections, and only previously registered political parties were allowed to register a candidate; voters could vote
in any polling station within their home municipality without being attached
to the specific station in their district to increase voter turnout. Finally, the
entire elections and voting procedure were affected by the COVID-19 pandemic
and took place under several restrictions.

The pandemic had a twofold impact on elections. The technical aspect concerned restrictions introduced according to epidemiological guidelines regarding pre-election campaigns, location and layout of polling stations, members
of polling stations commissions and employees as well as voting procedures,
while the political aspect concerned political participation and attitudes
toward the candidates.

According to the law, the submission of lists of candidates for the local elections of 2020 and 2021 took place for 120 days until election day (pre-election
campaign). Ahead of the emergency in the country, various political forces and
candidates were increasingly active during the pre-election campaign. While
in 2017, before Latvia's territorial reform had been implemented, there were
8.945 candidates running in the local government elections and 1.554 seats for
deputies, in the 2021 local elections, 5.599 candidates were running for one of
683 seats. This means that in the previous elections, nearly six candidates ran
for one seat, while in 2021, there were eight candidates. Thus, the epidemiology
did not discourage politicians from the elections. For the elections, the party
proposals were based on practical issues such as education, infrastructure, and
health care, but not on COVID-19 itself.

Municipalities played an essential role in figuring out how to keep their
communities safe during the pandemic. The emergency situation in Latvia
was lifted on 9 June 2020 (Cabinet Order No. 103 2020), and municipalities
were allowed to decide on the restrictions depending on the number of cases
in their region. The normal procedure of voting during the pandemic involved
voting at the polling stations. The Recommendations "Epidemiological Safety
Measures for the Containment of the Spread of COVID-19 Infection" (Cabinet
of Ministers of the Republic of Latvia, 2020) laid down the basic principles
and precautionary measures for the containment of the spread of COVID-19
infection as well as the requirements and restrictions for gathering, included,
among others, determining the maximum number of persons allowed at the
same time in the premises of the polling station; good ventilation and regular airing of polling stations; warning signs regarding keeping the right distance; hand disinfectants; obligatory wearing of protective face masks; using
the voter's own writing implements; placing a wastebasket and an additional
container for discarding used face masks at the polling station, etc. Similar

recommendations were given for local elections in 2021 (Central Election Commission, 2021). Above all, the voters had to have a face mask at polling stations, with the only exception to this being for individuals because of a *disability*, physical or mental health illness or condition, and children under the age of 7 (when attending the polling station with their parents). Voters had to temporarily remove their mask to show their face when giving their ID card. At the polling station, voters had to keep a distance of 2 meters. Moreover, according to the Recommendation, the election commission had to provide at least three reserve employees for each polling station and prepare a plan for the involvement of reservists in the ensuring of electoral process, in case members or employees of the polling station commission might not be present at the workplace due to sickness.

Voters who could not come to the polling station due to health conditions were allowed to vote via a ballot that had been mailed to the voter's home (off-site voting). An application for this method of voting needed to be submitted 5 days before the election day to the representatives of the nearest polling station, either delivered in person or sent by post or e-mail (secured by e-signature). This procedure for voting has, however, so far rarely been used - in the 2018 parliamentary elections, less than 17,000 individuals voted at home, which was only 1% of all voters. In the 2021 local elections, this procedure could also be used by voters in self-isolation or quarantine because of COVID-19 infection or the risks of infection. According to the Recommendations, members of the electoral commission should have been vaccinated against COVID-19, or they had to wear a face mask, protective coat, rubber gloves and, if possible, close-fitting safety glasses. The electoral commission took special precautionary measures when going to the voters, communicating with the voter by telephone to explain the voting procedure. The act of voting included 1. voting in the same place with the commission - a voter filled out their ballot paper, put election materials and an individual form into the ballot box, then a member of the polling station commission noted on the voters' list for voting at the voter's location that the voter had both voted and signed the voters' list form; 2. the electoral commission placed election materials (an individual form in which the voter signs regarding the receipt of election materials, a sealed ballot envelope, a set of ballot papers) in an easily accessible place for the voter (for example, at the door of the apartment), then a voter opened the door, took the ballot papers and the envelope, signed the list of voters, then opened the door and put the ballot into the ballot box.

When voting in hospitals and social care institutions, the electoral commission was obliged to cooperate with the management of the institution and in compliance with the quarantine restrictions and health protection measures

imposed by the institution. The Latvian soldiers of international military missions in Mali as well as individuals in prisons had the right to vote at their loca-
tions, where special polling stations were organized at that time. A voter who
wished to vote in prison had to submit an application to the prison administration no later than three days before the election day. An alternative voting
method was provided for voters in Ādaži and Jēkabpils, who had the opportunity to vote without getting out of the car, in so-called external polling stations. In this case, only one person could be in the vehicle during the vote. This
option was not available to voters in self-isolation or home quarantine because
of COVID-19.

It was also possible to vote abroad. In 2021, for the first time, voters eligible
to participate in municipal elections, who were staying abroad during elections, were allowed to apply for postal voting from abroad. Voters had to apply
for postal voting in advance – from 27 March to 24 April. According to the electoral register of 2021, a total of 150,000 Latvian voters lived abroad. On election
day, they could vote at one of the polling stations which were organized abroad
or by post if they had earlier applied for a postal vote. Polling stations abroad
were usually located in the Latvian diplomatic missions (embassies and consulates). This option may have the potential to increase the number of voters
in the future; according to data, in 2018 around 32,000 thousand individuals
used this method, which was 24% of eligible voters, whereas, as a result of
the program of cooperation between the government and the Latvian diaspora
for 2021–2023, encouraging citizens to participate in the elections from abroad
by improving and facilitating the registration system for postal voting, preparing and disseminating invitations for voters, providing information materials
on procedures for postal voting and voting abroad, it is expected that at least
50,000 people living and registered abroad will take part in the next parliamentary elections. Some politicians have also called for the possibility that voters
can choose the constituency in which their votes will be counted. Currently, all
Latvians who vote abroad vote for the Riga constituency, and they are not able
to vote for candidates representing the constituency where they used to reside.

Apart from the technical aspect of dealing with a pandemic, there were also
the political ones, which included an impact on the participation in elections
as well as the political preferences of voters. COVID-19 was an important reason for why people were unwilling to go to polling stations, illustrated by the
2020 Riga City Council Extraordinary Election, in which only 40% of Riga's
citizens voted, mainly due to people's fear for their own health and the possibility of contracting COVID-19 by going to the polls. In a pre-election survey carried out by the Central Election Commission in March 2021, 52% of
respondents indicated that COVID-19 had no influence on their decision to

vote. However, more than a third of respondents admitted that the COVID-19 pandemic negatively impacted their decision to participate in the elections, and more than half of respondents over the age of 64 hesitated over whether they should vote because of safety and health reasons (SKDS, 2021). While the state of emergency in Latvia was lifted on 7 April 2021, many restrictions were still in place during May and June. As a result, the voter turnout in the local elections in June 2021 was 34%, the lowest turnout in the Riga local elections since 1994 (58%). Moreover, the pandemic had a significant impact on the public mood and attitudes toward the ruling parties. The results of the "Latvian Barometer" survey in March 2021 indicated that 72% of respondents were dissatisfied with the government's reactions related to the pandemic, and 70% considered the economic situation as bad. Public distrust toward the government's decision-making was increasing at that time. Many government decisions aimed at limiting the spread of the virus have been incomprehensible to the public such as delayed deliveries, an absence of vaccination strategies, an ineffective information campaign, and a lack of confidence in the effectiveness of the vaccine. This has led to numerous demonstrations and protests by anti-vaxxers, which were, in fact, an act of expression of frustration and distrust of the government. Importantly, the low level of trust in the state authorities is not a new phenomenon – for several years now, Latvia has been among the countries which are characterized by low public support in relation to the political elite and – as a result – by frequent changes of government. Other factors include a political culture (broadly understood) characterized by considerable distrust toward the elite (and authorities in general) as well as lack of social awareness, which is lower in Latvia than in Western Europe due to dissatisfaction with the state of democracy in the country and the authorities' insufficient demonstration of taking responsibility for the society as a whole.

Finally, despite the opinion that municipal elections are not as important as parliamentary national elections, in reality, local elections still matter to political parties and candidates. To some extent, municipal elections can also affect the relationship between current coalition partners, and lead to changes in the government. Thus, theoretically, after the local elections, the government can face changes in the outline of the coalition.

While there is no place for a deeper analysis of the results of the municipality elections here, it is claimed that the results of local elections conducted in 2020–2021 confirmed that many areas elected parties that had already previously led the municipality. In the 2021 local elections, among the leaders were the Latvian Association of Regions and the *Union of Greens and Farmers*, but no party won a clear majority of the municipalities (LSM.lv 2021). This points to people's desire for stability because they preferred the old, already familiar leaders and did not trust the new ones. In part, it showed that, according to residents, municipality leaders have not worked badly. Additionally, it should be underlined that personality, not party membership, was important in municipal elections. At the same time, the results indicated that regional voters should not be ignored and that social, agrarian, and other local issues should be included in the governmental agenda.

13.4   Discussion

The analysis of the effectiveness of the electoral system and legal changes in this matter shows that Latvia has succeeded in improving the regulatory framework of the election process, its mechanism, and procedures. This includes determining the significant role of the institutions responsible for organizational processes as well as limiting electoral violations. Despite discussions regarding the normative basis, approaches and strategies for the development of electoral procedures have been continuing since the 1990s, when Latvia regained independence, there have been no serious violations of elections and both politicians and the public have accepted the election results. The exception to this was the 2006 elections to the Saeima when the results were questioned by the court on the basis of pre-election violations; however, it did not induce any violent protests and social objections toward the electoral commissions.

To some extent, Latvian elections have always been of interest for the international community as thousands of residents in Latvia have not been given Latvian citizenship, mainly representatives of Russian-speaking minorities (around 230,000 inhabitants in Latvia), who cannot participate in elections in the country. Thus, they are deprived of political rights and any real influence in the decision-making process in Latvia. They are not allowed to work in the civil service or occupy posts not only directly related to national security but also in the private sector, including state officials, diplomatic and consular corps, judges, lawyers, notaries, policemen, and soldiers (Kuczyńska-Zonik, 2017). After regaining its sovereignty, Latvian authorities introduced restrictive rules of naturalization based on the idea of 'ethnic democracy' to restore the interwar demographic situation of Latvia and to consolidate society in the nation-state. Latvia is still reluctant to grant automatic citizenship to all residents (however, this procedure is applied to non-citizens born in Latvia). As a result, the PE, CoE, UN High Commissioner for Human Rights as well as the OSCE High Commissioner on National Minorities have observed Latvia's citizenship policy (Institute on Statelessness and Inclusion, 2014; Reine, 2007) and elections conducted in the country to monitor whether the recommendations have been implemented.

One of the most serious problems affecting the Latvian electoral system concerns the low turnout and lack of public interest in elections. This is true for both Latvians voting in the country and those living abroad. This trend is exemplified particularly by the results of the 2014 and 2019 European Parliament elections when the turnout was 30% and 33%, respectively.[2] Thus, the 2014 PE elections started the discussions as to whether compulsory participation in the elections should be introduced. The majority of Latvians rejected this possibility, however, interesting results were obtained in an opinion poll in June 2021, when respondents were asked about their attitude toward mandatory participation in local government elections. 21% of interlocutors were for this proposal, while 74% were against it. The respondents were also asked if and how the citizens should be encouraged to participate in the elections. 25% of respondents claimed there should be an additional day of holiday, and 13% opted for a lottery prize for those who voted. 59% of respondents indicated that they did not support any of these solutions, as voting is a right and duty of citizens, which cannot be encouraged by receiving material benefits (SKDS, 2021b).

According to one of the explanations for why people are not interested in elections, it could simply be that everything is fine in people's lives. Therefore, there is no desire to go to elections and change anything. Others, on the other hand, did not go to the polling stations because they thought everything was bad anyway. There were no big issues in the context of the elections that could mobilize people. The COVID-19 pandemic then exacerbated this problem. But as Ieva Ilves, Advisor to the President of Latvia on Information and Digital Policy, said, "COVID-19 can be described as a force *majeure*, but it is also an opportunity. It catapulted the search for digital solutions to the very top of policy makers' agenda, but it also calls for ensuring democratic responsibilities such as privacy protection and building a trustworthy digital ecosystem." As a result, it was claimed that new technologies applied to the election process could be an effective tool during the pandemic crisis.

In the 2021 local elections, an online voter register at polling stations was used for the first time, which allowed voters to vote at any polling station in their municipality. Voters had the opportunity to vote at any of the polling stations in their constituency by showing their passport or ID card. Since the introduction of the eID card in Latvia, those voters who have only an identity card have been able to participate in the Saeima elections using a special

---

2   European Parliament elections are treated as secondary by voters in Latvia. The European election campaign remains on the margins of media and public attention.

voter card, which had to be received at the Office of Citizenship and Migration Affairs. Such a convoluted practice was seen as an additional administrative burden, and a reason not to participate in elections. Currently, voters could find out their electoral districts and polling stations in the district by using the e-service of the Office of Citizenship and Migration Affairs. Thanks to the online register, voters were able to use both passports and ID cards as individual documents for registration to vote at the polling station. Members of electoral commissions checked the passport or scanned the code of the voter's ID card using a mobile device to ensure that the voter was registered and to determine if he or she had already voted. According to a survey, 48% of individuals registered by the online register claimed it was convenient for them (SKDS, 2021b). Moreover, in 2021, additional amendments were introduced to allow Latvian citizens to vote in Saeima elections using their eID card (previously, residents in Latvia had been permitted to vote only with a valid passport). The Saeima elections are planned to be held in October 2022.

Latvia has already considered the possibility of introducing e-voting, and the discussion on this has continued since the 1990s. In late 2014, parliament rejected a public legislative initiative about e-voting because of negative opinions from experts, who said that there were no technological solutions that would make e-voting safe while keeping to the principle of a secret ballot as provided for in the Latvian Constitution. In 2018, the Ministry of Environmental Protection and Regional Development suggested the option of e-voting for municipal referenda. The Ministry did not exclude the possibility of traditional voting operating at the same time. Many experts emphasize that Latvia has already met the technical and organizational conditions for introducing electronic voting; it has good electronic infrastructure, widely available Internet, and enjoys a relatively high international position in the field of e-management. For several years, Latvia has been developing its e-government service consequently. However, there are some obstacles, for example, during the May 2019 PE elections, there was a significant system failure (LSM.lv, 2019a). According to the Elections Law in Latvia, in the case of PE elections, a voter can vote at any polling station in Latvia if there is an electronic register in order to check the exchange of information between the polling station where the voter is registered and any polling station where the voter is going to vote. As a result of the above-mentioned system failure, it was not possible to check if the voter had already voted because the information flow regarding the voter list was unavailable to polling stations in the country. The problems could not be solved quickly, so the next day, Saeima, considering that voters' rights to vote might be limited, extended the work of polling stations by four hours on Friday, the last day for early voting (LSM.lv, 2019b). The cost of this decision was 162,000 EUR. Furthermore, the Central Election Commission made a statement that the voters were able to vote only at the polling station where they had been registered. The system failure was not the only obstacle in those elections. A further notable issue was an administrative mishap in which almost half of Latvia's 1.3 million eligible voters failed to receive instructions specifying their assigned voting location.

The failure of the information system and, generally, low level of trust toward election security, have highlighted the need to intensify innovation and the development of new technologies in the electoral process in Latvia. So far, digital technologies in the electoral system have not been introduced significantly because the Central Election Commission has been rather sceptical about the changes. Therefore, new technologies have so far had little impact on the electoral process. Moreover, the lower priority of the technology development in the Latvian government's agenda compared to Estonia or Lithuania resulted mainly from the lack of political will and regulatory framework as well as the government's lack of readiness to use them (Zabašta, Rivža, 2010). In fact, during the pandemic crisis, it was extremely difficult to ensure universal and equal rights to the Internet for all residents. While a survey on the use of digital technologies in Latvian households has revealed that the share of households with Internet in 2020 reached almost 90% (as compared to 2019, connection increased by 4.3%), the largest share of regular Internet users were in urban regions (Riga, Zemgale) and the smallest were in Latgale, the least developed area in Latvia. Additionally, while 70% of Europe's population has basic digital skills, in Latvia only 43% of individuals have basic skills, with 24% above the basic level. To boost the digital transformation of the Latvian economy, it is important to further raise awareness of the importance of digitisation in the public and private sectors and to step up existing efforts to enable the full range of benefits to be reaped from the adoption of digital technologies by businesses.

Another question is the capability of the state to secure the system during the process of e-voting. New technologies may reduce the quality of the electoral process by interfering with the act of voting or changing the vote results, manipulation and attempts at foreign interference, or even cyberattacks, which undermine trust and confidence in the integrity of electoral processes. In Latvia, it is Russia who is claimed to interfere in its internal politics and try to destabilise the country's electoral system. Moreover, micro-targeting and behavioural profiling techniques derive data that is improperly obtained and is misused to direct divisive and polarizing narratives. This process opens up new attempts to manipulate the electorate. Further, some works (Cheeseman, Lynch, Willis 2018) have revealed that the costs of digital solutions are high and they do not improve the efficiency of the electoral process. Additionally, it is claimed that these technologies may create significant opportunities for corruption that vitiate their potential impact. Digital processes may be a source of mistrust and undermine international and domestic confidence in the policy-making process. The limited knowledge of many citizens and commentators about how digital processes actually work may mean that it is extremely difficult to differentiate false claims from plausible ones.

It should be underlined that the extension of voting methods to electronic voting does not translate easily into improved voter turnout, which is additionally influenced, among other things, by access to the Internet, trust in election procedures, or social habits. This is confirmed by research carried out in Estonia – D. Bochsler (2009), as well as K. Vassil and T. Weber (2013), stated that while the percentage of users voting electronically is growing, electronic voting does not affect the overall turnout. Consequently, the research results bring into question the issue of whether electronic voting is a remedy for the insufficient level of democracy in the state. Moreover, while digital technological development creates a wide range of electoral innovations for both the state institutions and the private sector, it may also undermine the legitimacy of the electoral process. For this reason, many officials and experts in Latvia are sceptical about the implementation of the innovations on a larger scale. Therefore, it is claimed here that Latvia is unlikely to follow Estonia's path as digital technologies are expensive and do not increase voter turnout enough. Latvia has to find its own balance between the effectiveness of the electoral process and the legitimacy of its electoral procedures.

13.5   Conclusions

The issue of adapting the system to the epidemiologic situation was taken very seriously in Latvia, so much so that both the extraordinary elections to Riga Council and municipality elections took place without any major obstacles. Recommendations and working principles for the election commissions and voters in a health crisis were determined so that the electoral process could continue. Furthermore, it has been recognised that this crisis could be a good "teacher", leading to the reassessment of new procedures in the electoral system. Latvia has introduced online voters registers and re-started discussion regarding electronic voting. The emergency situation also provided incentives for development in the e-direction. Those measures were expected to stimulate voter turnout, especially in the situation of the pandemic, when the mobility of citizens across their regions was limited. While the voters appreciated some modifications, the crisis has caused bigger concerns; whether and to what quality the electoral institutions have worked, and whether the established restrictions on human rights have been proportional. Moreover, taking into account previous electronic systems failures, which undermined social confidence in institutions, it seems that the Latvian government and society would not accept such digital technology solutions in the electoral process as they may imply several security risks, both for the electoral process and voters' personal data (Rodina, Lībina-Egnere, 2021). Additionally, it should be remembered that in the case of electronic voting, every citizen should have access to the Internet, otherwise voting via the Internet would be exclusive, and thus – would violate the principles of equality and freedom of elections.

Particularly, the so-called digital divide, which refers to the differentiation in effective access to modern information and communication technologies, should be underlined. Estonia is seen as a leading country in Central Europe in terms of digital public services. Apart from promoting a well-developed economy and information society, Lithuania, Latvia, and Estonia seek to limit social exclusion in the area of access to the Internet and, consequently, solve the problem of a digital divide (Wasiak, 2013). However, there are still some groups who are not able to take full advantage of new technologies including, among others, national minorities and ethnic groups, elderly people, people with lower levels of education, the unemployed, or people with low incomes. In addition, people with disabilities may face barriers in the use of both information and communication tools and e-services due to the nature of their disability and, therefore, they may also be at risk of exclusion (European Commission, 2004). In the case of Latvia, where the percentage of households with good quality Internet is the lowest in a region occupied by national minorities, changes to the voting options may induce a risk of technology exclusion of these minorities.

In contrast to Estonia, where an online voting option has been accessible since 2005, in Latvia and Lithuania the concept of electronic voting has been part of both academic discourse and public debate for a long time. Both of them have perceived this method as an instrument to increase voter turnout, especially among young people and citizens living abroad (Diržinskaitė, 2018) as, similarly to Latvia, data on electoral participation in Lithuania confirms a downward trend. Electronic voting was thus intended as a response to declining public involvement in elections. However, until now, fear of cyber threats, systems failure, vote manipulation, and the need to protect personal data have deterred both the Lithuanian and Latvian governments from implementing this voting method. In June 2020, the Lithuanian Seimas passed a law allowing people who vote abroad when "traditional voting in a foreign country is not possible", and people who remain isolated in Lithuania, to vote electronically

(Kuczyńska-Zonik, 2021). It seems that this is the first step toward implementing the online voting option in practice.

Generally, the low turnout in the Latvian elections has resulted from, above all, the low level of trust toward the state institutions and politicians. The lower the turnout, the lower the parliament's legitimacy, and the lower its authority in relationships with other public institutions. This was symptomatic particularly during the pandemic, when, according to public opinion, the government's response in Latvia to mitigating the pandemic's consequences was delayed, erratic, and inconsistent. There was neither information about the legitimacy of restrictions nor clear rules of conduct for services and institutions supervising compliance with the law. There was no extensive information campaign in the Russian language either. Therefore, strategic communication within society failed, reducing de facto trust in the government. Public opinion polls in Latvia taken in December 2020 indicated that the parliament and the government of Latvia were the least trustworthy (respectively 20 and 23%; in both cases, a drop by 7 percentage points compared to January 2020). In independent Latvia (after 1991), the lowest support level was recorded in April 2010 during a serious economic crisis, when only 7% trusted the Saeima and only 13% trusted the Cabinet of Valdis Dombrovskis. Since then, the most serious challenge for state authority has been the response to the pandemic. Therefore, it is not surprising that support for the government fell further during the second wave of COVID-19.

According to GlobSec, Latvia's society is one of the most dissatisfied with its system of governance (74%) in Central and Eastern Europe (Voices of Central and Eastern Europe, 2020). Moreover, as many as 76% of respondents do not believe that their needs are taken into account by state authorities. A low degree of trust is characteristic among people with primary and secondary education levels, Russian-speaking people, and citizens with low income as well as the residents of Latgale. These groups are also more likely to give up certain rights and freedoms for security. During times of crisis, feelings of dissatisfaction become the fuel for populist rhetoric and are used by politicians to promote their own political image and for agitation.

Above all, the introduction of significant changes in the election process with the use of new technologies may be successful. It should be preceded by an information campaign and education of voters at an early stage. The effectiveness of the electoral mechanism and the efficiency of the work of the electoral commission contribute to social stability and strengthen the credibility of state institutions.

References

Bochsler, D. (2009). Can the internet increase political participation? An analysis of remote electronic voting's effect on turnout. "DISC Working Paper Series 08". Center for the Study of Imperfections in Democracy (DISC). Budapest: Central European University.

Bol, D., Giani, M., Blais, A., Loewen, P. (2021). "The effect of COVID-19 lockdowns on political support: Some good news for democracy?". *European Journal of Political Research*, no. 60(2), pp. 497–505.

Cabinet of Ministers Republic of Latvia. (2020). Epidemiological Safety Measures for the Containment of the Spread of COVID-19 Infection. Retrieved from" https://www.mk.gov.lv/en/article/epidemiological-safety-measures-containment-spread-COVID-19-infection-adopted-10-july-2020?utm_source=https%3A%2F%2Fwww.google.com%2F.

Cabinet Order No. 103. (2020). Regarding Declaration of the Emergency Situation. Retrieved from: https://likumi.lv/ta/en/en/id/313191.

Central Election Commission. (2021). Recommendations for the Prevention of Infection COVID-19 at Polling Stations in the Elections of Local Government Councils in 2021. Retrieved from: https://www.cvk.lv/en/elections/local-elections/local-elections-2021/recommendations-for-the-prevention-of-infection-COVID-19-at-polling-stations-in-the-elections-of-local-government-councils-in-2021.

Cheeseman, N., Lynch, G., Willis, J. (2018). "Digital dilemmas: the unintended consequences of election technology". *Democratization*, no. 25(8), pp. 1397–1418.

Česnauskė, J. (2019). "Digital Economy and Society: Baltic States in the EU Context". *Economics and Culture*, no. 16(1), pp. 80–90.

DESI. (2020). The Digital Economy and Society Index 2020. Retrieved from: https://digital-strategy.ec.europa.eu/en/policies/desi.

Diržinskaitė, A. (2018). "Apolitiška karta: kodėl jauniems Lietuvos žmonėms neįdomi politika". *Politologija*, no. 4(92), pp. 3–28.

European Commission, (2004). Estonia's National Action Plan for Social Inclusion. Retrieved from: https://ec.europa.eu/employment_social/soc-prot/soc-incl/nap_incl_2004_ee_en_version.pdf.

European Commission, (2021). *eGovernment Benchmark 2019: trust in government is increasingly important for people*. 8 March. Retrieved from: https://digital-strategy.ec.europa.eu/en/library/egovernment-benchmark-2019-trust-government-increasingly-important-people.

GRECO, (2017). Fourth Evaluation Round Corruption prevention in respect of members of parliament, judges and prosecutors. Retrieved from: https://rm.coe.int/fourth-evaluation-round-corruption-prevention-in-respect-of-members-of/1680735150.

Helmane, I. (2020). "Vēlēšanas tiešsaistē – par un pret, LV portals. 19 October. Retrieved from: https://lvportals.lv/norises/321011-velesanas-tiessaiste-par-un-pret-2020.

Ikstens, J. (2014). "Brīvas un godīgas vēlēšanas". In J. Rozenvalds (Dd.), *Cik demokrātiska ir Latvija? Demokrātijas audits 2005–2014*, pp. 103–112, Latvijas Universitāte.

Ikstens, J. (2020). "Latvia: Political Developments and Data in 2019". *European Journal of Political Research Political Data Yearbook*, no. 59, pp. 225–233. DOI: 10.1111/2047 -8852.12294.

Jundzis, T. (2012). *"Vēlēšanu sistēma Latvijā un Taivānā: salīdzinoša analīze".* Latvijas Zinātņu Akadēmijas Vēstis, no. 66(4), pp. 4–13.

Karlovitz, T.J. (2020). "The Democratization of Technology – and Its Limitation". In T. Dirsehan (Ed.) *Managing Customer Experiences in an Omnichannel World: Melody of Online and Offline Environments in the Customer Journey*, pp. 13–25. Bingley: Emerald Publishing Limited. https://doi.org/10.1108/978-1-80043-388-520201004.

Karklins, R (2001). "Political participation in Latvia 1987–2001". *Journal of Baltic Studies*, no. 32 (4): 334–346.

Kuczyńska-Zonik, A. (2017). "Non-citizens in Latvia: Is it a real problem?". *Sprawy Narodowościowe*, no. 49.

Kuczyńska-Zonik, A. (2021). The Influence of New Technologies on the Election Process in Lithuania, *Przegląd Prawa Konstytucyjnego*, 6(64): 175–188, DOI 10.15804/ ppk.2021.06.14.

LATA. (2020), LATA un LU iestājas pret interneta vēlēšanām, 13 October. Retrieved from: https://www.lata.org.lv/post/lata-un-lu-iest%C4%81jas-pret-interneta-v% C4%93l%C4%93%C5%A1an%C4%81m.

Liepajniekiem.lv. (2020). *Eksperts: Vēlēšanās internetā jānodrošina balsu drošība un aizklātums, taču līdz šim nevienam nav izdevies to nodrošināt.* 14 October. Retrieved from: https://www.liepajniekiem.lv/zinas/sabiedriba/eksperts-velesanas-interneta -janodrosina-balsu-drosiba-un-aizklatums-tacu-lidz-sim-nevienam-nav-izde/.

LSM.lv. (2019a). Latvija izvēlas savus pārstāvjus Eiropas Parlamentā. Retrieved from: https://www.lsm.lv/raksts/zinas/latvija/latvija-izvelas-savus-parstavjus-eiropas -parlamenta.a320200/.

LSM.lv. (2019b). Traucējumu dēļ CVK aicina šodien iedzīvotājus doties vēlēt tikai uz savu iecirkni. 23 May. Retrieved from: https://www.lsm.lv/raksts/zinas/latvija /traucejumu-del-cvk-aicina-sodien-iedzivotajus-doties-velet-tikai-uz-savu-iecirkni .a320027/.

LSM.lv. (2021). ZZS un tās partijas gūst panākumus 15 pašvaldībās; Reģionu apvienība uzvar piecās vietvarās. 6 June. Retrieved from: https://www.lsm.lv/raksts /zinas/latvija/zzs-un-tas-partijas-gust-panakumus-15-pasvaldibas-regionu -apvieniba-uzvar-piecas-vietvaras.a407681/.

Millard, F. (2011). "Electoral-system change in Latvia and the elections of 2010". *Communist and Post-Communist Studies*, no. 44 (4), pp. 309–318.

Musiał-Karg, M. (2017). "Challenges of i-voting – practices, rules and perspectives. Examples from Estonia and Switzerland". *Przegląd Politologiczny*, no. 4, pp. 61–72.

OSCE. (2019). Latvijas Republikas 2018. gadas 6. oktobra parlamenta vēlēšanas DICB. Vēlēšanu izvērtēšanas misijas. Gala atskaite. 17 January. Retrieved from: https://www.osce.org/files/Latvia%202018%20parliamentary_final%20report_LTV.pdf.

Osóbka, P. (2016). *Saeima Parlament Łotwy*, Wydawnictwo Sejmowe: Warszawa.

Pabriks, A., Purs, A. (2002). "Latvia". In D.J. Smith, A.P. Pabriks, A. Purs, Th. Lane (Eds.) *The Baltic States. Estonia, Latvia and Lithuania*. London: Routledge.

Piątek, J. (2018). *"Technology "democratization". Peacetech – new quality of security management". Reality of Politics. Estimates - Comments – Forecasts*, no. 9, pp. 59–70.

Rodina, A., Lībina-Egnere, I. (2021). „The Latvian Parliament and the COVID-19 pandemic. E-Saeima, one of the first parliaments in the world ready to work in fully remote mode". In *The Parliament in the time of coronavirus Latvia*. Robert Schuman Foundation, Retrieved from: https://www.robert-schuman.eu/en/doc/ouvrages/FRS_Parliament_Latvia.pdf.

Saarts, T. (2011). "Comparative Party System Analysis in Central and Eastern Europe: the Case of the Baltic States". *Studies of Transition States and Societies,* no. 3, pp. 83–104.

Scott, J.S.C. (1999). *Seeing Like a State: How Certain Schemes to Improve the Human Condition Have Failed,* New Haven.

SKDS. (2021a). *Vēlētāju attieksmju pētījums 2021 LR pilsoņu aptauja 2021.gada marts.* Retrieved from: https://www.cvk.lv/uploads/files/Dokumenti/Atskaite_CVK_03 2021.pdf.

SKDS. (2021b). *Vēlētāju attieksmju pētījums 2021. Pēcvēlēšanu aptauja Latvijas iedzīvotāju aptauja 2021.gada jūlijs.* Retrieved from: https://www.cvk.lv/uploads/files/P%C4%93t%C4%ABjumi/Veletaju_attieksmju_petijums_CVK_072021.pdf.

Vassil, K., Weber, T. (2011). "A bottleneck model of e-voting: Why technology fails to boost turnout". *New Media & Society,* no. 13(8), pp. 1336–1354.

Voices of Central and Eastern Europe. (2020).

Wasiak, M. (2013). „Gospodarka oparta na wiedzy a wykluczenie cyfrowe. Analiza porównawcza nowych krajów członkowskich Unii Europejskiej". In M. Pokrzywa, S. Wilk (Eds.) *Wykluczenie społeczne. Diagnoza, wymiary i kierunki badań*, Rzeszów: Uniwersytet Rzeszowski, pp. 277–295.

WHO. (2020). WHO announces COVID-19 outbreak a pandemic. Retrieved from: https://www.euro.who.int/en/health-topics/health-emergencies/coronavirus-COVID-19/news/news/2020/3/who-announces-COVID-19-outbreak-a-pandemic.

Zabašta, A. Rivža, P. (2010). "Analysis of information and communication technology development in the Baltic Sea region states". *Economic Science for Rural Development*, no. 11, pp. 37–44.

CHAPTER 14

Elections under Special Supervision. Czech Republic 2020–2021

Elżbieta Lesiewicz

14.1 Introduction

The COVID-19 pandemic had a profound impact on governance and became a test for democracy. In response to the pandemic, many states have enacted new laws or declared states of emergency. Elections are one of the most important features of a democratic state. During the pandemic, electoral procedures had to ensure a balance between public health and individual freedom. Decision-making centers faced a difficult problem with the election cycle. The coronavirus pandemic caused unprecedented disruption to elections around the world. Regardless whether countries held elections on time or delayed them, their decisions had a significant impact on electoral processes. To ensure the credibility of elections and maintain public health, some countries decided to introduce new forms of voting. States that had elections scheduled during the pandemic included the Czech Republic, which held Senate by-elections in 2020, elections to regional councils and one third of the Senate in 2020, and elections to the Chamber of Deputies in 2021. These elections were accompanied by special measures to protect voters and electoral commissions from COVID-19 and to ensure the right to vote for voters in quarantine or otherwise isolated due to the disease.

The purpose of this study is to seek an answer to the question about the COVID-19 impact on the process of organization and implementation of elections in the Czech Republic, legal regulations, the principle of equality among competing parties, new voting methods, precautions and voting techniques under the sanitary regime, and topics raised by political parties in their election campaigns, and the outcome of the elections. In order to achieve the research objective, the research used the institutional and legal analysis which enabled to examine legal and institutional solutions applied in the Czech Republic during the pandemic. In addition, the chapter uses a systemic analysis and a decision-making method, which involve the examination of the research problem and related political processes from the point of view of the decision-making center. The decision-making method enabled us to analyze

© ELŻBIETA LESIEWICZ, 2024 | DOI:10.1163/9789004690622_016

causes and consequences of decisions made in the context of the pandemic crisis. The historical method was also helpful in the research process, as it supported the examination of the presence of particular parties and groupings on the Czech political scene. The motivation for considering this issue was that the topic is extremely relevant, as the COVID-19 pandemic, which has affected countries since 2020. The pandemic poses a major challenge for people involved in the electoral process, as their efforts need to focus on ensuring that democratic elections are secure for voters.

The present analysis is based on monographs and studies on changes in the Czech political system from the moment of their political transformation to the last elections in 2021 (Antoszewski 2007, Birch 2003, Bureś 2011; Koźbiał 2017; Charvát 2014; Czyżniewski 2014, 2018; Havlik, Kopeček 2009). Papers on Czech electoral law as well as the Czech constitutional system were also used (Skotnicki, 2000, 2018; Jirásková, Skotnicki 2013), together with articles that focus on elections during the pandemic (Jirásková, 2021). Moreover, the chapter refers to studies by various institutions and organizations on the socio-political situation faced by the government of Prime Minister Andrej Babiš (Institute of International Relations Prague, Centre for Eastern Studies, Institute of Central Europe, Masaryk Democratic Academy, Centre for Civil Liberties), as well as press articles and reports from major socio-political weeklies, dailies, and election campaign coverage by radio stations.

14.2   Legal and Organizational Changes Made in Response to the Pandemic

Elections in the Czech Republic are based on universal suffrage, secrecy, and equality of votes. Direct elections are held for five representative bodies, i.e. the Chamber of Deputies, the Senate, regional councils, municipal councils, and the European Parliament. Since 2013, also the president is elected in direct elections. The principles of electoral law are set out in the 1993 Constitution of the Czech Republic (Constitutional Act No 1/1993 Sb.). The electoral system differs from institution to institution. The Czech Republic does not have an electoral law regulated by the Electoral Code, but traditionally the electoral process of each body is regulated by a separate law.

The electoral system determines how seats are distributed in a representative body. There are essentially two basic electoral systems, the majority system and proportional representation system - with some modifications. The Constitution of the Czech Republic has introduced a majority system (in which the winner is usually the one who receives the majority of votes) for elections to the Senate and a proportional representation system for elections to the Chamber of Deputies and regional councils.

The COVID-19 pandemic, which has been ongoing since 2020, has significantly affected all areas of social and political life. The fight against the pandemic was undertaken by the Czech state by introducing a state of emergency, which is regulated by the Constitutional Act No 110/1998 - on the Security of the Czech Republic (Mareš, Novák, 2019). The government declared a state of emergency for the first time on March 12 and it lasted until May 17, 2020. For the second time, the state of emergency was declared on October 5 and lasted continuously until February 14, 2021 (Jirásková, 2021, p. 19). In relation to the pandemic, the government declared a state of emergency for the third time on November 25, 2021, and the designation ended on December 25, 2021. This involved a number of restrictions and limitations. Public and private events were banned, and the same applied to the public access to sports and cultural facilities, restaurants and some stores. The state border was closed and a curfew was declared preventing people under 65 from shopping in stores between 8 and 10 a.m. (*Nouzový stav...*). Four days after the state of emergency declared, the Central Crisis Team was established headed by Roman Prymula, the Deputy Health Minister and epidemiologist. On April 8, 2020, the Health Minister Adam Vojtěch declared that the uncontrolled spread of the coronavirus in the Czech Republic was stopped, and the country could prepare for the return to normal operation. As A. Vojtěch explained, quickly introduced restrictions helped the Czech Republic to regain a better epidemiological status than in Spain, Italy, USA, and Great Britain (*Vládní nesoulad...*). At the end of April 2020, the very mild progression of the pandemic enabled the government to take steps to relax state of emergency restrictions and introduce a smart quarantine. In late April and early May, the number of COVID-19 recoveries began to exceed the number of new cases. On May 11, the government allowed mass events to take place. On May 25, cafes, restaurants, zoos, castles and palaces were opened, and group events of up to 300 people were allowed both indoors and outdoors (*Rozvolnění od 25. Května...*).

14.2.1 *Senate by-Elections*

The aforementioned Constitutional Act No 110/1998 on the Security of the Czech Republic is also important in the context of elections, because if an extraordinary situation on the territory of the Czech Republic does not allow for elections on planned deadlines coinciding with the term of office of relevant bodies, such deadlines may be extended, but not longer than six months. Such a state of affairs occurred at the end of January 2020 when the President of the Senate died and elections had to be held. By the order of January 22,

2020, the President announced by-elections in constituency number 32 in Teplice, and he set the date for the election on March 27 and 28, 2020. However, due to the state of emergency that restricted freedom of movement within the territory of the Czech Republic, the election could not take place and on March 15, 2020, the government postponed the vote due to coronavirus-related emergency measures. At the same time, the Supreme Administrative Court (SAC) ruled that the government acted completely outside of its powers and jurisdiction while making the decision (*Nejvyšší správní soud...*). In consideration of the SAC's decision, the government adopted a new law, according to which elections should be held in June at the latest. By his order of May 6, 2020, the President of the Republic set a new date for by-elections in Teplice, with the first round on June 5 and 6 and the second round on June 12 and 13, 2020. In order to conduct the election after the state of emergency ended, the Ministry of the Interior issued new guidelines that set out the hygiene and epidemic prevention measures that were to be applied during the by-election (*Doplňovací volby do Senátu Parlamentu ČR...*).

14.2.2   Elections to Regional Councils and One-Third of the Senate

In the summer of 2020, the number of people infected in the Czech Republic began to increase. During the last weeks of July and the first week of August, the disease spread to cover almost the entire state. By the first week of September 2020, the Czech Republic was among the most affected countries in Europe in terms of the number of newly infected per million inhabitants. According to the electoral calendar and the decision of the President, regional council elections were set for October 2 – 3, 2020,[1] and one-third of the Senate[2] first and second election rounds for October 9 – 10, 2020. Typically, elections to the regional councils are held together with elections to the one-third of the Senate and usually coincide with local government elections and are always held in even years (*Volby do zastupitelstev kraju*).

In July 2020, the Interior Minister Jan Hamáček announced that people isolated due to an infectious disease could not participate in elections, because according to the law, quarantine was an obstacle to exercise the voting right (*Karanténa je překážka...*). This triggered protests among opposition parties. For example, Šárka Jelínková, the deputy chair of the Christian Democratic

---

1   In the Czech Republic, elections to regional councils, which represent 13 regions, are held once every 4 years.
2   The Senate, the upper house of the Parliament of the Czech Republic, has 81 senators, elected for 6 years with the exception that 1/3 of senators are elected every two years. Unlike the Chamber of Deputies, the Senate is partially renewed and cannot be dissolved.

Union - Czechoslovak People's Party (KDU-ČSL), stressed that the possible elimination of thousands of quarantined voters from the election could affect voting results. In her opinion, the government should have prepared special procedures that would make it possible to vote in quarantine in compliance with hygiene rules (*Jak se bude na podzim volit?*). Since the opposition demanded that people in quarantine be allowed to vote, the Ministry of Interior prepared a bill that would allow people in quarantine or isolation to participate in regional council and Senate elections while at the same time protecting public health from COVID-19 (*Lidé v karanténě budou*).

The new law was adopted under the state of emergency fast legislative process, with both the lower and upper houses of parliament approval of the government bill. The law was exceptional from a constitutional law perspective, as it regulated the 2020 regional and senate elections only (*Fišarová, Jirovec*).

Under the new law, three voting options were introduced for people in quarantine:
- voting from a car at a drive-in polling station; such polling stations (78) were set up in each county, and they were designed to accommodate motor vehicles and equipped by the military. Voters could vote from 7 a.m. to 3 p.m. on Wednesday during the election week,
- voting in a closed social service facility; if the county health department notified the county office about closures in their area, the county sent a special election commission. Voting took place from Thursday of election week at 7 a.m. to Friday until 6 p.m.
- voting in a special mobile ballot box; if a citizen in quarantine or isolation was unable to vote at the polling station, by 8 p.m. on Thursday of election week the citizen could make a request to the county office for a special election commission to arrive wearing a protective gear. The commission consisted of members of the drive-in team and arrived with a portable ballot box at the citizen's home. Voting lasted from 7 a.m. on Friday, the Election Day, until 2 p.m. on Saturday.

Special voting and counting methods were handled by a special election commission, consisting of three soldiers and a reporting officer appointed by the regional government (*Vláda schválila návrh zákona...*).

14.2.2.1   Elections to the Chamber of Deputies

The election to the Chamber of Deputies (consisting of 200 members elected every 2 years) also coincided with the pandemic. In December 2020, President Milos Zeman had already announced that the election would be held on October 8–9, 2021. He justified his decision by his intention to give the parties enough time to campaign (*Prezident republiky Miloš Zeman vyhlásil...*).

On April 16, 2021, the President of the Czech Republic announced the date of election to the Chamber of Deputies for quarantined persons. Pursuant to Act No 296/2021 Sb. on special voting methods for the 2021 elections to the Chamber of Deputies and amendments to certain laws, he determined that the voting at the polling station would take place on Wednesday, October 6, 2021, whereas the voting day at the residential premises would be Thursday, October 7, 2021. (*Prezident republiky vyhlásil termín voleb zvláštním...*). Under the law, voters quarantined or isolated due to COVID-19 were allowed to vote using special voting methods. In a similar manner to elections of one-third of the Senate and regional elections in 2020, the law introduced three voting options for those in quarantine and these were the same as for the elections for regional councils and one-third of the Senate (*Volby do Poslanecké sněmovny...*).

A few months before the elections to the Chamber of Deputies, the Constitutional Court caused a sensation by invalidating part of the electoral law. According to its ruling, the previous law violated the equality of the right to vote and the chances of candidates. The court found that the main problem with the law was that it divided the electoral territory into electoral units of different sizes without any basis in the Constitution and thus significantly distorted the strength of seats won in each region. A proposal to abolish the legislation, which was disadvantageous to smaller parties and their coalitions, was submitted by 21 senators from different coalitions in 2017. Jiří Šesták from the political grouping Mayors and Independents (STAN) spoke on their behalf. The senators pointed to the results of the previous parliamentary elections, in which, for example, the STAN movement, which scored just over five percent, needed more than twice as many votes as the victorious Action of Dissatisfied Citizens to win one seat (Ústavní *soud zrušil část volebního zákona...*).

On May 4, 2021, President Miloš Zeman signed an amendment to the electoral law. The Constitutional Court ruling abolished the previous method of converting electoral votes into parliamentary seats as unfair to less successful parties. Under the amended electoral law, a limit of 5% was set for a party or movement, 8% for a two-member coalition, and 11% for a multiple-member coalition. In the election to the Chamber of Deputies, voters could elect deputies in 14 regions. According to the new electoral law, the distribution of seats took place in two rounds. First, the Czech Statistical Office distributed seats in the regions among the electoral groups that got into the Chamber of Deputies. It did this using the so-called Imperiali quota. The total number of votes cast for winning parties was divided by the number of seats in the region plus two, and the parties had the number of their MPs according to their score in the region. The remaining undivided seats were then distributed nationwide in the second round using the so-called Hagenbach-Bischoff quota. Electoral groups received the seats in regions where they had the largest number of votes. The placement of a particular candidate depended on the party's list of candidates in the region and the preferential votes (*Nový volební zakon*).

In the context of the COVID-19 pandemic, another important act was the Pandemic Law No 94/2021 Sb., which replaced the state of emergency by introducing a milder pandemic law. On the day of its entry into force, i.e. February 26, 2021, the Czech Republic was put on the pandemic alert. One of the reasons for enacting the pandemic law, was the lack of parliamentary control over government's actions. During the state of emergency, the government did not have to inform the Chamber of Deputies about individual decisions or their effects, nor did it have to justify their decisions in detail, and such decisions could have been overturned by the Constitutional Court only. The pandemic law significantly strengthened the control exercised by the government. The government had to inform the Chamber of Deputies every two weeks about all actions and their changes. (*Pandemický zákon vs nouzový stav...*).

14.3   Election Campaign and Results during the Pandemic

14.3.1   *Senate by-Elections*

It is a cornerstone of democracy to have the government appointed through regular and periodical elections. However, there are situations when this regularity and the handling of elections are disrupted, for example, by the state of emergency, as it was the case in the Czech Republic during by-elections in constituency number 32 based in Teplice. The municipal office received ten applications for candidates submitted by political parties, but one application was rejected because one of the coalition parties did not have an authorized person acting on its behalf. There were seven men and two women among candidates, including mayors of three towns, two high school principals, a governor, a state councilor, and a former priest running for office (*Na Teplicku začali*).

The government made a significant contribution to the pre-election campaign when it postponed the vote on March 15, 2020 due to coronavirus emergency measures. However, the Supreme Administrative Court ruled that the government acted entirely outside its powers and jurisdiction in making such a decision. After a number of arguments (described in the Senate by-election section), the election date was finally set and the Ministry of Interior issued new special guidelines outlining sanitary measures to be used during the by-election. According to the guidelines, voters had to use hand sanitizer before entering a polling station, as well as they should wear a mask on their face that could only be removed for identification. Voters were also required to keep a two-meter distance between each other. This rule also applied to people waiting outside the polling station. Election commission members counting ballots had to be equipped with disposable gloves or frequently disinfect their hands. Voters who were in quarantine could not vote (*Kuk na komisi...*). The voter turnout was low in the first round of the Senate by-election (15.79% of eligible voters). The largest support was given to H. Hanza, the Mayor of Teplice and member of ODS (29.73%) and Z. Bergman, the principal of a high school and an independent candidate for a senator from the Senator 21 list (22.15%). Both of them went to the second round, in which H. Hanza won (57.17%). The turnout in the second round was 9.26% (*Doplňovací volby do Senátu Parlamentu ČR...*).

14.3.2   *Elections to Regional Councils and One-Third of the Senate*

Elections to regional councils and partial elections to the Senate took place in accordance with the electoral calendar despite a large increase in SARS-CoV-2 infections. The election campaign began with President Miloš Zeman's announcement of the election scheduled for April 2020. The announcement was very concise. In the Czech Republic, regional elections (as Senate elections) usually do not receive much public attention. Additionally, the decisive phase of the election campaign took place when the Czech Republic experienced the largest increase in daily SARS-CoV-2 cases and a change at the post of the Minister of Health. Increased activity by political groups became apparent in late August and in September. The Action of Dissatisfied Citizens, a political group of then Prime Minister A. Babiš, launched its campaign in September 2020 with the slogan "Whatever is done, pays off. Action instead of words" which was supposed to indicate the party's success to date (*Ukázaná platí...*). The Czech Pirate Party, on the other hand, built public support around the slogan "Now is the last chance to change the future". They stressed misuse of power by the then government and highlighted the upcoming threats the Czech people might face (e.g. climate change) (*Piráti a Starostové - program pro volby 2021*). Mayors and independent candidates (STAN) ran a so-called "garlic" campaign before the regional elections in the fall. They referred to garlic to draw attention to the fact that "regions need treatment" (*STAN zahájili kampaň do kraju...*). The election campaign also included references to the coronavirus pandemic. The first one to refer to it was the Czech Social Democratic Party (ČSSD), i.e. the coalition government party, whose campaign was launched on June 26, 2020 under the slogan "First the people, then the campaign". Such a choice was probably due to the increased popularity of the party's leader, Jan Hamáček, the Minister of the Interior, during the first wave of COVID-19 (*ČSSD zahájila kampaň...*). The success in limiting the spread of the coronavirus in spring 2020 was also planned to be used by the Action of Dissatisfied Citizens (ANO). Prime Minister A. Babiš repeatedly highlighted his and his own party's achievements in the fight against the pandemic. In mid-August 2020, based on the skeptical attitude of a large number of Czechs towards coronavirus, he criticized the idea of the then Minister of Health Adam Vojtěch regarding the renewed obligation to wear masks in closed spaces. At the same time, A. Babiš asked the media not to stimulate panic with their coronavirus reports. Considering a sharp increase in daily SARS-CoV-2 cases in September, the initial success of the ruling camp in the fight against the pandemic faded, and Prime Minister A. Babiš himself had to apologize to the public for his hasty declarations (*Wybory regionalne w Republice Czeskiej...*).

The ANO party of PM Andrej Babiš received the most votes in the regional council elections (21.83%). The ANO won in 10 of 13 self-governed regions and the city of Prague. The Czech Pirate Party came second with 12.3% and the Civic Democratic Party (ODS) third with 6.97% of public support. The Czech Social Democratic Party (ČSSD) and the Communist Party of Bohemia and Moravia (KSČM) recorded a decline in support, winning 4.93% and 4.76% of the vote, respectively. 34.6% of eligible voters participated in the elections, a very good result by Czech standards and circumstances caused by the coronavirus pandemic (*Wybory regionalne w Republice Czeskiej...*). The regional elections showed a progressive decline in public support for left-wing parties and parties that have a long history of presence on the Czech political scene, such as ČSSD and KSČM.

The 2020 elections to the Senate were held on October 2–3, 2020 (first round) and October 9–10, 2020 (second round). They elected 27 senators for a six-year term, thus renewing 1/3 of the *Senate. Mayors and Independent Candidates* (STAN) was the winner with 11 seats. The Civic Democratic Party won 5 seats, Christian Democratic Union-Czechoslovak People's Party 3 seats, and 2 seats by Tradition Responsibility Prosperity 09 (TOP 09), 2 Senators 21, and 1 seat each went to the Pirate Party, ANO, Party of Free Citizens, and the Democratic Club of Hradec Králové. In the first round of the Senate election, the turnout was 36.74%, while in the second round, it fell to 16.74% (*Volby do Senátu Parlamentu ČR konané v roce 2020*).

The elections were accompanied by strict hygiene measures. Premises were equipped with disinfectants to be used by voters and all interiors were regularly disinfected. Masks were required in polling stations and could be removed only when requested by the commission for identification. A few days before the election, on September 30, thanks to a special drive-in system, people in quarantine could vote from their cars. This solution was introduced under the pressure from the opposition. This voting did not cause any problems (*Korona-virové volby drive-in...*).

14.3.3 *Elections to the Chamber of Deputies*

On October 5, 2020, between the first and second rounds of the Senate election, the government again imposed a state of emergency. From October 8, cultural, social and sports events were suspended again. As of October 28, a curfew was introduced as well. Vaccination against COVID-19 began on December 27, 2020 (*Dva roky s koronavirem...*). In the context of the pandemic, the difficult and tense the situation in the Czech Republic was evidenced by the frequent changes at the post of the Minister of Health. This ministry was headed successively by Adam Vojtěch (13.12. 2017 - 21.09. 2020), Roman Prymula (21.09 - 29.10.2020), Jan Blatný (29.10.2020 - 7.06.2021), Petr Arenberger (7.06. 2021 - 26.05.2021), and Adam Vojtěch (26.05. 2021 - 17.12.2021) (Menšik, 2021).

The electoral campaign preceding the election to the Chamber of Deputies was relatively long, since President Miloš Zeman decided on the date of the election as early as December 2020. The decision aroused interest because the legislator stipulated that the elections were to be announced no later than 90 days before they were held. 20 political parties and 2 electoral coalitions declared their interest to run for election to the Chamber of Deputies. The campaign was largely dominated by COVID-19. The government immediately responded to the first wave of the pandemic with tough measures. However, the raging public health crisis exposed the state's inefficient public administration and its inability to plan and implement policies in a predictable and methodical manner. Moreover, the pandemic was politicized because of tensions within the fragile governing coalition. The government's ability to provide effective coordination of actions was undermined by Prime Minister A. Babiš reluctance to delegate responsibilities and his desire to be the only politician in the media spotlight. Some of the highest mortality rates in the world as a result of COVID-19 persisted in the Czech Republic for several weeks. This generated criticism of the government and its ability to exercise control. The political opposition questioned constitutionality of restrictions introduced during the state of emergency. This automatically translated into poll results. At the turn of 2020 and 2021, the party of Prime Minister A. Babiš was losing support. In the winter and spring of 2021, a significant number of voters withdrew their support to the ANO party as it failed to manage the crisis in the Czech Republic. Despite all the mistakes, eventually the government more or less managed to control the pandemic. As a result, the support for the ANO (Wasiuta) party began to increase from July 2021.

These elections were a kind of clash between the ANO party and two oppo-sition blocs, the liberal-centrist coalition of Pirates and the local government movement STAN, the center-right alliance SPOLU (Civic Democratic Party (ODS), Christian and Democratic Union - Czechoslovak People's Party (KDU-ČSL), and Tradition Responsibility Prosperity 09 (TOP 09)). In addition to the criticism of the government, these groupings were united by demands to fight oligarchy and corruption, transparency, extensive digitalization of public administration, equal opportunities, and environmental protection (Wasiuta).

The negative trend for the A. Babiš party began to reverse in April, when it was revealed that Russian military intelligence officers were responsible for the 2014 explosion of an ammunition depot in Vrbětice.[3] This caused a major stir in the country, which pushed pandemic management into the background. The Action of Dissatisfied Citizens also began to dictate the tone of the cam-paign and successfully improved its position in the polls with new social prom-ises. The party announced its plans to increase pensions, parental benefits, build housing, fight cancer, and protect the environment. The party of Prime Minister A. Babiš also ran a negative campaign, referring to the Czech Pirate Party as an extremist left-wing party, neo-communists, and "eco-fanatics. The Prime Minister also accused the Pirates of being open to migrants, arguing that "a vote for Babiš is a chance to protect national interests, our standard of living, and our culture and uniqueness" (Krzysztoszek, *Plevák*).

The election was held under stringent hygiene measures due to the COVID-19 pandemic as during the elections to regional councils and the Senate. On Sep-tember 27, 2021, the Ministry of Health issued an emergency measure to pro-tect the population and prevent the risk of COVID-19 infection (*Hygienická a protiepidemická ...*).

Thus, new rules were in place for the elections. Seats were divided accord-ing to the electoral clause which specified the percentage required to win seats in the Chamber of Deputies. An independent party had to achieve at least a 5% threshold. A two-member coalition had to reach at least 8% and a multi-member coalition needed at least 11%. In the end, the SPOLU coalition (ODS, TOP 09 and KDU-ČSL) with its electoral leader Petr Fiala won the 2021 election to the Chamber of Deputies with 27.79% of the vote, the ANO move-ment of Prime Minister A. Babiš came second with 27.12%, the Piráti a Staros-tové coalition with its electoral leader Ivan Bartos came third with 15.62%, and the SPD movement came fourth with 9.56%. For the first time in the history of

---

3   The explosions of two ammunition depots in Vrbětice occurred in October and December 2014. In April 2021, the Czech government publicized a justified suspicion that Russian intel-ligence officers were involved in the explosions.

the independent Czech Republic, the traditional parties čssd and ksčm did not get into the Chamber of Deputies. The turnout of 65.43% was the third highest in the history of the Czech Republic (*Volby do Poslanecké sněmovny 2021*).

The opposition's success should be attributed to their strategy to form a coalition. Coalition talks began after the 2020 local elections. Politicians were motivated by two factors. Firstly, no one alone stood a chance to defeat the ano, as its lead in November 2020 over the strongest party was 10 percentage points. Secondly, the House of Deputies, which close to the end of its term, included were 9 political groups, many of which could not count on getting beyond the 5 percent threshold again. Coalitions of spolu and Piráti a Sta- rostové were formed in December 2020. The independent state media also contributed to the opposition's success by publicizing information about the embezzlement of EU money by the prime minister, as well as reporting on the government's tragic management of the pandemic (Szyszko, 2021).

On November 8, 2021, after the coalition agreement was made, representa- tives of spolu (ods, kdu-čsl and top 09) signed another agreement with the second electoral coalition of the Czech Pirate Party and stan. Petr Fiala, the chairman of the Civic Democratic Party, was appointed prime minister.

14.4   Summary

The covid-19 pandemic has significantly affected electoral democracy around the world and challenged decision-making. Politicians faced the difficult task of responding quickly but reasonably to a situation of a high level of uncer- tainty regarding the prevention and impact of the pandemic. As a result, some national governments decided to postpone and others to hold elections. The latter had to take steps to reduce the risk of spreading the disease.

An example of a country whose government decided to hold elections during the pandemic was the Czech Republic. The exception was the by-election to the Senate following the expiration of the Senator Jaroslav Kubera's mandate in constituency number 32 in Teplice in 2020. From the original date of March 28, 2020, elections were postponed to June 5–6, 2020 due to the state of emer- gency imposed in the Czech Republic. The remaining elections to the regional councils and one-third of the Senate (October 2–3, 2020) as well as the Cham- ber of Deputies (October 8–9, 2021) were held as scheduled. The elections were accompanied by strict hygiene measures. Polling stations were equipped with disinfectants to be used by voters and interiors were disinfected regularly. It was required to wear facial masks, take temperature, keep social distance, and minimize the number of people in a polling station. Three alternative voting methods were also used for people in quarantine, as they could vote from a vehicle (drive-in) in specially designated areas, in social facilities, as well as using a portable ballot box. In the case of the Czech Republic, the pandemic did not affect voter turnout, and during the election to the House of Deputies, it was the highest since 1998 (65.43%). The pandemic had a limited impact on public support. Prime Minister A. Babiš declared success after the first wave of the pandemic in 2020. However, already in the autumn, the Czech Republic was on top among the European Union countries in terms of number of infections and deaths due to COVID-19. Nevertheless, the government managed to rebuild its support in summer of 2021. However, it lost the election by a small margin to the opposition ANO and SPOLU, which attracted respectively 27.12% and 27.79% of votes.

References

Antoszewski, A. (2007). „Systemy partyjne Europy Środkowej i Wschodniej". In K. Kowalczyk, & Ł. Tomczak (Eds.). *Czechy, Polska, Ukraina. Partie i systemy partyjne. Stan i perspektywy* (pp. 7–26)., Toruń: Wydawnictwo Adam Marszałek.

Birch, S. (2003). *Electoral Systems and Political Transformation in Post-Communist Europe*. Basingstoke–New York: Palgrave.

Bureš, J. (2011). "Československý parlament v roce 1989". In V. Doubek, M. Polášek et al. (Eds.). *Parlament v čase změny. Případové studie z vývoje českého a československého parlamentarismu* (pp. 123–148). Praha: Akropolis.

Charvát, J. (2014). "The Czech Party System Change since 2010: From Fragile Stability to Stable Fragility". *Revista de Stiinte Politice*, no. 41, pp. 141–154.

Czyżniewski, M. (2014). „Zmiana systemu partyjnego Republiki Czeskiej po wyborach do Izby Poselskiej w 2013 roku". *Studia Wyborcze*, no. 17, pp. 91–109.

Czyżniewski, M. (2018). „Wybory do Izby Poselskiej w 2017 roku jako wynik zmian politycznych w Republice Czeskiej". *Acta Universitatis Lodziensis. Folia Iuridica*, no. 84, pp. 135 –147.

ČSSD zahájila kampaň, sází na červený svetr. Hamáček ukázal billboard a ztuhl mu úsměv. Novinky.cz. Retrieved from: https://www.novinky.cz/volby/kraj/clanek/cssd -zahajila-volebni-kampan-opet-sazi-na-hamackuv-svetr-40333555.

Doplňovací volby do Senátu Parlamentu ČR 5. a 6. června 2020. Retrieved from: https:// www.teplice.cz/doplnovaci-volby-do-senatu-parlamentu-cr-5-a-6-cervna-2020/ms -28364/p1=28364.

Dva roky s koronavirem. Jaké byly a co všechno přinesly?). Retrieved from: https://
www.vecernikpv.cz/serialy/koronavirus/11238-dva-roky-s-koronavirem-jake-byly
-a-co-vsechno-prinesly.

Fišarová, L., Jirovec, T., „Volby do zastupitelstev krajů a do Senátu 2020". Retrieved from:
https://www.codexdata.cz/literatura/LT126944?amp=1.

*Hygienická a protiepidemická opatření při organizaci a v průběhu vol*eb. Retrieved from:
https://www.mzv.cz/telaviv/cz/konzularni_informace_viza/volby/hygienicka_a
_protiepidemicka_opatreni.html.

Havlik. V, Kopeček L. (2009). „Kształt i stabilność czeskich rządów: wpływ systemu partyjnego i wyborczego". *Wrocławskie Studia Politologiczne*, no. 10, pp. 59–77.

*Jak se bude na podzim volit? Senátoři opozice chtějí umožnit hlasování i lidem z
karantény.* Eurozpravy.cz. Retrieved from: https://eurozpravy.cz/domaci/politika
/podzimni-volby-lide-v-karantene-by-mohli-hlasovat-korespondencne-navrhuj
e-czernin.2be29ae5/.

Jirásková V (2021), „Wybory w dobie koronawirusa – Republika Czeska". *Studia
Wyborcze*, no. 31, pp. 17–34.

Jirásková V., Skotnicki K. (2009). *Parlament Republiki Czeskiej.* Warszawa: Wydawnictwo Sejmowe.

Karanténa je překážka ve výkonu volebního práva, vnitro a zdravotnictví vytvoří komisi.
Retrieved from: https://www.ceska-justice.cz/2020/07/karantena-prekazka-ve
-vykonu-volebniho-prava-vnitro-zdravotnictvi-vytvori-komisi/.

Koronavirové volby drive-in: Hlasování z auta nepřineslo žádné zácpy. Retrieved from:
https://www.idnes.cz/zpravy/domaci/volby-2020-senat-krajske-volby-korona
virus-COVID-19-hlasovani-karantena.A200930_063529_domaci_hm1.

Krzysztoszek, A., *Plevák* O., „Czechy. Premier Babiš startuje z przedwyborczą kam-
panią . Nie chce euro ani przyjmowania nielegalnych imigrantów". Euractiv.pl.
Retrieved from: https://www.euractiv.pl/section/grupa-wyszehradzka/news/czechy
-wybory-babis-unia-europejska-euro-imigranci/.

Koźbiał, K. (2017). „Ewolucja systemów partyjnych Czech i Słowacji po rozpadzie
Czechosłowacji. Analiza porównawcza". *Przegląd Politologiczny*, no 4, pp. 119–130

Kuk na komisi a nasadit roušku, velí pravidla k volbě Kuberova nástupce. Retrievd from:
https://www.idnes.cz/usti/zpravy/doplnovaci-volby-senat-teplice-kubera-rousky
-koronavirus-epidemie.A200602_115831_usti-zpravy_pakr.

Lidé v karanténě budou moci k volbám, vláda schválila návrh Ministerstva vnitra.
Retrieved from: https://www.mvcr.cz/volby/clanek/lide-v-karantene-budou-moci-k
-volbam-vlada-schvalila-navrh-ministerstva-vnitra.aspx.

Mareš, M., Novák, D. (2019). *Ústavní zákon* o bezpečnosti. *České republiky: Komentář.
Praha: Wolters Kluwer* ČR

Na Teplicku začali volit Kuberova nástupce v Senátu. Vybírají z devíti kandidátů. Retrieved
from: https://zpravy.aktualne.cz/domaci/na-teplicku-zacali-volit-kuberova
-nastupce-v-senatu/r~5070bc1ca72811eaa7deac1f6b22oee8/.

Menšik, J. (2021). "Vzpomínáte? Kdo všechno už za čtyři roky prošel vládou Andreje Babiše". Novinky.cz. Retrieved from: https://www.novinky.cz/domaci/clanek /vzpominate-kdo-vsechno-uz-za-ctyri-roky-prosel-vladou-andreje-babise -40361339.

Nejvyšší správní soud: Rozhodnutí vlády o odložení senátních voleb v Teplicích bylo mimo její pravomoc. Retrieved from: https://www.irozhlas.cz/zpravy-domov/nejvyssi-spravni -soud-doplnovaci-volby-do-senatu-jaroslav-kubera-teplice_2004011559_aur.

Nouzový stav. Retrieved from: https://www.mvcr.cz/clanek/zpravodajstvi-nouzovy-stav .aspx.

Nový volební zakon. Retrieved from: https://www.seznamzpravy.cz/tag/volebni-zakon -50503.

Pandemický zákon vs nouzový stav. Jak se má změnit boj s koronavirem? Retrieved from: https://www.rekonstrukcestatu.cz/archiv-novinek/pandemicky-zakon-vs-nouzovy -stav-jak-se-ma-zmenit-boj-s-koronavirem.

Piráti a Starostové - program pro volby 2021. Retrieved from: https://www.pirati.cz /program/.

Prezident republiky Miloš Zeman vyhlásil termín voleb do Poslanecké sněmovny. Retrieved from: https://advokatnidenik.cz/2020/12/28/prezident-republiky-milos -zeman-vyhlasil-termin-voleb-do-poslanecke-snemovny/.

Prezident republiky vyhlásil termín voleb zvláštním způsobem hlasování do Poslanecké sněmovny Parlamentu České republiky. Retrieved from: https://www.hrad.cz/cs /pro-media/tiskove-zpravy/aktualni-tiskove-zpravy/prezident-republiky-vyhlasil -termin-voleb-zvlastnim-zpusobem-hlasovani-do-poslanecke-snemovny-parlam entu-ceske-republiky-16097.

Proč se v Česku volí dva dny? Většina států to zvládne za pár hodin). Retrieved from: https://eurozpravy.cz/domaci/politika/202168-proc-se-v-cesku-voli-dva-dny -vetsina-statu-to-zvladne-za-par-hodin/.

Rozvolnění od 25. května: povoleny budou akce do 300 osob, do restaurací či na koupaliště jen s rouškou, „Hospodářské Noviny". Retrieved from: https://domaci .hn.cz/c1-66764250-zive-ministerstvo-predstavi-posledni-vlnu-rozvolnovani -tykat-se-bude-hotelu-ci-restauraci.

STAN zahájili kampaň do krajů. Vyhnat zlé duchy z úřadů jim má pomoci česnek. Retrieved from: https://www.novinky.cz/domaci/clanek/stan-zahajili-kampan-do -kraju-vyhnat-zle-duchy-z-uradu-jim-ma-pomoci-cesnek-40334876.

Skotnicki, K. (2000). *System konstytucyjny Czech,* Warszawa: Wydawnictwo Sejmowe.

Skotnicki, K. (2018). „Senat Republiki Czeskiej". *Przegląd Europejski,* no. 2, pp. 159–174.

Szyszko, J. (2021). „Czeski sukces. Jak opozycji udało się tam wygrać z populistami". Polityka.pl. Retrieved from: https://www.polityka.pl/tygodnikpolityka/swiat/213918 6,1,czeski-sukces-jak-opozycji-udalo-sie-tam-wygrac-z-populistami.read.

Ukázaná platí. ANO *zahájilo předvolební kampaň.* Retrieved from: https://www.novinky .cz/domaci/clanek/ukazana-plati-ano-zahajilo-predvolebni-kampan-40335248.

Ústavní soud zrušil část volebního zákona. Rychetský se snaží dostat Babiše z politiky, rozčiloval se premier, https://domaci.hn.cz/c1-66877650-ustavni-soud-zrusil-cast -volebniho-zakona-pro-poruseni-rovnosti-volebniho-prava.

Wasiuta, M. (2021) *Kontrofensywa Babiša. Czechy przed wyborami parlamenta- rnymi*. Ośrodek Studiów Wschodnich. Retrieved from: https://www.osw.waw.pl /pl/publikacje/komentarze-osw/2021-09-23/kontrofensywa-babisa-czechy-przed -wyborami-parlamentarnymi.

Wybory regionalne w Republice Czeskiej: umiarkowane zwycięstwo partii ANO. Insty- tut Europy Środkowej. Retrived from: https://ies.lublin.pl/komentarze/wybory -regionalne-w-republice-czeskiej-umiarkowane-zwyciestwo-partii-ano/.

Vláda schválila návrh zákona, který umožní volit lidem v karanténě. Retrieved from: https:// www.mvcr.cz/clanek/vlada-schvalila-navrh-zakona-ktery-umozni-volit-lidem-v- karantene.aspx.

Vladni nesoulad. Retrieved from: https://echo24.cz/a/SMEub/vladni-nesoulad-vojtech -chce-zakazy-zmirnovat-hamacek-by-kolednikum-ani-neotevrel.

Volby do zastupitelstev kraju. Retrieved from: https://www.mvcr.cz/volby/clanek/volby -do-zk-volby-do-zastupitelstev-kraju.aspx.

Volby do Senátu Parlamentu ČR konané v roce 2020. Retrieved from: https://www .volby.cz/pls/senat/serok?xjazyk=CZ&xrok=2020.

Volby do Poslanecké sněmovny Parlamentu České republiky v roce 2021. Retrieved from: https://www.mvcr.cz/clanek/aktualni-volby-do-poslanecke-snemovny-volby-do -poslanecke-snemovny-parlamentu-cr-8-a-9-rijna-2021.aspx?q=Y2hudWo9NA %3d%3d.

Volby do Poslanecké sněmovny 2021. Retrieved from: https://www.seznamzpravy.cz/p /vysledky-voleb/2021/parlamentni-volby.

Volby do Poslanecké sněmovny Parlamentu České republiky: kompletní přehled. Retrieved from: https://www.e15.cz/volby/volby-do-snemovny/volby-do-poslanecke -snemovny-parlamentu-ceske-republiky-kompletni-prehled-1375826.

CHAPTER 15

Does COVID-19 Really Matter? The Case of Landtags and Bundestag Elections in Germany in 2021

Kamil Glinka

15.1 Introduction

It is difficult to disagree with the statement that the COVID-19 pandemic poses a challenge to the functioning of a democratic state ruled by law. The spread of the SARS-COV-2 coronavirus "tests" democratic procedures, among which elections play a central role (Katz, 1997; Thomassen, 2014). Reading numerous reports and publications (Idea, 2022; Jäger, 2021; Landman & Di Splendore, 2020). proves that the scope of the COVID-19 pandemic's impact on the elections is wide, regardless of whether it is a legislative or executive election and whether it is local, regional or national elections (Birch et al., 2020). In other words, it is worth paying attention to the fact that the COVID-19 pandemic forces public authorities and institutions to adopt a specific model of action that is to limit, as far as possible, the destructive consequences of the COVID-19 pandemic (see Glinka, 2021; Onasz, 2021).

The elections held in those countries which the literature on the subject describes as consolidated democracies (Agh, 1993; Linz & Stepan, 1996; Schendler, 1998; Antoszewski, 2004) is a particularly interesting case. The unprecedented political, social and economic crisis in the form of the COVID-19 pandemic raises the question of whether the maturity and stability of democratic institutions that are characteristic of these countries is not subject to some kind of "disturbance". Moreover, it provokes the reflection on the potential impact of pandemic challenges and limitations on: (1) the technical dimension of the organization of elections, (2) the voter turnout, (3) the forms of participation in elections, (4) the election campaign and (5) the election results.

The analysis of the elections that took place in the Federal Republic of Germany (hereinafter: Germany) in 2021 is an attempt to answer the above-mentioned dilemmas[1]. Therefore, the elections to four landtags: Landtag

---

1   The statement about the consolidated form of the government of the Federal Republic of Germany is based not only on the extensive literature on the subject, primarily political

© KAMIL GLINKA, 2024 | DOI:10.1163/9789004690622_017

of Rhineland-Palatinate (Ger. *Landtag Rheinland-Pfalz*), Landtag of Baden-Württemberg (Ger. *Landtag von Baden-Württemberg*), Landtag of Saxony-Anhalt (Ger. *Der Landtag von Sachsen-Anhalt*), the Landtag of Mecklenburg-Vorpommern (Ger. *Landtag Mecklenburg-Vorpommern*) and the elections to the Bundestag are the subject of inquiries.

For the purposes of this paper, the following hypothesis is formulated: the COVID-19 pandemic is reflected in the elections to the Landtags and Bundestag in 2021. The impact of the COVID-19 pandemic on the elections to Landtags and Bundestag is manifested on the five levels. They are: (1) the technical dimension of the organization of elections, (2) the level of voter turnout, (3) the forms of participation in the elections, (4) the course of the election campaign and (5) the results of the elections (see Table 15.1).

It should be emphasized that the author's goal is not t carry out an in-depth and detailed analysis of the course of pre-election rivalry based on the use of marketing tools. There are two reasons for this. Firstly, a review of the available literature allows one to believe that the COVID-19 pandemic dominated the campaign discourse, both at the level of Landtags and at the level of the Bundestag. All political parties raised the problem of "fighting" the pandemic and presented their own proposals for solutions. Second, examining the relationship between the use of the COVID-19 pandemic theme during an election campaign and its impact on election results is a task that goes beyond the limited scope of this chapter.

The chapter consists of several parts: (1) Literature review and background, (2) Legal and organizational changes implemented in the context of the COVID-19 pandemic, (3) Analysis of elections, (4) Discussion and (5) Conclusions.

For the purposes of the chapter, the author applies the elements of comparative analysis, the analysis of the content of legal acts (acts of national law concerning election issues) and the statistical data analysis. Also the specialized reports on the organization of elections in the conditions of the COVID-19 pandemic are a valuable source of information.

15.2   Literature Review and Background

The literature on the subject devoted to the functioning of the German political system is extremely extensive. The most important directions of reflection

---

science, but also in reports published by specialized entities. For example, according to the Democracy Index from 2021 (DI = 8.67), Germany ranks high, fifteenth in the world, which allows it to be treated as a "full democracy" (Democracy Index, 2021).

TABLE 15.1   Operationalization of the research hypothesis

Analysis level	Characteristics
Technical dimension of the organization of elections	The COVID-19 pandemic requires, in a 'natural' way, the use of special, above-standard organizational solutions that are to increase the security of the elections, i.e. reduce the risk of contracting the SARS-COV-2 coronavirus while staying in a polling station.
Voter turnout	Fearing for their life and health, citizens resign from voting. Thus, the voter turnout is falling.
Forms of participation in elections	The risk of contracting the SARS-CoV-2 coronavirus translates into an increase in the percentage of voters deciding on the choice of postal voting.
Election campaign	Due to the undeniable impact on the functioning of the state and citizens, the COVID-19 pandemic is one of the main topics of election campaigns.
Election results	The political, economic and social crisis caused by the COVID-19 pandemic is reflected in the voting preferences of citizens who criticize the actions of the authorities in the field of "fighting" the pandemic. Therefore, there is a change in the existing political power structure in the Landtags and the Bundestag.

SOURCE: AUTHOR'S OWN WORK

include: the constitutional order of the state (see Goldman, 1974; Allen, 2001; Rudzio, 2018; Marschall, 2018), transformations of the party system (see Smith, 1993; Roberts, 1997; Poguntke, 2000, 2001; Gellner & Robertson, 2003; Green et al., 2011), the political leadership of the chancellors (see Klein, 1996; Wilkens, 2020), the reunification of Germany (see Zelnikov & Rice, 1997; Bozo et al., 2016; Rödder, 2020; Schabert, 2021), the role of Germany in the integration of the "old continent" and the functioning of Central Europe (see Novotná, 2015; Müller-Brandeck-Bocquet, 2021; Opiłowska & Sus, 2021). Among the numerous publications, there are also those that deal with the issue of the functioning of the German electoral system.

As Thomas Zittel argues, the German electoral system combines the solutions that are unique in the world (Zittel, 2017; cf. James, 2003; Bartl, 2003). Referred to as the mixed system, it is the result of a broad, cross-party compromise (Scarrow, 2001; Behnke, 2007).

It is worth noting that both the elections to the Landtags and the Bundestag are conducted on the basis of the rules of the majority and proportional system. While the half of the members of these chambers are elected in single-member constituencies (Ger. *Erststimme*), the other half- in multi-member constituencies (Ger. *Zweitstimme*). Therefore, each voter has two votes: one of them can be cast for a specific candidate (according to the logic of the majority system), and the other- on the list of a specific election committee (under the proportional system) (Niedermeyer, 2013; Rabbe & Linhart, 2015).

Although all the subsequent elections to the Landtags and the Bundestag are of interest not only to scientists, but also journalists and commentators of political life, the votes of 2021 attracted unprecedented attention. Both the votings took place during the COVID-19 pandemic (see Hyde, 2021). Moreover, the elections to the Landtags were perceived as a prognostic of the approaching elections to the Bundestag. They were a "measure" of support for the previous governments of the CDU/CSU and SDP coalition, including its activities aimed at counteracting the pandemic crisis. In other words, it was expected that the distribution of seats in union parliaments could be a "harbinger" of the changes in the national arena, i.e. the end of the CDU/CSU and SDP coalition led by Angela Merkel[2] (Mielke & Kuleßa, 2021).

15.3   Legal and Organizational Changes

Due to the dynamics of the spread of the SARS-CoV-2 coronavirus, Germany, like other Member States of the European Union, decided to introduce many far-reaching restrictions aimed at protecting the life and health of citizens. The limited framework of this chapter does not allow all the regimes to be characterized. Nevertheless, the most important restrictions in force in Germany include: a social distancing order, an order to cover the mouth and nose, the need to undergo tests for the presence of SARS-COV-2 coronavirus and undergo quarantine, no access to restaurants, cultural institutions, sports facilities and retail outlets for people who are unvaccinated or who do not have a current, negative result of the SARS-CoV-2 coronavirus test. It is also worth pointing to the most serious instrument of "fighting" the COVID-19 pandemic in the form of the so-called lockdown, which was introduced in Germany twice (see Narlikar, 2020).

---

2   Angela Merkel's pre-election declaration to resign as chancellor is a separate issue.

However, the scale of the restrictions was not the same across Germany. The COVID-19 pandemic has proved that individual federal states, and not only the Landtag of Rhineland-Palatinate, Landtag of Baden-Württemberg, Landtag of Saxony-Anhalt and Landtag of Mecklenburg-Vorpommern consequences of the spread of the SARS-CoV-2 coronavirus. Taking advantage of a wide range of autonomy understood as the right to decide on the directions of internal policy, trade unions regulated the functioning of sectoral areas (e.g. health care, social assistance, education, culture, public transport, labor market) in such a way as they considered justified and necessary.

When analyzing the legal and organizational changes related to the holding of elections to the Landtags and Bundestag, attention should be paid to at least three issues.

First, the election campaigns were special in many ways. As a result of the restrictions introduced, including banning the organization of public gatherings and mass gathering, the burden of the election was concentrated on the Internet space. Thus, competing political parties and candidates reached for the Internet, i.e. social media, blogs, forums and websites. On the other hand, traditional rallies and conventions as well as direct meetings with voters have been severely limited (Guardian, 2021; DW, 2021).

Second, the context of the organization of individual elections, despite the fact that they all fell within the COVID-19 pandemic, was not the same. The elections to the Landtag of Rhineland-Palatinate and the Landtag of Baden-Württemberg (March 14th) were organized during the so-called the second wave of the COVID-191 pandemic,[3] which was characterized by a sharp increase in the number of cases and a noticeable increase in the number of deaths. The elections to the Landtag of Saxony-Anhalt (June 6th) took place in a period when both indicators were clearly lower. On the other hand, the elections to the Landtag of Mecklenburg-Vorpommern, similarly to the elections to the Bundestag (September 26th), were conducted in conditions of "waiting" for the aggravation of the pandemic situation characteristic of the autumn and winter period. Moreover, it is worth noting that the elections to the Landtag of Rhineland-Palatinate, Landtag of Baden-Württemberg and Landtag of Saxony-Anhalt were held under lockdown conditions (see Figure 15.1). The condition for active participation in the elections of 2021 was compliance with the pandemic restrictions currently in force. These were the same restrictions as in

---

3   Using the term "COVID-19 pandemic wave" is problematic. It should be noted that there is no consensus on how to ultimately classify the increases in the number of cases and deaths characteristic of the spread of the SARS CoV-2 coronavirus. Researchers of the subject present relatively different approaches in this (see Glinka, 2021).

Confirmed cases

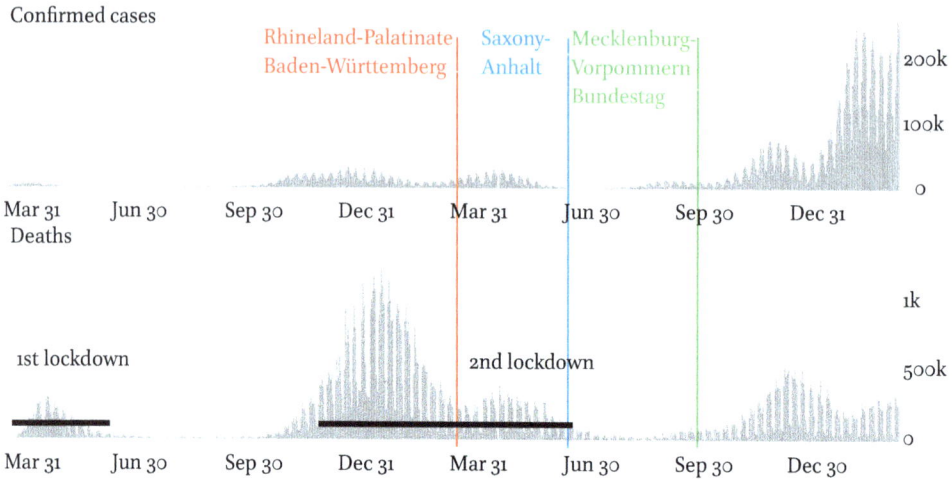

FIGURE 15.1   COVID-19 statistics and elections in Germany
SOURCE: WHO, 2022. RED REFERS TO LANDTAG OF RHINELAND-
PALATINATE AND LANDTAG OF BADEN-WÜRTTEMBERG ELECTIONS, BLUE
REFERS TO LANDTAG OF SAXONY-ANHALT ELECTIONS, GREEN REFERS TO
LANDTAG OF MECKLENBURG-VORPOMMERN AND BUNDESTAG ELECTIONS.
LOCKDOWNS ARE MARKED IN BLACK

other closed public spaces. Failure to comply with these restrictions was pun-
ishable by a fine. This does not mean, however, that no other, above-normative
solutions were introduced, which were also used by other Member States of
the European Union. These include, eg. lowering the threshold for the number
of signatures on the lists of support for election committees as well as extending the period of collecting signatures on these lists. However, these were solutions that were decided by the authorities of individual federal states.

Third, appearing in person at a polling station was not the only one form
of voting. All interested citizens could express their preferences by means of
postal voting. However, it is wrong to believe that the COVID-19 pandemic
has brought about any changes in this regard.[4] Postal voting has been present
in the German legal system for over sixty years, i.e. since 1957. Importantly,
starting from 2008, people choosing this form of participation in elections
do not have to justify their decision in any way. In other words, all citizens
are free to choose the form of voting (Müller-Török, 2020). It is worth noting

4   However, this does not change the fact that the ruling CDU/CSU and SPD coalition consid-
    ered in 2020 the possibility of holding elections to the Budestag in 2021 only in the form of
    postal voting (DW, 2020).

that compared to other European countries that allow voting without having to appear in person at a polling station (eg. Poland), such voting is relatively popular in Germany (see Musiał-Karg, 2020; Kapsa & Musiał-Karg 2020; Vashchanka, 2020).

15.4   Elections

15.4.1   *Turnout*

The analysis of the data presented in Figure 15.1 shows that Germany is in the group of thirty-seven countries in the world where an increase in the level of active participation in elections organized in the conditions of the COVID-19 pandemic has been recorded. The values in Figure 15.1 are cumulative. They cover all the elections, both to the Landtags and the Bundestag, that were held in 2020–2021. The cumulative turnout in 2018–2019 is the benchmark for the 2020–2021 election turnout level.

The analysis of the turnout level covering two consecutive elections leads to different conclusions. These are, on the one hand, the elections held in 2021 (elections to the Landtags and the Bundestag), and on the other hand, the elections held in 2016 (elections to the Landtags) and the elections held in 2017 (elections to the Bundestag).

It turns out that the increase in voter turnout was recorded only twice. While in the case of the Bundestag elections it was relatively small (an increase from 76,2% in 2017 to 76,6% in 2021, equal to 0,4%), in the elections to the Landtag of Mecklenburg-Vorpommern the level of active participation increased by almost 9% (an increase from 61,9% in 2016 to 70,8% in 2021, equal to 8,9%). The decline in voter turnout was observed three times. A decline of at or near 6,0% occurred during the elections in Rhineland-Palatinate (down from 70,4% in 2016 to 64,4% in 2021) and during the elections in Baden-Württemberg (down from 70,4% in 2016 to 63,8% in 2021). On the other hand, a significantly smaller decrease was characteristic of the situation in Saxony-Anhal (a decrease from 61,1% in 2016 to 60,3% in 2021, equal to 0,8%).

15.4.2   *Postal Voting*

Contrary to the changes in the level of voter turnout, which can be assessed as ambiguous, the percentage of citizens deciding on the correspondence form of voting has clearly increased. The increase concerned all four Landtag elections and the elections to the Bundestag. One can risk a statement that the COVID-19 pandemic led to the fact that the percentage of citizens voting by correspondence reached absolutely record values in 2021 (see Table 15.2).

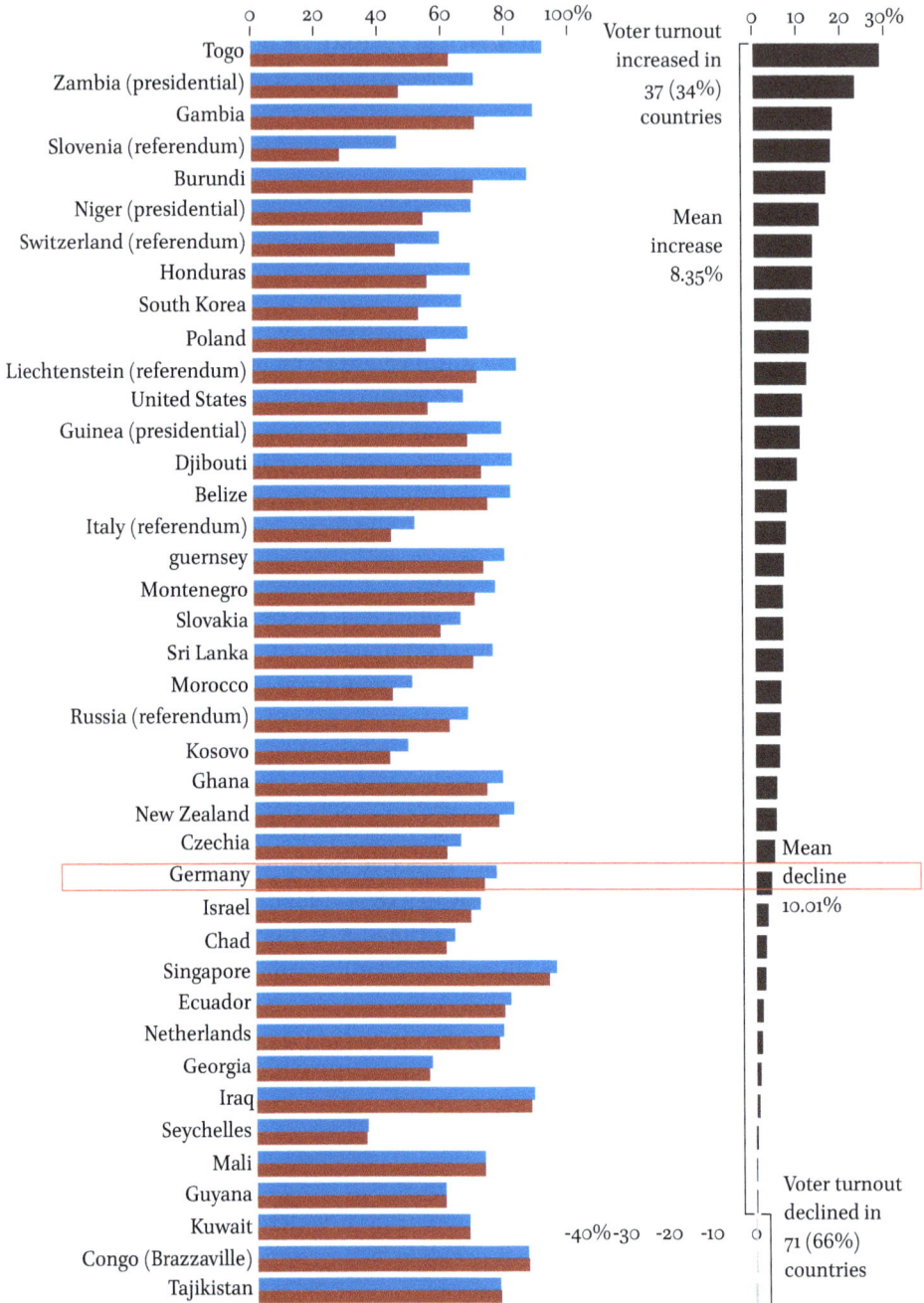

FIGURE 15.2   The voter turnout in Germany in comparison to other countries
SOURCE: IDEA, 2022. RED REFERS TO ELECTIONS 2018–2019, BLUE REFERS
TO ELECTIONS 2020–2021

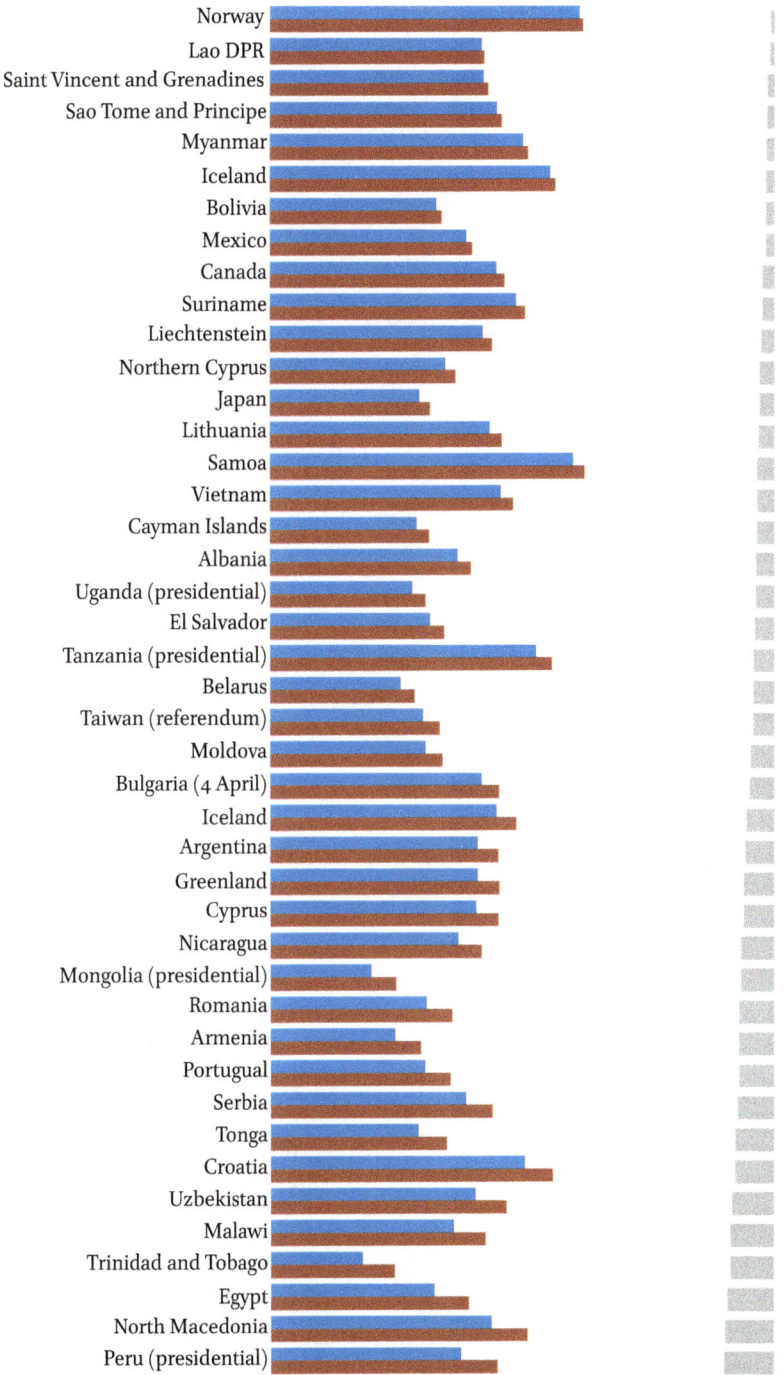

FIGURE 15.2   (*Continued*)

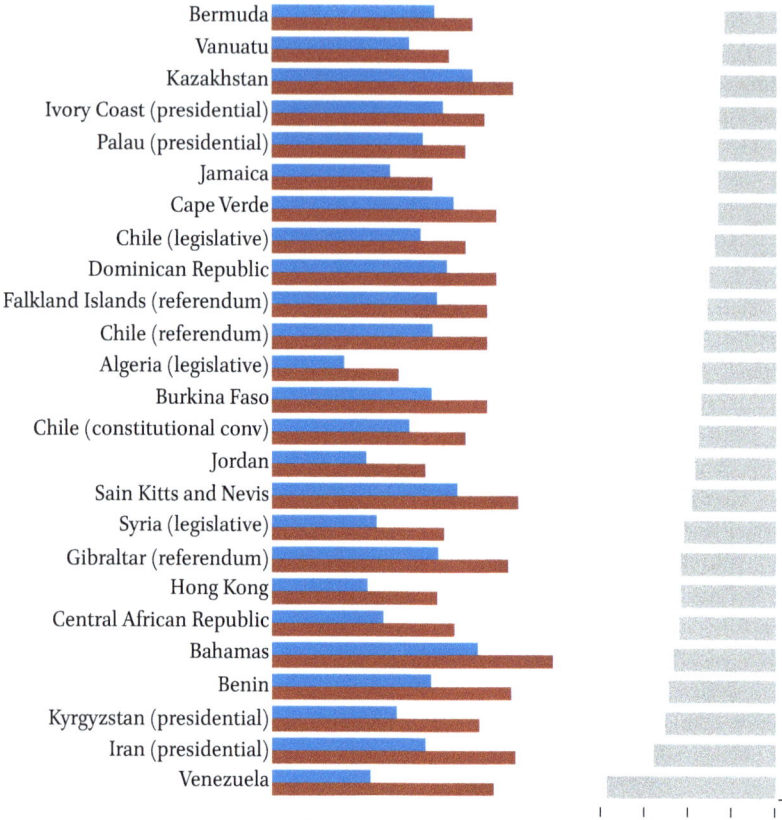

FIGURE 15.2   (*Continued*)

TABLE 15.2   Postal voting in elections in Germany

Elections	Percentage of postal votes by year	
	2016 or 2017	2021
Landtag of Rhineland-Palatinate	30,6	65,9
Landtag of Baden-Württemberg	21,0	51,3
Landtag of Saxony-Anhalt	13,7	29,1
Landtag of Mecklenburg-Vorpommern	20,0	34,5
Bundestag	28,6	47,3

SOURCE: RHEINLAND-PFALZ, 2021; BADEN-WÜRTTEMBERG, 2021; SACHSEN-ANHALT, 2021;
MECKLENBURG-VORPOMMERN, 2021; BUNDESTAG, 2021

As Daniel Hellmann notes: "Postal voting is a challenge to administrative capabilities. It opens up the possibility for several additional unwanted insecurities and managerial errors compared to in-person voting. This is not only true for states starting to adopt mail-in voting systems but also for states with a long-established tradition of postal voting such as Germany" (2021: 19; cf. Krimmer et al., 2021). Despite some organizational "stumbles", the postal voting procedure was well-organized. The increase of postal voters over 100% was recorded in the three federal states: Rhineland-Palatinate, Baden-Württemberg and Saxony-Anhalt. What is more, in the case of the elections to the Landtag of Mecklenburg-Vorpommern and the Bundestag, the percentage of citizens voting by mail increased by around 80%.

15.4.3   *Elections Campaign*

As it was signaled in the earlier part of the chapter, the COVID-19 pandemic was one of the most important, if not the most important topic of the election campaigns in 2021. Rival political parties and candidates formulated their own proposals to "fight" the pandemic crisis, starting with demands regarding the lockdown, quarantines and vaccinations, ending with the reorganization of the functioning of public transport, the labor market, the health care system, social welfare system, education, etc. The criticism of the current strategy of "fighting" the COVID-19 pandemic formulated by political opponents of the CDU/CSU and SPD coalition was a characteristic element of the campaign discourse. Importantly, party leaders and candidates running in the elections to both the Landtag and the Bundestag were the authors of the criticism.

Table 15.3 presents selected, but representative topics of the election campaigns before the elections of the Landtags and the Bundestag related to the COVID-19 pandemic.

It is worth noting that the COVID-19 pandemic was the source of at least a few campaign themes. In addition to the topics typical of all the analyzed elections - referred to as "common topics" - the so-called "different topics" became a part of campaign agenda.

The distinguishing features of the election campaigns in Rhineland-Palatinate and Baden-Württemberg could be observed not only in the so-called mask scandal, but also in the activity of the so-called nonconformist movement. While in the first case the accusations made against CDU deputies to the Bundestag worked in favor of the opposition groups, in the second case all the starting groups showed an unequivocally critical attitude towards the postulates put forward by the *Querdenken* (DW, 2021a, 2021b, 2021d, 2021e; BBC, 2021; StN, 2021).

The election campaigns for the Landtag of Saxony-Anhalt, like the campaign before the elections to the Landtag of Mecklenburg-Vorpommer,

TABLE 15.3   The COVID-19 pandemic as a topic of the elections campaigns in 2021

Elections (date)	Topic of elections campaigns	
	"Common"	"Different"
– Landtag of Rhineland-Palatinate (March, 14th 2021) – Landtag of Baden-Württemberg (March, 14th 2021) – Landtag of Saxony-Anhalt (June, 6th 2021) – Landtag of Mecklenburg-Vorpommern (September, 26th 2021) – Bundestag (September, 26th 2021)	– the criticism of the strategy of „fighting" against the COVID-19 pandemic implemented by the federal government by opposition parties and candidates – proposals for "rebuilding" the state after the COVID-19 pandemic crisis	– "mask scandal" (accusations that the Bundestag CDU deputies received remuneration in exchange for instructing the federal government to manufacturers of protective masks known to them) – nonconformist movement (Ger. *Querdenken*) against the restrictions on personal and civil liberties introduced as part of the "fight" against the COVID-19 pandemic – education reform (flexibility in the operation of educational and educational institutions) – remote work (change of labor law) – digitization of schools (the need to equip students and teachers with IT equipment and skills necessary to implement the education process under lockdown conditions) – obligatory vaccination against the SARS-COV-2 coronavirus – social support for people and companies affected by the COVID-19 pandemic

SOURCE: AUTHOR'S OWN WORK ON THE BASIS OF: GUARDIAN, 2021; DW, 2021A, 2021B, 2021C, 2021D, 2021E; BBC, 2021; NDR, 2021; MDR 2021; STN, 2021

were different from the campaigns carried out in Rhineland-Palatinate and Baden-Württemberg. A noticeably smaller number of pandemic topics was an element that diversified the campaign discourse. This does not mean, obviously, that the topics of this type did not engage public attention at all. However, they largely coincided with the topics of the election campaign to the Bundestag (MDR, 2021; NDR, 2021).

When analyzing the election campaign to Budestag, it should be noted that almost all political parties proposed digitization of schools. The FDP was the greatest advocate of this type of change. The proposals formulated by the FDP were so innovative that they assumed using the potential of artificial intelligence (AI) in order to optimize the education process. An important topic of the campaign was also the obligation to vaccinate against the SARS-CoV-2 coronavirus. The competing groups also stressed the need to provide social support to individuals and entrepreneurs affected by the COVID-19 pandemic. CDU was the spokesman for such solutions, who was losing in the polls, or rather her candidate for the office of chancellor – Armin Laschet. In line with the CDU's postulates, the catalog of those eligible for such assistance should include not only the elderly (retirees and pensioners), the disabled and the unemployed, but also all those who receive the minimum wage (DW, 2021c).

15.4.4   *Results*

The elections on March 14th, 2021 did not bring about any major changes in the structure of political competition. The existing coalitions retained their position in both federal states. In Rhineland-Palatinate it was a coalition of the SDP, FDP and the Greens. Malu Dryer from the SDP retained the post of prime minister (see Table 15.4). In Baden-Württemberg, in turn, the coalition formed by the Greens and the CDU strengthened its position. It should be emphasized in this context that the number of seats controlled by the Greens has increased – this is an increase from 47 in 2016 to as much as 58 in 2021. Winfried Kretschmann from the Greens retained the post of prime minister (see Table 15.5).

Contrary to the post-election balance of power in Rhineland-Palatinate and Baden-Württemberg, the results of the elections to the Landtag of Saxony-Anhalt (June, 6th 2021) resulted in the change in the existing balance of political forces. The coalition formed by the CDU, SDP and the Greens (the so-called Kenya coalition)[5] gave way to an agreement concluded by the CDU,

---

5   Kenya coalition refers to a governing coalition among the parties of the CDU/CSU), SPD and the Green Party. The name comes from the traditional colours of the parties (the CDU represented by black, the SPD by red and the Greens by green). These colours are also the colours of the Kenyan flag.

TABLE 15.4   2016 and 2021 elections to the Landtag of Rhineland-Palatinate - distribution of
              seats

	2016		2021
Political party	Number of seats	Political party	Number of seats
SDP	39	SDP	39
CDU	35	CDU	31
AfD	14	AfD	9
FDP	7	FDP	6
The Greens	6	The Left	10
–	–	Free Voters	6

SOURCE: RHINELAND-PALATINATE, 2016; 2021. THE POLITICAL PARTIES THAT MAKE UP
THE PARLIAMENTARY MAJORITY ARE MARKED IN GRAY

TABLE 15.5   2016 and 2021 elections to the Landtag of Baden-Württemberg - distribution of
              seats

	2016		2021
Political party	Number of seats	Political party	Number of seats
The Greens	47	The Greens	58
CDU	42	CDU	42
AfD	23	AfD	17
SDP	19	SDP	19
FDP	12	FDP	18

SOURCE: BADEN-WÜRTTEMBERG, 2016; 2021. THE POLITICAL PARTIES THAT MAKE UP THE
PARLIAMENTARY MAJORITY ARE MARKED IN GRAY

SDP and PFD (see Table 15.6). It is worth noting that Reiner Haseloff (CDU)
retained the position of prime minister.

When analyzing the results of the elections to the Landtag of
Mecklenburg-Vorpommern, it should be noted that while in the years 2016–
2021 the spearhead of the government was maintained by the SDP-CDU coalition (which was, in a sense, a "reflection" of the situation prevailing on the
national arena), the elections of 2021 transferred the change in the form of an
agreement between the SDP and Linke (see Table 15.7). However, the function

TABLE 15.6   2016 and 2021 elections to the Landtag of Saxony-Anhalt - distribution of seats

2016		2021	
Political party	Number of seats	Political party	Number of seats
CDU	30	CDU	40
AfD	25	AfD	23
The Left	16	The Left	12
SDP	11	SDP	9
The Greens	5	The Greens	6
–	–	FDP	7

TABLE 15.7   2016 and 2021 elections to the Landtag of Mecklenburg-Vorpommern - distribution of seats

2016		2021	
Political party	Number of seats	Political party	Number of seats
SDP	26	SDP	34
AfD	18	AfD	14
CDU	16	CDU	12
The Left	11	The Left	9
–	–	The Greens	5
		FDP	5

of prime minister was still held by the politics of the SDP: until 2017, Rewin Sellering, and from 2017, Manuel Schwesig.[6]

However, the elections to the Bundestag (September, 26th 2021) brought the most serious changes. The coalition formed by the CDU/CSU and the SDP (the so-called grand coalition) has lost its parliamentary majority. The helm of the government was taken over by the SPD, FDP and Greens (see Table 15.8).

---

6 The change in the position of prime minister was caused by Erwin Sellering's health problems. It was therefore not politically motivated.

TABLE 15.8   2016 and 2021 elections to the Bundestag - distribution of seats

2016		2021	
Political party	Number of seats	Political party	Number of seats
CDU/CSU	246	CDU/CSU	197
SDP	153	SDP	206
AfD	94	AfD	118
FDP	80	FDP	92
The Left	69	The Left	39
The Greens	67	The Greens	83

SOURCE: BUNDESTAG 2016; 2021. THE POLITICAL PARTIES THAT MAKE UP THE
PARLIAMENTARY MAJORITY ARE MARKED IN GRAY

Olaf Scholz (SDP) took the office of chancellor, replacing Angela Merkel
(CDU). One may be tempted to say that the Christian Democrats, ruling for fifteen years, suffered the consequences of a pandemic crisis, or rather social dissatisfaction with the way in which the pandemic was "managed". This does not
mean, obviously, that it was the only reason for the electoral failure. Certainly,
however, the COVID-19 pandemic did not make it easier for the Christian Democrats to fight to maintain the level of support from 2016.

15.5   Discussion

Although the organization of elections during the COVID-19 pandemic is a difficult undertaking that requires special precautions, the analysis shows that it
can meet all the democratic standards, from the principles of organizing an
election campaign to the freedom and secret of voting.

This does not mean, however, that the COVID-19 pandemic does not affect the
"celebration of democracy", whether it is a Landtag election or an election to the
Bundestag. On the contrary, it influences the choices, at least on several levels.

First, the COVID-19 pandemic has forced the adoption of "above-average"
organizational solutions related to the elections. Apart from the generally
applicable order to maintain social distance and cover the nose and mouth,
a number of minor regulations have been introduced, such as lowering the
required limit of signatures of the support for electoral lists, or extending the
period for collecting these signatures.

Secondly, voter turnout decreased, but not in all elections. As it
has been proved, in two cases (namely the elections to the Landtag of

Mecklenburg-Vorpommern and to the Bundestag), the percentage of people participating in the vote increased, which was in contrast to the concerns expressed by citizens about their own and their relatives' safety.

Third, one can risk a statement that the COVID-19 pandemic has strengthened the tendency to choose the postal form of voting. In absolutely every analyzed case, the increase in the number of citizens voting by mail was abrupt, even exceeding 100%.

Fourth, the crisis caused by the spread of the SARS-CoV-2 coronavirus was an important topic of election campaigns not only at the level of the Bundastag, but also the Landtags. In addition to the so-called common topics, public attention focused on the topics specific to individual campaigns. They were: the 'mask scandal', the nonconformist movement, the demand for digitization of schools and a project to support those citizens who were particularly affected by the pandemic crisis.

Fifthly, the pandemic crisis appears to have had an impact on changing the structure of political competition at the legislative level. In a few cases, the "ownership" of political parties changed, which led to the formation of new parliamentary majorities. A striking example of such a change is the defeat of the CDU/CSU and the formation of the government of the SDP, FDP and the Greens headed by Olaf Scholzt.

15.6   Conclusion

Taking into account the above, it can be concluded that the formulated hypothesis can be confirmed, but not fully.

First, it turns out that despite the fact that elections were held in such a special period as the COVID-19 pandemic, there was an increase in voter turnout in elections to Landtag of Mecklenburg-Vorpommern as well as Bundestag. It seems that this can be explained by the popularity of postal voting and the success of the social campaign that explained the advantages of choosing this form of voting. The increase in the turnout level may also be interpreted in terms of citizens' attachment to the institution of elections as a democratic form of political control.

Second, the pandemic crisis did not translate into a change in the existing balance of power in the two federal states. In other words, the opposition to the federal government coalitions in Rhineland-Palatinate and Baden-Württemberg, which after all conducted activities aimed at "fighting" the COVID-19 pandemic, were not held responsible for the failures accentuated by voters. The criticism was addressed to the federal government, despite the fact that the governments of Rhineland-Palatinate and Baden-Württemberg participated in agreeing on many key decisions, e.g. on the introduction of a lockdown. This situation can be explained not only by the efficiency of the election campaign and the effective use of political marketing tools, but also by the constant electoral preferences of the inhabitants of these two federal states.

Bearing in mind the above, one can risk a statement that the failure to fully confirm the hypothesis can be explained by the maturity of the German political system. It should be emphasized that all the analyzed elections met the highest democratic standards, proving that it is possible even in such a difficult situation as the COVID-19 pandemics.

The presented analysis seems to provoke further, in-depth research on the impact of the COVID-19 pandemic on the elections in the post-pandemic period. It is worth considering whether, and if so, to what extent, the post-pandemic "reconstruction" postulate becomes an element of political rivalry.

References

Ahg, A. (1993). "The „Comparative Revolution" and the Transition in Central and Southern Europe". *Journal of Theoretical Politics, 5*, 2. pp. 231–252. DOI: https://doi.org/10.11 77%2F0951692893005002004

Allen, Ch. S. (Ed.) (2001). *Transformation of the German Political Party System.* London: Berghahn Books.

Antoszewski, A. (2004). „Tranzycja polityczna". In A. Antoszewski, R. Herbut (Eds). *Leksykon politologii* (461–462). Wrocław: Atla 2.

Baden-Württemberg (2021). "Landtagswahl 2021: Erstmals mehr als 50 % Briefwahl. Baden-Württemberg: Nur in 30 Wahlkreisen ging die Mehrheit ins Wahllokal". *Baden-Württemberg Statistisches Landesamt.* Retrieved from: https://www.statistik-bw.de/Presse/Pressemitteilungen/2021099?msclkid=dfc3a491adf711eca69c7b0b15fffe1f

Bartl, A. (2003). *Electoral system in Australia and Germany – a comparative study.* Munich: GRIN Verlag.

Bawn, K. (1993). "The Logic of Institutional Preferences: German Electoral Law as a Social Choice Outcome". *American Journal of Political Science, 37* (4), 965–989. DOI: https://doi.org/10.2307/2111539

BBC (2021). "The anti-vax movement targeting German children". *BBC.* Retrieved from: https://www.bbc.co.uk/news/blogs-trending-56675874?msclkid=9925b8b3b50a11eca54c407d279b020f

Behnke, J. (2007). "The Strange Phenomenon of Surplus Seats in the German Electoral System". *German Politics, 16* (4), 496–517. DOI: https://doi.org/10.1080/09644000701652516

Behnke, J. (2007). *Das Wahlsystem der Bundesrepublik Deutschland. Logik, Technik und Praxis der Verhältniswahl.* Baden-Baden: Nomos.

Behnke, J. (2007). *Das Wahlsystem der Bundesrepublik Deutschland. Logik, Technik und Praxis der Verhältniswahl.* Baden-Baden: Nomos.

Birch, S. & Buril, F. & Cheeseman, N. & Clark, A. & Darnolf, S. & Dodsworth, S. &Garber, L. & Gutiérrez-Romero, R. & Tanja Hollstein, T. & James, T. S. & Mohan, V. & Sawyer, K. (2020). "How to hold elections safely and democratically during the COVID-19 pandemic". *The British Academy.* Retrieved from: https://www.thebritishacademy .ac.uk/publications/COVID-19-how-to-hold-elections-safely-democratically-during -pandemic/?msclkid=a702b315b4ed11eca6e4d219c055bfbe

Bozo, F. & Rödder, A. & Elise Sarotte, M. E. (2016). *German Reunification. A multinational history.* London: Routledge.

Bundestag (2021). "Wahlbeteiligung und Briefwahl". *Bundeszentrale für politische Bildung.* Retrieved from: https://www.bpb.de/kurz-knapp/zahlen-und-fakten /bundestagswahlen/341117/wahlbeteiligung-und-briefwahl/?msclkid=a027e11fad f711ec9a918b0d89fb01a8

Bundeswahlleiter (2017). "Bundestag election 2017". Retrieved from: https://www .bundeswahlleiter.de/en/bundestagswahlen/2017/ergebnisse/bund-99.html

Bundeswahlleiter (2021). "Bundestag election 2021". Retrieved from: https://www .bundeswahlleiter.de/en/bundestagswahlen/2021/ergebnisse/bund-99.html

Burkett, T. (1975). *Parties and Elections in West Germany: The Search for Stability.* London: C. Hene&Company.

Democracy Index (2021). "Democracy Index 2021: the China challenge". *Economist Intelligence.* Retrieved form: https://www.eiu.com/n/campaigns/democracy-index-2021/.

DG RI (2020). "Improving pandemic preparedness and management. Lessons learned and ways forward". *Directorate-General for Research and Innovation. European Commission.* Retrieved from:

DW (2020). Niemcy. Wybory do Bundestagu wyłącznie korespondencyjne?. *Deutsche Welle.* Retrieved from: https://www.dw.com/pl/niemcy-wybory-do-bundestagu -wy%C5%82%C4%85cznie-korespondencyjne/a-53351341?msclkid=1096bb79ad f611ec859e56c72612d95b

DW (2021a). "Schnelles Geld mit der Maskennot". *Deutsche Welle.* Retrieved from: https://www.dw.com/de/schnelles-geld-mit-der-maskennot/a-56815403?msclkid =ddc79d34a7c711eca794713565be0e2d

DW (2021b). „Koronawirus, maski i dwie dymisje". *Deutsche Welle.* Retrieved from: https://www.dw.com/pl/koronawirus-maski-i-dwie-dymisje/a-56819796

DW (2021c). "German election: Chancellor candidates face off over COVID, climate change and Afghanistan". *Deutsche Welle.* Retrieved from: https://www.dw.com /en/german-election-chancellor-candidates-face-off-over-COVID-climate-chan ge-and-afghanistan/a-59021944?msclkid=dc304b17b4ec11ecac1f2d24f41d816b

DW (2021d). "German mask scandal: 'Unforgivable violations of ethical standards'". *Deutsche Welle.* Retrieved from: https://www.dw.com/en/german-mask-scandal -unforgivable-violations-of-ethical-standards/a-56833018?msclkid=06846dd9b 50b11eca57481a3f8544a39

DW (2021e). "Meet Germany's 'Querdenker' COVID protest movement". *Deutsche Welle.* Retrieved from: https://www.dw.com/en/meet-germanys-querdenker-COVID -protest-movement/a-57049985?msclkid=99243b9ab50a11eca5f55a6cb51a51ef

Gellner, W. & Robertson, J. D. (Eds.) (2003). *The Berlin Republic German Unification and A Decade of Changes.* London: Routledge.

Glinka, K. (2021). "The biggest Polish cities in response to the first wave of the COVID-19 pandemic. The perspective of municipal self-government administration". *Przegląd Politologiczny, 2,* 47–69. DOI: http://dx.doi.org/10.14746/pp.2021.26.2.4

Goldman, G. (1974). *The German Political System.* New York: Random House.

Gordon, S. (1993), "Dimensions of Change in the German Party System" In S. Padgett (Ed.) *Parties and Party Systems in the New Germany* (87–95) Dartmouth: Aldershot.

Green, S. & Hough, D. & Miskimmon, W. (2011). *The Politics of the New Germany.* London: Routledge.

Guardian (2021). "The Guardian view on the German election results: negotiating a new era". *The Guardian.* Retrieved from: https://www.theguardian.com/commentisfree /2021/sep/27/the-guardian-view-on-the-german-election-results-negotiating -a-new-era?msclkid=dc2fe12ab4ec11eca75ada9f78b22707

Heinl, M. P., & Golz, S., & Bosch, Ch. (2021). "A Comparative Security Analysis of the German Federal Postal Voting Process". *The 22nd Annual International Conference on Digital Government Research, June, 198–207.* DOI: https://doi .org/10.1145/3463677.3463679

Hellmann, D. (2021). "Where the electoral shoe pinches. Postal voting problems in Germany between reality and perception". *Paper prepared for the ECPR Joint Session 2021. Panel "Early Voting and Electoral Integrity".* Retrieved from: https:// www.researchgate.net/publication/351839994_Where_the_electoral_shoe _pinches_Postal_voting_problems_in_Germany_between_reality_and_perception

Helms, L. (2006). "Germany: Chancellors and the Bundestag". In: N. D. J. Baldwin (ed.). *Executive Leadership and Legislative Assemblies.* London: Routledge. https://ec .europa.eu/info/sites/default/files/jointopinion_improvingpandemicpreparedness andmanagement_nov2020_0.pdf?msclkid=6bc3a288a70311ecad6127823d6a9792

Hyde, R. (2021). "Health in the 2021 German election". *The Lancet.* DOI: https://doi .org/10.1016/S0140-6736(21)02127-9

Idea (2022). "Global overview of COVID-19: Impact on elections". *International Institute for Democracy and Electoral Assistance (International IDEA).* Retrieved from: https://www.idea.int/news-media/multimedia-reports/global-overview-COVID-19 -impact-elections.

Jäger, M. (2021). *Die Zulassung von Parteien zur Bundestagswahl.* Berlin: Peter Lang.

James, P. (2003). *The German Electoral System.* London: Routledge.

Kapsa, I., & Musiał-Karg, M. (2020). *Alternatywne metody głosowania w opiniach Polaków. Postawy i poglądy względem wybranych form partycypacji w wyborach.* Poznań: Wydawnictwo Wydziału Nauk Politycznych i Dziennikarstwa UAM.

Katz, R. S. (1997). *Democracy and Elections.* Oxford: Oxford University Press.

Klein, H. (1996). *The German Chancellors.* London: Edition Q.

Krimmer, R. & Duenas-Cid, D. & Krivonosova, I. (2021). "Debate: safeguarding democracy during pandemics. Social distancing, postal, or internet voting – the good, the bad or the ugly?". *Public Money & Management, 41* (1), 8–10. DOI: https://doi.org/10.1080/09540962.2020.1766222

Landman, T. & Di Splendore, L. G. (2020). "Pandemic democracy: elections and COVID-19". *Journal of Risk Research, 23* (7–8), 1060–1066. DOI: https://doi.org/10.1080/13669877.2020.1765003

Linz, J. J., & Stepan, A. C. (1996). "Toward Consolidated Democracies". *Journal of Democracy, 7* (2), 14–33. DOI: https://doi.org/10.1353/jod.1996.0031

Marshall, S. (2018). *Das politische System Deutschlands.* Utb.

MDR (2021). "Haseloff als Ministerpräsident von Sachsen-Anhalt wiedergewählt". *MDR.* Retrieved from: https://www.mdr.de/nachrichten/sachsen-anhalt/landtagswahl/haseloff-wahl-ministerpraesident-dritte-amtszeit-100.html

Mecklenburg-Vorpommern (2021). "Zahlen zur Wahl in MV: Wahlbeteilung bei 70,8 Prozent – viele Briefwähler". *NDR.* Retreved from: https://www.ndr.de/nachrichten/mecklenburg-vorpommern/wahlen_mv_2021/Zahlen-zur-Wahl-in-MV-Wahlbeteilung-bei-708-Prozent-viele-Briefwaehler,landtagswahlmv360.html?msclkid=e03c5959adf811eca6538cc6eb8c9d8d

Mielke, G., & Kuleßa, P. (2021). "Vor der Bundestagswahl 2021: Auf dem Weg zu einer critical election?". *Forschungsjournal Soziale Bewegungen, 34* (3), 353–359. DOI: https://doi.org/10.1515/fjsb-2021-0052

Müller-Brandeck-Bocquet, G. (2021). *Deutsche Europapolitik. Von Adenauer bis Merkel.* Wiesbaden: Springer.

Müller-Török, R. (2020). "Wie sicher ist die Briefwahl in Deutschland? Eine kritische Betrachtung im Lichte der Europaratsempfehlung CM/Rec(2017)/5 zu E-Voting". In J. Beck, J. Stember (Eds.). *Der demographische Wandel: Zwischen Digitalisierung, Aufgaben-wandel und neuem Personalmanagement* (59–72). Baden-Baden: Nomos Verlagsgesellschaft.

Musiał-Karg, M. (2020). *Elektroniczne głosowanie w opiniach Polaków. Postawy i poglądy na temat e-voting.* Poznań: Wydawnictwo Wydziału Nauk Politycznych i Dziennikarstwa UAM.

Narlikar, A. (2020). "The Good, the Bad, and the Ugly: Germany's response to the COVID-19 Pandemic". *ORF Special Report.* Retrieved from: https://www.orfonline

.org/research/the-good-the-bad-and-the-ugly-germanys-response-to-the
-COVID-19-pandemic-66487/?msclkid=1d429e62b50911ec971a3f09b1fe8256

NDR (2021). Schwesig als Ministerpräsidentin von MV wiedergewählt NDR". Retrieved
from: https://www.ndr.de/nachrichten/mecklenburg-vorpommern/Schwesig-als
-Ministerpraesidentin-von-MV-wiedergewaehlt,koalitionmv156.html

Niedermayer, O. (2013). "Wahlsystem und Wählerverhalten". In: M. G. Schmidt, F.
Wolf, S. Wurster (Eds.) *Studienbuch Politikwissenschaft* (265–288). Wiesbaden:
Springer.

Novotná, T. (2015). "The Unification of Germany: A Case of the Transplantation
Model of Political Integration". In: T. Novotná (Ed.). *How Germany Unified and the
EU Enlarged. Negotiating the Accession through Transplantation and Adaptation*
(23–65). Cham: Palgrave Macmillan.

Onasz, M. (2021). "Quality of Democratic Election Process during the COVID-19 Pandemic: The Schedler's Chain of Democratic Choice Perspective". *Athenaeum. Polish
Political Studies*, 72 (4), 188–210. DOI: 10.15804/athena.2021.72.11

Opiłowska, E. & Sus, M. (2021). *Poland and Germany in the European Union. The Multidimensional Dynamics of Bilateral Relations.* London – New York: Routledge.

Poguntke, T. (2000). *Parteiorganisation im Wandel. Gesellschaftliche Verankerung und
organisatorische Anpassung im europäischen Vergleich.* Wiesbaden: Westdeutscher
Verlag.

Poguntke, T. (2001). "The German Party System: Eternal Crisis?". *German Politics*, 10 (2),
37–50.

Rabbe, J. & Linhart, E. (2015). "Wahlsystem-Effekte und die Rolle verschiedener
politischer Ebenen bei Wahlen in Deutschland". *Zeitschrift für Parlamentsfragen*, 46
(3), 608–621. DOI: http://www.jstor.org/stable/43977174.

Rheinland-Pfalz (2021). "Landstagwahl 2021". *Rheinland-Pfalz Statistische Analysen*, 54,
1–85.

Rhineland-Palatinate (2016). "Landesergebnis Rheinland-Pfalz – Endgültiges Ergebnis".
Der Landeswahlleiter Rheinland-Pfalz. Retrieved from: https://www.wahlen.rlp.de
/de/ltw/wahlen/2016/land/

Rhineland-Palatinate (2021). "Landtagswahl 2021: Endgültiges Ergebnis". *Der
Landeswahlleiter Rheinland-Pfalz.* Retrieved from: https://www.wahlen.rlp.de/de
/ltw/wahlen/2021/

Roberts, G. K. (1997). *Party Politics in the New Germany.* Landon – Washington: Pinter.

Rödder, A. (2020). *Geschichte der deutschen Wiedervereinigung.* München: C. H. Beck.

Rohrschneider, R. & Schmitt-Beck, R. (2019). *Parties and Voters at the 2013 German Federal Election.* London: Routledge.

Sachsen-Anhalt (2021). "Statistisches Landesamt Sachsen-Anhalt – Wahl des 8. Landtages von Sachsen-Anhalt am 06. Juni 2021", *Sachsen-Anhalt Die Landeswahlleiterin.*

Retrieved from: https://wahlergebnisse.sachsen-anhalt.de/wahlen/lt21/erg/kreis/lt .15.ergtab.php

Scarrow, S. E. (2001). "Germany: The Mixed-Member System as a Political Compromise". In S. M. Shugart & M. P. Wattenberg M. P. (Eds.), *Mixed-Member Electoral Systems: The Best of Both Worlds?* (55–69). Oxford: Oxford University Press.

Schabert, T. (2021). *France and the Reunification of Germany. Leadership in the Workshop of World Politics.* Cham: Palgrave Macmillan.

Schendler, A. (1998). "What is Democratic Consolidation?". *Journal of Democracy, 9* (2), 91–107. DOI: https://doi.org/10.1353/jod.1998.0030

Stimme (2021). "Kretschmann über schrittweise Lockerungen und mögliche Nachfolger". *Stimme.* Retrieved from: https://www.stimme.de/leben/wahlen/landtagswahl -2021/allgemein/kretschmann-ueber-schrittweise-lockerungen-und-moegliche -nachfolger-art-4453776

StN (2021). „Kretschmann nennt Corona-Pläne des Bundes „grob fahrlässig". *Sttutgarten Nachrichten.* Retrieved from: https://www.stuttgarter-nachrichten.de /inhalt.pandemie-kretschmann-nennt-corona-plaene-des-bundes-grob -fahrlaessig.978b5762-bff1-4263-915a-b5367c66c93e.html?msclkid=ef227518ab b411eca3cb4f56730a37a8

Thomassen, J. (2014). *Elections and Democracy. Representation and Accountability.* Oxford: Oxford University Press.

Vashchanka, V. (2020). "Political manoeuvres and legal conundrums amid the COVID-19 pandemic: the 2020 presidential election in Poland". *International IDEA.* Retrieved from: https://www.idea.int/sites/default/files/political-manoeuvres-and -legal-conundrums-2020-presidential-election-poland.pdf, checked on 3/20/2021

WHO (2022). "Germany. COVID-19 statistics". *World Health Organization.* Retrieved from: https://COVID19.who.int/region/euro/country/de

Wilkens, M. (2020). "The German Chancellors. Visual Strategies for the Image of the Head of State". In L. Cheles & A. Giacone (Eds.), *The Political Portrait. Leadership, Image and Power* (77–91). New York: Routledge.

Zelnikov, P. & Rice, C. (1995). *Germany Unified and Europe Transformed: Study in Statecraft.* Harvard: Harvard University Press.

Zittel, T. (2017). "Electoral System in Context: Germany". In E. S. Herron, & R. Pekkanen, & M. S. Shugar (Eds.), *The Oxford Handbook of Electoral Systems* (1–27). Oxford: Oxford University Press.

CHAPTER 16

The 2021 Parliamentary Elections in Bulgaria – A Long Farewell to Borisov

Jacek Wojnicki

16.1   Introduction

In Bulgaria – similarly to other countries around the world - the conduct of the 2021 parliamentary elections scheduled for April 2021 was greatly impeded by the COVID-19 pandemic. The analysis covers the evolution of the Bulgarian political scene in the period after 2020, which eventually led to the alternation of power, a key issue relating to the functioning of a democratic system. The scale of the socio-political crisis was vividly demonstrated by the fact that two consecutive parliamentary elections (in April and July 2021) ended with no possibility of forming a stable and effective executive government. A weak party system and volatile voter behaviour meant that a significant part of the Bulgarian electorate, critical of the policies of the political camp centered around Boyko Borisov, was unable to name a credible alternative. The problem was compounded by a growing dissatisfaction with the existing political elites and the socio-economic development of the modern Bulgarian state. The research question posed in this chapter is: how did the party system evolve in conjunction with the electoral process that led to the effective alternation of power in the Republic of Bulgaria in December 2021? How important in the above-mentioned process were new political factions, with an anti-establishment profile? In addition, the question involves the issue of the impact of the pandemic and the effectiveness or ineffectiveness of the state authorities in tackling the socio-economic consequences of the COVID-19 crisis.

The analysis employed several research methods: firstly, the comparative method was used to analyse several consecutive election campaigns to the National Assembly (in April, July, and the double presidential and parliamentary election campaign in November). Legal-institutional and historical-descriptive analysis was also used to describe the electoral system and the functioning of the analysed political and systemic institutions. The last research method employed was the decision-making method, in order to illustrate the decision-making process related to the formation of government coalitions and the shaping of the Bulgarian political scene.

16.2   Legal, Organizational Changes Made in the Context of Pandemic

The conduct of the election campaign ahead of the parliamentary election scheduled for April 2021 was greatly affected by the COVID-19 pandemic, as a result of which much of the agitation took place not directly in the form of gatherings and supporter rallies, but through traditional and social media. The ruling GERB's problem in the April campaign was the government's low efficiency in carrying out the vaccination process and a rise in COVID-19 infections in the country during the winter and spring of 2021. In the context of the fight against the coronavirus pandemic, BSP (Bulgarian Socialist Party) leader Kornelia Ninova declared an intensification of the vaccinations process and the start of talks with Russia and China on the purchase of their vaccines as a way out of the „vaccination trap" (Czarnecki, 2021).

The November vote, like the two previous ones in April and July 2021, was conducted with the use of appropriate voting machines and with adherence to strict COVID-19 sanitary rules (Manolova, 2021b). The COVID-19 pandemic powerfully exposed the weakness of the state structures, suffice it to recall that Bulgaria was at the very bottom of the list of EU countries for vaccination rates. By November 2021 (the date of the third election), just over 22% of the population had received at least two doses of a COVID-19 vaccine. Initially, the existing shortage was blamed on insufficient infrastructure, which prevented effective distribution of vaccines (Błaszczak, 2021). However, there were much bigger social problems related to the pandemic fight, notably conspiracy theories that were widespread in the public discourse and an effective disinformation campaign that had an extremely strong impact on the society. Another aspect was the lack of an integrated campaign to promote vaccinations while politicians avoided giving credible answers to questions about the need to introduce compulsory vaccinations. In November 2021, the fourth wave of the COVID-19 pandemic was sweeping through Bulgaria and the number of deaths was rising rapidly. Statistics indicated that Bulgaria was among the countries with the highest number of deaths per million inhabitants due to COVID-19. According to statista.com, in mid-November 2021, with 138.5 deaths, it was second only to the United Arab Emirates. In addition, analysts pointed out that the national health service was struggling to fulfil its basic duties, and fundamental problems included not only a lack of hospital beds, but also serious staff shortages among doctors and nurses. The systemic problems of the Bulgarian state health service should also be mentioned (Blaszczak, 2021).

16.3   The 2021 Elections' Context

In 2021, elections to the National Assembly were held three times, which is not common in established political systems. This testified to a serious socio-political crisis, an inability to form a stable government majority that would reflect the will of the Bulgarian electorate. While on one side of the political spectrum the situation was quite clear, with power in the hands of Citizens for European Development of Bulgaria (GERB) led by Boyko Borisov, an alternative to the existing system of power was only just emerging, a whole range of new political initiatives were springing up, some of which managed to transform themselves into classic parties. The socio-political crisis in the Republic of Bulgaria burst into the open in the summer of 2020 after the leak of recordings from a private Black Sea beach fenced off by an oligarch linked to the ruling camp. As a publicist writing about present-day Bulgaria pointed out: "when two years ago many countries ground to a pandemic standstill, Bulgaria pulsated with change. In 2020, Bulgarians took to the streets en masse to protest against Borisov's mafia and corruption abuses. The protesters were mainly young people: students of Western universities or workers who had returned to the country after the outbreak of the pandemic" (Siedlecka, 2022). This was a striking culmination of the process of mounting negative tendencies at the intersection of politics, economy and the mafia-criminal world, with Prime Minister Boyko Borisov becoming an emblematic symbol of these tendencies (Koseski, 2007; Ramet, 2012; Walkiewicz, 2018; Crampton, 2008; Engelbrekt, Kostadinova, 2020; Zloch-Christ, 1996).

The year's first parliamentary elections were called for 4 April 2021, a scheduled election after the end of the National Assembly's four-year term. With a rather low (by Bulgarian standards) turnout of less than 50% of those eligible to vote, the list submitted by the ruling GERB received the most votes – 25.8% (which translated into 75 seats). The second place went unexpectedly to There Is Such a People (INT), an anti-establishment party founded by tv showman Slavi Trifonov. The party's candidates won a total of 17.4% of the eligible votes, giving them 51 seats in the National Assembly. The main (until then) opposition party to Boyko Borisov's camp centred around the post-communist BSP, supported by the incumbent head of state Rumen Radev, received 14.8% of the votes cast (43 seats). The parliamentary mosaic was completed by two other parties – the Movement for Rights and Freedoms (DPS), representing the Turkish minority (10.4% of the vote and 30 seats) and Democratic Bulgaria (DB), formed as a coalition of parties describing themselves as centre-right and pro-European (9.3% - 27 seats) (Parties and Elections ... ; Gotev, 2021a; Manolov, 2021).

The results of the first parliamentary elections of 4 April 2021 meant, according to many analysts, a defeat for Bulgaria's existing political establishment (Seroka, 2021a). Despite the low turnout, both the ruling GERB and the post-communists from BSP, who had topped several polls, failed to mobilise a sufficient group of voters to ensure the ability to govern. The low turnout – even by Bulgarian standards – and the poor performance of the two main parties were primarily due to the COVID-19 epidemic (the Republic of Bulgaria was then in its third so-called 'lockdown' and the government's actions were generally assessed as largely ineffective by both experts and the public). It resulted in the demobilization of the older part of the electorate, and probably also of the voters involved in the public sector, a potential electorate of both GERB and BSP. Another factor worked against GERB, namely the economic consequences of the pandemic, which primarily affected the service sector (in 2020 alone, the tourism sector, very important for the country's economy, lost an estimated 800 million euros). Prime Minister Boyko Borisov's party was not helped by the propaganda game it played in the election period over the issue of North Macedonia's launch of accession talks with European institutions. It was aimed at capturing the nationalist electorate of BMPO (*Bulgarian* National Movement or WMRO-BND), but while its coalition partner did not make it into parliament as a result of these actions, GERB itself failed to improve its electoral result (Seroka, 2021a). In the April election, Borisov's centre-right party Citizens for European Development of Bulgaria (GERB) won 25.8% of the votes cast. This was about 7 percent less than in 2017 (i.e. in the previous election to the National Assembly). As a correspondent for a Polish daily commented: "If Borisov, who has ruled Bulgaria with short breaks since 2009, wants to remain as prime minister, he will be forced to look for a coalition partner" (Kokot, 2021).

However, it was not that simple, because even a coalition agreement with the Turkish DPS did not give GERB a majority in the Bulgarian parliament, and no other party wanted to form a parliamentary, let alone a governmental, alliance with Prime Minister Boyko Borisov. An alternative deal between the Socialists and the new ITN party also failed to materialise. In this situation, the head of state – pursuant to Article 99 point 5 of the Constitution of the Republic – orders the parliament's term to be shortened and appoints a caretaker government (Constitution of Bulgaria).

On 11 May 2021, President Rumen Radev signed a decree to shorten the term of parliament and order an early election. Bulgaria's caretaker government

was headed by reserve general Stefan Janev, the president's national security
adviser. Over the previous two decades, 61-year-old Yanev had held numerous
military posts at home and abroad – he headed the defence and security policy directorates in the defence ministry, was military attache in Washington,
served in leadership positions at the NATO Centre of Excellence for Defence
Against Terrorism in Ankara and worked at the NATO base in Mons. Several
ministers in the caretaker government, whose main task was to prepare new
elections, were members of the previous technical cabinet, appointed by President Radev in 2017. Yanev was Deputy Prime Minister and head of the defence
ministry in the previous technical cabinet. The composition of the caretaker
government was quite eclectic as it included representatives of both left-wing
and centre-right parties as well as experts, including several scientists and
businessmen, Harvard graduates. Yanaki Stoilov, a member of the leadership
of the Bulgarian Socialist Party, one of the authors of the current constitution
and a seven-term member of parliament since 1990, became minister of justice
(*Caretaker government*).

An important issue raised during the election campaign in the spring of
2021 was the growing discontent with the way the political camp symbolised
by Boyko Borisov and his party GERB exercised power (with some breaks since
2009). The socio-political crisis was aggravated by the fact that voters did
not find a worthy alternative on the Bulgarian political scene, seeing it neither in the post-communist BSP elite, nor in the fractured democratic power
elite. Thus, the July elections brought an unexpected success to the new party
„There is Such a People", founded by a tv and stage showman, who until then
had shown little ambition to participate in public life (Domaradzki, 2021).
As analysts of the Bulgarian political scene pointed out, a fierce and radical
political struggle was taking place in Bulgaria between the circle of the former
centre-right Prime Minister Boyko Borisov, who had ruled the Republic with
short breaks over the previous decade, and the new so-called protest parties
(Czarnecki, 2021.07.21).

The new political groups on the Republic's political scene shaped their electoral capital by demanding that not only the ruling GERB, but also the entire
Bulgarian establishment be removed from power (Pieńkowski, 2021). These
groups accused Borisov of creating an informal coalition supporting systemic
corruption together with the Turkish DPS, effectively controlled by oligarchs.
In turn, the post-communist BSP, which had held power alternately with GERB
in the Republic's recent political history, was accused of seeking to take over
and perpetuate these corrupt arrangements instead of eliminating them altogether. A breakthrough for the new political initiatives came with the mass

protests of the summer and autumn of 2020, which undermined in the eyes of the public the claims of the then head of government Boyko Borisov that the only alternative to GERB was a BSP rule. Meanwhile, the uncovering of a Russian spy network in both the Bulgarian Ministry of Defence and the National Assembly just two weeks before the July 2021 elections not only diminished support for the pro-Russian BSP, but also drove some GERB voters, who saw it as proof of the state's weakness under the rule of the political elite centred around Borisov, into the arms of new parties (Pienkowski, 2021).

President Rumen Radev was quite active in the new (spring) electoral campaign, seeking through the technical cabinet he appointed to expose as many corruption cases as possible during the rule of Boyko Borisov, who was in a sharp personal conflict with him (Seroka, 2021b) It should be added that the US administration was also active during the spring campaign. In June 2021, it sanctioned (under the so-called Magnitsky Act) seven Bulgarian citizens whom it accused of involvement in systemic corruption. Among those targeted were DPS-linked oligarch Delyan Peevski and a number of politicians and officials close to Borisov's government. The decisions of the Biden administration confirmed the allegations levelled by both investigative journalists and anti-corruption groups against the existing political and economic elites of the Republic of Bulgaria (Seroka, 2021a).

The second parliamentary election in the analysed period in Bulgaria took place on 11 July 2021. Compared to the spring poll, there was a certain shift in voter sympathies. The turnout – not only due to the holiday period, but also because of growing weariness of a part of the population with the socio-political crisis and due to distrust in the political elite – was only 42.2% of eligible voters. This time, it was the anti-establishment movement of a tv showman, There Is Such a People, that received the most votes (24.1% and 65 seats). GERB, running together with the Union of Democratic Forces (SDS), came second with 23.5% and 65 seats (including three for SDS). Meanwhile, the Socialists suffered another slump in popularity – the BSP's list received 13.4% of the vote, which translated into 36 seats. At the same time, there was a slight increase in support for the centre-right and pro-European coalition Democratic Bulgaria, with 12.6% of the votes cast (34 seats). The Turkish DPS maintained its stable support with 10.7% of the vote and 29 seats (Parties and Elections ...)

After the admittedly relative success, the leader of „There Is Such a People" proposed the formation of a minority cabinet, partly composed of ministers from the government of the former Tsar Simeon II (in office from 2001–2005). Slavi Trifonov was hoping to secure support from the Socialists and the Turkish

DPS for such a minority government. However, both the president and the parliamentary factions were quite sceptical of the political project that was put forward (Gotev, 2021b).

The Bulgarian president announced on 10 September 2021 that early parliamentary elections would take place on 14 November. Therefore, they would be held together with the first round of presidential elections. It should be noted that it was the third time that Bulgarians were called to the polls to elect MPs that year. It meant the dissolution of the parliament elected on 11 July, which was unable to produce a stable government (Wolska, 2021) The third and final attempt failed on 2 September 2021, when the Bulgarian Socialist Party (BSP) abandoned its attempt to form a new cabinet. The president was therefore given a mandate to call new early elections, while extending the life of the existing technical government led by Stefan Yanev. The National Assembly, which had been functioning since July 2021, with the largest number of deputies (but not an absolute majority) held by the anti-establishment party „There Is Such a People" led by popular tv showman Slavi Trifonov, was riven by deep divisions. The stalemate was further exacerbated by the fact that none of the parties expressed any real desire to cooperate with other factions in the National Assembly. Moreover, the parliament only managed to pass one law in two months – an amendment to that year's budget. It was a necessary step to release additional funds for expenses planned by the centre-right government of Boyko Borisov in order to tackle the COVID-19 pandemic (Wolska, 2021).

Analysts pointed out that the Bulgarian electorate supporting the isolation of GERB and DPS was represented by five parties, all of which had good chances of winning seats in the National Assembly. As for the anti-oligarchic parties – the case of Trifonov's „There is Such a People" and „Democratic Bulgaria" – the key demands relating to socio-political aspects were shared, which, however, did not eliminate significant ideological and policy differences, and lack of mutual trust. „This is a good background for quarrels, e.g. about the distribution of positions in the government, and opens them to attempts at manipulation by more experienced politicians from the political mainstream (GERB, DPS or the Bulgarian Socialist Party). Perhaps it will be different this time, because a good position of „We Continue the Change" may mean greater openness to political alliance with BSP, something that will change the position of, for example, Trifonov's party, which despite winning the previous elections was unable to win over potential coalition partners," concluded an analyst from the Centre for Eastern Studies regarding the situation in the Bulgarian parliament (Sieniawski, 2021).

The third parliamentary elections in the analysed year 2021 were held on 14 November, together with the presidential elections. Turnout dropped again, with just 39.1% of the votes cast. There were significant shifts, especially in the segment of the electorate opposed to the political camp represented by long-time Prime Minister Boyko Borisov. These enabled the formation of a fairly stable political arrangement – competitive to the political camp symbolised by GERB. The new faction We Continue the Change (Prodŭlžavame Promjanata – *PP*), founded by two former ministers, Kiril Petkov and Asen Vasilev, of the technocratic government, recorded the highest support. The PP list received 25.3% of the vote in the November poll, which gave it 67 seats. GERB came second with 22.4% of the vote (59 seats). The Turkish party DPS held a stable position on the political scene (12.8%, 34 seats). Three other parliamentary factions saw their popularity decline in comparison to the previous elections – the BSP socialists (10.1% and 26 seats), the anti-establishment ITN (9.4% and 25 seats) and Democratic Bulgaria (6.3% and 16 seats) (Parties and Elections ...).

12,990 district commissions were created within the Republic and 751 abroad in 68 countries. When it comes to candidates for elected state bodies, it should be noted that 22 candidates ran for the office of President, while 5,067 candidates ran for the National Assembly (with 240 statutory seats), put forward by 22 parties and 7 electoral coalitions. It was revealed during the campaign that 57 of them had links to the communist security services. Bulgarian law does

TABLE 16.1   Elections to the National Assembly in 2021

Party	Election I votes	Election I seats	Election II votes	Election II seats	Election III votes	Election III seats
GERB	25.8%	75	23.5%	65	22.4%	59
BSP	14.8%	43	13.4%	36	10.1%	26
INT	17.4%	51	24.1%	65	9.4%	25
PP	–	–	–	–	25.3%	67
DPS	10.4%	30	10.7%	29	12.8%	34
DB	9.3%	27	12.6%	34	6.3%	16

SOURCE: PARTIES AND ELECTIONS IN EUROPE. RETRIVED FROM: WWW.PARTIES-AND-ELECTIONS.EU/BULGARIA.HTML. * GERB – CITIZENS FOR EUROPEAN DEVELOPMENT OF BULGARIA; BSP – BULGARIAN SOCIALIST PARTY; ITN – THERE IS SUCH A PEOPLE; PP – WE CONTINUE THE CHANGE; DPS – MOVEMENT FOR RIGHTS AND FREEDOMS; DB – DEMOCRATIC BULGARIA

not prohibit former security service collaborators from running for office, it only requires that this information be made public (Manolova, 2021b).

As a publicist aptly concluded: "It cannot be denied, however, that Petkov and Vasilev won mainly thanks to voters who are professionally active, with higher education, from big cities, and people aged 18–30. Petkov's surprising success can be explained by the effect of a generational change in Bulgaria and the accompanying change in political imagination" (Siedlecka 2022). In September 2021, Petkov and Vasilev, who between May and August helped to expose many scandals and corrupt activities of the government of former Prime Minister Boyko Borisov, founded a new political party – under a rather general but flashy name – „We Continue the Change" (Manolova, 2021). Their main slogan during the election campaign was the fight against corruption and the issue of judicial reform. Petkov himself, who became a candidate for Prime Minister, quickly entered into talks with the centre-right coalition Democratic Bulgaria, the centre-left coalition Bulgarian Socialist Party for Bulgaria, and the winner of the previous July elections, the populist party „There Is Such a People". Negotiations began immediately after the official results were announced a few days after the vote. To avoid prolonging the growing socio-political crisis, President Rumen Radev called the inaugural session of the National Assembly at the first constitutionally possible date. At the same time, he expressed the hope that this time the parties striving to fight corruption would be able to overcome their differences and form a government (Manolova. 2021; Vygotska, 2021). A newly elected National Assembly – in accordance with the 1991 constitutional regulations – is convened for its first session by the President of the Republic no later than one month after the parliament is elected (Constitution of the Republic of Bulgaria, art. 75).

The parliamentary and presidential elections (held in November last year) significantly contributed to the strengthening of incumbent President Radev's position on the political scene (Seroka, 2021c). Although he failed to win re-election in the first round (49.4% of the vote), he was a clear favourite in the second round of voting, in which his main challenger, a GERB candidate, could only hope to win the votes of a part of the electorate of the other contenders. Rumen Radev, a former air force major general, was sharply at odds with the then Prime Minister Borisov during his entire first term (2016–2021). He raised allegations against the GERB leader of tolerating and encouraging corruption, nepotism and oligarchic schemes, casting himself as a defender of the interests of the so-called ordinary citizens of the Republic. As Rumen Radev was supported by the post-communist BSP, Bulgarian centre-right parties accused him of being pro-Russian. Although in his first term in office the president backed the Russian project to build a branch of TurkStream running through Bulgaria, it should be noted at this point in our analysis that the project enjoyed the support of almost the entire Bulgarian political class, including the political circles centred around Borisov. Simultaneously, general Radev was the initiator of Bulgaria's greater involvement in the Three Seas Initiative, primarily through the organisation of its summit in Sofia. At the same time, during the caretaker government of Stefan Yanev, appointed by the President (in May 2021), there was no warming of relations with Russia, as more Russian spies were detained (Seroka, 2021c).

At this point in our analysis, it is worth quoting two opinions relating to the public sentiment and expectations of Bulgarian voters towards the political elites. „There is a desire for change (...) so people are willing to vote for parties of change considered capable of forming a government," stressed Boriana Dimitrova, director of the opinion institute Alpha Research, adding „The two newcomers – Kiril Petkov and Asen Vasilev – are very enthusiastic but have little experience. I express concern that the next government coalition will be unstable." „It will be difficult to form a coalition between parties, of which the new party 'We Continue the Change' has gained so many voters" - said Ivan Krastev, a well-known Bulgarian political scientist and president of the Centre for Liberal Strategies in Sofia. The coalition „We Continue the Change" set out several priorities: putting an end to corruption and theft of state property, dismissing Prosecutor General Ivan Ghechev, not raising taxes but improving tax collection, necessary reforms in the health and education sectors, attracting foreign investment in advanced technologies; encouraging businesses to export, giving more freedom to small and medium-sized enterprises, a fair distribution of wealth and restoring citizens' trust in state institutions. The coalition was also unequivocally in favour of permanently anchoring the Republic of Bulgaria in the European Union and NATO (Deloy, 2021).

The political crisis in Bulgaria, which burst into the open in 2021, stemmed from the inability of parliamentary factions to form a stable government. „This is mainly due to the policy of isolating GERB and the Movement for Rights and Freedoms, which formally represents Bulgarian Turks. The latter is actually a party of the oligarchy and is seen as one of the symbols of corruption and oligarchisation of political and economic life in Bulgaria," emphasised Mateusz Seroka, Balkan analyst at the Centre for Eastern Studies (Sieniawski, 2021).

Stefan Yanev's caretaker government included two Harvard graduates – Kiril Petkov as Economy Minister and Asen Vasilev as Finance Minister. With an insight into their administrative structures, the ministers began to consistently expose the ins and outs of state capture. At the same time, seeking to hold the existing political and economic elites accountable, they did not act in haste, but pointed to the need for thorough analysis and serious systemic changes – including an effort to overhaul state structures in order to effectively stop draining the Republic's public finances. Petkov's and Vasilev's public activity strengthened their images as new breed of politicians – young, competent, honest and responsible, ones that had been in very short supply in Bulgarian public life after 1990 (Domaradzki, 2022; Milcheva, 2021).

As the Bulgarian anti-establishment formations were unable to form a stable and effective government over the period of several months in 2020/2021, an idea was born to form a new party, whose name, „We Continue the Change" (PP), directly referred to the style of politics represented by Petkov and Vasilev. The party, launched in September 2021, after less than two months emerged as the strongest faction in the National Assembly, receiving more than a quarter of the votes cast. Its co-chairs Petkov and Vasilev embarked on a mission to form the next cabinet (Domaradzki, 2022).

On 13 December 2021, the government led by Kiril Petkov received a vote of confidence in the National Assembly by a majority of 134 votes to 104. The coalition supporting the new cabinet was made up of four parliamentary factions – We Continue the Change (PP), Democratic Bulgaria (DB), the Bulgarian Socialist Party (BSP) and There is Such a People (INT). All the parties, despite many differences in terms of their programmes and ideology, shared the desire to break away from the pathological system of power symbolised by Prime Minister Boyko Borisov. Three of the coalition parties had been formed not long before, with the aim of tapping into the Bulgarian electorate's opposition to the iniquities of the post-communist transformation period and its support for radical socio-political changes. However, the governing process was shaping up to be quite arduous and exhausting, and the outlook for the governing team was – for various internal as well as external reasons – moderate (Todorov, 2022; Bulgarian Lawmakers) As a publicist rightly noted: "For some, Petkov is thus a hope for political decency and a guarantee of a more predictable Bulgaria than the one they have lived in over the past years. Others primarily want an end to the rule of insolent narcissistic men acting macho" (Siedlecka 2022).

Suffice it to recall that in early December 2021, the European Commission sent the new Bulgarian government a number of objections regarding the National Reconstruction Plan (NRP), which the Bulgarian authorities had presented to the EU institutions in mid-October. The objections mainly concerned the Bulgarian energy sector, as well as the need for reforms in the judicial system. It meant that a €6.5 billion tranche of EU funds, which the Bulgarian government hoped to receive, would be delivered at a much later date. In the area of judicial reforms, the EC expected the establishment of a control mechanism over the activity of the Prosecutor General. It should be noted here that Bulgarian judicial system regulations at that time practically did not provide for such supervision. The new Deputy Prime Minister A. Pekanov told the National Assembly that the Ministry of Justice had already devised a relevant mechanism. Judicial reform was one of the most important items in the new government's plans, which focused on the depoliticisation of the prosecutor's office, dismissal of the prosecutor general and creation of a powerful anti-corruption body in place of the existing commission (Lewicki, 2021).

16.4   Conclusion

The analysis looks at an attempt to recover from a serious socio-political crisis symbolised by the government of Boyko Borisov, which had significantly affected the development of the Bulgarian state since 2009. The case of the Bulgarian post-communist transformation has always been treated by many researchers as a specific model in comparison with other countries of the Central and Eastern European region. This was determined by multiple factors – a short tradition of democratic political institutions, an insufficient degree of socio-economic development compared to other countries in the region, strong influence of post-communist and mafia connections in the business and political world in the 1990s and beyond. All these tendencies were particularly exacerbated during the government of GERB and its leader Boyko Borisov. At this point, it is worth quoting the opinion of one of the leaders of democratic parties in Bulgaria, Christo Ivanov: Borisov does not have any views, he has simply realised that loyalty to European leaders ensures his impunity in the EU. That is why he quietly indulges in corrupt practices, manifesting a fake pro-Europeanism to the outside world. Even before Kaczyński and Orban came to power, he was dismantling the judiciary and restricting media freedom. Yet he managed to hide all this under the carpet because he was on good terms with Merkel. I am convinced that Borisov is worse than what you have in Poland and what is happening in Hungary (...) According to various public surveys, between 50 and over 70 percent of Bulgarian citizens believe that the government should step down and that the rule of law is threatened by the mafia which rules the country. No wonder that with such a public attitude, the protests are supported by all the opposition parties. We are talking about a really broad spectrum of political forces, which also include pro-Russian and Eurosceptic groups" (Cedro, 2020).

The sociopolitical developments in 2020 and then in 2021 were a direct expression of the growing public discontent with the actions of the Borisov government, identified with all the negative trends and phenomena described above. Support for GERB – despite some decline – was fairly stable and represented a quarter of the electorate, while the main problem was to build a credible and stable alternative to the ruling political camp. The anti-establishment party „There is Such a Nation" of tv showman Slavi Trifonov failed to handle the responsibility for the creation of a stable cabinet in July 2021, so the mission of forging a reformist faction passed to the new political movement „We Continue the Change". A situation where only the third parliamentary election held within eight months results in the formation of a stable government coalition is not common in democratic systems. Recently, a similar socio-political situation occurred in Israel. The coming months of 2022 will show how stable and effective is the newly formed structure of the Bulgarian political scene in the face of domestic and foreign challenges facing the Bulgarian state. This will depend on the success of the reform efforts of Kiril Petkov's cabinet and the durability of the government coalition formed in December 2021.

References

Błaszczak J. (2021), *Do trzech razy sztuka? Bułgaria w przededniu podwójnych wyborów*/ „Publikacje Instytutu Nowej Europy". Retrieved from: https://ine.org.pl/do-trzech -razy-sztuka-bulgaria-w-przededniu-podwojnych-wyborow/.

Bulgarian Lawmakers Confirm New Government After Months of Deadlock. 13.12.2021. Radio Free Europe/Radio Liberty. Retrived from: https://www.rferl.org/a/bulgaria -petkov-government-vote/31606371.html.

Cedro, M. (2020). „Bułgarski opozycjonista uderza w Tuska: wstyd mi za jego spotkanie z Borisowem". Dziennik Gazeta Prawna". Retrieved from: https://wiadomosci.dziennik .pl/polityka/artykuly/7845825,donald-tusk-christo-iwanow-bulgaria-opozycja -protesty.html.

Crampton, R. J. (2008). *Bulgaria*. Oxford: Oxford University Press.

Czarnecki, M. (2021.07.21). „Bułgaria po wyborach. Kto poprze rząd „bułgarskiego Kukiza"?. „Gazeta Wyborcza".

Czarnecki, Sz. (2021). „Bułgaria: kampania wyborcza w cieniu pandemii COVID-19" *Komentarze IEŚ*, no. 354 (51).

Deloy, C. (2021). "Legislative and Presidential Election in Bulgaria". Foundation Robert Schuman. The Research and Studies Centre o Europe, no. 956. Retrieved from: https://www.robert-schuman.eu/en/doc/oee/oee-1942-en.pdf.

Domaradzki, S. (2021.07.21). *„A kuku! Dlaczego showman Sławi Trifonow wygrał w Bułgarii wybory"*. *Polityka*, no. 31.

Domaradzki, S. (2022). „Bułgaria: harwardzki duumwirat". *Komentarze IEŚ*, no .495 (7).

Engelbrekt, K., Kostadinova, P. (Eds.) (2020). *Bulgaria's democratic institutions at thirty: a balance sheet*. Lanham: Lexington Books.

Gotev, G. (2021a). "Bulgarians vote for change, send three new parties to Parliament". Retrieved from: https://www.euractiv.com/section/elections/news/bulgarians-vote -for-change-sending-three-new-parties-in-parliament/ .

Gotev, G. (2021b). "Bulgaria's Trifanov makes 'take it or leave it' cabinet offer". Retrieved from: https://www.euractiv.com/section/elections/news/bulgarias-trifonov-makes -take-it-or-leave-it-cabinet-offer/.

Karp, J (Eds.) (2012). *Konstytucja Republiki Bułgarii. Seria: Konstytucja państw świata*. Warszawa: Wydawnictwo Sejmowe.

Kokot, M. (2021.04.05). „Po wyborach parlamentarnych w Bułgarii: o rządzie zadecy- duje satyryk i partie protestu", *Gazeta Wyborcza*.

Koseski, A., Willaume, M (2007). *Nowe kraje UE. Bułgaria. Rumunia*. Warszawa: Wydawnictwo Akademickie Dialog.

Manolov, R. "Slavi Trifanov: Bulgaria's miracle worker". Retrieved from: https://www .euractiv.com/section/all/news/slavi-trifonov-bulgarias-miracle-worker/.

Manolova, E. (2021a). „Wybory w Bułgarii: w nowym parlamencie znajdzie się siedem partii", Forsal.p. Retrieved from: https://forsal.pl/gospodarka/polityka/artykuly /8292851,wybory-w-bulgarii-w-nowym-parlamencie-znajdzie-się-siedem-partii .html.

Manolova, E. (2021b). „Bułgaria: wybory prezydenckie i przedterminowe wybory par- lamentarne". Serwis PAP. Retrieved from: https://www.pap.pl/aktualnosci/news %2C999216%2Cbulgaria-wybory-prezydenckie-i-przedterminowe-wybory-parla mentarne.html.

Milcheva, E. (2021). "Bulgarians put hope in 'Harvard tandem' to break political dead- look". Euractive.com. Retrieved from: https://www.euractiv.com/section/elections /news/bulgarians-put-hope-in-harvard-tandem-to-break-political-deadlock/

Parties and Elections in Europe. Retrived from: www.parties-and-elections.eu /bulgaria.html

Pieńkowski, J. (2021). „Wybory parlamentarne w Bułgarii – sukces partii antysyste- mowych", *Analizy PISM*, no. 31.

Ramet, P.S. (Ed.) (2012). *Polityka Europy Środkowej i Południowo-Wschodniej po 1989 roku*. Warszawa: Książka i Wiedza.

Seroka, M. (2021a). „Wybory parlamentarne w Bułgarii-zachwiana pozycja premiera Borisowa". *Analizy OSW*.

Seroka, M. (2021b). „Bułgaria-powyborcze pogłębienie kryzysu politycznego". *Analizy OSW*.

Seroka, M. (2021c). „Bułgaria po wyborach -wzmocnienie pozycji prezydenta Radewa". *Analizy OSW*.

Siedlecka, S. (2022.02.09). „Duet z Harvardu". *Polityka*, no. 7.

Sieniawski B. (2021). „Bułgaria: Trwa kryzys parlamentarny. Dziś trzecie w tym roku wybory. Czwarte już za kilka miesięcy?". Euractiv.pl. Retrieved from: https://www .euractiv.pl/section/demokracja/news/bulgaria-trzecie-w-tym-roku-wybory -parlamentarne-odbeda-sie-14-listopada/.

Todorov S., (2022). "Bulgaria in 2022: Can a New Government 'Continue the Change'?"; BalkanInsight. Retrieved from: https://balkaninsight.com/2022/01/04/bulgaria-in -2022-can-a-new-government-continue-the-change/.

Ushev, D. Gh. (2009). *Wähler und Parteien in Bulgarien: eine tiefgreifende Analyse der Wahltechnologien, Wahlakteure und Wählerverhalten bei den Parlamentswahlen in Bulgarien (1990–2008)*, Saarbrücken: VDM Verl. Dr. Müller.

Walkiewicz, W. (2018). *Bułgaria: dzieje polityczne najnowsze*, Warszawa-Białystok: Libra

Wolska, A. (2021). „Bułgaria: trzecie w tym roku wybory parlamentarne odbędą się w listopadzie". Euractiv.com. retrieved from: https://www.euractiv.pl/section /demokracja/news/bulgaria-trzecie-w-tym-roku-wybory-parlamentarne-odbed a-sie-14-listopada/.

Wójcicka, K. (2021). „Nowe rządy powstaną w Sofii i Bukareszcie", *Dziennik Gazeta Prawna*, Retrieved from: https://www.gazetaprawna.pl/wiadomosci/swiat/artykuly /8299193,nowe-rzady-powstana-w-sofii-i-bukareszcie.html.

Zloch-Christy, J. (Ed.) (1996). *Bulgaria in a time of change: economic and political dimensions*. Aldershot: Avebury.

Znepolski, J. (2019). *Bulgaria under communism*. London: Routlege.

CHAPTER 17

Non/elections in Pandemic Conditions. Parliamentary Elections in the Russian Federation in 2021

Natalia Kusa

17.1 Introduction

The 2018 presidential election in March was a great political event, probably every Russian knew about it. There were plenty of posters, information in the media, means of transport and public space in general, although Vladimir Putin himself did not actually run a classic campaign (understood as rallies, postulates, program, persuading voters, debates with opponents). In addition, their date was then set for the anniversary of the annexation of Crimea, so all over Russia, straight from the polling station, you could find a festival, concert or other event with free gadgets or snacks. On the other hand, in 2021, parliamentary elections were held by accident. They were not accompanied by any pro-turnout campaign that could be observed everywhere three years earlier. This election was not a display of the regime's strength and popularity, as United Russia has long enjoyed declining support, mainly systemically guaranteed (due to systemic counterfeiting, forced budgetary voices and the lack of an alternative). It was only about obtaining formal legitimation and avoiding protests from the opposition or voters who were deceived by fraud.

The parliamentary elections in 2021 took place under conditions that were significantly different from those in 2016, when the last parliamentary election took place. One of the main drivers of the change was the COVID-19 pandemic, which started in March 2020, with an exceptionally high death toll in Russia. However, what distinguishes Russia from other countries where the elections took place in a pandemic is the instrumental use of the restrictions introduced to limit the possibility of free participation in the elections. Comparing the elections in 2021 to the elections in 2016, one can see changes introduced on many levels. Within five years (although most of the measures were intensified just before the elections in 2021), the right to protest has been significantly reduced, the opposition has been dismantled, the main representatives of the opposition have been arrested, independent observation of elections has been prevented, online freedom of speech has been restricted and the non-democratic system of governance has been consolidated. Russia's 2021 parliamentary elections were exceptional not only because of the COVID-19 pandemic, and the pandemic itself served as the justification for the restrictions that made these elections virtually devoid of an element of competition and free choice.

The aim of the chapter is to analyze the factors that influenced the parliamentary elections in Russia in 2021 and the result of this election. The key will be to answer the following questions: how have the conditions for holding parliamentary elections in Russia in 2021 changed compared to 2016? What factors influenced the change in the conditions of the elections? How did the pandemic affect the elections, and how did the Russian authorities use the COVID-19 pandemic to increase their chances of winning?

The author of the chapter uses the method of institutional and legal analysis to analyze the factors that influenced the parliamentary elections in Russia in 2021 (analysis of laws and decrees regarding elections, the COVID-19 pandemic, the activities of the opposition, campaigning, voting; analysis of the activities of institutions and state bodies – the president of Russia, the government of the Russian Federation, parliament, political parties), the comparative method (comparison of the election conditions and the results of the parliamentary elections of 2016 and 2021) and the results of Russian public opinion polls.

17.2   Literature Review

When it turned out that the global COVID-19 pandemic, in addition to the health and safety of entire societies, also began to affect political processes, it also became the subject of interest in political science research. It quickly turned out that all preventive measures aimed at protecting the life and health of citizens also affect the functioning of political regimes, especially election processes. After the first decisions to cancel or postpone elections, researchers from around the world began to analyze the impact of the pandemic on electoral processes, including the impact of anti-pandemic actions taken by individual countries on the functioning of democratic and non-democratic systems. The impact of the pandemic and the reactions of individual governments to it over the entire electoral cycle, even creating the concept of pandemic democracy, was written by, e.g. Todd Landman and Luca Di Gennaro Splendore (Landman & Di Gennaro Splendore, 2020). Potential difficulties that may pose a challenge to governing bodies carrying out electoral processes in pandemic conditions have also become a topic of research (James, 2021). Researchers and practitioners also tried to compile a list of good practices that could help ensure the democratic nature of elections (Asplund & James, 2020), and analyzed the validity and effectiveness of alternative voting methods in a pandemic (Krimmer et al., 2021). Among the available studies, there were also some that analyzed not so much the impact of the pandemic on the elections, but the impact of the vote itself on the potential acceleration of the spread of the coronavirus (the case of the Czech Republic, Palguta et al., 2022).

The studies on the impact of the pandemic on political processes, especially election processes, also included analyzes of individual countries where elections during the pandemic took place or were postponed or canceled (Maizland, 2020; Maizland, 2020; Matlosa, 2021; Hamdani & Fauzia, 2021; Kim, 2020; Asplund, 2020). The International IDEA report (Asplund, 2020) also included an analysis of the pandemic parliamentary elections held in Russia in September 2021. However, this analysis focuses on the organizational aspects and changes introduced to the electoral process as a result of the pandemic. However, there are no studies in which the pandemic is analyzed in the context of political processes transforming Russia into a country devoid of opposition and alternative choices. This chapter aims to fill this gap.

In this chapter, the author, analyzing the case of Russia, refers to the concept of electoral authoritarianism (Gelman, 2013; Golosov, 2011; Levitsky, Way, 2010; Nadskakuła-Kaczmarczyk, 2017; Kusa, 2020), in which election is characterized by unequal rules of the game, which it is understood, i.a. high entry barriers (e.g. high barrier thresholds, complicated candidate registration procedures), unequal access of candidates to media and financial resources, the government's use of bureaucracy to increase the number of votes and election frauds (Gelman, 2013, p. 4). However, considering the events of recent years – also described in this chapter (including the attempted murder and imprisonment of Alexei Navalny, liquidation of the opposition, restriction of freedom on the Internet) – it also seems reasonable to refer to the concept of a totalitarian system, the symptoms of which were already observed in Russia since at least 2014 (Bäcker & Rak, 2018; Nadskakuła-Kaczmarczyk, 2016)

17.3 Legal and Organizational Changes Made in the Context of the Pandemic

The parliamentary elections in 2021 were not the first election event in the Russian Federation since the outbreak of the COVID-19 pandemic. Most of the solutions proposed in the parliamentary election had previously been tested during the Russian constitutional referendum held in July 2020 and during the regional elections held in September 2020.

The first under pandemic conditions was the so-called nationwide vote on constitutional amendments, which took place from June 25 to July 1, 2020. The course of this vote revealed, first of all, the regime's very poor preparation for organizing such an event under pandemic conditions, as well as the lack of adequate legal regulations. Under the pretext of concern for security related to the SARS COV-2 pandemic, the Russian government expanded the possibilities for early voting (in total, voting lasted a week), online and outside the polling station, as well as - practically without restrictions - at home (for this reason, during the voting, the Russian Internet was full of pictures of ballot boxes placed in buses, car trunks, on park benches). Thus, the least transparent means of voting were used, lacking effective control by observers, creating the widest scope for falsifying turnout and results (see Domanska, 2020a; European Commission For Democracy Through Law, 2021). The scale of falsification was extremely difficult to estimate under these conditions.

Shortly after the referendum, in September 2020, regional and local elections were held in Russia to elect, among others, governors, deputies of regional parliaments and local government representatives. The already tried-and-true multi-day voting and voting outside polling places were used again, the introduction of which was motivated by the coronavirus pandemic. As a result, electoral fraud was again committed on a scale that is difficult to estimate. According to Maria Domanska of the Center for Eastern Studies, "In early voting in some regions, up to more than 70% of all voters officially participated - its unprecedented scale served to falsify turnout and results." By contrast, according to the independent organization Golos, the number of reported violations was the highest in four years, and the election law the worst in the last quarter century (Domanska, 2020b).

Solutions related to the preparation for the holding of elections and referendums under pandemic conditions were introduced through various pieces of legislation, most often amendments to already existing acts – incl. Federal Law No. 67-FZ of June 12, 2002 "On the Fundamental Guarantees of Electoral Rights and the Right to Participate in a Referendum of Citizens of the Russian Federation", Federal Law No. 20-FZ of February 22, 2014 "On the Elections of Deputies to the State Duma Of the Federal Assembly of the Russian Federation" and the Code of Administrative Procedure of the Russian Federation. The largest scope of pandemic-related changes in election procedures was carried out by the Federal Law "On Amendments to Certain Legislative Acts of the Russian Federation" No. 267-FZ of July 31, 2020. As part of these amendments, several changes were introduced – justified by the COVID-19 pandemic – that influenced the procedure for holding parliamentary elections in 2021.

Firstly, as in the Russian constitutional referendum and in the 2020 regional elections, the voting time was extended in 2021 – this time from one to three days (*Федеральный закон О внесении …*, 2020). The change was argued by the COVID-19 pandemic – spreading the vote over three days was to reduce traffic at polling stations. However, the Russian opposition drew attention to the fact that the extended voting time may be beneficial for the authorities – this made it possible to more effectively mobilize the electorate dependent on the government (e.g. trips to polling stations organized by workplaces or offices, the more so as the elections also took place on a working day),[1] but at the same time, these activities were spread over three days, so they were not so visible to observers (Рожкова et al., 2020; *В Госдуме предложили …*, 2020). In addition, the three-day voting made it difficult to control the election process – doubts arose as to the safety of ballot boxes with votes at night (OSCE, 2021a, p. 6). The longer voting was also associated with the problem of ensuring a sufficient number of people to observe these elections (difficulties in finding people who would devote three days of observation, including working days).

The second innovation explained by the pandemic, also proven earlier, incl. during the constitutional referendum, were new forms of voting – online voting and voting outside the polling station (here the situations in which such voting can be carried out have been extended). Residents of seven Russian entities – two cities: Moscow and Sevastopol, as well as five oblasts: Nizhny Novgorod, Jarosław, Kursk, Murmansk and Rostov. The Murmansk Oblast and Sevastopol were chosen due to the anticipated numerous departures of the inhabitants of these regions during the elections, while in other oblasts electronic voting was already possible last year and, according to the authorities, it worked. In order to be able to vote electronically, Russians from eligible oblasts had to register in the system beforehand (from August 2 to September 13). Importantly, it was not possible to change the decision on how to vote on election day,[2] however, a person who resigned from electronic home voting despite prior registration could vote electronically at the polling station (special positions were to be created for such people). The possibility of electronic voting, especially in cities where the opposition is usually the strongest, was perceived as an attempt to

---

1 During the elections, about the employees of ministries, professional and conscript soldiers brought from units, and the queues of pupils and students brought from schools and universities, which were forced to vote, during the elections informed, e.g. independent Novaya Gazeta (*Россия впервые выбирает …*, 2021) and Meduza portal (*Явка – почти 17%…*, 2021).

2 During voting on the amendment to the constitution, the possibility of replacing electronic voting with classic voting at the premises was used for electoral fraud – loopholes in the system allowed for double voting.

increase the authorities' control over the voting process. Concerns were raised by the weak security system of the voting procedure, as well as the unreliable process of anonymizing votes (Кузнец & Ершов, 2021).

An additional provision, also already tested in 2020, was the possibility of voting outside the formally designated polling stations. However, this time, unlike in the case of the constitutional referendum, no use was made of the possibility of creating voting points on the streets, in parks, on housing estates or on buses.[3] However, there was an opportunity – already used during previous elections – the so-called early voting of citizens in hard-to-reach or remote areas who could cast their votes in mobile polls transported by committee members. This early voting ran from August 29 to September 16. Mobile ballot boxes have also been used in the context of a pandemic – the possibility of using this voting method has also been made available to citizens from all over Russia who, due to their health condition (including self-isolation due to COVID-19), could not go to the polling station (Asplund, 2020). In addition, the Russian authorities decided to use mobile ballot boxes to increase voter turnout without increasing the traffic at polling stations (and thus increasing the risk of the pandemic spreading), by sending members of precinct election commissions to popular places, e.g. in the Moscow region, mobile ballots appeared at the lake, near the church and at the stalls (*В Подмосковье создали ...*, 2021).

Thirdly, Russian authorities have decided to use the COVID-19 pandemic to make it difficult for citizens and organizations to observe the elections. This applied to both external and internal observers. The authorities of the Russian Federation, due to the sanitary and epidemiological situation in Russia, decided to reduce the permissible number of observers of OSCE's Office for Democratic Institutions and Human Rights (ODHIR) and its Parliamentary Assembly (OSCE PA) to 50 and 10, respectively. In response, the OSCE decided to cancel the observation mission (since it needed a team consisting of 80 long-term observers and 420 short-term observers), arguing that "the ability to independently determine the number of observers necessary for us to observe effectively and credibly is essential to all international observation" (OSCE, 2021b). The restrictions on the number of observers introduced by Russia

---

3 During the constitutional referendum, a large number of photos of voting points located in the strangest places appeared on the Russian Internet – in car trunks, buses placed on the streets or even benches in housing estates. Independent observers and the media criticized these actions, pointing to the inability to control such points, the questionable seriousness of the voting process and the numerous possibilities of counterfeiting (lack of control of the safety of the ballot box).

seem to have no justification, and it is certainly difficult to explain them as a pandemic, while in Russia itself at that time there were virtually no pandemic restrictions. On the other hand, the real effect of the lack of an observation mission is the lack of a report documenting electoral fraud and the undemocratic nature of the Russian elections. One of the few external organizations allowed to observe Russian elections was the Commonwealth of Independent States, which did not record any violations and concluded that all candidates had equal conditions to participate in the election (Asplund, 2020).

What is more, the Russian authorities decided – also often explaining it on the grounds of a pandemic – to significantly limit the possibilities of internal observation of the elections. The Golos social movement, which has been monitoring electoral frauds in Russia for years (previously as an independent organization, Golos), experienced the greatest difficulties. A month before the elections, Golos was entered on the list of the so-called foreign agents (Kusa, 2018; Kusa, 2020), which significantly hinders its functioning (Wolska, 2021). Election observation was also significantly impeded due to the resignation from the possibility of general election observation introduced in 2012 by the polling station monitoring system. So far, this possibility has been widely used by Russian citizens, but also by non-governmental organizations and foreign missions – in fact, after each election, there were videos documenting the moments when votes were poured into the ballot boxes or other forgeries committed by committee members. The universal transmission available on the Internet for everyone has been replaced by a portal where only members of election commissions, political parties, candidates in elections and selected organizations will be able to follow the images from cameras (Мельконьянц, 2021). And this means the end of general control of the election process and probably the intensification of the simplest falsifications – adding votes in favor of power, destroying opposition votes and multiple voting.

17.4 Other Factors Affecting the Parliamentary Elections

17.4.1 *Removal of Potential Opposition Candidates*
The Russian authorities have been preparing for the parliamentary elections at least from 2020. These long-term actions mainly consisted in the gradual removal of opposition entities that could take part in these elections. A pandemic has also been used for this purpose in some cases. Eliminated from participation in the elections, among others, Alexei Navalny, one of the most popular Russian oppositionists, who, even before the presidential elections in 2018, had built a nationwide network of election staffs, i.e. structures that

could be used to fight for votes in subsequent elections. Navalny has repeatedly organized thousands of protests throughout Russia, and even when he was arrested, he was also able to mobilize hundreds of thousands of Russians to oppose the Russian authorities. Therefore, more than six months before the elections, the Kremlin decided to permanently remove him from Russian political life and will probably not commit any more the mistake of allowing such a strong figure to participate in the elections, or even in public life. Therefore, the action of liquidating the opposition also covered other figures, including all people associated with A. Navalny, as well as his Foundation for Fighting Corruption (FBK) (it has been recognized as an extremist organization). Most of the associates and people who in any way announced that they would run in the elections were "neutralized" by the authorities – criminal cases were brought against them, most often related to the so-called sanitary accusations (accusations of violating the sanitary regime, calling for violations of this regime, deliberate spreading of an epidemic) (*Любовь Соболь вынесли ...,* 2021; *Обвиняемому по «санитарному ...,* 2021; Галямина, 2021). Pursuant to the regulations passed in 2020, citizens convicted under several articles of the Criminal Code, including the controversial article on repeated violations of the rules of street protests, were also eliminated from passive participation in elections (Колесников & Макаренко, 2021).

In addition, the removal of all candidates in any way related to the opposition or activities for the benefit of society is also intended to hinder the so-called intelligent voting initiated by Alexei Navalny. This mechanism was supposed to convince Russians to vote for anyone, except for a candidate of the ruling party, so as to deprive United Russia of the majority and introduce as many opposition representatives to parliament as possible (even if it is only a systemic opposition). Intelligent voting with – modest but still – success has been used in various local elections in recent years.[4] However, before the elections in 2021, the authorities decided to prevent all those who could count on

4 Researchers from the European University in St. Petersburg tried to calculate what support the opposition could gain thanks to the idea of the so-called intelligent voting. According to their study, smart voting in the regional elections in 2020 allowed for 5% of the votes in regional capitals and 7–8% in Moscow and St. Petersburg (however, it was not noticeable in rural areas). At the same time, the frequency of mentioning intelligent voting in social networks and in internet users' inquiries was low at that time (Турченко & Голосов, 2021). In 2021, smart voting was already extremely popular online and if it were a political party, it would rank third in terms of potential audience and engagement rates, right behind United Russia and the Communist Party of the Russian Federation (Голос, 2021).

public support, i.e. social activists, activists, people associated with Navalny, and the anti-system opposition from standing for election. Therefore, the symbolism of smart voting considered extremist, as a result of which the court banned search engines from displaying the phrase "smart voting" in search results, and Google and Apple were ordered to remove the application from stores (Голос, 2021; Asplund, 2020).

17.4.2 *Facade Opposition*

For several years now, the Russian authorities have been struggling with the problem of the weakening support for United Russia. The turning point here seems to be 2018 and the infamous pension reform that was passed in the shadow of the soccer world cup. The protests that were organized at that time (with great difficulties due to the limitations related to the championship) were held under slogans criticizing the Russian authorities, and above all the government, on which all responsibility for the changes was thrown. In July 2021, the activities of the Russian government were disapproved of by nearly half of Russians (49%), but at the same time the other half were in favor of the actions of the prime minister and his team (48%). On the other hand, the State Duma is assessed much worse – in July 2021, 56% of Russians did not accept its activities (the Duma was assessed worse only in 2018–2019, when the pension reform was passed and during the protests in 2011–2012), and only 40% praised it (Levada Analytical Center, 2021). Therefore, the Russian authorities, fearing that the support for United Russia would be low in the upcoming elections, decided to refer to measures that had already been used several times in the past. Inspired by the presidential administration, several new political parties were created in 2020 to use part of the electorate discouraged by United Russia. According to experts, these new parties can count on approx. 10–15% of the votes (although it is possible that the support will be lower) from groups that would definitely not vote for the party in power. New People, For Truth, Green Alternative and the Direct Democracy Party are to use the votes of, among others nationalists, anti-systemists and youth, and thus discourage these groups from voting for the opposition. It is possible that the Russian authorities also hoped that these parties would be selected as an alternative to United Russia under the so-called intelligent voting. An additional goal is to create the impression that new entities appear in the Russian party system (this is an offer for those who are discouraged by the constant victories of one party) and there is also room for those who do not want to vote for the so-called systemic opposition (Benedyczak, 2021). However, these entities were to be expected to drop out due to not exceeding the electoral threshold. The more so as the experiences of the last two decades show that the entry of a new entity into the Duma is practically impossible (only A Just Russia managed to do this in 2007).

17.4.3   *United Russia's New Electoral List*

In order to make the electoral lists of the outdated and repeatedly compromised power party more attractive, the Kremlin decided not only to create a few new entities that would attract new voters, but also to include well-known and well-liked personalities on the lists. Thus, the Russians – especially those from large cities or neighborhoods – could vote in the elections, i.a. for singer Victoria Daineko (recently created Green Alternative), singer Denis Maidanov (United Russia in the Moscow region), host of the animal and travel program Timofei Bazhenov (United Russia), journalist Yevgeny Popov (United Russia) or actor Vladimir Mashkov (United Russia) (*Звездный созыв ...*, 2021). There were quite a lot of such people on the lists in 2021, most of them used their popularity in the campaign, they were also often placed at the top of the lists as the so-called locomotives. All these activities were intended to mobilize voters to vote for the party in power (or the alleged opposition party) or to encourage participation in elections in general, especially younger people or residents of large cities.

17.4.4   *Internet and Media Control*

Although there has been no free media in Russia for over a decade (especially in the context of TV stations), the Internet has so far remained a certain sphere of freedom. However, after it was used on a mass scale for opposition activities and the organization of protests, the Russian authorities also decided to introduce a number of restrictions in this area. A large part of the regulations appeared in the wake of the post-election protests in 2011 and 2012, but the network was still used to coordinate opposition activities and as a space for relatively free criticism of the Russian authorities. While preparing for the next parliamentary elections, as early as 2020, the Russian authorities decided to increase the level of control over the Internet. It was important because due to the COVID-19 pandemic and numerous restrictions on mass rallies and direct meetings, the election campaign largely moved to the Internet (Asplund, 2020).

In December 2020, a package of laws was adopted that significantly impede access to independent information. Among them there was the act imposing high penalties on suppliers and owners of internet resources who refuse to remove banned information in Russia, as well as the regulation enabling linking the penalty for repeated refusal to remove banned materials with the revenues of the entity that provides the information (which means potential multi-million or even multi-billion penalties for e.g. Facebook or Youtube)

(*Госдума одобрила штрафы* ..., 2020). Additionally, Roskomnadzor was given the option to block foreign sites for "censorship" and "discrimination" of the Russian media. The Federal Communication Supervision Service will be able to partially or fully block sites or services that restrict socially significant information in Russia, including in connection with foreign sanctions against Russia (*Госдума разрешила блокировать* ..., 2020).

Importantly, these provisions are already used by Russian authorities and are mainly used to influence the content of international portals and platforms (for example, Roskomandzor slowed down traffic on Twitter as a penalty for not removing content that is undesirable in Russia). On an unprecedented scale, the Kremlin is blocking Russians' access to external information, the more so as most of the Russian independent news platforms had already been shut down. The parliamentary elections of 2021 can be considered one of the most "closed to the world" elections, and this at a time when virtually every Russian can access the network at any time.

The Russian authorities are also continuing their efforts to "clean up" Russia, especially the opposition side of the Internet. After many years of various point-based blockades of individual websites or services, this time the Kremlin operates widely, and the aim is to deprive Russians of access to independent, opposition or compromising content. As a result, the media and natural persons "acting as a foreign agent" of the Insider portal (investigative journalism and political analysis; the editor-in-chief was arrested) were added to the list (Михайлов & Савоченко, 2021); dozens of websites related to Alexei Navalny were blocked (including the main page collecting all information about the opposition, Navalny, investigations and finances); and the independent editorial office of Projekt.Media (which informed the Russian public about the activities of Russian mercenaries from the Wagner Group, investigations into the president's daughters or Kadyrov's second wife) was liquidated. And although each of these entities operated only online and had a limited audience (the message rarely reached the largest Russian cities), they were still considered a threat to the regime – the results of subsequent investigations can always lead to protests, especially in the largest cities with the greatest number of recipients of these media. So while in 2016 such activities were ignored, usually without commenting on the results of spectacular investigations (e.g. those concerning the most important persons in the state) and thus downplaying their importance, in the current tense situation the Kremlin decided that it was necessary to remove all potential sources of protest or social mobilization.

17.4.5   *Analysis of the Conduct of Elections*
Parliamentary elections in the Russian Federation were held on September 17–19, 2021. The turnout was 51.72% (which meant a result higher by nearly

4 percentage points compared to 2016). As expected, United Russia won the elections, gaining 324 seats, which gave it a constitutional majority. Representatives of four other parties also joined the State Duma – the Communist Party of the Russian Federation (57 seats), Just Russia (27 seats), the Liberal Democratic Party of Russia (21 seats) and New People (13 seats). Additionally, the new parliament included 5 independent deputies and one representative (single-member constituencies) of the Party of Growth, Homeland and Civic Platform (*Итоги выборов в Госдуму ...*, 2021). There were a number of recommendations in place at polling stations caused by the COVID-19 pandemic (including vaccination of committee members, ban on eating food, remote temperature measurement, masks and gloves, disposable pens, etc.) and not too many violations of these recommendations were recorded (Asplund, 2020).

Electronic voting aroused the most doubts, protests and accusations of forgery. The authorities did much to encourage Russians, especially from the largest cities, including Moscow, to participate in online voting to reduce queues at polling stations (and, according to independent organizations and opposition, to be more able to manipulate the result). Ultimately, over 2.6 million Russians (most of them from Moscow) took advantage of the online voting option. The results of the electronic vote in Moscow aroused the most controversy. Distrust and demands to repeat the vote (*КПРФ отказалась ...*, 2021) were caused by a delay in making the results of this voting available (only several hours after the end of the vote), closing the possibility of electronic votes being controlled by independent observers on the third day of voting, as well as results significantly different from the results recorded in traditional voting (in several districts the traditional voting was won by the candidates of the systemic opposition, but the results of the online voting gave victory to the candidates of United Russia) (Гонгальский, 2021; Шпилькин, 2021). The most active requests for the repetition of the vote were made by the Communist Party of the Russian Federation, which declared its non-recognition shortly after the election results were announced. The KPFR accused the authorities that the results of the electronic voting had been rigged, so that its candidates, leading in the traditional elections, ultimately lost after the votes in the electronic elections were counted. (*КПРФ отказалась ...*, 2021). The Russian authorities dropped all the charges and regarded the electronic elections as a great success, also in terms of turnout.

In fact, throughout the entire voting period, independent media and organizations reported numerous violations of the election law and fraud. The independent Novaya Gazeta kept informed about further violations, incl. about transported to Russia from the so-called Ukrainian Donetsk and Luhansk People's Republic of elections, queues of state administration employees forced

to vote, votes thrown into the ballot box, buying votes or prizes for voting
(*Выборы депутатов Госдумы ...*, 2021; *Выборы в России ...*, 2021). On the
other hand, the independent OVD-Info project devoted to political persecu-
tion in Russia reported that independent election observers were detained (i.a.
on charges of disseminating extremist symbols (intelligent voting), insulting
committee chairmen and disrupting their work, using foul language, etc.) by
the police and the services (ОВД-Инфо, 2021). The Golos social movement
drew attention to the fact that the Russians were deprived of the right to super-
vise the integrity of electronic voting, because the voting and vote counting
system is not transparent even to people with specialist knowledge in the field
of computer science. There were also many objections to voting with mobile
ballots, especially in voters' houses. Gołos informed that instead of compiling
a register of motions for house voting voluntarily submitted by voters, election
commissions used mainly lists provided to them by employees of the executive power and social insurance institutions. Some precinct election commissions showed an unrealistic number of voters voting at home (Голос, 2021b).
The analyzes of the independent Russian analyst Sergei Szpilkin (Шпилькин,
2021) show that about half of the votes for the victorious United Russia were
rigged votes, and the real electoral support for the ruling party was around
33%. The extra voices could result from, i.a. irregularities accompanying voting
by mobile ballot boxes.

17.5   Discussion

The Russian parliamentary elections held in September 2021 were – like many
previous elections – rigged. The scale of these electoral frauds perpetrated by the
Russian authorities was exceptionally high. According to experts, some of these
falsifications could result from changes introduced as a result of the COVID-19
pandemic, especially electronic voting and voting via mobile ballot boxes. Some
of the changes, such as impediments to election observers, infringed guaranteed by the Russian constitution the right of citizens to exercise control over
compliance with election procedures (an element of the constitutional right to
participate in the processes of exercising power). Erik Asplund and Toby James
(2020), when considering the issue of postponing elections due to a pandemic
or holding them in pandemic conditions, noted that elections conducted under
extraordinary conditions may be less free and less fair than they should be. In
addition, some governments, especially undemocratic ones, may use extraordinary measures introduced in the context of the pandemic to restrict the
activities of the opposition or independent media. Todd Landman and Luca

Di Gennaro Splendore (2020, p. 4) also pointed out that postponing or holding elections in pandemic conditions in authoritarian regimes may lead to abuse and further consolidation of the authoritarian system. Taking into account the above analyzes, it can be concluded that this is the situation in the Russian Federation. The Russian authorities have used measures and restrictions introduced in connection with the COVID-19 pandemic to make it difficult, or actually prevent the opposition from participating in the elections, and to rig them on an unprecedented scale. By giving the party power a constitutional majority and properly liquidating all opposition activities, the undemocratic regime of the Russian Federation was consolidated. Additionally, the arsenal of means that can be used to counterfeit subsequent elections has been expanded.

17.6   Conclusions

After the elections in 2016, when the party in power won the constitutional majority, and despite gigantic forgeries there were no mass protests, it seemed that not much could change in this system. However, the specificity of undemocratic systems lies in the fact that in crisis situations, such as a pandemic or an economic crisis, falsely legitimized authorities can easily become the target of criticism and outbursts of discontent. Therefore, the Russian government, aware of the fact that support for United Russia has been weakening for several years, undertook a whole series of measures aimed at conducting peaceful elections without protests, culminating in a stable victory for the ruling party, guaranteeing a constitutional majority. Virtually every election held in Russia after 2000 was recognized by international observation missions as violating the standards of democratic elections. Gradually, there were more and more of these violations, and the regime was more and more often classified as authoritarian (and even with totalitarian elements). In 2021, a number of techniques were added to the repertoire of standard techniques to "help" United Russia maintain full power – often justified by the COVID-19 pandemic – making these elections completely undemocratic. The lack of opposition, the inability to express opposition to the authorities, the inability to independently observe the elections, numerous electoral frauds and further obstacles to the functioning of independent media are the most important factors that influenced the elections to the State Duma in Russia in September 2021. In the months following the elections, it turned out that some of the solutions introduced in the context of the election worked well in the face of the war Russia waged against Ukraine, especially in the context of reporting this aggression to Russian citizens. The question that remains open is whether the measures introduced as a result of the pandemic will become a permanent element of Russia's election campaigns and elections, and whether Russia will continue to use them to make the elections a spectacle intended to simulate the universal legitimacy of the Russian government.

References

Asplund E. (2020) (Ed.). "Global overview of COVID-19: Impact on elections", International IDEA, 18 March 2020 (and updated), retrieved from: https://www.idea.int /news-media/multimedia-reports/global-overview-COVID-19-impact-elections.

Asplund E. & James T. (2020). "Elections and COVID-19: making democracy work in uncertain times". *Democratic Audit Blog.* Retrieved from: https://www.democraticaudit .com/2020/03/30/elections-and-COVID-19-making-democracy-work-in-uncertain -times/.

Asplund E. & James T. (2020). "Elections and COVID-19: making democracy work in uncertain times". *IDEA.* Retrieved from: https://www.idea.int/es/node/308409.

Bäcker R., Rak J. (2018). "The Change of Russian Political Regime from the "White Revolution" to Presidential Election (2012–2018)". *Przegląd Strategiczny*, no 11, pp. 143–155. DOI: https://doi.org/10.14746/ps.2018.1.10.

Benedyczak J. (2021). "Przygotowania władz Rosji do wyborów parlamentarnych". *PISM.* Retrieved from: https://pism.pl/publikacje/Przygotowania_wladz_Rosji_do _wyborow_parlamentarnych.

Domańska M. (2020a), "Farsa przy urnach. Głosowanie konstytucyjne w Rosji". Ośrodek Studiów Wschodnich. Retrieved from: https://www.osw.waw.pl/pl/publikacje /analizy/2020-07-02/farsa-przy-urnach-glosowanie-konstytucyjne-w-rosji.

Domańska M. (2020b), "Pandemiczne wybory w Rosji: nowe instrumenty manipulacji". Ośrodek Studiów Wschodnich. Retrived from: https://www.osw.waw.pl/pl /publikacje/analizy/2020-09-16/pandemiczne-wybory-w-rosji-nowe-instrumenty -manipulacji.

European Commission For Democracy Through Law (2021). *Russian Federation. Interim opinion on constitutional amendments and the procedure for their adoption.* Retrieved from: https://www.venice.coe.int/webforms/documents/?pdf=CDL-AD(2021)005-e.

Gelman V. (2013). "Cracks in the Wall. Challenges to Electoral Authoritarianism in Russia". *Problems of Post-Communism*, vol. 60, no. 2, pp. 3–10. DOI: https://doi .org/10.2753/PPC1075-8216600201.

Golosov G. V. (2011). "Regional Roots of Electoral Authoritarianism in Russia". *Europe– Asia Studies*, 63, no. 4, pp. pp. 623–639.

Hamdani F. & Fauzia A. (2021). "Legal Discourse: The Spirit of Democracy and Human Rights Post Simultaneous Regional Elections 2020 in the COVID-19 Pandemic Era".

Lex Scientia Law Review, vol. 5(1), pp. 97–118. DOI: https://doi.org/10.15294/lesrev .v5i1.45887.

James T. S. (2021), "New development: Running elections during a pandemic". *Public Money & Management*, vol. 41 no. 1, pp. 65–68. DOI: https://doi.org/10.1080 /09540962.2020.1783084.

Kim J. (2020), "Democracy, elections and pandemics: How South Korea ran parliamentary elections during the COVID-19 crisis". GLOBALCIT. Retrieved from: https://globalcit.eu/democracy-elections-and-pandemics-how-south-korea-ran -parliamentary-elections-during-the-COVID-19-crisis/.

Krimmer R., Duenas-Cid D. & Krivonosova I. (2021), "Debate: safeguarding democracy during pandemics. Social distancing, postal, or internet voting—the good, the bad or the ugly?. *Public Money & Management*, vol. 41 no. 1, pp. 8–10. DOI: https://doi.org /10.1080/09540962.2020.1766222.

Kusa N. (2018). "Zagraniczny agent w rosyjskim społeczeństwie. Normatywne ograniczenia w funkcjonowaniu organizacji pozarządowych w Federacji Rosyjskiej w latach 2012–2016". In Jakubowski J. & Pająk-Patkowska B. (Eds.), *Aktywność polityczna i jej przejawy we współczesnych państwach*. Poznań: Wydawnictwo Naukowe Wydziału Nauk Politycznych i Dziennikarstwa UAM.

Kusa N. (2020). *Z parlamentu i ulicy do internetu. Opozycja polityczna w putinowskim systemie władzy*. Poznań: Wydawnictwo Naukowe Wydziału Nauk Politycznych i Dziennikarstwa UAM.

Landman T. & Di Gennaro Splendore L. (2020). "Pandemic democracy: elections and COVID-19". *Journal of Risk Research*, vol. 23:7–8, pp. 1060–1066. DOI: https://doi.org /10.1080/13669877.2020.1765003.

Levada Analytical Center (2021). „Доверие политикам, одобрение институтов и положение дел в стране". *Levada*. Retrieved from: https://www.levada .ru/2021/07/30/doverie-politikam-odobrenie-institutov-i-polozhenie-del-v -strane-4/.

Levitsky S. & Way L. (2010). *Competitive Authoritarianism: Hybrid Regimes After the Cold War*. New York: Cambridge University Press.

Maizland L. (2020). "How Countries Are Holding Elections During the COVID-19 Pandemic". Council on Foreign Relations. Retrieved from: https://www.jstor.org/stable /resrep29836.

Matlosa K. (2021). "Elections in Africa During COVID-19: The Tenuous Balance Between Democracy and Human Security", *Politikon*, vol. 48:2, p. 159–173, https://doi.org /10.1080/02589346.2021.1913798.

Nadskakuła-Kaczmarczyk O. (2016). "Od „suwerennej demokracji" do twardego autorytaryzmu – wzmacnianie roli ośrodka kremlowskiego w Federacji Rosyjskiej". *Studia Politologiczne*, vol. 42, pp. 268–287.

Nadskakuła-Kaczmarczyk O. (2017). "Opposition in authoritarian regimes – a case study of Russian non-systemic opposition. *Środkowoeuropejskie Studia Polityczne*, no. 4, pp. 175–189.

OSCE (2021a). *Russian Federation, State Duma Elections 19 September 2021. ODIHR Needs Assessment Mission Report.* Warsaw: OSCE.

OSCE (2021b). "No OSCE observers for Russian parliamentary elections following major limitations". Retrieved from: https://www.osce.org/odihr/elections/russia/494488.

Palguta, J., Levínský & R., Škoda, S. (2022). "Do elections accelerate the COVID-19 pandemic?". *Journal of Population Economics*, vol. 35, pp. 197–240. DOI: https://doi.org/10.1007/s00148-021-00870-1.

Wolska A. (2021). "Rosja: Monitorujący wybory ruch społeczny „Głos" uznany za zagranicznego agenta". *Euractiv.* Retrieved from: https://www.euractiv.pl/section/demokracja/news/rosja-monitorujacy-wybory-ruch-spoleczny-golos-uznany-za-zagranicznego-agenta/.

"В Госдуме предложили отменить трехдневное голосование". 2020. *РБК.* Retrieved from: https://www.rbc.ru/politics/17/09/2020/5f6355229a7947fc035ac2c4.

"В Подмосковье создали более 500 мест для голосования — в палатках, на остановках, у храма и на берегу озера". 2021. *Novaya Gazeta.* Retrieved from: https://novayagazeta.ru/articles/2021/09/16/v-podmoskove-sozdali-bolee-500-mest-dlia-golosovaniia-v-palatkakh-na-ostanovkakh-u-khrama-i-na-beregu-ozera-news.

"Выборы в России. Первый день — только главное". 2021. *Novaya Gazeta.* Retrieved from: https://novayagazeta.ru/articles/2021/09/17/vybory-v-rossii-pervyi-den-tolko-glavnoe.

"Выборы депутатов Госдумы продолжаются. Онлайн – день третий". 2021. *Novaya Gazeta.* Retrieved from: https://novayagazeta.ru/articles/2021/09/19/vybory-deputatov-gosdumy-prodolzhaiutsia-onlain-den-tretii.

"Итоги выборов в Госдуму — 2021". *Ria Novosti.* Retrieved from: https://ria.ru/20210919/vybory_gosduma-1749875690.html.

"КПРФ отказалась признать результаты электронного голосования в Москве". 2021. *Meduza.* Retrieved from: https://meduza.io/news/2021/09/20/kprf-otkazalas-priznat-rezultaty-elektronnogo-golosovaniya-v-moskve.

"Явка — почти 17%, бюджетники стоят в очередях, Путин (возможно) голосует с помощью чужого телефона". 2021. *Meduza.* Retrieved from: https://meduza.io/feature/2021/09/17/yavka-9-byudzhetniki-stoyat-v-ocheredyah-putin-vozmozhno-golosuet-s-pomoschyu-chuzhogo-telefona.

"Госдума одобрила штрафы до 20% выручки за отказ удалять запрещенный контент в интернете". 2020. *Kommersant.* Retrieved from: https://www.kommersant.ru/doc/4626463.

"Госдума разрешила блокировать сайты и соцсети за цензуру". 2020. *Kommersant*. Retrieved from: https://www.kommersant.ru/doc/4627070.

"Звездный созыв. Кто из знаменитостей рвется в Госдуму". 2021. *Ria Novosti*. Retrieved from: https://ria.ru/20210804/vybori-1744215391.html.

"Любовь Соболь вынесли обвинительный приговор по «санитарному делу»". 2021. *Memorial*. Retrieved from: https://memohrc.org/ru/news_old/lyubov-sobol -vynesli-obvinitelnyy-prigovor-po-sanitarnomu-delu.

"Обвиняемому по «санитарному делу» оппозиционеру Ляскину на год запретили выходить из дома ночью". 2021. *Mediazona*. Retrieved from: https://zona.media /news/2021/08/06/year.

"Россия впервые выбирает Госдуму за три дня. Онлайн — день первый", 2021 *Novaya Gazeta*, retrieved from: https://novayagazeta.ru/articles/2021/09/17/rossiia -vpervye-vybiraet-gosdumu-za-tri-dnia-onlain-den-pervyi.

Галямина Ю. (2021). "Тысяча и один способ не пустить независимого кандидата на выборы". *Telegram*. Retrieved from: https://t.me/galyamina/2141?fbclid=IwAR2u Hif7Snjbl2ciIJC6BspkA9HcqLCoAQDa2wU-tiAOISwCnRVSlHoXNqk.

Голос (2021a). "Предвыборная агитация и административная мобилизация избирателей на выборах в единый день голосования 19 сентября 2021 года". *Golosinfo*. Retrieved from: https://www.golosinfo.org/articles/145472#2.

Голос (2021b). "Заявление по итогам наблюдения за выборами в единый день голосования 19 сентября 2021 года". *Golosinfo*. Retrieved from: https://www .golosinfo.org/articles/145498#2.1.

Гонгальский М. (2021). "Мандаты пользуются вбросом". *Novaya Gazeta*. Retrieved from: https://novayagazeta.ru/articles/2021/09/30/mandaty-polzuiutsia-vbrosom.

Колесников А. & Макаренко Б. (2021). "Дума-2021: четыре интриги выборов". *Moscow Center Carnegie*. Retrieved from: https://carnegie.ru/2021/05/31/ru-pub-84618.

Кузнец Д. & Ершов А. (2021). "Так все-таки были фальсификации на электронном голосовании — или власти просто мобилизовали на него больше своих сторонников?". *Meduza*. Retrieved from: https://meduza.io/feature/2021/09/24 /tak-vse-taki-byli-falsifikatsii-na-elektronnom-golosovanii-ili-vlasti-prosto -mobilizovali-na-nego-bolshe-svoih-storonnikov.

Мельконьянц Г. (2021). "УИК не для всех". *Novaya Gazeta*. Retrieved from: https:// novayagazeta.ru/articles/2021/07/15/uik-ne-dlia-vsekh.

Михайлов В., Савоченко А. (2021). "Уголовное дело о клевете высосано из пальца. Роман Доброхотов — об обыске и будущем The Insider". *Current Time*. Retrieved from: https://www.currenttime.tv/a/roman-dobrokhotov-ob-obyskah -i-budushem-the-insider/31383571.html.

ОВД-Инфо (2021). "Не менее 10 наблюдателей и членов комиссий задержали за первый день голосования". *Telegram*. Retrieved from: https://t.me/ovdinfolive /247.

Рожкова Е., Галанина А. Веретенникова К. & Винокуров А. (2020). "Госдуме дадут три дня". *Kommersant*. Retrieved from: https://www.kommersant.ru/doc/4500508.

Турченко М. & Голосов Г. (2021). *"Влияние «Умного голосования» на выборы 2020 года"*. *Riddle*. Retrieved from: https://ridl.io/vlijanie-umnogo-golosovanija-na -vybory-2020-goda/?fbclid=IwAR0LCg2aroOoxFdpSBX4kOPTYLxqeHLrsMvM1m LYbO6HhaObhtihdl-oZjA.

Федеральный закон "О внесении изменений в отдельные законодательные акты Российской Федерации" от 31.07.2020 N 267-ФЗ. Retrieved from: https://www .consultant.ru/document/cons_doc_LAW_358748/.

Шпилькин С. (2021). "«Электронное голосование — абсолютное зло» Независимый электоральный аналитик Сергей Шпилькин — о том, как власти скрывают данные о ходе и результате выборов". *Meduza*. Retrieved from: https://meduza.io/feature/2021/09/20/elektronnoe-golosovanie-absolyutnoe-zlo.

Шпилькин С. (2021). "От обнуления — к удвоению". *Novaya Gazeta*. Retrieved from: https://novayagazeta.ru/articles/2021/09/21/ot-obnuleniia-k-udvoeniiu.

CHAPTER 18

Local Elections during a Pandemic Time – A Case of Estonia

Maciej Górny, Oliwia Kowalik and Kamila Sierzputowska

18.1 Introduction

One of the main challenges of independent Estonia in 1991 was the development of a new electoral law and organization of free parliamentary and presidential elections, The firs actions after regaining independence were aimed at building new structures and state institutions that Estonia dis not have within the borders of the USSR. It should be emphasized that over the past twenty years since then, the Estonian electoral system has demonstrated the stability of the adopted solutions (including the prohibition clause, the election formula, the number and shape of constituencies). However, it was subject to reforms necessary in electoral legislation. The corrections to the electoral law that appeared over the years served to change three basic issues: 1) consolidating the party scene, 2) deepending the bond between voters and MPs, and 3) increasing the level of voter turnout (Mielewczyk, 2015). Currently, Estonia is a democratic parliamentary republic. A tripartite division of powers has been adopted, but with a predominance of legislation. Pursuant to the constitution of 3 July 1992, legislative power is vested in the unicameral Riigikogu. Five – adjective elections are held every four years on the first Sunday in March. Their organization and course are supervised by the National Electoral Commission together with poviat election committees, precinct election commissions and an electronic returning committee. The structure, competence and procedure of their appointment are specified in the Law on elections to the Riigikogu (Sagan, 2018). Due to the fact, that presidential elections are not universal, the head of state is elected by the 101 – person Riigikogu.

Estonia is divided into twelve constituencies, and the constituency boundaries correspond to the boundaries of fifteen Estonian counties. One constituency may include several counities, and the capital city Tallinn is divided into three constituencies. In the case of local elections, each municipality is an electoral constituency (except Tallinn, where there are eight constituencies). As in other Baltic states, the parties seem to be quite strongly leader – oriented and highly centralized. The emergence of new forces of Estonian political scene is

© MACIEJ GÓRNY ET AL., 2024 | DOI:10.1163/9789004690622_020

primarily the result of the emergence of Eurosceptic and anti – immigration attitudes, which increases the popularity of national – conservative groups (EKRE). Relative dissatisfaction was usually the result of unmet expectations of voters, but it only slightly contributes to the instability of the political scene or the election process itself. Elections in Estonia are held in accordance with international standards of free and fair elections.

Meanwhile, the appearance of COVID 19 in March 2020 has become a major challenge both for the conduct the security of the elections, and for the functioning of the state in general. The Estonian authorities, like the governments of most countries in the world, faced an unprecedented situation. The dynamically growing threat required rapid reactions to implement solutions that would enable the functioning of democratic election procedures under extraordinary circumstances. The principles of isolation and social distancing turned out to be a very demanding challenge, but necessary in order to ensure the safety of citizens during elections held in individual countries during a pandemic. In view of the necessity to introduce sanitary restrictions guaranteeing the safety of voters and election commissions, many countries decided to postpone their elections. According to the International Institute for Democracy and Electoral Assistance (IDEA), at least 80 countries and territories, between March 21, 2020 and February 21, 2022, decided to postpone their national and regional elections due to the threat of the SARS-CoV-2 coronavirus (IDEA, 2022). Many of them also decided to introduce a state of emergency to combat the epidemic threat more effectively or to adapt existing alternative voting methods and election procedures in such a way as to maximize safe electoral participation for citizens (Russack, 2021, p. 2).

Estonia, as the subject of the Authors' investigations, took similar decisions and actions. In addition, as one of the most digitally advanced countries in Europe, with a large electronic infrastructure and widely available free Internet, it has smoothly moved to remote operation. Switching to online public services, which before the pandemic in 99% were conducted online (e.g., e-cabinet, e-tax, e-health, e-residency, e-justice, e-police, e-school) did not pose a particular challenge. On the contrary, many years of experience in the use of new technologies in pandemic conditions, in a sense, strengthened Estonia`s position on the international arena.

According to the republic's election calendar, the first year of the pandemic (2020) did not include elections at any level. The presidential elections and local elections were planned only in 2021 (in October and November respectively). The chapter refers to the Estonian experiences, where the citizens have been offered the most diverse opportunities to participate in democratic processes. Estonia uses a wide range of alternative voting methods as well as simplified procedures which serve to minimize the risk of forced election absenteeism. In addition to the "traditional" methods, whereby citizens need to cast their votes in polling stations on election day, it is possible to vote in advance (both in special polling stations in public admiration institutions and via Internet voting). Basing on this one may state that Estonia is the world leader in this regard, since it is the first and thus far the only country in the world to use Internet voting extensively.

As Steve Kremer points out: "Estonia has, and it is a very tech-oriented country - it's often jokingly referred to as e-stonia for this reason. Its citizens have identity cards with electronic chips, which go some way to reducing the risk of voter coercion, as people are unlikely to hand over (something so personal) as their identify card. Of course, there's nothing to stop someone coming round to your house and forcing you to vote a certain way, but that type of coercion is hard to scale up" (Cartwright, 2019). Referring to the accusation expressed in the quoted statement, in fact i-voting facilitates the sale of votes and "family voting". Marcin Rulka rightly wrote that: "This does not, however, constitute an infringement of the principle of direct elections, since the persons who actually dispose of voters' votes in such a situation have not been formally authorized to do so they do not constitute a legal electoral body". At most, such a situation conflicts with the principle of equal elections. Formally, however, each voter has one vote, which materially has the same "strength" as the votes of other voters. To avoid situations where the environment forces the voter to vote for a particular candidate, Estonia has introduced the possibility of changing the vote (canceling the previous one) within 7 days of online voting or on the day of stationary voting. This solution also supports the implementation of the principle of freedom in expressing electoral preferences. It should be emphasized that i-voting does not affect, as well as postal voting, and home voting, the equality of active voting rights (Rulka, 2017, pp. 73–74).

Since its introduction, this method has been used in ten consecutive elections, the latest of which occurred during the pandemic, which was of particular importance in the era of threats to public health. Due to the manner in which the head of the state is elected (which is done by a unicameral parliament – the *Riigikogu*), only the local elections, which are universal, will be analyzed, as only in this case the could epidemic threat have had an impact on the course of the election process.

18.2   The State of Research

In recent years, there has been a growing interest among researchers in the issue of civic participation (Hacker & van Dijk, 2000; Norris, 2005; Kneuer,

2016; Lindner et al., 2016; Kapsa & Musiał-Karg, 2019). Of particular interest are the changes taking place in democratic processes caused by the use of modern technologies, not only in terms of civic participation, but also in electoral processes (Alvarez et al, 2009; Hall, 2012; Krimmer, 2012; Krimmer et al., 2016; Musiał-Karg & Luengo, 2021). In the available literature, many studies have been devoted to e-participation as well as electronic voting (Macintosh & Whyte, 2006; Trechsel, 2007; Krimmer, 2013; Krimmer, 2016; Musiał-Karg, 2018; Krok, 2020; Lindner & Aichholzer, 2020). Particularly noticeable in this regard is an increase in the research focusing on Estonia, a country whose wide-ranging electronic strategy, as well as favorable provisions in the electoral law have resulted in it being regarded as a global leader in terms of electronic voting (Musiał-Karg, 2017). Foreign researchers devote a great deal of attention to Estonian experiences in field of the implementation of ICT in democratic processes, as well as the consequences of the use of online voting (Alvarez et al, 2009; Laud, 2012; Vinkel, 2012; Krimmer & Volkamer, 2014; Solvak & Vassil, 2016; Vinkel & Krimmer, 2016). The recent years have also seen increased in interest in these issues among Polish researchers (Musiał-Karg, 2011a, 2011b; Kulikowska & Epa, 2015; Musiał-Karg, 2017; Skotnicki, 2018; Szwed, 2018; Zbieranek, 2018; Sierzputowska, 2020; Górny, 2021).

18.3   Methodology and Results

The aim of the present study is to determine the impact of the COVID-19 pandemic on the respective stages of the election process, i.e. the course of the election campaign, voter turnout, along with the political consequences, i.e. the results of the elections. The chapter aims to answer the following questions: To what extent did the pandemic affect the election process? What was the turnout in comparison to earlier local-level elections? To what extent did the country's authorities manage to hold the elections in this extraordinary situation? Did the use of modern technologies affect the level of the citizens' voting activity in the elections held during the pandemic?

The chapter mainly uses the method of critical analysis and institutional and legal analysis to identify documents of state institutions in the field of election procedures and mechanisms. This perspective allows us to present the course of the election process carried out during the pandemic.

On March 12, 2020, pursuant to Section 87 (8) of the Constitution of the Republic of Estonia (*Eesti Vabariigi põhiseadus*, 1992) in conjunction with Section 21 of the Act on threats (*Erakorralise seisukorra seadus*, 1996) the country introduced a state of "emergency" (eriolukord), on the basis of which limitations were imposed among others on activities of educational institutions, including organization of cultural events, as well as business activities business (Szwed, 2021, pp. 384–385). The end of the state of emergency came on May 17, 2020 (Webb et al, 2021), well ahead of the local elections scheduled for October 17, 2021.[1] Thus, it was not decided to postpone them, despite the fact that there was still a high risk posed by the SARS-CoV-2 virus. Political decision-makers were fairly unanimous on the matter – only the Estonian Center Party was willing to consider postponing the election (*Estonian municipal elections…*, 2021). It is worth noting here how the elections in question are conducted. Pursuant to Sections 155 and 156 of the Constitution, the local government units are municipalities and cities, while the representative body is the Council, elected in free, universal, equal, direct and secret elections, and pursuant to Section 1 (3) of the *Municipal Council Election Act* (*Kohaliku omavalitsuse volikogu valimise seadus*, 2002) also proportionally every 4 years. Municipal Councils appoint bodies of executive power. In elections to local councils, under the provisions of Section 156 of the Estonian Constitution, the right to vote is available to persons who have reached the age of 18 years and permanently reside in the territory of a given local government unit. Seats are distributed with the modified d'Hondt method. The numbers of seats in individual district depend on the number if inhabitants, with the exception of the capital city Tallinn, where the district are organized based on city district. Candidates for local authorities from 15 towns and 64 rural municipalities took part in the autumn elections. Apart from voting at the polling stations, citizens could also use alternative voting methods, which will be described below.

I-voting is a form of voting that is used universally, which is to say that it is available to all citizens. The situation is different with voting using the home ballot box, i.e. home voting. Under Section 52 of the *Municipal Council Election Act*, this method could be used by all voters unable to reach the polling station due to ill health or for any other valid reason. A declaration of such a desire can be done in writing – the voter must submit a letter to the office of a rural municipality, city government or voting district committee appropriate for the voter's place of residence by 2:00 p.m. on the voting day; by phone – the application can be submitted over the phone by calling the voting district committee on the day of the election between 09:00 a.m. and 2:00 p.m. The decision on eligibility for this type of voting is made by the voting district committee, which notifies the applicant of the outcome. Home voting is organized by at least two committee members.

---

1   Under Section 2 of the Municipal Council Election Act (2002): *Council elections shall be held on the third Sunday in October in an election year.*

The polling stations opened on Sunday, October 17, 2021, while the voting itself began on Monday, October 11. The election calendar was changed in relation to the previous years. One of the most important changes was abandonment of the three-day interval between early voting and the election day, which had sometimes been treated as a moment to eliminate possible irregularities in the system (Dyś-Branicka, 2016, p. 263). The authorities also decided to shorten the entire voting procedure to a full week,[2] so that it consisted of six pre-election days and the official election day. In the pre-election period, citizens of Estonia could exercise their right to vote electronically, with the use of modern technologies, and polling stations by means of early voting. Estonian *i-voting* is an alternative voting method which, when applied during a pandemic, helped to minimize the risk of infections. Citizens were able to participate actively in elections from their own homes, without the need of going to a polling station. An additional solution, which Estonia also used in previous years, was early voting at polling stations, as mentioned above. From Monday to Thursday, at least one polling station was made available in each voting district, which was open from 12.00 a.m. to 8.00 p.m. From Friday, all polling stations in all districts were opened at the same hours. In the context of the developing COVID-19 pandemic, early voting could help maintain social distancing as Estonian citizens had the opportunity to vote throughout the week. The contributing factor here was the fact that on the election day proper (Sunday) some voters did not have to go to the polling stations due to having voted earlier. This solution allowed avoiding situations that took place in other countries, where long lines of citizens who wanted to vote in elections were formed in front of polling stations, increasing the risk of contracting the SARS-CoV-2 virus.

Due to the extraordinary circumstances related to the pandemic, exceptional electoral procedures were introduced, which resulted in voters no longer being tied to a specific polling station according to their place of residence. In the elections under discussion, voting was possible at any polling station in the voting circuit / municipal district competent for the place of residence. Voters could cast their votes for 7 days, as shown in the table on the next page:

Voting via the Internet was possible between October 11 and October 16, i.e. throughout the full so-called pre-election period. It will be the subject of the subsequent section. A significant obstacle in the procedure of general elections in the world was quarantine. In most countries, it resulted in the citizens' inability to vote, as election procedures were not adapted to emergency

---

2   In 2019 the collection of votes lasted from the Thursday preceding the election week until Sunday – the election day.

TABLE 18.1   The 2021 local elections calendar Estonia

LOCAL GOVERNMENT COUNCILS ELECTIONS 2021

Mon 11.10	Tue 12.10	Wed 13.10	Thu 14.10	Fri 15.10	Sat 16.10	Sun 17.10.2021
ADVANCE VOTING						ELECTION DAY
Voting at polling places of administrative centres 12.00–20.00				Voting at all polling places 12.00–20.00		Voting at all polling places 9.00–20.00
Online voting						
Mon 9.00…				…Sat 20.00		
Voting at the location of voter 9.00–20.00				Home voting 9.00–20.00		

SOURCE: LOCAL ELECTIONS 2021 (2021). VALIMISED. RETRIEVED FROM: HTTPS://WWW
.VALIMISED.EE/EN/LOCAL-ELECTIONS-2021

situations. An entirely different situation could be observed in Estonia, where, thanks to the methods of alternative voting introduced in previous years, it was possible to ensure that every citizen could vote. On the government website, anyone interested could find information about the three possible ways of participating in the elections in the time of isolation. The first of these was remote voting, i.e. voting with the use of the Internet (i-voting). The second option available to quarantined people was voting from home in their own election district. A citizen interested in this method could apply by phone, providing the information indicated on the website. Home voting, according to the calendar presented above, took place from Friday to Sunday in the election week, and the applications had to be submitted no later than by 2 p.m. on Sunday. This solution made voting possible even for those citizens who were sent into isolation at the last minute but had not taken advantage of the possibility to vote in the pre-election period. The last option was voting in a place of residence that was in a different election district. The principle was similar to that of home voting; however, it was only available in the pre-election period, i.e., from Monday to Thursday, and applications needed to be submitted in writing by 2 p.m. on Monday (Local elections 2021, 2021).

Analyzing the organization of the local elections, it can be concluded that they were conducted in a well-thought-out manner, and alternative voting methods played the most important role in the face of an emergency by protecting the citizens. Statistical data show that Estonian citizens readily use alternative methods of voting in elections, 72 percent of voters decided to vote in the pre-election period, which is an increase of almost 10 percent in comparison to the 2019 parliamentary elections. The figure below shows the distribution of votes on individual days in the pre-election week, according to the voting method selected.

The majority of those participating in elections decided to vote electronically, and the turnout of i-voters for all votes cast in local elections was 46.58%, which shows that almost every other Estonian decided to vote online. During the election week, it is worth noting that from Monday to Thursday the number of votes averaged around 60,000 per day, trending notably upward on Friday and Saturday. Ultimately, as many as 423,443 votes were cast in the electronic and early voting.

Analyzing data from previous years, however, it is hard to say that the COVID-19 pandemic has significantly increased interest in electronic voting. Based on i-voter turnout data for all votes cast in the election, it is not apparent that turnout will increase in 2021. An increase in i-voter turnout can be seen over several years in which it has increased significantly; however, despite

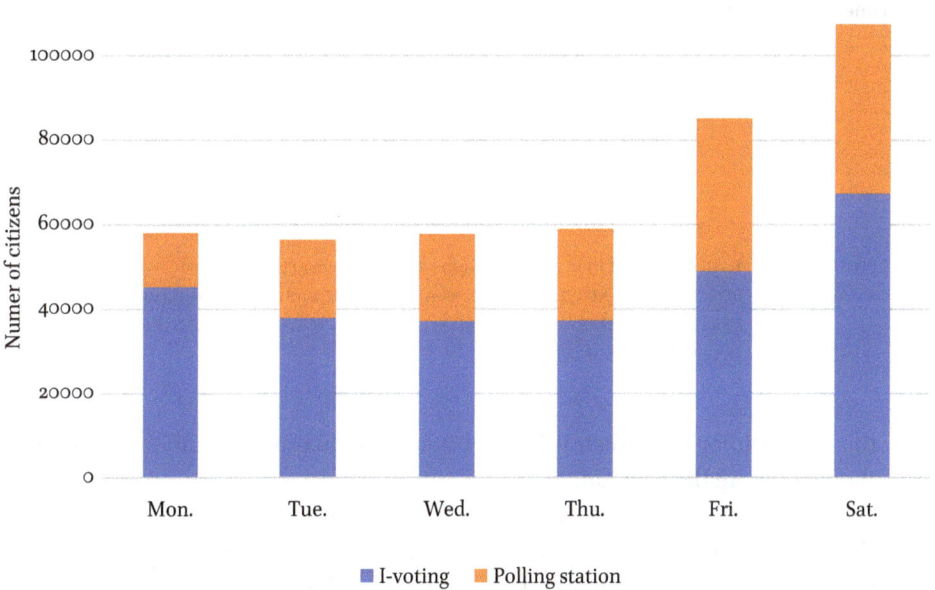

FIGURE 18.1   Advance voting in local election 2021
SOURCE: THE AUTHORS' OWN ELABORATION BASED ON VOTER TURNOUT STATISTICS (2021). VALIMISED. RETRIEVED FROM: HTTPS://KOV2021 .VALIMISED.EE/EN/PARTICIPATION/INDEX.HTML

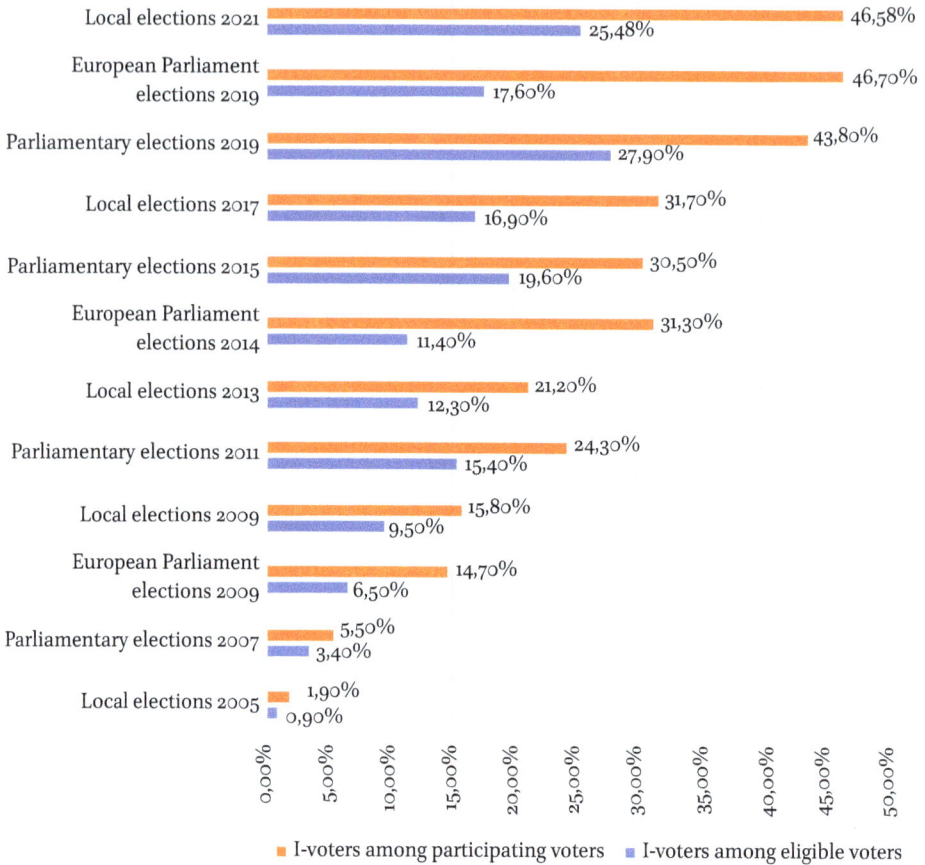

FIGURE 18.2   I-voter turnout in general elections in Estonia (2005–2021)
            SOURCE: THE AUTHORS' OWN ELABORATION BASED ON VALIMISED
            STATISTICS. RETRIEVED FROM: HTTPS://WWW.VALIMISED.EE/EN/ARCHIVE
            /STATISTICS

the epidemiological threat, it has not increased as much as one might have thought before the election.

When analyzing the distribution of the votes by voting method selected, it should be noted that 159,470 votes were cast on the election day itself, which is only 27% of all the votes. About one percent of the voters chose to vote with home ballot box (this method has been described in one of previous paragraphs). The overall turnout was 54.7%, slightly above the level of the last local elections in 2017 (53.3%). In relation to this, we should emphasize that citizens

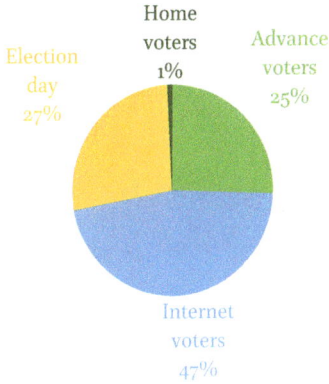

FIGURE 18.3   Percentage of votes based on the voting method
SOURCE: THE AUTHORS' OWN ELABORATION BASED ON VOTER TURNOUT
STATISTICS (2021). VALIMISED. RETRIEVED FROM: HTTPS://KOV2021
.VALIMISED.EE/EN/PARTICIPATION/INDEX.HTML.

actively participated in these elections, despite the state of emergency. It can certainly be said that Estonians are increasingly willing to use methods of alternative voting which gave a sense of greater security in a pandemic situation certainly and, above all, allowed all citizens to participate in the elections, regardless of their health or being under quarantine.

One of the most important aspects of local voting in 2021 was the subsequent increase in citizen interest in early voting, that is, before the official election day. As you can see, more than 70% of votes were cast before Sunday, meaning that more than 2/3 of citizens decided to take advantage of the opportunity to vote early in the election. Early voting certainly helped to avoid long queues that could form on election day if all citizens decided to vote at the polling station. From the perspective of ensuring protection and security of citizens, this solution, just after e-voting, can be considered an interesting way in which the state can conduct elections during emergency situations. However, such a high interest of Estonians in alternative methods that were available before the official election day is not entirely due to the sense of danger itself, nor the impact of the whole COVID-19 pandemic. Looking at the graph below, which also presents a trend line, one can see that the increase from 2021 falls within this trend line, calculated based on previous data from previous years. Therefore, it is hard to tell if the 5pp increase is a result of the COVID-19 pandemic or a trend that has remained the same in Estonia for several years.

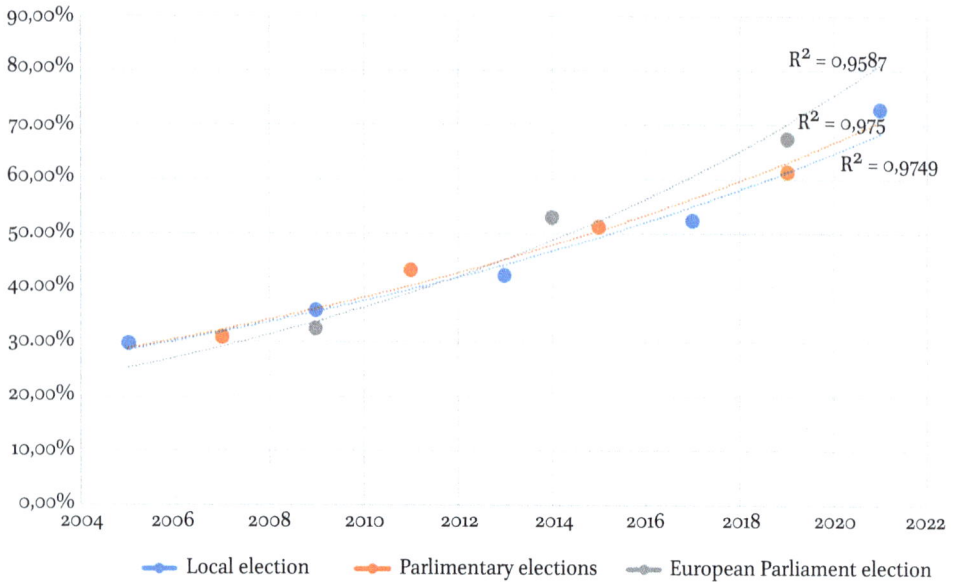

FIGURE 18.4   Percentage of advance poll votes from total votes (%)
SOURCE: THE AUTHORS' OWN ELABORATION BASED ON VALIMISED STATISTICS.
RETRIEVED FROM: HTTPS://WWW.VALIMISED.EE/EN/ARCHIVE/STATISTICS

18.4   Conclusions

The COVID-19 pandemic and its consequences have invariably posed a global challenge to modern democracies. Since its beginning in March 2020, national governments were obliged to make immediate decisions, based on which many new solutions were introduced to improve the functioning of each country. The achievements of Estonia to date, which, even before the outbreak of the pandemic, had been successively introducing investments enabling efficient remote operation, gave the citizens improved possibilities of participating in the election process.

The present analysis allows the formulation of several conclusions. Firstly, as the republic's authorities had previously made alternative voting opportunities (including i-voting) available to its citizens, the country coped very well with holding elections in the state of emergency. It is also noticeable that Estonians are increasingly willing to use alternative methods of voting; however, it cannot be concluded that the significant increase in voting during the pre-election period (early Internet voting) was entirely the result of the pandemic. Undoubtedly, as the analyzed voter turnout in the 2021 local elections shows, despite the implementation of Internet voting, which seemed to be the most convenient method, many Estonians are still attached to the traditional form of participation in elections.

In summary, the example of Estonia shows that it is possible to conduct general elections effectively during a pandemic, while completely minimizing the risk to public health. In such a situation, however, the election process should be based on proven voting methods and possible improvements of the election procedures functioning thus far. In conclusion, the example of Estonia shows that it is possible to successfully hold general elections in a pandemic while completely minimizing the risk to public health. In such a situation, the election process should, however, be based on proven voting methods and possible improvements to the existing election procedures. Meanwhile, it should be keep in mind that each process of introducing alternative voting, e.g. voting by correspondence or i-voting, is a long-term process, requiring a strategy for its implementation, due to the necessary changes of a socio-political, normative-organizational, infrastructural (technological) nature. Hence, the implementation of any method of e-voting depends on regulatory and management issues, the existing socio-political framework and the level of technological development of the country. The efficient functioning of Estonian i-voting is primarily a consequence of the long-proven functioning of alternative election procedures, as well as a high level of public trust. The success in minimizing threats in the era of pandemic elections is also confirmed by the experience of Lithuania, which in 2021 introduced drive-thru voting as a pandemic adaptation of the classic method of voting in polling stations. On the other side we have Poland with its attempts to hold presidential elections in the format of *all-postal voting*, which ended in failure due to the organizational disorder resulting from marginal use of this alternative voting method in preceding years.

Meanwhile, Estonia, which commonly uses ICT tools in government administration, found itself in the reality of the pandemic with no major disruptions, thus strengthening its position on the international arena.

References

Alvarez, R. M., Hall, T. E & Trechsel, A. H. (2009). "Internet Voting in Comparative Perspective: The Case of Estonia". *Political Science and Politics,* 42(3), pp. 497–505. https://dx.doi.org/10.1017/S1049096509090787

Applegate, M., Chanussot, T. & Basysty, V. (2020). "Considerations on Internet Voting: An Overview for Electoral Decision-Makers", Retrieved from: https://www .ifes.org/sites/default/files/considerations_on_internet_voting_an_overview_for _electoral_decision-makers.pdf

Cartwright, J. (2019), 'Online voting isn't ready for high-stakes elections'. Retrieved from: https://ec.europa.eu/research-and-innovation/en/horizon-magazine/online-voting -isnt-ready-high-stakes-elections

Dyś-Branicka, I. (2016). „E-voting jako alternatywna procedura głosowania na przykładzie Estonii – szanse i zagrożenia". Retrieved from: http://www.repozytorium.uni.wroc.pl /Content/79494/05_01_I_Dys-Branicka_E-voting_jako_alternatywna_procedura _glosowania.pdf

Eesti Vabariigi põhiseadus (RT 1992, 26, 349). Retrieved from: https://www.riigiteataja .ee/akt/115052015002

"Estonian municipal elections shouldn't be postponed, most parties say"(2021). Baltic News Network. Retrieved from: https://bnn-news.com/estonian-municipal-elections -shouldnt-be-postponed-most-parties-say-223403

Erakorralise seisukorra seadus (RT I 1996, 8, 165). Retrieved from: https://www.riigite ataja.ee/akt/106052020005

Górny, M. (2021). "I-voting – opportunities and threats. Conditions for the effective implementation of Internet voting on the example of Switzerland and Estonia". Przegląd Politologiczny, no. 1/2021, pp. 133–146. DOI: http://dx.doi.org/10.14746 /pp.2021.26.1.9

Hacker, K. L. & van Dijk, J. (2000). Digital Democracy: Issues of Theory and Practice. London: Sage.

Hall, T. E., (2012). "Electronic voting. The World of Political Science: The Development of the Discipline Book Series". In N. Kersting (Eds.), Electronic Democracy, pp. 153–176. Berlin- Toronto: Barbara Budrich Publishers.

IDEA (2022). "Global overview of COVID-19: Impact on elections". Retrieved from: https://www.idea.int/news-media/multimedia-reports/global-overview-COVID-19 -impact-elections

Kapsa, I. & Musiał-Karg, M. (2019). "Citizen e-Participation as an important Factor for Sustainable Development". European Journal of Sustainable Development, 8(3), pp. 210–220. https://dx.doi.org/10.14207/ejsd.2019.v8n3p210

Kneuer, M. (2016). "E-democracy: A new challenge for measuring democracy". International Political Science Review, 37(5), pp. 666–678. https://dx.doi .org/10.1177/0192512116657677

Kohaliku omavalitsuse volikogu valimise seadus (RT I 2002, 36, 220). Retrieved from: https://www.riigiteataja.ee/akt/117112017007

Krimmer, R., Volkamer, M., Barrat, J., Benaloh, J.; Goodman, N.; Ryan, P.Y.A. & Teague, V. (Eds.) (2016). Electronic Voting: First International Joint Conference, E-Vote-ID 2016, Bregenz: Springer.

Krimmer, R. (2016). "Constitutional Constraints for the Use of ICT in Elections". *Expert Electoral Review*, Special Issue 2016, pp. 28–35. Retrieved from: https://www. researchgate.net/publication/301220032_Constitutional_Constraints_for_the_Use _of_Information_and_Communication_Technologies_in_Elections

Krimmer, R. & Volkamer, M. (Eds.) (2014). *6th International Conference on Electronic Voting EVOTE2014*, Tallinn: TUT Press.

Krimmer, R. (Ed.) (2013). *Handbook for the Observation of New Voting Technologies* (*NVT*). Warsaw: OSCE/ODIHR.

Krimmer, R. (2012). "The Evolution of E-voting: Why Voting Technology is Used and How it Affects Democracy". Dissertation at Tallinn University of Technology.

Krok, E. (2020). *Partycypacja Obywatelska.*Toruń: Dom Organizatora.

Kulikowska, M. & Epa, E. (2015), „Perspektywy uregulowania powszechnego dostępu do Internetu i elektronicznego głosowania w Polsce". *Studia z Zakresu Nauk Prawnoustrojowych. Miscellanea*, vol. 5, pp. 75–93.

Laud, P. (Ed.) (2012). *Information Security Technology for Applications 16th Nordic Conference on Secure IT Systems,NordSec 2011*. Tallinn: Springer.

Lindner, R. & Aichholzer, G. (2020). "E-Democracy: Conceptual Foundations and Recent Trends". In L. Hennen, I. van Keulen, I. Korthagen, G. Aichholzer, R. Lindner & R. Nielsen, Ø (Eds.), *European E-Democracy in Practice*, pp. 11–45. Cham: Springer.

Lindner, R., Aichholzer, G., Hennen, L. (Eds.). (2016). *Electronic democracy in Europe. Prospects and challenges of e – publics, e-participation and e-voting.* Cham: Springer.

"Local elections 2021" (2021). *Valimised.* Retrieved from: https://www.valimised.ee/en /local-elections-2021.

Macintosh, A. & Whyte, A. (2006). *Evaluating how e-participation changes local participation.* Retrieved from: http://www.gov2u.org/publications/Evaluating_ePartici pation.pdf

Mielewczyk, J. (2015). „Geneza i ewolucja ustawodawstwa wyborczego w Republice Estońskiej o 1991 roku". *Studia Politicae Universitatis Silesiensis* no.15.

Musiał-Karg, M. & Luengo Ó. G. (Eds.) (2021). *Digitalization of democratic processes in Europe. Southern and Central Europe in a Comparative Perspective.* Cham: Springer.

Musiał-Karg, M. (2018). „Analiza doświadczeń związanych z wykorzystaniem głosowania internetowego (i-voting) w wybranych państwach", *Zeszyty Prawnicze Biura Analiz Sejmowych Kancelarii Sejmu*, no. 1(57), pp. 46–68. https://dx.doi.org/10.31268 /ZPBAS.2018.03

Musiał-Karg, M. (2017). "Challenges of i-voting – practices, rules and perspectives. Examples from Estonia and Switzerland". *Przegląd Politologiczny*, no. 4, pp. 61–72. https://dx.doi.org/10.14746/pp.2017.22.4.6

Musiał-Karg, M. (2011a). „*Internetowe głosowanie w E-stonii na przykładzie wyborów w latach 2005–2009". Przegląd Politologiczny*, no. 3, pp. 99–118.

Musiał-Karg, M. (2011b). "*The Theory and Practice of Online Voting. The Case of Estonia (selected issues)*". *Athenaeum. Polish Political Science Studies*, no. 29, pp. 180–198.

Norris, P. (2005). "The impact of the Internet on Political Activism: Evidence from Europe". *International Journal of Electronic Government Research*, no. 1(1), pp. 19–39. https://dx.doi.org/10.4018/jegr.2005010102.

Rulka, M. (2017), „E-voting a zasady prawa wyborczego. Analiza porównawczoprawna". *Przegląd Sejmowy no. 3(140)*.

Russack, S. (2021), "Introduction: COVID and democracy", In S. Russack (Ed.) *The effect of COVID on EU democracies*. Retrieved from: https://epin.org/wp-content /uploads/2021/05/The-effect-of-COVID-on-EU-democracies.pdf

Sagan, S. (2018), Ustrój państwowy Republiki Estonii. Rzeszów: Wydawnictwo Uniwersytetu Rzeszowskiego.

Sierzputowska, K. (2020). "Estonian Way to the Digital State : Determinants of the Development of the Republic of Estonia". *Athenaeum. Polskie Studia Politologiczne*, no. 68, pp. 160–176. https://dx.doi.org/10.15804/athena.2020.68.11.

Skotnicki, K. (2018). „Instytucja i-votingu w wybranych krajach". *Zeszyty Prawnicze Biura Analiz Sejmowych Kancelarii Sejmu*, no. 1(57), pp. 71–85. https://dx.doi.org/10.31268 /ZPBAS.2018.04

Solvak, M. & Vassil, K. (2016). *E-voting In Estonia: Technological Diffusion and Other Developments Over Ten Years (2005–2015)*. University of Tartu & Estonian National Electoral Committee, Tartu.

Szwed K. (2021). „Regulacja stanów nadzwyczajnych w Republice Estońskiej a pandemia COVID-19". *Przegląd Prawa Konstytucyjnego*, no. 4 (62), pp. 375–387. https:// dx.doi.org/10.15804/ppk.2021.04.24,

Szwed, K. (2018). „Pozycja ustrojowa rządu republiki Estonii oraz jego rola w tworzeniu nowoczesnego państwa. *Polityka i Społeczeństwo*. no. 2 (16), pp. 83–98. https://doi .org/10.15584/polispol.2018.2.6.

Trechsel A. H. (2007). *E-voting and Electoral Participation*. In C. de Vreese (Ed.), *Dynamics of Referendum Campaigns, An International Perspective*, Palgrave. London.

Vinkel, P. Krimmer, R. (2016). "The How and Why to Internet Voting An Attempt to Explain E-stonia". *International joint conference on electronic voting*, Cham: Springer.

Vinkel, P. (2012). Internet Voting in Estonia. In Laud P. (Ed.) *Information Security Technology for Applications 16th Nordic Conference on Secure IT Systems,NordSec 2011*. Tallinn: Springer.

"Voter turnout statistics" (2021). Valimised. Retrieved from: https://kov2021.valimised .ee/en/participation/index.html

Webb, E., Winkelmann, J., Scarpetti, G., Behmane, D., Habicht, T., Kahur, K., Kasekamp, K., Köhler, K., Miščikienė, L., Misins, J., Reinap, M., Slapšinskaitė-Dackevičienė, A., Võrk, A. & Karanikolos, M.(2021), "Lessons learned from the Baltic countries' response to the first wave of COVID-19". *Health Policy.* https://dx.doi.org/10.1016/j.healthpol.2021.12.003

"When will other countries join Estonia in voting on the internet?", *E-stonia.* Retrieved from: https://e-estonia.com/when-will-other-countries-join-estonia-in-voting-on-the-internet/

Zbieranek, J. (2018). „Głosowanie przez internet (i-voting) w wybranych państwach". *Zeszyty Prawnicze*, no. 1(57), pp. 9–45. https://dx.doi.org/10.31268/ZPBAS.2018.02

PART 3

Electoral Turbulence in Poland

From Disastrous Reform and Failed Election to Safeguarding
Democracy: Poland as a Unique Case Study

∴

Guarantees of Universal Suffrage in the Era of Elections Held during the Pandemic

Krzysztof Skotnicki and Joanna Kielin-Maziarz

19.1 Introduction

Elections in a democratic state are conducted on the basis of many principles, with the principle of universality always being mentioned in the first place both in legal acts, including primarily in constitutions, as well as in legal and political literature on the subject. This is understandable not only because it has been shaped in this way historically, but above all because of its importance. Power in a democratic state belongs (or is exercised, depending on the wording used in the Basic Laws) to the collective sovereign, who is most often referred to as a nation or a people. It is also understandable that the primary way in which such a sovereign exercises this power is through representatives who must be elected in some way, and elections are such a way. However, it will be possible to speak of a real representation of the sovereign only if the right to select the representative body or bodies through which the sovereign's authority is exercised belongs to the widest possible circle of persons, since it is evident that, even in view of age, not everyone can do so. Having an active right to vote depends on the fulfillment of several conditions (censuses), which are usually: having citizenship of a given country, a certain number of years of age (usually 18, although currently in some countries it is beginning to be reduced), having full legal capacity, as well as full public or electoral rights. It should be remembered, however, that in order for persons entitled to vote during the elections of representative bodies to be able to exercise this right, certain conditions must be created for this, otherwise the universality of elections will be a fiction. Nowadays, many such guarantees are known and used: the date, day or days of voting, registers and lists of voters, the creation of a significant number of polling stations, including those adapted to the possibility of voting in them by sick, disabled or elderly people, the creation of special polling stations for voters staying in hospitals, other health care institutions, social care homes, prisons, abroad, on seagoing ships on election day, the so-called alternative ways of voting, which include voting by proxy, postal voting and various ways of remote voting (so-called e-voting), are also becoming more and more popular (Skotnicki, 2000).

The SARS-CoV-2 pandemic has posed a number of new challenges for the modern world, including those related to the conduct of elections of representative bodies. It has become obvious that they cannot take place on the basis of the existing rules, that it is necessary to postpone them in time, or to modify or even introduce new guarantees enabling them to be carried out (Johnson, A.F., Pollock, W., Rauhaus, B. (2020). 249–264; Landman, T., Di Gennaro Splendore, L. (2020). 1060–1066; Bertoli, S., Guichard, L., Marchetta, F. (2020, June). The aim of the study is to present how this problem was solved in Poland and to consider whether all actions taken at that time were appropriate and effective. The thesis that is subject to verification is that after the initial very flawed regulation of the Act of April 6, 2020 on the special rules for holding general elections for the President of the Republic of Poland ordered in 2020 (*Ustawa z dnia 6 kwietnia 2020 ...*), the solution contained in the act of June 2, 2020 on special rules for the organization of general elections for the President of the Republic of Poland, ordered in 2020, with the possibility of postal voting (*Ustawa z dnia 2 czerwca 2020 ...*), was worked out, which allowed for a relatively safe conduct of presidential elections on June 28 (1st round) and July 12, 2020 (second round). The issues raised in the chapter have not been, so far, the subject of a broader study, but have appeared more as an element of broader legal and political considerations regarding the restriction of human and civil liberties and rights in the era of the COVID-19 pandemic, or research devoted to elections during this pandemic (see: *Dylematy polskiego prawa ..*, 2021; Musiał-Karg, 2021). First of all, we examine legal acts, mainly the already mentioned one. At the same time, we use the legal-dogmatic method, which serves us to exegesis the regulations we are interested in. We also analyse the results of the 2020 presidential election, in which the statistical method is helpful. To a small extent, we also show how attempts were made to guarantee the universality of elections in other countries, using in this case the legal-comparative method.

19.2   Legal Background and Possible Scenarios

Considerations should begin with a reminder that, in accordance with Article 127(2) of the Constitution of the Republic of Poland of 1997, in 2020 the term of office of President Andrzej Duda, elected in 2015, was coming to an end and there was a need to order the election of the President of the Republic of Poland. Therefore, on the basis of Article 128(2) of the Constitution of the Republic of Poland and Article 289(1) and Article 290 of the Electoral Code

(*Ustawa z dnia 5 stycznia 2011 ...*), the Marshal of the Sejm, on 5 February 2020, issued a decision on ordering the election of the President of the Republic of Poland setting their date for 10 May 2020 and specifying the electoral calendar for them (*Postanowienie Marszałka ...*, item 184).Thus, the election was ordered before the SARS-CoV-2 virus, which causes an acute infectious disease of the respiratory system, referred to as COVID-19, arrived in Poland. In connection with the appearance of this disease, the Minister of Health first issued regulations of March 13, 2020 on the declaration of an epidemic emergency in the Territory of the Republic of Poland (*Rozporządzenie Ministra ...*, item 433), and after a week a regulation of March 20, 2020 on the announcement of the state of epidemic in the Republic of Poland and the introduction of lockdown (*Rozporządzenie Ministra ...*, item 491). In this situation, it became obvious that the ordered presidential elections, as well as the Senate by-elections or local government by-elections or early elections and local referendums will not be able to take place in the way provided for in the Act of 5 January 2011 – Electoral Code or the act of 15 September 2000 on local referendum (i.e. *Obwieszczenie Marszałka ...*, item 741). On the one hand, it has become problematic to conduct an election campaign, and on the other hand, and even more importantly, to hold a vote.

In this situation, the simplest solution seemed to be to postpone the election (Grzybowska-Walecka & Wojtas-Jarentowska, 2020; Musiał-Karg, 2021, pp. 32–33); this could be done by introducing one of the states of emergency (state of natural disaster or state of emergency),[1] which, according to Article 228(7) of the Constitution, would automatically lead to the extension of the term of office of the incumbent President and postpone the presidential and local elections not only for the duration of this state, but also 90 days after its completion.[2] In Poland, however, such a step was not decided and in this situation, on March 22, 2020, in several municipalities, there were conducted by-elections to municipal councils or early elections of the mayor.[3] It should

---

1   This is what the Czech Republic, for example, has done. For more details, see: Jirásková, 2021, pp. 17–34.

2   The subject of the study makes us ignore the legal problems arising in such a case (independent of political ones) resulting from the lack of precision of the regulations in the Basic Law and the Electoral Code regarding such a situation, which m.in do not allow to answer the question whether the elections would be continued or started anew, i.e. whether new candidates can be proposed).

3   These were by-elections to the following councils: Pątnów commune (Łódź Voivodeship), Strzelce Wielkie Commune (Łódź Voivodeship), Smyków Commune (Świętokrzyskie Voivodeship) and the City Council in Biała Piska (Warmian-Masurian Voivodeship) and early elections of the mayors of Wierzchlas Commune (Łódź Voivodeship) and Jarosław

be remembered, however, that at that time there were no regulations directly referring to the conduct of elections during the pandemic, hence, with the growing state of epidemic threat, first of all, the election commissioners asked for appropriate recommendations of the State Sanitary Inspection, which recommended limiting the number of people staying in polling stations, keeping a two-meter distance from themselves, as well as equipping the premises of precinct election commissions with containers with disinfecting liquid, creating the possibility of voting by voters using disposable pens, the work of members of election commissions wearing gloves, as well as airing polling stations and disinfecting door handles. The course of these elections was also treated as an experiment before the presidential election and a test of turnout in a situation of fear of infection.The fears were well founded. For example, in the second round of the election of the Mayor of the Commune of Jarosław, the turnout was 28.44%, while in the first round (8 March) it was 49.29%, and in the election of the Mayor of the Commune of Wierzchlas – 9.48% (*Obwieszczenie Komisarza Wyborczego* ...). Already on 24 March 2020, the Minister of Health issued a regulation amending the regulation on the announcement of the state of epidemic in the territory of the Republic of Poland (*Rozporządzenie Ministra Zdrowia* ..., item 522), which provided for the period from 25 March 2020 to 11 April 2020 inter alia a ban on movement (added § 3a paragraph 1) and a ban on gatherings (added § 11a paragraph 1); this gave rise to postponing the dates of local elections.

In our opinion, postponing elections in a state of epidemic can be treated as a guarantee of universal elections, as it leads to a situation in which voters participate in the act of voting without fear of contamination.

19.3   Holding the Elections - Legal Analysis

The most important problem was the holding of the election of the President of the Republic of Poland on May 10, 2020. The first move to do this was to expand the circle of voters who could vote by post. This was done by the Act of March 31, 2020 amending the Act on special solutions related to the prevention, prevention and combating of COVID-19, other infectious diseases and crisis situations caused by them, and some other acts (the so-called first anti-crisis shield amending the so-called special coronavirus law) (*Ustawa z*

Commune (Podkarpackie Voivodeship). During the by-elections, however, voting did not take place everywhere, because only one candidate was nominated in a single-mandate constituency (the so-called non-contentious elections).

dnia 31 marca 2020 ...). It amended the Electoral Code and allowed voting by correspondence to voters subject to compulsory quarantine, isolation or isolation at home on the voting day, as referred to in the Act of 5 December 2008 on preventing and combating infections and infectious diseases in humans (*Obwieszczenie Marszałka ...,* item 1239; *Ustawa z dnia 31 lipca 2019* ... ; *Ustawa z dnia 23 stycznia 2020* ... ; *Ustawa z dnia 2 marca 2020* ...) and those who they turned 60 on the day of voting at the latest (added to § 1a in Article 53a of the Electoral Code). It was a significant change, as it should be remembered that postal voting into the Polish electoral law system was introduced by the Electoral Code, but only for voters abroad. However, even before its entry into force, when it was amended by the Act of 27 May 2011, this method of voting was made possible for people with disabilities, understood as "voters with limited physical, mental, mental or sensory fitness, which makes it difficult for them to participate in elections " (added point 11 in Article 5 of the Electoral Code) (*Ustawa z dnia 27 maja 2011* ...). The amendment to the Electoral Code on July 11, 2014 (*Ustawa z dnia 11 lipca 2014* ...), which opened the possibility of postal voting during all elections except for local elections (although such a proposal was also submitted), went even further. This solution, for fear of falsification, was criticized by parliamentarians of right-wing groups and after they came to power, there was even a bill to abolish this way of voting. Following numerous voices of opposition, including the National Electoral Commission, the National Electoral Office, the Commissioner for Human Rights and the communities of people with disabilities, the amendment to the Electoral Code finally left the possibility of voting by mail by voters with severe or moderate disabilities with severe or moderate disabilities within the meaning of the Act of 27 August 1997 on vocational and social rehabilitation and employment of disabled persons (new wording of Article 53a § 1 of the Electoral Code) (*Ustawa z dnia 11 stycznia 2018* ..., art. 5 point 25).

However, the existing legal situation did not guarantee the certainty of holding presidential elections in 2020. The ruling majority therefore decided, despite the so-called legislative silence, to pass an episodic law, which was to ensure the election of the Head of State within the already set deadline. There is a dispute as to whether this was permissible. It is emphasized that the state of epidemic is functionally identical to the state of emergency, in particular the state of natural disaster, and some restrictions even exceed it. Its establishment is therefore a circumvention of the Constitution (Garlicki, 2020, p. 461), which in Art. 128 sec. 6 inter alia excludes changes to the electoral law in emergency states. Therefore, such a solution was unacceptable (Piotrowski, 2021, pp. 169–170). In our opinion, due to the spread of the pandemic, it was permissible, but it required the agreement of the most important, including opposition, parliamentary political parties. We also look at it differently from the perspective of two years since those events. The lack of talks and the discrepancy of positions meant that this did not happen, and the rulers undertook legislative actions on their own.

In this situation, there was great legal chaos. The Act of 16 April 2020 on special support instruments in connection with the spread of the SARS-CoV-2 virus (*Ustawa z dnia 16 kwietnia 2020 ...*) suspended in Article 102 a number of provisions of the Electoral Code, including, above all, the competences of the National Electoral Commission in determining the template of the ballot paper and ordering the printing of cards. At the same time, work began on the Act on special rules for conducting general elections for the President of the Republic of Poland ordered in 2020 (*Ustawa z dnia 6 kwietnia 2020 ...*), which, in violation of a number of procedural rules, was enacted on 7 May 2020 (Skotnicki, 2021, pp. 139–157), and entered into force only on 9 May 2020, i.e. on the eve of the elections. Undoubtedly, this was not conducive to legal certainty, and it is also difficult to talk about the existence of guarantees for the universality of elections, when in the few weeks preceding the elections, it was not known whether they would take place on the prescribed date and on what basis. On the one hand, all the time, in accordance with the electoral calendar, elections were held on the basis of the Electoral Code, while depriving the National Electoral Commission of determining the template of ballot papers and ordering their printing, and on the other hand, work was underway on a new law regulating these elections, and even actions were taken in accordance with this project, i.e. without the applicable legal basis, e.g. election packages were printed.

The election of the President of the Republic of Poland on May 10, 2020, of course, did not take place. However, it should be analyzed whether the act passed just before that date actually guaranteed voters to participate in voting.

There is no doubt that the purpose of passing this law was not only to hold elections of the President of the Republic of Poland at all costs and as soon as possible, but also to create a guarantee for the universality of voting. Therefore, Article 2 stipulates that the presidential elections already ordered will be conducted only by postal voting. In the "Explanatory Memorandum" of the bill, it was explicitly emphasized that this would exclude "the potential risk of getting sick, existing with the obligation to cast votes at the polling station" (*Poselski projekt ...*). However, the question arises whether the proposed solution was a real guarantee of universal elections.

Postal voting is, as commonly known, one of the so-called alternative methods of voting and as such is recognized in Poland as compliant with the Constitution. This was stated by the Constitutional Tribunal in its judgment of 20 July

2011 (*Wyrok*). It should be remembered, however, that this judgment referred to a situation in which the choice of the method of voting depended on the will of the voter, who independently decided whether he wanted to do it on general terms at the polling station of the ward electoral commission or otherwise. At that time, the Tribunal stressed that the voter, deciding "to vote outside the premises of the ward electoral commission, consciously resigns from [...] the guarantee of the secrecy of the vote created by the State, while assuming the obligation to organise for itself the appropriate conditions to ensure the secrecy of the vote" (*Wyrok*). The mentioned act deprived the voter of the possibility of making such a choice by introducing only the so-called *all-postal voting* (Musiał-Karg & Kapsa, 2021, pp. 6–8). Thus, it was not a real guarantee of universality of voting. Postal voting was not particularly popular in Poland. For example, during the 2015 presidential election, 42,814 electoral packages were sent during the first round out of a total of 14,993,468 ballot papers issued (*Obwieszczenie Państwowej Komisji Wyborczej z dnia 11 maja 2015 ...*), and in the second round 56,854 electoral packages were sent out of 16,956,615 ballot papers issued (*Obwieszczenie Państwowej Komisji Wyborczej z dnia 25 maja 2015 ...*). A similar interest in postal voting took place during the 2015 Sejm elections, when every voter could vote by mail; 45,538 packets were sent out of a total of 15,563,499 ballot papers issued (*Obwieszczenie Państwowej Komisji Wyborczej z dnia 25 maja 2015 ...*). It is difficult to predict what this results from, but it seems that it is largely due to the voter's distrust, whether the vote cast in this way will actually be delivered and counted, or even whether it will not be falsified.

Such concerns were also formulated after the announcement of exclusive postal voting in the presidential election on May 10, 2020. However, they were also significantly deepened by other solutions established by the Act of 6 April 2020.

The first doubt arose from the fact that voters were not sure whether they would receive election packages. This was due to the fact that the Act in Article 3(1) entrusted the task of their delivery to an operator designated within the meaning of the Act of 23 November 2012 – Postal Law, i.e. a single-member company of the State Treasury – Poczta Polska S.A. The problem does not concern this entity, but the fact that delivery was to be made (from 7 days to the day falling before the day of voting) "directly to the voter's mailbox or to the voter's address indicated in part A of the electoral register". Apart from the issue of providing Poczta Polska S.A. with data from the electoral registers, which in itself raises many doubts, it was primarily supposed to be an ordinary shipment without the obligation to confirm its receipt. So the voter was not sure whether she would reach him. It was uncertain whether the deliverer would deliver it, especially when he knew or guessed the voter's political views. There was also a question of what to do if more or less election packages are delivered to a given address than voters staying at that address.

Article 4 of the Act provided that at the latest on the day of its entry into force, a voter may apply to the commune office for inclusion in the electoral register, and at the same time referred to matters not regulated in it to the Electoral Code. Even in a situation in which this law would enter into force earlier than 9 May 2020, due to the time of the complaint process, it was quite illusory to guarantee the universality of elections.

The Act in Article 5(1) then imposed on the voter the obligation to complete and sign the declaration of personal and secret voting contained in the election package and to send it back together with the completed ballot paper to the ward electoral commission. Without this, the vote cast was not thrown into the ballot box and was not counted. Previous experience shows that voters make many mistakes when filling out declarations, which means that their votes are not taken into account when determining the results of voting and election results. Of course, the statements could not be resigned, nor was there a technical and organizational possibility for the voter to receive an already completed statement, which he should only sign. However, it was clear that many votes cast would contain errors in statements (e.g. no PESEL- Universal Electronic Population Registration System number entered), and thus these votes would not be taken into account. Undoubtedly, this significantly weakened the guarantee of universality of this vote.

Serious doubts must also be raised by the method of transferring the vote by post to the precinct electoral commission. Up to a certain point, the procedure envisaged was the same as the one in force before. The voter was to first fill out a ballot paper and put it in an envelope for a ballot paper, which he then had to seal. The next step was to put this envelope and the statement of personal and secret voting in the return envelope. In this case, however, the electoral law of 6 April 2020 no longer required it to be sealed. The most questionable, however, is that pursuant to Art. 5 sec. 2 return envelopes were to be placed in person or through another person "in a specially prepared for this purpose mailbox of the operator designated in the commune in which the electoral register is listed" and in Warsaw in the district in which the electoral register is listed (Article 5(3) of the Act). The requirements to be met by such a box were to be determined, in a regulation, by the minister competent for state assets. It was never released. The introduced solution did not answer many questions, in particular how many such boxes are to be prepared, how many places are to be where they are to be exhibited, how they will be protected, for example, against destruction or theft and how their location will be notified to voters.

The act also provided that the return envelope was to be placed in this mailbox "not earlier than at 6.00 and no later than 20.00 on the voting day", but who was to watch over it? Envelopes for the municipal precinct election commission were to be delivered by the operator who provided the mailbox for return envelopes. However, was it certain that all return envelopes would actually be delivered there? Despite the fact that the answers to some of these questions were to be provided by a regulation issued by the minister competent for state assets in consultation with the minister competent for health (Article 6(1) of the Act), the established solution can hardly be considered a real guarantee of universal elections. In this situation, it was understandable that many voters would be so confused that they would resign from participating in the elections, including for fear of contracting the virus.

A separate problem was the possibility of handing over the return envelope by "another person". The compatibility of this solution with the principle of immediacy of the election is questionable, and there was no guarantee that the envelope would actually be thrown into this box, which was very likely in a situation where the person fulfilling the request knew or guessed the content of the voter's vote who asked him for such a favor. It is also understandable that the status of such a „other person" was absolutely unclear legally (*Opinia o ustawie ...*).

Many similar doubts were also raised by the manner of handing over election packages and return envelopes in the case of voters remaining in compulsory quarantine on the day of voting, in isolation or isolation at home, in social welfare homes, in health institutions, prisons or detention centers.

The Electoral Act of 6 April 2020 also provided for the possibility of voting by post abroad. The most serious problem in this case was the requirement for a voter abroad to inform the competent consul of his intention to vote by mail by the 14th day before election day. This made it unrealistic for this group of voters to participate in the elections, and on the day the Sejm rejected the Senate's position, as well as the entry into force of the law itself, it was of course impossible, which only more clearly shows the chaos prevailing at that time.

The assessment of the electoral law of 6 April 2020 must therefore be unequivocally critical. It did not guarantee that elections would be held in accordance with the principle of universal elections, and it also raised legitimate doubts as to its compatibility with other principles, such as the principle of equality or the principle of fairness. In the literature on the subject, this law is fully justified in indicating "did not become – fortunately – the basis for the implementation of the electoral process; we didn't witness the events when election packages would be passed on nobody knows who by and who to" (Balicki, 2021, p. 203).

19.4   Legal Aspects of Further Electoral Regulations

Due to the fact that the presidential elections were not held on May 10, 2020, work was immediately started on a new law regulating the procedure for their conduct. This led to the adoption (again in violation of the legislative procedure) of the Act of 2 June 2020 on specific rules for the organization of general elections for the President of the Republic of Poland ordered in 2020 with the possibility of voting by mail (*Ustawa z dnia 2 czerwca 2020 …*). The very next day, the Marshal of the Sejm ordered these elections, setting them for June 28, 2020 (*Postanowienie Marszałka …,* item 988). The legal basis for this ordinance is art. 128 sec. 2 of the Constitution, Art. 293 § 2 of the Electoral Code and Art. 15 sec. 1 of the act passed the day before; there are serious doubts as to the admissibility of adopting this provision, but considerations on this subject differ from the subject of this study (Piotrowski, 2021, pp. 168–169).

The new presidential electoral law adopted the traditional method of voting at the premises of the precinct election commission as the basic method of voting, while postal voting, as its title already indicates, was an alternative chosen only by the voter (Article 2 (1) of the Act). The only exception was in the case of voting abroad, when "Due to the epidemic situation in the host country, it is allowed to indicate the territorial jurisdiction of the consul of the oblasts where only correspondence voting is possible" (Article 2 (4), second sentence, of the Act) . On the other hand, voting by post was not possible in the country in separate voting precincts established in health centers, nursing homes, student houses or student housing complexes, prisons and detention centers, as well as in external departments of such a facility and detention center, and in voting precincts established on Polish sea-going ships and also in the event of a disabled voter granting a power of attorney to vote (Article 2 (2) of the Act).

The law established relatively early maximum deadlines for the notification of an intention to vote by correspondence. In Poland, this had to be reported to the election commissioner through the office of the commune in which you were entered on the electoral roll, up to 12 days before election day, and in the case of voters subject to compulsory quarantine, isolation or isolation at home on the day of voting – up to 5 days before on election day, and the voter who started such quarantine, isolation or isolation at home after that date could do so even up to 2 days before election day; abroad, the notification of such an intention to the consul had to take place by the 15th day before the election day (Article 3 (1) and (2) of the Act). There was also a lot of freedom in the manner of submitting the notification, as it could be done orally, in writing or in electronic form via the service provided by the minister responsible for computerization (Article 3 (3) of the Act).

Election packages were delivered to voters by municipal offices, which did so via Poczta Polska S.A. with the participation of at least two of its employees, with the application of the provisions on registered mail (Article 5 (2) and (5) of the Act), they could be delivered by employees of municipal offices and collected in person (Article 5 (3) and (4) of the Act) . The voter should receive the election package no later than 5 days before election day, and in the case of voters who, due to quarantine, isolation or home isolation on the voting day, expressed their will to vote by correspondence in the period from 12 days before election day, even no later than 2 days before the voting day (Article 5 (1) of the Act). Abroad, election packages were sent by consuls as unregistered items, but if it was declared in the notification of the intention to vote by correspondence, it was also possible to collect them in person (Article 6 (2) and (3) of the Act). Importantly, voters received completed declarations on personal and secret voting, which they only had to sign, as well as self-addressed return envelopes. On request, they also received an overlay for the voting card prepared in the Braille system.

In the country, there was a general rule according to which return envelopes were sent back by the voter to the appropriate ward electoral commission via Poczta Polska S.A. The Act in Article 8(4) imposed on this operator the obligation to place in each commune a mailbox in a rounded up number resulting from the quotient of the number of voters who reported in a given commune the intention to vote by mail and the number 750. The voter himself addressed the return envelope. Until the 2nd day before the election day, it was also possible to personally deliver the return envelope: in the country – to the municipal office, and abroad – to the consulate.

The interest in postal voting during the presidential elections both in the first round on June 28, 2020 and during the re-election on July 12, 2020 (second round) was significant and definitely higher compared to the earlier elections to the Sejm and Senate in 2019 or the presidential elections in 2015. In the first round, due to the desire to vote by post, election packages were sent to 536 821 voters, out of the total number of 19,026,600 voters who were issued with voting cards; 483,898 return envelopes were sent back, and 462,807 envelopes with ballots were thrown into the ballot boxes (*Obwieszczenie Państwowej Komisji Wyborczej z dnia 30 czerwca 2020...*). The re-elections were even more popular. Election packages were sent to 704,111 voters; 614,631 return envelopes were sent back, and 593,269 envelopes with a ballot paper were thrown into the ballot boxes (*Obwieszczenie Państwowej Komisji Wyborczej z dnia 13 lipca 2020 ...*). For comparison, during the presidential election in 2015, 56,845 election packages were sent to voters in the first round, and 40,720 return envelopes were returned (*Obwieszczenie Państwowej Komisji Wyborczej z dnia 27 października*

2015 ...). According to the Office of the Spokesperson of the Ministry of Foreign Affairs, in 2020, over 387,000 citizens expressed their willingness to participate in the presidential election in the first round, of which over 343,000 were voters voting by mail. For comparison, in 2015, 196,121 voters were entered in the electoral rolls during the first round of voting, including 34,021 voting by mail (*Podsumowanie wyborów prezydenckich* ...).

Voting at the premises of the precinct election commission as the primary method of casting a vote during the pandemic meant that in order to ensure the universality of elections during the COVID-19 pandemic, it was necessary to provide voters and members of precinct election commissions with special conditions protecting against infection. The Act in Art. 16, therefore, imposed on the minister competent for health matters to define, by means of a regulation, personal protection measures for members of precinct election commissions, as well as detailed rules of sanitary safety at the polling station. This act was the Regulation of the Minister of Health of June 15, 2020 on the list of personal protective equipment related to combating the COVID-19 epidemic for members of precinct election commissions and detailed rules of sanitary safety at the polling station (*Rozporządzenie Ministra Zdrowia ...*, item 1046). It envisaged, inter alia, equipping polling stations with liquid for hand disinfection, prohibition of covering the table at which committee members were sitting with cloth or other absorbable material, washing with liquid for disinfecting door handles, light switches or other surfaces and objects touched by voters and commission members, members of the election commission received gloves, masks and helmets, were required to sit at a distance of at least 1.5 m from each other, rooms should be aired for at least 10 minutes per hour (without interrupting the vote), voters over 60 with young children or pregnant women were served first. It should be noted that there were generally no major problems with equipping polling stations with disinfectants and other required things, and often they were not even used, which allowed municipalities to allocate them to other tasks related to counteracting the pandemic. There was also no significant increase in the number of coronavirus cases, which does not mean that due to the infection, it was not necessary to replenish the constituency of the precinct election commissions before the next elections; however, it was not common.

When presenting guarantees of universal suffrage during the COVID-19 pandemic, it should also be noted that by-elections to municipal councils are still held (although sometimes, due to the submission of only one candidate, there is no need to vote), the election of the mayor in the event of the expiry of his mandate or local referendums. Unfortunately, no special provisions have been issued in this regard. Only on 27 May 2021 merely the Guidelines of the Chief Sanitary Inspector on the safe implementation of the elections of the authorities of the territorial self-government units during the term of office and local referenda recommended to be carried out from the second decade of June 2021 have been issued (*Wytyczne Głównego Inspektora Sanitarnego* ...), which have not made changes from the previous practice . In practice, opinions were consulted on this matter or requests were made for appropriate recommendations by district sanitary and epidemiological stations. Voting at polling stations is also carried out in the same way as it was during the presidential elections in 2020. Most importantly, the budget allocated by the National Electoral Office for the conduct of these elections and referenda provides funds for the purchase of disinfectants, masks, etc. In our opinion, however, this should not be done on the basis of a certain practice or even the guidelines of the Chief Inspector. Sanitary, but a special legal regulation should be issued, for example extending the validity of the aforementioned Regulation of the Minister of Health of 15 June 2020 on the list of personal protective equipment related to combating the COVID-19 epidemic for members of ward electoral commissions and detailed rules of sanitary safety at the polling station.

19.5   Conclusions

Summing up the analysis carried out, it should be stated that an unambiguous assessment of the guarantee of universal suffrage during the elections and referendums in Poland is not possible. Especially at the beginning of the pandemic, striving at all costs to hold presidential elections was not the right solution and it was possible to resort to the institution of a state of emergency, in particular a state of natural disaster, allowing all elections to be postponed to the period of this state and 90 days after its completion.

Conversely, the desire to hold presidential elections in 2020 as soon as possible meant that little attention was paid to them. The idea of carrying them out in the episodic act of April 2, 2020 only by correspondence voting was not consulted with various entities in a deserving manner, there was no broader consent to it of various political forces and, above all, it was so disastrously constructed that it is difficult to speak in in this case that it was a real guarantee of universal elections. It was not certain whether the election packages would reach the voters, the obligation was imposed on the voter to fill in declarations of the right to vote, which due to, for example, providing the PESEL number gave rise to the risk of not taking into account the ballot paper sent in the return envelope, and it was not known where the operator's mailboxes would be for voting. It is good that the elections carried out on the basis of this regulation did not take place.

The episodic law of 2 June 2020 was undoubtedly devoid of these defects, at least to the extent that its predecessor did. Voting by post was an alternative to traditional voting at the polling station of the ward electoral commission and the voter decided on the choice of voting method. One can have some doubts about the detailed solutions, which, however, does not undermine the overall positive assessment. However, it should be remembered that this method of voting was not introduced in Poland due to the COVID-19 pandemic, because it was already known earlier. To such a wide extent, it was used out of necessity, because just a little earlier in 2018 the possibility of voting in this way was strongly limited, and even its liquidation was proposed. It is also worth noting that, in the current content of the Electoral Code, only a few voters have such a possibility to vote, and there is no guarantee that before the parliamentary elections in 2023, the old age limit for voters who can vote in this way will not be restored. In our opinion, such a significant increase in the number of voters voting by mail should also be assessed with some caution. The question arises whether it resulted from the fear of infection or more from the desire to participate in elections of particular political importance in connection with the Polish constitutional crisis.

In the study, we did not refer to proxy voting and voting on the basis of certificates of voting rights, because their use is not related to the pandemic.

Undoubtedly, the lack of an attempt to reach for other ways of voting in Poland should be assessed negatively. We mean not only *e-voting* or *i-voting*, which are used with varying degrees of success in other countries (especially positively in Estonia), about which the Polish literature on the subject is already relatively rich (Więckowska, 2002, p. 36; Czaplicki, 2005, p. 42; Preisner, 2007, p. 205; Rzucidło, 2013, p. 68; Skotnicki, 2018, p. 68; Musiał-Karg, 2018), but also some ad hoc solutions, such as the creation of 78 special polling stations in the Czech Republic in connection with the pandemic (e.g. in the vicinity of sports stadiums or hospitals), in which eligible voters could, two days before the election, while observing hygiene measures, throw ballot papers into the ballot box without getting out of the car (the so-called early voting) (Jirásková, 2021, p. 26). These are our recommendations for the future (Pyrzyńska, Skoczylas, 2020, p. 233; Florczak – Wątor, 2021, p. 294; Morley, 2023, p. 367; Téglásie, Nagy, p. 1246)

The situation in which by-elections in municipalities, the election of the mayor in the case of the office vacant, and local referenda are conducted without special legal regulations guaranteeing their universality, but only on the basis of the guidelines of the Chief Sanitary Inspector and in accordance with a certain practice that itself it does not raise any comments in itself. Therefore, also in this case, we recommend taking appropriate legal action, preferably adopting an appropriate amendment to the Electoral Code authorizing the minister responsible for health to issue a special regulation for this purpose.

References

Balicki, R. (2021). „Głosowanie korespondencyjne w polskim porządku prawnym – zmienne dzieje regulacji". In: J. Ciapała, A. Pyrzyńska (Eds.), *Dylematy polskiego prawa wyborczego*. Warszawa: C.H. Beck.

Bertoli, S., Guichard, L., Marchetta, F. (2020, June). *Turnout in the Municipal Elections of March 2020 and Excess Mortality during the COVID-19 Epidemic in France*. Bonn: Institute of Labor Econmics. Retrieved from: http://ftp.iza.org/dp13335.pdf.

Czaplicki, K.W. (2005). „Głosowanie elektroniczne (e-voting) – wybrane zagadnienia". In: F. Rymarz (Ed.), *Demokratyczne standardy prawa wyborczego Rzeczypospolitej Polskiej. Teoria i praktyka*. Warszawa: Krajowe Biuro Wyborcze.

Ciapała, J. & Pyrzyńska, A. (2021). *Dylematy polskiego prawa wyborczego*. Warszawa: C.H. Beck.

Florczak-Wator, M. *"States of Emergency in Poland and Their Impact on the Protection of Human Rights in Times of COVID-19 Pandemic."* Romanian Journal of Comparative Law, vol. 12, no. 2, 2021.

Garlicki, L. (2020). *Polskie prawo konstytucyjne. Zarys wykładu*. Warszawa: Wolters Kluwer Polska.

Grzybowska-Walecka, K. & Wojtas-Jarentowska, K. (2020). *Lockdown w demokracjach w czasach pandemii COVID-19*, Raport, Konrad Adenaer Stiftung, https://www.kas.de/documents/279510/8099243/Raport+Lockdown.pdf/8eb86ae7-2a6c-7e06-6506-0b76386b2494?version=1.0&t=1610026523952

Jirásková, V. (2021). „Wybory w dobie koronawirusa – Republika Czeska", *Studia Wyborcze*, vol. XXXI, pp. 17–34.

Johnson, A.F., Pollock, W., Rauhaus, B. (2020). Mass Casualty Event Scenarios and Political Shifts: 2020 Election Outcomes and the U.S. COVID-19 Pandemic. *Administrative Theory & Praxis*, 42(2), pp. 249–264.

Landman, T., Di Gennaro Splendore, L. (2020). Pandemic Democracy: Elections and COVID-19. *Journal of Risk Research*, 23(7–8), 1060–1066.

Morley M.T., *"Election Emergencies: Voting in Times of Pandemic"*, *Washington and Lee Law Review* 80, (359), 2023.

Musiał-Karg M. & Kapsa I. (2021). "Debate: Voting challenges in a pandemic—Poland", *Public Money & Management*, vol 41 no 1, pp. 6–8, https://doi.org/10.1080/0954096 2.2020.1809791.

Musiał-Karg M. (2018). „Analiza doświadczeń związanych z wykorzystaniem głosowania internetowego (i-voting) w wybranych państwach", *Zeszyty Prawnicze BAS no.* 1(57), pp. 46–68, https://doi.10.31268/ZPBAS.2018.03

Musiał-Karg M. (2021). „Głosowanie korespondencyjne podczas pandemii COVID-19. Doświadczenia z polskich wyborów prezydenckich w 2020 r.", *Przegląd Prawa Konstytucyjnego*, no. 2(60), pp. 31–48, DOI 10.15804/ppk.2021.02.02.

Obwieszczenie Komisarza Wyborczego w Przemyślu z dnia 23 marca 2020 r. o wynikach przedterminowych wyborów Wójta Gminy Jarosław, przeprowadzonych w dniu 8 marca 2020 r. oraz w dniu 22 marca 2020 r. Retrieved from: https://przemysl.kbw.gov .pl/uploaded_files/1584962751_obwieszczenie-o-wynikach-wyborow.pdf.

Obwieszczenie Marszałka Sejmu Rzeczypospolitej Polskiej z dnia 4 kwietnia 2019 r. w sprawie ogłoszenia jednolitego tekstu ustawy o referendum lokalnym. Dz. U. 2019 poz. 741.

Obwieszczenie Marszałka Sejmu Rzeczypospolitej Polskiej z dnia 6 czerwca 2019 r. w sprawie ogłoszenia jednolitego tekstu ustawy o zapobieganiu oraz zwalczaniu zakażeń i chorób zakaźnych u ludzi. Dz. U. 2019 poz. 1239.

Obwieszczenie Państwowej Komisji Wyborczej z dnia 11 maja 2015 r. o wynikach głosowania i wyniku wyborów Prezydenta Rzeczypospolitej Polskiej. Dz. U. z 2015 r. poz. 650.

Obwieszczenie Państwowej Komisji Wyborczej z dnia 25 maja 2015 r. o wynikach ponownego głosowania i wyniku wyborów Prezydenta Rzeczypospolitej Polskiej. Dz. U. z 2015 r., poz. 725.

Obwieszczenie Państwowej Komisji Wyborczej z dnia 27 października 2015 r. o wynikach wyborów do Sejmu Rzeczypospolitej Polskiej przeprowadzonych w dniu 25 października 2015 r. Dz. U. z 2015 r. poz. 1731.

Obwieszczenie Państwowej Komisji Wyborczej z dnia 13 lipca 2020 r. o wynikach ponownego głosowania i wyniku wyborów Prezydenta Rzeczypospolitej Polskiej. Dz. U. z 2020 r. poz. 1238.

Obwieszczenie Państwowej Komisji Wyborczej z dnia 30 czerwca 2020 r. o wynikach głosowania i wyniku wyborów Prezydenta Rzeczypospolitej Polskiej, zarządzonych na dzień 28 czerwca 2020 r. Dz. U. z 2020 r. poz. 1163.

Opinia o ustawie z dnia 6 kwietnia 2020 r. o szczególnych zasadach przeprowadzania wyborów powszechnych na Prezydenta Rzeczypospolitej Polskiej zarządzonych w 2020 r. (druk senacki nr 99). Retrieved from: https://www.senat.gov.pl/gfx/senat/pl /senatekspertyzy/5487/plik/oe_292.pdf.

Piotrowski, R. (2021). *Ważność wyborów prezydenckich w świetle Konstytucji RP.* In: J. Ciapała, A. Pyrzyńska (Eds.), *Dylematy polskiego prawa wyborczego.* Warszawa: C.H. Beck.

Podsumowanie wyborów prezydenckich za granicą, 29.06.2020. Retrieved from: https://www.gov.pl/web/dyplomacja/podsumowanie-wyborow-prezydenckich-za -granica.

Poselski projekt ustawy o szczególnych zasadach przeprowadzania wyborów powszechnych na Prezydenta Rzeczypospolitej Polskiej zarządzonych w 2020 r. Sejm Paper No. 328/IX term.

Postanowienie Marszałka Sejmu Rzeczypospolitej Polskiej z dnia 5 lutego 2020 r. w sprawie zarządzenia wyborów Prezydenta Rzeczypospolitej Polskiej. Dz. U. 2020 poz. 184.

Postanowienie Marszałka Sejmu Rzeczypospolitej Polskiej z dnia 3 czerwca 2020 r. w sprawie zarządzenia wyborów Prezydenta Rzeczypospolitej Polskiej. Dz. U. 2020 poz. 988.

Preisner, A. (2007), „e-Voting – przyszłość demokracji? (szkic kilku niełatwych kwestii)". In: S. Grabowska, R. Grabowski (Eds). *Międzynarodowa Konferencja Naukowa nt.: Prawo wyborcze do parlamentu w wybranych państwach europejskich. Rzeszów 3–4 kwietnia 2006 roku.* Rzeszów: Wydawnictwo Uniwersytetu Rzeszowskiego.

Pyrzyńska A., Skoczylas D., "Elections during COVID-19 Pandemic in the Light of Democratic Values and International Standards of Human Rights Protection", European Research Studies Journal Volume XXIII, Special Issue 2, 2020.

Rozporządzenie Ministra Zdrowia z dnia 13 marca 2020 r. w sprawie ogłoszenia na obszarze Rzeczypospolitej Polskiej stanu zagrożenia epidemicznego. Dz. U. 2020 poz. 433.

Rozporządzenie Ministra Zdrowia z dnia 20 marca 2020 r. w sprawie ogłoszenia na obszarze Rzeczypospolitej Polskiej stanu epidemii. Dz. U. 2020 poz. 491.

Rozporządzenie Ministra Zdrowia z dnia 24 marca 2020 r. zmieniające rozporządzenie w sprawie ogłoszenia na obszarze Rzeczypospolitej Polskiej stanu epidemii. Dz. U. 2020 poz. 522.

Rozporządzenie Ministra Zdrowia z dnia 15 czerwca 2020 r. w sprawie wykazu środków ochrony osobistej związanej ze zwalczaniem epidemii COVID-19 dla członków obwodowych komisji wyborczych oraz szczegółowych zasad bezpieczeństwa sanitarnego w lokalu wyborczym. Dz. U. 2020 poz. 1046.

Rzucidło, J. (2013). „Perspektywy głosowania za pośrednictwem Internetu w Rzeczypospolitej Polskiej", *Studia Wyborcze*, vol. XV.

Skotnicki, K. (2018). „Kilka słów o i-votingu". In: R. Balicki & M. Jabłoński (Eds). *Dookoła Wojtek … Księga pamiątkowa poświęcona Doktorowi Arturowi Wojciechowi Preisnerowi.* Wrocław: Wydział Prawa, Administracji i Ekonomii Uniwersytetu Wrocławskiego.

Skotnicki, K. (2000). *Zasada powszechności wyborów. Zagadnienia teorii i praktyki.* Łódź: Wydawnictwo Naukowe Uniwersytetu Łódzkiego.

Skotnicki, K. (2021). *Państwo prawa a tryb uchwalenia w 2020 r. ustaw regulujących wybory Prezydenta RP.* In: J. Ciapała, A. Pyrzyńska (Eds.), *Dylematy polskiego prawa wyborczego.* Warszawa: C.H. Beck.

Téglási A., Nagy A., *"Elections in Hungary and in other countries under special legal order: Especially during the pandemic"*, Zbornik radova Pravnog fakulteta Novi Sad 2021, 55(4).

Ustawa z dnia 5 stycznia 2011 r. – Kodeks wyborczy. Dz.U. 2011 nr 21 poz. 112.

Ustawa z dnia 27 maja 2011 r. o zmianie ustawy – Kodeks wyborczy oraz ustawy – Przepisy wprowadzające ustawę – Kodeks wyborczy. Dz. U. 2011 nr 147 poz. 881.

Ustawa z dnia 11 lipca 2014 r. o zmianie ustawy – Kodeks wyborczy oraz niektórych innych ustaw. Dz. U. 2014 poz. 1072.

Ustawa z dnia 11 stycznia 2018 r. o zmianie niektórych ustaw w celu zwiększenia udziału obywateli w procesie wybierania, funkcjonowania i kontrolowania niektórych organów publicznych. Dz. U. z 2018 r. poz. 130.

Ustawa z dnia 31 lipca 2019 r. o zmianie niektórych ustaw w celu ograniczenia obciążeń regulacyjnych. Dz. U. 2019 poz. 1495.

Ustawa z dnia 23 stycznia 2020 r. o zmianie ustawy o działach administracji rządowej oraz niektórych innych ustaw. Dz. U. 2020 poz. 284.

Ustawa z dnia 2 marca 2020 r. o szczególnych rozwiązaniach związanych z zapobieganiem, przeciwdziałaniem i zwalczaniem COVID-19, innych chorób zakaźnych oraz wywołanych nimi sytuacji kryzysowych. Dz. U. 2020, poz. 374.

Ustawa z dnia 31 marca 2020 r. o zmianie ustawy o szczególnych rozwiązaniach związanych z zapobieganiem, przeciwdziałaniem i zwalczaniem COVID-19, innych chorób zakaźnych oraz wywołanych nimi sytuacji kryzysowych oraz niektórych innych ustaw. Dz. U. 2020 poz. 568.

Ustawa z dnia 16 kwietnia 2020 r. o szczególnych instrumentach wsparcia w związku z rozprzestrzenianiem się wirusa SARS-CoV-2. Dz. U. 2020 poz. 695.

Ustawa z dnia 6 kwietnia 2020 r. o szczególnych zasadach przeprowadzania wyborów powszechnych na Prezydenta Rzeczypospolitej Polskiej zarządzonych w 2020 r. Dz. U. 2020 poz. 827.

Ustawa z dnia 2 czerwca 2020 r. o szczególnych zasadach organizacji wyborów powszechnych na Prezydenta Rzeczypospolitej Polskiej zarządzonych w 2020 r. z możliwością głosowania korespondencyjnego. Dz. U. 2020 poz. 979.

Więckowska, E.M. (2002). *„Wpływ nietradycyjnych technik głosowania na frekwencję podczas wyborów i referendów"*, Studia Wyborcze, vol. XIV.

Wyrok Trybunału Konstytucyjnego z dnia 20 lipca 2011 r. Sygn. akt K 9/11 (OTK ZU 6/A/2011, item 61).

Wytyczne Głównego Inspektora Sanitarnego w sprawie bezpiecznej realizacji wyborów organów jednostek samorządu terytorialnego w toku kadencji i referendów lokalnych rekomendowanych do przeprowadzenia od drugiej dekady czerwca 2021 r. – materiał archiwalny. Retrieved from: https://www.gov.pl/web/gis/wytyczne-glownego-in spektora-sanitarnego-w-sprawie-bezpiecznej-realizacji-wyborow-organow-jednost ek-samorzadu-terytorialnego-w-toku-kadencji-i-referendow-lokalnych-reko mendowanych-do-przeprowadzenia-od-drugiej-dekady-czerwca-2021-r.

CHAPTER 20

The Impact of the Experience from Elections during the COVID-19 Pandemic on the Desirable Direction of Changes in Polish Electoral Law

Agata Pyrzyńska

20.1 Introduction

The COVID-19 pandemic has significantly influenced electoral processes of many countries (Birch et al., 2020, p. 6; Picchio & Santolini, 2022, p. 2–3), contributing to changes in legislation, often causing postponement of voting days and other activities from the electoral calendar (International IDEA, 2022; Vashchanka 2020, p. 5; Maizland, 2020; Tatarczyk & Wojtasik, 2023, p. 620). This is also true for Poland, where the term of office (laid down in the Constitution) of the then president expired during the pandemic. In effect, an election for the head of the country became one of the leading subjects in parliamentary debates and among public life commentators in the first half of 2020. This should not be surprising given the importance of elections for the entire political system and the Polish President's status in this system. Striving to hold a vote during the pandemic while not declaring the state of emergency meant that significant amendments to legislation had to be made (OSCE/ODIHR, 2020a, p. 1). Unfortunately, given the circumstances, the regulator's legislative actions were hasty, whereby citizens' (voters') sense of legal certainty was shaken (OSCE/ODIHR, 2020b, p. 6). A permanent state of concern about procedures in place entered the scene, also among election organizers. Contrary to numerous doubts reported by constitutionalist circles, the parliament first passed the Act of 6 April 2020 on special rules for holding elections to the office of the President of the Republic of Poland ordered for 2020 (*Ustawa z dnia 6 kwietnia 2020 r ...*). This act entered into force the day before the vote, which, combined with other circumstances in law and in fact, made it impossible to hold the balloting on 10 May 2020. On 2 June 2020 another act on special rules for holding elections to the office of the President of the Republic of Poland ordered for 2020 allowing correspondence voting was passed (*Ustawa z dnia 2 czerwca 2020 r ...*). Despite numerous opposing voices (Matczak, 2020a), this law became a direct basis for holding elections for the head of the state in 2020 while omitting many regulations of the Electoral Code (EC). It needs to be emphasized that the procedure for those new laws was contrary to the legislative blackout rule safeguarded by judicial decisions of the Polish Constitutional Tribunal and the legislation of the Council of Europe (Skotnicki, 2021, p. 142; Venice Commission, 2002; Clerfayt, 2005, p. 26; Kalandadze, 2020). What is more, new rules for holding presidential elections in 2020 were laid down not by means of a systemic amendment to the Electoral Code, preceded by a thorough and weighted debate, but by an episodic act, which in the context of electoral matter deserves stern criticism.

However, we cannot overlook the fact that presidential elections were not the only votes that took place in this special time in Poland. Despite exceptionally difficult circumstances, electoral administration and local governments had to handle a few hundred additional electoral processes (*Terminarz wyborów ...*, 2022) which were held at the local level because terms of office of municipal, county and regional councillors expired (by-elections) and so did terms of office of executive bodies in municipalities (early elections) (Kielin-Maziarz & Skotnicki, 2022, p. 178). However, regardless of their unquestionable political importance, these elections were treated rather differently by the legislator than the head-of-state choosing. In fact, they were organized on the basis of laws then in force, included in the Electoral Code, and thus did not take into account the special circumstances of the time of a pandemic. It caused many practical problems which could only be solved through special engagement of election organizers and a close cooperation with health inspection authorities.

In the light of the above, elections held in the time of the COVID-19 pandemic are undoubtedly an excellent basis to review electoral law measures laid down for extraordinary situations. The aim of this chapter is to examine which legislative solutions caused organizational difficulties in the pandemic reality and to determine whether the experience from electoral practice has a chance to translate into the Polish legislator's specific actions to ensure the holding of fair and democratic elections should similar circumstances occur in the future. As has been previously said, the Polish legislator mainly focused on adopting adequate measures for presidential elections that were particularly important from the political point of view. Failure to address the question of organizing and holding mid-term local government appointments (by-elections or early elections) in the time of the pandemic must be seen as a serious oversight. I must also point out that the legislative actions so far have been ad hoc, whereby they are largely not comprehensive and systemic solutions that could be applied in future electoral processes. Meanwhile, we cannot rule out that extraordinary situations, not necessarily caused by the COVID-19 pandemic, will not surface in the future. The method of interpretation of applicable laws is used in this study to review and assess current regulations in force and so is the method of analysis of views of legal scholars and commentators, helpful in formulating *de lege ferenda* postulates.

20.2   Selected Areas of the Polish Electoral Law that Require the Legislator's Response

One of the most noticeable changes in electoral law in the time of the pandemic in Poland was undoubtedly the introduction of correspondence voting as an alternative to traditional appearance at a polling place (Musiał-Karg, 2022, p. 22). This solution was laid down in the June 2020 Act and may be applied to presidential elections. Under this law, the right to exercise correspondence voting was granted to all voters save for those who voted in separate polling districts created in health care establishments, social assistance homes, halls of residence, prisons or detention centres. Moreover, correspondence voting could not be exercised on board of Polish see-going vessels and by voters with disabilities if they had not given anyone a power of attorney to vote. Finally, the act prescribed a disputed solution that allowed for correspondence voting to be prohibited in countries on the territory of which there were no organizational, technical or legal possibilities to hold voting by post (RPO, 2020; Matczak, 2020a, p. 13). As electoral practice has shown, postal vote, leaving aside the assessment of its individual components, turned out to be a necessary solution that strengthens the implementation of the principle of universal elections. In the first round of the 2020 presidential elections, voting packages were sent to 536,821 persons (*Obwieszczenie Państwowej Komisji Wyborczej z dnia 30 czerwca 2020 r....*), whereas in the second round it was 704,111 packages (*Obwieszczenie Państwowej Komisji Wyborczej z dnia 13 lipca 2020 r. ...*). A few detailed questions deserve attention when talking about correspondence voting.

We must first emphasize the need to bring back, as a rule, universal correspondence voting. As we know, the solution adopted in pandemic circumstances in the June 2020 Act is not a *novum* in the Polish legal order. Universal correspondence voting was already introduced in 2014 (*Ustawa z dnia 11 lipca 2014 r...*) and applied to all voters in 2015 presidential elections. Unfortunately, a controversial amendment to the Polish electoral law under the act of 11 January 2018 on amending certain acts to increase citizens' participation in the election process, in the functioning and reviewing of certain public bodies (*Ustawa z dnia 11 stycznia 2018 r ...*) reduced the personal scope of this measure solely to voters with severe or moderate disabilities. The amendment drafter claimed then that "correspondence voting significantly increases the risk of irregularities" (Sejm, 2017) but failed to tell how it was to happen in fact (Balicki, 2021, p. 200). What is more, he did not quote any information that could reliably confirm allegations against this form of voting. Meanwhile, it is obvious that with adequate regulations that safeguard correct conduct (Venice Commission, 2002), correspondence voting today is a certain standard of institutional guarantees of the principle of universal elections (Jackiewicz, 2016, p. 280; Zbieranek, 2011, p. 95; Kowalska, 2020, p. 37; Musiał-Karg, 2021, p. 46). A return to the universal form of correspondence voting in 2020, in extraordinary pandemic conditions, must be seen as an appropriate approach. Giving ballotters the option to vote by post meant higher turnouts and also directly strengthened the freedom of choice, which was not forced by the need to juggle health security and health of voters and their exercising their "civil obligation". Nevertheless, given the gravity of the constitutional principle of universal elections, the Polish legislator should review the wording of the Electoral Code to reinstate correspondence voting as a form available to all citizens, not only as an alternative in the extraordinary circumstances that surrounded the 2020 presidential elections. The special importance of this postulate may be evidenced by the fact that it resounds in the circles of Polish legal scholars and political scientists, and also in the opinion of the central electoral authority, that is the National Electoral Commission (*Informacja Państwowej Komisji Wyborczej z 25 lutego 2021 r....*, p. 12).

When talking about correspondence voting during the pandemic, we cannot overlook one more issue. The episodic 2020 law regulated in a particular way the situation of persons who were quarantining, in isolation or self-isolating at home before the vote day. Pursuant to Article 3(1) of the act, these voters could declare their intent to vote by post no later than 5 days before the election day, with the proviso that if the quarantine or isolation started after that day, the voter could declare their intent to vote by post no later than 2 days before the vote (Article 3(2)). Given the dynamic epidemic situation in Poland, this solution must be seen as legitimate. At the same time, it is worth juxtaposing this regulation with measures laid down in the Electoral Code which, as pointed out in the introduction, were applied in the time of the pandemic in other types of balloting, including mid-term local elections (by- and early elections). Admittedly, in the beginning stages of the pandemic the legislator saw that the Code needed to regulate the extraordinary situation of persons that were quarantining, in isolation or self-isolating at home on the day of the vote. Nevertheless, it is difficult to agree that the option taken then fully satisfies the needs of electoral practice. Pursuant to Article 53b(1) of the Electoral Code in connection with Article 53a(1a) thereof, introduced to the Electoral Code under the Act of 31 March 2020 on amending the act on special solutions related to the prevention, counteracting and combating of COVID-19, other infectious diseases and crisis situations caused by them, as well as certain other acts, the said group of voters may declare their intent to vote by post no later than five days before the election. Given such a time frame, a question arises about the situation of voters who are ordered to quarantine or self-isolate later than 5 days before the election day. Contrary to what was the case in the 2020 presidential elections, in the light of current provisions they will be deprived of the possibility to participate in the voting. As a consequence, this deadline clearly violates the principle of the universal right to vote by disregarding the extraordinary circumstances of some citizens. As we may conclude, organizational considerations stood behind the adoption of this time frame. Admittedly, preparation of voting packages and their distribution on days directly before the election day does require considerable effort from elections' organizers (district electoral commissions, election officers or staff of municipal offices). Still, it is not impossible. Since extending the time frame for declaring an intent to vote by post to 2 days before the election was possible in the 2020 presidential elections, which by default were a much greater organizational challenge than local elections held in one polling district (by-elections) or in one municipality (early elections), it seems that it should not be too difficult a task in local elections either. Therefore, we must conclude that the main problem in this case is that the Polish legislator does not show a systemic approach to the amended regulations and that there is no perspective on the needs of electoral practice. This is quite surprising since mid-term local elections are not separate cases, but quite the contrary - a few hundred have been held in the time of the pandemic. Therefore, the legislator should take immediate legislative actions to change the deadlines laid down in the Electoral Code during which quarantining or isolating voters are allowed to declare their intent to vote by post. As shown above, this would undoubtedly provide a guarantee for a bulk of ballotters by setting additional safeguards for them to exercise their right to vote.

When analysing the subject matter of correspondence voting it is also worth noting that the legislator should, taking the June 2020 Act as a model, modify the Code's procedure for declaring intent to vote by post. *De lege lata*, pursuant to Article 53b(1) of the Electoral Code in connection with Article 53b(2a) EC, the entitled persons shall declare their intent to vote by post to the election commissioner who will then pass this declaration on to an election officer. The procedure under the June 2020 Act seems much more efficient and adequate for electoral practice needs. This procedure stipulates that the declaration shall be presented to the election commissioner "via the municipal office". This mode means that the procedure was shortened and the staff of the delegation of the National Electoral Office, already burdened with an array of electoral tasks, do not have to be involved in additional steps.

The next problem that surfaced in the course of organization of elections in the time of the pandemic was the question of creating separate polling districts, located mainly in health care establishments and social assistance homes. Pursuant to Article 12(4) EC, an election commissioner shall create a separate polling district if at least 15 voters are present in it on election day. At the same time, the legislator allowed for such a district not to be established "in justified cases on request of persons in charge of a given unit". Undoubtedly, creating such districts provides a guarantee of the principle of universal elections, quoted here a few times already (Buczkowski, 1998, pp. 115–116). The aim of creating separate districts is to ensure that voters who are staying in health care establishments and social assistance homes due to their condition, age or disability are able to vote in their place of current residence (Kisielewicz & Zbieranek, 2018, p. 83). Nevertheless, the dilemma whether establishing such districts is not too great a risk for hospital patients or residents of social assistance homes appeared numerous times at elections held during the pandemic. Therefore, we must bear in mind that these persons, as a rule, had weaker immunity and often had concurrent conditions. The media often reported on new SARS-CoV-2 "outbreaks" in hospitals or social assistance homes, where the number of infections usually grew rapidly. This is why electoral commissioners often faced an uneasy choice in by-elections and early elections: allowing voters to exercise their constitutional right to elect by creating a separate district or restricting this right by invoking Article 12(4) EC *in fine*. It seems that from the formal and legal point of view, not creating a district as prescribed in Article 12(4) EC *in fine* in these extraordinary circumstances of the pandemic was justified as long as the manager of such an entity submitted a relevant request. Creating a polling district in a hospital or a social assistance home meant that members of a district electoral commission, i.e. "visitors", had to enter its premises and neither the manager of the place nor the electoral authority could verify their health or vaccination status. This, in turn, could pose a risk of bringing coronavirus to persons especially vulnerable to infections and its quick transmission. Bearing in mind the danger associated with the lack of detailed regulations on the procedure to appoint district commissions in separate districts, it is worth referring to the regulation laid down in the episodic June 2020 Act applied in presidential elections. The legislator prescribed a certain solution which, at least presumably, was to minimise the threat to the voters' health when carrying our elections in separate districts. Pursuant to Article 20(3) of this act, upon a request of the manager of a health care establishment or a social assistance home, employees of such an establishment may be appointed to a district electoral commission established there. This seems like a reasonable solution since, as previously mentioned, it reduced the risk of infection as preparation for the voting was to be done by persons who were already in day-to-day contact with such patients or residents. It is a pity that the Polish legislator failed to see the need to adopt similar regulations in the Electoral Code, including in its provisions applied in local mid-term elections. Such an extraordinary procedure for appointing commissions in separate districts seems a noteworthy solution, both in the context of extraordinary situations and typical conditions. The staff of establishments in which separate districts may be created know very well the specifics of contact with such residents and should as a rule care for the safety of those in their charge. As it seems, these considerations should stand in favour of adopting solutions applied pursuant to the June 2020 Act, also to the Electoral Code.

When discussing the subject matter of the impact of the COVID-19 pandemic on Polish electoral law, we should also address the issue of how candidates or lists of candidates are given support. At the moment, the Electoral Code prescribes that a candidate or a candidate may be put forward if the initiative has enough public support (Article 296 EC, Article 210(1) EC, Article 265(1) EC, Article 343 EC, Article 427(1) EC, Article 457(3) EC and Article 465 EC), expressed by voters' signatures placed on paper lists. As pointed out by K. Urbaniak, this is to prevent "nonsensical" candidates from running, i.e. persons without a political background and who do not enjoy minimum public backing (Urbaniak, 2016, p. 37). This method of confirming candidates' support in the Polish legal order, though not indiscriminately, has been functioning for years and has been, in a way, a "legacy" element of the Polish electoral procedure. The pandemic period has shown, nevertheless, that collecting the legally prescribed number of signatures in traditional form is not always possible or at least straightforward due to objective though unpredictable reasons. During the 2020 presidential elections, electoral committees did on occasions try to use circumstances beyond their control, related to limited inter-personal contact and travel restrictions introduced by regulations, to justify their failure to collect the required number of signatures. Interestingly, extraordinary circumstances have even impacted the Supreme Court's approach to relaxing its rigour for the procedure of collecting signatures to show support for candidates put forward in the last 2020 presidential elections, which was demonstrated in particular in its controversial decision of 23 March 2020.[1] Such facts are a

---

1   This refers to the case when the Electoral Committee of presidential candidate Sławomir Grzywa. Despite not having the required 1,000 signatures for the presidential elections

postulate for the legislator to consider allowing electronic gathering of support signatures for candidate lists, as an alternative. Such a solution does not seem impossible today, given the recent dynamically progressing digitisation of many public authorities and institutions. A more universally accessible ePUAP (a platform for public authority's communication with citizens) or the use of the features of the trusted profile could become good tools to support the procedure. A system developed directly by election organizers (National Electoral Office in cooperation with the National Electoral Commission) could be another solution. Admittedly, it requires more time for appropriate development and implementation, but stays under the control and moderation of independent electoral administration. As may be assumed, digitisation of at least some electoral steps, along with the developing system of safeguards, is unavoidable. It is worth noting here the recent steps (postulated for a long time now; Rakowska-Trela, Rulka, 2011) to launch the Central Voters Register (Pietrzak, 2021, p. 25). Its implementation will undoubtedly open new possibilities also in digitisation of the process of collecting support signatures. It should be noted here that the postulate to introduce electronic collection of support signatures is also expressed by stakeholders directly interested in using this procedure. After the last presidential election a petition was filed to amend the act of 5 January 2011 - Electoral Code, to allow expression of support for candidates or candidate lists in Polish presidential elections and in parliamentary elections in the electronic form (as an alternative to the traditional model; Sejm, 2021). Unfortunately, despite a positive opinion of the Sejm's Bureau of Research (Biuro Analiz Sejmowych, 2021), the postulate contained in the petition to take legislative actions to introduce an electronic system of collecting signatures was not approved by the Petitions Commission, which decided in general that given its significance in the election process, this issue cannot be processed upon a petition. However, taking into account the experience of the time of the pandemic and also the fact that similar circumstances may recur in the future, this question must be treated as open and this postulate must be seen as an opportunity to minimise negative incidents associated with collecting support signatures in a traditional manner (early signature collection, formal defects when placing support signatures, etc.).

---

ordered for 10 May 2020, the Committee had to be notified by the National Electoral Commission following the Supreme Court decision of 23 March 2020, I NSW 4/20 (LEX no 2944354). The Supreme Court claimed that collecting the requisite number of signatures in the course of the pandemic "was an unrealistic feat (...), made difficult by objective factors justified by extraordinary circumstances entirely independent of the electoral proxy". These "extraordinary circumstances", the Court believed, included the occurrence of a state of a real threat of the SARS-CoV-2 pandemic (Pyrzyńska, 2021, p. 395ff).

Finally, somehow to sum up the discussion on the imperfections of the regulation of the electoral law revealed in the course of the COVID-19 pandemic,
we must address one more important question. It is the constitutional order
to hold elections during the state of emergency. Pursuant to Article 228(7) of
the Constitution of the Republic of Poland of 2 April 1997, during a period of
introduction of extraordinary measures, as well as within the period of 90 days
following its termination, the term of office of the Sejm may not be shortened,
nor may a nationwide referendum, nor elections to the Sejm, Senate, organs
of local government nor elections for the Presidency be held, and the term of
office of such organs shall be appropriately prolonged. The aim of this regulation is to safeguard the functioning of elected authorities against changes made
to them as a result of extraordinary situations. It is also intended to disallow
a situation where in the face of extraordinary circumstances the absence of
relevant authorities will preclude effective counteraction against the emerged
threat (Prokop, 2005, pp. 39–41) and also to protect citizens against recourse to
extraordinary measures to manipulate the electoral procedure (Trybunał Konstytucyjny, 1998). Admittedly, no extraordinary measures were introduced in
2020 when the presidential election was due pursuant to the requirements of
the basic law, despite numerous calls from constitutionalists (Matczak, 2020b;
Szcześniak, 2020). Nevertheless, the circumstances and the then debate once
again showed the previously noted problem of a lack of provisions detailing
the constitutional regulation on how to proceed with the electoral process
initiated before the announcement of introduction of extraordinary measures. Regulations in force at the moment do not say directly what effect the
introduction of extraordinary measures has on elections (K. Skotnicki's belief
seems convincing - he claims that the electoral process does not get annulled
but suspended; Skotnicki, 2020, p. 37–38, Eckhard, 2014, p. 785). They are also
silent on how exactly the "reopening" or "re-launching" of the electoral process
must proceed after the extraordinary measures are withdrawn and after the
lapse of 90 days during which no electoral steps must be taken. As it seems, to
ensure legal certainty and to protect voters and participants of electoral rivalry
alike, it seems necessary to specify questions related to the electoral calendar
in the "re-opened" part of the electoral process, though this will surely not be
an easy task from the legislative point of view.

20.3   Conclusions

The pandemic period revealed numerous flaws of Polish electoral law regulations in extraordinary situations. Firstly, the legislator did not give sufficient

focus to all types of elections in the time of the pandemic. While presidential elections (important from the political point of view) were held on the basis of a special regulation adopted as an episodic act, a few hundred electoral actions in mid-term local elections had to be conducted under practically unmodified general rules. This caused numerous organizational difficulties and also undermined the guarantee character of the measures in force. This situation confirms a trend, noticeable for quite a long time now, where the legislator lacks a systemic approach to amended laws, which in turn affects the quality of the electoral process. The example of numerous local elections held mid-term perfectly shows that the legislator did not deem it necessary to rely on certain proven measures laid down in the June 2020 Act in elections organized according to the code-prescribed procedure (e.g. the question of how to appoint district electoral commissions in separate districts created in health care establishments and social assistance homes). The time of the pandemic has also shown that there are areas of electoral law at which the legislator must take a fresh look (e.g. digitisation of collection of support signatures on candidate lists). The electoral practice in the time of the COVID-19 pandemic also reminded us about having to undertake a debate on the statutory regulation that specifies how to proceed with the open electoral process in the event of introduction of extraordinary measures after the elections are ordered. It seems that the legislator should take appropriate relevant legislative steps as soon as possible so that possible amendments to electoral law are not accused of infringing the rules of correct legislation, in particular the legislative blackout principle.

References

Balicki, R. (2021). "Głosowanie korespondencyjne w polskim porządku prawnym – zmienne dzieje regulacji". In: J. Ciapała & A. Pyrzyńska (Eds.), *Dylematy polskiego prawa wyborczego* (pp. 191–207), Warszawa: C. H. Beck.

Birch, S. & Buril, F. & Cheeseman, N. & Clark, A. & Darnolf, S. & Dodsworth, S. & Garber, L. & Gutiérrez-Romero, R. & Hollstein, T. & James, T. S., & Mohan, V. & Sawyer, K. (2020). *How to hold elections safely and democratically during the COVID-19 pandemic*. London: The British Academy.

Biuro Analiz Sejmowych (2021). "Opinia dotycząca petycji nr BKSP-144-IX-346/21 w sprawie zmiany ustawy – Kodeks wyborczy polegającej na umożliwieniu wyrażania poparcia dla kandydatów lub list kandydatów w formie elektronicznej". *Sejm Rzeczypospolitej Polskiej*. Retrieved from: http://orka.sejm.gov.pl/petycje.nsf/nazwa /IX-346/$file/IX-346.pdf.

Buczkowski, J. (1998). *Podstawowe zasady prawa wyborczego*. Lublin: Wydawnictwo UMCS.

Clerfayt, G. (2005). "The European electoral heritage and the Code of Good Practice in Electoral Matters". *Science and technique of democracy. European Standards of Electoral Law in Contemporary Constitutionalism*, no. 39, pp. 22–28. Retrieved from: https://www.venice.coe.int/webforms/documents/default.aspx?pdffile=CDL -STD(2004)039.

Czaplicki, K.W. & Dauter, B. & Jaworski, S.J. & Rymarz, F. & Zbieranek, J. (2018). *Kodeks wyborczy. Komentarz*. Warszawa: Wolters Kluwer.

Eckhardt, K. (2014). "Konstytucyjny zakaz przeprowadzania wyborów w czasie trwania stanu nadzwyczajnego – kilka wątpliwości". *Gdańskie Studia Prawnicze,* volume XXXI (no. 1), pp. 781–786.

International IDEA (2022). "Global overview of COVID-19: Impact on elections". *International IDEA*. Retrieved from: https://www.idea.int/news-media /multimedia-reports/global-overview-COVID-19-impact- elections.

Informacja Państwowej Komisji Wyborczej z 25 lutego 2021 r. o realizacji przepisów Kodeksu wyborczego oraz propozycje ich zmiany (ZPOW-502-1/21). (2021). Państwowa Komisja Wyborcza. Retrieved from: https://pkw.gov.pl/uploaded_files/1613491481 _2-1-21-informacja.pdf.

Jackiewicz, A. (2016). "Głosowanie korespondencyjne oraz głosowanie przez pełnomocnika jako alternatywne metody głosowania w świetle polskiego kodeksu wyborczego". *Białostockie Studia Prawnicze*, vol. 20/A, pp. 273–283. DOI: 10.15290/ bsp.2016.20A.19.

Kalandadze, N. (2020). "Switching to all-postal voting in times of public health crises: Lessons from Poland". *International IDEA*. Retrieved from: https://www.idea.int /news-media/news/switching-all-postal-voting-times-public-health-crises-lessons -poland.

Kielin-Maziarz, J. & Skotnicki, K. (2022). "Restrictions on the Right to Vote in the Pandemic during the Election of the President of the Republic of Poland in 2020". *Białystok Legal Studies/ Białostockie Studia Prawnicze*, vol. 27, no. 2, pp. 177–192. DOI: 10.15290/bsp.2022.27.02.10.

Kowalska, M. (2020). "Alternatywne formy głosowania w polskim prawie wyborczym". *Przegląd Europejski*, no. 2, pp. 35–48. Doi: 10.31338/1641-2478pe.2.20.3.

Maizland, L. (2020). "How Countries Are Holding Elections During the COVID-19 Pandemic". *Council on Foreign Relations*. Retrieved from: https://www.cfr.org /backgrounder/how-countries-are-holding-elections-during-COVID-19-pandemic.

Matczak, M. (2020a). "Opinia w sprawie zgodności z Konstytucją RP rozwiązań legislacyjnych zawartych w ustawie z dnia 12 maja 2020 r. o szczególnych zasadach organizacji wyborów powszechnych na Prezydenta RP zarządzonych w 2020 r. z możliwością głosowania korespondencyjnego (Druk senacki nr 118)". Senat Rzeczypospolitej

Polskiej. Retrieved from: https://www.senat.gov.pl/gfx/senat/pl/senatekspertyzy/5510/plik/oe-295.pdf.

Matczak, M. (2020b). "Opinia w sprawie zgodności z Konstytucją RP rozwiązań legislacyjnych zawartych w ustawie z dnia 6 kwietnia 2020 r. o szczególnych zasadach przeprowadzania wyborów powszechnych na Prezydenta Rzeczypospolitej Polskiej zarządzonych w 2020 r. (Druk senacki nr 99)". Senat Rzeczypospolitej Polskiej. Retrieved from: https://www.senat.gov.pl/gfx/senat/pl/senatekspertyzy/5486/plik/oe_290_1_1.pdf.

Musiał-Karg, M. (2021). "Głosowanie korespondencyjne podczas pandemii COVID-19. Doświadczenia z polskich wyborów prezydenckich w 2020 r.". *Przegląd Prawa Konstytucyjnego*, no. 2, pp. 31–48. DOI: 10.15804/ppk.2021.02.02.

Musiał-Karg, M. (2022). "Postal Voting In the 2020 Presidential Election – How Did Electoral Participation Evolved During the COVID-19 Pandemic?". *Przegląd Politologiczny*, no. 4, pp. 17–26. DOI: 10.14746/pp.2022.27.4.2.

Obwieszczenie Państwowej Komisji Wyborczej z dnia 30 czerwca 2020 r. o wynikach głosowania i wyniku wyborów Prezydenta Rzeczypospolitej Polskiej, zarządzonych na dzień 28 czerwca 2020 r. (2020). Państwowa Komisja Wyborcza. Retrieved from: https://prezydent20200628.pkw.gov.pl/prezydent20200628/statics/prezydent_20200628_obwieszczenia/uploaded_files/1593587233_obwieszczenie-002.pdf.

Obwieszczenie Państwowej Komisji Wyborczej z dnia 13 lipca 2020 r. o wynikach ponownego głosowania i wyniku wyborów Prezydenta Rzeczypospolitej Polskiej. (2020). Państwowa Komisja Wyborcza. Retrieved from: https://prezydent20200628.pkw.gov.pl/prezydent20200628/statics/prezydent_20200628_obwieszczenia/uploaded_files/1594724319_obwieszczenie-pkw-20200713-1915.pdf.

OSCE/ODIHR (2020a). "Poland, Presidential Election, 28 June 2020: Statement of Preliminary Findings and Conclusions". OSCE Office for Democratic Institutions and Human Rights. Retrieved from: https://www.osce.org/files/f/documents/4/9/455728.pdf.

OSCE/ODIHR (2020b). "Republic of Poland, Presidential Election, 28 June and 12 July 2020. Special Election Assessment Mission Final Report". OSCE *Office for Democratic* Institutions and Human Rights. Retrieved from: https://www.osce.org/files/f/documents/6/2/464601.pdf.

Picchio, M. & Santolini, R. (2022). "The COVID-19 pandemic's effects on voter turnout". *European Journal of Political Economy,* np. 73, pp. 1–15. DOI: https://doi.org/10.1016%2Fj.ejpoleco.2021.102161.

Pietrzak, M. (2021). "Wybrane doświadczenia związane z organizacją wyborów w latach 2018–2020 z perspektywy Krajowego Biura Wyborczego". In: J. Ciapała & A. Pyrzyńska (Eds.), *Dylematy polskiego prawa wyborczego* (pp. 15–28). Warszawa: C.H. Beck.

Prokop, K. (2005). *Stany nadzwyczajne w Konstytucji Rzeczypospolitej Polskiej.* Białystok: Temida 2.

Pyrzyńska, A. (2021). "Glosa do postanowienia Sądu Najwyższego z dnia 23 marca 2020 r. (I NSW 4/20)". *Przegląd Prawa Konstytucyjnego*, no. 2, pp. 395–406. DOI: 10.15804/ ppk.2021.02.24.

RPO (2020). Pismo Rzecznika Praw Obywatelskich z dnia 21 maja 2020 r. do Przewodniczącego Komisji Ustawodawczej Senatu RP, VII.602.9.2020.JZ.

Rakowska-Trela, A. & Rulka, M. (2011). *Centralny elektroniczny rejestr wyborców podstawą reform prawa wyborczego*. Warszawa: Instytut Spraw Publicznych.

Sejm (2017). "Uzasadnienie do poselskiego projektu ustawy o zmianie niektórych ustaw w celu zwiększenia udziału obywateli w procesie wybierania, funkcjonowania i kontrolowania niektórych organów publicznych *Druk sejmowy nr 2001)". *Sejm Rzeczypospolitej Polskiej*. Retrieved from: https://www.sejm.gov.pl/sejm8.nsf /druk.xsp?nr=2001.

Sejm (2021). "Petycja w sprawie zmiany ustawy z dnia 5 stycznia 2011 r. Kodeks wyborczy (Dz.U. z 2020 r. poz. 1319) w zakresie umożliwienia wyrażania poparcia dla kandydatów lub list kandydatów w wyborach Prezydenta RP oraz w wyborach do Sejmu i Senatu w formie elektronicznej". *Sejm Rzeczypospolitej Polskiej*. Retrieved from: https://www.sejm.gov.pl/Sejm9.nsf/agent.xsp?symbol=PETYCJA&NrPetycji =BKSP-144-IX-346/21.

Skotnicki, K. (2010). "Opinia na temat skutków prawnych wprowadzenia stanu klęski żywiołowej". *Zeszyty Prawnicze BAS*, no. 3, pp. 35–40.

Skotnicki, K. (2021). "Państwo prawa a tryb uchwalania w 2020 r. ustaw regulujących wybory Prezydenta RP". In: J. Ciapała & A. Pyrzyńska (Eds.), *Dylematy polskiego prawa wyborczego* (pp. 139–158). Warszawa: C. H. Beck.

Szczęśniak, A. (2020). "Co z wyborami? Prof. Piotrowski: Tylko bez stanu wyjątkowego. Przecież nie będziemy do koronawirusa strzelać". *OKO.press*. Retrieved from: https://oko.press/co-z-wyborami-prof-piotrowski-koronawirus/.

Terminarz wyborów i referendów w trakcie kadencji 2018–2023. (2022). Państwowa Komisja Wyborcza. Retrieved from: https://pkw.gov.pl/uploaded_files/1644864035 _terminarz-wyborow-w-trakcie-kadencji-2018-2023-wow-14022022.pdf.

Trybunał Konstytucyjny (1998). Wyrok Trybunału Konstytucyjnego z 26 maja 1998 r., K 17/98, LEX nr 33149.

Tatarczyk, D. & Wojtasik, W. (2023). "The Incumbency Advantage during the COVID-19 Pandemic: Examining the 2020 Polish Presidential Election". *East European Politics and Societies and Cultures*, vol. 37, no. 2, pp. 608–626. DOI:10.1177/08883254221085307.

Urbaniak, K. (2016). "Prawne i praktyczne aspekty obowiązku zbierania podpisów jako element prawa zgłaszania kandydata w wyborach prezydenckich. Uwagi de lege lata i de lege ferenda". *Studia Politologiczne*, no. 42, pp. 35–55.

Ustawa z dnia 5 stycznia 2011 r. - Kodeks wyborczy. Dz.U. 2020 poz. 1319 ze zm.

Ustawa z dnia 11 lipca 2014 r. o zmianie ustawy - Kodeks wyborczy oraz niektórych innych ustaw. Dz.U. 2014 poz. 1072.

Ustawa z dnia 11 stycznia 2018 r. o zmianie niektórych ustaw w celu zwiększenia udziału obywateli w procesie wybierania, funkcjonowania i kontrolowania niektórych organów publicznych. Dz.U. 2018 poz. 130.

Ustawa z dnia 6 kwietnia 2020 r. o szczególnych zasadach przeprowadzania wyborów powszechnych na Prezydenta Rzeczypospolitej Polskiej zarządzonych w 2020 r. Dz.U. 2020 r. poz. 827.

Ustawa z dnia 2 czerwca 2020 r. o szczególnych zasadach organizacji wyborów powszechnych na Prezydenta Rzeczypospolitej Polskiej zarządzonych w 2020 r. z możliwością głosowania korespondencyjnego. Dz.U. 2020 poz. 979.

Vashchanka, V. (2020). "Political manoeuvres and legal conundrums amid the COVID-19 pandemic: the 2020 presidential election in Poland". *International IDEA*, pp. 1–16. Retrieved from: https://www.idea.int/sites/default/files/political-manoeuvres-and-legal-conundrums-2020-presidential-election-poland.pdf.

Venice Commission (2002). Code of the Good Practice in Electoral Matters. Guidelines and Explanatory Report, adopted by the Venice Commission at its 52nd session (Venice, 18–19 October 2002) CDL-AD (2002) 23 rev/ Strasbourg, 23 May 2003. Venice Commission. Retrieved from: https://www.venice.coe.int/webforms/documents/default.aspx?pdffile=CDL-AD(2002)023rev2-cor-e.

Zbieranek, J. (2011). "Alternatywne procedury głosowania w Polsce na tle państw Unii Europejskiej". *Studia BAS*, no. 3, pp. 93–120.

CHAPTER 21

The Course of the Election Process in Poland during the COVID-19 Pandemic

Ryszard Balicki

21.1   Introduction

Nowadays, elections are treated as an obvious element of citizens' participation in exercising power. However, their role in a given state depends on the adopted systemic regime. This was indicated by Dieter Nohlen, who stressed that "the elections in various political systems are understood differently already at the definition level. It makes a fundamental difference whether the voter chooses between several parties and its decision may be free, or whether one party can vote only because others could not put up their candidates" (Nohlen, 2004, p. 24). In a democratic state they are treated as the "driving force of democracy" (LeDuc et al., 2002, p. 1), it is often emphasized that "the free elections conducted according to the rules which allow honest and faithful consideration of the will of the voters can be considered one of the foundations of a democratic system" (Łączkowski, 2009, p. 51). The role of elections in hybrid regimes -, i.e. in countries that are no longer democracies, but have retained some institutions referring to democratic models (Balicki, 2020) - is different. The rulers do not give up this attribute of the legality of their power, however, the elections held are not rival elections, and the rulers cannot lose them (Antoszewski, 2016, p. 139). In these countries, the entire system of exercising power is geared to protecti the dominant position of the ruling party, and elections are one of the important elements of this structure.

Regardless of the political model operating in the state, elections are an institution so desirable that - as it is emphasized in the literature - already at the end of the previous century "they were held in almost every country in the world" (Hermet et al., 1978, p. VII). Therefore, it is important that their organization is properly prepared and that they can be conducted irrespective of external circumstances that may occur. The experience of the COVID-19 pandemic caused by the SARS-CoV-2 virus in 2020, however, has shown that this is not the case. In many countries, it has become necessary to postpone the dates of the scheduled elections (Musiał-Karg, 2021, pp. 32–33), or to carry them out under conditions different from the previous ones (Krimmer et al., 2021).

Poland also faced a similar dilemma, in which the presidential elections were to take place in 2020. The Polish case is particularly interesting, as the date of the scheduled presidential elections coincided with the peak of the disease. This chapter aims to demonstrate the impact of the pandemic on the possibility of holding elections. The necessity to ensure realistic (but also safe) conditions for making decisions by the sovereign is the responsibility of public authorities. The study is devoted to showing the changes in election law taking place in Poland in 2020 from the legal perspective.

21.2   The Socio-Political Context

Poland's democratic experience is very limited. After the fascinating stage of the First Republic of Poland - the Polish model of democracy, embodied in the form of the noble republic - a tragic period came, in which the Polish state disappeared from the map of Europe. Poland regained its independence in 1918, then became a republic and started building its democratic identity (Balicki, 2018). The emerging democracy, however, did not have time to strengthen itself. Already in 1926, there was a *coup d'etat* and the seizure of power by authoritarian military circles (Rothschild, 1962). The period after the Second World War also prevented the establishment of a democratic state. Poland then became part of the bloc of communist states operating under the control of the USSR (Balicki & Ławniczak, 2014). Only the political transformations of 1989 allowed Poland to begin the process of abandoning real socialism. Despite the difficulties encountered, the goal seemed obvious - a political system based on the patterns of liberal democracies, where it is the sovereign, in democratic elections, that could make the most important decisions. Over the past years, the weaknesses of the Polish democracy have been noticed many times, but a particular regression took place after 2015. At that time, there was an exceptional situation, considering Polish political experience. Not only were the double elections (presidential and parliamentary) won by representatives of one political option, but also, due to the wrong election strategy of the left-wing parties, for the first time it was possible to form a government without the necessity to conclude coalition agreements.

The concentration of power in the state in the hands of a single political force cannot, in itself, be considered as an element contributing to the destruction of the constitutional model of government. In such a situation, however, it becomes particularly important to respect the democratic mechanisms of the political system, or more broadly - the principles of political and legal culture.

Unfortunately, the decisions made by the ruling party in Poland (Prawo i Sprawiedliwość [Law and Justice]), and especially the laws adopted, have repeatedly led to the violation of the constitutional guarantees appropriate for liberal democracy, preventing (or hindering) the possibility of arbitrary power.

A consequence of the negative changes in the political life was also a growing internal conflict and deepening social divisions, fueled both by direct decisions by the rulers and decisions made by the authorities subordinate to them

21.3   The Applicable Election Law

The constitutional regulation of the election law is not a matter highly valued by the doctrine of the Polish constitutional law. In the literature on the subject, the abandonment of including it in a separate editorial unit is particularly criticized (Banaszak, 2012, p. 269). In line with the adopted convention, constitutional regulations cover only the basic principles of election law, while detailed issues were included in the Act of 5 January 2011 - Electoral Code (*Ustawa z dnia 5 stycznia 2011* ...). Such a situation, especially in view of the necessary vagueness of the constitutional regulation, may favour the instrumentalisation of the election law (Banaszak, 2013, p. 33).

Despite the doubts raised above, the adoption of the Electoral Code - the first comprehensive regulation of election law in Poland - should be appreciated. The previous legal status - apart from the constitutional regulation - included five separate electoral laws (ordinances) regulating the issues of elections to individual bodies. These acts were adopted in the period from 1990 to 2004 (and amended many times later), and as a consequence did not constitute a coherent and stable legal system. On the contrary, this state introduced "a lot of complications and troubles both for voters and members of the election commissions" (Skrzydło, 2011, p. 16).

The enactment of the Electoral Code was therefore a reaction to the long-held postulate of adopting a comprehensive regulation of electoral law (Buczkowski, 1998, p. 362; Rymarz, 2007; Uziębło, 2011, p. 7). The main reason for the adoption of the Code was the necessity to facilitate the application of election law standards and the introduction of new, uniform institutional solutions to facilitate voting (alternative forms of voting); (Balicki, 2021). However, an equally important premise was the desire to ensure the stability of the electoral law (Patrzałek & Skrzydło, 1997, p. 11), because so far the practice in this area has been highly criticized (Sokala, 2001, p. 11). Unfortunately, this goal was not achieved - changes to the Electoral Code were frequent, and proposals for its amendments were submitted even more frequently. The literature on the subject states that in the years 2011–2016 the Code was changed on average every 137 days, and the proposed amendments were submitted every 50 days (Sieklucki, 2020, p. 290).

The basic principles for the election of the President of the Republic of Poland are set out in art. 127 of the Constitution. According to its content, the head of state in Poland is currently elected in universal, equal, direct, and secret voting. This solution is a consequence of a modification made in 1990, because when the presidential office was reactivated to the Polish political system (in 1989), it was decided that the election would be made by both houses of parliament acting as the Zgromadzenie Narodowe (National Assembly) (Górecki, 1996).

Article 127 of the Constitution also specifies the content of the passive electoral law - a candidate for the office of president must be a Polish citizen, be 35 years of age at the latest on the day of the elections and enjoy full electoral rights to the Sejm. The candidate's application must be supported by 100,000 citizens who have active voting rights to the Sejm.

The elections for the President of the Republic of Poland are held in two rounds. In the first round, a candidate who has obtained more than half of the valid votes (absolute majority) may be elected. However, if none of the candidates obtains such support, the second round of elections is held on the fourteenth day after the first. Two candidates who received the highest number of votes in the first round are taking part in it.

The Constitution of the Republic of Poland also refers to a situation in which one of the two candidates who are to participate in the re-voting withdraws their consent to stand, loses the right to vote or dies. In accordance with the regulation contained in art. 127 sec. 5, in such a case, the voting is postponed for another 14 days, and the candidate who obtained the next number of votes in the first round goes to the final vote. However, this solution seems to be unjustified. In such a situation, we only seem to follow the rules of democracy. Admittedly, the candidate with the highest (consecutive) support goes to the next vote, but at the same time we ignore the political views of the supporters of the candidate who no longer stands, and who had greater support in the first round. It seems that it would be justified in such a situation to repeat the election so that all voters could express their position.

Article 128 of the Constitution stipulates that the term of office of the president is 5 years, and this office may be held only twice. The constitutional regulation also specifies the procedure for launching the election process, both in connection with the typical expiry of the term of office of the President of the

Republic of Poland, as well as in the event of emergency situations (vacancy of office). In both cases, the election is ordered by the Marshal of the Sejm.

The term of office of the head of state in Poland begins with the oath before the National Assembly. This oath is an essential element to commence the term of office of the President of the Republic of Poland, however, the session of the National Assembly itself is not covered by the formal requirements, in particular, there is no requirement for a certain number of members of the National Assembly to participate (Maroń, 2012).

21.4   The Course of the Election Process in 2020 (Part One)

On February 5, 2020, the Marshal of the Sejm issued a decision ordering the election of the President of the Republic of Poland (*Postanowienie Marszałka Sejmu ...*, item 184.), with the date of voting in the first round set for May 10, 2020. Along with the ordering of the elections, the election calendar was announced and the election campaign was formally launched.

However, the circumstances meant that the elections were not conducted according to the originally planned rules. In November 2019, the first cases of a new viral disease were diagnosed in the Chinese city of Wuhan (Hubei province). Originally, this virus was limited and only affected Wuhan, but in January 2020 it spread to a significant territory of China, and in February its outbreaks began to spread to other countries (South Korea or Italy).

On March 4, 2020, a month after the official start of the election campaign, the first coronavirus patient was diagnosed in Poland, and from that moment it was the fight against the pandemic that became a dominant element in public discussion and had a significant impact also on events related to the elections. On March 11, 2020, the World Health Organization declared a pandemic - that is, an epidemic of an infectious disease, present at the same time on different continents, the outbreaks of which arise independently of each other. Three days later, on March 14, 2020, in connection with SARS-CoV-2 virus infections, an epidemic threat was introduced in Poland (*Rozporządzenie Ministra Zdrowia ...*, item 433), and then – from March 20, 2020 – the state of the epidemic (*Rozporządzenie Ministra Zdrowia ...*, item 491).

However, due to the fact that the government did not introduce any of the constitutionally defined states of emergency, the formal necessity of holding elections in accordance with the previously specified date did not change.

These circumstances became the basis for the National Electoral Commission to point out that "in accordance with the content of art. 228 sec. 7 of the Constitution of the Republic of Poland, the elections for the President of the Republic of Poland cannot be held only during the state of emergency and within 90 days after its termination, and the term of office of this body is then extended accordingly. Decisions to introduce one of the constitutionally described states of emergency may only be taken by the state organs authorized to do so in the Polish Constitution. The National Electoral Commission expects that the decisions made will guarantee the possibility of actual implementation of the constitutional election rights of citizens" (*Informacja z 27 marca 2020 ...*).

At the same time, the National Electoral Commission, taking into account the state of epidemic in the country, appealed to all of the authorities and public administration, as well as to all election committees for cooperation in election matters, considering both the health and life of voters and the good of the Republic of Poland. The position of the NEC also resulted from an analysis of the experiences of other countries where, in order to avoid the transmission of the virus among voters and members of election commissions (as in France, during the first round of elections on March 15, 2020), it was decided to postpone the election date (Italy, Great Britain or Chile), or their organization by postal elections (elections in Bavaria).

The ruling party in Poland decided to prepare and pass a law on special solutions related to the prevention, counteraction and combatting of COVID-19, other infectious diseases and the crisis situations caused by them. It was this legal act that was intended to provide the rulers with the necessary tools to combat the pandemic.

In the following weeks, this act was amended several times, including on March 28, 2020. Then, at 4.25 am (sic!), The Sejm adopted - to the surprise of many - the amendment to the Electoral Code. At that time, the right to vote by correspondence was extended to people who were in "compulsory quarantine, isolation or isolation at home" on the day of voting, and for voters who turned 60 on the day of the elections at the latest (*Ustawa z dnia 31 marca 2020 ...*). As it turned out, this was the first of many sudden and surprising regulations concerning the elections.

A week later - on April 6 - the Sejm adopted the law on special rules for holding the presidential elections in 2020. In accordance with the content of the law adopted by the Sejm, elections based on it would not - in practice - be organized by the National Electoral Commission, but by undefined structures subordinate to the Minister of State Assets with the dominant role of Poczta Polska S.A., and voting would be possible only by correspondence voting (Musiał-Karg & Kapsa, 2021).

It should be emphasized that not only the content of the above-mentioned act, but also the process of its adoption violated the basic standards of law.

The Sejm session transcript shows that the entire legislative process was completed within a few hours, i.e. faster than the so-called urgent procedure (*Sprawozdanie Stenograficzne z 9. posiedzenia Sejmu ...*). And the content of art. 123 sec. 1 of the Constitution clearly states that the urgent procedure may not be adopted (inter alia) bills on elections. The undisputed intention of the legislator was that the parliamentary work on laws regulating issues that are so fundamental from the point of view of a democratic state of law should be conducted in a manner that would prevent it from being rashly passed (Skotnicki, 2021, pp. 148–149).

On April 18, 2020, the Act on special support instruments in connection with the spread of SARS-CoV-2 virus came into force (*Ustawa z dnia 16 kwietnia 2020 ...*). Pursuant to art. 102 of this Act, during the period of an epidemic threat or an epidemic, when the general elections for the President of the Republic of Poland were held in 2020, the application of the provisions of the Electoral Code was suspended in some matters, including to the issue of voting by correspondence, and - what is very important - the powers of the National Electoral Commission to determine the pattern of the voting card and to manage its printing. So, a dozen or so days before the election date, Poland was faced with a far-reaching legal problem. As the chairman of the PKW [NEC] said in an interview: "On the one hand, the Election Code is in force. This is combined with the change that came into force last Friday, that certain tasks are no longer performed by the PKW [NEC], including the fact that they do not order printing of cards. And this is overlapped by the third level, i.e. the act on correspondence voting, which is being processed in the Senate"(*Przewodniczący Państwowej Komisji ...*). The election process was plunged into legal and organizational chaos.

In connection with the above, the National Electoral Commission [NEC] in its information of April 9 emphasized that "the elections are the moment when the sovereign can express his opinion and decide in whose hands he will entrust their fate. However, in a democratic country, elections are not only about voting, it is a complicated mechanism in which both the voters, the candidates and the public administration bodies organizing the election process participate. This process, due to its significance and complex shape, must be based on clear and unambiguous norms derived directly from the Constitution. The regulations in force in the state have to guarantee that the rules of political competition will be clear and equal for everyone, and that the results of the elections will fulfill the will of the nation. To achieve this goal, the election law must be stable, and in particular the process of its modification cannot raise any legal doubts. The National Electoral Commission upholds its appeal contained in the position announced on March 27, 2020, addressed to the authorities and public administration and election committees, for the necessary cooperation in the organization and holding of elections, taking into account both the health and life of voters and the good of the Republic of Poland, and, as a consequence, taking decisions that will guarantee the possibility of actual implementation of citizens' constitutional electoral rights"(*Informacja Państwowej Komisji Wyborczej z dnia 9 kwietnia 2020 ...*).

On May 6, 2020, the Sejm rejected the resolution of the Senate from the preceding day, in which the Senate entirely rejected the law on special rules for holding general elections for the President of the Republic of Poland ordered in 2020. This complex decision-making process meant that for four days before the date of elections set by the Marshal of the Sejm, the legal status on the basis of which they were to be held was not established. The act of 6 April did not enter into force until 9 May, so one day before the scheduled vote!

Fortunately, this act did not become the basis for the implementation of the election process, but an unprecedented event took place - the elections were not held at the previously announced date. The NEC drew attention to this, emphasizing that, although it "undertook all activities related to the conduct of the elections for the President of the Republic of Poland, ordered by the Marshal of the Sejm of the Republic of Poland on May 10, 2020, to which it was obliged by law," but depriving the National Electoral Commission of legal possibilities printing ballots made it impossible to vote in the election of the President of the Republic of Poland on 10 May 2020. For this reason, the NEC informed "the voters, election committees, candidates, election administration and local government units that voting on May 10, 2020 cannot be held" (*Komunikat Państwowej Komisji Wyborczej z dnia 7 maja 2020 ...*).

21.5   The Course of the Election Process in 2020 (Part Two)

On the evening of May 10, 2020, the National Electoral Commission adopted Resolution No. 129/2020 on the impossibility of voting for candidates in the election of the President of the Republic of Poland, and decided that this fact was equivalent to the effects provided for in art. 293 § 3 of the Act - Election Code, there is no possibility to vote due to the lack of candidates, and - as a consequence - it is required to order the election again (*Uchwała Nr 129/2020*).

The adoption of the above resolution was preceded by a discussion of the members of the PKW [NEC] and a detailed analysis of the unprecedented situation in which Poland found itself due to the failure to vote. The solution to the problem was complicated due to the lack of regulations which could be applied to the circumstances in question, both in the provisions of the Polish

Constitution and in the Election Code. In this situation, PKW [NEC] considered that the reference to the content of art. 293 § 3 of the Election Code is the only basis for starting the - lawful - procedure for re-ordering elections.

The election of the President of the Republic of Poland was finally held on June 28 and July 12, 2020, and the basis for their implementation were the provisions of the Electoral Code and the Act of June 2, 2020 on special rules for the organization of general elections for the President of the Republic of Poland, ordered in 2020 with the possibility of postal voting (*Ustawa z dnia 2 czerwca 2020 ...*).

This act provided for the possibility of postal voting for all interested parties, however, it took the form of an alternative voting to the traditional voting at a polling station. The exception concerned voters residing in 20 countries where the epidemic situation did not allow for the classic form of voting, and those voters in the country who lived in communes where the National Electoral Commission, at the request of the minister competent for health, ordered voting only by correspondence (*Uchwała nr 197/2020 ...* ; *Uchwała nr 198/2020 ...*). In the elections, in the second round of the voting, Andrzej Duda, the previous president, was re-elected.

21.6   Conclusions

It is undisputed that the COVID-19 pandemic was a sudden and unforeseen event, but such a finding cannot justify the lack of appropriate legal instruments that could allow for the elections. Since the SARS-CoV-2 virus appeared for the first time, the occurrence of an epidemic (including viral) threat should not come as a surprise. States should be prepared for such a situation. In the Polish political system, the only possible reaction would be to introduce one of the three constitutional defined states of emergency. In 2020, due to the political conditions, the rulers did not want to use this path. In such a case, it was necessary to prepare the elections in accordance with the extraordinary sanitary regime. There was no - unlike in some other countries - legal grounds to decide on postponing the elections. In order to achieve this goal, it became necessary to amend the election law, or to withdraw from its application once and to pass extraordinary provisions. In both cases, there has to be a violation of the desired standard of electoral law, i.e. the breach of the so-called legislative silence (Jakubowski, 2015; Kaczmarczyk, 2021). This element of stability of the electoral law, formulated both in the Code of Good Practice in Electoral Matters of the Venice Commission (defined as the period of the year before the elections) and in the jurisprudence of the Constitutional Tribunal (defined as the requirement of six months before the beginning of the election process), is not, however, absolute. As it is emphasized in the jurisprudence of the Constitutional Tribunal, the legislative silence may be broken in the event of extraordinary circumstances requiring an amendment to the election law (*Wyrok*, K31/06). There is no doubt that the pandemic was such a circumstance. However, even in such a case, the process of amending the election law has to be conducted with full respect for the principles of good legislation, as well as with the aim of achieving the broadest possible consensus of political forces. Otherwise, there may always be an accusation of taking actions aimed at increasing the chances of a given candidate or the ruling party (Garlicki, 2020, p. 156).

References

Antoszewski, A. (2016). *Współczesne teorie demokracji*. Wydawnictwo Sejmowe.

Balicki, R. (2018). "How reborn Poland became a republic". *Przegląd Prawa Konstytucyjnego* (6(46)), 15–24. https://doi.org/10.15804/ppk.2018.06.01

Balicki, R. (2020). "Elections in Hybrid Regimes". *Przegląd Prawa Konstytucyjnego*, (6(58)), 159–166. https://doi.org/10.15804/ppk.2020.06.12

Balicki, R. (2021). „Głosowanie korespondencyjne w polskim porządku prawnym - zmienne dzieje regulacji". In J. Ciapała & A. Pyrzyńska (Eds.), *Monografie Prawnicze. Dylematy polskiego prawa wyborczego*. Warszawa: Wydawnictwo C.H. Beck.

Balicki, R., & Ławniczak, A. (2014). „Instytucjonalne aspekty PRL jako kolejnego wcielenia państwowości polskiej". In: M. Grzybowski & B. Naleziński (Eds.), *Państwo demokratyczne, prawne i socjalne: Księga jubileuszowa dedykowana profesorowi Zbigniewowi Antoniemu Maciągowi* (pp. 81–93). Kraków: Krakowskie Towarzystwo Edukacyjne - Oficyna Wydawnicza AFM.

Banaszak, B. (2012). *Prawo konstytucyjne* (6th ed.).Warszawa: C.H. Beck.

Banaszak, B. (2013). „Jakie zmiany w Konstytucji RP są potrzebne?". In: S. Bożyk (Ed.), *Aktualne problemy reform konstytucyjnych*. Białystok: Temida 2.

Buczkowski, J. (1998). *Podstawowe zasady prawa wyborczego III RP*.

Garlicki, L. (2020). „Europejskie standardy rzetelności wyborów (Komisja Wenecka i Europejski Trybunał Praw Człowieka)". *Przegląd Konstytucyjny* (4), 142–185.

Górecki, D. (1996). „Ewolucja przepisów dotyczących trybu wyboru prezydenta w polskim prawie konstytucyjnym". *Przegląd Sejmowy* (2(14)), 9.

Hermet, G., Rose, R., & Rouquié, A. (1978). "Preface". In: G. Hermet, R. Rose, & A. Rouquié (Eds.), *Elections Without Choice*. Palgrave Macmillan UK.

Informacja Państwowej Komisji Wyborczej z dnia 9 kwietnia 2020 r. Retrieved from: https://pkw.gov.pl/aktualnosci/informacje/informacja-panstwowej-komisji -wyborczej-z-dnia-9-kwietnia-2020-r

Informacja z 27 marca 2020 r. Retrieved from: https://pkw.gov.pl/aktualnosci/informacje /panstwowa-komisja-wyborcza-informuje

Kaczmarczyk, M. P. (2021). „Implementacja Kodeksu Dobrej Praktyki w Sprawach Wyborczych w polskim prawie wyborczym". In: M. Zubik & J. Podkowik (Eds.), *Aktualne wyzwania prawa wyborczego.* Warszawa: UW. https://doi.org/10.31338/uw .9788323552598. pp. 63–76

Komunikat Państwowej Komisji Wyborczej z dnia 7 maja 2020 roku. Retrieved from: https://pkw.gov.pl/aktualnosci/wyjasnienia-stanowiska-komunikaty/komunikat -panstwowej-komisji-wyborczej-z-dnia-7-maja-2020-roku

Jakubowski, P. (2015). "Cisza legislacyjna — zasada prawa wyborczego w Rzeczypospolitej Polskiej". *Przegląd Sejmowy* (4(129)), 9–23.

Krimmer, R., Duenas-Cid, D., & Krivonosova, I. (2021). "Debate: safeguarding democracy during pandemics. Social distancing, postal, or internet voting—the good, the bad or the ugly?", *Public Money & Management, 41*(1), 8–10. https://doi.org/10.1080 /09540962.2020.1766222

LeDuc, L., Niemi, R. G., & Norris, P. (2002). „Introduction: Comparing Democratic Elections". In: L. LeDuc, R. G. Niemi, & P. Norris (Eds.), *Comparing democracies 2: New challenges in the study of elections and voting* (2nd ed.). Sage.

Łączkowski, W. (2009). "Prawo wyborcze a ustrój demokratyczny". *Ruch Prawniczy, Ekonomiczny I Socjologiczny, LXXI* (2), 51–64.

Maroń, G. (2012). „Instytucja przysięgi prezydenta w polskim porządku prawnym", *Przegląd Prawa Konstytucyjnego* (2), 159–191.

Musiał-Karg, M. (2021). „Głosowanie korespondencyjne podczas pandemii COVID-19. Doświadczenia z polskich wyborów prezydenckich w 2020 r.", *Przegląd Prawa Konstytucyjnego, 60*(2), 31–48. https://doi.org/10.15804/ppk.2021.02.02

Musiał-Karg, M., & Kapsa, I. (2021). "Debate: Voting challenges in a pandemic—Poland", *Public Money & Management, 41*(1), 6–8. https://doi.org/10.1080/0954096 2.2020.1809791

Nohlen, D. (2004). *Prawo wyborcze i system partyjny: O teorii systemów wyborczych.* Warszawa: Wydaw. Nauk. „Scholar".

Patrzałek, A., & Skrzydło, W. (1997). "Cele i zasady kodyfikacji prawa wyborczego w Polsce". *Przegląd Sejmowy* (2(19)), 9–21.

Postanowienie Marszałka Sejmu Rzeczypospolitej Polskiej z dnia 5 lutego 2020 r. w sprawie zarządzenia wyborów Prezydenta Rzeczypospolitej Polskiej. Dz. U. 2020 poz. 184.

Przewodniczący Państwowej Komisji Wyborczej Sylwester Marciniak w wywiadzie dla PAP. Retrieved from: https://pkw.gov.pl/aktualnosci/informacje/przewodniczacy -panstwowej-komisji-wyborczej-sylwester-marciniak-w-wywiadzie-dla-pap

Rothschild, J. (1962). "The Military Background of Pilsudski's Coup D'Etat", *Slavic Review, 21*(2), 241–260. https://doi.org/10.2307/3000631

Rozporządzenie Ministra Zdrowia z dnia 13 marca 2020 r. w sprawie ogłoszenia na obszarze Rzeczypospolitej Polskiej stanu zagrożenia epidemicznego. Dz. U. 2020 poz. 433.

Rozporządzenie Ministra Zdrowia z dnia 20 marca 2020 r. w sprawie ogłoszenia na obszarze Rzeczypospolitej Polskiej stanu epidemii. Dz. U. 2020 poz. 491.

Rymarz, F. (2007). „O wyższy poziom legislacji i stabilizację polskiego prawa wyborczego". In: F. Rymarz (Ed.), *Iudices electionis custodes (sędziowie kustoszami wyborów): Księga Pamiątkowa Państwowej Komisji Wyborczej* (pp. 145–154). Kraj. Biuro Wyborcze.

Sieklucki, D. (2020). „Zmiany i projekty zmian w polskim systemie wyborczym po uchwaleniu Kodeksu wyborczego", *Politeja, 13*(4 (43)), 289–309. https://doi.org /10.12797/Politeja.13.2016.43.12

Skotnicki, K. (2021). „Państwo prawa a tryb uchwalania w 2020 r. ustaw regulujących wybory Prezydenta RP". In: J. Ciapała & A. Pyrzyńska (Eds.), *Monografie Prawnicze. Dylematy polskiego prawa wyborczego* (pp. 139–157). Warszawa: Wydawnictwo C.H. Beck.

Skrzydło, W. (2011). „Kodyfikacja prawa wyborczego w Polsce – zakres i znaczenie", *Przegląd Prawa Konstytucyjnego, 7*(3), 15–30. https://doi.org/10.15804/ppk.2011.03.01

Sokala, A. (2001). *Ordynacja wyborcza do Sejmu Rzeczypospolitej Polskiej i do Senatu Rzeczypospolitej Polskiej z dnia 12 kwietnia 2001 roku* (Wyd. 1). Tow. Nauk. Organizacji i Kierownictwa Stowarzyszenie Wyższej Użyteczności „Dom Organizatora".

Sprawozdanie Stenograficzne z 9. posiedzenia Sejmu Rzeczypospolitej Polskiej w dniu 6 kwietnia (trzeci dzień obrad). Retrieved from: https://orka2.sejm.gov.pl/StenoInter9 .nsf/0/8E10DCFB24EF9825C1258545005118FA/%24File/09_c_ksiazka_bis.pdf

Uchwała nr 129/2020 Państwowej Komisji Wyborczej z dnia 10 maja 2020 r. w sprawie stwierdzenia braku możliwości głosowania na kandydatów w wyborach Prezydenta Rzeczypospolitej Polskiej. Dz.U. 2020 poz. 967. Retrieved from: https://pkw.gov.pl /uploaded_files/1589173994_uchwala-nr-129.pdf

Uchwała nr 197/2020 Państwowej Komisji Wyborczej z dnia 19 czerwca 2020 r. w sprawie zarządzenia głosowania wyłącznie korespondencyjnego na terenie gminy Baranów w wyborach Prezydenta Rzeczypospolitej Polskiej zarządzonych na dzień 28 czerwca 2020 r. M.P. 2020 poz. 544.

Uchwała nr 198/2020 Państwowej Komisji Wyborczej z dnia 19 czerwca 2020 r. w sprawie zarządzenia głosowania wyłącznie korespondencyjnego na terenie gminy Marklowice w wyborach Prezydenta Rzeczypospolitej Polskiej zarządzonych na dzień 28 czerwca 2020 r. M.P. 2020 poz. 545.

Ustawa z dnia 5 stycznia 2011 r. - Kodeks wyborczy. Dz.U. 2011 nr 21 poz. 112.

Ustawa z dnia 31 marca 2020 r. o zmianie ustawy o szczególnych rozwiązaniach związanych z zapobieganiem, przeciwdziałaniem i zwalczaniem COVID-19, innych chorób

zakaźnych oraz wywołanych nimi sytuacji kryzysowych oraz niektórych innych ustaw. Dz. U. 2020 poz. 568.

Ustawa z dnia 16 kwietnia 2020 r. o szczególnych instrumentach wsparcia w związku z rozprzestrzenianiem się wirusa SARS-CoV-2. Dz. U. 2020 poz. 695.

Ustawa z dnia 2 czerwca 2020 r. o szczególnych zasadach organizacji wyborów powszechnych na Prezydenta Rzeczypospolitej Polskiej zarządzonych w 2020 r. z możliwością głosowania korespondencyjnego. Dz. U. 2020 poz. 979.

Uziębło, P. (2011). "Wprowadzenie do kodeksu wyborczego", *Przegląd Prawa Konstytucyjnego* (3(7)).

Wyrok Trybunału Konstytucyjnego z dnia 3 listopada 2006 r. Sygn. akt K 31/06. Dz. U. Nr 202, poz. 1493.

CHAPTER 22

Postal Voting of Poles abroad – The Case of the 2020 Presidential Election

Izabela Kapsa and Magdalena Musiał-Karg

22.1 Introduction

The President of the Republic of Poland is elected every five years in a general election. Due to the expiring term of the then President, the next elections were scheduled for spring 2020. Under applicable law, the election date was announced in early February, about a month before the first COVID-19 case was registered. However, the pace of the pandemic in Poland indicated that the peak of the incidence would take place at the end of April, i.e. a few days before the scheduled presidential election. Despite the coincidence of both dates, it was finally decided to hold presidential elections on May 10, 2020, but based on specific legal provisions - in the form of all-postal voting. As it soon turned out, both Poland's minimal experience in using this alternative voting method and the legal and time constraints meant that the actions taken by the ruling body were ineffective, and it was impossible to hold elections within this timeframe in a pandemic. As a result, adopting a special law proved to be the case, which laid down specific rules for holding these elections at a new date. According to them, Poles in the country voted in person at polling stations under a sanitary regime (except for high-incidence constituencies), and voters voting outside the country - voted by post.

The most important limitation that contributed to the difficulties in organising the electoral process in Poland during the COVID-19 pandemic was the lack (a small number) of alternative voting methods. The attempt to introduce all-postal voting failed a few weeks before the voting date. The postponement of the election date to the end of June 2020 and the maintenance of postal voting for Poles voting outside the country and in districts where the epidemic suddenly and significantly worsened made it possible to hold these elections. However, many voters voting by post required extra effort to participate in these elections.

In this chapter, the authors present an analysis of postal voting in the presidential elections in Poland in 2020 from the perspective of voters from abroad. The analysis is based on the results of a survey conducted among Poles after the first and second rounds of elections to answer the following research questions: How was the election process abroad - from registration to postal voting? What problems arose in connection with the postal voting in these elections? To what extent were Poles voting abroad in the 2020 presidential election satisfied with the postal voting? What are their views on this voting method? In order to answer these questions, the authors analysed the quantitative and qualitative responses of the respondents. In addition, they presented the political and legal context of the presidential election during the pandemic in Poland and the previous experience of postal voting in the country.

22.2   Background

Under Art. 128 of the Polish Constitution (1997) and Art. 289 of Electoral Code (*Ustawa*, 2011), the election of the President of the Republic of Poland is ordered by the Marshal of the Sejm, considering the time limits arising from both legal acts. The election of the President of the Republic of Poland takes place after obtaining an absolute majority of votes, the date of the election is the date of the first round of voting, and if none of the candidates obtains the required majority of votes, the second round of voting takes place 14 days later. In August 2020, the term of office of President Andrzej Duda was about to expire. Hence, on February 5, 2020, i.e. less than a month before the first case of COVID-19 was reported, the next election was set for May 10, 2020. The election process continued despite subsequent cases and despite the forecasts for the peak of the first wave of the pandemic in Poland in the last days of April 2020.

An attempt to get out of the problematic situation, aimed at holding elections despite the pandemic, was the adoption of the so-called "anti-crisis shield". In addition to other pandemic regulations, it introduced the possibility of postal voting for people over 60 and people in quarantine (*Ustawa*, 2020a). Then the Act on special rules for holding presidential elections was introduced, according to which postal voting was the only form of voting for all voters (*Ustawa*, 2020b). The first legal Act was adopted on March 31, 2020, and the second one on April 6, 2020, i.e. during the election process and the ongoing election campaign. However, the parliament's actions were widely criticised because, according to the judgments of the Constitutional Tribunal, significant changes to the Electoral Code may be introduced no later than six months before the first election procedures (*Wyrok*, 2011; Venice Commission, 2002). Concern over these plans was expressed by organisations and institutions such as the OSCE Office for Democratic Institutions and Human Rights, the European

Commission, the Venice Commission, the National Electoral Commission and the Ombudsman. In addition to formal irregularities, the election process was also characterised by organisational chaos, preventing the holding of elections on the scheduled date (more: Musiał-Karg & Kapsa, 2021). Ultimately, based on the announcement of the National Electoral Commission, no voting took place on May 10, 2020 (Announcement, 2020).

The next step was the adoption of a new law setting out specific rules for the organisation of the presidential elections in 2020 (*Ustawa*, 2020c). Under the provisions of this Act, voting was to be held in person at polling stations. However, on-demand postal voting was also possible. Apart from voters optionally using this voting method in the country, it was the only voting method for voters voting abroad and in those municipalities or parts thereof where the epidemic situation suddenly and significantly worsened (this solution was applied in two municipalities in the country). The due date was set for June 28, 2020; in terms of the number of cases, much safer than initially planned. Of course, in the case of a personal vote, guidelines were prepared regarding the obligation to maintain social distancing, covering the mouth and nose, or disinfectant use. The challenge, however, was to prepare for postal voting, with which Poland had little experience so far.

The possibility of postal voting on demand for Poles voting abroad was introduced in the Electoral Code of 2011. Since then, the groups of citizens who could use this voting form have been changed several times. After the amendment to the Electoral Code of May 27 2011, this alternative voting method was also made available to all persons with a significant or moderate degree of disability. Furthermore, the amendment to the Electoral Code of July 11, 2014, extended the possibility of postal voting, granting this right to every voter. Interestingly, a year after this amendment, presidential and parliamentary elections were held in Poland, in which postal voting was available to all eligible. However, as it turned out, there was little interest in this voting method among voters (Kapsa & Musiał-Karg, 2020; Musiał-Karg, 2021).

What's more, voters who voted by post made many mistakes, making their votes invalid. Consequently, another change was introduced in 2018, abolishing universal postal voting, leaving this possibility only to people with a severe or moderate degree of disability. Thus, until 2020, postal voting was not successfully practised in Poland. Nevertheless, it was the only possibility for many voters to vote, which significantly increased the number of votes cast (Table 22.1 includes figures).

At the outbreak of the COVID-19 pandemic, Poland had a limited catalogue of alternative voting methods, of which postal voting was not particularly popular (voting by proxy was also available). Nevertheless, the Polish government

TABLE 22.1   Voting by post in the general elections in Poland in 2015 and 2020

	Elections to the Sejm	Elections to the Senate	Presidential elections 2015		Presidential elections 2020	
			I round	II round	I round	II round
Entitled to vote	30629150	30629150	30688570	30709281	30204684	30268460
Vaild votes cast	15595335	15593033	15023886	16993169	19026600	20047543
Number of election packages sent	45538	45538	42814	56845	536821	704111
Number of return envelopes received	39958	39952	35053	40720	483898	614631
Share of sent election packages in relation to all eligible voters	0,149%	0,149%	0,14%	0,185%	1,78%	2,33%
Share of postal votes among all votes cast	0,242%	0,243%			2,43%	2,96%

SOURCE: NATIONAL ELECTORAL COMMISSION, WWW.PKW.GOV.PL, 20.01.2022

made efforts to hold presidential elections scheduled for 2020, relying on specific legal solutions. In addition, pursuant to a special act, the possibility of
postal voting was introduced for voters voting outside the country and those
subject to quarantine. However, the previous experience with postal voting
and the limited time to prepare for elections using this method may have
raised concerns and curiosity among researchers as to the characteristics and
course of this voting.

22.3   Methodology

To obtain answers to the research questions, the authors made a quantitative
and qualitative analysis of the respondents' answers to the questionnaire,
which was conducted online twice – after the first and the second round of
voting in the presidential elections. The questionnaire contained open and
closed questions relating to the voting process – from registration to voting
and statements containing various opinions on voting by post. The survey was
addressed to Poles voting abroad. Social media, mainly Facebook, distributed
the survey information and invitation to complete it. The existing groups asso-
ciating members of the Polish Community in various countries and through
the group established in response to the change in electoral law in the 2020
presidential election - "Polonia has NO choice" stamped their role, too. By
sharing survey information with their friends, members of these groups also
increased the scope of the survey to people who did not belong to Facebook
groups. Therefore, membership in groups was not a significant factor here.

   502 respondents took part in the first round, and 760 respondents in the second round. About 20% of the respondents from the second questionnaire also
participated in the first one. In both surveys, the majority of respondents were
women. The largest age group were people aged 35–44. In terms of education,
people with higher education were the majority. When it comes to the country
of residence, the most numerous group were Poles living in Great Britain (in
both rounds, more than half).

   Moreover, it was possible to find respondents staying in other European
countries (e.g. in Germany, Norway, Spain, Ireland and France) and in the USA
in similar but much smaller proportions. Refer to Table 22.2 for the characteristics of the group of respondents. Individual votes are not included in the table;
however, respondents also voted in such countries as Turkey, Canada, Brazil
and Japan.

   The analysis in this chapter includes a quantitative analysis, mainly descriptive statistics of the studied variables, and a qualitative analysis of respondents'

TABLE 22.2   Descriptive statistics of respondents' demographic characteristics and country of residence

	I round		II round	
Sex				
	N	%	N	%
man	103	20,52	121	15,92
woman	399	79,48	639	84,07
Age				
	N	%	N	%
18–24 years	15	2,99	24	3,16
25–34 years	124	24,70	199	26,18
35–44 years	249	49,60	376	49,47
45–54 years	82	16,33	108	14,21
55–65 years	23	4,58	47	6,18
over 65 years	9	1,79	6	0,79
Education				
	N	%	N	%
no education	1	0,20	0	0
primary / lower secondary	0	0	8	1,05
vocational	21	4,18	56	7,37
secondary / post-secondary	146	29,08	282	37,11
higher education	334	66,53	415	54,47
Country of residence				
	N	%	N	%
Great Britain	271	53,98	435	57,24
Norway	46	9,16	4	0,52
Germany	44	8,76	52	6,84
Spain	38	7,57	41	5,39
Ireland	20	3,98	13	1,71
USA	13	2,59	10	1,32
France	12	2,39	68	8,95

SOURCE: OWN STUDY

answers to open-ended questions about their experiences with the election process.

22.4   Results

The first issue examined was analysing the election process from voters' perspectives. Given the limited time to prepare elections using the postal voting method, it was particularly demanding to carry out registering voters in the electoral register efficiently and provide them with election packages on time to enable them to vote in the elections.

The first part of the study included questions about the various stages of the election process - how efficient the registration process was and the receiving/sending back of the election package. Should problems at any stage of the election process arise, respondents had the opportunity to describe the nature of the problems they were experiencing.

As for the registration process - the intention of postal voting abroad was reported to the consul by the 15th day before election day (for the first round); in most cases, it proceeded smoothly. However, as many as 11.75% of respondents reported problems registering in the voter register. These problems mainly related to technical issues: the website on which one had to register was either not working or "crashing"; registration failed despite providing correct data; the voter was not entered into the register despite receiving an e-mail confirming the registration; no possibility to register from a mobile device; the form did not accept personal data. There were also procedural issues, such as the lack of a valid passport or the need to provide data not included in the passport.

In the second round of elections, which took place two weeks later, the obligation to register in the electoral roll only applied to those who were not registered in the register at the first round. Despite this, 15.52% of the respondents still had problems registering in the electoral register. Problems again concerned technical issues, such as the lack of or difficult access to the website, difficulties in approving the application via an activation link or the inability to enter data via a smartphone. In addition, some people reported no contact with the diplomatic mission, which they tried to establish in the event of technical problems, or the need to re-register despite registering for the first round of voting. As a result of these problems, some people were not entered into the electoral roll and could not vote.

Although most of the voters registered on time, not all of them managed to vote. Out of all surveyed in the first round of the elections, only 85.46%

indicated they had received the election package within the time limit for voting. 8.76% of the respondents did not receive it (despite successful registration), and 4.78% received it after the due date. In the second round, 87.76% indicated that they had received an election package in time for voting. However, 7.89% of the respondents did not receive it, and 4.34% received it after the deadline. In both rounds, a dozen or so per cent of the respondents who had registered in the electoral roll could not vote because they had not received the election package within the time limit for voting. Moreover, 4–7% of the respondents failed to register. Despite the actions taken and the expressed will to vote, all these voters did not participate in the elections (the percentage/figures are presented in Table 22.3).

The second important aspect of the election process was postal voting itself. Again, it should be noted that the vast majority of voters did not notice any irregularities in voting. However, some respondents pointed to other errors or irregularities they noticed during the vote.

22 respondents (4.38% of the total) reported errors in the first round and 40 (5.26%) in the second. The most common errors reported were: missing (or different colours of) a stamp on the ballot paper, no ballot card or statement,

TABLE 22.3   Data on the difficulties reported by respondents as to the course of the election process during the 2020 presidential election

| | Presidential elections 2020 | | | |
| | I round | | II round | |
	number	% of the total	number	% of the total
Problems with registering in the electoral register	61	11,86%	118	15,52%
Received the election package after the deadline	24	4,66%	33	4,34%
Did not receive an election package	42	8,17%	60	7,89%

SOURCE: OWN STUDY

damaged documents or a transparent envelope for the ballot paper. These mistakes are definitely linked to the short time available for diplomatic missions to prepare elections using this voting method.

Some respondents also reported the late delivery of the election package as an error. For this reason, only 40% of the respondents (in the first round of voting) indicated that they knew that their election package reached the diplomatic mission in time; in the second, it was 34%. 77% of respondents in the first round and the same in the second round sent the package by post, 6% (in the first round) and 7.37% (in the second round) of the respondents delivered it in person, and 8.76% (in the first round) and 5.29% (in the second round) used commercial or social courier services. The respondents additionally provided data on the costs incurred for sending the election package to the polling station. Costs (and, of course, also the currency) differed depending on the country of stay, but it is worth mentioning their range: from € 1.55–26; £ 7–8; NOK 20–25.

The lack of certainty about the delivery of the election package to the diplomatic mission also translated into a relatively high level of doubts about whether the vote was accepted. Only about 30% of the respondents in the first round and 25% in the second round said there were no such doubts. Also, about 33% of those surveyed in the first round and 35% in the second round had no doubts that their vote was secret (this issue could have been related to both the voting method and the type of voting envelope used by the election commission).

The study also decided to examine the assessment of postal voting as a means of participating in elections and respondents' level of satisfaction with postal voting in these particular elections.

In their assessment of the postal voting, respondents' satisfaction was relatively low in both voting rounds -some fewer people were definitely satisfied and somewhat satisfied than those who were dissatisfied. The difference was even more significant in the second round: over 35% were satisfied in the first round, while almost 45% were dissatisfied; in the second, 33% were satisfied, while almost 50% were dissatisfied. However, it is fascinating to have far less critical opinions of respondents on the statements made for the study concerning postal voting to participate in elections and resolve the best possible solution for the time of a pandemic. Interestingly, during the first round of voting, there was a similar number of supporters and opponents of postal voting as a method of participating in the elections. In the second round, the latter increased by approximately 10%. When assessing postal voting as a suitable method during a pandemic, more respondents believed this to be accurate than those who disagreed with it.

TABLE 22.4 Opinions on postal voting

	I round					II round				
	5	4	3	2	1	5	4	3	2	1
I am satisfied with the postal voting in the first round of the 2020 presidential elections.	10,16%	25,1%	20%	21,51%	23,31%	12%	21%	18,42%	16%	32,76%
I believe that postal voting is a good form of participation in elections.	18,87%	22,57%	18,29%	20,82%	19,45%	18,42%	17,37%	17,63%	18,55%	28,03%
I believe that during a pandemic postal vote is the best form of voting.	28,4%	27,82%	22,18%	12,26%	9,33%	25%	21,31%	23,81%	12,24%	17,63%

5 - Absolutely. 4 - Probably yes. 3 - It's hard to say. 2 - Not really. 1 - Definitely not.
SOURCE: OWN STUDY.

22.5   Discussion

Among the many countries where national or subnational elections or referendums were to be held during the pandemic, at least 80 countries and territories decided to postpone them, at least 160 decided to hold elections, and at least 65 held elections that were initially postponed due to concerns related to COVID-19 (IDEA, 2022). In response to the dilemmas of the governments of those countries that decided to hold elections, several research positions appeared regarding the rules of their organisation. The discussion was taken, among others, by Robert Krimmer, David Dueñas-Cid and Juliia Krivonosova (2020), who presented three scenarios for countries that decided to hold elections during the COVID-19 pandemic: carry on but add health protection, postal voting or i-voting. In Poland, attempts were made to use the second scenario, but the first time (at the initially planned date) without success, and the second time (at the delayed date and on special terms) with some difficulties.

Both on the first scheduled date of the elections and the presidential elections postponed to the end of June, organisational weaknesses and time constraints emerged, which hampered the smooth and democratic voting by post. A reliable legislative process regarding the elections, including the guarantee of respect for democratic electoral standards and principles (universality, secrecy, directness), was not successfully completed. The ability of postal service providers in other countries (for Poles voting abroad) to properly handle and deliver postal items (election packages) to voters turned out to be a challenge (Musiał-Karg & Kapsa, 2020). Furthermore, due to problems with registration in the electoral roll and the failure to receive the electoral package within the time limit for voting, some significant problems emerged for democratic standards. The indicated situations prove that it was impossible to guarantee the elections' universality (López-Pintor, 2010). There were also doubts about the possibility of maintaining the secrecy of voting (reported by respondents participating in the survey, transparent envelopes that made it possible to read the vote).

The survey revealed the respondents' doubts about the delivery of the election package to a diplomatic mission and whether the vote was taken into account. These doubts were confirmed by the data of the National Electoral Commission, according to which the share of envelopes with votes that were thrown into the ballot box (in relation to the packages issued) amounted to 86.21% in the first round of elections and 84.26% in the second round. Delays in delivering an election package or the lack of an electoral package despite registration in the electoral register, on the one hand, made it impossible for these people to participate in the elections. On the other hand, it significantly undermined voters' confidence in both this voting method and the democratic nature of the election process. The same applies to invalid votes, which according to SEC data, amounted to 4.41% in the first round and 3.50% in the second. In addition, respondents participating in the survey reported irregularities regarding the lack of a stamp or documents in the electoral package, which could also affect the recognition of the vote as invalid.

Another critical aspect of the election process concerned the transfer of the burden of responsibility for voting effectiveness (understood as acceptance of the vote by the election commission) onto voters, as evidenced by the mobilisation of the so-called social couriers. They organised themselves to deliver electoral packages to the commission. Given the information about the late delivery of election packages to voters, many people shared their concerns about the possibility of returning the package in time. It was then that Poles living in different parts of the world began to organise themselves on their own so that as many votes as possible reached the district electoral commissions. The so-called social couriers quickly appeared, collected voters' packages, and handed them over to diplomatic missions.

22.6   Conclusions

Despite the pandemic conditions, the Polish government showed great determination to organise the presidential elections - first in the form of all-postal voting on May 10, 2020 (which failed), and then in a hybrid version - in June (1st round) and July (2nd round). However, both the dynamics of the pandemic and the too hasty and erroneous handling of special legal regulations translated into organisational chaos and legal doubts, which made it impossible to conduct elections on the first scheduled date. A solution was adopted as a result. According to the solution, a new time limit was used to vote in a hybrid manner - in person in the country (except for districts excluded from this form of voting due to the high incidence of disease) and by post abroad, due to the short time for preparation of postal voting and little experience so far. Unfortunately, this voting method caused many irregularities, and some voters were excluded from the election process.

The analysis of the results of empirical research of voters voting by post outside Poland leads to the following conclusions. First, due to technical problems (and other problems in the voter registration process), some voters, despite their expressed willingness to participate in the elections, did not vote. In addition, despite their successful registration in the electoral roll, successive groups did not receive an election package in time for voting. Finally, others were unsure whether their vote had reached the polling station and was considered. In this situation, some voters took over the responsibility for the effectiveness of voting (understood as the vote accepted by the election commission), as evidenced by the mobilisation of the so-called social couriers who organised themselves grassroots to deliver election packages to the commission (Turkish, 2020; Next Citizens ..., 2020).

Interestingly, despite the low level of satisfaction of the respondents with the presidential election, their opinions on postal voting as a voting method and in the specific conditions of the pandemic were much less critical. Such opinions on postal voting in a country where the previous experience with alternative voting methods was limited may constitute an incentive for the government to improve the process of organising elections using this method. Therefore, the method is expected to remain in the electoral code longer.

References:

IDEA (2022). "Global overview of COVID-19: Impact on elections". Retrieved from: https://www.idea.int/news-media/multimedia-reports/global-overview-COVID-19-impact-elections

Kapsa, I. & Musiał Karg, M. (2020). *Alternatywne metody głosowania w opiniach Polaków. Postawy i poglądy względem wybranych form partycypacji w wyborach*. Poznań: Wydawnictwo Naukowe UAM - Wydział Nauk Politycznych i Dziennikarstwa UAM.

Komunikat (2020). „Komunikat Państwowej Komisji Wyborczej z dnia 7 maja 2020 roku". Retrieved from: https://pkw.gov.pl/aktualnosci/wyjasnienia-stanowiska-komunikaty/komunikat-panstwowej-komisji-wyborczej-z-dnia-7-maja-2020-roku.

Krimmer, R., Dueñas-Cid, D. & Krivonosova, J. (2020). "Debate: safeguarding democracy during pandemics. Social distancing, postal, or internet voting—the good, the bad or the ugly?". *Public Money & Management, 41* (no. 1), pp. 8–10. DOI: 10.1080/09540962.2020.1766222

López-Pintor, P. (2010). "Assessing Electoral Fraud in New Democracies A Basic Conceptual Framework, IFES White Paper". Retrieved from: https://www.ifes.org/sites/default/files/rlp_electoral_fraud_white_paper_web.pdf.

Musiał-Karg, M. & Kapsa, I. (2021). „Debate: Voting challenges in a pandemic – Poland". *Public Money & Management, 41* (no.1), pp. 6–8. DOI: 10.1080/09540962.2020.1809791

Musiał-Karg, M. & Kapsa, I. (2020). „All-postal voting (powszechne głosowanie korespondencyjne) w wyborach prezydenckich w Polsce w 2020 r. O tym, jak nie procedować w czasie pandemii?" In K. Hajder, M. Musiał-Karg & M. Górny (Eds.), *Konsekwencje pandemii COVID-19: Państwo i społeczeństwo* (135–145). Poznań: Wydawnictwo Naukowe Wydziału Nauk Politycznych i Dziennikarstwa UAM.

Musiał-Karg, M. (2021). „Głosowanie korespondencyjne podczas pandemii COVID-19. Doświadczenia z polskich wyborów prezydenckich w 2020 r.". *Przegląd Prawa Konstytucyjnego*, 2(60), pp. 31–48. DOI 10.15804/ppk.2021.02.02

Konstytucja Rzeczypospolitej Polskiej (1997). Retrieved from: https://www.sejm.gov.pl/prawo/konst/polski/kon1.htm.

Starzewski, Ł. (2020). „Następni obywatele, głównie z zagranicy, skarżą się, że nie mogli głosować na Prezydenta RP – choć chcieli". Retrieved from: https://bip.brpo.gov.pl/pl/content/nastepni-obywatele-glownie-zagranicy-skarza-sie-rpo-ze-nie%C2%Aomogli-glosowac.

Turecki, K. (2020). „Pomoc dla Polonii. Kurierzy społeczni dostarczą karty do konsulatów". Retrieved from: https://wiadomosci.onet.pl/tylko-w-onecie/wybory-2020-polacy-za-granica-kurierzy-spoleczni-dostarcza-karty-do-konsulatow/cgyhzjo

Ustawa (2011). „Ustawa z dnia 5 stycznia 2011 r. - Kodeks wyborczy". Dz.U. 2011 nr 21 poz. 112.

Ustawa (2020a). „Ustawa z dnia 31 marca 2020 r. o zmianie ustawy o szczególnych rozwiązaniach związanych z zapobieganiem, przeciwdziałaniem i zwalczaniem COVID-19, innych chorób zakaźnych oraz wywołanymi nimi sytuacji kryzysowych oraz niektórych innych ustaw". Dz.U. 2020 poz. 568.

Ustawa (2020b). „Ustawa z dnia 6 kwietnia 2020 r. o szczególnych zasadach przeprowadzania wyborów powszechnych na Prezydenta Rzeczypospolitej Polskiej zarządzonych w 2020 r." Dz.U. 2020 poz. 827.

Ustawa (2020c). „Ustawa z dnia 2 czerwca 2020 r. o szczególnych zasadach organizacji wyborów powszechnych na Prezydenta Rzeczypospolitej Polskiej zarządzonych w 2020 r. z możliwością głosowania korespondencyjnego". Dz.U. 2020 poz. 979.

Venice Commission (2002). Code of good practice in electoral matters. Opinion 190/2002:
https://www.venice.coe.int/webforms/documents/default.aspx?pdffile=CDL-AD(2002)023rev2-cor-e. 2.05.2020.

Wyrok (2011). „Wyrok Trybunału Konstytucyjnego z dnia 20 lipca 2011 r.", K 9/11.

CHAPTER 23

Was It a "Youthquake"? The Increase in Electoral and Political Participation of Polish Youth during the COVID-19 Pandemic

Radosław Marzęcki

23.1 Introduction

Since the beginning of the democratic changes in 1989, young people have been considered the most demobilized group of Polish voters. The patterns of their electoral activity also had some consequences, as political parties or candidates are usually less interested in the electorate, which shows weaker loyalty and low readiness to participate in elections, and is additionally relatively small in number. Therefore, they were less often than older groups targeted by political promises made in election campaigns. Meanwhile, during the presidential elections that took place in July 2020 we could observe an unprecedentedly high level of turnout among the youngest voters, which for the first time in history exceeded the engagement rate of the oldest voters. Social surveys also confirmed unprecedented upward trends in the level of youth interest in politics. There are many indications that these phenomena are not coincidental. Once again, young people marked their influence in the public space a few months later, taking part in mass protests against the tightening of the abortion law. In November, up to one million young people, mostly women, demonstrated. The scale of this involvement was so large that predictions were made in public discourse that it could become a kind of generational experience for young citizens. The beginning of 2021 also saw the historically highest rate of young people's identification with left-wing views, which is the result of an upward trend that has progressed consistently since 2015.

The main aim of the chapter is to systematize and coherently describe the most important trends in the patterns of political and electoral participation of young Polish citizens during the pandemic. These include: (1) a dramatic increase in the turnout rate during the presidential elections, which for the first time in history exceeded the engagement rate of the oldest voters; (2) a significant increase in interest in politics; (3) mass participation of young people in social protests against tightening the abortion law, despite the restrictions in force limiting the right to organize gatherings; (4) the highest ever rate of identification of young people with left-wing views. Taking into account their nature and dynamics, the chapter interprets them as a manifestation of 'youth-quake', i.e. a multidimensional change in the political and electoral participation of young citizens, which has a significant impact on political processes.

23.2   Young People Participate "Differently". Literature Review

Although scholarly descriptions of youth involvement in public and political affairs are more often critical in tone, a detailed socio-political portrait of a young citizen is by no means clear-cut. Usually, the attitudes towards politics of younger and older generations are confronted (García-Albacete & Lorente, 2019; Grasso, 2014; Quintelier, 2007). The most frequent accusations include political and electoral passivity (Blais, Gidengil & Nevitte, 2004; Franklin, 2004; Berman, 1997), no interest (García-Albacete, 2014; Pirie & Worcester, 1998) and low level of knowledge about public affairs (Park, 1999), indifference or lack of connection to the rest of the community in which they live. Youth's growing alienation from traditional politics is also pointed out (Dermody, Hanmer-Lloyd & Scullion, 2010), or even active rejection of politics (Farthing 2010). An important thread in this narrative is the anxiety about effects this 'youth participatory deficit' (Bečević & Dahlstedt, 2021) will have bfor the foundations of democracy in the future (Marzęcki, 2020, p. 34; Loncle et al., 2012; Walther et al., 2020). 'Crisis of democracy' is spoken of in the context of declining rates of political participation in many late-modern societies (Crozier, Huntington & Watnuki, 1975; Macedo, Alex-Assensoh & Berry, 2005), and young citizens – due to their particularly low level of political participation – are sometimes considered a special threat (Furlong & Cartmel, 2012; Henn & Foard, 2012; Dalton, 2008; Zukin et al., 2006; Fahmy, 2006; Wattenberg, 2002). Concerns about the future stem primarily from an understanding of the role that the youngest generation of citizens plays in any society (Plutzer, 2002). Metaphorically speaking, it is "the lens in which the various problems and tensions of the system are focused. [Youth] is a barometer of change and social mood" (Szafraniec, 2011, p. 11). Proper identification of young people's aspirations, interests, problems and intentions allows for better planning of specific policies, anticipating various phenomena or avoiding destructive social conflicts. The basic structure of man's personality, their fundamental values (including participatory and political orientations), are crystallized before adulthood and are subject to relatively little change thereafter (Inglehart 1977; 1990; 1997; 2018). Therefore, pessimistic indicators of conventional youth participation are treated by some researchers as a harbinger of further intensification of these negative trends, and the signaled 'crisis of democracy' or 'crisis of youth' means something more serious – 'crisis of the future' (Kirbiš et al., 2017, p. 184).

On the other hand, it is difficult to overlook scientific works whose conclusions may serve as a counterargument in the discussion on political engagement of youth. Researchers agree that young people may feel alienated (have a sense of marginalization and rejection by political elites), but it is also indicated that their absence from the functioning of traditional institutions is not necessarily the result of apathy (lack of knowledge, interest and motivation for political action) (Loader, 2007; Marsh, O'Toole & Jones, 2007). On the contrary, young people are interested in politics and believe in the democratic process, but the fact that they are excluded from formal politics and institutions makes them 'engaged sceptics' who are neither apolitical nor apathetic (Henn & Foard, 2014; Henn, Weinstein & Wring, 2002; Phelps, 2012). Without a doubt, young citizens are disillusioned with political parties and the weakness of the agenda of issues that are at the center of mainstream political discussions. They tend to be concerned with issues that established politics usually ignores (Beck & Beck-Gernsheim, 2002, p. 158) resulting in the disavowal of politicians through non-support. Many young people feel disillusioned with what politics offers, but this should not be misinterpreted as a lack of interest in politics in general (Loader, Vromen & Xenos, 2014). It is worth distinguishing between the processes taking place in relation to conventional participation (voting, political party membership, reading newspapers, etc.) and unconventional participation, and above all, recognizing the role and importance of youth presence within new, alternative forms of participation (Giugni & Grasso, 2021). In this view, young people do not sink into apathy, but choose other forms of politics that seem more meaningful to them (Norris, 2002; Sloam, 2013). Forms of youth political engagement are often referred to as 'novel' (Farthing, 2010), 'innovative' (Giugni & Grasso, 2021) or 'creative' (García-Albacete & Lorente, 2019) and include, among others, political consumerism and e-democracy. Some researchers note that the transformation of youth participation patterns consist in displacement of traditional models of representative democracy as the dominant cultural form of engagement by alternative approaches increasingly characterized through networking practices (Loader, Vromen & Xenos, 2014, p. 143). Youth's traditional relationship with politics is gradually replaced by a more personalised politics of self-actualisation through digital networking or consumer activism (Vromen, Xenos & Loader, 2015, p. 82). Sarah Pickard uses the term 'Do-It-Ourselves (DIO) politics' to show that participants bypass electorally focused political structures and take political and civic initiatives by acting together online and offline within various private and public arenas:

a family, a peer group, a community, locally, regionally, nationally or globally (Pickard, 2019, p. 391). Such activities are often mediated or facilitated by digital channels of expression, particularly social media, and are primarily aimed at making the world fairer, greener and more peaceful. Social media can have enormous potential not only to mobilize but also to broaden political participation (Xenos, Vromen, Loader, 2014).

The scepticism expressed by young people towards those who represent them, rather than being seen as a sign of apathy, could be viewed as a fully legitimate democratic attitude of reflectively engaged citizens, aware of their personal situation and position in the political system (Loader, Vromen & Xenos, 2014, p. 148). In attempting to accurately describe patterns of youth political participation, we should go beyond both disengaged paradigm (youth is passive and lacks political interest), and engaged paradigm (youth are active in new ways). This is the essence of what Rys Farthing (2010) calls 'the politics of youthful antipolitics', because both engagement and disengagement occur simultaneously in young people's attitudes. Referring to the concept of 'freedom's children' (Beck & Beck-Gernsheim, 2002) claims that young people live with a freedom that was entirely unknown to earlier generations, representing radically unpolitical model of citizenship (Farthing, 2010, p. 188). Therefore, in unusual activities of radically unpolitical young people we can see a kind of rationality. The young generation's rejection of politics is its way of negotiating new freedoms of a risk society (Farthing, 2010, p. 188) and in this sense represents a new and particular form of political influence. Non-action becomes the deepest challenge for political elites (p. 190), which often place youth on the margins of their plans and visions. On the other hand, specific acts of participation can be seen as a kind of fight by those who feel excluded (e.g., due to class, gender, ethnicity, race or age) for the recognition of their right to be 'full citizens' (Fitzgerald et al., 2010).

The change in the model of participation is that regular engagement is being replaced by the activities referred to as 'micro-political' or 'cause-oriented', in which young people act not towards the state, but towards specific issues (Farthing, 2010; Pattie, Seyd & Whiteley, 2004). They engage in an individualized rather than a collective way, getting involved in ad hoc issues-based campaigns (rather than long-term organizational commitment) (Vromen, Xenos & Loader, 2015, p. 82) and can be referred to 'standby citizens', who make their willingness to act in the public or political sphere dependent on their own momentary motivation or the appearance of suitable external circumstances (García-Albacete & Lorente, 2019; Amnå & Ekman, 2013). Research findings show that younger people in particular are more likely to participate in protest activities: from signing online petitions and peaceful demonstrations to violent riots (Renström, Aspernäs & Bäck, 2021; Gauthier, 2003; Sloam, 2016). This tendency wanes with age (Melo & Stockemer, 2014).

23.3   Pandemic as "Politicized Times"

It is important for the concept of 'standby citizens' that the context of action can play an activating role. Not only journalistic, but also scientific descriptions of youth participation patterns in public life often take as a point of reference groundbreaking events from the past, which constitute empirical confirmation of the thesis that young people can change the 'course of history', using their quantitative and symbolic potential in confrontation with the hegemonic socio-political order, guarded by political elites (usually dominated by older generations). The archetypal example is the student revolt of 1968. Some researchers see in the structural (political or economic) conditions of socialization in youth the sources of attitudes that may become fixed in subsequent years of a person's life (García-Albacete & Lorente, 2019, p. 3). Gema García-Albacete uses such an example, citing the activity of the young generation of the late 1960s and early 1970s. She argues that these people, living in 'more politicized times', strongly and permanently internalized norms of political activity. Similarly, she explains the attitudes of contemporary youth who, living, studying and working in 'less politicized times', adapt to reality through a relatively low level of participation in public or political life (García-Albacete, 2014, p. 234). The factor of politicization as a determinant of motivation to participate and engage in politics, especially in the intergenerational aspect, was also considered by other researchers (Grasso et al., 2019). Their main premise is the thesis that generations growing up in specific periods (political and historical) assimilate specific political values and behaviors (Mannheim, 1928) and in this sense "the characteristics of an epoch tend to mould their imprint on those 'coming of age' in that period" (Grasso et al., 2019, p. 201). Similarly, depoliticization is "a major factor alienating the public, and particularly younger generations, from politics" (p. 203). Research on British youth shows that the political contexts in which different political generations have grown up differ significantly in terms of the extent of politicization and the contestation of ideas. Generations socialized in the turbulent 1960s and 1970s are even described as 'the protest generation' (Jennings, 1987). The next generation ('Thatcher's Children'), growing up in the era of the neoliberal market economy (1980s and 1990s), when there was more emphasis than before on individualism and self-reliance over collective pursuits, already represents a weaker level of motivation for political action. Even less motivated is the Millennial

generation ('Blair's Babies') entering adulthood at the turn of the 20th century, socialized in an era of technocratic governments that avoided ideological
disputes by arguing that all political issues had already been resolved (Grasso
et al., 2019).

The pandemic crisis – due to its multidimensional social impact – is sometimes compared to the global financial crisis of 2007–2008. In its aftermath,
satisfaction with and trust in political institutions declined, protests increased,
and parties in power lost many voters (Della Porta et al., 2017). During the
post-crisis period, young people's political interest and participation remained
higher than before, while adults generally participated at similar levels
(García-Albacete & Lorente, 2019). At the same time, it was emphasized that
the economic crisis affected different social groups unevenly, and young people were the most harmed (Standing, 2011). Greater unemployment, limited
life opportunities, and higher risks of poverty and debt were both sources of
alienation and frustration, reflected in political anger manifested in many high
cost types of political participation (e.g. protest movements) (Giugni & Grasso,
2021). However, the point is not just that more young people were affected by
the crisis, but that young people were more strongly affected by the crisis,
and the effects on them are more long-lasting (O'Higgins, 2010). According to
grievance theory, political mobilization (including the propensity to participate in protests) may be a function of a sudden deterioration in subjective
well-being (an increase in relative deprivation) (Grasso & Giugni, 2016). The
economic impact of the COVID-19 pandemic (GDP in the EU fell by more than
14% on average) is just one dimension of the negative experiences of young
people over the past two years. According to the report of the European Parliament's Committee on Employment and Social Affairs on the social and economic impact of the global COVID-19 crisis, the most vulnerable sectors of the
economy are: retail, catering, hospitality and tourism, i.e. those which employ
many young people (Konle-Seidl, Picarella, 2021). However, the impact of the
pandemic on young people is systematic, deep and disproportionate, it particularly affects young women (Barford, Coutts & Sahai, 2021) and brings up
fears about the future (ILO, 2020). Young people indeed feel the main victim
of the pandemic, which has significantly changed their typical lifestyles, negatively affected the quality of education, reduced mobility, weakened social
ties, and made 'unlucky entrants' out of those who completed their education
during the crisis, making it difficult to start a career. In fact, the medium- and
long-term negative effects of this unlucky entry into the labor market will not
only be economic, but above all of social and health nature (Schwandt & von
Wachter, 2020; von Wachter, 2020). On the other hand, Ivan Krastev argues
that the pandemic may have implications for the future of democracy, as it

has weakened young Europeans' trust in the political system (Krastev, 2020; Krastev & Leonard, 2021). It has determined new social and generational divisions, in light of which the young are more likely than the old to blame governments for the continuing effects of the pandemic and to challenge the official arguments used to justify restrictions. Additionally, it is signaled that young citizens in recent years have played a leading role in the growing number of mass protests around the world, "fighting for change in governance structures, economic inequalities, democratic inclusion, response to climate change, and more", while restrictions to counter the pandemic resulted in limitations on the right of assembly (UNFPA & IFRC, 2020, p. 9). This does not mean, however, that the causes of the earlier mobilization of young people were effectively 'silenced' at the same time.

23.4   Youth Electoral Participation in Pandemic Times

From the perspective of the passing time, it seems reasonable to ask to what extent such politicization of the young generation took place during the COVID-19 pandemic? Undoubtedly, the political responses of young Poles during this period indicate an increase in rates of political participation. The pandemic significantly reshaped their attitudes toward politics, and the first sign of this was the results of a survey conducted in June 2020 for the National Democratic Institute among 16–29 year olds in the Visegrad Group countries (NDI, 2020). A significant proportion of respondents declared that the pandemic crisis had increased their level of interest in politics and public affairs: in Poland: 52%, Czech Republic: 51%, Slovakia: 65% and in Hungary: 53%. Therefore, we can hypothesize that during the pandemic period in Poland we experienced a multidimensional change in political participation of young citizens – it concerned conventional and unconventional forms of involvement and had a significant impact on political processes, although still – due to the numerical predominance of older age groups of voters – not on the political status quo. To diagnose the socio-political attitudes of young Poles, a detailed analysis of secondary data from public opinion surveys was carried out, mainly of systematically archived data from exit polls conducted in 2015–2020 by Ipsos and surveys carried out by The Public Opinion Research Center (CBOS) on significant manifestations of youth political engagement during the COVID-19 pandemic.

The first more robust evidence of a change in this sphere turns out to be the level of turnout during the pandemic presidential elections in July 2020. However, a retrospective look at the Polish elections of recent years shows young voters in an unfavorable light. In 2015–2019, the lowest turnout was always observed among the youngest voters (18–29 years old). The most active were usually voters aged 40–49 (Table 23.1).

In 2020, however, there was an unprecedented level of turnout among the youngest voters (18–29 according to Ipsos data), which for the first time since 1989 exceeded the engagement rate of the oldest voters (60 years and older). It is interesting that this happened twice: during the first, but also during the second round of elections, when many young people had already lost the main motive for which they had voted two weeks before, i.e. the desire to support

TABLE 23.1   Turnout by age group of voters in 2015–2019, in percent

	2015 (Parliamentary election)	2015 (Presidential election, 2nd round)	2018 (Local election)	2019 (EP election)	2019 (Parliamentary election)
Total voter turnout (PKW)[a]	50.92	55.34	54.96	45.68	61.74
Total voter turnout (exit poll)	51.6	56.1	51.3	43.4	61.1
18–29 years (exit poll)[b]	43.7	48.2	34.8	27.6	46.4
30–39 (exit poll)	52.3	58.3	51.3	37.8	60.3
40–49 (exit poll)	58.8	64.8	64.9	47.6	75.7
50–59 (exit poll)	56.7	60.5	54.3	53.9	59.6
60 years and older (exit poll)	49.9	52.6	54.7	48.0	66.2

SOURCE: OWN COMPILATION BASED ON NATIONAL ELECTORAL COMMISSION (PKW) AND IPSOS DATA (EXIT POLL)

a Shown to verify the reliability of exit poll data.

b Ipsos collected data on the age of respondents using predefined age brackets (e.g. 18–29 years), therefore it is not possible to recode the data into other categories (e.g. 18–24 years).

TABLE 23.2   Young voters' (18–29 years) support for candidates in the 2020 presidential election, in percent

	First round	Second round
Rafał Trzaskowski	24.3	63.7
Szymon Hołownia	22.9	–
Krzysztof Bosak	22.1	–
Andrzej Duda	20.0	36.3
Robert Biedroń	6.2	–
Władysław Kosiniak-Kamysz	2.0	–
Stanisław Żółtek	0.8	–
Marek Jakubiak	0.6	–
Waldemar Witkowski	0.5	–
Paweł Tanajno	0.4	–
Mirosław Piotrowski	0.2	–

SOURCE: OWN COMPILATION BASED ON IPSOS DATA

their own leader (Table 23.2). Based on official population statistics, we can determine that as of the moment of the 2020 presidential election, there were 2.73 million people aged 18–24 (about 9% of those eligible to vote), while those aged 18–29: 5.19 million (about 17% of those eligible). We can estimate that about 3.32 million young voters aged 18–29 participated in the first round, of which about 1.85 million voted for candidates who did not qualify for the second round. Another 200,000 more young voters participated in the rerun vote.

While the weaker motivation of voters aged 60 and older should not come as a surprise given the climate of epidemiological threat that accompanied the candidates' competition at the time (after the failed attempt to organize the election by correspondence way), it is worth noting two other facts that do not allow us to underestimate the significance of youth involvement in the electoral process. Firstly, the distance between turnout levels achieved by particular age cohorts has been significantly reduced (Table 23.3). Finally, the disparity in the level of turnout between the group of 20- and 30-year-olds was levelled off. In 2015, it was 8 p.p., and it increased significantly in subsequent elections. Secondly, the reduction of intergenerational differences was primarily the result of a record increase in the participation rate precisely in the group of the youngest voters (by almost 21 p.p.), which brings certain associations

TABLE 23.3   Voter turnout by age group in 2019 and 2020, in percent

	Parliamentary election (2019)	Presidential election (2020, 1st round)	Presidential election (2020, 2nd round)	The difference between 2019 and 2020 (2nd round) – percentage points
18–29 years	46.4	64.0	67.2	+20.8
30–39	60.3	64.6	66.2	+5.9
40–49	75.7	69.6	74.6	−1.1
50–59	59.6	72.3	75.3	+15.7
60 years and older	66.2	55.4	61.9	−4.3

SOURCE: OWN COMPILATION BASED ON IPSOS DATA

with the phenomenon of political 'intensification' of young people, already observed earlier, e.g. in Great Britain, and referred to as the 'youthquake'.

The term 'youthquake' (as a combination of youth and earthquake) was named the 2017 word of the year by the editors of the Oxford English Dictionary. It means "a significant cultural, political, or social change arising from the actions or influence of young people" (Oxford English Dictionary, 2017) or "the surge in political awareness, engagement, activism and electoral turnout of young people" (Pickard, 2019, p. 1). In practice, it has been perpetuated as an illustration of record high levels of voter turnout (up from 43% in 2015 to 64%, an increase of 21 p.p.) among young people (18–24) in the British 2017 General Election. This activity resulted from the politicization of Young Millennials, being the consequence of the dominance of austerity politics and the rise of authoritarian-nationalist forms of populism in the aftermath of the global financial crisis. An additional source of discontent among young people was the fact that "cultural or postmaterial issues, such as environmental protection, national identity and immigration, have become more contentious and prominent" (Sloam & Henn, 2018, p. 7). More universally, we can say that 'youthquake elections' require a minimum of one of three conditions: (1) an increase in youth turnout; (2) a marked change in youth support for a political party or the emergence of a new party with broad youth support; (3) a significant increase in the number or intensity of youth political activities (Sloam & Henn, 2018, p. 8). It is also an indicator of 'youthquake elections' that changes in the patterns of voting preferences violate the political *status quo*. The results

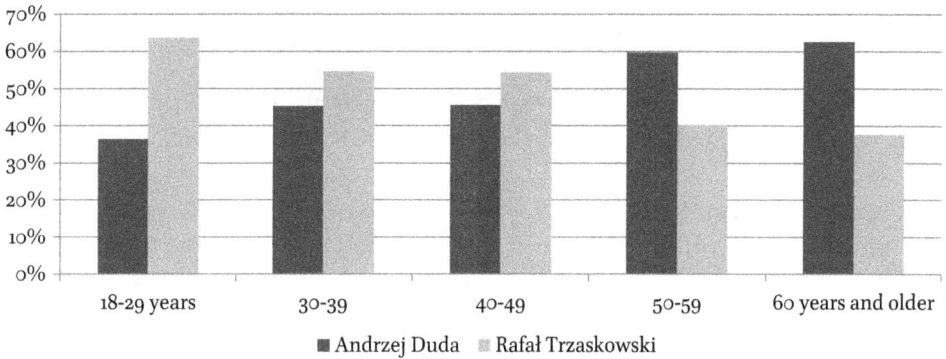

FIGURE 23.1   Support for candidates in the second round of the 2020 presidential election by
age group (in percent)
SOURCE: OWN COMPILATION BASED ON IPSOS DATA

of the second round of the presidential elections in Poland presented by age groups show the existence of a strong intergenerational divide in Polish society (Figure 23.1), although still the preferences of older voters are decisive due to their quantitative predominance in the social structure (those aged over 60 were 9.78 million; they constituted about 32% of people eligible to vote). However, the results of the second round of the presidential elections were a symptom of the reevaluation of youth preferences on the 'Left-Right' scale. Trzaskowski initiated a more liberal discourse (in the worldview dimension), while Duda appealed to conservative voters.

Symptoms of 'youthquake' can also be found in survey results of The Public Opinion Research Center (CBOS) implemented in the post-election period. At the beginning of 2021, increasing trends in the level of youth interest and declarations of participation in the elections were noted (CBOS, 2021a). While those declaring a 'medium' level of interest (meaning following only major events) prevailed among both general respondents and those aged 18–24, the period between 2019 and 2020 saw an increase in the percentage of people who are interested in politics to a high or very high degree (closely following everything that happens in politics). At the same time, the number of people rating their interest as little or none decreased. This conclusion applies primarily to the youngest group of respondents. The report emphasizes: "we are dealing with a significant increase – the percentage of young Poles declaring very high interest in political life has doubled (from 2% to 4%), and in declarations of high interest we observe an unprecedented jump of 5 percentage points (from 9% to 14%). The current level of interest in politics among Poles aged 18–24 is also the highest in the history of our research" (CBOS, 2021a). An indicator of

the stronger 'politicization of the times' in which we currently live may additionally be manifested by declarations of intention to participate in elections.
These, too, reached levels not seen in the entire history of surveys conducted
by CBOS after 1989, although an upward trend was already visible from 2014.
On the scale of the entire society, the year-on-year increase amounted to 3 p.p.,
reaching 79% of respondents convinced that they would definitely go to the
ballot box. In the case of young respondents aged 18–24, there was a jump of as
much as 10 p.p. compared to the previous year (from 67% to 77%). It is worth
bearing in mind, however, that survey declarations regarding participation in
elections are usually inflated.

23.5   Youth Protests in Pandemic Times

The increase in political engagement among young citizens during the pandemic is not just down to voter activism and interest in politics. Fall 2020 saw a
significant increase in both the number and intensity of youth political protest
activities, despite the pandemic restriction on freedom of assembly in place at
the time (Figure 23.2). This was a direct social reaction to the Constitutional
Tribunal's (CT) verdict of October 22, 2020, declaring certain provisions of the
Act on Family Planning, Protection of the Human Fetus and Conditions for
Permissibility of Termination of Pregnancy to be inconsistent with the Polish
Constitution. The repealed article allowed abortion in a situation where there

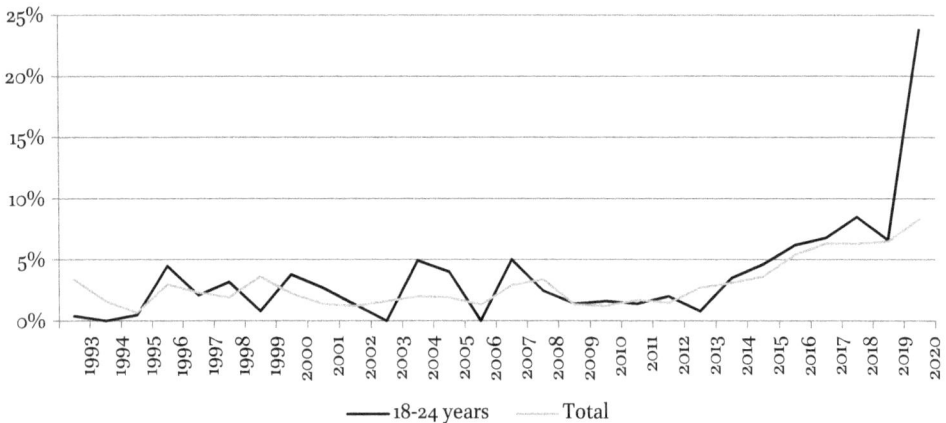

FIGURE 23.2   Participation in strikes and demonstrations 1993–2020
SOURCE: OWN COMPILATION BASED ON CBOS, 2021B

is a "high probability of severe and irreversible impairment of the fetus or an incurable disease threatening its life".

According to Article 57 of the Polish Constitution, everyone is guaranteed the freedom to organize peaceful assemblies and participate in them. The limitation of this freedom may be determined by law. Regardless of this, restrictions in the fight against COVID-19 were introduced primarily in regulations issued by the Minister of Health, which was met with strong criticism, among others from NGOs. Since the beginning of October 2020 – i.e. during the protests against the CT verdict known as the Women's Strike – the limit for participants of assemblies was 5 people. Despite these restrictions, numerous assemblies have been held primarily as so-called spontaneous assemblies held in connection with a sudden event related to the public sphere that don't need to be approved or notified. During the protests, the police indiscriminately checked and detained persons participating in them. Demonstrations and protests often had a mass character and went far beyond the limit indicated in the regulation. According to the Helsinki Foundation for Human Rights, one of the largest protests of the Women's Strike in Warsaw was attended by 100,000 people, accompanied by many smaller protests across approximately 600 Polish cities, towns and villages (HFHR, 2021, p. 3).

The wave of protests that swept through Poland at that time was more precisely diagnosed by CBOS in a survey conducted in November 2020. On this basis, it can be concluded that participation in protests was associated with a higher than average interest in politics and electoral participation. Additionally, a closer observation of the social base of these protests reveals the operation of a mechanism of normative change, described as a consequence of the socialization of young generations in conditions significantly different than the older generations of parents of contemporary 20- and 30-year-olds (Inglehart, 1977; 1990; 1997). The divergence in attitudes, views and axiology of younger and older generations, increasingly visible in the light of survey results, is the result of different socialization contexts of children and parents. Normative change affects society as a whole to varying degrees, but usually accelerates with each new generation. It is, however, difficult to observe in the short term. Perhaps that is why the scale of the protests following the CT ruling, but also the demographic structure of the demonstrators, came as a surprise to many. The CBOS survey shows that 8% of respondents declared their participation in the demonstrations. This means that a total of about 2.5 million adult Poles protested across the country in October and November 2020. For comparison, participation in the so-called 'black protests' in 2016, which had analogous reasons, was declared by 3% of respondents at that time (then

TABLE 23.4   Participation and support for protests after the Constitutional Tribunal ruling
                on October 22, 2020 by age group, in percent

Age of respondent	Percentage of respondents declaring participation in protests after the Constitutional Tribunal ruling	Percentage of respondents declaring support for protests after the Constitutional Tribunal ruling
18–24 years	28	74
25–34	15	70
35–44	9	72
45–54	8	65
55–64	2	58
65 years and older	1	49

SOURCE: OWN COMPILATION BASED ON CBOS, 2020A

the reason was the decision of the Sejm to refer to work in committees the draft law tightening the regulations allowing abortion). The survey data clearly show that in 2020 there were protests whose driving force was the involvement of younger age groups above all (Table 23.4). Participation in demonstrations was declared by 28% of respondents aged 18–24 (actually about 764 thousand people) and 15% of those aged 25–34 (about 799 thousand people). It should be noted that these were definitely more often young women. Participation in the protests was confirmed by 41% of women and 18% of men aged 18–24.

Observing the political attitudes of young people during the pandemic, we notice the fourth – after the increase in electoral engagement, interest in politics and protest activity – phenomenon which contradicts the commonly formulated earlier thesis of a depoliticized young generation. This is how we should understand the information about the historically (after 1989) highest index of identification with left-wing views among young people (18–24 years old) (Figure 23.3). This index in 2020 reached a previously unobserved level: 30% (in 1990 it was 29%, in turn, in 2000: 25.1%) and was the result of a sharp increase compared to 2019, when it was 17%. Additionally, it reached an even higher value in the first half of 2021: 33% (while for the Right: 21%). It is worth noting that declarations of left-wing sympathies among the youngest voters have remained at a relatively low level (not exceeding 20%) since 2002, clearly lower than identifications with the Right. The largest gap between

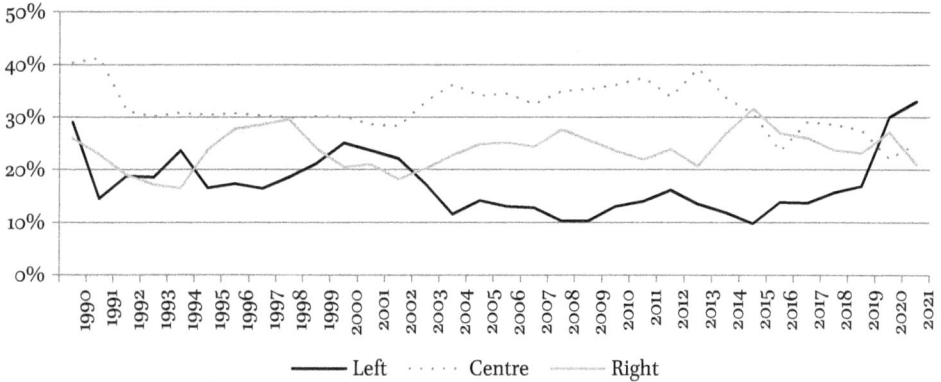

FIGURE 23.3   Declared political views in age group 18–24 years
SOURCE: OWN COMPILATION BASED ON CBOS, 2021A.
DATA FOR 2021 ARE FROM THE FIRST HALF OF THE YEAR ONLY

identification with the Left and the Right occurred in 2015 (21.8%). Since then, we have observed a steady increase in left-wing sympathies among young Poles. The current distribution of ideological preferences in this age group is almost a complete reversal of the distribution of self-identification in the whole society, where right-wing views are declared by 35% of respondents, and left-wing views – 22% (CBOS, 2021a).

Young Poles have repeatedly previously expressed their dissatisfaction by supporting protest movements such as ACTA (2012), 'black protests' (2016), against justice reforms (2017) or more regularly as the Youth Climate Strike. Their mass mobilization on an unprecedented scale that followed a successful attempt to tighten abortion laws has become a pretext for discussing whether it will prove to be a kind of collective experience, forming a new political generation. Young Poles are undoubtedly already different from their parents' generation: they express a decidedly more liberal worldview, they are also 'specific' in terms of behaviors within the broadly understood sexuality and morality, but also religiousness (CBOS, 2021c). An indicator of the generational specificity of the young here is primarily the speed with which these processes are occurring in younger age groups, which are liberalizing and secularizing much faster than older groups (CBOS, 2021d).

These differences of opinion have also been an important backdrop to the social protests. Growing frustration, distrust, and anger toward political elites revealed a political dispute interpreted in an intergenerational pattern. Politicians, most often representing the older generation, became the object of criticism; the protesters accused them of condescension and lack of understanding of the problems of young people. The Polish term 'dziaders' (in a sense, the equivalent of the term 'boomer') gained popularity, used in many meanings: colloquial, humorous or insulting, e.g. "a person, especially a man, whose behavior, views, tastes and manner are perceived by the speaker as outdated or even anachronistic, and who (in the opinion of the speaker) is not able to cope with the modern social reality" or "a person, especially a man (no matter how old he is), who condescendingly refers to women (and thinks of them that way), convinced that he is right" (OJUW, 2022). The long-lasting strikes, demonstrations and protests, which were a reaction to the restriction of abortion law in Poland, had a much broader overtone: often anti-government, anti-party, or anti-political in general. Therefore, apart from the direct cause of the protests, one should also look for indirect causes. Many works on youth involvement in protest movements emphasize that the main motivation is distrust towards political leaders, and youth demonstrations often adopt moralistic rhetoric. Young protesters tend to present their motivations in terms of fighting for 'rights and freedoms' and are less likely to exhibit ideological self-identification (Erpyleva, 2021). Some researchers have found that motivations for protest actions among young people stem from the need to belong to a social group. Social ties may be a determining factor, and young people are more likely than older people to actively encourage friends to participate in protest actions. They themselves are also particularly sensitive to such encouragement. Younger generations are making a more pronounced shift toward postmaterialistic, self-expression-oriented values. Thus, in individualistic cultures, they may be more strongly motivated to take political action, as they gain the opportunity to self-represent their identities and the acceptance of others. Finally, it is emphasized that participation in protest activities is a manifestation not only of ideological sympathies, but it "can also be completely detached from the political outcome of the action, and solely have a social function" (Renström, Aspernäs & Bäck, 2021, p. 783), while the performative nature of protests is particularly attractive to a certain type of participants: young people who seek the approval of desired social groups (Renström, Aspernäs & Bäck, 2021). Therefore, in a sense, we were dealing with an attempt (and a need at the same time) to 'temporarily' recreate a non-pandemic/pre-pandemic reality in which social bonds are not limited by anything. Mass protests in the period of the pandemic could also have been a specific radical form of opposition to making such important decisions for the society in an unfair way, i.e. by taking advantage of both formal and legal restrictions, as well as the natural fear of the virus among potential protestors (in October 2020, the so-called second wave of the pandemic began in Poland, with its peak at the turn of the first and second decade of November).

23.6   Conclusions

This chapter has attempted to systematize and coherently describe the most important trends in the patterns of political participation of young Poles during the COVID-19 pandemic. Many indicators of their political engagement after 1989 led to the conclusion about a depoliticized, apathetic, and alienated young generation whose electoral votes are of diminishing value to political elites. It seemed that pandemic times would only deepen their distance from politics. Meanwhile, in practice, we observed an actual political 'awakening' of the young generation, which is importantly evidenced by secondary data from public opinion polls in Poland. We observed a record high turnout of young citizens in the 2020 presidential election, a noteworthy increase in interest in politics, mass social protests driven by young people, especially young women, and finally – we noticed a dynamically progressive increase in identification with the Left. The chapter makes a number of assumptions that mandate the appreciation of unconventional forms of political participation by young people. Nevertheless, the youthquake phenomenon was seen in light of both traditional and alternative forms of political engagement. Based on different theoretical concepts, it was concluded that the pandemic was an important factor in the politicization of young people's attitudes, making them aware of how many aspects of their everyday lives are determined by politics. The strength of their mobilization is evidenced by the massive scale of protests, despite the restrictions in place and the natural sense of danger associated with the next wave of the pandemic. It did not turn out to be the only factor determining the processes described here, but it certainly became an important catalyst for changes that had been taking place in the young generation for a long time. In this sense, they as 'standby citizens' were 'activated' because they felt a corresponding motivation reinforced by external circumstances. In addition to the pandemic, the 2020 election campaign (in which, among other things, the LGBT community was very strongly criticized) and the public debate about the form of the presidential election (mail or traditional) were important motivating factors. Many young people treated the act of voting as an expression of disagreement with a certain type of persuasion used by politicians of the ruling party involved in the campaign of Andrzej Duda's campaign (according to polling data, the young are relatively more likely to accept extending the scope of rights for LGBT people). The reasons for this 'awakening' include the general negative attitude of young voters towards the ruling party (PiS), which strengthened its position after the victory in 2019, but also a poor assessment of current decisions on how to counteract the pandemic (the sanitary regime had a particularly negative impact on the well-being of young people) or tightening the abortion law. Researchers using the term 'youth-quake' in the British or American context emphasize that it has meant a rise in cosmopolitan-left sentiment (socially liberal and economically Left politi-cal parties) (Sloam & Henn, 2018). The events in Poland should be interpreted in a similar way, but here the cultural aspect was more strongly emphasized. The rebellion of the young is aptly summarized by Elżbieta Korolczuk (2021, p. 72), writing that it is "saturated with ideas of radical democracy and femi-nism", and "the mass mobilization may indicate that a new left-wing populism has emerged in response to the right-wing populism of the ruling coalition, understood as opposition to what is happening in Poland and as a demand expressed by the people who want to have an impact on the world". For many of them, participation in the protests constituted 'prior contact' with politics, which, as an experience of living in politicized times, may facilitate their polit-ical engagement in the future (McAdam, 1990). Young people who are just entering adulthood still tend to search for their own political identity, their voting preferences are prone to more random impulses, and their awareness of their own interests will change with the new social roles in which they will engage. Therefore, it is necessary to constantly monitor the views and values of the young generation, using both secondary and primary social research for this purpose, also formulating more practical recommendations for the insti-tutions responsible for conducting youth policy, abandoning the value-based approach in favor of a more constructive one, since young people are indeed not a 'threat' but the 'future' of democracy.

References

Amnå, E., & Ekman, J. (2013). "Standby citizens: Diverse faces of political passiv-ity". *European Political Science Review*, 6(2), 261–281. DOI: https://doi.org/10.1017/S175577391300009X.

Bäck, E. A., Bäck, H., & García-Albacete, G. M. (2013). "Protest activity, social incentives, and rejection sensitivity: Results from a survey experiment about tuition fees". *Contention: The Multidisciplinary Journal of Social Protest*, 1(1), 1–15.

Barford, A., Coutts, A., & Sahai, G. (2021). *Youth employment in times of COVID*. ILO: Geneva.

Bečević, Z., & Dahlstedt, M. (2021). "On the margins of citizenship: Youth participation and youth exclusion in times of neoliberal urbanism". *Journal of Youth Studies*. DOI: https://doi.org/10.1080/13676261.2021.1886261.

Beck, U., Beck-Gensheim, E. (2002). *Individualization. Institutionalized individualism and its social and political consequences*. London: Sage.

Berman, E. M. (1997). "Dealing with cynical citizens". *Public Administration Review*, *57*(2), 105–112. DOI: https://doi.org/10.2307/977058.

Blais, A., Gidengil, E., & Nevitte, N. (2004). "Where does turnout decline come from?". *European Journal of Political Research*, *43*(2), 221–236. DOI: https://doi.org/10.1111 /j.1475-6765.2004.00152.x.

CBOS (2020). *O dopuszczalności przerywania ciąży i protestach po wyroku Trybunału Konstytucyjnego* [*On the admissibility of abortion and protests after the verdict of the Constitutional Tribunal*]. Retrieved from: https://www.cbos.pl/SPISKOM .POL/2020/K_153_20.PDF.

CBOS (2021a). *Zainteresowanie polityką i poglądy polityczne młodych Polaków na tle ogółu badanych* [*Interest in politics and political views of young poles compared to the general population*]. Retrieved from: https://www.cbos.pl/SPISKOM .POL/2021/K_016_21.PDF.

CBOS (2021b). *Młodzi Polacy a poczucie wpływu na sprawy publiczne i zaangażowanie w protesty* [*Young poles and the sense of influence on public affairs and involvement in protests*]. Retrieved from: https://www.cbos.pl/SPISKOM.POL/2021/K_095_21.PDF.

CBOS (2021c). *Ważne kwestie społeczno-polityczne w opiniach młodych Polaków* [*Important socio-political issues in the opinions of young Poles*]. Retrieved from: https://www .cbos.pl/SPISKOM.POL/2021/K_093_21.PDF.

CBOS (2021d). *Religijność młodych na tle ogółu społeczeństwa* [*Religiosity of young people compared to the general population*]. Retrieved from: https://www.cbos.pl/SPISKOM .POL/2021/K_144_21.PDF.

Crozier, M., Huntington, S. P., & Watnuki, J. (1975). *The crisis of democracy: Report on the governability of democracies to the trilateral commission*. New York: New York University Press.

Dalton, R. J. (2008). *The good citizen: How a younger generation is reshaping American politics*. Washington: CQ Press.

Della Porta, D., Fernández, J., Konki, H., & Mosca, L. (2017). *Movement parties against austerity*. Cambridge: Polity Press.

Dermody, J., Hanmer-Lloyd, S., & Scullion, R. (2010). "Young people and voting behaviour: Alienated youth and (or) an interested and critical citizenry?". *European Journal of Marketing*. *44*(3/4), 421–435. DOI: https://doi.org/10.1108/03090561011020507.

Erpyleva, S. (2021). "Active citizens under eighteen: Minors in political protests". *Journal of Youth Studies*, *24*(9), 1215–1233. DOI: https://doi.org/10.1080/13676261.2020.18 20973.

Fahmy, E. (2006). *Young citizens: Young people's involvement in politics and decision making*. Burlington: Ashgate.

Farthing, R. (2010). "The politics of youthful antipolitics: Representing the 'issue' of youth participation in politics". *Journal of Youth Studies*. *13*(2), 181–195. DOI: https:// doi.org/10.1080/13676260903233696.

Fitzgerald, R., Graham, A., Smith, A., & Taylor, N. (2010). "Children's participation as a struggle over recognition. Exploring the promise of dialogue". In B. Percy-Smith & N. Thomas (Eds.), *A handbook of children and young people's participation. Perspectives from theory and practice* (293–305). London: Routledge.

Franklin, M. N. (2004). *Voter turnout and the dynamics of electoral competition in established democracies since 1945.* Cambridge: Cambridge University Press.

Furlong, A., & Cartmel, F. (2012). "Social change and political engagement among young people: Generation and the 2009/2010 British election survey". *Parliamentary Affairs, 65*(1), 13–28. DOI: https://doi.org/10.1093/pa/gsr045.

García-Albacete, G. (2014). *Young people's political participation in Western Europe: Continuity or generational change?.* Basingstoke: Palgrave Macmillan.

García-Albacete, G., & Lorente, J. (2019). "The post-austerity youth. Political attitudes and behavior". *Revista Internacional de Sociología, 77*(4), 1–19, DOI: https://doi.org/10.3989/ris.2019.77.4.19.004.

Gauthier, M. (2003). "The inadequacy of concepts: The rise of youth interest in civic participation in Quebec". *Journal of Youth Studies, 6*(3), 265–276. DOI: https://doi.org/10.1080/1367626032000138255.

Giugni, M., & Grasso, M. T. (2021). "Youth and politics in times of increasing inequalities". In M. Giugni & M. T. Grasso (Eds.), *Youth and politics in times of increasing inequalities* (1–26). London: Palgrave Macmillan.

Grasso, M. T., & Giugni, M. (2016). "Protest participation and economic crisis: The conditioning role of political opportunities". *European Journal of Political Research, 55*(4), 663–680. DOI: https://doi.org/10.1111/1475-6765.12153.

Grasso, M. T., Farrall, S., Gray, E., Hay, C., & Jennings, W. (2019). "Socialization and generational political trajectories: An age, period and cohort analysis of political participation in Britain", *Journal of Elections, Public Opinion and Parties, 29*(2), 199–221, DOI: https://doi.org/10.1080/17457289.2018.1476359.

Grasso, M. T. (2014). "Age, period and cohort analysis in a comparative context: Political generations and political participation repertoires in Western Europe". *Electoral Studies, 33*, 63–76. DOI: https://doi.org/10.1016/j.electstud.2013.06.003.

Henn, M., & Foard, N. (2012). "Young people, political participation and trust in Britain". *Parliamentary Affairs, 65*(1), 47–67. DOI: https://doi.org/10.1093/pa/gsr046.

Henn, M., & Foard, N. (2014). Social differentiation in young people's political participation: The impact of social and educational factors on youth political engagement in Britain". *Journal of Youth Studies, 17*(3), 360–380. DOI: https://doi.org/10.1080/13676261.2013.830704.

Henn, M., Weinstein, M., & Wring, D. (2002). "A generation apart? Youth and political participation in Britain?". *The British Journal of Politics and International Relations, 4*(2), 167–192. DOI: https://doi.org/10.1111/1467-856X.t01-1-00001.

HFHR (2021). "Impact of the coronavirus pandemic on the criminal justice system". *Helsinki Foundation for Human Rights.* Retrieved from: http://www.hfhr.pl/en.

ILO (2020). "Youth & COVID-19: Impacts on jobs, education, rights and mental well-being". *International Labour Organization.* Retrieved from: https://www.ilo .org/wcmsp5/groups/public/---ed_emp/documents/publication/wcms_753026.pdf.

Inglehart, R. (1977). *The silent revolution: Changing values and political styles among Western publics.* Princeton: Princeton University Press.

Inglehart, R. (1990). *Culture shift in advanced industrial society.* Princeton: Princeton University Press.

Inglehart, R. (1997). *Modernization and postmodernization: Cultural, economic, and political change in 43 societies.* Princeton: Princeton University Press.

Inglehart, R. (2018). *Cultural evolution, people's motivations are changing, and reshaping the world.* Ann Arbor: Cambridge University Press.

Jennings, M. (1987). "Residues of a movement: The aging of the American protest generation". *American Political Science Review, 81*(2), 367–382. DOI: https://doi .org/10.2307/1961957.

Kirbiš, A. Flere, S., Friš, D., Tavčar Krajnc M. & Cupar T. (2017). "Predictors of conventional, protest, and civic participation among Slovenian youth: A test of the civic voluntarism model". *International Journal of Sociology, 47*(3), 182–207. DOI: https:// doi.org/10.1080/00207659.2017.1335518.

Kitanova, M. (2020). "Youth political participation in the EU: Evidence from a cross-national analysis". *Journal of Youth Studies, 23*(7), 819–836. DOI: https://doi.org /10.1080/13676261.2019.1636951.

Konle-Seidl, R., & Picarella, F. (2021). "Youth in Europe: Effects of COVID-19 on their economic and social situation". *Policy Department for Economic, Scientific and Quality of Life Policies Directorate-General for Internal Policies.* Retrieved from: https://www .europarl.europa.eu/RegData/etudes/STUD/2021/662942/IPOL_STU(2021)662942 _EN.pdf.

Korolczuk, E. "Bunt młodych" ["Youth rebellion"]. In P. Kosiewski (Ed.), *Język rewolucji* [*The language of revolution*] (71–74). Warszawa: Fundacja im. Stefana Batorego.

Krastev, I. (2020). "The seven early lessons of the global coronavirus crisis". *The New Statement.* Retrieved from: https://www.newstatesman.com/world/europe/2020/03 /coronavirus-early-lessons-global-crisis.

Krastev, I., & Leonard, M. (2021). Europe's invisible divides: How COVID-19 is polarising European politics". *European Council on Foreign Relations.* Retrieved from: https://ecfr.eu/publication/europes-invisible-divides-how-COVID-19-is-polarising -european-politics/.

Loader, B. (2007). *Young citizens in the digital age. Political engagement, young people and new media.* London: Routledge.

Loader, B., Vromen, A., & Xenos, M. A. (2014). "The networked young citizen: Social media, political participation and civic engagement, information". *Communication & Society*, 17(2), 143–150. DOI: https://doi.org/10.1080/1369118X.2013.871571.

Loncle, P., Cuconato, M., Muniglia, V., & Walther, A. (2012). *Youth participation in Europe. Beyond discourses, practices and realities*. Bristol: Policy Press.

Macedo, S., Alex-Assensoh, Y. & Berry, J. M. (2005). *Democracy at risk: How political choices undermine citizen participation and what we can do about it*. Washington: Brookings Institution Press.

Mannheim, K. (1928). *The problem of generations essays on the sociology of knowledge*. London: Routledge.

Marsh, D., O'Toole, T., & Jones, S. (2007). *Young people and politics in the UK*. Basingstoke: Palgrave Macmillan.

Marzęcki, R. (2020). "Constructive emotions? Patriotism as a predictor of civic activity in Poland". *Italian Political Science Review/Rivista Italiana di Scienza Politica*, 50(1), 33–51. DOI: https://doi.org/10.1017/ipo.2019.15.

McAdam, D. (1990). *Freedom summer*. Oxford: Oxford University Press.

Melo, D. F., & Stockemer, D. (2014). "Age and political participation in Germany, France and the UK: A comparative analysis". *Comparative European Politics*, 12, 33–53. DOI: https://doi.org/10.1057/cep.2012.31.

NDI (2020). *Youth Attitudes on Politics and Democracy in Central Europe*. Retrieved from: https://www.ndi.org/sites/default/files/NDI_Youth2020_FINAL_0.pdf.

Norris, P. (2002). *Democratic Phoenix: Reinventing political activism*. New York: Cambridge University Press.

O'Higgins, N. (2010). "The impact of the economic and financial crisis on youth employment: Measures for labour market recovery in the European Union, Canada and the United States". *Employment Working Paper No. 70*. Geneva: ILO.

OJUW (2022). „Dziaders". *Obserwatorium Językowe Uniwersytetu Warszawskiego*. Retrieved from: https://nowewyrazy.uw.edu.pl/haslo/132-dziaders.html.

Oxford English Dictionary (2017). "Word of the year: Youthquake". Retrieved from: https://en.oxforddictionaries.com/word-of-the-year/word-ofthe-year-2017.

Park, A. (1999). "Young people and political apathy". In R. Jowell, J. Curtice, A. Park, K. Thomson, L. Jarvis, C. Bromley & N. Stratford (Eds.), *British social attitudes. The 16th report. Who shares new labour values?* (23–40). Aldershot: Ashgate.

Pattie, C., Seyd, P.A., & Whiteley, P. (2004). *Citizenship, democracy and participation in contemporary Britain*. Cambridge: Cambridge University Press.

Phelps, E. (2012). "Understanding electoral turnout among British young people: A review of the literature". *Parliamentary Affairs*, 65(1), 281–299. DOI: https://doi.org/10.1093/pa/gsr056.

Pickard, S. (2019). *Politics, protest and young people political participation and dissent in 21st century Britain*. London: Palgrave Macmillan.

Pirie, M., & Worcester, R. M. (1998). *The millennial generation*. London: Adam Smith Institute.

Plutzer, E. (2002). "Becoming a habitual voter: Inertia, resources and growth in young adulthood". *American Political Science Review, 96*(1), 41–56. DOI: https://doi.org/10.1017/S0003055402004227.

Quintelier, E. (2007). "Differences in political participation between young and old people". *Contemporary Politics, 13*(2), 165–180. DOI: https://doi.org/10.1080/13569770701562658.

Renström, E. A., Aspernäs, J., & Bäck, H. (2021). "The young protester: The impact of belongingness needs on political engagement". *Journal of Youth Studies, 24*(6), 781–798. DOI: https://doi.org/10.1080/13676261.2020.1768229.

Schwandt, H., & von Wachter, T. (2020). "The long shadow of an unlucky start". *Finance & Development, 57*(4), 16–18.

Sloam, J. (2013). "Voice and equality: Young people's politics in the European Union". *West European Politics, 36*(3), 1–23. DOI: https://doi.org/10.1080/01402382.2012.749652.

Sloam, J. (2016). "Diversity and voice: The political participation of young people in the European Union". *The British Journal of Politics and International Relations, 18*(3), 521–537. DOI: https://doi.org/10.1177/1369148116647176.

Sloam, J., & Henn, M. (2018). Youthquake 2017: The rise of young cosmopolitans in Britain. London: Palgrave Macmillan.

Standing, G. (2011). *The precariat: The new dangerous class*. London: Bloomsbury.

Szafraniec, K. (2011). *Młodzi 2011* [Youth 2011]. Warszawa: Kancelaria Prezesa Rady Ministrów.

UNFPA & IFRC (2020). "COVID-19: Working with and for young people". Retrieved from: https://www.unfpa.org/sites/default/files/resource-pdf/COMPACTCOVID19-05.pdf.

von Wachter, T. (2020). "The persistent effects of initial labor market conditions for young adults and their sources". *The Journal of Economic Perspectives, 34*(4), 168–194.

Vromen, A., Xenos, M. A., & Loader, B. (2015). "Young people, social media and connective action: From organisational maintenance to everyday political talk". *Journal of Youth Studies, 18*(1), 80–100. DOI: https://doi.org/10.1080/13676261.2014.933198.

Walther, A., Batsleer, J., Loncle, P., & Pohl, A. (2020). *Young people and the struggle for participation. Contested practices, power and pedagogies in public spaces*. London: Routledge.

Wattenberg, M. (2002). *Where have all the voters gone?*. Cambridge: Harvard University Press.

Xenos, M. A., Vromen, A., & Loader, B. (2014). "The great equalizer? Patterns of social media use and youth political engagement in three advanced democracies". *Information, Communication & Society, 17*(2), 151–167. DOI: https://doi.org/10.1080/13691 18X.2013.871318.

Zukin, C., Keeter, S., Andolina, M., Jenkins, K. & Delli Carpini, M.X. (2006). *A new engagement? Political participation, civic life, and the changing American citizen.* Oxford: Oxford University Press.

CHAPTER 24

Political Communication during the 2020 Presidential Election Campaign in Poland: The Role of Medical Experts

Agnieszka Łukasik-Turecka

24.1 Introduction

The 2020 presidential election campaign in Poland was described as the strangest and longest (Maciuszczak, 2020) since 1989—a breakthrough year of the Polish political system.

The official beginning of the presidential election campaign in Poland took place on February 5, in accordance with the decision of the Marshal of the Sejm of the Republic of Poland to order presidential elections on May 10 (*Postanowienie Marszałka …*, 2020a). More than a month later, on March 20, a state of epidemic was introduced covering the entire territory of the Republic of Poland by ordinance of the Minister of Health (*Rozporządzenie Ministra …*, 2020). The government regulation published shortly afterwards indicated restrictions, orders, and bans concerning citizens in connection with the epidemic (*Rozporządzenie Rady….*, 2020). In such a situation, the possibility of a standard election campaign, as well as the organization of an election, were uncertain.

The preparations for postal voting, initiated by the government, were criticized in the public sphere. The criticism concerned the inability to prepare the entire proposed procedure in such a short time, which was to consist in voting only by correspondence. On May 7, i.e., 3 days before the elections, the National Electoral Commission announced that it was not possible to hold the elections on May 10 (PKW, 2020), therefore the Marshal of the Sejm announced a new election date for June 28 (*Postanowienie Marszałka...*, 2020b). Both the traditional and the correspondence method were considered as possible forms of voting. However, it should be emphasised that both the original idea of organising all-postal voting and then the idea of holding a hybrid version of voting in the 2020 presidential elections raised many objections from both election law specialists, international organisations and doctors (Musiał-Karg, Kapsa, 2020, pp. 6–8).

In practice, this decision significantly extended the presidential election campaign in Poland, although not for all candidates did it mean an extension of the campaign struggle. Rafał Trzaskowski, one of the two most important candidates, had a much shorter official election campaign than Andrzej Duda. Trzaskowski became the official candidate of the Civic Coalition on May 15, replacing the previous candidate of this political alliance, Małgorzata Kidawa-Błońska.

Failure to hold the elections on the first date, as well as the change of the candidate for the office of the President of the Republic of Poland in the case of one of the most important political formations in Poland, are not the only features that characterize the abovementioned election campaign. There was also the notable fact that, apart from the most important actors in the process of political communication, which during such a period are always candidates for the presidency of the Republic of Poland, another type of political actor appeared—medical experts. One can even talk about the intensified presence of doctors and virologists in the Polish media and public space from spring 2020. The reason was that the presidential election campaign in Poland took place during the first wave of the COVID-19 pandemic.

In the first days and weeks of the pandemic, the media statements of medical experts concerned only the area of medicine, as they spoke about topics related to the SARS-CoV-2 virus and the COVID-19 pandemic. The thematic scope of statements by medical experts began to expand over time. The media statements of medical experts ceased to concern only topics related to the virus and the health of Poles, and more and more often concerned the activities of the Polish authorities and also included an assessment of these activities. The constant presence of medical experts in the Polish media and public space during the pandemic, as well as the high level of trust placed in them by the Poles, contributed to a strong positioning of these actors on the political scene (Łukasik-Turecka, 2021a).

24.2   Literature Review

Political communication refers to the flux of information and trade of messages between political actors, citizens, and the media. Each of them accords to the creation of political public spheres. Research on political communication has historically concentrated on publicly visible forms of mass communication which involved organised actors who dealt with fundamental political issues under the conditions of liberal democratic nation-states (Esser, Pfetsch, 2020, pp. 336–337).

As Frank Esser and Barbara Pfetsch state, these conditions are no longer justifiable. Today, political communication is in many ways characterised by a combination of public and personalised communication, mass media and social media, and established and non-established communicators (2020, p. 337).

A large number of different types of actors participate in the political process, and they are not only the representatives of the political and administrative elite. Actors are also representatives of economic life, culture, science, the health service, education, and the judiciary. A special type of actor of political communication are experts (Michalczyk, 2020, pp. 229–230), regardless of the period in the election calendar: whether it is a period of a formal election campaign or an inter-election period.

In the literature on the subject, various typologies of experts can be found depending on the adopted criterion. Based on whether an expert's work is visible to the public or not, we can distinguish between overt and covert experts. The first group consists of experts who appear in the media, are known to the public and considered reliable and objective by them. Stanisław Michalczyk, however, undermines this credibility, writing about the bias of experts in commenting on issues and problems, and in this group he additionally distinguishes right-wing, left-wing, liberal, etc. "experts" (2020, p. 231).

The second group consists of those who work in offices and related staff, preparing reports for other political actors (Michalczyk, 2020, pp. 230–231). These are what Ulrich Sarcinelli writes about when he refers to them as the 'new elite in the grey area of democracy' (2011, p. 179). He stresses that today no political actor can succeed on the political stage without the ability to communicate through the media. He points out that political communication is one of the skills that political elites operating in a media society must develop and nurture. Political actors in the media market constantly have to vie for media attention due to the expansion of the media system, the increase in the number of providers and the growing complexity of the media offer. This is why, Sarcinelli emphasises, it is so important to look at this group of people who have such a strong influence on the functioning of politicians on the political scene (2011, pp. 179–180).

The range of positions of these types of actors is wide: they include press officers, speechwriters, image and political consultants. These experts are valuable to political elites primarily because they know the logic of the media system and use this knowledge for their organisation or their clients (Sarcinelli, 2011, p. 180).

The adoption of another criterion, namely the degree of the expert's involvement in the process of communication between the ruling and the ruled, makes it possible to distinguish three types of experts: an ordinary intermediary, an expert-translator, and an expert helmsman. An ordinary intermediary is a silent partner in the communication of others and acts as to relay a message, while an expert-translator is not only a channel for transmitting information, but also processes and interprets it. The highest form of expert involvement in the process of communication between the ruling and the ruled is an expert helmsman who leads and is not limited to being only an intermediary in the transmission of information (Kurczewska, 1997, pp. 251–254).

The typology of experts, prepared for political scientists appearing in the media, was developed by Ewa Marciniak, who discussed the types of roles of experts in political communication. The first type is a typical expert, knowledgeable in a given field and trying to smuggle at least one category or scientific concept into the media. The second type is a guide to the world of complicated politics (sometimes the world of a political game), and the third is an arbiter who has to decide and tell the truth: who lost and who won. As Marciniak emphasizes, these three types often occur simultaneously and overlap (Łukasik-Turecka, 2021b, pp. 137–138).

A media expert is defined by such terms as: an independent commentator, a specialist representing the authority of science, and a person functioning in a symbiotic relationship with the media. This kind of symbiosis between media and media experts is based on the fact that thanks to the medium, the expert gains recognition, and thanks to the experts, the medium becomes an attractive relay (Nosal, 2009, p. 89).

The literature on the subject also includes a description of the areas of expert activity. Przemysław Nosal includes among them: reporting; explaining what is happening; interpreting and commenting; assessing, forecasting; and instructing (2009, pp. 92–95).

The activities of media medical experts who appeared in the Polish pandemic reality in March 2020 in connection with the COVID-19 pandemic can be included in the abovementioned areas.

According to Nosal, the first area of activity—reporting the events one witnesses—is the most elementary function of an expert. Due to their competence, it is the expert who is the only one who can reliably report the course of events (2009, p. 92). During the entire period of the pandemic in Poland, medical experts reported to the media the events taking place in hospitals, emergency stations, or intensive care units.

An expert, as emphasized by Nosal, not only reports empirically tangible events, but also explains what is happening, and explains the mechanisms and rules governing them. Their task is to make the media message more understandable (2009, p. 92). This function was performed by medical experts in

Polish media—they explained the way in which the pandemic spread, why there were more infections in a given part of the country and less in others, why they were also ill, etc.

Experts are not limited to being impartial observers and narrators. They also interpret phenomena. Nosal emphasizes that due to the knowledge an expert has, their interpretation may be much more valuable than the interpretation of the event made by a person who is not backed by the authority of science (2009, p. 93). Medical experts in Poland interpreted and commented in the media on everything related to the SARS-CoV-2 virus and the COVID-19 pandemic.

Experts are also entrusted with the substantive assessment of both the entire social system and its individual segments (Nosal, 2009, p. 93). In the case of medical experts in Poland, we can easily find this type of activity during the COVID-19 pandemic: evaluation in the media of actions taken by the government in the field of health protection, decisions made regarding the purchase of medical equipment, introducing or not introducing restrictions, complying with their recommendations, opinions issued by the Medical Council, etc.

Forecasting is another area of expert activity. It is they who, based on their knowledge, should make predictions about a given phenomenon. We also expect this from medical experts. It was medical experts who provided information on the end of a given wave of the virus, information on new variants, introduction or lifting of restrictions, information on subsequent lockdowns, what will happen due to the Omicron variant, etc.

Scientific knowledge and authority entitle experts to formulate advice, suggestions, and instructions on how to proceed regarding a given issue (Nosal, 2009, p. 94). This is another area of activity of experts, including medical experts.

The role of media experts, in this case virologists, was strongly recognized during the COVID-19 pandemic. In Poland, however, we were dealing not only with the popularization of expert knowledge in the media, but with a situation in which the medical expert became one of the leading actors in political communication.

24.3   Research Framework

The aim of the research was to show whether, and if so, how, medical experts' presence in the media in connection with the COVID-19 pandemic influenced the content of the political messages of the main candidates for the presidency of the Republic of Poland during the 2020 election.

Before starting the research, three questions were asked: 1) Did the political messages of the main candidates for the office of the President of the Republic of Poland in the analyzed period contain information about the COVID-19 pandemic and the SARS-CoV-2 virus? If so, what topics did they cover? 2) Were the statements of the main candidates for the office of the President of the Republic of Poland on the same topics as those from the statements of medical experts? If so, what were they? 3) Did the main candidates for the office of the President of the Republic of Poland refer in their statements to the statements of medical experts in the media? If so, what topics did they cover?

The period between March 20, 2020 and July 11, 2020 was chosen as the research period. Although the official beginning of the presidential election campaign in Poland took place on February 5, 2020, and the first case of COVID-19 was diagnosed in Poland on March 4, 2020, the date of the beginning of the research period was March 20, 2020, when the state of epidemic was announced in Poland.

The main methods used in the research were content analysis (qualitative), secondary data analysis and also the comparative method. Due to the fact that the restrictions related to the pandemic caused the candidates to focus on remote communication strategies, including social media, instead of in-person meetings, the messages in this type of media were analyzed. The subject of the analyses were materials published on the official channels on Facebook and Twitter of the two main candidates for the office of the President of the Republic of Poland (Andrzej Duda and Rafał Trzaskowski), as well as the media statements of selected medical experts.

The basis for my research were the results of Małgorzata Adamik-Szysiak's research on the degree of exposure of references to the COVID-19 pandemic in the messages published by the main candidates for the office of the President of the Republic of Poland in social media (2021) and her own research.

24.4   Results

The starting point for the research were the interesting results of the quantitative and qualitative analysis by Małgorzata Adamik-Szysiak (2021), regarding the degree of exposure of references to the COVID-19 pandemic in the messages published by the main candidates for the presidency of the Republic of Poland in social media. The almost identical research period (from March 26 to July 11, 2020) made it possible to use the results of these studies to conduct analyses of the potential impact of experts on the content of the political messages of the main candidates for the presidency of the Republic of Poland during the 2020 elections. The research conducted by Adamik-Szysiak shows that in the 2020 presidential campaign, in the posts of all candidates on Facebook, references to the COVID-19 pandemic were found in only 14% of posts before the first round of the election, and there was only a trace of this topic in the second round—less than 1% posts. The data obtained from the study of candidates' posts on Facebook was confirmed by surveys of the candidates' tweets published in the same period (2021, p. 116). These results are all the more surprising as before the first round of the election, the pandemic was the dominant topic in media coverage—36%, and in the period before the second round, this topic was much less discussed—7% of communications (Adamik-Szysiak, 2021, p. 120). As the author notes, if not for the knowledge about the first wave of the pandemic, including numerous restrictions and limitations, from such a low number of references to the pandemic in the posts of the two most important candidates for the presidency of the Republic of Poland it would be difficult to conclude that the campaign was overshadowed by an active coronavirus pandemic (Adamik-Szysiak, 2021, pp. 117–118).

Referring to the communication strategies implemented in social media by the main candidates in the presidential election (A. Duda and R. Trzaskowski), Adamik-Szysiak emphasized that the issues related to COVID-19 were of secondary importance, despite the fact that the topic was an important thread both in media messages and the discussions of Internet users (2021, p. 122).

The analysis of the results of the research carried out for the purposes of this chapter showed that the political communications of the two main candidates for the office of the President of the Republic of Poland in the analyzed period rarely contained content about the COVID-19 pandemic and the SARS-CoV-2 virus. Messages that contained pandemic-related content covered only a few topics. In the case of Andrzej Duda, they concerned:
- appreciating the work of the public services and various social groups in the fight against the coronavirus
- a promise that in the second term of office he would not sign any law that would allow the privatization of public hospitals
- no possibility of overcoming the crisis after the pandemic in the event of selecting a counter-candidate
- no obligatory vaccinations against the coronavirus
- the sound budgetary situation despite the pandemic crisis, and

– the need to quickly recover from the post-pandemic crisis and return to normal.

Andrzej Duda's competitor, Rafał Trzaskowski, in his posts on the pandemic raised the following topics:

– appreciating the work of the public services and various social groups in the fight against the coronavirus
– the need to improve the health service
– highlighting values such as solidarity in the difficult time of the pandemic
– the need for vaccinations in connection with the coronavirus, including criticism of the incumbent president
– charges against the minister of health regarding a lack of information on the epidemic situation
– accusations against the incumbent president that Poles were left without help and information during the pandemic.

The statements of the two main candidates for the office of the President of the Republic of Poland very rarely dealt with topics that matched those included in the statements of medical experts. The underlying reason was that any pandemic-related topics were rarely mentioned in the lead candidate communications. Vaccination was a topic that was covered both lead candidates and medical experts. President Andrzej Duda spoke in favor of making coronavirus vaccinations optional. His counter-candidate asked in his statements whether the incumbent president was against immunization and described the president's statement as strange and incomprehensible. Other topics, such as face masks, sometimes appeared in the candidates' statements, but usually in a different context than the experts referred to them, for example Rafał Trzaskowski accused the health minister of buying masks from his friend.

The main candidates for the office of the President of the Republic of Poland very rarely referred in their statements to the statements of medical experts in the media. The most visible reference is to vaccination topics in the last phase of the election campaign. It was in reaction to President Andrzej Duda's statement that there was no need to introduce compulsory vaccinations that his opponent emphasized that, according to experts, vaccinations were undeniably needed.

The research presented a completely different phenomenon. With very rare cases of the statements of media experts in the media being mentioned in the statements of candidates, media statements of medical experts referring to statements of candidates or, more broadly, those of the government, were more often noted. In late May and early June 2020, when the Polish government was implementing the next stage of lifting restrictions related to the SARS-CoV-2 epidemic, citizens were informed that they no longer had to wear masks on the streets, and Prime Minister Mateusz Morawiecki said that the pandemic was under control. In response to this, there were media statements from such medical experts as, among others, Prof. Włodzimierz Gut, Prof. Krzysztof Simon, and Dr Paweł Grzesiowski, questioning the Prime Minister's words about the pandemic being under control (Lurka, 2020a; Lurka, 2020b; Stelmach, 2020).

A similar situation occurred after Andrzej Duda's media statements regarding vaccination against the coronavirus. He presented his position on vaccination both on social media and during an election debate organized by public television. To the statement of the incumbent president that he was not a supporter of any compulsory vaccinations (Lurka, 2020c). Dr Paweł Grzesiowski responded that not only epidemic safety was neglected in the election campaign, but the basis of public health, i.e., preventive vaccinations, was violated (Lurka, 2020d).

24.5   Discussion

The fact that candidates for the presidency of the Republic of Poland rarely published content related to the pandemic was probably related to their willingness to conduct a positive campaign. Both candidates wanted as many voters as possible to vote on election day, so they did not want to arouse fear of the pandemic among their potential voters. Moreover, in the spring of 2020, there was widespread hope that the pandemic would last no longer than a few months, so the presidential candidates did not seem to take the pandemic into account when plotting the prospects for the next 5 years. Therefore, the topics discussed in the entries about the pandemic most often concerned thanks to the services and appreciation of the good situation despite the crisis, or accusations against the opponent and his staff. Nevertheless, the results of the analysis are surprising, given the fact that the entire election campaign took place during the first wave of the pandemic.

Due to the fact that the candidates rarely spoke about the pandemic, they also rarely took up topics that matched to those of medical experts. Vaccines were a topic that emerged from both candidates and experts. During the first wave, in Poland there was a discussion regarding the possible inclusion of vaccines against coronavirus in the compulsory vaccinations. As a result, the candidates had to respond to this proposal just before the elections, taking into account the statements of their own electorates.

The main candidates for the office of the President of the Republic of Poland, apart from in rare cases, did not refer to medical experts' media statements in their own statements. The observed opposite phenomenon of medical experts referring to the statements of the main candidates for the presidency of the Republic of Poland, as well as other politicians from the ruling staff, caused the experts to become active actors of political communication. The role of medical experts grew with the months of the pandemic, and also after the elections were completed (Łukasik-Turecka, 2021a).

24.6   Conclusions

The analysis of the results of research on the potential impact of experts on the content of political messages of the main candidates for the presidency of the Republic of Poland during the elections of 2020 showed that despite the ongoing pandemic and the growing role and recognition of medical experts, health issues were marginalized in the messages of the candidates for the office of the President of the Republic of Poland. The political messages of the candidates for the office of the President of the Republic of Poland in the analyzed period contained little content on the COVID-19 pandemic and the SARS-CoV-2 virus. The messages were usually positive (thanks to the doctors, appreciation for the work of physicians, etc.); there was a lack of information about disturbing content, and if any, it was in the context of a warning against choosing a competitor considering the difficult times after the pandemic.

In the statements of candidates for the office of the President of the Republic of Poland, it was rare to find topics that matched those of medical experts. The candidates did not make any reference to the statements of medical experts in the media; on the contrary—it was medical experts who referred to the candidates, mainly Andrzej Duda and politicians of the ruling staff, often criticizing them.

In situations where the messages dealt with the same issues, very often politicians and medical experts drew contradictory conclusions: we control the pandemic (politicians) vs. we are not yet in control of the pandemic (experts); restrictions (politicians) vs. we should not put up with restrictions (experts); we should not introduce compulsory vaccinations against coronavirus (one of the main presidential candidates) vs. the lack of compulsory vaccinations is a disregard for epidemic safety and a violation of the basis of public health (experts).

Since spring 2020, in connection with the COVID-19 pandemic, we have had an intensified presence of medical experts in the Polish public and media space. The thematic scope of the experts' statements clearly indicates that in the analyzed period, we were dealing with actors not of public but political communication. Analysis of the media content, both the analysis carried out for the purposes of this chapter and the one carried out by Adamik-Szysiak (2021), indicates the duality of topics in the media space in the analyzed period: the preferred topic for politicians is campaign activity (mainly reporting campaign activities), and for experts, the pandemic (health). Despite the competition, the main candidates mirrored the message; they followed the same leads, they referred to the same issues.

In conclusion, despite the election campaign taking place during the first wave of the coronavirus, and despite the fact that health always ranks among the highest in the hierarchy of values of Polish society (CBOS, 2020), the topic of the pandemic in the messages of the presidential candidates was definitely marginalized. The fact that medical experts began to appear extremely frequently in the analyzed period in the Polish public and media space had little impact on the subject of statements of the candidates for the presidency of the Republic of Poland.

References

Adamik-Szysiak M. (2021). "Pandemia COVID-19 w strategiach komunikowania w mediach społecznościowych głównych kandydatów w wyborach prezydenckich w Polsce w 2020 roku". *Media Biznes Kultura, vol. 2 (11)*, pp. 109–122. DOI: https://doi.org/10.4467/25442554.MBK.21.017.15158.

CBOS. (2022). "Komunikat z badań: Wartości w czasach zarazy", cbos.pl. Retrieved from: https://www.cbos.pl/SPISKOM.POL/2020/K_160_20.PDF.

Esser F., Pfetsch B. (2020). „Political communication". In D. Caramani (Ed.). *Comparative Politics* (pp. 336–358), New York: Oxford University Press.

Kurczewska J. (1997). *Technokraci i ich świat społeczny*. Warszawa: Wydawnictwo IFiS PAN.

Lurka K. (2022a). "Prof. Włodzimierz Gut: Pandemia nie jest opanowana". *termedia.pl*. Retrieved from: https://www.termedia.pl/mz/Prof-Wlodzimierz-Gut-Pandemia-nie-jest-opanowana,38133.html.

Lurka K. (2022b). "Prof. Krzysztof Simon: Epidemia wcale nie jest opanowana". *termedia.pl*. Retrieved from: https://www.termedia.pl/mz/Prof-Krzysztof-Simon-Epidemia-wcale-nie-jest-opanowana,38239.html.

Lurka K. (2022c). "Andrzej Duda: Nie jestem zwolennikiem szczepień obowiązkowych". *termedia.pl*. Retrieved from: https://www.termedia.pl/mz/Andrzej-Duda-Nie-jestem-zwolennikiem-szczepien-obowiazkowych,38626.html.

Lurka K. (2022d). "Dr Grzesiowski o wypowiedzi prezydenta". *termedia.pl*. Retrieved from: https://www.termedia.pl/mz/Dr-Grzesiowski-o-wypowiedzi-prezydenta,38641 .html.

Łukasik-Turecka A. (2021a). "Медицинские эксперты как новые участники политической коммуникации в Европе во время пандемии COVID-19 на примере Польши и Латвии", *Wschodni Rocznik Humanistyczny, vol. XVIII*, pp. 123– 132. DOI: 10.36121/aturecka.18.2021.4.123

Łukasik-Turecka A. (2021b). "Sprawozdanie z webinarium pt. «Eksperci w mediach – interpretatorzy, tłumacze rzeczywistości czy aktorzy komunikowania politycznego?". *Studia i Analizy Nauk o Polityce*, vol. 1, pp. 137–139, DOI: https://doi .org/10.31743/sanp.12248

Maciuszczak T. (2020). "Wybory prezydenckie 2020. Najdziwniejsza i najdłuższa kampa- nia wyborcza po 1989 roku. Wywiad z Wojciechem Magusiem". dziennikwschodni.pl. Retrieved from: https://www.dziennikwschodni.pl/wybory-prezydenckie/wybory -prezydenckie-2020-najdziwniejsza-i-najdluzsza-kampania-wyborcza-po-1989 -roku,n,1000269016.html.

Michalczyk S. (2020). "Aktorzy i instytucje komunikowania politycznego: systematyka problematyki". In A. Cieślikowa & P. Płaneta (Eds.). *Od modernizacji do mediosfery: meandry transformacji w komunikowaniu: prace ofiarowane dr. hab. Ryszardowi Filasowi* (pp. 229–252), Kraków: Instytut Dziennikarstwa, Mediów i Komunikacji Społecznej Uniwersytetu Jagiellońskiego.

Musiał-Karg M., Kapsa I. (2021). „Debate: Voting challenges in a pandemic – Poland". *Public Money & Management*, vol. 41, nr 1, pp. 6–8. DOI https://doi.org/10.1080 /09540962.2020.1809791

Nosal P. (2009). "Kultura ekspercka w mediach" . *Teraźniejszość-Człowiek-Edukacja*, vol. 4 (48), pp. 89–103.

PKW. (2022). "Komunikat Państwowej Komisji Wyborczej z dnia 7 maja 2020 roku", pkw.gov.pl. Retrieved from: https://pkw.gov.pl/aktualnosci/wyjasnienia-stanowiska -komunikaty/komunikat-panstwowej-komisji-wyborczej-z-dnia-7-maja-2020 -roku?beta=false.

"Postanowienie Marszałka Sejmu Rzeczypospolitej Polskiej z dnia 5 lutego 2020 roku w sprawie zarządzenia wyborów Prezydenta Rzeczypospolitej Polskiej". (2020a). *pkw.gov.pl*. Retrieved from: https://pkw.gov.pl/uploaded_files/1580912925_Postano wienie_Marszalka_Sejmu_Rzeczypospolitej_Polskiej_z_dnia_5_lutego_2020_r_w _sprawie_zarzadzenia_wyborow_Prezydenta_Rzeczypospolitej_Polskiej.pdf

"Postanowienie Marszałka Sejmu Rzeczypospolitej Polskiej z dnia 3 czerwca 2020 r. w sprawie zarządzenia wyborów Prezydenta Rzeczypospolitej Polskiej". (2020b). *pkw.gov.pl*. Retrieved from: https://www.pkw.gov.pl/uploaded_files/1591262885 _d20200000098801.pdf

"Rozporządzenie Ministra Zdrowia z dnia 20 marca 2020 roku w sprawie ogłoszenia na obszarzeRzeczypospolitejPolskiejstanuepidemii",(2020).*www.gov.pl*.Retrievedfrom: https://www.gov.pl/web/rpa/rozporzadzenie-ministra-zdrowia-z-dnia-20-marca -2020-r-w-sprawie-ogloszenia-na-obszarze-rzeczypospolitej-polskiej-stanu -epidemii

"Rozporządzenie Rady Ministrów z dnia 31 marca 2020 r. w sprawie ustanowienia określonych ograniczeń, nakazów i zakazów w związku z wystąpieniem stanu epidemii", (2020). *www.jablonna.pl.* Retrieved from: https://www.jablonna.pl/pliki /aktualnosci/2020/marzec/Rozporzadzenie%20z%2031%20marca.pdf

Sarcinelli U. (2011), „Politische kommunikation in Deutschland: Zur Politikvermittlung im demokratischen System". Wiesbaden: Springer-Verlag.

Stelmach M. (2020). "Dr Paweł Grzesiowski: Jeszcze daleko do wygaśnięcia epidemii". *termedia.pl.* Retrieved from: https://www.termedia.pl/mz/Dr-Pawel-Grzesiowski -Jeszcze-daleko-do-wygasniecia-epidemii-,38195.html

Positions of the Main Political Parties in Poland on the Presidential Election during the COVID-19 Pandemic

Piotr Chrobak

25.1   Introduction

The election of the President of the Republic of Poland ended in Poland with the so-called a two-year election marathon, which began with elections to the local government in autumn 2018, followed by elections to the European Parliament in spring 2019, and elections to the Sejm and Senate of the Republic of Poland in autumn. The election of the President of the Republic of Poland was scheduled for spring 2020 (*Postanowienie Marszałka Sejmu RP z dnia 5 lutego 2020...*). It seemed that both politicians and voters were already knackered of the three campaigns mentioned, which could made the election of the head of state the least interesting. However, with the coronavirus pandemic, it happened otherwise. As a result of this extraordinary situation, the presidential election was accompanied by a number of changes and events that significantly determined the dynamics of this election campaign, i.e. failure of conducting voting on time, introduction of new solutions in electoral law less than six months before the elections, and replacement of the presidential candidate from the largest opposition party in the newly ordered elections.

This chapter aims to analyze the positions and actions taken by PiS and PO RP and their candidates towards the organization of the election of the President of the Republic of Poland during the COVID-19 pandemic. PiS is the largest and by far the dominant party in the United Right (ZP) coalition that exercises power in Poland. Thus, it is PiS that practically manages the government's activities. On the other hand, the PO RP, which is part of the Civic Coalition (KO), is the largest and most important opposition grouping. Before the ZP took over power in 2015, the Platform (together with the minority coalition partner - the Polish People's Party) exercised power in the country for two terms. The aforementioned groups were analyzed, as they are the two most important parties in Poland (their domination has lasted since 2005), and moreover, it was ultimately the candidates from these groups that decided who would sit in the seat of the head of state. It is about President Duda, who is running for re-election, supported by PiS and Kidawa-Błońska, and then about Trzaskowski, i.e. candidates proposed by the PO.

Taking into account the threat to health and even life caused by the pandemic, the following research hypothesis was formulated: Parties and their candidates want to hold elections even during a pandemic, if their contenders have a real chance of victory. To verify this hypothesis, the following research question was posed: How did the political environment (major political parties) perceive the issues of organizing pre-planned elections in the context of the growing COVID-19 pandemic? In order to answer them, it is necessary to analyze what positions were presented by the above-mentioned political groupings and their candidates regarding the organization of elections during the pandemic. The analysis was ran with the use of a comparative method, regarding the similarities and differences between the aforementioned parties and their candidates, both before the first and subsequent conducted elections, as for the organization of the election of the head of state and the conducting of the election campaign during the COVID-19 pandemic.

25.2   Background

The election of the President of the Republic of Poland in 2020 took place during the coronavirus pandemic - SARS-CoV-2, which reached Poland in March 2020. The panic that COVID-19 caused around the world was caused by a significant threat to health and even life, in the absence of medicine because the doctors knew little about it. To slow down its spread, the vast majority of countries began to introduce various types of restrictions, sometimes causing a number of controversies, as discussed in more detail by Sylwia Frach (2021), Olga Hałub-Kowalczyk (2020), and Martinas Maluzinas (2021a). In addition, individual countries have taken steps to protect the functioning of their economies, as reported by, inter alia, Magdalena Mikołajczyk (2021).

Similar to Poland, other countries also had to decide whether elections should be held in such dangerous conditions. A number of publications have been devoted to the analysis of electoral processes during the COVID-19 pandemic. About the elections and the procedure to be followed in order for the elections to take place in pandemic conditions, wrote, inter alia, Toby S. James and Sead Alihodzic (2020), Erik Asplund, Bor Stevense, Toby S. James and Alistair Clark (2020) and Robert Krimmer, David Duenas-Cid and Iuliia Krivonosova (2020). About the elections in France were writing, among others, Simone Bertoli, Lucas Guichard and Francesca Marchetta (2020), Tommaso Giommoni and Gabriel Loumeau (2020) as well as Laurent Bach, Arthur

Guillouzouic and Clément Malgouyres (2021). The presidential election in the USA was carried by: Emily Chen, Herbert Chang, Ashwin Rao, Kristina Lerman, Goeffrey Cowan and Emilio Ferrara (2021), Thad Kousser, Seth Hill, Mackenzie Lockhart, Jennifer L. Merolla and Mindy Romero (2021), as well as Richard L. Hasen (2020). The elections in Canada were analyzed by: Holly Ann Garnett, Jean-Nicolas Bordeleau, Allison Harell i Laura Stephenson (2021). On the other hand, the parliamentary elections in Lithuania were described by Martinas Malužinas (2021b) and Aleksandra Kuczyńska-Zonik (2021).

Initially, before the outbreak of the pandemic, 10 candidates applied for the highest office in Poland: Robert Biedroń (MEP, Chairperson of the Spring of Robert Biedroń), Krzysztof Bosak (Member of the Polish Parliament, member of the Confederation of Freedom and Independence), Andrzej Duda (President RP, non-party, before he sat in the chair of the head of state in 2015, he was a deputy to the European Parliament and a member of PiS), Szymon Hołownia (journalist, wrote for: "Gazeta Wyborcza", "Rzeczpospolita", "Wprost", "Tygodnik Powszechny" and "Newsweek Polska", he was also a presenter on Religia.tv and TVN, non-party, after the elections, the creator and leader of Poland 2050 Szymon Hołownia), Marek Jakubiak (entrepreneur, member of the Federation for the Republic of Poland, in 2015–2018 Member of the Polish Parliament associated with the Kukiz'15 club, from November 2018 until the end of his term of office he remained a non-attached MP), Małgorzata Kidawa-Błońska (MP and Deputy Speaker of the Sejm of the Republic of Poland, member of the PO RP), Władysław Kosiniak-Kamysz (Member of the Sejm of the Republic of Poland, president of the PSL), Mirosław Piotrowski (lecturer at the College of Social and Media Culture, member of the Real Europe Movement - Europa Christi), Paweł Tanajno (entrepreneur, non-party) and Stanisław Żółtek (entrepreneur, member of the Congress of the New Right and Polexit) (*Obwieszczenie PKW z dnia 15 kwietnia 2020...*). The election rivalry between them lasted practically until May 8, that is, until the election silence was to be announced.

The pandemic (and the accompanying fierce conflict between the ruling coalition and opposition parties) so complicated the preparations for the elections that holding them on the scheduled date, i.e. on May 10, turned out to be very difficult, and as a result, the voting was not held (*Uchwała PKW nr 129/2020...; PKW ZPOW-421-24/20...*). In such circumstances, an attempt to force voting could lead to a violation of the constitutional provisions on the election of the head of state (Rakowska-Trela, 2021). Furthermore, it was influenced not only by the fear of the coronavirus among the public, but also by the fears of some local authorities as to the possibility of safe organization and conduct of voting (Czapiewski, 2021, pp. 61–62). The new voting date was set for June 28 (*Postanowienie Marszałka Sejmu RP z dnia 3 czerwca 2020...*). The elections were held in accordance with the provisions of the Electoral Code (*Ustawa z dnia 5 stycznia 2011...*) and a specially passed act enabling voting by correspondence (*Ustawa z dnia 2 czerwca 2020...*).

Not conducting to vote on May 10 led to a situation where, as a result of the decreeing of new regulations (*Ustawa z dnia 2 czerwca 2020...*), the possibility of adding new candidates or replacing the existing ones, provided that 100 thousand. signatures, which the staff had a week for. However, candidates who collected the required number of signatures in the previous not-held elections and were registered, did not have to - interestingly - collect them again. Also those candidates who collected an insufficient number of signatures in the previous elections and were not registered, then if they decided to stand for new elections, it was enough - by the decision of the Supreme Court (*Postanowienie Sądu Najwyższego z 12 czerwca 2020...*) - that they would only collect the missing signatures. In this situation, the candidacy of Waldemar Witkowski from Unia Pracy (UP) could be registered. The aforementioned legal solutions aroused a number of controversies (Pyrzyńska, 2021).

The Civic Platform - as the only party - took advantage of this possibility and on May 15 it replaced its candidate for Rafał Trzaskowski (Rafał Trzaskowski kandydatem..., 2020.05.15). The decision was probably influenced by the fact that during the campaign conducted during the coronavirus pandemic, the Platform candidate began to lose support very quickly due to, inter alia, the series of mistakes made by herself, her staff and the party leaders. It seems that at first they were not able to adapt to the campaign conducted during very difficult pandemic conditions. Only after the replacement of the candidate and personnel changes in the election staff, which brought a new strategy and tactics, Trzaskowski entered an equal fight with Duda (Sondaż dla..., 2020.07.10).

Eventually, 11 candidates took part in the re-scheduled elections in 2020. Witkowski (the director of the Hipolit Cegielski Housing Cooperative, a member of UP) joined the aforementioned contenders, and Trzaskowski (President of Warsaw, vice-president of the PO RP) replaced Kidawa-Błońska (*Obwieszczenie PKW z dnia 12 czerwca 2020...*). The election was not carried out by the exclusive correspondence voting, for which the government was in favor, only in a hybrid manner, i.e. traditionally and by post (Musiał-Karg, 2021, pp. 40–46).

As in the first vote none of the candidates won more than half of the valid votes cast, the second round was to decide who would sit in the seat of the head of state. The winner of the first round was Duda with a majority of over 13% of the votes, compared to Trzaskowski, who was on a close second (*Obwieszczenie PKW z dnia 30 czerwca 2020...*). The vote was held again on July 12. After a very fierce and even competition, the winner was Duda, who won 10,440,648 votes (51.03%) and defeated Trzaskowski with a difference of 422,385 votes (2.06%), who obtained 10,018,263 votes (48.97%). Thus, the incumbent president was re-elected (Chrobak, 2021, pp. 92–95). The interest in the elections in the first vote was 64.51%, while in the second vote 68.18% (*Obwieszczenie PKW z dnia 13 lipca 2020…*). It should be noted that in spite of the ongoing pandemic, the government undertook pro-turnout measures, including on financial or material rewards (e.g. by funding a fire engine) for municipalities in which the turnout was the highest in the country (Piękoś, 2020, pp. 218–222).

25.3   Positions and Actions of PiS and PO RP and Their Candidates Regarding the Elections during the COVID-19 Pandemic

The growing fear of coronavirus infection and the restrictions introduced had a significant impact on the planning, organization and the course of the elections itself (*Jak koronawirus…*). The subject of the coronavirus has dominated the subject of the election campaign. There was practically no information service that did not mention COVID-19 in its material (Bartoszewicz, 2020, p. 66). The situation got even more complicated when it turned out that the voting date was most likely to coincide with the expected peak of the disease. Then the date of voting became one of the dominant topics of public debate. The leaders of individual parties, candidates for the office of the President of the Republic of Poland and experts (mainly medical) debated whether the vote should be held on time or whether it should be moved by introducing one of the states of emergency. Here appeared another problem. Supporters of postponing the elections could not agree on when they should be postponed. Most often it was talked about autumn 2020 or spring 2021. However, no one could have predicted what the pandemic situation would be at that time. As it turned out, in the fall of 2020, there was a second wave of infections, and in the spring of 2021, a third wave, etc.

The approach to the date and form of voting was assessed differently. The biggest differences occurred depending on whether politicians from the ruling coalition or the opposition spoke. It should be noted that opinions among politicians in the ruling coalition and among the opposition were also divided. Some opposition MPs were accused of acting on the border of the law or even illegally. One of the charges against the correspondence form of the elections was the reference to the provision that forbade introducing changes to the election law less than six months before voting (*Prawnicy o…*).

It should be pointed out that the positions on the COVID-19 pandemic expressed by PiS, and thus the government co-created by this party, and announced by President Duda from this party, were – which should not be surprising in such a situation - convergent. Similarly to the positions presented by the PO RP, its presidential candidate Kidawa-Błońska and the Parliamentary Club Koalicja Obywatelska - Civic Platform, Nowoczesna, Inicjatywa Polska, Zieloni (KP KO).

25.4   The Position of PiS, the Government and Andrzej Duda

Like other countries, the Polish government also took the position that the introduction of restrictions would help limit the spread of the coronavirus. Therefore, from March 13, it was forbidden to organize gatherings of more than 50 people, and from March 24, they were completely forbidden, with few exceptions (*Rozporządzenie Ministra Zdrowia z dnia 13 marca 2020...*; *Rozporządzenie Ministra Zdrowia z dnia 24 marca 2020...*). The first restriction limited meaningfully the conduct of the election campaign, while the second made it practically impossible, as it eliminated any possibility of direct contact with voters.

The restrictions were ordered by virtue of the introduced state of epidemic threat, and then the state of the epidemic, as well as the specially enacted "Act on preventing and combating infections and infectious diseases in humans", aimed at better adapting the regulations to combating the coronavirus pandemic (*Ustawa z dnia 5 grudnia 2008...*; *Ustawa z dnia 2 marca 2020...*). Here a problem appeared whether the introduction of restrictions allowing for far-reaching restrictions on the constitutional rights and freedoms of an individual should be based on extra-constitutional emergency states, such as an epidemic emergency and an epidemic, or whether one of the constitutional emergency states, i.e. a state of disaster, should not be introduced disaster (Uziębło, 2021). However, the introduction of a state of natural disaster would postpone the elections by several months, which PiS did not want to agree to.

The above problem did not only concern the conduct of the election campaign, but was of much broader significance. As a result of the introduced restrictions, some enterprises were closed, including from the gastronomic industry. Kindergartens were also out of service, and schools and universities switched to remote teaching. In this way, the government wanted to limit the possibility of transmission of the virus. However, restricting the freedom of economic activity (by prohibiting or restricting the conduct of economic activity involving a given type of goods or services) was a restriction of some constitutional freedoms and rights (Uliasz, 2021, pp. 176–188). In this situation, there were also voices (not only of the PO RP, but also of experts) that the aforementioned restrictions limiting human rights should be introduced under the provisions "on a state of natural disaster", provided for in the Constitution of the Republic of Poland, and not under the Act " on the state of the epidemic". Since the latter is not included in the constitution, it could not serve as a legal basis (Gajda, 2020, pp. 19–26). Justyna Węgrzyn also writes about the fact that the government should introduce a state of natural disaster (2021, pp. 148–158). Krzysztof Urbaniak and Monika Urbaniak (2021, pp. 331–339) and Agata Ludera-Ruszel and Karol Piękoś (2021, pp. 318–327) have a similar opinion. An even more serious problem was related to the restriction of religious practices. Piotr Stanisz notices that: "establishing restrictions on the freedom to manifest religion through acts of worship in regulations issued by the Minister of Health and the Council of Ministers is an activity outside the scope of statutory authorizations and is inconsistent with the Polish constitution. According to the Constitution of the Republic of Poland, passing a law is the only permissible form of introducing restrictions on the freedom to manifest religion, and this rule does not recognize exceptions even in emergency situations" (Stanisz, 2021, pp. 144). Therefore, according to the scholar, changes to the effective law should be made so that, in the event of emergencies, restrictions can be made according to the prevailing situation (Stanisz, 2021, pp. 144–161).

The constitution does not actually dictate in what situations one of the three states of emergency should be introduced, but leaves it to the judgment of people in power. In this particular case, the problem was that both PiS and President Duda were determined and able to hold the elections on the original date, so there was no question of introducing a state of national calamity. On the other hand, the greatest problem was ensuring the safety of both voters and members of electoral commissions. For this purpose, the government put forth voting only by correspondence (*Ustawa z dnia 6 kwietnia 2020...*). It should be noticed that this form of voting has never been practiced before, so it required - in pandemic conditions and under time pressure – to make a lot of preparations. It seems that PiS was leading up to elections at all costs, as it was afraid that due to the introduced restrictions, the ratings of both President Duda and the party itself might deteriorate, which could prevent it from being re-elected. It is worth to notice that the pre-pandemic survey gave Duda victory even in the first vote, and after the outbreak of the pandemic, they indicated a possible victory, but only in following vote (Roguska, 2020; Feliksiak, 2020; Pankowski, 2020; Cybulska, 2020a; Głowacki, 2020a).

25.5 The Position of the PO RP and Małgorzata Kidawa-Błońska

The subject related to COVID-19 was given a lot of attention by both the PO RP and its candidate for the office of president (Bartoszewicz, 2020, pp. 69).

After the first case of COVID-19 was confirmed in Poland, Kidawa-Błońska announced on March 4 the appointment of a coronavirus threat monitoring team. As the threat spread, campaigning became more and more dangerous, so on March 10, she announced on Twitter and Facebook that out of concern for the safety and health of participants, large open meetings as part of the presidential campaign were adjourned until further notice (Spotkania otwarte..., 2020.03.10). At the same time, she appealed for the coronavirus not to be used for political purposes. After those declarations, Kidawa-Błońska's election campaign clearly stopped, which certainly had an impact on the polls. Although it should be noted that the candidate tried to run the campaign via the Internet. She organized a number of videoconferences, incl. with local government officials from the West Pomeranian Voivodeship, Silesia, Łódź and with chosen local government officials from all over Poland, devoted to the epidemic situation (Raport Kidawy: Problemy samorządów..., 2020.03.20).

However, on March 26, KP KO appealed to Prime Minister Mateusz Morawiecki to introduce a state of national calamity, instead of an epidemiologic (Wprowadźmy stan..., 2020.03.26). After the government has consistently refused, the Civic Platform together with its presidential candidate began to appeal at the end of March to stop campaigning and postpone the elections for a later date (Kidawa-Błońska apeluje o..., 2020.03.29; Wybory w czasie...). According to Kidawa-Błońska, in an emergency of life or health caused by the coronavirus, the vote on May 10 should not take place, and the elections should be held when it is safe for people to do so. Then, she called on all voters to boycott the vote and stay home after the government continued the election process. This position may have been influenced by the getting worse results of Kidawa-Błońska in election polls, which in April indicated that she would not even enter the second round (Głowacki, 2020b). The Civic Platform could reckon that the postponement of the elections would increase the chances of its candidate, as the restrictions introduced by the government and supported by the President would result in a decline in support for Duda.

To underline its determination, on March 31 Kidawa-Błońska abeyed running the campaign and called on other candidates to do so, although it did not receive a broader response (Wybory w czasie...). At the same time, in the Sejm forum, she was expressing her critical position towards the government as to the continuation of preparations for the vote (Rząd uprawia...). To pay an attention to the fact that voting may not be common, she was pointing to possible problems with the participation of Poles living abroad who, due to the restrictions, could have problems reaching the polls (Małgorzata Kidawa-Błońska wysyła...). However, despite the abeyance of the campaign, along with other candidates, on April 22, she took part in the debate on "Climate

Crisis: Scenarios for Poland", organized by Kantar Polska and Global Compact Network Poland. This kind of behavior could be disorientating for voters, who could not be certain whether Kidawa-Błońska was participating in the campaign or adjourns it, especially since in the following days she continued to criticize the government for further work on the organization of elections (Oni wybory...). At the same time, it was constantly losing support in election polls (Sondaż: 10 maja...; Sondaż: Duda...). It should be emphasized, that due to the restrictions introduced, running the campaign was actually very difficult and could be limited to the Internet and also press conferences.

Major criticism of the PO RP against PiS was caused by the announcement by Prime Minister Morawiecki and Deputy Prime Minister and Minister of State Assets Jacek Sasin of the commencement of preparations for voting only by correspondence, with the help of the Polish Post. The Civic Platform together with Kidawa-Błońska were strongly against this form of voting. Then, it was officially announced on what date, in their opinion, the vote should be postponed. It was postulated that the elections to be prepared by the PKW (and not by any other institution) should be held only on May 16, 2021. It was proposed to prepare for a mixed mode by then, i.e. voting in the traditional form, as well as by correspondence and via the Internet (Bezpieczne wybory...).

As the government continued its preparations, the Platform, in order to prevent voting in the above-mentioned form, on April 21, as KP KO, requested the Supreme Audit Office to conduct an inspection at the Chancellery of the Prime Minister, the Ministry of State Assets, Polish Post S.A. and Polish Security Printing Works S.A. in the field of establishing the legality (according to politicians from the PO RP, the act to which the government referred to correspondence voting was a non-binding legal act, because it was not accepted by the Sejm and the Senate), advisability, reliability and thriftiness of actions taken (*Wniosek do NIK*...).

As the PO RP was determined to make it impossible to hold elections, PiS took all steps to run it. In this situation, on May 4, the CP KO appealed to the Chairman of the PKW to become involved in an attempt to solve the crisis that affected the organization of the elections. It was arguing over the legal chaos to which - according to KO - the coalition in power had caused, wishing to hold the elections on 10 May at all costs (Apel do Przewodniczącego..., 2020.05.04). It should be pointed out that on May 7, the PKW in its announcement informed that under the Act of April 16 (*Ustawa z dnia 16 kwietnia 2020*...), inter alia, the competences of the PKW in terms of establishing the model of voting cards and ordering them to be printed. It was found that the legal regulation in force deprived the PKW of the tools necessary to perform its duties, and therefore the vote on May 10 - according to PKW - could not take place (*Komunikat PKW z dnia 7 maja 2020...*). In this situation, on May 8, KP KO filed a motion for a vote of no confidence in Minister Sasin, caused by his actions in the organization of the election of the President of the Republic of Poland. According to KO, the actions of Minister Sasin led to absolute electoral, constitutional and democratic chaos in Poland (Składamy wniosek...). In turn, on July 8, he submitted to the Marshal of the Sejm a programme of resolution on the appointment of an Investigating Committee to investigate the correctness and legality of actions taken by public authorities and institutions in the implementation of purchases and contracts for services or supplies in connection with counteracting COVID-19 (Komisja śledcza...).

At this point, it should be pointed out that the idea of voting in correspondence form only was criticized not only by the PO RP. Also, a large number of experts were critical of it. Maciej Onasz interchanged and analyzed a number of disadvantages related to the attempts to carry it out (Onasz, 2021, pp. 202–203. See also: Musiał-Karg, 2021). Anna Rytel-Warzocha also wrote about irregularities in the provisions of the act which is to introduce correspondence voting. The author points out that if the voting were held on the basis of the rules of the aforementioned act, it could threaten, inter alia, universality and secrecy of elections (Rytel-Warzocha, 2020, pp. 105–111). Rush in the works and the resulting mistakes or threats, contained in the above-mentioned the act, as well as the very rapid pace of its decreeing and immediate entring into force, on the one hand shows how much the coronavirus has complicated the possibility of voting, and on the other hand shows the determination of the state authorities to meet the constitutional deadlines regulating the time in by which the election of the head of state should be carried out. Also, the political games that attended this act did not have a positive impact on its final shape. Eventually, it turned out to be impossible to conduct a vote based on the provisions of the aforementioned act, which in turn led to the lack of voting within the prescribed period.

Maciej Onasz notices that the pandemic had an impact on decreasing the democratic standards according to which the election process should take place. He points out that before the first, ultimately failed, voting, conducting an election campaign in the form of, inter alia, the organization of election rallies and other types of mass meetings with voters was limited, or even impossible, due to people's fear of infection of the coronavirus, and then by politicians giving up this form of contact, and as a consequence of the introduced restrictions (Onasz, 2021, pp. 198–200). Interestingly, after the announcement of the new election date, both before the first and the re-voting, both the candidates and voters did not show such fears.

25.6   Candidates' Positions in New Elections

Both PiS and President Duda, from the very beginning of the pandemic, took the position that elections should be held in spring 2020 and took all the actions to make this happen, despite the rising threat from the coronavirus. On the other hand, the PO RP and Kidawa-Błońska practically from the end of March, consistently were striving to move them, arguing that, inter alia, the fact that campaigning is very difficult and voters will be able to become infected with COVID-19 through their presence at the polling station or - when the postal vote has been announced - through contact with the envelope (Gąbka, 2020). The position of the PO RP regarding the conduct of elections during the pandemic changed when Kidawa-Bońska, who had very low support in election polls, was replaced by Trzaskowski, who enjoys the highest support among all opposition candidates (Cybulska, 2020b, c).

In their programs, both Trzaskowski and Duda referred to the coronavirus pandemic, in chapters devoted to, inter alia, economy, health or science (NOWA SOLIDARNOŚĆ..., 2020; Plan Dudy..., 2020). In the case of Duda, the issues related to the coronavirus practically coincided with the position of the government. In the struggle for the votes of farmers, President Duda thanked them that during the pandemic there was no short supply of food, while emphasizing the high quality of Polish agricultural products (Kasińska-Metryka, 2021, pp. 115).

On their websites, both PO RP and Trzaskowski were encouraging to take part in the elections, both in the first and in the second vote. Trzaskowski was also encouraging to report to act as a person of trust in election commissions (Wybory prezydenckie..., 2020.06.23; II tura..., 2020.07.06). There were no more warnings about infecting the coronavirus and no messages encouraging people to stay at home and avoid large crowds, which could be found on the website of both the PO RP and Kidawa-Błońska before May 10 (#pakietbezpieczeństwa...).

Both Trzaskowski and Duda posted on their websites numerous photos of outdoor meetings with voters. We can see there crowds and tightly gathered people who not only did not keep their distance from one another, but the vast majority of them did not wear protective masks, which showed that the safety rules regarding the coronavirus left a lot to be desired at the meetings of both candidates (Dziękuję za Waszą..., 2020; Multimedia..., 2020).

It is worth to notice that when it turned out that the elections would be held, the topic of the coronavirus was not so much discussed, and the candidates returned to the old rhetoric and divisions in politics, invariably running on the line of the PO RP versus PiS and KO versus the ZP. Each side in the aforementioned fight used, inter alia, a series of stereotypes in our politics (Ludwiniak, 2020, pp. 354–356).

25.7   Similarities and Differences

Summarizing both election campaigns regarding the analyzed candidates and their supporting parties, one can mention the similarities and differences between the approach to the organization of elections between Duda and Kidawa-Błońska, and then Trzaskowski, and between Kidawa-Błońska and Trzaskowski, see Tables 25.1 and 25.2.

Analyzing the activities of Duda and Kidawa-Błońska, and then Duda and Trzaskowski, it can be seen that in the first case, the candidates have more differences than similarities, while in the second case, the situation is the opposite. President Duda consistently was striving for elections the whole time. In turn, the PO RP first tried to postpone them, and when it failed, it led to the replacement of the candidate and conducted the campaign with the new candidate.

Comparing the approach to the elections by Kidawa-Błońska and Trzaskowski, we can see almost the same differences. Kidawa-Błońska did her best to prevent the conduct of elections on the original date. The main reasons were that campaigns were prevented and the risk of infection COVID-19. On the other hand, Trzaskowski fully developed his campaign, and there was no question of encouraging a boycott, but on the contrary, he encouraged voters to participate in the vote. Opposite to PiS, there is a lack of consistency in the approach to the organization of elections on the part of the PO RP.

25.8   Conclusions

It is a common opinion that one of the conditions for the safe conduct of elections during a pandemic is, inter alia, good cooperation in their organization, between the party in power and the opposition, and with the institutions responsible for their organization. In addition, the existing solutions regarding their organization should be used – possibly improved and adjusted – ensure their clarity and avoid new, so far unproven solutions (Birch et al., 2020). As it

TABLE 25.1   Similarities and differences in the activities of PiS and PO RP and the candidates for the
office of the President of the Republic of
Poland they support

Candidate and supporting party	The first failed elections with a vote on May 10, 2020	
	Differences	Similarities
A. Duda PiS (including the government)	– striving to run elections in spite of the pandemic – willingness to conduct an exclusive correspondence vote – running an election campaign – encouraging participation in elections	– due to the escalation of the pandemic, abandoning direct voting at the polling station
M. Kidawa-Błońska PO RP (including KP KO)	– efforts to move elections to spring 2021 due to the pandemic – criticism of exclusive correspondence voting – mixed system voting in spring 2021 – abeyance of running campaign due to the threat of COVID-19 infection – calling for a boycott of the elections	

Candidate and supporting party	The second elections were conducted with voting on June 28 and July 12, 2020	
	Differences	Similarities
A. Duda PiS (including the government)	– striving to run the elections in spite of the pandemic from the outset	– conducting the election campaign despite the threat of a pandemic – nonadherence with the restrictions during election rallies – agreement to vote in the mixed system
R. Trzaskowski PO RP (including KP KO)	– despite prior opposition, taking part in new elections	

SOURCE: OWN STUDY

419 POLITICAL PARTIES IN POLAND AND THE PRESIDENTIAL ELECTION

TABLE 25.2 Similarities and differences in the activities of Kidawa-Błońska and Trzaskowski

Candidate and supporting party	Differences	Similarities
M. Kidawa-Błońska PO RP (including KP KO)	– efforts to postpone elections due to the pandemic to spring 2021; – abeyance of the campaign due to the threat of COVID-19 infection – adherence the restrictions while conducting the election campaign (until it was abeyance) – exhorting for a boycott of elections – exhorting to stay at home to minimize the risk of infection of COVID-19 – no inciting to report to election board as a person of trust – warning that envelopes may carry a coronavirus	– criticism for exclusive correspondence voting – mixed voting
R. Trzaskowski PO RP (including KP KO)	– no pursuit to postpone elections – conducting the election campaign in spite of the threat of COVID-19 infection – nonadherence with the restrictions during election rallies – encouraging participation in elections – brak apeli o pozostanie w domach, aby zminimalizować ryzyko zarażenia COVID-19 – inciting to report to election board as a person of trust – no warnings that envelopes may carry a coronavirus.	

SOURCE: OWN STUDY

turned out, when organizing the election of the President of the Republic of Poland, there was no cooperation beyond the divisions on the PiS (including the government), PO RP (along with other opposition parties), PKW and local government authorities. In addition, attempts were made to make too large changes in the voting method, which was supposed to, inter alia, have a negative impact on their clarity. As a result, all this made it impossible to vote on 10 May. However, as a result of later cooperation, elections were held with voting in June and July. It means that not so much the pandemic turned out to be an impediment preventing voting on May 10, but the fierce long-term political conflict between PiS and PO RP, which led, among others, to to use the pandemic in political struggle.

It is also worth to note that if in Poland, besides direct voting at a polling station, there were other methods of voting, e.g. via the Internet, or postal voting would be more popular, there would be no problem with the organization of the voting process itself in emergency situations, such as the COVID-19 pandemic (Landman & Di Gennaro Splendore, 2020). However, it should be remembered that the election process includes not only the voting itself, but the entire preparation stage, requiring the involvement of many people who, along with voters and candidates, were at risk of being infected with COVID-19 (James, 2021).

The vote itself was carried out safely, as there was no rapid increase in getting ill after the elections (Vashchanka, 2020). However, the problem was with the election campaign. First restrictions meant that not all candidates could fully conduct the campaign. On the other hand, the sitting president, due to his office, was much more often shown in the media, which could not but meant his popularity (Strzelecki, 2020). All this shows that, in a situation where we cannot ensure not only safe voting, but also equal campaigns for all election campaigns, postponing elections should be considered (James & Alihodzic, 2020; Asplund & James, 2020).

When analyzing the approach of the government and President Duda to the COVID-19 pandemic, a certain twofold approach can be noticed. On the one hand, the ruling camp undertook a range of measures to limit the spread of the coronavirus, and on the other - as it turned out - it wanted to hold elections at all costs. According to the government, it was possible to introduce a number of necessary restrictions which, according to the opposition and some experts, offended against the regulations, including the Constitution of the Republic of Poland, and at the same time it was possible to observe the actions of the government, continuing preparations for the elections, against inter alia opinion of a large part of the medical community (Musiał-Karg & Kapsa, 2021). It is hard not to get the impression that one of the crucial factors that decided that

PiS wanted to hold elections on time was the high support enjoyed by President Duda in the polls and the fear that as a result of the protracted pandemic and the need for the government to make unpopular decisions, the support of may decrease.

The attitude of the largest opposition party was also interesting. First, the Civic Platform and the entire KO criticized the government very strongly for continuing preparations for the elections. The more Kidawa-Błońska lost in the polls, the more criticism rose. However, when the election date was postponed by only 6 weeks, which made it possible to replace Kidawa-Błońska with Trzaskowski and actually fight for victory, there was no boycott of the election campaign and no more incitement to stay at home during the voting day.

By analyzing, inter alia, the way of organizing election rallies – including photos posted on the websites – both Duda and Trzaskowski, it can be seen that both parties and their candidates, in order to achieve victory, largely discounted the safety rules aimed at preventing the infection of COVID-19. In this way, the health and even the lives of people gathered at the rallies were at risk. The main political players had the impression that "the end justifies the means." With an eye to everything, it should be noticed that the hypothesis has been positively verified, as it turned out that both analyzed parties, when their candidates had a real chance of winning, agreed to run elections during the pandemic.

Referring to the results, it can be stated that both the pandemic and decision about the organization of the elections and the fight against the coronavirus, which were publicized by the opposition, did not affect President Duda's supporters enough to endanger his re-election. Although it should be noted that he only won in the second round, after a very close fight.

References

„II tura wyborów prezydenckich już w niedzielę". 2020.07.06. Retrieved from: www .platforma.org.

„Apel do Przewodniczącego Państwowej Komisji Wyborczej". 2020.05.04. Retrieved from: www.platforma.org.

Asplund, E., Clark A., James T.S. & Stevense B. (2020). "People with COVID-19 and those self-isolating must not be denied the vote". *LSE COVID 19 Blog*. Retrieved from: https://blogs.lse.ac.uk/COVID19/2020/10/23/people-with-COVID-19-and-those-self -isolating-must-not-be-denied-the-vote/.

Asplund, E. & James, T.S. (2020). "Elections and COVID-19: making democracy work in uncertain times". Retrieved from: https://www.democraticaudit.com/2020/03/30 /elections-and-COVID-19-making-democracy-work-in-uncertain-times/.

Bach, L., Guillouzouic, A. & Malgouyres, C. (2021). "Does holding elections during a COVID-19 pandemic put the lives of politicians at risk?". *Journal of Health Economics*, volume 78.

Bartoszewicz, M. 2020. „Rama interpretacyjna „pandemii COVID-19" a wybrane zasady propagandy politycznej – propozycja zestawienia zakresu użyteczności". *Acta Politica Polonica*, no 2.

Bertoli, S., Guichard, L. & Marchetta, F. (2020). "Turnout in the Municipal Elections of March 2020 and Excess Mortality During the COVID-19 Epidemic in France". *IZA – Institute of Labor Economics*.

"Bezpieczne wybory". 2020.04.20. Retrieved from: www.platforma.org.

Birch, S., Buril, F., Cheeseman, N., Clark, A., Darnolf, S., Dodsworth, S., Garber, L., Gutiérrez-Romero, R., Hollstein, T., James, T.S., Mohan, V. & Sawyer, K. (2020). "How to hold elections safely and democratically during the COVID-19 pandemic". *The British Academy*. London, doi.org/10.5871/bac19stf/9780856726507.001.

Chen, E., Chang, H., Rao, A., Lerman, K., Cowan, G. & Ferrara, E. (2021). "COVID-19 misinformation and the 2020 US presidential election". *The Harvard Kennedy School Misinformation Review* 1, no. 7, DOI: 10.37016/mr-2020-57.

Chrobak, P. (2021). „Wybory Prezydenta Rzeczypospolitej Polskiej na Pomorzu Zachodnim na tle kraju w 2020 roku". In T. Czapiewski & M. Siedziako (Eds.), *Kronika Szczecina 2020. Miasto w cieniu pandemii*. Szczecin.

Cybulska, A. (2020a). „Kto wygra wybory prezydenckie - przedwyborcze prognozy Polaków na progu kampanii wyborczej". *Komunikat z badań*, CBOS, no 26.

Cybulska, A. (2020c). „Preferencje przed I turą wyborów prezydenckich 2020". *Komunikat z badań*, CBOS, no 76.

Cybulska, A. (2020b). „Preferencje w wyborach prezydenckich na przełomie maja i czerwca". *Komunikat z badań*, CBOS, no 64.

Czapiewski, T. (2021). "Local Government in the Process of Organizing General Elections During the Pandemic – The Experience of the 2020 May Elections in Poland". *Przegląd Prawa Konstytucyjnego*, no 6 (64).

„Dziękuję za Waszą energię". (2020). Retrieved from: www.trzaskowski2020.pl.

Feliksiak, M. (2020). „Oceny działalności parlamentu prezydenta i władz samorządowych". *Komunikat z badań*, CBOS, no 9.

Frach, S. (2021). „Retoryka strachu w czasie pandemii COVID-19. Przypadek Emmanuela Macrona". *Athenaeum. Polskie Studia Politologiczne*, no 70 (2).

Gajda, A. 2020. "Restrictions on Human Rights and Freedoms During the Time of Epidemic in Poland". *Przegląd Prawa Konstytucyjnego*, no 5 (57).

Garnett, H.A., Bordeleau, J-N., Harell, A. & Stephenson, L. (2021). "Canadian Provincial Elections during the COVID-19 Pandemic". *International Institute for Democracy and Electoral Assistance*. Stockholm.

Gąbka, A. 20.05.2020.. „PO ostrzegała przed „kopertami śmierci", teraz chce zbiórki podpisów. Hipokryzja". Retrieved from: www.tvp.info.pl.

Giommoni, T. & Loumeau, G. (2020). "Lockdown and Voting Behaviour: A Natural Experiment on Postponed Elections during the COVID-19 Pandemic". Available at SSRN: https://ssrn.com/abstract=3659856 or http://dx.doi.org/10.2139/ssrn.36 59856.

Głowacki, A. (2020b). „Preferencje w potencjalnych korespondencyjnych wyborach prezydenckich". *Komunikat z badań*, CBOS, no 54.

Głowacki, A. (2020a). „Preferencje w wyb. prezydenckich w pierwszej połowie marca". *Komunikat z badań*, CBOS, no 35.

Hałub-Kowalczyk, O. (2020). "New Challenges for the Right to Privacy During the COVID-19 Pandemic – The Outline of the Problem". *Przegląd Prawa Konstytucyjnego*, no 5 (57).

Hasen, R.L. (2020). "Three Pathologies of American Voting Rights Illuminatedby the COVID-19 Pandemic, and How to Treat and Cure Them". *Election Law Journal*, Volume 19, Number 3, DOI: 10.1089/elj.2020.0646.

"Jak koronawirus wpływa na płuca?". 2020.03.28. *Rzeczpospolita*.

James, T.S. (2021). "New development: Running elections during a pandemic". *Public Money & Management*, volume 41, issue 1, DOI: 10.1080/09540962.2020.1783084.

James, T.S. & Alihodzic, S. (2020). "When Is It Democratic to Postpone an Election? Elections During Natural Disasters, COVID-19, and Emergency Situations". *Election Law Journal: Rules, Politics, and Policy*, Volume 19, Number 3, DOI: 10.1089 /elj.2020.0642.

Kasińska-Metryka, A. (2021). "The President – creator or prisoner of his own image? Psychopolitical determinants of the functioning of the Head of State exemplified by the Polish Presidency of Andrzej Duda". *Studia Politologiczne*, no 61.

Kazimierczuk, A. 28.03.2020. „Duda o terminie wyborów: może być nie do utrzymania". *Rzeczpospolita*.

„Kidawa-Błońska apeluje o bojkot wyborów prezydenckich i zawiesza kampanię". 29.03.2020. *Rzeczpospolita*.

„Komisja śledcza ds. nieprawidłowości przy zamówieniach związanych z COVID-19". 06.07.2020. Retrieved from: www.platforma.org.

Komunikat PKW z dnia 7 maja 2020 roku. Retrieved from: www.pkw.gov.pl.

Kousser, T., Hill S., Lockhart, M., Merolla, J.L. & Romero M. (2021). "How do Americans want elections to be run during the COVID-19 crisis?". *Research and Politics*, DOI: 10.1177/20531680211012228.

Krimmer, R., Duenas-Cid, D. & Krivonosova, I. (2020). "Debate: safeguarding democracy during pandemics. Social distancing, postal, or internet voting—the good, the bad or the ugly?". *Public Money & Management*, DOI: 10.1080/09540962.2020.1766222.

Kuczyńska-Zonik, A. (2021). "The Influence of New Technologies on the Election Process in Lithuania". *Przegląd Prawa Konstytucyjnego*, no 6 (64).

Landman, T. & Di Gennaro Splendore, L. (2020). "Pandemic democracy: elections and COVID-19". *Journal of Risk Research*, vol. 23, nos. 7–8, DOI: 10.1080/13669877 .2020.1765003.

Ludera-Ruszel, A. & Piękoś, K. (2021). "Restrictions in Freedom of Business Activity and Worker Rights. Comparative Analysis of Provisions in Force During the 1st Wave of COVID-19 Pandemic and Constitutional Regulations on the State of Emergency". *Przegląd Prawa Konstytucyjnego*, no 6 (64).

Ludwiniak, M. (2020). „Stereotypy polityków w kampaniach wyborczych". *Studia Politologiczne*, no 55.

Malużinas, M. (2021a). "Lithuanian Democracy under the State of Emergency: will the COVID-19 pandemic affect the assessment of the state of democracy in the country? – system analysis". *Athenaeum. Polskie Studia Politologiczne*, no 72 (4).

Malużinas, M. (2021b). „Wybory parlamentarne w czasie pandemii COVID-19. Przykład wyborów litewskich w 2020 r.". *Athenaeum. Polskie Studia Politologiczne*, no 69 (1).

„Małgorzata Kidawa-Błońska wysyła interpelację do Premiera Morawieckiego ws. głosowania Polonii". 16.04.2020. Retrieved from: www.kidawa2020.pl.

Mikołajczyk, M. (2021). "State policy towards labour market changes caused by COVID-19". *Athenaeum. Polskie Studia Politologiczne*, no 71 (3).

„Multimedia". (2020). Retrieved from: www.andrzejduda.pl.

Musiał-Karg M. (2021). „Głosowanie korespondencyjne podczas pandemii COVID-19. Doświadczenia z polskich wyborów prezydenckich w 2020 r.". *Przegląd Prawa Konstytucyjnego*, no 2 (60).

Musiał-Karg M. & Kapsa I. (2021). "Debate: Voting challenges in a pandemic – Poland". *Public Money & Management*, no 41 (1).

„NOWA SOLIDARNOŚĆ Program Rafała Trzaskowskiego 2020". (2020). Retrieved from: www.trzaskowski2020.pl.

Obwieszczenie PKW z dnia 15 kwietnia 2020 r. o kandydatach na Prezydenta RP w wyborach zarządzonych na dzień 10 maja 2020 r.

Obwieszczenie PKW z dnia 12 czerwca 2020 r. o kandydatach na Prezydenta RP w wyborach zarządzonych na dzień 28 czerwca 2020 r.

Obwieszczenie PKW z dnia 30 czerwca 2020 r. o wynikach głosowania i wyniku wyborów Prezydenta RP, zarządzonych na dzień 28 czerwca 2020 r., Dz.U. 2020, poz. 1163.

Obwieszczenie PKW z dnia 13 lipca 2020 r. o wynikach ponownego głosowania i wyniku wyborów Prezydenta RP, Dz.U. 2020, poz. 1238.

Onasz, M. (2021). "Quality of Democratic Election Process during the COVID-19 Pandemic: The Schedler's chain of democratic choice perspective". *Athenaeum. Polskie Studia Politologiczne*, no 72 (4).

„Oni Wybory. My Życie – Małgorzata Kidawa-Błońska i Rafał Trzaskowski o działaniach samorządu w obliczu koronawirusa". 2020.04.23. Retrieved from: www.kidawa2020.pl.

„#pakietbezpieczeństwa – działania gospodarcze w związku z koronawirusem". 18.03.2020. Retrieved from: www.platforma.org; www.kidawa2020.pl.

Pankowski, K. (2020a). „Preferencje w pierwszej turze wyborów prezydenckich na progu kampanii wyborczej". *Komunika z badań*, CBOS, no 23.

Piękoś, K. (2020). "Selected Pro-Turnout Initiatives of Province Self-Governments on the Example of the Second Round of Presidential Elections in Poland in 2020". *Przegląd Prawa Konstytucyjnego*, no 6 (58).

PKW ZPOW-421-24/20. Wyjaśnienia dotyczące postępowania komisarzy wyborczych i organów gmin w związku z zakończeniem wyborów Prezydenta RP zarządzonych na dzień 10 maja 2020 r.

"Plan Dudy". (2020). Retrieved from: www.andrzejduda.pl.

Postanowienie Marszałka Sejmu RP z dnia 3 czerwca 2020 r. w sprawie zarządzenia wyborów Prezydenta RP, Dz.U. 2020, poz. 988.

Postanowienie Sądu Najwyższego z 12 czerwca 2020 r., sygn. akt I NSW 61/20.

Postanowienie Marszałka Sejmu RP z dnia 5 lutego 2020 r. w sprawie zarządzenia wyborów Prezydenta RP, Dz.U. 2020, poz. 184.

„Prawnicy o nocnych zmianach w Kodeksie wyborczym: haniebne i bandyckie głosowanie". 28.03.2020. *Rzeczpospolita*.

Pyrzyńska A. 2021. „Warunki rejestracji kandydata na Prezydenta RP w wyborach zarządzonych na 28.06.2020 r.". *Państwo i Prawo*, no 2.

„Rafał Trzaskowski kandydatem na Prezydenta RP". 15.05.2020. Retrieved from: www.platforma.org.

Rakowska-Trela, A. (2021). „Wybory prezydenckie 2020". *Państwo i Prawo*, no 9.

„Raport Kidawy: Problemy samorządów w obliczu niewydolnych działań rządu w walce z koronawirusem". 20.03.2020. Retrieved from: www.kidawa2020.pl.

Roguska, B. (2020). „Preferencje partyjne w styczniu". *Komunika z badań*, CBOS, no 8.

Rozporządzenie Ministra Zdrowia z dnia 13 marca 2020 r. w sprawie ogłoszenia na obszarze Rzeczypospolitej Polskiej stanu zagrożenia epidemicznego, Dz.U. 2020, poz. 433.

Rozporządzenie Ministra Zdrowia z dnia 24 marca 2020 r. zmieniające rozporządzenie w sprawie ogłoszenia na obszarze Rzeczypospolitej Polskiej stanu epidemii, Dz.U. 2020, poz. 522.

Rytel-Warzocha, A. (2020). "Postal Voting as an Ultimate Rescue Measure for Presidential Election During the COVID-19 Pandemic in Poland". *Przegląd Prawa Konstytucyjnego*, no 5 (57).

„Rząd uprawia propagandę i zajmuje się wyborami zamiast zająć się realną pomocą dla Polaków – parliamentary speech of Małgorzata Kidawa-Błońska". 6.04.2020. Retrieved from: www.kidawa2020.pl.

„Składamy wniosek o odwołanie ministra Jacka Sasina". 8.05.2020. Retrieved from: www.platforma.org.

„Sondaż: 10 maja Andrzej Duda wygrałby w I turze". 30.03.2020. *Rzeczpospolita.*

„Sondaż: Duda wygrywa w pierwszej turze, Kidawa-Błońska ostatnia". 24.04.2020. *Rzeczpospolita.*

„Sondaż dla „Wiadomości": 0,62 pkt. proc. przewagi Dudy". 10.07.2020. *Rzeczpospolita.*

„Spotkania otwarte Małgorzaty Kidawy-Błońskiej zawieszone ze względu na zagrożenie koronawirusem". 10.03.2020. Retrieved from: www.kidawa2020.pl.

Stanisz, P. (2021). „Ograniczenia wolności kultu religijnego w czasie pandemii COVID-19: między konstytucyjnością a efektywnością". *Przegląd Sejmowy*, no 3 (164).

Strzelecki, M. 22.03.2020. "Virus Crisis Boosts Polish President Before Vote Under Lock-down". *Bloomberg*, Retrieved from: <https://www.bloomberg.com/news/articles /2020-03-22/virus-crisis-boosts-president-before-vote-in-locked-downpoland>.

Uchwała PKW nr 129/2020 z dnia 10 maja 2020 r. w sprawie stwierdzenia braku możliwości głosowania na kandydatów w wyborach Prezydenta RP.

Uliasz, R., (2021), „Wolność działalności gospodarczej a pandemia COVID-19. Uwagi w kontekście konstytucyjnego zakazu naruszania istoty wolności i praw (art. 31 ust. 3 zd. 2 Konstytucji RP)", *Przegląd Prawa Konstytucyjnego*, no 5 (63).

Urbaniak, K. & Urbaniak, M. (2021). "Limitation of Human and Civil Rights and Free-doms During the Pandemic in Poland". *Przegląd Prawa Konstytucyjnego*, no 6 (64).

Ustawa z dnia 5 grudnia 2008 r. o zapobieganiu oraz zwalczaniu zakażeń i chorób zakaźnych u ludzi, Dz.U. 2019, poz. 1239.

Ustawa z dnia 5 stycznia 2011 r. Kodeks wyborczy, Dz.U. 2020, poz. 1319.

Ustawa z dnia 2 marca 2020 r. o szczególnych rozwiązaniach związanych z zapobieganiem, przeciwdziałaniem i zwalczaniem COVID-19, innych chorób zakaźnych oraz wywołanych nimi sytuacji kryzysowych, Dz.U. 2020, poz. 374.

Ustawa z dnia 6 kwietnia 2020 r. o szczególnych zasadach przeprowadzania wyborów powszechnych na Prezydenta RP zarządzonych w 2020 r., Dz.U. 2020, poz. 827 (repealed).

Ustawa z dnia 16 kwietnia 2020 r. o szczególnych instrumentach wsparcia w związku z rozprzestrzenianiem się wirusa SARS-CoV-2, Dz.U. 2020, poz. 695.

Ustawa z dnia 2 czerwca 2020 r. o szczególnych zasadach organizacji wyborów powszechnych na Prezydenta RP zarządzonych w 2020 r. z możliwością głosowania korespondencyjnego, Dz.U. 2020, poz. 979.

Uziębło, P. (2021). „Odpowiedzialność organów władzy państwowej i ich członków za niekonstytucyjne ograniczenia praw i wolności jednostki w czasie stanu zagrożenia epidemicznego i stanu epidemii". *Przegląd Konstytucyjny*, no 1.

Vashchanka, V. (2020). "Political manoeuvres and legal conundrums amid the COVID-19 pandemic: the 2020 presidential election in Poland". *International Institute for Democracy and Electoral Assistance*, Stockholm.

Węgrzyn, J. (2021). „Realizacja normy programowej wynikającej z art. 68 ust. 4 Konstytucji RP w stanie epidemii COVID-19 (uwagi ogólne)". *Przegląd Prawa Konstytucyjnego*, no 3 (61).

„Wniosek do NIK ws. organizacji wyborów". 22.04.2020. Retrieved from: www.platforma.org.

„Wprowadźmy stan klęski żywiołowej!". 26.03.2020. Retrieved from: www.platforma .org.

„Wybory prezydenckie już w niedzielę". 23.06.2020. Retrieved from: www.platforma .org.

„Wybory w czasie epidemii byłyby działaniem zbrodniczym – Małgorzata Kidawa-Błońska zawiesza kampanię i wzywa do bojkotu wyborów 10 maja". 31.03.2020. Retrieved from: www.kidawa2020.pl.

CHAPTER 26

Polish Political Leaders' Views on Holding the Presidential Election during the COVID-19 Pandemic

Quantitative and Qualitative Analysis of Parliamentary Speeches

Jakub Klepański and Maciej Hartliński

26.1   Introduction

The presidential election is one of the most important political events in a democratic state. The way it is organized and the level of citizens' participation have a fundamental impact on the level of legitimacy of power. That is why its effective and legitimate conduct during the pandemic should be a priority, essentially when it comes to observing all the regulations related to the electoral law resulting from the Constitution and other legal acts.

When face-to-face contact was considerably limited, public institutions did not function on their regular basis and the world adopted the remote mode of work and education, the presidential election was approaching in Poland. Urgent and intense like never before, the matter of electoral engineering emerged as one of the most important issues in public debate. It assumed the form of various proposals of holding the election (Flis & Marcinkiewicz, 2020). Numerous proposals collided with the existing law to a greater or lesser extent (Michalak, 2020; Szczepański, 2020; Rakowska-Trela, 2020). Wishing to adapt to the current conditions, the government was determined to organize the election by mail (Flis & Ciszewski, 2020; Tatarczyk & Wojtasik, 2022), yet it had to reconcile its actions – both aiming at conducting the election as well as rising to the challenges of managing the COVID-19 pandemic (Lipiński, 2021; Piontek & Ossowski, 2021). As a consequence of the confusion engendered by the pandemic, the election did not finally take place on the originally scheduled date of 10 May 2020. Eventually, the first round was held on 28 June 2020 and the run-off on 12 July 2020 (Sula, Madej & Błaszczyński, 2021).

The aim of this study is to analyse the activity of Polish political leaders participating in parliamentary debate in relation to holding the presidential election during the pandemic, especially in the context of the discussion on failing to organise it on the originally established date. The main research question concerns the policies and views of political leaders on holding the election during the pandemic. It is crucial to determine what proposals in favour of organising the election when observing the law and ensuring the safety of citizens were made by the most important politicians in the country.

Methodology-wise, quantitative and qualitative analyses were employed to compare the activity of particular political leaders and the content of their proposals. A generative statistical model of Latent Dirichlet Allocation (LDA) useful for discovering topics present in documents was applied. The primary source material included speeches of political leaders in the Sejm. The scrutiny encompassed a total of 548 speeches made by leaders of all political parties and presidents of parliamentary clubs and parliamentary circles present in the Polish Parliament of the 9th Term, which was elected in 2019.

The study consists of five parts. After introducing the key aspects of the study, attention will be focused on the assumptions behind the research process, thus a review of the most important themes from the literature of the subject and a detailed description of the research assumptions will be provided. In the next step, quantitative and qualitative analyses are to be conducted. Such a structure of the study will make it possible to draw conclusions based on the conducted research.

26.2   Research Design

Public speeches contain important clues allowing one to recognise the values politicians cherish and thus they play an important political role. Consequently, they are a key element of democracy, showing ideological diversity a plethora of proposals for solving political problems (van Dijk, 1997; Triadafilopoulos, 1999).

Parliamentary discourse is an excellent source of knowledge about policies and views of political leaders. The words they say in the parliament, in many cases, quickly become widely disseminated by the media and reach citizens. They are understood to be an official position of a given politician and often of the party they represent. This allows citizens to relate their own individual views to those put forward by political leaders and their parties (Ilie, 2015).

The importance of parliamentary discourse has been recognised by numerous scholars (van Dijk, 1993; 2004; Bayley, 2004; Martin, 2011). Having considered their analyses, it can be concluded that this type of political activity is a crucial element of democracy. It is not uncommon for policies and views to contradict each other, thus triggering debate and confrontation of different visions.

As mentioned earlier, public speeches constitute exceptionally valuable research material that can be analysed from several perspectives. Research on speeches by American presidents has been undertaken exceptionally often (Lewis, 1997; Gunawan, 2010; Ping & Lingling 2017; Hidayat & Nababan & Djatmika 2019; Liu, 2012). The distinctive feature of such studies consists in their high level of methodological diversity. This makes them extremely valuable and inspiring in building the research process followed in the present study.

The research technique that was applied involves searching for keywords in speeches, and is derived from Shaul Shenhav's (2004) research. The purpose of this process is to learn about the context of the speech, to determine the specifics of the language used and to identify the narrative technique employed by a given politician.

Quantitative analyses studying parliamentary discourse can be exemplified by the work of Martin G. Søyland and Emanuele Lapponi (2017). Based on constructed linguistic classifiers, the positions and statements of political parties in Norway were examined. The aim of the study was to determine the level of polarisation of the political scene in the country. The study showed that the use of such innovative quantitative methods is risky and must be employed judiciously and carefully. It turned out that parties that are ideologically close to each other are not confused more often than those that are more distant from each other.

Automated topic models are increasingly often used in parliamentary speech research. One of the most commonly employed ones – also used in the following research – is Latent Dirichlet Allocation, also employed in a study of speeches by New Zealand MPs (Curran et al., 2018). The results indicated how the popularity of given topics changed over time. In addition, the authors of the study diagnosed the links between topic trends followed by political parties in their speeches and particular social, economic and legislative events. Moreover, they identified which parties played a dominant role in the discourse and which parties participated only in debate on a given topic.

A model derivative of the LDA was used by Agnieszka Kwiatkowska (2017) in her research on parliamentary discourse. Using the STM (structural topic model) method, the author measured the level of language radicalisation in the Polish parliament. The results based on automated algorithms indicated that Polish MPs often used radical language, although this had become increasingly noticeable in recent years.

The authors of the present study aimed to verify the level of interest in the topic of the 2020 presidential election visible in the scrutinised speeches. For this reason, they employed the topic modelling technique of Latent Dirichlet Allocation (Blei & Ng & Jordan, 2003). This is a popular method used in text analysis research, and results it yields are considered highly reliable (Jelodar et al. 2019; Curran, 2018; Calvo-González & Eizmendi & Reyes, 2018; Kaleru & Dhanikonda, 2018; Yano & Cohen & Smith, 2009; Zirn & Stuckenschmidt, 2014).

The LDA topic modelling consists in processing the content of the studied material by linking co-occurring words according to certain parameters (e.g. frequency) and language specificity. The application of LDA algorithms allowed for the automated determination of ten most important topic profiles in the studied speeches. The analysis was conducted using the R language in the RStudio environment.

Prior to this stage of analysis, the speeches were pre-processed to maximise the precision of the study. This included: removal of Polish characters, numbers and punctuation marks; removal of everything that is not the speech itself from the transcript (e.g. comments from the floor, utterances of the Speaker of the Sejm, descriptions of the situation in the chamber, etc.); removal of stopwords – a majority of pronouns, prepositions, conjunctions, numerals, etc., that is words irrelevant to the study. This preliminary modelling facilitated compiling a suitable corpus of data prepared for analysis in the R language. At this point, it should be noted that the empty databases of J. Gowin and P. Kukiz were discarded as neither of the politicians took part in the parliamentary debate during the period under scrutiny.

The main research question of the present study concerns determining the attitude towards holding the election during the pandemic presented by political leaders in Poland. Specific questions refer to the following dilemmas: How often did politicians of the parties forming the government and of the opposition parties express their views on the 2020 presidential election? Are there any correlations between party affiliation and frequency of participation in parliamentary debates on the topic under scrutiny? What statements and demands concerning the 2020 presidential election were voiced by the leaders in question?

The research process was divided into two main stages: quantitative analysis, which allowed for a comparison of undertaken activity, and qualitative analysis, which made it possible to identify particular demands voiced by political leaders concerning the conduct of the 2020 election during the pandemic. The method of critical discourse analysis was used to carry out a comparative study of these positions and their descriptions in the current socio-political context.

In order to achieve the research objective, the undertaken analysis included 548 speeches delivered in the Sejm of the Republic of Poland by selected political leaders during parliamentary sessions since the beginning of the 9th term (12 November 2019) until the date of the swearing-in of President of the

Republic of Poland Andrzej Duda for the second term (6 August 2020). This timeframe overlaps with the beginning of the COVID-19 pandemic in Poland, thus obviously the presidential election took place during it. The analysis encompassed the speeches of leaders of all political parties and chairpersons of parliamentary clubs and parliamentary circles that were represented in the Sejm of the Republic of Poland of the 9th term (2019–2023)[1] during the period under scrutiny (i.e. 12 November 2019 – 6 August 2020).[2]

26.3   Quantitative Analysis

The conducted analysis shows ten most frequently co-occurring linguistic relations, each consisting of ten words. On the basis of the presented results, it can be concluded that the LDA method helped to identify the most frequent topics in the examined speeches as each of the figures contains at least one keyword. On their basis, the following topic profiles were identified, and they correspond to numbers 1–10 in Figure 26.1: State; Security; Economic policy; Judiciary; State budget; Politics; Society; Elections and health; Women's rights; The left, social policy.

The results presented above allow one to conclude that during the period under scrutiny politicians spoke relatively frequently about the upcoming election. An interesting situation occurred in profile "8," where the algorithm ranked the keywords "elections" and "health" within the same topic profile. On

---

1   The Union of European Democrats party is an exception. Its chairperson, Elżbieta Bińczycka, did not win an MP's seat in the 2019 parliamentary elections. Therefore, no speeches by a politician of this party were included in the research.

2   The analysed speeches of politicians concerned only the period in which they served as president or chairman of their party. Jarosław Kaczyński (chariman of Law and Justice), Jarosław Gowin (chariman of Agreement), Zbigniew Ziobro (chairman of United Poland), Ryszard Terlecki (chairman of the parliamentary club – Law and Justice), Borys Budka (chairman of Civic Platform, chairman of the parliamentary club – Civic Coalition), Cezary Tomczyk (chairman of the parliamentary club – Civic Coalition from 25 september 2020 to 22 july 2021), Adam Szłapka (chariman of Modern), Barbara Nowacka (chairman of Polish Initiative), Małgorzata Tracz (women co-chariman of Green Party; Marek Kossakowski, Wojciech Kubalewski as co-chairmen are not counted. They were not memebers of the parliament), Krzysztof Gawkowski (charimen of the parliamentary club – Left), Włodzimierz Czarzasty (chairman of Left Democratic Alliance), Adrian Zandberg (one of the leaders of the Left coalition, co-founder and the most recognizable politician of the Together party, in the parliamentary elections he obtained the best election result among all members of this party – over 140 thousand votes), Władysław Kosiniak-Kamysz (chairman of Polish People's Party), Paweł Kukiz (chairman of Kukiz'15), Jakub Kulesza (chairman of the parliamentary club – Confederation), Janusz Korwin-Mikke (chairman of KORWiN), Grzegorz Braun (chairman of Confederation of the Polish Crown), Robert Winnicki (chairman of National Movement).

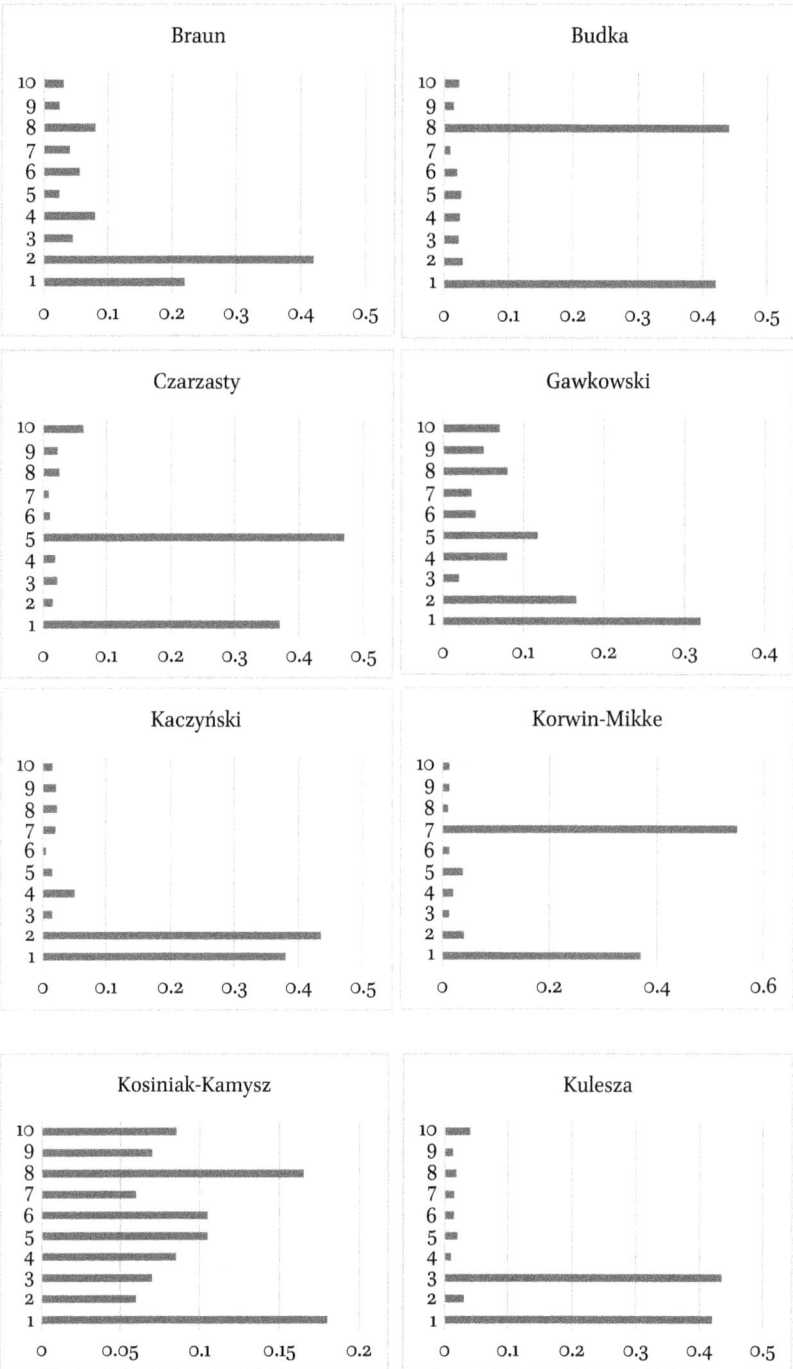

FIGURE 26.1   Frequency of topic profiles in speeches of leaders under scrutiny

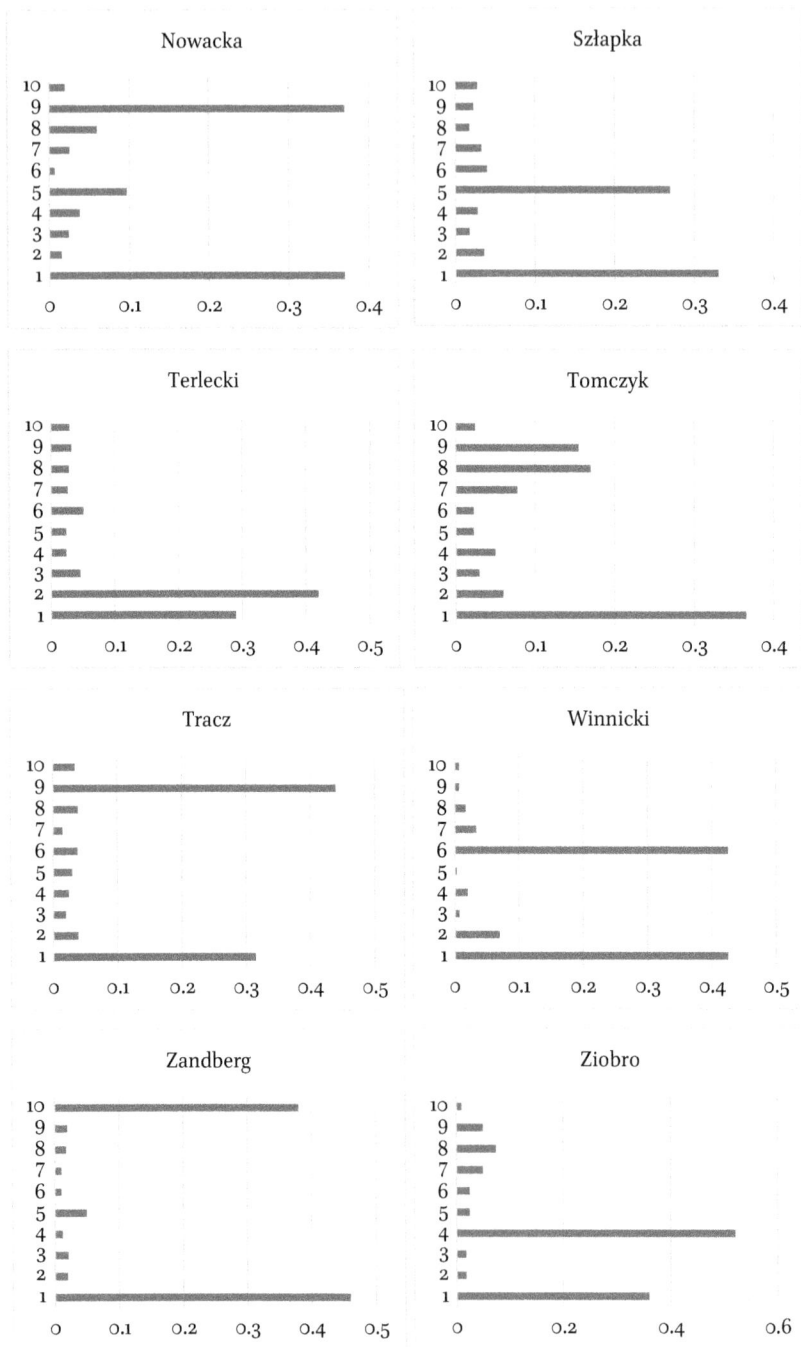

FIGURE 26.1   (*Continued*)

this basis, it can be supposed that politicians spoke about the election mainly in the context of the health-related situation in the country.

From the perspective of the present research, "Elections and health" proves to be the most important topic profile. The results clearly show that politicians who – according to the algorithms – most often spoke about the election or the health-related situation in the country are B. Budka, W. Kosiniak-Kamysz, A. Szłapka and C. Tomczyk. It is worth accentuating the low level of involvement of politicians from the currently ruling coalition (J. Kaczyński, R. Terlecki, Z. Ziobro, J. Gowin did not make any statement in the period under scrutiny).

Moreover, the results depicted in Figure 26.1 represent topic interests of individual leaders. Based on that, it can be concluded that their parliamentary discourse during the period under scrutiny was highly diversified in this matter.

From the perspective of the study, "elections" and "president" are the most important keywords. These two keywords served as a tool in the next stage of the research, which consisted in highlighting speeches in which the politicians under scrutiny directly referred to the topic of the 2020 presidential election. For the purpose of this analysis, the words "election" and "president" were traced in each speech (in the entire corpus of data).

Using this method allowed for the search of keywords employed in several linguistic forms. Additionally, in order to ensure the maximum precision of this part of analysis, all the speeches highlighted by the search engine were also checked for their subject-matter content. This was aimed at diagnosing whether a given speech in which the search engine had identified the phrase in question actually referred to the topic of the presidential election. Thanks to this step, a special sub-corpus of data was created in which only speeches by leaders directly relating to the topic under scrutiny were collected.

Out of a total of 5233 speeches delivered at the sessions of the Sejm of the Republic of Poland during the analysed period, 548 were delivered by political leaders. The total $\%_1$ index is 10.47, which corresponds to the percentage of leaders in parliamentary discourse during the analysed period. It can therefore be concluded that every tenth speech was delivered by the politicians distinguished in the study.

On average, every tenth speech of the leaders in question concerned the analysed topic. This is evidenced by the collected results – out of the 548 speeches mentioned above, 59 addressed topics related to the 2020 presidential election in Poland. The total value of the $\%_3$ index was 0.11.

Leaders in question spoke relatively most often during the 11th session of the Sejm ($\%_1 = 14$; $\%_2 = 3.65$). Based on the quoted variables, it can be seen that out of 20 speeches of the leader, on average 3 were related to the analysed topic. From the 2nd to the 7th session of the Sejm of the 9th term, the participation of leaders in parliamentary debate can be described as low.

Interest in the presidential election as a topic increased considerably from the 8th session (26–27 March 2020). Significantly, it was the time the election campaign was beginning. The heightened level of interest in this issue continued until the 15th session of the Sejm (22–24 July), but the levels of particular indicators were unstable.

In terms of the number of speeches delivered, G. Braun (Confederation of the Polish Crown) was the most active of all leaders, with a total of 144 speeches at the Sejm in the period under investigation (this is over 26.2% of all leaders' speeches). The total value of the variable $\%_1$ is 2.75, which analogically is the highest result among the investigated politicians. In turn, the leaders with the lowest number of speeches in the Sejm in the specified period are: J. Gowin and P. Kukiz (both of them did not speak even once during the period under scrutiny). Interestingly, leaders of the party which is part of the so-called United Right (J. Kaczyński, J. Gowin, Z. Ziobro, R. Terlecki) made speeches on

TABLE 26.1   The number of speeches given by leaders on the 2020 presidential election

	J. Kaczyński	R. Terlecki	Z. Ziobro	J. Gowin	B. Budka	A. Szłapka	B. Nowacka	M. Tracz	C. Tomczyk	W. Czarzasty	A. Zandberg	K. Gawkowski	W. Kosiniak-Kamysz	P. Kukiz	J. Korwin-Mikke	G. Braun	R. Winnicki	J. Kulesza
session 1	0	0	0	0	0	0	0	0	0	0	0	0	0	0	0	0	0	0
session 2	0	0	0	0	0	1	0	0	0	0	0	0	0	0	0	0	0	0
session 3	0	0	0	0	0	0	0	0	0	0	0	0	0	0	0	0	0	0
session 4	0	0	0	0	0	0	0	0	0	0	0	0	0	0	0	0	0	0
session 5	0	0	0	0	0	0	0	0	0	0	0	0	1	0	0	0	0	0
session 6	0	0	0	0	0	0	0	0	0	0	0	0	0	0	0	0	0	0
session 7	0	0	0	0	0	0	0	0	0	0	0	0	0	0	0	0	0	0
session 8	0	0	0	0	0	0	0	0	0	0	0	0	0	0	0	0	0	0
session 9	0	0	0	0	6	0	0	1	0	0	0	1	3	0	1	1	0	0
session 10	0	0	0	0	0	0	0	0	0	0	0	1	0	0	0	0	0	0
session 11	0	0	0	0	8	1	1	1	0	0	0	5	3	0	0	3	0	2
session 12	0	0	0	0	2	0	1	1	0	1	0	1	2	0	0	2	1	1
session 13	0	0	0	0	0	0	0	0	0	0	0	0	0	0	0	0	1	0
session 14	0	0	0	0	3	0	1	0	0	0	0	0	0	0	0	1	0	0
session 15	0	0	0	0	0	0	0	0	0	0	0	0	0	0	1	0	0	0

SOURCE: OWN CALCULATIONS BASED ON DATA FROM PARLIAMENTARY SPEECHES

the topic in question very rarely in comparison to leaders of opposition parties, as they spoke only 16 times altogether. Those who made the greatest number of speeches were B. Budka (LWW = 19) and W. Kosiniak-Kamysz (LWW = 9).

The leaders of the coalition forming the parliamentary majority (J. Kaczyński, R. Terlecki, Z. Ziobro, J. Gowin) did not speak about the elections even once in the analysed period.

26.4   Qualitative Analysis

Before commencing the present analysis, it was necessary to read the content of the identified 59 speeches by leaders in which they made references to the topic of the 2020 presidential election. Then, the positions and statements of each leader in the context of the topic under analysis were identified, followed by their comparative analysis.

Starting the qualitative analysis from the speeches of the government coalition party leaders, it should be noted that none of them (that is J. Kaczyński, R. Terlecki, Z. Ziobro as well as J. Gowin) spoke about the presidential election in the Polish parliament during the period under scrutiny. Thus, it is impossible to determine their positions. Nevertheless, the lack of participation of the United Right leaders in the debate on such an important topic is an intriguing phenomenon. However, it is difficult to pinpoint unequivocally what caused such an attitude on the part of these leaders.

On the other hand, the politician who spoke most often (among the analysed ones in the selected period) about the 2020 presidential election is B. Budka. In April 2020, then the leader of Civic Platform, he often urged the Parliament to postpone the presidential election, originally planned for 10 May, 2020, due to the coronavirus pandemic: "(...) Forget about the election on 10 May. Let's focus on working together, let's do something good together for Poland and Poles, and then, when the epidemic is over, there the right time for the election will come. The sooner you understand this, as Prime Minister Gowin did, the better for you, but also the better for Poland."

When it was proposed that the presidential election be held by mail, B. Budka opposed this solution vehemently, questioning its legitimacy: "(...) It is shameful that you are trying to compromise the Polish electoral system. The post office is not capable of delivering mail on time at the moment because there are not enough postmen, and you want to hold the election by mail. Do you want only one electoral commission in each municipality and only one in each district in Warsaw? This will be embarrassment in front of the whole Europe and the whole of Poland. (...) What legitimacy will there be for a person to come to power in this way, in a way that is morally crude and fraudulent, and finally in a way that generations will remember as aimed solely at granting you the power? Madam Speaker, Honourable Members, this bill is obscene (...)". In his speeches, the politician repeatedly called for introducing a state of natural disaster in the country and consequently, postpone the election: "(...) The only constitutional right of the government and the right of this majority to postpone the election in accordance with the Constitution was to declare a state of natural disaster (...)."

After the election, assessing the campaign and the election process, B. Budka said: "(...) Ladies and Gentlemen, you used the state administration to make the election not equal and not universal. You have committed many abuses which, in our opinion, could have affected the election result (...)." In support of his thesis that the election was unfair, he argued that the state institutions had been involved in promoting A. Duda, unequal financial limits for candidates had been adopted, and A. Duda had been favoured in the public media.

In turn, the leader of the Nowoczesna (Modern) party, A. Szłapka, spoke twice on the issue of the presidential election. The politician said that the Polish state was compromised by the fact that the election of 10 May 2020 did not take place. He criticised the government for failing to impose a state of natural disaster, which would have legitimised the postponement of the election date: "(...) The election was supposed to be held in Poland on 10 May. It was not held. It simply did not take place. And two days after that date we still do not know when the election is to take place or under what conditions. We face chaos: chaos related to the pandemic, chaos related to the economy, constitutional chaos. Mr. Prime Minister, we are in chaos. Do you really still believe that there were no grounds for imposing a state of natural disaster? (...)." It can be stated that the position of A. Szłapka on the subject in question is the same as the one expressed by B. Budka.

B. Nowacka, the leader of Inicjatywa Polska (Polish Initiative), which is part of the Civic Coalition, in her statements criticised the possibility of holding the election by mail the way it had been proposed by the government: "(...) A question to Law and Justice (PL. PiS) MPs: When will you put an end to these Sasinaria [Jacek Sasin is a minister in the Law and Justice government responsible for the electoral process, and his activity is believed by the opposition to be the essence of Law and Justice incompetence in relation to the 2020 election; Sasinaria is a term coined to refer to that] (...) Madam Minister, Article 14 is scandalous. You are replacing Minister Sasin with Speaker Witek. It looks more pleasant, but she is still not the National Electoral Commission, and you yourself said that this body should have full control over the electoral process. Why do you want to act against small municipalities? Why don't you help them organise electoral commissions in safe conditions? It is the poorest municipalities that will suffer because of your regulations. You are the ones who failed to prepare the election, and the money should go to small municipalities instead of sponsoring Mr Sasin's whims. And the third thing. How are you going to support postal workers? (...)."

When the election process was over, Nowacka decided to voice a summary of the activities undertaken by the ruling parties. Her words are very similar to those of B. Budka, although in addition she paid special attention to the involvement of government members in A. Duda's campaign: "(...) Elections are a special occasion. (...) You have ruined this celebration, Ladies and Gentlemen of Law and Justice. You ruined it in an undignified and disgusting way, because this election was neither fair nor equal. Yet it was a success of the citizens, those who went to the polls despite contempt and hatred shown on public TV, despite the leaflets distributed by the Polish Post Office. (...) Are you not ashamed that for several months we have been watching a campaign of hatred, excluding not only Rafał Trzaskowski, but every person who dares to think differently than you? These were ministers and prime ministers, not ordinary politicians, who participated in the presidential campaign of Andrzej Duda. The prime minister – 200 campaign meetings, the president's office – also involved in the campaign. (...) Shame on you. You have ruined this celebration of democracy (...)."

The last politician from the Civic Coalition whose speeches are included in the analysis is M. Tracz, the leader of the Green party. In speeches in which she referred to the topic of the election, she criticised the government for seeking to organise it – originally – on 10 May, without taking into consideration the unfolding pandemic: "(...) I am ashamed that today we, MPs of the Sejm, are discussing the bill introducing changes to the electoral law. I am ashamed standing in front of Polish women and men who are facing new challenges day by day, who are now losing their jobs or closing down their businesses, who are losing their livelihoods. I am ashamed standing in front of the healthcare workers who are putting their lives at risk on the front line fighting this epidemic. I am ashamed that we are not dealing with the problems of Polish women and men that are affecting them here and now. Instead, we are dealing with the selfish interests of one party and one candidate – a party and a candidate who, as we can see, do not care for human health and life, the health and life of their voters, postal workers, electoral commission workers (...)."

Moreover, the MP openly criticised the government for not imposing a state of natural disaster, as well as for seeking to organise the election by mail: "(...) Today, once again, instead of dealing with the economic crisis, the health crisis, the social crisis, we are dealing with a constitutional crisis, a crisis of democracy that you, the United Right government, have caused. A crisis which could have been avoided if you had listened to the opposition, which had been calling on you to declare a state of natural disaster for two months. But you preferred, in your obstinacy, in your arrogance, to go ahead with the election in May. And for this task you chose the worst organiser under the sun – Minister Sasin. He did not organise the election for you, yet along the way he had broken the law several times, he had spent millions of zlotys, and all that will be left of him is a new CEO of the Polish Post Office and several tonnes of waste paper. Where are these packages? 33 million election packages. Who is looking after them now? Why are there 10% more of them than the number of all the voters?"

The results of the analysis of the Civic Coalition leaders' positions and statements reveal that their views on the subject of the 2020 presidential election are identical and concern the same issues. They are based on criticism of the government's actions, especially on the following levels: failure to introduce a state of natural disaster; pursuit of elections by mail; calling into question fairness and equality of the election because of the involvement of state institutions in A. Duda's campaign. At the same time, there was not a single element in the scrutinised speeches in which these politicians supported the solutions proposed by the government.

The next politicians whose statements undergo scrutiny are leaders of the Left coalition: W. Czarzasty, A. Zandberg and K. Gawkowski. A. Zandberg did not speak about the presidential election in the period under analysis, while W. Czarzasty spoke only once on the topic. Like leaders of the Civic Coalition, he also openly criticised the idea of holding it by mail: "(...) Minister Sasin printed ballots without any procedure, without any legal basis, and finally lost them. He does not know where 30 million ballots are. All this cost us 68 million PLN. (...) Mr. Prime Minister, there are articles for this in the Penal Code: articles 231 and 296 of the Penal Code (...)." Unlike leaders of the Civic Coalition though, Czarzasty did not speak about other aspects, such as the introduction of a state of natural disaster. He also chose not to summarise the election process after the election was finally held.

K. Gawkowski spoke much more extensively on the examined topic than W. Czarzasty. The politician clearly criticized the government for focusing too much on issues related to organizing the election instead of fighting the pandemic. He also voiced the need to introduce a state of natural disaster, which would mean postponing the election: "(...) For a week, you have not submitted a single bill, a single proposal that could clearly show how you will help employees and entrepreneurs. (...) We demand that a state of natural disaster be introduced. It is a constitutional way of postponing the election, quickly and effectively. It is also fully justified in the state we are in, the epidemic state. Don't even think of introducing a state of emergency, because people will come after you sooner than you think. Postpone this election and start dealing with what is truly important (...)." Moreover, Gawkowski repeatedly criticised

the idea of holding the election by mail, highlighting problems with its legitimacy: "(...) The truth is that Law and Justice MPs are happy to talk about the
election on TV, but in the Sejm they do not want to discuss it. What are you
afraid of? Are you afraid the OSCE says that the election will be undemocratic,
or are you afraid of the decision announced by the head of the National Electoral Commission, who said that the elections will not be free? You persuade
local government institutions to break the law, you print ballots to manipulate
the result, and cases concerning the legitimacy of the election are dismissed by
the prosecutor in no time (...)."

On the basis of the utterances quoted above, it ought to be concluded that
leaders of the Left were highly critical of the government's actions regarding
the organisation of the 2020 presidential election, focusing on similar issues as
the Civic Coalition politicians.

The leader of the Polish People's Party, W. Kosiniak-Kamysz, himself a candidate in the presidential election of 2020, relatively often commented on its
organisation and course. The politician repeatedly stressed that in the face of
the unfolding COVID-19 pandemic, the presidential election should be of lesser
importance and it should be postponed: "(...) It is not the election date that is
important for Poles today. It is their health and life, place of work, whether they
can ensure security for their family, health security and social security. People
worry about such matters, they talk about them at home (...)." In a speech of 6
April 2020, W. Kosiniak-Kamysz criticised the government's efforts to organise
the election by mail. "(...) If this election is to be conducted fairly and carefully, such changes should not be introduces (...), changes which should not
be introduced in the Electoral Code 6 months before the elections, let alone
14 days from the date of submission of this bill for consideration by the High
Chamber. (...) No conditions to perform the process fairly and safely have been
kept. Therefore, I once again make a motion – this time to reject the bill in its
entirety, a bill that serves only to solidify the current power, and not to conduct
fairly the electoral process, as it has already been violated by the lack of an
election campaign (...)." Additionally, the PSL leader called for the introduction
of a state of natural disaster, which would allow for the postponement of the
election date: "(...) The election is to be held in 4 days, and Poles do not know
who, where, when, how, in what way.... They don't know how the voting will
proceed. A state of natural disaster must be declared because the candidates
are not to blame for the current situation. It is not even the fault of the coronavirus pandemic. It is the fault of bad decisions, taking away the competences of
the National Electoral Commission, the lack of cooperation with local governments and the failure to introduce a state of natural disaster not to postpone
the election, but to acknowledge the very fact (...)."

W. Kosiniak-Kamysz also expressed a highly critical opinion on the government's actions regarding the presidential election. His views on this matter included the following postulates: postponing the originally planned election date; introducing a state of natural disaster; calling into question the legitimacy of holding the election by mail. The politician closely related his views to the coronavirus pandemic unfolding in Poland. Unlike leaders of the Civic Coalition, he chose not to voice his opinion to sum up the electoral process after its conclusion.

The leaders of the Confederation party, J. Korwin-Mikke, G. Braun, R. Winnicki, J. Kulesza, are the last group of politicians whose statements need to be analysed within the previously defined scope. J. Korwin-Mikke was not as radically opposed to the idea of holding the election by mail as leaders of the other opposition parties. He stated that the idea itself was relatively rational, but the way the process was organised was controversial, which made it impossible for him to support the bill: "(...) We do not trust PiS. We don't believe PiS will proceed with this election honestly, so we will vote against the bill. The idea itself is not idiotic, but in the case of an idea of those people, it is at least irresponsible, let's be clear – most likely criminal (...)." What he said did not fit into the relatively uniform narration of the other opposition parties, also when it comes to the postponement of the original election date of 10 May 2020: "(...) What right do you have to accuse PiS that the election was not held on 10 May? You did everything possible to ensure that the election was not held on 10 May. You are responsible for this, not PiS. Let us say this clearly and openly (...)."

In the statements of G. Braun no references to all the issues raised by the above presented politicians were identified. The leader of the Confederation of the Polish Crown did not call for the introduction of a state of natural disaster, but he had reservations about the government's policy of imposing restrictions which aimed at preventing the development of the pandemic: "A question to the absent minister, the prime minister, this whole crew: If the reasons, which you have maintained for the past weeks and months, why it is not possible to hold the election in the planned manner, so to speak, in the real world, with voting at polling stations, as I understand it, have apparently ceased to exist, they are no longer there, then what are the reasons public life in Poland, public space, other buildings, not necessarily polling stations, should continue to remain closed? What is the legal basis and what is the scientific basis for such administrative decisions, with the implementation of which Minister Szumowski still threatens the nation?" In other speeches in which he addressed the subject under investigation, he promoted the Confederation candidate, Krzysztof Bosak, and the website that was supposed to be a safeguard for the fairness of the election: "(...) Before you put such a tick in the box next to the name of Krzysztof Bosak, the best candidate for President of the Republic of Poland... Before you do so, go to www.pilnujwyborow.pl, and keep an eye on the election. Keep an eye on it, don't sleep, so that they don't steal you, Dear Poles, because here, admittedly, from time to time, an alliance is formed across divisions, yet an alliance formed to get a better share of the spoils (...)."

R. Winnicki also did not elaborate on his position on such issues as the election by mail, change of its date, introduction of the state of natural disaster. In the few speeches in which he referred to the issue of election in any way, the promotion of K. Bosak's candidacy can only be found: "(...) As far as the Institute of National Remembrance is concerned – unfortunately, it does not fully fulfil its tasks, which Krzysztof Bosak as a presidential candidate also has spoken about several times, pointing out that although the provisions of the act on the IPN explicitly state that it is supposed to defend a good name of Poland and Poles, for example, there are no regularly responding English-language accounts in the IPN's social media that would continually carry out this kind of work (...)."

In the speeches of J. Kulesza, the chairman of the Confederation parliamentary circle, one can find criticism towards the government for the failed attempt at organising the election by mail: "(...) I understand that the accusation is that the Civic Platform, following the example of other states, did not waste millions of zlotys on a vaccine that was unnecessary. You would have wasted it, just as you have wasted 68 million zlotys on printing ballots (...)." However, like other politicians of the Confederation, he was not radically critical of the government's actions concerning the analysed issue. What is more, he supported the proposal to organise the election in a hybrid mode, i.e. partly stationary and partly by mail: "(...) I am very happy that we are finally giving citizens a choice. Whoever is not convinced about remote voting, comes to the polling station. Those who are concerned about their health have the option of voting by mail. Let us extend that choice. Perhaps there are people who are also afraid of receiving the electoral package from their postman, because we know that the virus can linger on paper. Let us also introduce the possibility of voting via the Internet (...)."

The above indications prove that the Confederation's leaders did not criticize the government's actions in the context of the 2020 presidential election on so many levels as leaders of the Civic Coalition, the Left and the Polish Coalition. Unfavourable voices regarding the government's undertakings were found in their speeches, yet their context was slightly different than that of the views presented by the other politicians of the opposition parties.

The Table 26.2 presents a comparative analysis of the positions and declarations of the leaders whose speeches were subjected to qualitative analysis.

TABLE 26.2   Leaders' positions in the context of the 2020 presidential election

Parliamentary Club	Party	Leader	Position
Law and Justice	PiS	J. Kaczyński	–
	PiS	R. Terlecki	–
	SP	Z. Ziobro	–
Agreement		J. Gowin	–
Civic coalition	PO	B. Budka	Changing the election date from 10 May, 2020; Opposing the election by mail; Introducing a state of natural disaster; Calling into question the fairness and equality of the election
	Modern	A. Szłapka	Changing the election date from 10 May, 2020; Introducing a state of natural disaster
	IP	B. Nowacka	Opposing the election by mail; Calling into question the fairness and equality of the election
	Green	M. Tracz	Changing the election date from 10 May, 2020; Opposing the election by mail; Introducing a state of natural disaster
	PO	C. Tomczyk	–
Left	SLD	W. Czarzasty	Opposing the election by mail
	Together	A. Zandberg	–
	Spring	K. Gawkowski	Introducing a state of natural disaster; Opposing the election by mail
PSL-Polish coalition	PSL	W. Kosiniak-Kamysz	Changing the election date from 10 May, 2020; Opposing the election by mail; Introducing a state of natural disaster; Calling into question the fairness and equality of the election
Kukiz'15	Kukiz'15	P. Kukiz	–

TABLE 26.2   Leaders' positions in the context of the 2020 presidential election (*Cont.*)

Parliamentary Club	Party	Leader	Position
	KORWiN	J. Korwin-Mikke	Undermining confidence in the government to hold the election properly; Blaming the opposition for postponing the 10 May, 2020 election
	KKP	G. Braun	Criticism of pandemic restrictions; Promoting the presidential candidate
Confederation	RN	R. Winnicki	Promoting the presidential candidate
	KORWiN	J. Kulesza	Criticizing the government for the failed attempt at organizing the election by mail; Supporting the idea of organising the election in a hybrid mode.

SOURCE: AUTHORS'S ANALYSIS BASED ON PARLIAMENTARY SPEECHES

26.5   Conclusions

Following the research process designed in line with the selected method, it was possible to answer the main research question and identify the positions of political leaders towards holding the presidential election during the pandemic. This allowed for providing a comparison between individual politicians and the parties or coalitions they represent.

Politicians of parties forming the government took part in the parliamentary debate much less frequently during the period in question. Moreover, they did not speak on the subject of the 2020 presidential election even once. On the other hand, leaders of opposition parties took the floor often, and B. Budka, W. Kosiniak-Kamysz and W. Czarzasty relatively most often mentioned the examined topic in their utterances.

The analysis based on the LDA model determined that the election topics were strongly related to health issues. The qualitative analysis confirmed these findings – the abovementioned leaders talked about the election mainly in the context of the COVID-19 pandemic.

The results of the research indicate that the discourse on the 2020 presidential election did not involve leaders of the parties forming the government at the time. Leaders of the Civic Coalition, the Left and the Polish Coalition presented similar positions on the organisation of the election. Most of the statements on the subject were related to the issue of the coronavirus pandemic, as already indicated by the results of the quantitative research. Leaders of the Confederation were not as firm critics of the government's activities on the same issues as leaders of the Civic Coalition, the Left and the Polish Coalition, although they also expressed negative opinions on the activity of the government (in the context of the election and the pandemic, among others). The issues most frequently discussed by the leaders in question were: postponement of the original election date of 10 May 2020 due to the pandemic, inter alia by means of introducing a state of natural disaster; criticism of the organisation of the election by mail; questionable equality, secrecy and fairness of the electoral process. Opposition party leaders criticised the government in almost every speech on the election topic. Their main positions and demands were: postponing the original date of the election planned for 10 May 2020, introducing a state of natural disaster, rejecting the bill of holding elections by mail, and calling into question the equality of the election campaign.

References

Bayley, P. (2004). "Introduction. The whys and wherefores of analysing parliamentary discourse". In P. Bayley (Ed.) *Cross-Cultural Perspectives on Parliamentary Discourse* (1–44). Amsterdam: John Benjamins.

Blei, D. M., Ng, A. Y., & Jordan, M. I. (2003). "Latent Dirichlet Allocation", *Journal of Machine Learning Research*, 3, 993–1022.

Calvo-González, O., Eizmendi, A., & Reyes, G. (2018). "Winners Never Quit, Quitters Never Grow. Using Text Mining to Measure Policy Volatility and Its Link with Long-Term Growth in Latin America". *Policy Research Papers*, 8310, 1–35.

Curran, B., Higham, K., Ortiz, E., & Filho, D. V. (2018). "Look who's talking: Two-mode networks as representations of a topic model of New Zealand parliamentary speeches", *PLoS One*, 13(6), https://doi.org/10.1371/journal.pone.0199072.

Flis, J., & Ciszewski, W. (2020). „Nieudane samobójstwo polityczne – ustawa o powszechnym głosowaniu korespondencyjnym w wyborach prezydenckich 2020". *Studia Socjologiczno-Polityczne. Seria nowa*, 12, 99–120. DOI: 10.26343/0585556X20705

Flis, J., & Kaminski, M. (2022). "Multi-player electoral engineering and COVID-19 in the polish presidential elections in 2020". *Mind & Society*, 1–8. https://doi.org/10.1007/s11299-022-00287-7

Gunawan, S. (2010). „Style of Obama's Inauguration Speech". *K@ta*, Vol. 12(1), 92–107. DOI: 10.9744/kata.12.1.92-107.

Hidayat, T. N., Nababan, M. R., & Djatmika, D. (2019). "The Shift Process in Transitivity system on Obama's and Trump's Inauguration Speech: A Translation Study". *Humaniora*, 31(2), 211–220. DOI: https://doi.org/10.22146/jh.34901

Ilie, C. (2015). "Parliamentary Discourse". In K. Tracy, C. Ilie, & T. Sandel (Eds.), *The International Encyclopedia of language and social interaction*, 1–15. Chichester: Wiley Blackwell.

Jelodar, H., Wang, Y., Yuan, C., Feng, X., Jiang, X., Li, Y., & Zhao, L. (2019). "Latent Dirichlet allocation (LDA) and topic modeling: models, applications, a survey". *Multimedia Tools and Applications*, 78, 15169–15211. DOI: https://doi.org/10.1007/s11042-018-6894-4.

Kaleru, S., & Dhanikonda, S. R. (2018). „Exploratory Data Analysis and Latent Dirichlet Allocation on Yelp Database". *International Journal of Applied Engineering Research*, 13(21), 15035–15039.

Kwiatkowska, A. (2017). „'Hańba w Sejmie' – zastosowanie modeli generatywnych do analizy debat parlamentarnych". *Przegląd Socjologii Jakościowej*, 2, 82–109. DOI: https://doi.org/10.18778/1733-8069.13.2.05

Lewis, D. (1997). "The Two Rhetorical Presidencies: An Analysis of Televised Presidential Speeches 1947–1991". *American Politics Research*, 25(3), 380–395. DOI: https://doi.org/10.1177/1532673X9702500307

Lipiński, A. (2021). "Poland: 'If We Don't Elect the President, the Country Will Plunge into Chaos'". In: G. Bobba & N. Hubé (Eds.), *Populism and the Politicization of the COVID-19 Crisis in Europe* (115–129). Cham: Palgrave Macmillan.

Liu, F. (2012). "Genre analysis of American Presidential Inaugural Speech". *Theory and Practice of Language Studies*, 2(11), 2407–2411. DOI: 10.4304/tpls.2.11.2407-2411

Martin, D. J. (2011), *Communicating Vision. A Linguistic Analysis of Leadership Speeches*, Dissertations. 561. https://digitalcommons.andrews.edu/dissertations/561

Michalak, B. (2020). *Koronawirus a wybory prezydenckie. Czym grozi głosowanie podczas epidemii?*. Warszawa: Fundacja Batorego.

Ping, K., & Lingling, L. (2017). "Application of Interpersonal Meaning in Hillary's and Trump's Election Speeches". *Advances in Language and Literary Studies*, 8, 28–36. DOI: https://doi.org/10.7575/aiac.alls.v.8n.6p.28

Piontek, D., & Ossowski, S. (2021). "The "Non-Campaign" and the "Non-Elections" on the Internet in the 2020 "Spring" Presidential Election Campaign in Poland". In M. Musiał-Karg, & Ó.G. Luengo (Eds.), *Digitalization of Democratic Processes in Europe. Studies in Digital Politics and Governance* (57–73). Cham: Springer.

Rakowska-Trela, A. (2020). *Wybory prezydenckie 2020. Kontekst prawny*. Warszawa: Fundacja Batorego.

Shenhav, S. (2004). "Once Upon a Time There Was a Nation: Narrative Conceptualization Analysis. The Concept of 'Nation' in Discourse of Israeli Likud Party Leaders". *Discourse & Society*, 15(1), 81–104. DOI: https://doi.org/10.1177/0957926504038947

Sula, P., Madej, M., & Błaszczyński, K. (2021). "In the shadow of plagues: 2020 presidential elections in Poland". *Przegląd Politologiczny*, 2, 27–45. DOI: 10.14746/pp.2021.26.2.3

Szczepański, D. (2020). "Proposals for Constitutional Changes in the Presidential Election Campaign in Poland in 2020". *Przegląd Prawa Konstytucyjnego*, 6(58), 191–201. DOI: https://doi.org/10.15804/ppk.2020.06.15

Søyland, M. G., & Lapponi, E., *Party Polarization and Parliamentary Speech*, http://folk.uio.no/martigso/workingpapers/soyland_lapponi_ecpr2017.pdf

Tatarczyk, D, & Wojtasik, W. (2022). "The Incumbency Advantage during the COVID-19 Pandemic: Examining the 2020 Polish Presidential Election". *East European Politics and Societies*. DOI: https://doi.org/10.1177/08883254221085307

Triadafilopoulos, T. (1999). "Politics, Speech, and the Art of Persuasion: Toward an Aristotelian Conception of the Public Sphere". *The Journal of Politics*, 61(3), 741–757. DOI: https://doi.org/10.2307/2647826.

van Dijk, T. A. (1997). "Discourse analysis as ideology analysis". In C. Schoaffner & A. L. Wenden (Eds.), *Language and Peace* (229–245), Amsterdam: Harwood.

van Dijk, T. A. (1993). "Principles of critical discourse analysis". *Discourse & Society*, 4(2), 249–283. DOI: https://doi.org/10.1177/0957926593004002006

van Dijk, T. A. (2004). "Text and context of parliamentary debates". In P. Bayley (Ed.), *Cross-Cultural Perspectives on Parliamentary Discourse* (339–372). Amsterdam: John Benjamins.

Yano, T., Cohen, W. W., & Smith, N. A. (2009). *Predicting Response to Political Blog Posts with Topic Models*, In Proceedings of Human Language Technologies: The 2009 Annual Conference of the North American Chapter of the Association for Computational Linguistics (477–485). Boulder: Association for Computational Linguistics.

Zirn, C., & Stuckenschmidt, H. (2014). "Multidimensional Topic Analysis in Political Texts". *Data & Knowledge Engineering*, 90, 38–53. https://doi.org/10.1016/j.datak.2013.07.003.

Conclusion: Elections in Extraordinary Situations

Magdalena Musiał-Karg and Izabela Kapsa

The COVID-19 pandemic was not the first, nor will it probably be the last world-wide health issue. Undoubtedly, it has disrupted practically every area of public and social life. The global spread of the disease had a profound impact on the delivery of public services as well as the routine procedures and events in democratic states, including elections. In the wake of the COVID-19 pandemic, the world witnessed unprecedented disruption to the electoral process, with nations grappling to balance the fundamental principles of democracy with the need to protect public health. The book is an invaluable resource, shedding light on the complexities and dilemmas faced by governments, election officials, and citizens during the trying time.

Under normal circumstances, the organization of elections is a complex undertaking that requires adequate time, proper planning and consideration of all legal rules, and much effort by institutions and officials in charge. Elections during the pandemic brought a lot of challenges and had transformative effects on the intricate relationship between democratic processes and public health. This inspired the authors to examine the impact of pandemics on electoral systems, voter behavior, and the overall democratic structure of societies. Since traditional voting at polling stations could not guarantee social distance, election officials rushed to find measures to protect both the integrity of elections and public health. At that time, many countries had no specific guidelines as they lacked any similar experience. In many parts of the world, these difficulties the situation was exacerbated by a growing sense of uncertainty and fear of unpredictable consequences of the virus. Self-isolation and social distancing became a challenge for contemporary democracies and electoral procedures. The pandemic has shown that the implementation of democratic and safe elections can be demanding, sometimes even impossible.

The research problem discussed in the book refers to holding elections in extraordinary situations. Due to an abrupt spread of SARS-CoV-2 many governments decided to introduce major restrictions (related to social distancing) and postpone their parliamentary, presidential, or local elections and referendums scheduled for 2020 and 2021. States where elections coincided with the pandemic had to make important choices as to when the polling should take place, what measures put in place to reduce the risk of infection, and how to mitigate the potential impact of election-related tensions that may be exacerbated by the pandemic and restrictions associated with it.

This historical health crisis made governments realize that a variety of legal, technical, and health issues and implications should be considered when deciding whether to proceed with elections or not. Additionally, constitutional arrangements had to be made to ensure that democratic institutions could operate as they would in normal circumstances and to secure people's fundamental rights and freedoms. Officials around the world struggled to designate sufficient funding to implement security measures, new alternative voting methods (i.e. expanding mail-in voting) and inform the public about the changes.

The book aims to answer the questions of how to eliminate the impact of the pandemic on the organization of elections, and how to build framework conditions, define requirements, and provide solutions in countries where elections were to be held during the pandemic or a similar unpredictable and unexpected situation. The analysis of some European countries provides an insight into different legal and practical solutions, and shows how these countries organized safe and democratic elections in the emergency situation and ensured integrity of the electoral process.

During the global health crisis, the specifics of popular voting, conditions, and the conduct of elections attracted scientific studies. This contributed to the current discussion on aspects of electoral systems, electoral regulations, and campaigns and alternative voting methods. Consecutive chapters of the book discuss issues and reflections, and provide insights in several contexts related to the health crisis. Consequently, the authors reflect on various topics related to elections during the pandemic, including democratic standards and proper organization of voting. At the same time, they attempt to determine whether such threats can affect the course or outcome of elections.

The book begins a theoretical discussion on different aspects of elections when held in extraordinary situations, as well as other conditions and factors affecting democracies, political actors and societies. These include alternative voting procedures that can support the principle of universal suffrage during a pandemic and the right to free and universal elections. All of them are presented the context of international standards and the right to participate in free elections (based on OSCE reports). In some countries, electoral laws adopted or proposed for adoption during the COVID-19 pandemic reduced sovereignty in a way described in the theory of neo- and quasi-militant democracy. While examining specific circumstances of the election during the pandemic, the book refers to the radical criticism of democratic states and general elections as expressed in anarchist political thought and populist governance, as well as disinformation and its role in the electoral process.

The empirical part corresponds with theoretical issues raised in the book and relates primarily to legal and organizational issues, election management in health crises, as well as the implementation of alternative voting methods, including the extended postal voting, online registration systems, and the establishment of temporary polling stations. It also examines the effectiveness and potential pitfalls to highlight both success stories and areas for improvement. The case studies presented also consider political communication, electoral resilience, as well as the defense of democracy and its values in the context of electoral systems. Particular attention is paid to the broad implications for democracy and governance. The book raises critical questions about long-term effects of disrupted electoral processes, legitimacy of governments, and the trust among citizens. The authors reflect on the potential erosion of democratic norms and the rise of authoritarian trends amidst uncertainty.

According to IDEA (2023), from 21 February 2020 until 21 February 2022 at least 80 countries and territories across the globe decided to postpone national and subnational elections due to COVID-19. At least 160 countries decided to hold national or subnational elections whereas 65 countries and territories held elections that were initially postponed due to the pandemic. The authors analyze countries that decided to proceed with elections that were initially postponed due to the pandemic. These include, for example, Serbia where general elections (originally scheduled for April 26, 2020) were moved to June 21, 2020; Czech Republic with their Senate by-elections (originally scheduled for March 27–28 and April 3–4 2020) moved to June 5–6 and June 13, 2020; Latvia which moved extraordinary elections to the Riga Council (originally scheduled for April 25, 2020) to August 29, 2020; Italy where national referendum (originally scheduled for March 29, 2020) was organized in September 20–21, 2020 and Poland where presidential elections (originally scheduled for May 10, 2020) were moved to June 28 and July 12, 2020.

The book provides examples of elections and referendums held amid COVID-19, i.e. the national referendum (August 30, 2020) and parliamentary elections (February 7, 2021) in Liechtenstein; parliamentary elections in Lithuania (October 11, 2020); elections to regional councils and the Senate by-elections, as well as the election to the Chamber of Deputies in the Czech Republic (October 2–3, 2020 and October 8–9, 2021); parliamentary elections (April 4 and July 11, 2021), as well as early parliamentary elections together with the first round of presidential elections (November 14, 2021) in Bulgaria; Municipal Council elections in Latvia (June 5, 2021); elections to Landtags and Bundestag (between March and September 2021) in Germany; parliamentary elections in Russia (September 17–19, 2021), and local elections in Estonia (October 17, 2021).

The analysis of these examples provides an insight into special health security procedures implemented in all countries. Serbia, for instance, implemented the state of emergency and restrictions to movement and assembly. On the election day, polling stations were equipped with masks and gloves to protect citizens from the spread of COVID-19. The Czech Republic introduced the obligation to wear masks, undergo temperature checks, keep social distance, and reduce the number of people at polling stations. Three alternative voting methods were also in place for people in quarantine as they could vote from their cars (drive-in) in specially designated places, in social facilities, as well as using a portable ballot box. Latvia applied special measures as they defined the maximum number of people allowed at the polling station, thorough ventilation of polling stations, and warning signs were placed to remind about keeping the right distance, together with hand disinfectants, obligatory facial masks, personal voter's writing implements, wastebaskets and additional containers for used facial masks at polling stations, etc. Liechtenstein introduced general sanitary recommendations, such as obligatory facial masks indoors, traffic organization so new coming voters did not interact with those leaving the polling station. Lithuanian Sanitary introduced safety procedures, such as social distancing, extended group of voters entitled to vote at home, longer polling station opening hours, and mobile polling stations.

Apart from sanitary restrictions in polling stations, Italy also applied voting at home. Based on the decision of a medical doctor, a patient could vote at home upon a visit by the special electoral commission. Poland introduced postal voting for voters under quarantine and those voting abroad. Bulgaria used voting machines to reduce the number of people in polling stations and introduced stricter hygiene rules. In Germany, elections were held under lockdown so voters had to comply with generally applicable restrictions. Russia extended voting over several days, voting outside the polling station and online voting. Estonian voters were no longer assigned to specific polling stations according to their place of residence. Thus, voting was possible at any polling station in the voting or municipal district relevant for their place of residence. Quarantine was a significant obstacle in general elections in the world. In most countries, it prevented citizens from voting, as election procedures were not adapted to such emergency situations. However, Estonia applied an entirely different setup. Alternative voting methods introduced several years

earlier helped to ensure that every citizen could vote. The government website provided full information about three possible ways of participating in the
election.

Additionally, most of the states had to introduce special legal measures even
if the elections were held on time. Serbia implemented changes to the electoral law shortly before elections. Several important measures included the
introduction of voter lists and observers to counteract any abuse of the process. Other changes also included lowering the electoral threshold from 5% to
3% (in general and local elections). The Czech government declared the state
of emergency three times and also applied new rules in elections to regional
councils where seats were divided according to the electoral clause, 5% for one
party and 8% or 11% for coalitions of two or more parties. In line with legislative changes in Lithuania, a special electoral district was created for citizens
residing permanently or temporarily outside the country. They also created
a pool of electoral commission members and special conditions to support
the submission of preliminary reports on financing political campaigns. Additional measures were adopted to help voters with disabilities and register candidates, as well as alternative methods of voting, voting abroad including.

In Poland, the government was determined to organize the presidential
election, initially in the form of all-postal voting on May 10, 2020 (which failed),
and then in a hybrid setup in June (1st round) and July (2nd round). Apart from
sanitary restrictions to in-person voting, the hybrid election also included the
option to vote by mail for quarantined and for those voting from abroad. In
Italy, the Minister of the Interior and the Minister of Health introduced operational and preventive procedures for members of election commissions and
voters, while trying to reconcile constitutional electoral rights and health security. This also included hygiene guidelines for polling stations and counting
votes, as well as providing safe access to polling stations. Yet another example
is Bulgaria which adopted dedicated regulations. Apart from strict COVID-19
sanitary rules, the country introduced voting machines. Russia amended their
election laws to extend the voting period to three days and use online voting
and voting outside polling stations. On top of that, they reduced the permitted
number of observers due to sanitary and epidemiological constraints.

Latvia, Liechtenstein, Germany and Estonia did not adopt special legal solutions regarding elections. The use of alternative voting methods or the postponement of elections helped to avoid the need to change the electoral law
in excess of generally applicable sanitary restrictions. There were some minor
changes to lower the number of signatures on support lists filed with election
committees as well as to extend the period of collecting such signatures in Germany. Finally, Estonia abandoned the three-day interval between early voting

and the election day, which was treated as a period to eliminate possible irregularities in the system.

In the context of social and political processes, some societies accepted decisions made by their states (Czech Republic, Latvia, Liechtenstein, Italy) and voting procedures adopted (Germany, Estonia), while in other countries decisions made in connection with the pandemic highly polarized politicians and societies (Serbia, Russia, Poland). In some countries voter turnout remained unchanged (Czech Republic), in others it was reduced (Bulgaria, Italy) or increased (Russia).

Electoral campaigns in all countries used both traditional and electronic media. In many countries, the access the then ruling parties and politicians had to public media helped them to dominate the discourse in these communication channels. This generated criticism and dissatisfaction of the opposition (Serbia, Bulgaria, Russia, Poland) and pandemic-related decisions became subject of political dispute (Czech Republic, Germany). The COVID-19 pandemic became the lead political topic in such countries as Serbia and Czech Republic, while in Latvia, Lithuania and Germany, economic and social issues, natural environment, and health and crisis management prevailed.

Certainly, the book highlights that the COVID-19 pandemic was a significant factor that greatly influenced the electoral process in many countries. Not only did the pandemic change electoral calendars, but also electoral laws, procedures, election agendas of political parties and their candidates, election campaigns and, above all, public attitudes. These, in turn, depended on the phase of the pandemic, number of infections and deaths in the country and the world. On top of this, government policies, management of the health crisis, and media reports played their major role. Consecutive chapters offer numerous examples to support this assumption. Although some countries managed to implement safe voting procedures during the pandemic, others could not hold elections as originally planned for organizational reasons. The analyses also indicate that right-wing populism hindered the response to COVID-19 in some countries. In countries ruled by populist governments, politicians presented an anti-science approach and often marginalized arguments and opinions expressed by experts on security measures to be adopted during voting.

Based on the evidence presented in the book, the topic seems to be extremely valid, interesting and relevant. It encompasses many aspects of a modern state, including the operation of political institutions, the role of electoral bodies, the political and electoral system, and, finally, legal solutions applied in particular countries. Issues related to elections held during or after natural catastrophes or human-inflicted crises have been subject to research into challenges to modern democracies, especially in the context of the development of electoral systems.

Modern democracies may face many challenges. An example is the pandemic which took the entire international community by surprise, because it was unpredictable regarding its scope and duration, as well as social, demographic, economic and political ramifications. Undoubtedly, each country's experience with elections during COVID-19 is important and extends far beyond any future pandemic and issues related to the management and organization of elections. The book discusses the case of Lithuania and its effort to bring the country fully in line with OSCE commitments and other international obligations and standards as regards democratic elections. The same applies to Poland which was requested to implement numerous recommendations to improve elections. Whether solutions and patterns suggested continue to be implemented in the future in the political practice still remain an open question.

The thorough analysis of real experience in this book can be a source of valuable lessons and recommendations to ensure resilience and integrity of the election process during future pandemics or crises. However, this book can provide a benchmark for the future rate and direction of changes to be made to the election process to make it resilient to emergencies from the perspective of states, political actors, and representative democracies in the post-COVID-19 era. We believe that the book may serve as a valid and insightful guide for policymakers, election administrators, researchers, and citizens interested in understanding the intricate dynamics between public health and democratic processes. We hope that the book will inspire, facilitate, and encourage other researchers to explore and take a critical approach to issues raised.

Index

www.ingramcontent.com/pod-product-compliance
Lightning Source LLC
Chambersburg PA
CBHW072039020426

42334CB00017B/1330